Homer's Odyssey

Homer's Odyssey

My Quest
For Peace
and Justice

By Homer A. Jack
Edited by Alex Jack

One Peaceful World Press • Becket, Mass.

Dedicated

To those, living and dead, of many world religions, or none, and living on all continents who made my passage through life exciting and perhaps useful, especially—

To my parents, Alex and Cecelia Jack,

To my wives, Esther Williams and Ingeborg Kind,

To my children, Alex and Lucy and their partners, Gale and Stan,

To my grandchildren, Michael, Molly, Jon, and Masha,

To my step-children, Renate, Sigrid, and Marianne
and their families,

And to so many more.

Homer's Odyssey
© 1996 by Alex Jack

For information on mail-order sales, wholesale or retail discounts, distribution, translations, and foreign rights, please contact the publisher:

One Peaceful World Press
P.O. Box 10
Leland Road
Becket, MA 01223
U.S.A.

Telephone (413) 623-2322
Fax (413) 623-8827

First Edition: May 1996
10 9 8 7 6 5 4 3 2 1

ISBN 1-882984-13-7
Printed in U.S.A.

Cover Photo: Homer at a WCRP conference in New Delhi
Spine: Homer as minister of the Unitarian Church of Evanston
Back Cover: Homer speaking at the United Nations

INTRODUCTION

MY FATHER'S SON

British Parliamentarian and disarmament advocate, Philip Noel-Baker, received the Nobel Peace Prize in 1959. He opened his address at Oslo by asking: "Why has it (the Nobel Prize) come? I have been of all men the most fortunate of all. I was my father's son." By this he meant that he walked in the footsteps of his father who was not only a parliamentarian but also a peace advocate, working mightily to prevent World War I.

I, also, have been "the most fortunate of all," for I was also my father's—and mother's—son. They worked for peace and justice and early on they taught me to do the same. Indeed, this autobiography may not be as interesting as it might have been just because in these two decisive areas, I have not evolved.

In choosing the title for this book, I went to the dictionary to find the meaning of odyssey: "1. An extended adventurous wandering. 2) An intellectual or spiritual quest." My life, like many others, has truly been a wandering quest. I must confess that it has not always been easy to spend three score and ten years plus with the name of Homer—the Greek poet! Yet I know preciously little about the original Homer. My mother told me that I was given the name simply because my parents were looking for one which couldn't easily be shortened—no nickname. For that reason, I have had to endure the burden of bearing the name Homer, a minor difficulty shared by the few other Homers I have known. How, over the years, I have avoided knowing so little about the Greek Homer, and never preached a sermon about him, is surely a subject for psychoanalysis.

I have contemplated writing my life story for many years. I lived through a large swath of the twentieth century and have been involved in some peace and justice movements. I have no illusions that

I made any personal difference on even one key national or international decision, and yet the actions of citizens are cumulative and are never useless.

When I "retired" in 1987, my wife and I intentionally moved to Swarthmore, Pennsylvania, so I would have easy access to my personal and organizational papers in the Swarthmore College Peace Collection. Some of these materials were deposited and indexed there for several decades. My first task was to write the history of the World Conference on Religion and Peace (WCRP). I finished the first draft in 1989 and began work on the autobiography. I completed only about a quarter of the manuscript when President Bush began to threaten war with Iraq. I pushed everything aside and tried to help prevent the conflict and, once it started, help bring about an armistice. Finishing my last anti-war campaign in mid-1992, I then spent the next year finalizing my WCRP history for publication, which came off the presses in May 1993.

I was about to resume work on the autobiography when I was hospitalized for tests in June 1993 and found I had pancreatic cancer and it had spread. My days were numbered, less perhaps if I adhered to a more healthful diet. My son, Alex, had worked for many years as a macrobiotic author and teacher. Indeed, he brought me the newly revised edition of his book, *The Cancer-Prevention Diet*, co-authored with Michio Kushi, the Japanese-born educator and leader of the macrobiotic community and longtime supporter of world government, when I returned from the hospital. Dana Greeley, my friend and colleague in the Unitarian Universalist Association and WCRP, had turned to macrobiotics at Alex's suggestion when he was diagnosed with terminal colon cancer in 1985, and according to his wife, Debby, lived at least six months longer than expected, and he passed away peacefully at home.

Between mouthfuls of brown rice, miso soup, vegetables, and seaweed, I resumed work on my autobiography. By mid-June, I realized my time was probably limited. I knew my energy was definitely lessening. I decided to turn my autobiography into an autobiography/anthology. Instead of trying to write several dozen more chapters, I would try to find in the archives selected essays, sermons, addresses, and other writings that would possibly describe my life better than a warmed-over description several decades later. What would be lost would be the perspective of history and experience, but what would be gained would be the freshness and immediacy of the original moment. In any case, I had no choice. Thus the anthology portion of this book.

I have not hesitated to prune these essays and speeches to save space. Where I have not had time to do so, I have asked my son—a professional editor—to do so, and in a way not to sacrifice too much flavor. To lighten the burden for the reader, I am not using endnotes or giving full bibliographical citations, but invite the interested reader to refer to the bibliographical note at the end of this book regarding my archives and further research.

Also, for the sake of simplicity, I will often use the term, Unitarian, when I should write Unitarian Universalist. These two denominations were parallel in the U.S. until they merged in 1961. Though my longest ministry was with the Unitarian Church of Evanston, the first church I served was actually the tiny Universalist Church of Litchfield, Illinois, in 1942-42, so I am not biased against Universalists.

I will try not to use sexist terms. I will also try to be politically correct in other sensitive areas. It is hard to know what word to use for black Americans—Negroes, colored, African-Americans? I tend to go back and, especially in essays and speeches from the 1940s, '50s, and '60s, let the original—usually Negro—stand in its historical context.

I am grateful for all who helped me with the huge task of preparing this volume, including the staff of the Swarthmore College Peace Collection, especially Eleanor Barr; my son, Alex, who remains my editor and publisher; Ingeborg, my wife and encourager, especially at the end; and those individuals and foundations who may contribute financially to its publication.

I do not know the fate of this manuscript. I have tried to make arrangements toward that end, but I may have to help in some way from the grave. I have confidence that ultimately it will be published in some form. I hope *Homer's Odyssey* will be worth reading and a challenge, not only to my grandchildren, but also to several generations who I earnestly hope will become world citizens.

Homer A. Jack
Swarthmore, Pennsylvania
June 28, 1993

EDITOR'S NOTE

Homer—as he was universally called, even by his children—died several weeks after writing the introduction to this book. As he indicated, he completed only about a quarter of the text—the early period from his birth and growing up in Rochester in the '20s and '30s through his race relations work in Chicago in the '40s, the early years in Evanston in the '50s, and material on his family and associates.

In editing the rest of the text, I have followed his general outline and anthology selections, but have added a prologue consisting of several key moments in his life that shaped his future and the future of modern society.

Modesty—in standing up for what he believed in—was not one of Homer's virtues. But I think he was genuinely too modest about his own contribution to history. For example, a Homeric epic could be written about how the United States and Soviet Union ended atmospheric nuclear testing in the late '50s and early '60s, featuring President Kennedy, Premier Khrushchev, Pope John XXIII, Prime Minister Nehru, Albert Schweitzer, Bertrand Russell, Norman Cousins, and Homer—who as director of SANE did as much as anyone to orchestrate this breakthrough—as well as a Greek chorus representing world public opinion and the spirits of Gandhi, Einstein, and victims of the atomic bombing of Hiroshima and Nagasaki from the next world. The Partial Nuclear Test-Ban Treaty of 1963 was the crowning achievement of the Kennedy Administration and the turning point in reversing the nuclear arms race. The seeds of détente, the nuclear freeze movement, and eventually the end of the Cold War were sown in this accord.

Characteristically, in the material that he left for his autobiography, Homer barely mentions his own role in helping to end nuclear testing. Nor does he describe the first Freedom Ride in the Deep South which he participated in in 1947, his visit to Montgomery, Alabama, in 1956 to support the boycott of segregated buses led by a young clergyman named Martin Luther King, the Cuban Missile Crisis, and other historic events. Instead his selections focused primarily on the complex, unheralded, and—frankly dull—disarmament and human rights issues that he patiently worked on for several decades at the United Nations. Homer—who received a Ph.D. in biology and then abandoned science "to work with men rather than mice"— remained enough of an evolutionist to know that social change comes primarily through small, incremental steps rather than bold, dramatic ones. Yet for the sake of the ordinary reader, I have emphasized the energy and passion of Homer's younger days. The specialist who wishes to plumb the depths of his disarmament and human rights work in his mature and elder years is directed to the bibliography at the end, especially to Homer's own books in recent years describing these issues in detail.

As editor, I have also condensed selections on socialism, communism, and anti-communism, a subject dear to Homer's heart—and liver. For nearly a half century, Homer "fought"—vociferously but nonviolently—against the double-standard of the communists and their supporters in the labor, civil rights, and peace movements who judged the U.S. by different moral and ethical criteria than the U.S.S.R. The collapse of the Soviet Union from within—the repudiation of its totalitarian ethic by its own people—has largely vindicated the position taken by Homer, ACLU founder Roger Baldwin, pioneering civil libertarians John Haynes Holmes and Donald Harrington, and other liberals. The partisan debate that Homer, as well as these others, was drawn into during that era—like literary or scientific priority disputes—seems largely arcane and irrelevant to those on the perimeter or now living in a different age. However, I have included Homer's essay on a visit to Moscow in 1938. He never changed the views he expressed in this short eyewitness account of Stalin's Russia, and the essay is published here for the first time.

I have also taken license as an editor—and son—to conclude Homer's story with a chapter on his last days and an appreciation of his life, as he once wrote about his father.

The format and typography of this volume, including the front and end matter, are modeled on *The Gandhi Reader*, an autobiographical anthology of Gandhi's life and writings that Homer compiled in the mid-1950s. I trust he would approve of these editorial decisions, especially this last one.

In bringing this work to completion, I am grateful for help and support from many people and many quarters: especially to Gale, my wife, for help with research, typing, copy editing, and proofreading and her patience and encouragement through the entire project; to Esther, my mother, for her gracious support and encouragement; to Masha and Jon, our children, for their love and enthusiasm; to Lucy, my sister, for her insight and inspiration; to Michael, my nephew and Homer's grandson, for help with typing and to Molly, my niece and Homer's granddaughter, for her cheerful presence; to George H. Williams, my uncle, for his reminiscences and encouragement; and to Ingeborg Jack, Homer's wife, for biographical material, help with locating documents, and photographs. Special thanks to Astrid Lindberg of Evanston and Rev. Frank Robertson of the Unitarian Church of Evanston for research assistance related to Homer's Evanston ministry; to George M. Houser for reviewing sections on race relations and the African freedom movement; and to the Swarthmore College Peace Collection for maintaining Homer's archives in such splendid condition. I am indebted to Paul Aicher and the Topsfield Foundation, Charles Bloomstein and the Joyce Mertz-Gilmore Foundation, and Yoshihiro Ohno of the Niwano Peace Foundation for their grants and help in defraying the cost of publication; and to my colleagues at One Peaceful World and the Kushi Institute.

Through this book, I hope that Homer's strong, prophetic voice will be heard in the new century and contribute to humanity's endless dream of a world of enduring peace and justice.

Alex Jack
Becket, Massachusetts
August 6, 1995

Contents

Part III: Parish Minister (1948-1954)

Part IV: World Traveler (1955-1959)   205

Part V: Peace Leader (1960-1964)   255

Part VI: Denominational Official (1965-1969)   311

PRINCIPAL CHARACTERS

Adams, James Luther (1901-1994). Unitarian minister, professor at Meadville and Harvard Divinity School, and Homer's mentor.

Cousins, Norman (1912-1990). Editor, world government leader, founder and co-chairman of SANE, and principal intermediary in achieving the Partial Test-Ban Treaty.

Dulles, John Foster (1888-1959). Secretary of State during the Einsenhower Administration who practiced nuclear brinksmanship and opposed decolonization and non-alignment.

Einstein, Albert (1879-1955). German-born scientist, philosopher, and peace promoter.

Eisenhower, Dwight D. (1890-1969). U.S. President who warned against "the military-industrial complex."

Fromm, Erich (1900-1980). Viennese-born psychoanalyst, author, and board member of SANE.

Gandhi, Devadas (1900-1957). Editor of the *Hindustan Times* and Gandhi's son.

Gandhi, Manilal (1892-1966). Leader of the Indian community in South Africa and Gandhi's son.

Gandhi, Mohandas (1869-1948). Father of modern India who developed the philosophy of nonviolent direct action (*satyagraha*) in South Africa, perfected its methods in India, and opposed untouchability and other forms of discrimination.

Greeley, Dana McLean (1908-1986). President of the Unitarian Universalist Association and a principal founder of WCRP.

Holmes, John Haynes (1879-1964). Unitarian minister of the Community Church in New York, author, and social activist.

Houser, George (1915-). Methodist minister, a founder of CORE, and director of the American Committee on Africa.

Jack, Alexander (1878-1943). Rochester artist, photoengraver, socialist, and Homer's father.

Jack, Alex (1945-). Editor, author, macrobiotic teacher, and Homer's son.

Jack, Cecelia Davis (1886-1976). Rochester suffragist, homemaker, and Homer's mother.

Jack, Esther Rhys Williams (1916-). Social worker, homemaker, librarian, and Homer's wife 1939-1971.

Jack, Ingeborg Kind (1927-). German-born homemaker, Quaker, human rights activist, and Homer's wife 1972-1993.

Kennedy, John F. (1917-1963). U.S. President and architect of the 1963 Partial Nuclear Test-Ban Treaty.

Khrushchev, Nikita (1894-1971). Soviet premier who encouraged the final negotiations of the Partial Test-Ban Treaty.

King, Martin Luther, Jr. (1929-1968). Baptist minister, Gandhian disciple, and leader of the modern civil rights movement.

McCarthy, Joseph R. (1908-1957). Senator from Wisconsin whose reckless attacks on suspected communist and leftists gave rise to the McCarthy Era in the early 1950s.

Muste, A. J. (1885-1967). Minister, pacifist, and elder spokesman of the peace movement during the Vietnam War.

Narayan, Jayaprakash (1902-1979). Indian statesman, freedom fighter, and leader of the independence movement for Bangladesh.

Nehru, Jawaharlal (1890-1964). Prime Minister of India, first world leader to call for an end to nuclear testing, and head of the non-aligned movement.

Niwano, Nikkyo (1906-). Japanese founder and president of Rissho Kosei-kai and a founder and leader of WCRP.

Noel-Baker, Philip (1889-1982). British MP, Olympic athlete, disarmament expert, and Nobel Peace laureate.

Pickett, Clarence (1884-1965). Director of the American Friends Service Committee, a founder and co-chairman of SANE, and social activist.

Russell, Bertrand (1872-1970). British mathematician, philosopher, author, and leader of the campaign for nuclear disarmament.

Rustin, Bayard (1910-1987). A founder of CORE, adviser to Martin Luther King, and organizer of the March on Washington.

Schweitzer, Albert (1875-1965). Alsatian-born humanitarian-philosopher-physician and Nobel Prize laureate who lived for a half century in Africa and toward the end of his life spoke out against atomic tests and war.

Scott, Michael (1907-1983). Anglican priest who led the struggle against apartheid while exiled from his native South Africa.

Spock, Benjamin (1903-). Physician and writer who became a

spokesman for SANE and a leader of the peace movement.

Stevenson, Adlai E. (1900-1965). Governor of Illinois, twice Democratic presidential candidate, and U.S. Ambassador to the U.N.

Thomas, Norman (1884-1968). Leader of the Socialist Party in America and national peace leader.

Williams, David Rhys (1890-1970). Minister of the Unitarian Church of Rochester, social activist, literary detective, and Homer's mentor and father-in-law.

Williams, Lucy Adams (1890-1969). Homemaker, family historian, and Homer's mother-in-law.

Williams, Lucy Isabel Jack (1947-). Nurse, mother, and Homer's daughter.

GLOSSARY

ACLU   American Civil Liberties Union; human rights organization founded by Roger Baldwin and others, 1920-

ACOA   American Committee on Africa; New York-based group supporting the African freedom movement, 1952-

AFSC   American Friends Service Committee; Quaker relief, social service, and peace education organization, headquartered in Philadelphia; 1917-

Ahimsa   Nonviolence (*a*, privative; *himsa*, violence—Sanskrit). Traditional precept in Hinduism, Buddhism, and Jainism.

Apartheid   The doctrine and system of racial separation that prevailed in South Africa, 1948-1994.

BAC   Black Affairs Council; organization devoted to black empowerment within the Unitarian Universalist denomination in the late 1960s

Bandung   Indonesian mountain resort city; site of the 1955 Asian-African Conference that marked the final decolonization of the modern world.

Belgrade   Capital of Yugoslavia; site of the 1961 First Non-Aligned Conference.

CCARRD   Chicago Council Against Racial and Religious Discrimination; local anti-discriminatory alliance; 1944-1950s

CNVA   Committee for Non-Violent Action; Gandhian peace

group based in New York that organized civil disobedience at nuclear testing sites in the 1960s

CORE   Congress of Racial Equality; civil rights organization founded in Chicago that organized the first sit-ins and freedom rides against segregation; 1941-

FOR   Fellowship of Reconciliation; international association of religious pacifists; 1914-

Harijans   A term given by Gandhi to the untouchables (*hari*, God; *jan*, people—Sanskrit).

IARF   International Association for Religious Freedom; assembly of liberal churches including the Unitarian Universalists, Brahmo Samaj, and Rissho Kosei-kai.

Jim Crow   Fabric of laws, customs, and beliefs upholding segregation in South and North from Reconstruction through the 1960s.

Lambaréné   City in Gabon (formerly French Equatorial Africa) near Dr. Albert Schweitzer's hospital.

Montgomery   City in Alabama where a boycott of segregated buses in 1955-56 led by Martin Luther King, Jr. launched the modern civil rights movement.

NAACP   National Association for the Advancement of Colored People; civil rights organization; 1909-

NGO   Non-Governmental Organization or its observer working within the United Nations community; term refers both to the group itself and to an individual spokesperson or official.

Non-Alignment   Doctrine of identifying with neither the Eastern nor Western bloc during the Cold War; articulated by Prime Minister Nehru of India, President Tito of Yugoslavia, and other predominantly Third World leaders.

Reverence for Life   Ethical doctrine developed by Doctor Albert

21

Schweitzer based on the insight: "I am life that wills to live in the midst of life that wills to live."

SANE   National Committee for a Sane Nuclear Policy; peace group in the forefront of the campaign to end nuclear testing and achieve disarmament; 1957-1988; became SANE/Freeze, 1988-1993; Peace Action, 1993-

Satyagraha   Truth force or soul force (*sat*, truth; *agraha*, firmness— Sanskrit); nonviolent direct action developed by Gandhi and practiced by many individuals and groups after his time. (*Satyagrahi*: Male practitioner of satyagraha. *Satyagrahini*: Female practitioner of satyagraha.)

SCLC   Southern Christian Leadership Conference; civil right organization founded and led by Martin Luther King and Ralph Abernathy; 1957-

SNCC   Student Nonviolent Coordinating Committee; Southern-based civil rights and community organizing network that grew increasingly militant; 1960-1969

UUA   Unitarian Universalist Association; liberal religious denomination that evolved from the merger of the American Unitarian Association and the Universalist Church; headquartered in Boston; 1961-

WCC   World Council of Churches; international association of Protestant and Reformed churches; 1948-

WCRP   World Conference for Religion and Peace; multireligious organization that lobbies at the U.N., sponsors social action projects, and holds a global assemblies; 1969-

WRL   War Resisters League; radical pacifist anti-war, anti-draft group based in New York; 1923-

WSP   Women's Strike for Peace; a leading peace organization in the 1960s; 1961-

WPC   World Peace Council; international organization sympathetic to Soviet foreign policy; 1950-.

PROLOGUE

ALL STAND TOGETHER

DEFINING MOMENTS

"Tell me, Muse, of the man of many ways, who was driven
far journeys after bringing down Troy's sacred citadel.
Many were those cities he saw, whose minds he learned of,
many the sorrows he endured in his heart on the wide sea,
struggling for his own life and the homecoming of his
companions."   — The Odyssey, Book I

Most of Homer's life was devoted to establishing racial justice and preventing nuclear war—the two most intractable problems of the latter half of the twentieth century. He largely adopted the outlook and methods of his heroes Gandhi and Schweitzer—*Satyagraha* or truth force and Reverence for Life. The material in this section shows Homer in the prime of his life as a minister and a social activist. The description of his first visit to Dr. Schweitzer's African hospital presents a moving portrait of a contemporary peaceable kingdom. The dramatic account of Martin Luther King's inaugural campaign in Montgomery, Alabama, depicts the triumph of nonviolence and Gandhian values. As director of SANE, Homer's incisive recommendations during the Cuban Missile Crisis thread the eye of an ideological needle, offering insights that are still applicable to world crises today. The birth of WCRP—the World Conference on Religion and Peace—in the ancient city of Kyoto, Japan, unifying religious leaders from East and West, represents the fruition of an age-old dream of a spiritual parliament of humanity.

Photograph: Homer in the mid-1950s

1 LAMBARENE
(1952)

VISIT TO DR. SCHWEITZER'S HOSPITAL

In June 1952, Homer spent two weeks visiting Albert Schweitzer in Lambaréné, then part of French Equatorial Africa, now the Gabon, en route to South Africa where he joined in and reported on the struggle against apartheid. A warm friendship developed between the old philosopher and the young clergyman, and Schweitzer invited Homer to visit him on three other occasions at his jungle clinic (1957, 1958, and 1962) and twice at his home in Günsbach in Alsace. Among all the people he met in his life and travels, Homer said that Schweitzer made the deepest personal impression. The description of Homer's first visit with Schweitzer originally appeared in the Saturday Review of Literature.

I have just spent a fortnight as the guest of Albert Schweitzer in his jungle hospital at Lambaréné, French Equatorial Africa. It has been an unforgettable experience, well worth the expense, time and risk involved. In the midst of a midwestern snowstorm last winter I resolved to visit Lambaréné if Dr. Schweitzer would have me. I wrote him and received a cable, "Expect you Lambaréné May." Late in April I left the States, after taking injections over a six-week period for protection against tropical diseases. The journey required a total of four weeks—a week by boat to France and then almost three weeks by small steamer from Bordeaux to Port Gentil at the mouth of the Ogowe. Lambaréné is less than three days from New York City by air—with lucky connections—but I chose the longer way

25

partly because I wanted to travel the route Dr. Schweitzer took when he first went to Africa and—since he has never flown from France to Africa—has taken again so often.

Across the Bay of Biscay and down along the hump of west Africa I went, stopping at countries well known to stamp collectors: Senegal, French Guinea, the Ivory Coast, Dahomey and the Cameroons. At Port Gentil I was met by Dr. Ladislas Goldschmid, who worked longer for Albert Schweitzer than any other physician and is now practicing in Port Gentil. Through the foresight of Dr. Schweitzer, I was taken by native boatmen in a timber merchant's pinasse on the 24-hour journey up the river. Dodging the dreaded tsetse flies, I stood on the little boat reliving the April day in 1913 when Dr. and Mrs. Schweitzer first came up this broad river and were so impressed with its "antediluvian scenery" of papyrus clumps, bright-flowering creepers, and vast network of tree roots. I saw an occasional monkey clambering on the palm trees, but not one hippo, not even a crocodile.

Schweitzer at Home

At twilight we reached the tiny town of Lambaréné, situated on a large island in the Ogowe. Two and a half miles upstream at a fork in the river lay the Hopital d'Albert Schweitzer. Once at the primitive landing, I was led several hundred yards uphill, and there, in a blue work apron and white helmet, was Albert Schweitzer! He looked remarkably like recent photographs: a large man with big nose, full mustache, and a broad, infectious smile. He greeted me warmly and took me into his small study-bedroom. He showed me his two pet antelopes in a cage behind the bookcase and then led me to my room at one end of the building housing European patients. Immediately he made me feel completely at home. I have been one of his hospital family for the past two weeks, not working as hard as any of them but occasionally trying to do my share as a foreman of fifteen Africans who cut and haul wood in the jungle half a mile behind the hospital.

The most stimulating experience here for the visitor is mealtime, for then he is seated directly opposite *le grand docteur* as the Africans call him. About five minutes after the dining hall bell rings, Albert Schweitzer comes in, puts his helmet on top of the piano, and takes his seat at the center of the long table, flanked by his two longtime helpers, Emma Haussknecht and Matilda Kottmann. (Mrs.

Schweitzer, unable any longer to endure the tropical climate, is living in Europe.) The other staff members, including two physicians and three nurses, and occasional guests complete the circle. This is the big meal at the hospital and the cuisine is excellent, with many tropical foods and some things imported from Europe or America. A typical meal may include slices of fresh papaya, baked plantain (oversized bananas), meat in season, vegetables and salad from the hospital gardens, and a dessert of fruit. Dr. Schweitzer eats several helpings of soybeans at each meal and always cuts off part of the bread and stuffs it in his pocket for the animals. (This is a common practice of staff members and usually all but the visitor go out of the dining room with pockets or even a plate full of leavings for some favorite animals.)

The conversation, when Dr. Schweitzer is in the mood, is even better than the food. Often he is introspective and tells about his experiences in youth and about the early years at the hospital. Usually he spoke to me in short sentences, which Mlle Emma patiently translated into English. When on rare occasions she got a word wrong—he understands English but almost never speaks it—he would ask her to make a more accurate translation.

Almost An Intellectual

Many of our conversations dealt with race relations and colonialism. He told me the oft-repeated story of how, one day, he asked a well dressed African lounging around the hospital to give him a hand with some logs he was carrying. The man replied, "I'm an intellectual and don't drag wood about." Keeping on with his work Dr. Schweitzer replied, "You're lucky. I, too, wanted to become an intellectual, but I didn't succeed." For all his problems, Dr. Schweitzer evidences a sense of proportion. He once wrote, "Those who now speak in unfriendly terms about the natives may have come out to Africa full of idealism, but in the daily contest have become weary and hopeless, losing little by little what they once possessed of spirituality."

The noon and evening meals are preceded by a short blessing, given by Dr. Schweitzer, and the evening meal is always followed by a short worship service. After the dishes have been cleared away, Mlle Emma passes out the hymn-books and gives the Bible to the doctor. He takes a pair of tarnished glasses out of his shirt pocket, finds the scripture reading with the help of faded notes fastened together with string, and puts the bookmark at the Lord's Prayer. He selects an appropriate hymn, reads the first line, gives the number, and gets up and walks around the table to the upright piano to accompany the singing. Then by the light of a kerosene lamp with a home-made green shade, he reads a passage from Scripture, followed by the Lord's Prayer. This constitutes the evening service, which, by its sheer simplicity and the spirit of its leader, creates a worshipful experience deep in the African jungle. There is no chapel here, but on Sunday mornings the European nurses take turns leading a worship service in the open space between the hospital buildings. Also on Sunday mornings there is a worship service in the largest of the leper villages.

Today the visitor to Lambaréné is more conscious of Schweitzer the musician than of Schweitzer the philosopher, the theologian, or even the physician. There are few outward evidences here of his many achievements as a philosopher and theologian and he no longer practices medicine at the hospital, though he still keeps up with every detail, participates in difficult diagnoses, and is present at difficult childbirths (as he was for a Caesarean operation at three o'clock one morning during my stay). Almost every evening after supper, and frequently for a half-hour before 7:30 breakfast, he can be heard practicing on the specially built piano with pedal attachments which the Paris Bach Society gave him in 1913. One Saturday evening while I was there, the hospital's newly acquired record player was connected to the single electric line, and for half an hour ten of us, including Dr. Schweitzer, listened to the new long-playing records (to be released in the United States this autumn) of his performance on the organ in the little church of his native Günsbach in Alsace. As he listened he often closed his eyes, occasionally asking Mlle Emma to turn the volume up or down. The music was by Bach, Mendelssohn, and César Franck. One evening he invited me to sit on the piano bench with him while he practiced. For an hour I watched his fingers replaying difficult passages from Bach. Occasionally he paused to pencil directions above the notes by the light of the kerosene lamp. His two pet antelopes rustled in the cage just beyond the piano. As I left his study to go to my room in the bright light of the full tropical moon, I could hear traditional musicians across the river competing with the *le grand docteur* on their tom-toms.

The most important innovation in recent years is the three leper villages a half-mile from the main hospital buildings. The recent development of better drugs—the sulfones—to help arrest this disease prompted Dr. Schweitzer to bring the lepers to a place where they could be easily reached for treatment. More than 300 lepers—among them some small children—live in these villages in houses of bamboo and palm leaves. Their condition demands the full-time services of a physician and their daily rations alone tax the resources of the hospital.

Both in the leper villages and in the main hospital, the antiseptic-conscious American is at first shocked at the primitive and unsanitary living arrangements of the patients. It has been Dr. Schweitzer's aim, however, to simulate as much as possible the conditions of the native villages. The people flock to his hospital because they feel at home there. Ambulatory patients, including some lepers, contribute toward the expense of their food by working on the hospital plantation or at various maintenance jobs. Dr. Schweitzer has always tried not to charge the full cost of treatment to Africans whose bills will be paid by white employers, for fear that they would tend to delay the visit of the sick to the hospital.

Another change at Lambaréné is the inevitable one of personnel. Today, for the first time, there is an American physician here. But most of the staff are from Alsace, Switzerland, and Holland. Some of these people have been working here for long periods with only short leaves. Staff members volunteer their services, receiving only their passage, board and room, and a little spending money. Dr. Schweitzer is generous at heart—as the visitor well knows—but he is also one of the most frugal of men. He uses every old envelope and every old nail and will make the franc or dollar stretch to unbelievable lengths. But he never economizes with medicines, and despite his many old-fashioned ways, he believes in making use of the very latest medical discoveries.

Supervises Every Detail

To the visitor, it seems that three-quarters of the time and energy Dr. Schweitzer and the staff give to the hospital is spent getting work out of the native people for the operation of the institution. Every morning *le grand docteur* assigns some women to gather palm nuts and some men to help with the new building. Often he has to settle a minor—or major—palaver. One wishes that this man who so embodies love and the reverence for life could be put in an environment where he could build a truly utopian medical community through the use of love, instead of cajoling and threatening. Indeed,

Dr. Schweitzer is so busy supervising the essential housekeeping of this establishment of more than 600 souls that there is never the free time he—and the world—wishes he might have. Visitors to whom he gives time generously to discuss everything from Gandhi to television do not lighten his burden either. He also has an extensive correspondence and, with the help of his assistants, painstakingly writes thank-you letters to all who send contributions to the hospital. When he is in Günsbach he has even less time for creative activity. It is said that his greatest block of undisturbed time is the three-week voyage to and from Africa. He would like to make a second visit to America, but first he wants to finish certain books he is writing. To those who know him best, there is simply no possibility of his ever leaving Lambaréné permanently.

As I pack up to leave Dr. Schweitzer and his hospital and begin the three-day journey by canoe, mail truck, and railroad to Brazzaville, I am grateful that I have had this privilege. During my time here, I have got to know the ever burdened staff and even some of the goats, pigs, dogs, cats, ducks, and birds which roam at will over the hospital grounds. Most of all, I have begun to know Albert Schweitzer and the great institution he has so lovingly nurtured. This is only one of many hospitals operated by devoted Christians to help sick people in many parts of the world. Yet Albert Schweitzer's hospital is different in that it is run by no mission board but is the personal project and responsibility of one man. The question many ask is "What will happen to the hospital when Albert Schweitzer dies, as even he must some day, despite his amazing vigor at seventy-seven?" The immediate answer and perhaps the ultimate one lies with concerned Americans of all faiths and denominations.

Dr. Schweitzer once wrote: "Those who have learned by experience what physical pain and bodily anguish mean, belong together all the world over . . . in the fellowship of those who bear the mark of pain. On them lies the humanitarian task of providing medical help in the colonies." One sees this humanitarian task at Lambaréné, where forty cents will buy fresh fish for the anemic bodies of five of six leper children. There is one thing for certain: Dr. Schweitzer will never retire, and he will end his tremendously versatile life in his beloved Lambaréné.

2 MONTGOMERY
(1956)

GANDHI WALKS IN ALABAMA

In the early 1940s and 1950s, Homer helped introduce Gandhian philosophy and techniques to the American people through the Congress of Racial Equality (CORE), which he helped found as a young Unitarian seminarian and minister, and through his books, The Wit and Wisdom of Gandhi *and* The Gandhi Reader. *In March 1956, he journeyed from his pulpit in Evanston, Illinois, to Montgomery, Alabama, to support the city-wide boycott of segregated buses by the black community. The nonviolent campaign, led by Martin Luther King, Jr., a twenty-seven-year-old Baptist preacher, launched the modern civil rights movement. In a sermon to his congregation back in Evanston, Homer described King and his wife as "fearless and consecrated" and perceptively observed that the protests might be "the beginning of Civil War II" in America. Later that summer, Dr. King invited Homer to preach on Gandhi at the Dexter Avenue Baptist Church in Montgomery. Homer's eyewitness dispatches from Montgomery for the* Hindustan Times *and* Indian Opinion *(founded by Gandhi in 1903) introduced news of this nonviolent revolution to India and—still today—offer a unique perspective on this historic event.*

Montgomery, Alabama—Mahatma Gandhi is walking the streets of this city of the Deep South. There are no spinning wheels, no Gandhi caps, no copies of *Harijan*, and no Viceroy, but it is a Gandhian movement just the same.

Montgomery is a city of 125,000 persons in what is referred to as the "Deep South" of America. It is where racialism is most severe, where Negroes have suffered the longest. The present Gandhian protest started—as all Gandhian campaigns have done—with a long-standing, just grievance. On December 1, 1955, a forty-year-old Negro seamstress, Mrs. Rosa Parks, refused to move from her seat on a Montgomery bus. Three other Negro passengers—all men—moved from the middle of the bus to the back, but Mrs. Parks was tired—of her day's work and of forty years of an American *apartheid*. So she refused to obey the driver's order to move so that several white passengers who had just boarded the bus could be seated. The driver stopped the bus and Mrs. Parks was arrested for breaking the segregation laws. (This had echoes of the day in 1893 when Mohandas Gandhi himself faced segregation en route to Pretoria.)

Mrs. Parks' arrest caused the Negro clergymen of Montgomery to ask for a one-day protest by the 50,000 Negroes in Montgomery who constituted about 75 percent of the passengers on the bus system. As a result, almost no Negroes rode the buses. This protest was so successful, and so unusual for the South, that it has continued, and Montgomery's Negroes have avoided the giant yellow buses ever since.

Mild Demands

In the meantime, a strong Negro organization, led by clergymen, has evolved, called the Montgomery Improvement Association. It made three mild demands: 1) more courtesy by the white drivers; 2) ultimately Negro drivers on routes into preponderantly Negro residential areas; and 3) seating in the buses on a first-come, first-served basis, with Negroes beginning from the back and whites from the front. Significantly, the Negroes did not ask the total end of segregation on these public carriers.

The unity, restraint, and organization of the Negro community in Montgomery have seldom before been equaled in the South—or North. And the white community of Montgomery is baffled, as the British overlords of India were. The whites in Montgomery have, in their floundering, done almost everything to ensure the success of this protest (the Negroes prefer not to call it a boycott). They have intimidated the Negroes, even with violence, and have harassed the car-pools. They even indicted almost 100 leaders, including two dozen preachers, on an old state law against conspiracy to boycott. But whatever the white city commissioners do seems only to result in a new unity, a new fearlessness on the part of the Negro community and its leaders. It is the Salt March all over again.

Just how Gandhian is the Montgomery protest? Not only was Mrs. Parks' original refusal to move on that huge yellow bus a spontaneous reaction on her part, but the whole protest movement itself seems, from what I can determine, also spontaneous. Although Dr. Martin Luther King, Jr., the young leader of the protest, told me that he knew of Gandhi when studying in theological school, he certainly cannot be considered a full-blown Gandhian. But the leadership of the Montgomery protest soon discovered that what they were doing was what Gandhi did in South Africa and India. They naturally stumbled upon Gandhian attitudes and techniques used more recently in the defiance campaign in South Africa in 1952 and in the mass *satyagraha* in Portuguese Goa in 1955.

The Negro leaders in Montgomery repeatedly emphasize that they don't hate anybody—the bus company, the city commissioners, or the white community in Montgomery. But they say they are just going to avoid the buses until their grievances are met. They don't even hate those who have used violence against them. The leaders warn their own people not to use violence, although there were reports of some violence against the buses on the very first day of the protest. Love and nonviolence are the cornerstones of this movement—and fearlessness follows. Also, as with Gandhi himself, this protest combines religion and politics. It is probably no accident that this movement sprang from within the Negro churches of Montgomery.

The Negro church, at the moment, is still almost the only institution in the South, except the National Association for the Advancement of Colored People, which is beyond the reach of the white man. Heretofore, the church has been escapist and the practical, rational Negro in the South has not reached for it. But today, with tension rising in the South and with more able leadership in the churches, the church is fulfilling almost a revolutionary role. Thus the twice weekly rallies of the movement in Montgomery are squarely within the churches.

The mass meetings are not unlike Gandhi prayer meetings. A theme song has been adopted for the duration of the protest. Its tune is "Old-Time Religion." Its words:

> We are moving on to vict'ry,
> We are moving on to vict'ry.
> We are moving on to vict'ry,
> With hope and dignity.

We shall all stand together,
We shall all stand together,
We shall all stand together,
'Til every one is free.

We know love is the watchword,
We know love is the watchword,
We know love is the watchword,
For peace and liberty.

Black and white all are brothers,
Black and white all are brothers,
Black and white all are brothers,
To live in harmony.

We are moving on to vict'ry,
We are moving on to vict'ry,
We are moving on to vict'ry,
With hope and dignity.

Immediately after his house was bombed, Dr. King told his neighbors who had assembled, some reportedly with weapons to protect him: "Don't get panicky. Don't do anything panicky at all. Don't get your weapons. He who lives by the sword shall perish by the sword. Remember that is what God said. We are not advocating violence. We want you to love our enemies. I want you to love your enemies. Be good to them. Love them and let them know you love them. I did not start this boycott. I was asked by you to serve as your spokesman. I want it to be known the length and breadth of this land that if I am stopped this movement will not stop. For what we are doing is right. What we are doing is just. And God is with us."

Gandhian Technique

At one of the prayer meetings, Rev. Ralph D. Abernathy said: "Our method is one of passive resistance, of nonviolence, not economic reprisals. We have nothing against the bus company. It can run buses as long as it wants to—but it will run them without Negroes until it gives us justice. Let us keep love in our hearts, but fight until the walls of segregation crumble."

Some leaders are studying the sage from Sevagram. They are conscious that their movement has been likened to Gandhism (in headlines across America) and they are determined to study Gandhism and to adopt some of his techniques. They are conscious, too, that other Negro communities—in the South and even in the North where segregation is less—are watching their movement carefully, for this could spread among Negroes as pro-segregation talk is spreading among whites in the South just now.

What of American Gandhians? They are looking at this movement with amazement. CORE, the Committee of Racial Equality, was founded in 1941 in an effort to adapt Gandhism to the American race relations scene. It has had some important successes, chiefly in the North, but occasionally in border cities as Baltimore, Washington, and St. Louis. Once CORE made a foray into the South and contributed substantially to the lessening of segregation on interstate bus transportation. As hard as CORE tried, and lack of funds prevented it from trying very hard, CORE never made significant progress in the middle or deep South. And now arises this movement, spontaneously and with no relation to CORE, and yet increasingly going the Gandhian way!

Impact of the Protest

This protest has had a tremendous impact across America. Many newspapers have sent special reporters to witness the protest and write long stories. Many Northern newspapers have published sympathetic editorials. A great number of religious, labor, and other groups especially in the North, have sent funds to the protest, for their expenses are heavy with legal expenses for their trial. A group of clergymen called for a nationwide day of prayer on March 28 in sympathy with the protest, the nearest thing in America today to an Indian *hartal* [boycott]!

There is a blanket of silence towards the protest from the white citizens of Alabama. Most whites apparently do not want even this lessening of segregation, although they ride vertically with Negroes without segregation in Montgomery's elevators! Intimidated are those whites who are in favor of this slight lessening of segregation as demanded by the Negroes at this time. There is a pervasive totalitarianism gripping the South, even Southern liberals, including those in Montgomery. The only white individual who

35

has openly aided the protest and helped raise funds and consistently used his automobile for the car pool is the Rev. Robert S. Graetz, a twenty-seven year old minister of an all-Negro Lutheran church in Montgomery.

Walk with God

What will be the outcome? The protest has been a success in putting economic pressure on the bus company. Whatever the outcome of the court trials of the 100 leaders, the protest is sure to benefit. If they are convicted, they will become martyrs and will go to jail willingly—after appealing their conviction. If they are set free by the court, they will be vindicated. Compromise is always possible, but the city fathers are increasingly under pressure not to compromise for they are told that if they "let go" in Montgomery, it will be "harder to hold the color line" in Birmingham or Atlanta.

After the protest is settled, one can only hope that the Negroes of Montgomery will use their new-found tool of nonviolent resistance and tackle some of the other basic areas of segregation in their city.

When the 100 leaders were arrested, there was a "walk with God" pilgrimage and the major car pools were suspended for a day and virtually the whole Negro population walked to the center of Montgomery. Those who saw the pilgrimage said they will never forget the stirring sight as, when the Negroes came toward the center of the city, slouches straightened and fatigue faded and, even in the old, the stance was one of dignity, no longer of defeat.

One old lady sat on a bench, and rubbed her feet, saying, "Before my soul was tired, even if my feet were not; but now my feet are mighty tired, but at least my soul is free."

If you asked her what *satyagraha* was, she wouldn't know. But somehow she's gotten the magic of the method if she knows not the name.

3 NEW YORK
(1962)

THE CUBAN MISSILE CRISIS

*The Cuban Missile Crisis is widely regarded as the most dangerous event
of the Cold War. In October 1962, President Kennedy issued an ultimatum
for the Soviets to remove offensive missiles stationed in Cuba and ordered
U.S. ships to blockade the island and stop and search incoming Soviet vessels. For several days, the world teetered on the brink of nuclear war. Ultimately, Premier Khrushchev backed down and World War III was narrow-
ly averted. At the time of the crisis—and for the duration of Kennedy's
presidency—Homer was executive director of SANE, the nation's foremost
peace group, which he had helped found with Norman Cousins and Clarence Pickett in 1957. During this period, Homer helped coordinate the international campaign for an end to nuclear testing and the arms race.
Homer gave the following speech in the immediate aftermath of the confrontation. In July 1963, in the face of rising public opinion against nuclear testing and the behind-the-scenes diplomacy of Norman Cousins,
SANE's chairman, President Kennedy and Premier Khrushchev signed the
Partial Test-Ban Treaty outlawing atmospheric atomic and hydrogen bomb
tests—the crowning arms control agreement of the Cold War and the beginning of détente. Several months later, President Kennedy was assassinated in Dallas.*

The Cuban missile crisis has been a traumatic experience for
the American people and their government, for the Soviet government if not perhaps for many of the Soviet people, and for other
peoples and governments throughout the world.

If I were President, how would I have handled the crisis? First, I would have tried to normalize relationships before October 23—when the ultimatum was issued—by 1) publicly not allowing another Bay of Pigs, 2) not allowing subsequent raids, 3) taking up the offer of Cuban President Dorticos on apropos items, 4) getting some trade going with Cuba, and 5) allowing travel between our two countries. Secondly, when the missile bases were discovered, I would have taken the problem to the U.N. Security Council and then to the General Assembly, asking for an inspected withdrawal. Needless to say, I would not have instituted a military quarantine or engaged in a nuclear showdown. And needless to say, I am not President, so this approach was not tried. Luckily, the world survived—this time.

Five Dangers

I would like to discuss the Crisis—which is not yet finished—by evaluating the dangers and the opportunities and then suggesting specific actions which could be taken, especially by the U.S. Government, to move a world which was on the brink of nuclear war to a world which could be on the brink of nuclear peace.

It is said that any crisis is a mixture of dangers and opportunities. Let me discuss the dangers first. The first danger growing out of the Cuban missile crisis is the growth of the "hard line" here in the United States. I fear that the popular lesson of the crisis to the American people is this: The President used force to stand up to the Russians and, as a result, the Russians backed down. From this "lesson" has flowed and flowered the hard line. We hear it expressed in various ways: "You can't trust the Russians." "The Russians have broken every treaty they have ever signed." "Strength is the only language the Russians know." "Negotiation with the U.S.S.R. is appeasement." This strengthening of the hard line in public opinion is one of the most dangerous results of the Cuban missile crisis.

And this brings us to the second danger. The hard-line is bound to influence American foreign policy in other spheres. A hard-line public opinion is bound to result in a hard-line Administration. At present, just now, it can be said that the President is politically and militarily left of the country, certainly of much of his own Administration or so it is made to appear to many of us. Once the politicians catch their breath after the elections, there will be overwhelming pressures for the Administration to repudiate its no-invasion pledge of Cuba and, across the world, for the Administration to "hold fast" and not negotiate over Berlin.

A third danger is the enhancement of the hard line within the Kremlin. The Soviet Union may not be a mirror image of the United States in all areas. But the shipment of forty-two missiles from Cuba back to the Soviet Union—and all this retreat implies—may result in liquid political fuel for what we know to be remaining neo-Stalinist elements within the Central Committee of the Kremlin. Even if Khrushchev might survive, his soft-line might not. And the dangers to the world of a hard Soviet line are as overwhelming, indeed more so, as the dangers of a hard American line.

This leads to a fourth danger: the necessity for the Soviet Union to show the world that she also has repudiated any "no win" policy. If she is bravely licking her wounds over Cuba, inevitably she will open new wounds in a political area of her own choosing. Will it be Berlin and Germany? Or will it be in the Middle East? We can almost anticipate a crisis somewhere, soon, with the Soviet Union holding the strategic advantages we admittedly held in the Cuba arena.

A fifth and final danger has to do with Cuba itself. If the delicate, continuing negotiations among our country, the Russians, and the Cubans falter, there could still be the possibility of armed clashes, even an invasion, by the U.S. of the island of Cuba. The probability lessens each day, but the possibility still remains.

So much for the five dangers growing out of the Cuban missile crisis, and there are others. To name several: 1) the use of news as weaponry by the Administration and 2) the lessening of tolerance for opposing foreign policy views.

Five Opportunities

Now let me enumerate an equal number of opportunities. The first opportunity arising from the Cuban missile crisis has to do with American public opinion and peace. Many millions of Americans, during that last week of October, realized that they were on the brink of nuclear war and for the first time they looked beyond the brink and saw the meaning of nuclear war, saw it as they never saw it during the fallout shelter debates of a year ago. The Cold War has been brought back to our backyard. These millions of Americans have not yet become active citizens for peace, but their moment of truth must somehow be used so they can be allies in the movement

39

for a world of peace plus justice. The crisis, for all its dangers, could give the peace movement its greatest opportunity.

The second opportunity has to do with the United Nations. During those seven days that shook the world, almost ended our world, we saw the U.N., and especially the office of the Secretary-General, rise before our very eyes. The mediation efforts of U Thant were among the U.N.'s finest hours. That week demonstrated that the U.N., with all its imperfections and weaknesses, can contribute mightily to mediation and peace. Khrushchev backed down, but the U.N. helped him to do so. But for the grace of God, Kennedy could have been in Khrushchev's shoes, might well be there some day soon, and the U.N. might be the instrument needed for even the U.S. to back down more gracefully.

A third opportunity growing out of the Cuban missile crisis is the nuclear disengagement of the whole of Latin America. A week after President Kennedy's October 22 speech, Brazil submitted a resolution to the First Committee of the U.N. urging an atom-free Latin America with verification. The U.S., in somewhat of a change in position, has indicated that she will vote in favor of the Brazilian resolution, although some of the Latin American states want the resolution to imply that no nuclear warheads will be transported through the Panama Canal and that no nuclear warheads will be stored in Puerto Rico. In any case, the chances appear good that the Brazilian resolution will be approved by the General Assembly sometime during Thanksgiving week, although the approval of a resolution by the General Assembly does not in itself even bring the Latin American area close to nuclear disengagement.

A fourth opportunity growing out of the Cuban missile crisis is a greater possibility for agreement between the U.S. and the U.S.S.R. on a test-ban treaty and ultimately on general and complete disarmament. I will discuss this possibility in a few moments.

A final opportunity presented by the Cuban missile crisis is a greater degree of cooperation among the peace movements in the U.S. If the crisis shook the American people, it also shook the American peace organizations—all of them, and their number and isolation are legion. During the crisis they worked more closely than ever before. After the crisis they came together, evaluated their weakness, and made two resolves: to work between crises to prevent crises by becoming much more political, and to work during crises by setting up a National Peace Council—only roughly equivalent to the President's National Security Council—to meet daily both in New York and Washington.

Organizational and Individual Action

The Cuban missile crisis may have frozen some attitudes in the U.S., but it has also opened receptivity of many as millions of Americans went to the brink and looked into the hell of nuclear war. This is a moment for a vast education campaign to reach new people. Suggestions for organizational and individual action follow.

1. Convene between now and December 15 (or early in the New Year) an all-day workshop on "A Breakthrough to Peace: Lessons from the Cuban Crisis." Try to elicit the widest possible sponsorship. Have panel discussions on Cuba, Berlin, Disarmament, Nuclear Testing, and other issues. National religious, labor, and general organizations might be approached if they are represented in your community. Perhaps the workshop can end with an open public meeting.

2. Visit your congressmen and two senators in a representative delegation before they return to Washington early in January. Give them a copy of the SANE policy statements and any others resulting from the Cuban missile crisis.

3. As issues arise in the next few weeks and months, write letters to the editor of your local newspaper emphasizing various facets in SANE's interim or 1963 policy statements.

Now is the time to prevent a second nuclear crisis!

4 KYOTO
(1970)

A NEW WORLD'S PARLIAMENT
OF RELIGIONS

In October 1970, four hundred religious leaders, drawn from ten world faiths and thirty-nine countries, met in Kyoto, the sacred city and former capital of Japan, for the inaugural session of the World Conference on Religion and Peace (WCRP). The gathering—the spiritual heir to the World's Parliament of Religions in Chicago in 1893—issued a Declaration on behalf of the world's religious community on the Vietnam War, disarmament, racial harmony, and other international issues. Homer served as Secretary-General for the assembly and for subsequent assemblies in Leuvan, Belgium; Princeton, New Jersey; Sydney, Australia; and (as Emeritus Secretary-General) Nairobi, Kenya. In 1979, Chinese religious leaders, representing a quarter of the world's people, joined an international gathering for the first time, and the Conference became truly international. The six-day gathering in Kyoto, as Homer notes below in an excerpt adapted from his book on the history of WCRP, has continued into its third decade. During this time, WCRP has served as the spiritual conscience of the world on matters relating to peace and disarmament, racial and religious equality, and economic development and social justice.

The World Conference opened in Kyoto on Friday, October 16, 1970, with participants arriving at the impressive International Conference Hall. Shri R. R. Diwakar, the acting chairperson, called the inaugural plenary meeting to order promptly at 9:30 a.m. The opening ceremony consisted of a Buddhist meditation service featuring a number of Buddhist priests and a massed choir. The 400 participants—delegates, fraternal delegates, observers, and members of the secretariat—sat at desks. The balconies were filled with 2,000 visitors from various religious groups in Kyoto, Osaka, and Kobe.

The Lord Abbot Kosho Ohtani, honorary president of the conference and head of the Higashi Honganji sect of Jodo Shin Buddhism, greeted the delegates. He recalled that "Japan is the only country that has been victimized by an atom bomb,"and that "ours is a nation that has absolutely discarded all aggressive war potential through the promulgation of a 'peace constitution.'" President Nikkyo Niwano of Rissho Kosei-kai also offered greetings on behalf of the Japan Religions League, the host of the conference representing the five major religions of Japan. He felt that "the time has arrived when religions, instead of antagonizing each other because of what we once thought was a religious conviction, should cooperate with each other to contribute to the cause of mankind and world peace."

Bishop John Wesley Lord, chairperson of the conference nominating committee, proposed a list of permanent conference officers. The slate was elected unopposed. Then Archbishop Angelo Fernandes of New Delhi gave the presidential address. He ended with the question, "Could a summit meeting of the world's topmost religious leaders point one day to the formation of a world body—a sort of parliament of world religions, with the independence and impartiality of a judiciary—unhesitatingly and fearlessly proclaiming and upholding what is in the interest of the common good of all peoples?" He added that "the answer depends on you and what you make of the conference." Sir Zafrulla Khan, president of the International Court of Justice in the Hague, and a Muslim from Pakistan, gave an address called "The Fundamental of Peace." He based his address "entirely on the Qur'an," for the reason that "the values inculcated by a faith must be discovered in its scriptures." He observed that "the essence of the problem of peace is that the individual must be at peace with himself and with mankind [and] in consequence of putting himself at peace with his Maker." Then several messages to the conference were read, including those from Secretary-General U Thant of the U.N. and from Prime Minister Eisaku Sato of Japan.

The afternoon plenary meeting began with an Islamic prayer service. As Secretary-General, I gave an address on the topic "Making This the Best We Know." Following a procedural session, participants divided into groups representing the major world religions: Buddhism, Christianity, Hinduism, Islam, Judaism, Shintoism, Sikhism, Zoroastrianism, other Japanese religions, and other non-Japanese religions. Their task was to explore their hopes for the conference.

The opening banquet was held in the Kyoto Grand Hotel with the Japan Religions League as host. Participants were welcomed by the Reverend Nenkai Inada, chairman of the League's board. The response of the participants was given by Metropolitan Philaret of Kiev, head of the U.S.S.R. delegation. There was also entertainment, including a demonstration of flower arrangements and a Japanese dance, *Fujimusume*.

On Saturday, October 17, the third plenary meeting was opened with a Jewish prayer service. President Niwano was chairperson. Dr. Hideki Yukawa, the 1949 Nobel laureate in physics, spoke on "The Creation of a World without Arms." He declared that "the phrase, 'the total destruction of the human race,' ceased to sound hyperbolic and now its actual possibility can by no means be ignored." Then Professor R. J. Zwi Werblowsky of the Hebrew University of Jerusalem gave an address on "Between the Crossfires: Some Reflections on Religion, Peace, and Human Rights." He insisted that "neither the concern for human freedom and social progress nor the desire for peace are the monopoly of religions." They may share these concerns, "but they have no cause to claim a special role for themselves." Each participant then joined one of the three commissions (on disarmament, development, and human rights). That afternoon, the fourth plenary meeting opened with a Christian prayer service. Professor Mahmud Husain, dean of the University of Karachi, was chairperson. Dr. Eugene Carson Blake, general secretary of the World Council of Churches, gave an address on development. An address was also given on "Religion and Peace" by Shri Jagadguru Gangadhar Rajayogeendra, a Hindu from India. Sessions of the commissions then resumed.

After a tea break, a plenary session was convened to hear a panel on techniques of peace action. Those speaking were Dr. Blake, Dr. Ralph D. Abernathy, president of the Southern Christian Leadership Conference (and a close co-worker of Martin Luther King, Jr.), and the Venerable Thich Thien Minh, vice-president of the executive council of the Unified Buddhist Church of Vietnam. Dr. Abernathy made an "Appeal to the Religious People of the World." Thich Thien Minh discussed "Nonviolent Action from a Vietnamese Buddhist Viewpoint."

On Sunday, October 18, participants met in their respective commissions all day. In the evening, most participants met in simultaneous groups arranged according to their nationality—especially the Japanese, Indians, Americans, and Soviets.

Monday, October 19, was "tour day." Participants visited four religious places: Nishi Honganji temple, Tenrikyo headquarters, Todaiji temple, and Heian Jingu shrine. At the International Conference Hall, some of the rapporteurs and other participants and members of the secretariat spent the day drafting reports. In the evening the conference follow-up committee held an open hearing on whether to continue the work of the evolving organization after the conference adjourned. The steering committee also met.

Tuesday, October 20, began with the final meeting of the participants in their respective commissions with five simultaneous panels on education for peace, communication for peace, legislation for peace, direct action for peace, and interreligious cooperation for peace. The fifth plenary meeting, opened with a Shintoist prayer service, was chaired by Bishop Lord. Archbishop Dom Helder P. Camara of Brazil gave an address on "Religions and the Need for Structural Changes in Today's World." He explained that, "just as in poor countries, the rich classes maintain their wealth at the expense of the misery of millions of fellow men, the rich countries derive their wealth from the underdevelopment and misery of the poor ones." He added that, "in the long run, what they pretend to give back in the form of technical and financial aid is merely a drop of water which, on no account, makes up for the tremendous losses inflicted on the underdeveloped countries." Then Archbishop Camara confessed that "we Christians are among the most responsible for this negative state of affairs," although it would be "easy to continue the illusion of listing the benefits which we, through the Christian message, have brought to men." But if one went "into the heart of the problem, we shall find that 20 percent of humanity holds in their hand 80 percent of the resources of the earth and, for our shame, the privileged 20 percent—who do not succeed in overcoming their own selfishness and in finding their way toward justice and love, which would lead toward peace—are, at least in their origin, Christians." Archbishop Fernandes read a message to the conference from Pope Paul VI.

On the final day, Wednesday, October 21. Dr. Dana Greeley, former president of the Unitarian Universalist Association, chaired the sixth plenary meeting, which began with a Hindu service. Discussion began on the three commission reports. The Vietnamese delegation presented a six-point proposal. The closing plenary meeting was chaired by Archbishop Fernandes, with Mr. William P.

Thompson, a Christian, and Mr. Sunao Miyabara, a Buddhist, as parliamentarians. As at the inaugural meeting, every seat in the balcony was filled with members of local religious groups. The meeting opened with a Zoroastrian prayer service. The debate on commission reports continued and all were adopted, including a separate resolution on South Africa. The only heated debate took place on the Middle East portion of the report of the human rights commission.

Dr. Harold A. Bosley of the conference message committee presented the Kyoto Declaration, which was approved. In the closing segment, the Venerable Thich Nhat Hanh gave a summary and critique of the conference, entitled "Saved by Man." Archbishop Fernandes made some concluding remarks and the Reverend Nenkai Inada bid participants farewell from the Japan host committee. The plenary session concluded with a Sikh prayer service and a reception at the Conference Hall.

The religious enumeration of delegates showed ninety-two Christians, thirty-eight Buddhists, twenty-three Hindus, nineteen Shintoists, and eighteen Muslims. Representatives from other religions included seven Jews, three Baha'is, three Sikhs, two Zoroastrians, one Jain, one Confucian, and ten members of other Japanese and non-Japanese religions. In addition to the 219 delegates and fraternal delegates, there were 106 observers, speakers, guests, members of the secretariat, aides, and spouses. Of these, seventy-five were Japanese. However, there were still other categories of participants: 264 members of the press, 150 Japanese volunteers, 200 daily visitors, eleven honorary sponsors, 100 professional employees, and fifteen secretaries. Thus the grand total of persons involved in the conference was 1,065—not including the several thousand in the balconies during the opening and concluding meetings.

A special effort was made to ensure that religious leaders from socialist states would attend. In the end, they came from the U.S.S.R., Mongolia, Bulgaria, the German Democratic Republic, Poland, and Rumania. None came from China, North Korea, or North Vietnam, although a cable containing warm greetings arrived from the Vietnam United Buddhist Association in Hanoi.

The greatest achievement was that the conference was held— and successfully. Several hundred religious leaders, from a wide range of religions and nationalities, assembled for the express purpose of discussing the relation between religion and peace. The decades-old dream that world religions might help make world peace more possible was beginning to be fulfilled.

A final achievement of the conference was its continuation as an organization. Nobody wanted the experiment to stop. The final plenary session overwhelmingly agreed that the work of the conference should continue and that some of the insights articulated at Kyoto would be transmitted to the U.N. What was initially thought of as a six-day meeting has continued for more than two decades.

The Kyoto Declaration

The World Conference on Religion and Peace represents an historic attempt to bring together men and women of all major religions to discuss the urgent issue of peace. We meet at a crucial time. At this very moment we are faced by cruel and inhuman wars and by racial, social, and economic violence. Man's continued existence on this planet is threatened with nuclear extinction. Never has there been such despair among men. Our deep conviction that the religions of the world have a real and important service to render to the cause of peace has brought us to Kyoto from the four corners of the earth. Bahai, Buddhist, Confucian, Christian, Hindu, Jain, Jew, Muslim, Shintoist, Sikh, Zoroastrian, and others—we have come together in peace out of a common concern for peace.

As we sat down together facing the overriding issues of peace we discovered that the things which unite us are more important than the things which divide us. We found that we share:

• A conviction of the fundamental unity of the human family, and the equality and dignity of all human beings;

• A sense of the sacredness of the individual person and his [and her] conscience;

• A sense of the value of the human community;

• A realization that might is not right; that human power is not self-sufficient and absolute;

• A belief that love, compassion, selflessness, and the force of inner truthfulness and of the spirit have ultimately greater power than hate, enmity, and self-interest;

• A sense of obligation to stand on the side of the poor and the oppressed as against the rich and the oppressors; and

• A profound hope that good will finally prevail.

Because of these convictions that we hold in common, we believe that a special charge has been given to all men and women of religion to be concerned with all their hearts and minds with peace and peacemaking, to be the servants of peace. As men and women

47

of religion we confess in humility and penitence that we have very often betrayed our religious ideals and our commitment to peace. It is not religion that has failed the cause of peace, but religious people. This betrayal of religion can and must be corrected.

In confronting the urgent challenges to peace in the second half of the twentieth century, we were compelled to consider the problems of disarmament, development, and human rights. Clearly peace is imperiled by the ever-quickening race for armaments, the widening gap between the rich and the poor within and among the nations, and by the tragic violation of human rights all over the world. In our consideration of the problems of disarmament we became convinced that peace cannot be found through the stockpiling of weapons. We therefore call for immediate steps toward general disarmament, to include all weapons of destruction—conventional, nuclear, chemical, and bacteriological. We found that the problems of development were aggravated by the fact that the resources spent on research, and on the manufacture and stockpiling of such weapons, consume a grossly inordinate amount of the resources of mankind. We are convinced that these resources are urgently needed instead to combat the injustices that make for war and other forms of social violence. Any society in which one out of every four children dies is in a state of war. While development of itself may not bring peace, there can be no lasting peace without it. Therefore we pledge our support to the effort of the United Nations to make the 1970s a decade of development for all mankind.

The social convulsions clearly evident in the world today demonstrate the connection between peace and the recognition, promotion, and protection of human rights. Racial discrimination, the repression of ethnic and religious minorities, the torturing of political and other prisoners, legalized and de facto denial of political freedom and equality of opportunity, the denial of equal rights of women, any form of colonialist oppression—all such violations of human rights are responsible for the escalation of violence that is debasing human civilization.

While we of this Conference speak for ourselves as persons brought together from many religions by our deep concern for peace, we try also to speak for the vast majority of the human family who are powerless and whose voice is seldom heard—the poor, the exploited, the refugees, and all who are homeless and whose lives, fields, and freedoms have been devastated by wars. We speak to our religions, the ecumenical councils and all interfaith efforts for peace, to the nations, beginning with our own, to the United Nations, and to men and women outside established religions who are concerned about human welfare.

To one and all, beginning with ourselves, we say that the point of departure for any serious effort in human enterprise—educational, cultural, scientific, social, and religious—is the solemn acceptance of the fact that men and all their works are now united in one destiny. We live or die together in the struggle for peace. We cannot honestly denounce war and the things that make for war unless our personal lives are informed by peace and we are prepared to make the necessary sacrifice for it. We must do all in our power to educate public opinion and awaken public conscience to take a firm stand against war and the illusory hope of peace through military victory. We are convinced that religions, in spite of historic differences, must now seek to unite all men in those endeavors which make for true peace. We believe that we have a duty transcending sectarian limits to cooperate with those outside the historic religions who share our desire for peace.

We pledge ourselves to warn the nations whose citizens we are that the effort to achieve and maintain military power is the road to disaster. It creates a climate of fear and mistrust; it demands resources needed for the meeting of the needs of health, housing, and welfare; it fosters the escalation of the arms race that now threatens man's life on earth; it sharpens differences among nations into military and economic blocs; it regards peace as an armed truce or a balance of terror; it dismisses as utopian a truly universal concern for the welfare of all mankind. To all this we say "No!"

We desire to convey our concern for peace to the United Nations. The achievement and maintenance of peace requires not only a recognition of the existence of the United Nations, but, even more, support for and implementation of its decisions. We urge universal membership in the United Nations, a more just sharing of power and responsibility in its procedures. We urge the member nations to accept its leadership in resolving issues that have led or may lead to conflicts.

It is our hope that this Conference will help us see and accept our responsibility as men and women of religious faith for the achievement of true and lasting peace.

PART ONE 1916-1941

YOUNG NATURALIST

THE ROCHESTER YEARS

"One touch of nature makes the whole world kin."
—Shakespeare

Rochester, New York—city of industry, invention, and independent political thought—was home to Homer, his parents, and his immigrant grandparents. For nearly three-quarters of a century, the Jack family struggled, advanced, and eventually thrived in this pleasant upstate city on Lake Ontario. Though he left his native city in 1940 and seldom returned, Rochester's natural beauty, sense of civic responsibility, and multicultural environment left its mark on Homer's outlook and development.

Photograph: Homer with pet rabbits, early 1920s

5 ROCHESTER
(1916-1933)

GROWING UP IN THE FLOWER CITY

Perspective 1916: The World War took a great toll in Europe. President Woodrow Wilson won reelection on a platform including, "He kept us out of war." Albert Einstein announced his general theory of relativity. Rabindranath Tagore won the Nobel Prize in Literature. Frank Lloyd Wright completed the Imperial Hotel in Tokyo. News was broadcast by radio for the first time. Twenty-two U.S. states voted for prohibition. The first birth control clinic in the U.S. was opened by Margaret Sanger. The Saturday Evening Post *bought its first illustration by Norman Rockwell. The first mechanical refrigerator was marketed. Popular songs in the U.S.A. included "Roses of Picardy" and "La Cucaracha."*

Born in 1916, I was in some ways an average American boy, growing up in the 1920s, and graduating from high school in the Depression year of 1933. In other ways, I may have been different. My parents were involved with American socialism and I was an only child. Also Rochester was perhaps not the average American city. It was better.

My mother and father were fascinating people, even to many besides myself, and they were supportive, often doting, parents. They early encouraged my interest in nature which was also their interest. With precocious enthusiasm, I pursued this hobby. My formal education through high school was undistinguished, except once toward the end of primary school, I took from school what I felt useful. I had friends, but still was something of a loner. In the background were my mother's and father's families in a city both conservative and tolerant.

53

Kodak and Xerox City

I was born—on May 19—actually not in Rochester, but in Greece—a suburb of Rochester, in a private clinic. My parents were born in Rochester and lived their entire life there. Rochester was early a flour milling town, because of water power from the falls of the Genesee River and hence "The Flour City." When milling went West, the city became known as "The Flower City." Actually, Rochester today is known the world over as the birthplace of two worldwide products, Kodak—when I grew up—and today Xerox. Perhaps Rochester should be called the Kodak and Xerox City, but of course it is the birthplace of much more.

When I was born, my parents' small home was at 12 Aldern Place. I was their only child. At the time, my father—Alexander, a commercial artist—was thirty-eight. My mother—Cecelia, although everybody called her Sis—was thirty. In a manuscript written in 1933, I recalled my parents using the usual words to describe me: "a bouncy, blue-eyed, blond baby boy." (I soon outgrew my blue eyes and my blond hair.) Photos show me lying on my stomach on the kitchen table.

I have only a few early memories of our first home which, incidentally, is still standing. My father painted the kitchen yellow, and I still remember drippings of yellow paint all over the place, including kitchen utensils, years after. Also my mother once tried to dry some plums in the oven to make prunes. The pungent smell of burnt plums continues in my mind to this day. I early helped my father with the small garden. When I was asked what I would like to be when I grew up, my answer was, "Joe, a farmer!" My father and I early called each other, for some reason, "Joe." The name stuck until he died.

We had no dogs or cats then—never a cat—but for awhile we did have two huge rabbits. They were housed in a wooden shed, which we called a Kendrick, since that was the first name of a family friend, Professor Kendrick P. Shedd! In that period a large barn-like complex visible from our house went up in flames at night. My parents awoke me to watch. It was a horrifying sight for a half-awake youngster. This was the era just before electric refrigerators. I remember well the ice-man coming to the house in a horse-drawn vehicle. We placed a four-sided card in the front window: 25, 50, 75, or 100 pounds.

We lived not far from Edgerton Park with a small zoo. It acquired a baby elephant. My parents always encouraged me to eat apples, and I had one in the pocket of my sheepskin coat the day Sally arrived at the zoo. I gave her my apple and my picture appeared in a Rochester newspaper—for the first time. Also my parents would take me nearby to the site of the old Erie Canal which no longer was used for traffic after the Barge Canal was built. The Erie contained small ponds with fat, squirming tadpoles, and I collected these polywogs in a jar for our aquarium at home.

290 Crosman Terrace

During the economic boom of the mid-1920s, my parents decided to build a house and sell our home on Aldern Place. My father wanted to be as close to nature as possible within the confines of Rochester. We bought a lot on the new extension of Crosman Terrace, with the backyard bordering on Pinnacle Hill. An architect was hired, and probably the original design was fairly common for the time. My father insisted on his imprint: some stone outside as well as inside, a special stone fireplace. The greatest innovation was rough plaster walls inside. To watch the house at 290 Crosman Terrace being built, we drove across the city sometimes every evening. I can still smell the cut lumber and the wet plaster.

My father was especially concerned about the backyard, working to preserve and utilize the steep hill on our lot up Pinnacle Hill. Most of the hill itself had recently been a Catholic cemetery, although shortly before our house was completed, the graves overrun by bushes were removed. The whole wooded hill was something of a young boy's—and lovers'—paradise. I made a tree house with two boys living next to us: Ellis and Selden Ring. My father took care that the slice of the hill on our property would be as natural as possible. We lugged stones seemingly for years in our Ford, from far-away abandoned country fences. My father replanted many wild flowers, including a few yellow lady-slippers. For annuals, we went at five o'clock on Saturday mornings in early spring to the wholesale market near the New York Central tracks where we bought flats of cosmos, pinks, and pansies.

In our new home, at the age of ten, I promptly set up a series of childhood businesses: companies mostly of my imagination, but each with a business card which I printed on the foot press my father purchased for me. The Jackson Stamp Company grew out of the urging of my father to collect stamps as he, intermittently, had done. The Jackson Travel Company consisted mostly of travel brochures from travel agencies downtown. I still remember the colored brochures of Bermuda. (That is one place I have yet to visit.) There was, for real, the Jackson Printing Company in our basement, where I printed the namecards from real type—decades before desktop publishing.

In this period, not as much for money as to keep up with some of my schoolmates, I became a door-to-door salesman. For awhile it was magazines: *Literary Digest, Colliers,* and *Saturday Evening Post.* We received what seemed then big prizes for every new subscription. I never had a newspaper route, perhaps because my father sold newspapers for many years as a young boy and probably did not want his son to duplicate his experiences, even in the then-suburbs. Also for awhile I did sell, house to house, rolls of toilet paper! I forgot why, but that was apparently what several of my friends did in our neighborhood at the time.

One of my hobbies—when I was ten years old and which did not last long—was to collect autographs of well-known people. I would write, and in those days I often would receive a reply, sometimes with a photograph as well as the autograph. These still repose in my papers: signed photos of Harold Lloyd, Charles Chaplin, and Mary Pickford. There are also letters from state governors and federal cabinet members and also from pianist Ignace Paderewski, socialist Eugene V. Debs, Vice-President Charles Dawes, First Lady Grace Coolidge, and song writer Irving Berlin. The nicest came from Helen Keller, the blind leader, who precisely printed: "Peace hath higher tests of manhood than ever battle knew."

Five or six houses up the street lived a widow, Lillian Renckert, and her three daughters. Since I was an only child, these girls, with two cousins, served as sisters. I went to the Renckert home often. I learned tennis from Ijain, slightly older than myself, and at five on a spring morning she would throw gravel on my upper bedroom screen. I would dress quickly and we would walk 15 minutes to Cobbs Hill for several sets of tennis on the empty courts. We would return home in time for school. Also I explored Pinnacle Hill, with bones occasionally uncovered in the overgrown, abandoned, open grave sites. I knew the location of the first spring flowers, especially the rare trailing arbutus. I also went to Cobbs Hill to skate on the wide waters of the old Erie Canal. I remember, when I must have been all of ten years old, a striking girl, my age, with a new red leather jacket. I did not have the courage to talk to her even once, let alone skate with her. But how I admired her—from afar!

Primary School

My primary school days were uneventful. I began kindergarten at School No. 34, a mile or so from our first home. I cried when my mother dragged me to kindergarten that first day, but soon I was building castles with blocks. After we moved to Crosman Terrace, School No. 35 was just down the steep hill on Laburnum Crescent. Going down to school was much more fun—and fast—for my nine-year-old legs than coming home. I remember the frequently waxed school floors—the clean smell—but more the tiny store opposite on Field Street. There I bought wondrous things for one penny each: candy, gum, picture cards, and stickers. Alas, the store has disappeared and the two-storied school building has been replaced.

It was at No. 35 School that I learned about American Indians. The Rochester Savings Bank not only made us little capitalists—there was time for weekly savings deposits right in the classroom to teach each of us how to save—but it issued all kinds of booklets on early Rochester and the Seneca Indians. We learned much about those indigenous peoples and made replicas of their villages. At home my father helped me make miniature log cabins, log houses, and wigwams. He loved such work, and I closely watched. The settlement of early Rochester was painstakingly described, the city having been founded about a century before I was born. Later, a wealthy friend of my father, printer Charles Bluntaugh, showed us his remarkable collection of first editions of that curious volume, *Mary Jemison: White Woman of the Genesee*.

In my last year in grammar school I was named valedictorian—"standard bearer." This was the only academic honor I ever received—never as Phi Beta Kappa. Being standard bearer was a mixed blessing, since I had to put up the American flag every morning on the outside flagpole. My opposite was Betty Bullen, a physician's daughter living just down Crosman Terrace. For being standard bearer, my parents gave me my first wristwatch and a dog. I loved Rexie, a brown shepherd. In my urban living, I never have had as many dogs—or cats—as I would have liked.

Wider Horizons

My parents purchased our first auto around 1922. This made possible Easter vacation and summer trips. They wanted me to see "the world." They early took me to Canada—just beyond nearby Niagara Falls, and then to the Adirondack Mountains, Boston, New York City, and Washington. Twice my parents took with us girls my age—Helen Renckert, and Ruth Schlosberg, who lived on Laburnum Crescent. They shared the experience and kept me company, in lieu of a sister.

In the Adirondacks we made the two-day climb to the top of Mt. Marcy, the highest mountain east of the Mississippi River. My father and a brother and a friend climbed Marcy some twenty-five or thirty years earlier, walking all the way from Rochester. This time my Uncle Emanuel and his two children, David and Esther, came along. It was a family project always remembered later. In Boston, we made the usual tourist visits, but cut short our trip when there were predictions of violence. It was the week of August 1927 and Sacco and Vanzetti were executed on the twenty-third for alleged murder during a robbery, but many felt then—and to this day—that they were framed.

We visited New York several times, staying usually with my Aunt Celia and Uncle Emil, and cousins Robert and Frances, in Brooklyn. We went also to Washington at cherry blossom time. I was impressed that my father was a personal friend of our congressman, Meyer Jacobstein. They sold newspapers together as boys. The Congressman gave us choice seats to the Congress and tickets to visit the White House. These several trips I still remember: garnet mines in the mountains, the poets' homes in New England, Chinatown in New York, and first seeing the Lincoln Memorial.

During my youth, my parents bought a modest summer cottage at 47 Braddock Street at Charlotte, one block from Lake Ontario and ten miles north of Rochester. We stayed there for several summers. One windy night on the beach I saw the police recover the body of a drowned person. I have never forgotten. Another time I was bitten by the dog of a neighbor—the head of Fanny Farmer's Candies, then a Rochester concern. Mostly I remember watching the coal ferry going from Charlotte toward Canada. Another country! Very often I looked out on the lake, hoping that the sky might part and I might actually be able to see a foreign country.

Cultural Advantages

Rochester has always been known to possess more cultural advantages than most American cities of its size. I was exposed to some. I remember, as a child, going to the new Eastman Theater for Saturday morning movies and to Saturday afternoon plays for children. Later, I stood in line for gallery tickets to see Broadway plays at the Lyceum Theatre, next to the Seneca Hotel. In this period the University of Rochester moved to its new campus on the Genesee River. We inspected the campus before it opened and marvelled at the spacious Rush Rhees Library.

My father took me, fairly regularly, to the Rochester City Club luncheons in the old Powers Hotel on Saturday noons. A wide variety of nationally known persons spoke. I was one of the few youngsters present. I interviewed poet Carl Sandburg after his speech for my high school paper. Sports are part of culture. My father took me to the new stadium of the newly-named Rochester Red Wings, in the days of Rip Collins, before he went to the major league. We did not go to baseball games often, but enough so that baseball to this day remains my favorite spectator sport. I remember listening to the World Series one autumn in our car radio as we were going east of Rochester to buy a gallon of apple cider. (To this day, the World Series means cider-time.) Occasionally I went with friends to the professional basketball games in the East Main Street Armory. My first suit with long pants I wore to one of those games. Rochester was to my unfolding consciousness both a conservative and a radicalizing experience. I early learned of the Establishment: not only Eastman Kodak, but the several large banks, the prominent civic leaders, and its conservative influences. Much later, I got to know Frank E. Gannett, the publisher who tried to run for the U.S. Presidency on the Republican ticket. His company owned both Rochester newspapers and much later established *U.S.A. Today.*

Mostly, I was exposed to the small but for me decisive counter-culture. Rochester was always home to unusual social reformers. During the Civil War it was home of the noted anti-slavery leader, Frederick Douglass (1818-1895), born a slave. I knew this, but I did not know a single black during all my boyhood in Rochester. We did learn to be concerned about Indians, if not blacks, but I did not know a single Indian either. Most had long left the Genesee Valley.

Rochester was also the longtime home, if not birthplace, of Susan B. Anthony (1820-1906). My father knew Miss Anthony and some of her close friends. She was a household word, and my mother was an early and active suffragist. Indeed, one of Miss Anthony's closest companions, Gertrude Blackall, was very much a friend of our family. In later life she kept moving from one furnished room to another, and my father always dutifully helped move her belong-ings, mostly papers, with our auto. Miss Blackall died in the 1930s.

Another radical Rochesterian (but whose home was curiously paid for by John D. Rockefeller) was Walter Rauschenbusch (1861-1918). A Baptist, like Rockefeller, he was a teacher at the Rochester Theological Seminary. My father knew Rauschenbusch and my parents often talked about this leader of the Social Gospel Movement in America who was also a socialist.

Monroe High School

I entered Monroe High School, a six-year combination of junior and senior high, in the autumn of 1928. Monroe was about a half-hour walk from our Crosman Terrace home. Often my father took me to school by auto on his way to work. Usually I walked home, often meandering for an hour or more down Monroe Avenue, passing favorite stores and the Monroe Public Library. Few of our friends had two family autos in those days and, in any case, my mother never drove. In this period, and earlier, my parents tried to interest me in music. They were not heavy-handed, so I dutifully went along, if hardly enthusiastic. I first studied violin at the age of seven, in class and then with a private teacher, but without spectacular success. Also my parents urged me, and again I did not resist, to take private voice lessons. I hardly reached any recital level. In junior high I switched from violin to bass violin and then to tuba. Thus I soon was able to join the school orchestra and band. My chief memory, besides losing lots of saliva at tuba, was being close to the stage for school assemblies and plays. I never touched string or brass instruments after I reached university.

Somehow my musical experiences in high school did not prepare me to be even modestly interested in music as a listener. I never—to this day—collected records or tapes and have too seldom gone to concerts or operas. I rather like jazz and other modern music, but once removed. Music has never been a hobby; something happened to my relationship to music in those high school days. My ignorance of music, my lack of understanding and appreciation of it, is one of the failings of my life.

Girls/Women

My two female cousins living in Rochester—Doris and Eunice—became also my sisters, together with the three Renckert girls living down the street. While living at our summer place near Lake Ontario, some of my boyfriends and I took two girls our age far into the fields to "pick strawberries." I had just read *What Every Boy Should Know*. In the strawberry fields we discovered our differences, but scarcely more! Some years before acquiring a driver's license, I took my cousin Doris in our auto for a long ride, absenting ourselves from a family dinner. We were severely reprimanded when we returned.

Also at the Allegany School of Natural History, when I was age fourteen, I first "went out" with a woman. We rode in the rumble seat several times, going to Bradford, Pennsylvania—to buy boxes of apricots! We also got soaked several times on field trips. She was a student at Bryn Mawr College, almost five years my senior. Nothing came from our encounter; indeed, both of us knew more about the mating habits of red newts as would-be biologists.

Early Writing

Neither my father nor mother was a writer, yet I seemed to like to write, early on. Age thirteen, I devoted my summer to learn typing and stenography at a commercial business school. I have been a fast typist ever since, but quickly forgot shorthand from disuse. In high school, I wrote a column, "Seriously Speaking," in the school newspaper, *Monroe Life*. I was editor of the school literary magazine, *Kaleidoscope*. At that period I was a better magazine editor than an essayist; the two examples of my magazine writing which were printed are hardly timeless. One had to do with how the giraffe got a long neck.

Also in high school, I was invited to join the Pencil Pushers Club of aspiring writers like myself. We met once or twice a month, on Friday evenings at one or another student's homes, to read our writings, but equally for socializing. I remember walking around Cobbs Hill reservoir after Pencil Pushers on many a Friday night. This was the most important extracurricular activity during my last two years at high school. My future wife, Esther Williams, attended regularly. Some of the friends I met there became life-long, such as

Joseph Delibert and Leon Hollerman. Joe was a year ahead of me and studied engineering at Cornell where I later saw him occasionally. He went to work all his life for Babcock and Wilcox, a manufacturer of boilers. I would later often meet him for lunch at the Cornell Club of New York. Leon became a professor of economics in California and an expert on the Japanese economy. Once we saw each other in Tokyo.

Occasionally I would go with less literary students. This was the era of Prohibition. My parents were teetotalers. In part perhaps to separate myself from them, I went occasionally with John Adler and Phil Bettette to illegal places—speakeasies—to buy beer. I never told my parents, but in time they must have suspected.

In this period, my interest in world affairs accelerated. I joined Agora, the school debating club. I defended the proposition: "The U.S. should recognize the present Soviet Government of Russia." I began my side of the debate by suggesting that "I am not here as a paid agent of the Soviet Government; I am not here as a propagandist of communism; I am here as an earnest and sincere student of the truth." Then I put the onus directly on my country:

"The blame for the origin of the present ill-feeling between the governments lies entirely with America; the government of Russia fulfills the requirements for recognition." After making numerous debating points, I declared that U.S. recognition "might temper the spirit of rigid dictatorship and might gradually permit a more democratic form or spirit to prevail." I was almost seventeen years old when I participated in this debate. Yet was I wrong in urging recognition?

Now, almost sixty years later, when "Russia" has become Russia again, I still believe it has been advantageous to America and to world peace that we recognized the Soviet Union when we did— only a few months after that debate. However, I never gave myself any credit for President Roosevelt's decision!

Symbols are often as important as facts. During my high school years I somehow acquired the reputation of being radical. Perhaps it was the red corduroy pants I occasionally wore or even my all out support for socialist Norman Thomas. When the 1933 school yearbook, *Monrolog*, appeared just before graduation, the doggerel next to my photograph read:

Comrades all (alas, alack!)
Are Lenin, Marx, and Homer Jack.

During my last year in high school, the 1932 presidential campaign was in full swing. Roosevelt was challenging President Hoover, but I was unabashedly for Norman Thomas. One night we put large posters of Thomas' picture on the front of Monroe High. However, I took little part in high school politics. In the last year there, I began to read the *Nation* and the *Saturday Review* regularly. In that last year of high school, I wrote a brief manuscript entitled, "16 Full Years: An Autobiography." On the title page I added: "This is a manuscript which has not been reread by the author, but which has just been written—and let written." I have learned better since, yet that fragment is very revealing of my mood as I finished high school in 1933: "But life is so futile, so paradoxical, so meaningless! The explanation of this would go into what I have received from sixteen full years. But this would require a much different atmosphere and disposition than I am in, at present."

A Young Naturalist

As long as I can remember, my parents were members of the Burroughs-Audubon Nature Club, a Rochester organization with a tenuous relation to the National Audubon Society. Almost every other Friday evening my parents attended its lectures, often with slides, at the Rochester Museum. This was the real church for my family and for any—at the time—premature conservationists.

On Saturday afternoons, except in deep winter, there were also Burroughs-Audubon nature hikes. Our leaders included Milton Baxter, a telephone engineer turned botanist, and Fred Boughton, a bearded bachelor and mushroom expert. Bergen Swamp was one favorite, and the rattlesnakes we occasionally cornered there were more afraid of us than we were of them! On Saturday, May 21, 1927, just before one Audubon hike, we heard on the radio that Lucky Lindy had just landed in France. (Some months later I went with my father to the Rochester Airport where we saw Lindbergh on his nation-wide, victorious, barnstorming tour.)

The Burroughs-Audubon Nature Club whetted my appetite for nature study, more than for "pure" science. Initially, I wanted to become a geologist and go to Yale. In high school, I was president of the Science Club. The Wards Natural Science Establishment was located in Rochester and this was a source for geological and biological teaching materials. Once Wards had a giant fire and friends on the staff let me pick over their smoke-damaged minerals. My father often took me on fossil-collecting expeditions. Trilobites were my favorites, at Nine-Mile Creek south of Buffalo and at an outcrop south of Syracuse. An alcove off the bedroom of our new Crosman Terrace home was reserved for my nature collections, especially geological.

Burroughs-Audubon was a direct route to my attending, for two summers, the Allegany School of Natural History, some 150 miles south of Rochester, in Allegany State Park. This was a teacher-training summer school of the University of Buffalo, affiliated with the Buffalo Museum. Somehow I was admitted in 1930, despite being the only high school student enrolled. I studied botany, entomology, and geology. I eagerly returned for a second summer where I made a survey of the fungi of the area. I made many friends among the students and faculty. Later, my botany teacher, Dr. Robert B. Gordon of Ohio State University, became director, succeeding Dr. Robert Coker of the University of North Carolina. Dr. Gordon wrote, "You were the only high school student in the class, but your work in field botany would have been credible to any college boy."

Allegany led me to the University of Michigan Biological Station near Cheboygan. The first summer there I was again the only high school student in the class. I attended for three summers, the last in 1934 when I did some research in plant ecology. This led to my giving a paper to a meeting under the auspices of the American Association for the Advancement of Science (AAAS). My father accompanied me to their annual meeting in December 1934 when I delivered the paper before a joint meeting of the Botanical Society of America and the Ecological Society of America. My eight minutes on the program was entitled "Precipitation Retention" and dealt with the water absorbed by the common lichen, reindeer moss. Much more noticed was the Gibbs Lecture the day after mine when Albert Einstein discussed "An Elementary Proof of the Theorem Concerning the Equivalence of Mass and Energy." He was followed around by journalists since this may have been Einstein's first use of English at a large scientific gathering. It is said that an advertisement appeared in the personal columns of a Pittsburgh newspaper: "Albert, I know you can do it. Frau Einstein." As for my own paper, I "did it" and this was reflected in one sentence in the magazine, *Science*, for February 1, 1935, and a slightly longer article in *Ecology*. My first published work appeared in *Aquarium News*, a Rochester publication. In an essay "A Biologist's Pond-ering," I wrote, "Nature has been in the aquarium business long before glass—nay, even man—was invented!"

6 ROCHESTER
(1916-1933)

MY PARENTS AND HERITAGE

My Father

My father, Alexander—the eldest of nine brothers and sisters: Elizabeth (Rappl), Emma (Bloom), Sarah (Higbee), Louis, Emanuel, Celia (Berman), Frances (LaBarr), and Leo—was born on April 25, 1878, in Rochester, New York. His father, Gustave, a glazier, was born in 1843 in Austria and came to the United States and Rochester in 1873—just ten years after Abraham Lincoln issued the Emancipation Proclamation freeing the slaves. His mother, Fanny, was born in 1854 in Germany. She also came to Rochester in 1873 and soon married his father.

My first complete recollection of my father goes back to our home on Aldern Place. My father was short, prematurely gray. He was a foot or more shorter than my mother, but he was tall to me, then, as he would help me "take care of the yard"—rake the sand pile, clean out the rabbit pen, and tidy up the refuse from the three great lombardy poplars in front of our house. We worked in the yard together; and his purpose was much more to cultivate me and give me an early introduction to nature than beautify the grounds. Poking around that small yard, I gathered my first distinct picture of Alex—white-thatched, humorous, and with his black four-in-hand tie. As an artist, Alex wore this hand-tied, flowing, black bow tie all his life.

My father's family—growing to thirteen children, nine of

whom survived—had a difficult time. Being the oldest boy, my father had to find work, and by the time he was eight, he left public school and spent most of his time selling newspapers in Rochester. His was a downtown route, but he would sell papers, too, on the horse-drawn streetcars, as they would slowly rise up the Main Street hill.

It was during these long, newspaperboy days that my father first met up with Unitarianism. Down Cortland Street, almost to Court, there was the Boys' Evening Home supported by the Unitarian Church. Alex went there, as did his paper-selling friends. There they found friendship, a library, and classes, under the genial supervision of Dr. William Channing Gannett, minister of the Unitarian Society of Rochester and a famous hymn writer. There my father discovered his talent for drawing. He attended one of these art classes and soon took home drawings of flowers and figures. The Boys's Evening Home, especially during the winters when cold winds blew in from the lake, became competition for his home of three brothers and five sisters. But Alex took home most of his earnings from the papers and then would go from Wait Street, across Main to Courtland and classes at the Boys' Evening Home.

Soon Alex graduated from being a carrier to working in the circulation department of the newspaper. It was not a desk job, but involved bundling the papers for the out-of-town subscribers. (Later, every time in college I received a package from home, there would be the expert packaging and tying Alex learned during his *Union-Advertiser* days.) As he rose slowly in the newspaper world, so he rose with his art, too. Soon he became an instructor in the Boys' Evening Home and then, for awhile, teacher in the State Industrial School for Boys up in Edgarton Park. Then one day his newspaper work and his art merged, and he became a cartoonist for the newspaper. As a sports cartoonist, afternoons in spring and summer would find him up in the press box of the old ball park. For it was a cartoon a day for him during the whole baseball season.

However, eventually the publisher began dictating just what political sides my father should take in his other cartoons. One day my father refused to draw a cartoon making fun of the efforts to curtail drinking—the devastating social effects of which he must have seen close up from his life on the streets. On principle, my father resigned. He was married by now and couldn't live on pure art. Still, he had made a good many friends around town and decided to go into the commercial art business for himself.

He acquired a partner, Ed Weaden, and established the Lincoln

Photo Engraving Company—that was about the time I was born. The office was above the bus depot in the Sullivan Building on South Avenue, opposite what is now the Rochester Public Library. Some afternoons, after high school, I would walk through the new Sears Roebuck store and go to the center of Rochester to my father's office. I loved his huge table, with piles of drawings and photographs. He had a small drawing board near the window. Back in other rooms, Ed did the photo-engraving, and the place was covered with so-called dragon's blood, a fine reddish powder. I watched the photography and the etching, in strong-smelling acid, and even then I realized that this was no vocation for me. Now, of course, photo-engraving is ancient history, supplanted by new scanning and printing techniques.

Occasionally my father would ask me to deliver a package, a half-tone or drawing, to some of his customers: B. Forman, National Clothing, Edward's, or McCurdy's. On my way back to his office, I would occasionally stop at the White Tower. I can still smell, and taste, those wonderful, five-cent hamburgers. Cost-wise, it was more than half a century ago.

My father had several hobbies or small businesses. When radio became popular, around 1920, and many Americans built their own crystal sets, my father collaborated with a friend to make a wall chart of radio symbols. He tried to sell this orange chart by mail order. Hundreds were around our house, but I doubt if many were sold. Also he started another venture—Japanese Art Prints. He made a limited edition of three Japanese floral prints on rice paper. The set depicting plum blossoms, hydrangeas, and wisteria sold for 50 cents postpaid! Again, hundreds were stored all over our home. It was more of a hobby than a business. My father also intermittently collected stamps. He encouraged me and soon I had my own album. Yet it was not until the 1970s that I became a serious stamp collector, beginning with U.N. issues. My father was a chess player and early he taught me. One summer when I was in Michigan, we played chess by mail, and he designed a postcard with a chess board imprinted.

This description of my father does not do justice to his personality. He gave a touch of ingenuity, uniqueness, art, beauty, and humor to everybody and everything he touched. These attributes have skipped me entirely, if not perhaps others in my generation.

My mother was the family letter-writer. She wrote often—and distinctly. I almost never received a letter from my father. However, in the archives I found one dated August 31, 1941. My parents had just returned from a short trip to New York, staying with his sister, Ceila. He wrote: "We sure enjoyed our trip to New York City. The folks tried to please us in every way and succeeded." I had just started studies at Meadville Theological School and earlier wrote that I would find a part-time job. (I became an early-morning janitor in the University of Chicago administration building, cleaning the offices of the executive staff, including that of President Robert M. Hutchins.) My father continued in that letter: "It is pleasing to us that Homer will seek a boss [a job] during his vacations so he too can truly talk about the working class and incidentally collect a little fodder." (As a matter of fact, this was only the third time I ever tried to collect "fodder"—begin to pay my own way while in undergraduate and graduate schooling.)

This letter from my father was written after Hitler had taken over the Low Countries, but several months before Pearl Harbor. My father observed: "The Russians are not such pushovers as the other countries were and before they (the Germans) know it they will die of too many victories like that brave warrior who yelled at his captain, 'I caught an enemy.' When the captain yelled back, 'Bring him in,' the brave warrior yelled back, 'He won't let me.'"

My father and mother were Jewish by birth. The family name was Jacubowitz, but was Americanized in the early 1920s to Jack. My father and mother were not religious. Indeed, socialism was their religion. They never attended, or joined, a synagogue. They believed in "assimilation," which at the time—the end of the nineteenth century—was a popular method for Jews both in Europe and America to deal with persistent anti-Semitism. My parents approved my becoming, toward the end of my father's life, a Unitarian clergyman. Shortly after entering theological school, I sent my father the popular pamphlet, *Are You A Unitarian Without Knowing It?* He wrote, "After reading it we came to the conclusion that even a deep red radical could subscribe to it without calling it spiritual propaganda."

My Mother

My mother, Cecelia Davis, was born on February 2, 1886, in Rochester, New York. Her grandparents, Hirsch and Temer (or Theresa) David, came from Latvia. They lived in the town of Vindau, outside Riga. (At various times in history, Latvia was ruled by Russia, Sweden, Finland, and other conquerors.) Hirsch David was a distiller, perhaps of vodka. They had five sons and three daughters, all born in Vindau. The second son was Morris, my mother's father. Two of the David sons went from Vindau to Odessa to study distilling, but soon left by ship for America. An uncle lived in New York, but for some reason they went on to Rochester. The Davids spoke German, although in school they learned Russian.

Soon the parents and the six other siblings, including my grandfather, went to Rochester where they Americanized their name to Davis. In Rochester, Morris met Christiana (or Dina or Tina) Rubens, who also was born in Latvia. They married, probably in the early 1880s, and had five children: Libby (Schuler), Cecelia (Jack), Jennie (Leve), Rose (Berger), and Harry. Morris was a cigar maker; one brand was MSD, his initials! My grandmother marched with the bloomer girls and rarely stayed home to cook. My great-aunt Sarah, Morris' sister, was also socially active. Her best friend was Emma Goldman, the anarchist and women's rights leader who had emigrated from Lithuania because of anti-Semitism and settled in Rochester. She met her husband, Harry Henschel, at Emma's wedding.

My mother, Cecelia—many called her Sis—was tall and, from old photographs, beautiful. She had minimal formal schooling and soon worked as a bookkeeper at McCurdy's department store. She became involved in the socialist movement where she met my father. I was their only child.

My mother was a homemaker during her married life. She never had an outside job, but kept the books for my father's small partnership, the Lincoln Photo Engraving Company. She was active in parent-teacher's affairs, an officer of the Burroughs-Audubon Nature Club, and in feminist and peace activities.

My parents had their own ideas about public (and private) health. They were, for long periods, vegetarians. Also they distrusted most physicians. They did not believe in inoculations and found a physician in Syracuse who gave me a false vaccination certificate. My parents were vociferous non-smokers and teetotalers. However, my mother made the best home-made root beer. She would make ten tall bottles at a time, put them in our dark cellar for a period, and this process resulted in the drink having almost an alcoholic kick.

The Era of Debs

I was born into the era of Eugene V. Debs. Both of my parents during the first two decades of the twentieth century were ardent socialists. Debs was their leader and the beloved hero of most socialists in the U.S.A. He was a charismatic figure and "rank-and-file" socialists actively identified themselves with the "Abe Lincoln of Labor." In the first decade of my life—1916 to 1925—Debs was more of a public figure than any other in our Rochester household during my most impressionable years.

Eugene V. Debs was born in Terre Haute, Indiana, in November 1855. His parents were Alsatians who came to America in the early 1850s. (Just a century later I heard Albert Schweitzer say—and it is written in his biographies—that he was a cousin of Debs' mother. Indeed, Jean-Paul Sartre was also a cousin. Schweitzer apparently approved Debs more than Sartre, for Schweitzer commented: "Yes, Sartre and I were cousins, but neither one of us admits [it].")

Debs left school early and worked on the railroads. He soon became a union official. He was imprisoned for breaking a federal injunction in the Pullman strike of 1895, despite having Clarence Darrow as his lawyer. In prison for six months, he began reading Karl Marx and other socialist literature. He helped found the Socialist Party of America just after the turn of the century. Debs ran for U.S. president five times, first in 1900. His last attempt was in 1920 when he received almost one million votes despite being in prison under the Espionage Act for criticizing World War I. He died in 1926.

Debs was primarily a public speaker and represented the Socialist Party both to its members and the American public. He exuded warmth and integrity to my parents and to many non-socialists. He was America's most beloved radical hero—even today. Debs occasionally visited Rochester on his incessant lecture tours. For example, during his election campaign in October 1908, in the "Red Special" barnstorming train, he visited Rochester. I am sure my parents attended—eight years before I was born. Also in September 1918, Debs was in Rochester, opposing the war and demanding that Americans already in prison for opposing the war be released.

What kind of socialist was Debs—and therefore my parents? Debs strongly opposed World War I and that is why he was in prison in 1920-21, although he was tried seven months after the war ended. My parents also opposed that war. I was less than one year old when the U.S. went to war in 1917 and thus grew up in that anti-war environment. My parents had several socialist friends in Rochester who were persecuted during that war. Also I have vague memories that my father was economically hurt for being a socialist, but I retain no details.

Debs was also clear about the communist schism within the Socialist Party. While he helped establish the Industrial Workers of the World (IWW or Wobblies), he belatedly realized their anarchistic and violent character and repudiated them. The American communists, who founded their own party several years after the Russian Revolution, hoped that Debs might join. Yet Debs in Atlanta jail, when some visitors told of a recent visit to Russia, agreed that it was not a workers' paradise. (Debs never visited Soviet Russia or other parts of Europe.) In 1922, Debs declared, "The Communist Party has no place in America." Debs was frequently, in that period, heckled at meetings by communists. Also he sent a cable to Lenin protesting any execution of social revolutionaries on trial in Moscow. My parents probably followed Debs in not welcoming the Communist Party, but like many American socialists they probably welcomed the birth of Soviet Russia and watched sympathetically from afar.

In addition to opposing war and violence (and, toward the end of his life, communism), Debs strongly supported racial justice. He did not hesitate to attack Booker T. Washington "backed by the plutocrats," but he increasingly became militant, remarking: "It makes all the difference whether God Almighty gave you a white skin or a black one." Again, my parents agreed with Debs and went out of their way to oppose bigotry.

Debs and the Socialist Party never could decide whether to modify American capitalism or—nonviolently—overthrow it. The relatively slender constituency was too divided for Debs and other leaders to make a clear decision. However, Debs in his popular rhetoric was an agitator. He declared: "Intelligent discontent is the mainspring of civilization. It is agitation or stagnation." There was little stagnation in Debs or his followers, even in Rochester.

This was powerful conditioning for an only child just before and during the 1920s. Often I heard my parents repeat the words uttered by Debs after he was sentenced in 1919: "While there is a lower class, I am in it; while there is a criminal element, I am of it; and while there is a soul in prison, I am not free."

Religion and Politics

There is an admonition in some cultures to leave religion and politics alone if one wants tranquillity. My parents left religion alone, but not politics. There was little tranquillity. Both my parents were Jewish. Yet at least my father's family did not observe Jewish religious customs or go to synagogue or temple. Their parents came to America for economic reasons and also to escape European anti-Semitism. My parents, if not their parents, felt that assimilation would lessen anti-Semitism. Assimilation was difficult but an increasing solution among Jews, especially before Zionism became popular and before the Nazi Holocaust occurred.

Many American Jews were swept up by American cosmopolitanism. They were Americans first, decreasingly Jewish. Financier Henry Morganthau, Sr., declared: "We have fought our way through to liberty, equality, and fraternity, and no one shall rob us of these gains. I refuse to allow myself to be called a Zionist. I am an American." Justice Louis D. Brandeis, who never joined a synagogue or Jewish fraternal order, condemned—before he was convinced of Zionism—those Jews who tended "to keep alive differences of origin or classify men according to their religious beliefs."

Journalist Walter Lippmann in an unpublished article wrote as "one of those assimilated creatures to whom the Jewish past has no very peculiar intimate appeal, who find their cultural roots where they can, have no sense of belonging to the Chosen People, and tremble at the suggestions that God has imprudently put all his best eggs in one tribal basket."

I do not know the thinking of my grandparents or even, sad to say, my parents on their personal strategy of fighting anti-Semitism. They seemed to have sought acceptance in American society through submergence of their Judaism rather than through affirmation of it. They found a safety net, a security blanket, in the American and international socialist movement to which they could give their ultimate loyalty and escape their Jewish identity. Socialism became their church, a secular religion.

My mother and father independently discovered the socialist movement in Rochester at the turn of the century no doubt for a variety of reasons. They attended lectures and other events at the Labor Lyceum on St. Paul Street, near the Bausch and Lomb factory. This was part of the German Turnverein movement, dispensing gymnastics but also offering a venue for socialist meetings. The Labor Lyceum became their club. My parents apparently found each other there. Indeed, I remember the Labor Lyceum in my early youth, chiefly as a source of pamphlets on various aspects of socialism and a place where long, boring meetings occurred. Thus I grew up, without synagogue, "without religion." I was Jewish by culture, but not by religion.

By the time I was in Junior High School I got to know George Williams, son of David Rhys Williams, the minister of the First Unitarian Church of Rochester. The Williams family, and especially their two older children, George and Esther, invited me to attend the Young People's Class on Sunday noon at their church. I gradually attended, taking the long walk late Sunday morning.

My parents were noncommittal at my sampling Unitarianism, but they admired the work of the Unitarian Church in the community for decades and especially the civic leadership of David Rhys Williams. They certainly created no obstacles for me. My parents never hid their Jewish origins, but they never emphasized them either. (There was a Menorah and a Star of David on my grandparents' gravestone at Mount Hope Cemetery, but it is not known if that was their choice or that of one of their children.) I do know that my father suffered from anti-Semitism in Rochester; if I learned how, I have long since conveniently forgotten.

7 ITHACA • RICHMOND
(1933-1937)

A COSMOPOLITAN EDUCATION

Perspective 1933: Franklin Delano Roosevelt became President with 15 million Americans out of work. Adolph Hitler became Chancellor of Germany. The U.S. and the U.S.S.R. established diplomatic relations. Fiorello La Guardia elected Mayor of New York City. Forty-two American blacks were killed during 1933 by lynch mobs. Gasoline sold for 18 cents a gallon and eggs for 29 cents a dozen in the U.S.A. James Hilton published the novel, Lost Horizons. *Ah,* Wilderness *by Eugene O'Neill was produced on Broadway. Popular songs included "Only A Paper Moon," by E. Y. Harbsurg and "Stormy Weather" by Ted Koehler. Former President Calvin Coolidge and novelist John Galsworthy died.*

Cornell University, founded in 1865, was—and is—one of the best universities in the U.S.A. Although earlier I said I wanted to go to Yale University—when as a boy I was studying geology—I never seriously applied there, since by 1933 I was interested in a career in botany. Cornell had a top botanical department and, if I were lucky, I could attend as a resident of New York State virtually without tuition. My parents never questioned my expenses for education, even though our family always was middle class.

In September 1933 my mother and father took me on the three-hour drive southeast of Rochester to Ithaca, and the college campus "far above Cayuga's waters." I had been allocated a room in the relatively new Baker Dormitory, a three-story stone building just below the student union, Willard Straight Hall. My parents helped

74

move my possessions from the auto to my bare room. In those days, students had clothes; today they have electronic gear! Soon I said good-bye to my parents as they drove back to Rochester.

On the first Monday morning of school, representatives of half a dozen of Cornell's forty-five fraternities came to my dormitory room. "Can you come to our house for dinner?" I went to one for supper, another for lunch, still a third for breakfast. I was being "rushed." Actually those fraternities gave me nearly all my meals that first week, but I worked for them. That first night after supper I was taken to an upper room and questions were flung at me: "Is your father working? Can you pay the $200 initiation fee? Are you a football man?" (The answer to that last question seemed obvious!) Soon I also learned to ask questions: "How much of a mortgage does your house have?" What does it cost each member when you have a house party?" ($25 to $125 each!) "Who are your famous alumni?" (A Phi Beta Kappa back in 1898 and four football captains in as many years.) Despite my dour reactions, one or two invited me to pledge. I never did join a fraternity at Cornell—or anywhere. The one fraternity which I would have eagerly joined was Telluride, but it was a mystery then—and still today—how members were invited. I had several friends there, some of the intellectual leaders of the student body. Telluride is still on campus, funded by a mining foundation in Colorado.

I made very few friends in Baker Dorm. Willard Straight was too big and impersonal. I was told of Llenroc Lodge (Cornell spelled backwards!) which was a cooperative eating club. I went not so much for the savings as for the friendships—mostly non-fraternity/sorority students. At Llenroc I indeed made some friends. In addition to taking two courses in botany, every Saturday that first autumn I went to the inlet of Cayuga Lake to do some work on aquatic ecology. Dr. Robert B. Gordon of Allegany School and Ohio State encouraged me to continue my private research, but the water was chilly in September and October and I really had no plan. I got cold and wet and felt sorry for myself. Along came Nellie, a red-haired freshman, who cheered me up. She came from a farm south of Syracuse and was also an Ag student. We started dating and went to movies and dances.

Opposing ROTC

I had to take the prescribed freshman courses, much more than two courses in botany: economics, biology, English, public speaking, two courses in chemistry, and "drill." I soon found myself, hardly realizing, that I was in the Reserve Officer Training Corps (ROTC) every Thursday afternoon. It was compulsory for every male. I had to buy a uniform—grey riding suit, black tie, black coat, black high top boots. Between a big brute from Buffalo and a little one from Dobbs Ferry, I would hear: "Company, hun, two, three, four." For two and one-half hours we marched in hot, itchy suits in the large field house. We carried heavy rifles, lay on our bellies, heard lectures on national defense by the resident general. I had become a soldier without quite knowing it! I petitioned to get out. The Secretary of the University sternly replied that all students at the University must, by order of the Trustees, take military drill. The only exception was not conscience but physical disability, with a physician's excuse. I continued drilling for the rest of that term, but did not take ROTC the second term in my freshman year—or ever.

During the second term of my freshman year, I joined other students in an on-going campaign against ROTC. Cornell had a history of both faculty and student opposition to compulsory military training. An earlier report declared that there was "no legal necessity to have compulsory drill" at Cornell and "it was not an adequate substitute for physical training." In the summer of 1933, just before I entered, the Trustees of Cornell after two years' debate, denied the request of both faculty and students to make ROTC optional. Their excuse was the "present unsettled economic and social conditions of the country and the world." Harvard, Yale, Stanford, and Princeton all thought otherwise and made military training optional.

This action of the Trustees brought student response. On May 31, 1934, when the ROTC year came to a climax with a mass drill at the field house, some of us students outside Bailey Hall rallied against military training, opposing Cornell's effort to prepare hundreds of new soldiers "to sacrifice life, home, happiness to new empires ór to break strikes." We formed our own Optional Drill Corps (ODC) using as a "Co-ed Regiment" theme song,"I Didn't Raise My Boy to Be a Soldier." ODC held meetings at Willard Straight Hall every Wednesday evening, called "sham battles." We issued a manual on "What Every ODC Officer Should Know." Cornell hosted a Conference on War and Fascism in April. In retrospect, that may not have been the best national auspices. My father at the time designed a flier, printed in orange and black, entitled, "Join Company B." The text read: "Stay Neutral. Be here while they fight over there. Be here when the fight is over." I distributed these widely.

Earlham College

At the end of my freshman year at Cornell, I had sufficient credits to begin my junior year. A few students at that time would spend a junior year in Europe. I wanted to get away from a large university and also I wanted to get around ROTC I felt that, if I spent a year away, plus my advance credits, I might just get by with only one term of military training. Professor Loren Perry, a Quaker, recommended that I go to the small Quaker college, Earlham. I was admitted. Earlham was at Richmond, Indiana, and by now my parents had given me an auto. In early autumn, 1934, I drove to Indiana. I lived in a student dormitory, Bundy Hall, not as modern as Baker Dorm, and I ate in the college cafeteria. The Biology Department was at the time in the basement of Bundy.

I took animal morphology and histology, but Earlham gave me a chance to widen my intellectual horizons. I took Spanish, psychology, creative writing with that conservative Quaker, E. Merrill Root, and philosophy with Thomas Kelly. Since the student body was much smaller than at Cornell, I quickly got to know a number of students, especially those in my dorm. Often we went by auto to the ice-cream shop several blocks away for malts—probably twenty cents then! We attended movies in town. I got to know more "town girls" than co-eds.

I wrote a column in the school newspaper, but took little part in school affairs since I was a newcomer. My column was wide-ranging, and I recounted in some detail my experiences in refusing to join a Cornell fraternity and in being forced to take ROTC. I did a lot of reading that year, and first became a regular reader of *Time*. Also I read regularly the Broadway magazine, *Variety*. I drove home for Christmas vacation, in the days before interstate highways, and the strip along Lake Erie was icy in December.

In a letter to Professor Millard S. Markle of Earlham, written in November 1935, after I returned to Cornell, and with some perspective, I tried to recapture my feelings about Earlham. The college was snug, secure, unpretentious. There was a somewhat strained fellowship between its faculty and students. I could now better understand Earlham's "small college" attitude and ideals. What I received from my one-year visit was an understanding of the workings and advantages of a small liberal arts college. It had as legitimate a place under the educational sun as a large university. The paramount advantage was in orienting its students for life, and how to act to get along with people. Also Earlham helped its students more than Cornell to determine how and what to study for one's life work. What more important, what more essential, advantages could any educational institution offer?

I also recalled the Biology Department in Bundy basement—its achievements and importance inversely proportional to its quarters, directly proportional to its modern, abundant equipment and its personnel. I reluctantly admitted to Professor Markle that my contact with his department did not further stimulate my interest in botany as such. Rather, it stimulated an interest in something more worthwhile: pedagogical procedure and organization in both college and university, including botany departments. I predicted that, if things remain as they were, I would work for a doctorate on just that subject: some phase of educational research as applied to college. (My prediction of 1935 came true through 1940.)

Cornell Cosmopolitan Club

After a year at Earlham, I decided not to go for a fourth summer to the biological station in Michigan. I was doing too much too soon. I decided to spend the summer in Rochester. My parents, in the meantime, had sold the Crosman Terrace house and moved to a more modest one on Finch Street, not far from our original neighborhood adjoining Lake Avenue.

My health—teeth problems—was such that some of my professors worried about my retreat from activity. Professor Gates wrote me on August 1, 1935, from Michigan: "One of the things which you need to learn is to take life more easily and to do things without using up so much excess energy." I still need that warning—more than half a century later!

At Cornell once more, I realized that I did not want to live in a dormitory again. When I was a freshman I admired—from afar—the Cornell Cosmopolitan Club. It was located off campus, in "collegetown," and there were rented rooms, mostly for foreign students, but a few for Americans. I applied early for a room—and got one.

I think I learned more at the Cosmo Club than on campus during my senior year or during the next year when I was working for a master's degree. I suddenly was thrown into truly an international world which I had not experienced: Turgut Bilsel of Turkey, Tom Boon-Long of Siam, W. L. Chia of China, Costa Couvaras of Greece,

78

H. M. Desai of India, Fevzi Errera of Turkey, Abdul Khayyat of Iraq, C. B. Patel of India, P. Rimkus of Lithuania, Sardar Singh of India, S. Y. Tang of China, and L.A. van Melle of Holland. Americans also were associated with the Cos Club: Mary and Jay Bryant who were the faculty advisers, Nelson Foote, Earl Sasser, Igor Roodenko, Art Danforth, and others. A few of these classmates I have kept in touch with ever since, especially Singh, Sasser, Roodenko, and Foote. Tom Boon-long I saw in Thailand after fifty years, just before his death in 1989.

Food was only intermittently served at the Club, and some of us helped organize a cooperative dining club on nearby Dryden Road. I was among the group that helped with making policy, if not food. Our cafeteria beat the prices at the commercial restaurants and Willard Straight Cafeteria.

Life at the Cosmo Club was not all study. Once I wrote to Sardar Singh, who left the club for a long trip to the Midwest, recounting life in his absence: "Yesterday and last night some of us went to Syracuse for a banquet-dance at the Syracuse University Cosmopolitan Club. We went in my car, arriving at Syracuse at 3:00 p.m. We enjoyed life around the town, ate at the banquet, met other Cornellians there, went to the dance, and came sailing into Ithaca at 4 a.m. this morning, after which we slept until about 1:00 this afternoon. We ate at the co-op, attended a meeting of its board of directors, returned to Cos Club to read the Sunday *New York Times*, fooled away time writing letters and straightening up our room (a usual Sunday afternoon occupation). In a little while there will be the usual tea, then we may eat at the co-op and go to the movies. You see, Singh, life goes here pretty much the same, despite the fact that you are nowhere to be seen."

My work at the University that year centered around the Nature Study Department, headed by Professor E. Laurence Palmer. I took his courses and generally became a member of his team. I took courses in vertebrate zoology, conservation, methods of education, nature literature, and free-hand drawing. I also managed to take a few liberal arts courses, especially one on war by Professor Needham and one on the French Revolution by Carl Becker.

In this period I learned a great deal about libraries from Professor Albert Hazen Wright, my zoology professor. He had a feel for books and he gave a valuable seminar on library resources.

I received my bachelor's degree (B.S.) at Cornell's sixty-eighth commencement in June, 1936—age twenty—with my proud parents in attendance. That summer I did not go back to Michigan. I did make a short visit to Allegany School and also visited the Williams family at their cottage near Westfield, along Lake Erie.

One of my closest friends, older than I, was H. M. ("His Majesty") Desai, an agriculturist from Gujarati in India. When he left Cornell and the U.S.A in August 1936, I sent him a good-bye letter to the Europe-bound boat: "We can always be under the illusion that we might meet again, someday, but we may never do so." We did not! I returned to Cornell in the autumn of 1936 and enrolled for a master's degree, again in nature study and zoology.

I had to write a thesis. Given my experiences at the Allegany School and the Michigan Biological Station, I proposed to write a dissertation on the biological field stations of the United States. Professor Palmer concurred. I devised a questionnaire and sent it to the hundred or more stations in the U.S.A. Then I decided to visit those in the Eastern U.S. for a first-hand survey. I did this in the early summer of 1937, driving 4,000 miles in sixteen states and visiting twenty-five field stations from the Mississippi to New England. I finished typing the thesis by August.

At Wood's Hole, Massachusetts, I decided to hire a boat to take me to the nearby uninhabited Penikese Island on Buzzards Bay. It was a former leper colony and then became the site of the Anderson School of Natural History established by Louis Agassiz (1807-1873) of Harvard. The opening of the School was an American event and was telegraphed to New York newspapers. All I could do was trace the building lines of the old laboratory, but the legend motivated me to write several articles about this historic field station, called by some "one of the greatest influences on science teaching in America."

Earlier I faced the problem of finding employment. These were hard times—between Depression and war—for colleges and universities. I wrote my share of letters for fellowships and other positions, but received no offers. I began to look to other teaching. Living at the Cosmo Club, my appetite was strong to go abroad to work. I heard of the Near East College Association. I wrote for openings; one was at Athens College in Greece. I drove to Syracuse to be interviewed by a faculty member on leave. He offered me a job to teach English outside Athens. Knowledge of modern or ancient Greek was not required. This was more of a high school than college. I was delighted with the prospects, but this meant I had to finish my master's thesis and board ship for Europe early in September.

8 ATHENS • VIENNA • MOSCOW
(1937-1938)

EUROPE ON THE EVE OF WAR

Perspective 1938: In March, Adolf Hitler made Anschluss (union) with Austria. In early summer, Germany confiscated "degenerate art" and called up one million reservists. In August, London warned Hitler that an attack on Czechoslovakia could mean world war. In September, Italy expelled all Jews entering since 1919, and France and England signed a pact with Hitler and Mussolini allowing Germany to take Sudentenland, with Neville Chamberlain declaring that the accord will bring "peace in our time." On November 9—Kristallnacht—Jewish shops were wrecked in Germany and Austria.

I left for Greece on September 8, 1937. My parents, and many friends, were at the dock in New York City to see me off on the *Queen Mary*—or at least to see the great ship. My father designed a going-away card, with a picture of that Queen of the Seas.

I had high expectations for my first trip to Europe, at the age of twenty-one. The eleven-day voyage was uneventful. I met a Syrian trader, living north of the Arctic Circle in Alberta, who was on a visit home. We had some good walks, and talks, as we in third class explored this great ocean liner. I disembarked in France, spent a night in Paris, and then took the train to Venice. There I took a gondola to an Italian vessel which took me to Greece, going through the narrow Corinth Canal. Soon I was in Piraeus and took the long taxi ride to Athens College in a suburb, facing the great 3,000-foot Hymettus mountain range. It was from these mountains that much of the marble used in building the Acropolis was mined. On one of my first nights, I visited those ancient ruins. It was really a wonderful sight, those majestic, simple columns in the shadow of the moon, and so high up from the rest of Athens. The city of Athens itself was in parts very dirty, yet neon signs were everywhere, and some of the houses were beautiful examples of modernistic architecture, although donkeys laden with milk cans or vegetable baskets passed in front of these cubic houses.

My roommate was also a newly arrived American teacher, David G. Farrelly of Springfield, Massachusetts. He spent much time that year writing to his girlfriend in America, Betty Jane. We became good friends and went around Athens and occasionally through Greece. During Christmas vacation, we crossed the Mediterranean to Egypt by boat, going "deck" or fourth class. Often we entered first class to visit a Greek friend, Edwin Saltiel, a Jewish businessman who was consul in Athens for Japan.

We explored Cairo and then took a train to Luxor. There I bought a cobra, after intricate bargaining with a snake-charmer, and took it by train back to Cairo and Alexandria. There I persuaded an American sailor to take the snake—live—to New York and ship it to Cornell. (When I returned to Ithaca more than a year later, I learned that the cobra died somewhere between Hoboken and Ithaca. I was shown the snake in alcohol and a label crediting me with collecting it in Egypt!) In a letter to my parents I observed that "the antiquities did not move me nearly as much as the Egyptian people—so many people and so poor." This was my very first visit to what was later called "the Third World."

David and I also went on an Easter cruise to the Greek islands. That cruise cost $50 and I wrote my parents: "I think it will be worth the price." On the *S.S. Hellas* we went to the monastery peninsula of Mr. Athos, Santorini, Delos, Rhodes, and Crete. We also spent a day in Istanbul and saw some of our Egyptian diplomatic friends who were now working in Turkey. Years later David became a professor of government in California and I read an article of his in the *Nation* magazine. We corresponded once or twice, but I never saw him after I left Athens.

To describe Athens College as a boarding school for rich Greeks and especially Greek-Americans would not be accurate, but students of all ages could live in its one, huge building. We teachers had to maintain order—from the primary school boarders to those in their last year. Although I taught English in English, I had not majored in English or in teaching English as a second language. Thus I learned the night before I taught—*Macbeth*, Sinclair Lewis' *Arrowsmith*, and W. H. Hudson's *Green Mansions* and his *Far Away and Long Ago*.

The work at Athens College started with breakfast at 8:00 a.m. and the first class at 8:45. The second period was free, for me, and then there were three other classes. The boys—there were no girl students—would rise when I entered the classroom and say in English, "Good Morning, Mr. Jack." The teaching was not easy, and almost every night I had papers to correct. I had to supervise the dorms one or two nights a week and also, for several afternoons, monitor work for younger students in the fields, mostly containing rocks and lizards. I wrote my Cornell friend, Nelson Foote, that "the only difference between being a student and a teacher is that the teacher works over his desk the night after an examination rather than the night before!" I was, however, quite free on weekends except for the occasional one when I was on duty and thus the teacher responsible if anything should happen to the several hundred resourceful, resident students.

I still had considerable time on my hands. I wrote a Turkish friend who had returned home from Cornell: "I find myself amply rewarded for the semi-drudgery of school life by my frequent excursions around Athens and elsewhere." Three or four late afternoons a week I took the 15-minute bus ride to downtown Athens. At Constitution Square I would go to a table at Zonars, a sidewalk care opposite the Grand Bretagne Hotel. My choice was always the Buffalo Special, an ice-cream sundae appropriated by Zonars from relatives in Buffalo! Soon a close-knit group developed, consisting of Ayoub el Shahat, Hafez Amer, El Amrousi—all of the Egyptian Embassy; Connie Hadjilia, a Greek journalist; and Mohammed Wali Khan, apparently the Foreign Minister of Afghanistan until he was exiled with the King in 1932. After political talk during the year before the formally declared war in Europe, we adjourned to a cheap restaurant near the Acropolis for more talk, always paying for the meal of Wali Khan. This was a precious association in which I increasingly participated for more than six months.

During the ten months in Greece, I carried on a vigorous correspondence. I wrote regularly to my parents, addressing them as "Alexensis" [Alex and Sis]—kind of taxonomic nomenclature. I told them of my forthcoming trip to Egypt and that it might cost $75! I wrote that "it is hard to save money and that they might have to help me out somewhat." Of course, they did. I wrote to some of my friends made at the Cosmo Club, especially Nelson Foote who later became a well-known sociologist, but at the time was an impoverished socialist and pacifist. I sent a cable to the silver jubilee of the Burroughs-Audubon Nature Club and a long report on my botanical observations. Before describing the natural history of Greece, I catalogued the familiar sights and smells of Monroe County that I missed and made me homesick:

New England asters wet with heavy frost; rain-soaked, rotting Clavaria mushrooms with snails eating the slime; the autumn foliage on a cloudless afternoon reflected in the blue waters of a deep lagoon; garter snakes basking in the Indian summer warmth before their great sleep until hepatica-time; the crackle of leaves under my feet as I scramble up a steep bank in search of a vireo nest made conspicuous by a sudden leaf-fall; the idle recreation of plucking stick-tights from my breeches; the smell of burning leaves and the bluish haze therefrom which encircles small villages; the search for bittersweet along rocky fences; sandbanks with withered, silvery mullein on the talus slopes; and the peat-bog with cotton-grass fluttering and cranberries riding on the sphagnum. Yes, one doesn't appreciate the robin until it leaves for the winter!

After describing some of the flora and fauna, I described my personal quarters:

I have a praying mantis in my room; it makes a nice pet. I let it loose, at intervals, to romp over my cyclamen plant or a bunch of big, yellow chrysanthemums. The name of this insect is supposedly taken from the ecclesiastical posture of its front legs when at rest, but when busy, this creature is satanic, and the *a* in praying becomes as quickly an *e* as its enemy becomes its breadbasket. Then there is a fat, black spider in a jar on my desk. It must have built many miles of web since first being introduced in my fruit-jar. I feed it flies, live ones, and they are not hard to find at this season.

I wish I might describe, in detail, my cage with three lizards on my bookcase—a nice, fat green one, one with a pink belly, and a lazy fellow, brown and white. All have broken tails: all were caught by my anxious students who pulled the lizards' tails, only to become embarrassed, as the lizards scampered off, leaving the students holding the tails—and the bag.

With persistence, they did catch these sly creatures, in their present, mangled condition.

After cataloguing the chestnut, olive, and other edible trees, I concluded on an idealistic note, "I am now making arrangements with the active Animal Protection Society here to petition the Ministry of Agriculture to proclaim such shrines as the Acropolis as bird sanctuaries. The Greeks love nature, and perhaps such a thing as this will show them the way, will touch off their imagination, and, once again, there will be a golden age for birds in Greece."

I sent a cable to a surprise party for my parents on their twenty-fifth anniversary on May 9. I urged my parents to make their first trip to Europe and visit me. They did not—then or ever. Social life in Athens seemed continuous. At the Thanksgiving Party of the U.S. Embassy I met Cleta Olmstead, daughter of a University of Chicago archeologist. We went out together for several weeks. Also I attended the functions of the Anglo-Hellenic Club, where I sometimes met the parents of my students.

Jack-O-Lantern

I have the natural instinct of letting go of friends with reluctance. My two years at the Cosmopolitan Club resulted in so many friendships and new insights that I found it hard to separate myself completely from two dozen friends I made from literally around the world. Thus to deal with a kind of homesickness, but also my penchant for journalism, I wrote and mimeographed a two-page newsletter in 1938 from Athens. Called *Jack-O-Lantern*, the first issue contained news from twenty "alumni."

The second newsletter was sent from Ithaca in April 1939. Although most of us were members of the dining co-op, all of us occasionally ate at nearby Johnny's Restaurant and I reported that it had the "same waitresses, same white table-tops, same menu: soup, chops, french fries, pie, milk—and 45¢ check." I ended the two pages this way: "If World War prevents the next edition of this *Lantern* from appearing, let's plan a CC Club reunion in the Old World or, if the conflict becomes particularly devastating, in the Other World."

The third issue was mailed in May 1940—eight months after war began. I had to announce the death, but not from war, of the first of our number, Turgut Bilsel of Turkey who was teaching at a new normal school in Afghanistan. At the bottom of each newsletter

I listed the Bureau of Missing Persons, the names of those who had not written me and told of their jobs, personal life, and new addresses. At the end I wrote: "It is an awful feeling, this list getting larger and larger and not knowing that many of the nineteen persons listed we'll never see—nay, never hear from again." I added that eight are technically in countries at war, and at least one has been a soldier since his days at Cornell.

Number four, I believe the last *Jack-O-Lantern*, was written on September 5, 1941. The price was still "an annual note to compiler." I wrote that, by continuing our contacts, we will be doing our part to keep alive the flickering flame of international goodwill during these perilous moments in history."

My agenda for Europe went beyond teaching at Athens College. On this first trip I wanted to see something of the continent. Also I made plans with Professor Palmer to do field work in Europe toward my doctorate, visiting European field stations. I had originally agreed to work at Athens College for three years, but several factors truncated the sojourn to one year. I was itching to finish my doctorate, European war appeared to many to be on the horizon, and the situation at Athens College itself was hardly ideal. Also the Metaxis dictatorship vexed me, more than perhaps most faculty, although some were secretly already in the anti-fascist underground. Farrelly went back to the U.S. that summer, hoping to return, but did not.

When I finished my work at Athens College at the end of June 1938, I had all of Europe before me. The limits were not time, but money. I estimated the costs of my four-month study-tour would be $500. I applied unsuccessfully for travelling fellowships and finally wrote my parents that with my savings of $300, I would need only $200 from "the Jack Foundation." My parents had no "foundation," but were always generous with our limited finances. That was never a major worry, for them or myself, since I tended to be frugal.

My one date was the meetings of the British Association for the Advancement of Science at Cambridge University in August. Thus I decided on a clockwise tour: Italy, France, Britain (including Cambridge), the Netherlands, Germany, Austria, Scandinavia, the Soviet Union, Rumania, and back to France to take a boat to return to America. I figured the trip would take four months. In the end it took six, and I arrived home just before New Year's Day 1939.

My main objective was to visit several dozen biological field stations. In doing so, I naturally tried to understand the people and the country. I visited Naples and Rome and field stations in a few other Italian cities; Monaco (known for its oceanographic institute as well as its gambling); and some institutions in southern France. Then I went up to Switzerland before crossing into England. In a hotel on the top of Jungfrauhoch, 11,300 feet up, I met a fellow traveler in the reading room. We talked about conservation and modern education for several hours. I asked him for his name and found he was the famous Dale Carnegie, author of the bestselling *How to Make Friends and Influence People*. "He practiced what he preached," I wrote my parents, "but I read his book in Greece, too, so I quite made friends with him, and I was interested to see how much a writer and popular radio man as he sees the value of the popularization of science into nature-study." The British Association meetings in Cambridge were rich in experiences with scientific personalities. I delivered my paper on July 18 and afterwards met physicist J. D. Bernal—with whom I was to have heated ideological battles in another decade—and author Julian Huxley.

I then visited field stations in the Lake Country, before crossing to Holland. I soon entered Germany and visited an oceanic station on the fortified island of Helgoland. After several weeks in Germany and Austria, seeing Nazi rule firsthand, I trembled for the future of Europe. In a letter home dated August 10, 1938, I warned:

> Hitler is here to stay—despite the wishful thinking of right thinking people everywhere. The average German thinks of Hitler really as a God, knows he can do no wrong, and sincerely believes he is helping their country. Funny part about it, in some things he is.

I described some of the economic policies that contributed to full employment and that redressed some of the wrongs imposed on Germany at the end of World War I. Then I addressed political problems, including the terrible takeover of Austria.

> The Jewish problem is rather interesting—more than that, tragic. You walk down the streets of Vienna and every shop has a sticker on the window "Aryan." Large stores and tiny stalls with Fineberg's or Goldman's are either closed, or their signs are painted out, and another sign says, under new management. Every Jew, since two or three weeks ago, has been dismissed from not only ownership of a business, but all employment. Pensions have been stopped in most cases. Many have been taken to concentration camps. Long lines are pathet-

ically waiting at the British and American legations. Worst of all there's an exhibition in town—*Der ewige Juden* (the eternal Jew). You can get a reduced ticket on the tram if you go and see it. All this is tragic, but more tragic, still, is that every person one talks to more or less believes in what Hitler's doing to the Jews. I've talked to college professors and shopkeepers and they affirm, upon persistent questioning, that there might be good Jews, but that they were crowding the professions and they're getting their due. That's the sad part of Germany.

On the Oriental Express this morning from Germany, I rode and talked with a family fleeing from Austria. They're going to Uruguay—after their relatives paid $1500 for a visa. He was a furrier before the Anschluss, and was only allowed to take 40 marks (or $16.00) out of the country. I have seen and heard a lot more, but this will give you, I hope, enough to think about for the time being.

Visit to Stalin's Russia

From Austria, I went by train to Scandinavia and then by train again to the Soviet Union under Stalin. My visit to the Soviet Union was, however, more to find out for myself about the real workings of communism than about my thesis. Had I found what I was probably seeking—a new society—the visit may well have made me a communist. My memory of that visit to Stalin's Russia is now quite vague. The hardship, oppression, and glumness of the people converted me—but against Russian communism if not against Marxism. The long railroad journeys in cold November, life in Moscow's Metropole Hotel, a brief stay in a Soviet hospital—these and other experiences shriveled whatever predisposition I had toward Russia from my socialist mother's milk! Forever after, I remembered this experience. However predisposed I may have been toward communism, the experience was counterproductive.

Those who visited the motherland of communism were seeking a validation of their hopes—a society which would give employment to all. More important, they were searching for something to fill the nagging, yawning vacuum which the U.S.A. was already no longer filling, and which eluded all but the most ardent religionists. Some of us went to Moscow hoping to find a society that worked, and not only materially. Even in 1938 it was apparent in the capital city that that society did not. Yet some political pilgrims of that period found what they were looking for, however much they occasionally had to close their eyes. Thus persons of all classes and conditions returned from Russia captivated, eager to tell all how much better socialist society was. They were ready to risk all to spread communism worldwide and do so in the raging civil war in Spain or in their labor unions in New York or Chicago. Somehow this secular religion did not move me—in Moscow or in the weeks and years since. I was singularly unsmitten.

Following are excerpts from an essay (amplified with remarks in a letter to my parents) that I wrote in the heat of disillusionment shortly after my 1938 visit. It was only rediscovered by me in my archives in 1992, published here for the first time:

There are many fascist tendencies in the U.S.S.R. First is the propaganda for the head of the government. Walk through Berlin or Vienna. Most store windows and certainly every restaurant and home will contain a lithographed portrait of Hitler, some as big as life and done in oils. Go to the *tabik*, the corner cigar store, and there you can buy picture postcards of Hitler in various poses—feeding a fawn or coyly playing with little girls (Goebbels' daughters). Listen to a speech in Germany and it will invariably end with "Heil Hitler."

Let us haul down the swastica and see what lies behind the hammer and sickle. The trimmed mustache broadens into a Stalinoid one, and this grinning face is everywhere—in every home, factory, school. In one kindergarten I saw a scrapbook of his pictures. In the so-called "Lenin corner" of a textile factory, I noticed a large statue of Stalin embracing two children. I asked the guide the reason for the statue: "Because Stalin loves children." That was the same answer I received when I asked about Hitler and children on a postcard in Germany. The Stalin theme is used at the conclusion of many speeches. Translated passages from reports given in the Supreme Soviet almost invariably end with "Long Live Stalin."

The Museum of the Revolution in Moscow contains more pictures of Stalin actually than of Lenin. Stalin is shown playing a part equal to that of Lenin in liberating the proletariat. In fact, the popular name of the party in power is the Lenin-Stalin Party. If Stalin has done so much good and the people like him so vigorously for this, why is it necessary to build up consciously all this propaganda for him and falsify history? It looks pretty much as if the dictatorship of the proletariat had turned out to be one of a Georgian proletarian. Germany and Italy freely admit their Duce and Führer. The Russian government, however, does not admit the primacy of Stalin.

Another fascist tendency in Russia is the supreme position of the army. The best-dressed men in Germany and Italy are those in the army. In Russia the men of the Red Army are not only the best dressed, but often the only nicely dressed men in the country. Half the travelers and occupants of hotels seem to be from the armed forces. One can feel the tremendous strength of the country that is being sucked up and used by the army. It is evidenced by this reply in the department stores: "We do not have this item; the army supply must first be filled." From every corner one hears commands nearer to boastfulness than pride about the army—a strange Hitleroid affectation. Children in kindergarten are given toy tanks, and in one school I saw a whole table of plastic-like war figures. In the higher grades, I saw a whole art exhibit given over to pictures of war.

A third fascist tendency is the importance of the party in control. In Russia the Communist Party is the sole party, and as such it probably exerts an important influence. They train their future members when young. Practically all children are Octobers or Pioneers. The only reason they wear no more than red kerchiefs is that there are no complete uniforms to be had, as there are—and are worn—in Germany. Later the select Pioneers become Young Communists. Is this where Hitler borrowed his Young Nazi idea from? It is not easy to ascertain the exact privileges of party membership. The Intourist guides emphatically say there are no privileges—but these same guides call a new political prison in Leningrad the Office of Home Affairs! Certainly the majority of important office-holders are party men. Whether they received their positions because of, or despite, their party affiliation is difficult to determine. It is known, however, that for certain positions a worker must be vouched for by at least two party members. This smacks of the ward-boss if not the fascist system. In Russia party members do not wear pins as in Germany or Italy. It is not easy to decide whether this is a curse or a blessing.

Another fascist tendency is the desire of the state to increase its population. Certainly no sane government, realizing the great want and unbelievably low standard of living of the people, would desire more mouths to feed, a rise in the birth rate. Yet the bounty system for large families is in effect in Russia, and can result in war-fodder, as in Germany and Italy.

Perhaps the last important fascist tendency is the intolerance toward, and the suppression of, any opposition. In Germany, they are quick to call any opposition Marxist, Jewish, communist. In Russia, the word for them is Japanese-, German-, Trotskyite-wreckers. In the new Soviet constitution there are lovely guarantees of freedom of speech and the press. But when all the speeches are on the same note and all the newspaper articles are as stereotyped as in Germany, it is hard to find where this freedom is. There is freedom to worship "our Stalin" and there is freedom to quote his words, but there is not license to read *Mein Kampf* or even find the *London Times* in all of Russia. If communism can stand up, ideologically and intellectually to fascism or capitalism, why is there the necessity for the absolute absence of all foreign newspapers and books? It is often treason for Russians to speak to foreigners. I was only able to talk to one person in all of Russia, besides my guides. This person said it would go hard on him if he were seen talking to a foreigner—and then declined to talk. In no other country are foreigners treated as lepers. Even pictures are not allowed. I was "arrested" for taking moving pictures in the street in Odessa. They took my film "for developing." They developed it, all right, but scratched off the emulsion!

It is inconceivable that there is that degree of unanimity in Russia as is evidenced by the tone of the people. They have a catechism, and though it may differ from that of Nazism or the Catholic Church, it still is a catechism. They are told what to believe.

I am also a little disappointed in the people. After all, it has been twenty-one years since the beginning of communism, but the people are quite capitalistic. Money is the big thing. Tipping is still a fashion. Theft has increased. In Europe guests in hotels leave their shoes outside their room door for shining each night. I did that the first night in Leningrad. The very next day I was warned—never do that, there is too much chance that your shoes will be taken. I expected that communism might change the Soviet people, but it didn't, or perhaps they are worse than before.

I overlook, of course, the good things. I know about them, and have taken them for granted, and perhaps they are more important than what I have mentioned above. The common ownership or socialization of everything is good. So is the emphasis on education and science. Yet for some reason I feel no longer any great enthusiasm for Russia. Russia perhaps will be a great country someday—but quite in the future. And so, after my visit from the hot to the cold, from Germany through Russia, I arrive at this conclusion, which was not possible before ever coming to Europe: that America isn't a bad place to live in. I most certainly would rather live in it than in Russia.

Totalitarianism

In retrospect, I am surprised I was so relatively "non-political" during my 16 months in Europe. This was just one year before the beginning of World War II. In Greece, General Ioanan Metaxas (1871-1941) was premier. His was a fascist dictatorship. I have tended to glamorize my role there in buying mimeograph stencils—as a teacher—and slipping them to my Greek faculty friends at College for use in the underground. This was tame anti-fascism indeed. And how many stencils could I ever have purchased? They could not, and did not, bring Metaxas down.

I must have spent ten or more days in Mussolini's Italy. I saw the symbols of El Duce. I was not impressed, but I made no study of fascism while there and certainly showed no significant opposition. I passed through Nazi Germany again on my return from the east. Again, I saw all the Nazi paraphernalia. I was stunned more than I was energized to take any action in opposition. However, despite the Munich agreement, the gathering clouds were unmistakable:

> Now that the war crisis is over, what do you think will happen? Enduring peace? Not quite, for both England and Germany started increasing their defenses actually before the ink dried on the documents at the Munich conference. Germany was certainly the victor over England at the Czech crisis. Now in pride, Germany's taking one more step—colonies. In all the streetcars, there are signs: "Where are our colonies?" That's the way—when one campaign ends, another begins. The people are told the world's against them. They believe it, work so much harder for Hitler. And you can be sure that will very much be in the news for the next six months. I could go on, but I'm afraid I've said more than I ought to—in a letter mailed in Germany—already.

I was in Austria three times, all after the Anschluss of March, 1938, when Hitler took over the country. However, I had a legitimate excuse for my being oblivious to the political environment of Austria. I developed a crush on Nancy Horton, a young woman I had met on the voyage, but nothing came of my infatuation. In Salzberg, we visited the exhibit of "Degenerate Art." The several hundred paintings were assembled by Hitler and Goebbels to suggest that modern German art was subversive and anti-German. The artists included George Grosz, Paul Klee, Wassily Kandinsky, and Marc Chagall. Some rank today as the finest of the century. Indeed, in the 1990s one-half of these paintings were reassembled and displayed to acclaim in Los Angeles and Berlin. Hitler was correct in thinking that modern art threatened his legitimacy.

Two of my three visits came before Kristallnacht—November 9, 1938. I visited Vienna for a week about a month afterwards. I remember walking up Mariahilferstrasse and seeing signs on some stores indicating that they were *Judenfrei*—free of Jews. I remember talking to some Austrian friends of Nancy who were outspokenly anti-Nazi. I saw overt anti-Semitism, with sadness. On my last train out of Austria and Germany, en route to Paris, I somehow finally spoke my mind about Hitler in the third class compartment. There was an argument of rising decibels, overcoming the noise of the train, and I had to leave the compartment in some fear. But I arrived in Switzerland the next day unharmed.

Another political environment to which I was subjected was on the *President Harding* en route from France to the U.S.A. Third class was filled with Americans returning from serving in Spain with the Abraham Lincoln Brigade. Most passengers were so seasick during that late December crossing that we stayed pretty much in our rooms. However, I did get into arguments with some of those "veterans" on the Spanish issue. I was not at all pro-Franco, but I realized even then that the Brigade had several political agendas.

The December crossing on the *President Harding* was rough. I hardly left my cabin. We arrived in New York just before New Year's. Today, after more than one-half century of world travels, this European sojourn of 16 months was the longest period I have ever been away from the U.S.A.

9 ITHACA
(1939-1940)

MARRIAGE AND THE MINISTRY

I returned to Cornell in February 1939. Professor Palmer was agreeable that I write my doctoral thesis on "The Biological Field Stations of the World," using the material I collected from my visits to these institutions in Europe. However, I was fast losing interest in this project, but I had the wit to realize that any thesis is better than no thesis. I was close enough to receiving a Ph.D. not to allow anything to deflect me.

I wanted and needed a job and I wanted to work in a more challenging field. As I would quip long afterwards, "I became more interested in men than mice, in humanity than science." Indeed, one of the two minor subjects for my doctorate reflected this shifting interest. While my major was still science education, and one minor was zoology, the other minor was sociology. I was somehow becoming increasingly disenchanted with "science." I learned more about the philosophy and indeed the methodology of science subsequently in theological school than during all my years in science at Cornell.

My shift of interest from science to politics was reflected in two book reviews I wrote in 1939 for *Areopagas*, the Cornell journal of opinion. After reviewing two volumes by J. D. Bernal and Robert Lynd, I ended with this paragraph: "Will all scientists face the fundamental problems of society or will they find themselves in the words of W. H. Auden 'lecturing on navigation while the ship is going down?'"

My problem was not only intellectual. It was practical. After too many years of schooling, and only one job for one year in Greece, I needed the prospect of more permanent employment. Also world war was obviously approaching. On top of this, I was even thinking about marriage Put all these strands together—and I was in a quandary.

In Ithaca, I also felt that I should no longer completely depend upon my parents for funds for education. I tried to get part-time employment. I worked in one or two private homes for my room and board, doing household chores and yard work. Therefore I did not go back to the Cosmo Club to live. In those days, I spent much time in my cubicle in Fernow Hall and diligently wrote and typed my thesis. Also I had to brush up on German and French to pass my language requirements for the doctorate. I had some course work to finish and some oral examinations to take. All of these problems converged upon me during the spring term. By September, world war came.

Then I had to register for the draft. I did so on October 16, 1940 at Board 543 on Dewey Avenue in Rochester. The one continuing evidence of my work for a doctorate was that my thesis, greatly abridged, was published after the war. I long had correspondence with Dr. Frans Verdoorn, the enterprising publisher of *Chronica Botanica* in Leiden. Indeed, I visited him there in 1938. About a year later, Verdoorn emigrated to Waltham, Massachusetts, and *Chronica Botanica* was published there. In the summer of 1945 he published, in elegant form, a special issue of my *Biological Field Stations of the World*. I dedicated the volume to my parents "who sought in every possible way to give (me) the opportunity for study and travel." Indeed, I visited seventy-nine stations in eighteen countries in North America, Europe, and Africa for this purpose.

Esther Rhys Williams

In the late 1920s I met Esther Rhys Williams. She was the daughter of David and Lucy Williams. He was minister of the First Unitarian Church of Rochester. They lived in a parsonage on Highland Parkway and had three children: Esther, George, and David. I met George first at a Burroughs-Audubon Nature Club event. He was interested in birds and shrubs, and so was I. Somehow I was never an inveterate bird-watcher, perhaps because of weak eyes, but I was a great trees-and-shrubs boy. George and I got together and we often identified rare shrubs in the arboretum at nearby Highland

Park. Once we hitchhiked to Cornell University to size up its Botany Department. (George went to St. Lawrence University and, in time, became Professor of Church History at Harvard, a long vocational distance from botany; indeed, over time, he also became the father-in-law of my daughter!)

Through George I was gradually introduced to the Williams family. (My parents independently came to know David Rhys Williams for his leadership of liberal projects in Rochester.) George went to East High School, but Esther went to Monroe. She was in a class behind me, and active in school affairs. She was the lead in several high school plays—which I watched at close hand, since I played bass in the school orchestra. She was president of Pencil Pushers, the writing club, while I was vice-president. We also both worked on *Kaleidoscope*, the literary magazine, Esther as poetry editor and myself as managing editor.

During my two final years at Monroe, I admired Esther—but at a distance. I really never went out with her during all those high school years, although we moved in the same social circle, and indeed I attended the young people's society at the Unitarian Church, largely through the urging of George and Esther. We took an English course together and studied the *Odyssey* for which we had to give a presentation. My father helped me prepare a beautiful map of the Aegean with all the Greek islands, and Esther—along with my other classmates—was as jealous as Athena when the golden apple was awarded to Aphrodite! Esther went on to Oberlin as I went to Cornell—but she graduated Phi Beta Kappa (the National Honor Society) while I did not.

I kept my eye on Esther, if from afar, and several times wrote to our mutual friend, Joseph Delibert—then working near her in Ohio—wondering whether I should keep in contact with her. On Nov. 8, 1936, I wrote Joe, "I hardly ever think of Her, yet why do I quite naturally write the pronoun with a capital H?" Earlier that year I wrote him that I had dinner with the family: "After a typical Williams dinner with more politics than food (not actually) and after a profound discussion on the proof of immortality with her father, then I had a jocund and at times even a blithe talk with her."

Esther and I really saw very little of each other until I came back from Europe at the end of 1938. In Berlin I received a letter from her informing me that she was a social case worker in training in Cleveland. I sent her an immediate reply. In early 1939, back at Cornell, my interest in Esther increased. We began to see much of each other, despite her being in Cleveland and I being in Ithaca, and became engaged. We were married by her father in his Unitarian Church in November 1939. Ours was a big wedding. My parents were pleased and so were Esther and I.

Family friend Professor Kendrick P. Shedd composed a song for us, "A Graeco-Persian Romance," with echoes of the Homeric epic, which went in part:

Old Homer wrote the Odyssey.
　　Ulysses was his theme.
For ten blue years he wandered
　　In a constant waking dream.
A-longing for old I T H A C A,
　　His rocky home supreme—
Hurrah for the dream of old Homer!

Oh, Esther was a charming maid
　　Who wore the Persian crown;
She saved a people from grim death
　　And won a vast renown.
Thereafter she left Asia for
　　Our good old Monroe town—
Hurrah for the modern QUEEN ESTHER!

Refrain:

Hurrah! Hurrah! for HOMER and his bride!
Hurrah! Hurrah! for ESTHER at his side!
　　Oh, may they have, great happiness
　　Through all life's time and tide . . .

The next day, literally, we drove to Ithaca where we set up housekeeping in a small apartment in college town, almost opposite the Cosmo Club. Esther rather easily found a job as a secretary to a professor in the University. I continued to finish my Ph.D. thesis. Within a year, I received my degree. Since I could not find a job, we moved to Rochester. By then my parents were wintering in Florida. We moved into my parents' small house on Finch Street.

Since I was unemployed, and since my father gave up his business—retired—we decided to make a grand tour. Neither of my parents had been to Mexico or California; neither had Esther or I. So we took the long trip, over several months, down the East Coast, around Florida, through Mexico—pioneering then by auto—

through Arizona and visiting the Grand Canyon and Yosemite Park, up California to San Francisco, and then overland again to Rochester. It was a thrilling slice of North America and all four of us enjoyed it. Somehow we traveled in good humor. This may have been one high point in my parents' lives—a long trip with their son, married and with his wife. Before returning to Rochester, we stopped in Chicago where I paid my first visit to the Meadville Theological School where Unitarian ministers were being trained.

We reached Rochester at the end of April 1940 and our national efforts to involve the U.S. in the European war were growing. Two months earlier the Rochester Citizens' No-War Committee had been formed. I gave almost full time during the month of May to this group, editing the first number of *Rochester No-War News* which came out on May 10 to coincide with a large no-war rally featuring Senator C. Wayland Brooks of Illinois. Some three thousand persons attended. The purposes of our committee were to 1) keep America out of a foreign war; 2) resist war propaganda and hysteria; 3) work for world reconstruction; and 4) maintain and strengthen democracy at home. A number of prominent clergy sponsored this local effort, including David Rhys Williams. The national effort brought together strange bedfellows. I acknowledged this in a letter to Joseph Delibert: "I am willing to swallow my pride and unite with all kinds of people against war, whatever their motive may be." These included Charles A. Lindbergh and Norman Thomas, Hugh Johnson and John Haynes Holmes and Harry Emerson Fosdick. I was astounded to receive a note from Sheddy, who was ousted from the faculty of the University of Rochester two generations before for opposing World War I. He strangely supported the U.S. going to war, writing: "So if it means war for us, then let it be so. This foolish idea that this is Britain's war, not ours, is silly and suicidal."

In the meantime my father-in-law, David Rhys Williams, kept urging me to go to theological school, first to become a minister, but at least to avoid the draft. My interest in the ministry antedated World War II by four years. I contemplated entering the ministry seriously enough to warrant Dr. Sidney Snow, president of Meadville, having breakfast with me in September 1935 between trains in Rochester as he journeyed from his summer home in Vermont back to Chicago. Nothing tangible came of that encounter, but I did renew contact with him in the spring of 1941 about entering Meadville. He and the faculty approved the application. My move from science to theology was the end of my professional work in science and the beginning of my career as a social activist.

PART TWO 1941-1948

GANDHIAN DISCIPLE

THE CHICAGO YEARS

"Ah me, what are the people whose land I have come to this time,
and are they violent and savage, and without justice,
or hospitable to strangers, with a godly mind?"
— The Odyssey, Book VI

The towering moral figure of Mohandas Gandhi dominated Homer's consciousness in the early 1940s. In a letter to President Roosevelt in 1942, Gandhi warned, "I venture to think that the Allied declaration that the Allies are fighting to make the world safe for the freedom of the individual and for democracy sounds hollow, so long as India and, for that matter, Africa are exploited by Great Britain, and America has the Negro problem in her own home." Through the '40s and '50s—the era spanning World War II, the bombing of Hiroshima and Nagasaki, the beginning of the nuclear arms race, the genesis of the modern civil rights movement, and the decades of Asian and African independence—Chicago served as the hub of Homer's life and travels. Chicago was then the nation's second largest city—the counterweight to New York, the capital of finance, fashion, and home of the Yankees, the perennial World Series champions. Chicago's star waned in the next generation following Mayor Daley's crackdown on dissent at the 1968 Democratic Convention and as Los Angeles surpassed it in population and cultural innovation. But at midcentury, the city on Lake Michigan— as the pulsating heart of the Midwest, the terminus of the black exodus from the South, and the gateway to the West—was the epicenter of the American Dream.

Photograph: Delegation from the American Unitarian Association, including Homer (left), at White House with President Harry S. Truman (right)

10 CHICAGO
(1940s-1950s)

PARIS OF THE PRAIRIES

Ordinarily Homer would never boast about splitting the atom or founding the Communist Party. But in this essay—a paean to Chicago, where he lived longer than any other metropolitan region—he does both! Published originally as the first of a two-part article in the Indian Messenger, *the organ of the Brahmo Samaj, the essay introduces the Windy City to Indians en route to Chicago for a meeting of the IARF—International Association for Liberal Christianity and Religious Freedom. Homer's portrait vividly captures the energy and excitement of the city in which his own early dreams and ambitions were launched.*

The German statesman, Prince Bismark, exclaimed to the nineteenth century, "I wish I could go to America if only to see that Chicago." He never did, but such diverse world figures as Rudyard Kipling, Jawaharlal Nehru, and Albert Schweitzer have managed to visit "that Chicago." The foreign visitor might select New York for its cultural richness, Washington for its international atmosphere, Cincinnati or Rochester for their civic virtue, Boston or Philadelphia for their historical flavor, Miami or Los Angeles for their climate, but why Chicago?

Chicago is a wonderful town, first of all, because of its unabashed, unselfconscious extravagance. Chicago architect and planner, Daniel H. Burnbam said, "Make no little plans: they have no magic to stir men's blood and probably themselves will not be realized. Make big plans; aim high in hope and work, remembering that a noble and logical diagram once recorded will never die, but long after we are gone will be a living thing, asserting itself with growing intensity. Remember that our sons and grandsons are going to do things that would stagger us. Let our watchword be 'order' and our beacon 'beauty.'"

Chicago's watchword has not always been order, and Chicago's beacon has not always been beauty, but Chicago made no little plan even before Burnham. Everything about Chicago tends to be, not merely large or early, but the biggest and the first. What other city, for example, could reverse the direction of a large river? But Chicago did just that to the Chicago River, and for good reason, since it wanted to prevent the pollution of Lake Michigan, a pollution which, before the river was turned in 1871, caused 1,500 deaths to Chicagoans each year. Indeed, the name Chicago comes from "Checegou," an Indian designation for the river, meaning strong or powerful. And the strong here referred to the strong-smelling wild garlic or leek growing along the stream!

What other city in America, or in the world, can match Chicago as a transportation center and thus a mercantile center? Chicago is the rail, air, highway, and inland waterway center of a continent. With its twenty truck railroads, passenger trains arrive and depart at the rate of more than one a minute. With its thirteen airlines, eleven with foreign routes, Chicago's Midway airport alone witnesses the landing or take-off of an airplane every 90 seconds, the busiest airport in the world. With its strategic location between the Great Lakes and the Mississippi River, Chicago receives more ships, handling more cargo than both the Panama and Suez canals combined. The Board of Trade is the world's largest grain market. The Merchandise Mart is the world's largest building in square feet. With its 15,000 manufacturing concerns, the county of Cook has the greatest dollar industrial output of any county in any nation, and with the most diversified industry. More steel, more plastics, more diesel locomotives, more meat, more candy, more electronic equipment are produced in Chicago than anywhere in the whole wide world.

Chicago is extravagant in its tragedy as well as in its triumphs. Its panics, its jobless, its riots can only be recorded in superlative terms. The Chicago Fire of 1871 started in the cowbarn behind Patrick O'Leary's house and promptly consumed 17,000 buildings, a record before aerial blockbusters. The great Iroquois Theatre Fire in 1903 killed 602 persons. The Great Lakes excursion steamer, *Eastland*, overturned in the Chicago River in 1915 killing 812 persons.

There were still other Chicago superlatives: the first Pullman car, the first refrigerator car, the first atomic chain reactor, the first skyscraper, the world's largest hotel, America's largest convention city, the greatest pile of medical facilities, and the greatest collection of theological seminaries. It is this quantity, if not necessarily the quality, that makes Chicago a fascinating town.

Chicago is, secondly, a wonderful town because of its people. Its opportunities have attracted people even more than ideas. Founded in 1833, Chicago grew to more than a million in fifty years. Chicago is the youngest of the world's great cities. Chicago, at the age of twenty-seven, was as large as Athens. Chicago, at the age of forty-five, caught up with Rome. At fifty, Chicago was as Vienna or Constantinople. Today Chicago is the sixth largest city of the world, only surpassed by Tokyo, London, New York, Shanghai, and Moscow—in that order—and easily surpassing Buenos Aires, Berlin, Paris, and Bombay. Today metropolitan Chicago with its suburbs in six counties and in parts of three states, has a total population of 6 million. With the new Cal-Sag harbor and industrial development, sociologists are talking of 8 million inhabitants by 1980.

It is not, however, so much the total number of people but the waves of peoples who have come and made Chicago. First it was the American Indians who settled Chicago, but they never liked the swamps and they have only come again recently when the office of Indian Affairs began resettling them from Western reservations to the City. After the early Indians came the French explorers followed by the enterprising Easterners who arrived to develop this likely frontier and incorporated the city in 1830. Then followed wave upon wave of European immigration. By 1900 Chicago had more Scandinavians and Dutch than any other city in America, and also the nation's largest Polish, Lithuanian, Bohemian, Croatian, and Greek settlements. During and after the first and second world wars came the Negroes, almost 750,000 today, and also the Japanese-Americans and Mexican-Americans and Puerto Ricans. Until a few years ago, many of these ethnic islands were well developed and charming—with their stores, newspapers, restaurants, clubs, and churches. Even today one can still go to "Little Athens" near Harrison and Halsted streets and buy Greek pastry or to Milwaukee Avenue for Polish food or to Belmont Avenue for some Swedish bread. These centers are beginning to disappear as the third generation has moved way out, even into the suburbs. This is the Chicago, the American way—this mobility.

It has been these people from all nationalities, from all religions, with all kinds of names who have given Chicago its brains—a Fermi—and its mayors—a Czermak. It is these waves of people who have made Chicago an exciting town.

Thirdly, Chicago is a wonderful town because it has mirrored the social problems—and growth—of America. There are certainly better cultural opportunities in some other American cities. There are certainly better universities in New England. There are certainly better social movements—organizations—in New York. Somehow the major battles that made America have been fought or mirrored in Chicago.

Much of the native radicalism that was American began right in Chicago. It was the city where labor pioneer Eugene V. Debs fought with capitalist pioneer, George M. Pullman. It was where Gov. John P. Altgeld, "the eagle forgotten," pardoned some of those convicted of the Haymarket riot. It was the city where Upton Sinclair wrote his novel *The Jungle* and put some humanity into the meatpackers and into their stockyards. It was in Chicago that Jane Addams founded her social settlement, Hull House. (Indeed John Galsworthy's play, *Justice*, was first performed on the stage of Hull House with Theodore Roosevelt in the first night audience.) The social settlement movement flourished in Chicago not only with Hull House but also with Graham Taylor's Chicago Commons and Jenkin Lloyd Jones' Abraham Lincoln Center, settlements which attracted the young musician Benny Goodman and the young writer Richard Wright. It was in and near Chicago where the American Communist Party was really born (although the Chicago Association of Commerce does not usually broadcast this fact), and it was Chicago where Sewall Avery had to be carried out of his plush mail-order house office for resisting a government labor relations decree. It was here that the American dynasties were founded: McCormick, Armour, and Swift, and also the maverick millionaires, Samuel Rosenwald, Marshall Field, and Anita McCormick Blaine.

It was in Chicago that a new type of university was born, the University of Chicago. The early students were to sing, "John D. Rockefeller, wonderful man is he, gives all his spare change to the U. of C." And this spare change of a non-Chicagoan totalled $35 million in his lifetime. It was largely through this magnificent university that Chicago was measured, chronicled, and dissected by social scientists, from its Gold Coast to its taxi dance halls, from its homeless men to its black ghetto. No city in the world has spawned as many outstanding volumes of sociological surveys.

It was in Chicago that the muckrakers found their muck, Lincoln Steffins writing about Charles T. Yerkes and the others. It was Chicago that produced Michael "Hindy-Din" Kenna and John "The

104

Bath" Coughlin, two first-ward aldermen more crooked than Wacker Drive. Chicago produced Al Capone and captured John Dillinger, those authentic gangsters, and Charles Yerkes and Samuel Insull, those authentic robber barons. It was two Chicagoans who received the Nobel Peace Prize, the world's highest honor, Charles Dawes from Evanston and Jane Addams from Halsted Street. It was Chicago where the 1927 Kellogg Peace Pact was born, conceived by attorney Salmon O. Levinson, and where FDR made his "Quarantine speech" portending the Second World War.

It was Chicago where Abraham Lincoln was first nominated for the presidency in the Wigwam in 1860 and where William Jennings Bryan made his "Cross of Gold" oration in 1896. It was where Clarence Darrow practiced law and defended Leopold and Loeb. It was where Big Bill Thompson, mayor, threatened to "punch King George in the snout," and where what called itself the World's Greatest Newspaper was published. Chicago was the site of the 1886 Haymarket Riot and the 1919 Negro-white riots.

Chicago was where Louis Sullivan and Dankmar Adler designed the Auditorium and Frank Lloyd Wright planned his first houses and Mies van der Rohe put up huge, stilt-like, lake front apartments, where the skyscraper idea originated and where city planning flourished.

Chicago was—and is—a great city, a microcosm of our rapidly changing world.

11 CHICAGO • LITCHFIELD • LAWRENCE
(1941-43)

UNITARIAN RADICAL

Perspective 1941: Franklin Delano Roosevelt was inaugurated as President for the third time and he asked Congress to support lend-lease to supply allies (at war since 1939). Germany bombed the House of Parliament in London. France sent 5,000 Parisian Jews to labor camps. Hitler's associate, Rudolph Hess, landed in Scotland. Germany attacked the Soviet Union on June 30, voiding the August 1939 Nazi-Soviet non-aggression pact. Roosevelt and Churchill off Newfoundland signed the Atlantic Charter. The German Army massacred Ukrainians, including many Jews, at Babi Yar. Japan attacked Pearl Harbor and the U.S. declared war on Japan and two days later on Germany and Italy. (The only vote in the U.S. Congress against the war was Jeannette Rankin who also opposed the U.S. going to war in 1917). Arthur Koestler's Darkness at Noon *was published and Richard Wright's* Native Son *played on Broadway. The U.S. population was 132 million, U.S.S.R. 181 million, India 389 million, and China about 500 million.*

Once I decided to attend theological school, and was accepted, I was eager to go. I did not want to waste a summer before the autumn opening of Meadville Theological School, and found that I could attend summer school at the University of Chicago and begin to take courses toward my ministry degree. Also my father-in-law, David Rhys Williams, was to deliver the baccalaureate sermon at the graduation ceremonies of Meadville early in June. That appeared to be a good time to leave Rochester and travel with the family to Chicago, staying there for the several weeks until summer school began. This was one of several schools for training Unitarian ministers. It was established in the 1860s at Meadville, Pennsylvania, but transferred to the University of Chicago community in order to be in proximity with a great university and its Divinity School. Meadville was a small school, with perhaps thirty students and three full-time faculty. Meadville was one of half a dozen theological schools comprising the Federated Theological Faculty, and we students were encouraged to take many courses in the University, including its Divinity School.

We found housing in the Divinity School Apartments on Maryland Avenue, in Hyde Park, just a few blocks from campus. Esther soon found a clerical job with Billings Hospital. I had a fair amount of correspondence just before going to Meadville, and shortly afterwards, about my switch in career. I did not gradually decide to change careers. I did it so quickly, at least outwardly, so that some of my closest friends expressed surprise at my studying for the ministry. I wrote an old friend of our family, Kendrick P. Shedd, that the real reason I wanted to enter the ministry was that "much more thought and time should be devoted to human relations than to pure science at this stage in the development of civilization." While I did not pretend that I could contribute very much to either, I would at least "feel better inside if I can do something, if only little, to change the social order for the better, than to continue to identify the species of oaks or orchids." I wrote that it was almost as if I had to decide to enter the Communist Party or the liberal church.

I chose the latter because there is more potential for social change coming from the liberal pulpit than most realize." I was willing "to take the risk and find out."

My friend, Nelson Foote, wrote from a new job in Washington on the very eve of my attending theological school that "the Unitarian church is decadent and no longer a leader in liberal thought." He urged me to teach, not preach. He felt that the ministry was "an easy way out of your quandary." I should strike out boldly and courageously for myself, since I had the imagination to be a good radio or newspaper reporter. He closed by admitting that, while most of my friends would "snort" if they heard of my switch, they would "on second thought admit that you would probably make a go of it, if you got started." Nelson, incidentally, came to Cornell as a devout Christian and left as an aspiring sociologist skeptical of all religion. Cornell had the opposite effect on me.

Trying to justify my new career to my senior professor at Cornell, Dr. Palmer, I wrote early in my theological studies that I go about the University of Chicago campus with the Holy Bible under my arm, not the Holy Gray—*Gray's Manual of Botany*. Yet I wrote him that we scrutinize parts of the Bible as closely as we used to dissect zoological specimens.

Litchfield Universalist Church

All Meadville students had to do field work during their studies for a degree. During my first year—1941-42—I did field work at Olivet Church, a small Presbyterian Church on the Near North Side of Chicago. Rev. Alva Tompkins was the minister, and I knew him when I was a student at Cornell and he was one of the chaplains there. My year with Al was uneventful. I seldom preached, but worked with his Sunday School. That the church was Presbyterian, not Unitarian, concerned me little, for Al was a person deeply involved with social issues and indeed his parsonage was often the site of Fellowship of Reconciliation meetings for all of Chicago.

My second year at Meadville turned out to be my final year, since by going to school in summer, I could take three years in two under the University of Chicago plan. Actually, graduation included a thesis, and I never finished one—on "Denominational Social Action"—until several years later. That second year I was assigned field work at the Universalist Church in Litchfield, Illinois. I became its minister, with all the rights and privileges of the office, including $15.00 a week for my weekends there, of which $9.00 was needed for the long roundtrip journey to southern Illinois, about 300 miles each way!

I would leave every Saturday morning, take the bus to Engelwood and then the Illinois Central train four or more hours south. I would stay with Mrs. Davis, an elderly widow who had a nice house. En route I would prepare my sermon and, once in Litchfield, attempt to squeeze in as many as two parish calls on Saturday evening. My congregation consisted of seven persons when I started and the climax was around Christmas when President Snow of Meadville came down with me and some twenty-two persons attended.

I learned many aspects of the ministry at Litchfield, and in my field work report I listed: publicity, preaching, visiting, and other pastoral work. I also made the weekly postcard (by hectograph) that was sent to all church families. My field work involved occasional preaching at other churches, such as in Little Hickory, Illinois, and attending the Illinois State Universalist Convention. My sermons included "Is Religion an Instinct?" "The Church Assesses Pearl Harbor," "Dare We Be Thankful Today?" "Between the Lines of History," and "Malvern: The British Church Militant."

My first year as a theological school student was decidedly mixed. I found that Meadville gave me a great opportunity to work on social issues, but I failed miserably on family affairs. My wife moved out on me after the first year. I moved into the Meadville men's dormitory just opposite the school's academic building on Woodlawn Avenue at 57th Street. The reasons for our separation were mixed. I simply did not pay enough attention to her. Also she was carrying the financial burden as I was ostensibly going to school, but spending increasing time on race relations and other issues. Black/white relations for me became more important than marital relations.

Unitarian Church of Lawrence

In the late summer of 1943, I began the intricate process of finding a post as full-time minister. I wrote to several denominational officials that "I am a socialist and pacifist, but hoped that these philosophies would, if anything, make me more tolerant and understanding." In the early autumn I spent six weeks in Boston—the Holy See of Unitarianism—attending a seminar for new ministers and dealing with placement officials of the American Unitarian Association. A classmate, Vilmar Bose, who was spending a summer working for the Socialist Party, was asked by the denominational officer in charge of the ministry: Has your summer work convinced you that you would be better off (working) through secular rather than religious channels?

Dr. Charles H. Lyttle of Meadville wrote me in September that he was recommending me for the ministry of the Unitarian Church of Lawrence, Kansas, since its leader, Leona Handler, was leaving for further training.

Dr. Lyttle strongly recommended the church to me: "The congregation is very progressive in thought and very open-minded and experimental and the church is closely linked with the local cooperative." Curtis Reese, head of the Western Unitarian Conference, wrote me that it was a grand opportunity.

I took a train to Kansas and candidated for the pulpit during the last ten days of October, 1943. One of my sermons was "A More Balanced Liberalism." The church was established in 1856 by the first governor of Kansas. It had its own building some blocks from the large University of Kansas (KU), but the latter in 1943 was only a shadow of itself because of war. I also learned that there were about fifty members of the church and twenty-five "prospects." The budget was about $2,000 a year, including my salary of $843. Its principal income was interest from a trust fund and a subsidy from the Unitarian Association for college work.

After returning to Chicago, I received a call to become its minister. I drove back to Lawrence and began on November 21. The attendance during the first four Sundays was thirty-six, forty-two, thirty-five, and thirty. I confided to one of my Meadville classmates and several of us were writing to each other, and at that time I especially wrote to Dick Kuch at Rockford and Paul Henniges at Long Beach—that the church was "a mess." I did what I could to try to reduce the church's debt, $400—a big amount at that time—and to straighten out the office. More important, the leading layperson, Prof. Florence B. Sherborn, a child study expert, became ill with cancer. We managed to publish her booklet, "The Challenge of Modern Science to Liberal Religion," but not until after her death.

I worked hard to build up the church the best way I could—through college youth. Because of war, most of the students at KU were women. We started a Saturday Evening Club. It was three-hyphenated: inter-racial, inter-denominational, college-age. This turned out to be my most successful innovation.

Lawrence was then a town-and-gown community of 15,000 persons. Like most of America—North and South, East and West—it was a racist town. Negroes were not allowed to join the KU football team. Negroes could not join the University Choir because "their voices are different." Negroes could not eat in the private dining room of the town's only hotel, the Eldridge, even for a ministers' breakfast. This was "John Brown's town" in what before the Civil War was called "Free Kansas." The town was also "violently" anti-Roosevelt (Franklin D.) and anti-labor.

I delivered a series of sermons on race relations entitled "Brothers Under the Skin." I tried to befriend the local NAACP and help the ailing co-op store. I even edited their bulletin to increase sales!

I also spoke out on the war. In a sermon, "Dare We Be Thankful Today?," given on Thanksgiving Sunday in the middle of World

War II, I listed seven points to be grateful for: 1) the maintenance of civil liberties in the U.S.; 2) the churches were not at war; 3) the domestic economy was more democratic; 4) discrimination against Negroes was breaking down—slowly; 5) the world had grown smaller and more cosmopolitan; 6) the enemy was showing us our sins and making us better; and 7) the forces that were making for utter destruction could be transformed to forces for utter construction. I also preached on a religious response to the strategic bombing of civilians on both sides, resulting in widespread massacres.

Reunion and Renewal

During my second year as a Meadville student, Esther and I were civil to each other and I saw something of her since she stayed in the University (Hyde Park) area. She had taken a new, higher paying job with the Metallurgy Department of the University. Metallurgy was a name to divert attention from its real purpose; it turned out to be part of the Manhattan Project which made the first atomic bomb. Esther had no notion of the scope of "Metallurgy," although she was secretary to the personnel administrator and, thanks to her initiative, desegregated his office by convincing him to hire a young Negro typist. After I went to Kansas, Esther and I fitfully corresponded and at some point she moved to Boston. Soon I wanted a reconciliation, but one of her uncles felt she should get a quick divorce and that she did. The more she became remote, the more I wanted her nearer—again as a wife. Finally, in mid-summer, 1944, she consented to remarry me. We got as quick a marriage—in Indiana—as she earlier got a divorce. We rented an apartment in the Hyde Park area, on Ellis Avenue. By then I was working with the Chicago Council and had decided to stay in that job, partly because of the increased salary which I needed to pay for the increased responsibilities of having a wife again. So I resigned from the Lawrence Church. Esther and I drove to Lawrence where, between sermons on two successive Sundays in September, I helped the church open its 1944-45 church year without me as minister. Some members expressed sorrow that I was leaving after only one year as their minister; others were relieved if only because their budget would be more balanced without the salary of a full-time minister!

Looking backwards, I must admit that several of us students at Meadville were an unruly, radical crowd—if three or four students (out of perhaps fifteen full-time students) could be considered

111

a crowd. No wonder President Snow died a year later! In the two full years I was resident at Meadville, I managed—with others—to take the following initiatives. We tried to unionize the small staff, three or four Negroes. We sent greetings as a student body in the form of an advertisement in the May Day issue of the U.S. communist newspaper, the *Daily Worker*. We picketed the British Consulate on Michigan Avenue as part of Mohandas K. Gandhi's call for worldwide protests for "Quit India Day." We devoted an entire chapel service (held every Friday afternoon) to the plight of Robert Chino, a young Chinese-American who refused to be drafted and was treated badly in Chicago Federal Court.

Our student radicalism had at least two sources. One was our uneasiness with America's involvement in World War II. This was the period just before and after the Japanese attack on Pearl Harbor. Many of us held various degrees of pacifism, although other Meadville and University of Chicago students did not.

In Kansas I became secretary of the Unitarian Pacifist Fellowship, a national society of fifty ministers and 150 laymen who, on religious grounds, pledged not to participate in war. Back in Chicago, I had fears of being drafted if I left the full-time parish ministry. I vowed indeed not to go into the army, if drafted, but go either to Civilian Public Service camp as a conscientious objector, or perhaps to prison. Thus I tried frankly to quickly find a strong vocational connection with organized religion even while working for the Chicago Council which, I realized, would not qualify as a religious institution in the eyes of most draft boards. I soon put together a job as Minister for Radio of the Chicago Unitarian Council. I printed an impressive letterhead, but the job was unsalaried. All I did was direct a weekly, 15-minute radio program which was aired early every Sunday afternoon. I also did some joint publicity for the eight Unitarian churches in the area which united for this purpose. (The Universalist churches were not yet involved.) I felt that this work might not be entirely persuasive to my draft board in Rochester and sought even more solid church connections.

I wrote to Preston Bradley in October, 1944, suggesting I might become Minister of Inter-Racial Relations of People's Church since he was Chairman of the Chicago Council. He never replied! (Although it was a Unitarian Church and Bradley was a liberal and it was very much his church, that proposal at the time would hardly have been acceptable.)

12 CHICAGO
(1942)

THE BEGINNINGS OF CORE

Perspective 1942: Twenty-six countries in Washington issued a declaration of the United Nations against the German/Italian/Japanese Axis. Nehru succeeded Gandhi as head of the Indian National Congress. One hundred and ten thousand Japanese-Americans were interned on the West Coast of the U.S. Nazis began sending Jews to Auschwitz in Poland. Negro recruits were allowed in the U.S. Navy for the first time. Churchill and Roosevelt in Washington agreed to develop the atomic bomb. The Indian National Congress launched its "Quit India" campaign led by Gandhi. The first controlled nuclear chain reaction was achieved at the University of Chicago. Popular songs included "White Christmas" and "Praise the Lord and Pass the Ammunition."

In the autumn of 1942, I began attending a meeting of the University of Chicago group or "cell" of the Fellowship of Reconciliation (FOR). This was a Christian pacifist group, founded in England in 1914 and in the U.S. in 1915. In the late 1930s, with war fever and pacifist reaction growing, the FOR had an office in New York City and groups in a number of cities and college campuses. A. J. Muste (1885-1967), a clergyman briefly turned Trotskyite and then minister of the Labor Temple in New York City, was called in 1940 to become Secretary of the American FOR. (His co-secretary was John Nevin Sayre, a relative of President Woodrow Wilson.) In the summer of 1941, Muste hired two young national staff members: James Farmer to be Race Relations Secretary and Bayard Rustin to be Youth Secretary. He also hired George M. Houser to be part-time

113

Youth Secretary in the Chicago area.

Houser came to the Chicago Theological Seminary from Danbury Federal Correctional Institution, where he and seven other students at Union Theological Seminary in New York refused a year earlier to register for the draft and accept ministerial exemption. They spent ten months in jail. Born in Cleveland, Houser, at age three, went to the Philippines with his missionary parents and in 1935-36 was an exchange student in China. In Chicago, Houser, age twenty-five, was eager to establish a network of FOR cells. Occasionally, representatives from the different cells would gather at the near North Side parsonage of the Rev. Alva Tompkins, minister of Olivet Institute Presbyterian Church (where I was doing my weekend field work for seminary).

That FOR Group began discussing three issues: 1) opposing the draft and the growing effort by President Roosevelt to enter the existing world war, 2) helping India become independent, and 3) understanding the racism we saw all about us in the University neighborhood of Hyde Park. Soon Pearl Harbor was bombed on Sunday, December 7, and America entered the war. While we continued to oppose the war and help CO's (conscientious objectors), we somehow were challenged by the racism at our doorstep and what we might do to confront it directly, especially in wartime. We increasingly believed in nonviolence and, if we could not put it to use on the battlefields of Asia and Europe, we wondered if we could do so in the neighborhoods of Chicago, and especially Hyde Park, Woodlawn, and Kenmore. We began to read Richard Gregg's *The Power of Non-Violence*—one of the first American studies of Gandhian nonviolence. We also used a new volume, *War Without Violence*, by Krishnalal Shridharani, an Indian who studied at Columbia University. His doctoral thesis became this book which "Americanized" the techniques of *satyagraha* or nonviolent direct action which Mohandas K. Gandhi evolved in South Africa and was at the time still continuing in India.

Shridharani was not an arm-chair observer. At the age of twenty, he participated in Gandhi's Salt March of 1931 and was imprisoned. He wrote in his book, "Satyagraha is to be employed only when anything, except violence and war, is more desirable than the existing state of affairs." He quoted Gandhi who, in a speech in England also in 1931, said: "The conviction has been growing upon me that things of fundamental importance to the people are not secured by reason alone, but have to be purchased with their suffering." Gandhi added that "nobody has perhaps drawn up more petitions or espoused more forlorn causes than I, and I have come to this fundamental conclusion that if you want something really important to be done you must not merely satisfy the reason, you must move the heart also." Gandhi concluded, "The appeal of reason is more to the head, but the penetration of the heart comes from suffering. It opens the inner understanding in men."

Housing Discrimination in Chicago

We in Chicago, and especially the cell at the University of Chicago campus, suddenly realized that we had to appeal more than to reason; we had to penetrate the heart of the racists who were our neighbors. Thus we realized that the Saturday afternoon studies of Gandhism were insufficient; we had to act. We early concluded that housing segregation was the most serious problem confronting Chicago's Negroes and perhaps one of the most vulnerable. It appeared to be based on the existence of racial restrictive covenants or deeds on property preventing it from being sold or occupied by Negroes. How could a combination of legal and direct action break these nefarious instruments that, we soon found, were even supported by the University of Chicago?

It was decided to establish a cooperative house for men in a racially restrictive area. This was to become a university version of a Gandhian ashram. A house was rented at 4853 Kenwood Avenue, owned by Mrs. Edgar Lee Masters, widow of the author of the *Spoon River Anthology*. A lease was signed by some whites and then ten blacks and whites moved into Men's Interracial Fellowship House on January 1, 1942. (I was involved in the project, but was not one of the residents because I lived with my wife in an apartment for theological students owned by the University.)

Soon the presence of the Negroes was questioned, but no action was taken by the owner. However, all ten were forced to leave after six months because the lease could not be renewed. A number of persons were involved in this effort, including James Farmer, Alvin Cannon, James R. Robinson, Hugo Victoreen, and Russell Smith. We were greatly aided by Dr. Arthur G. Falls, and his wife, Lillian. He was a physician and she was a social worker. They became our advisers and gave us insights about Chicago's large black ghetto—"the Southside."

Simultaneous to this activity, James Farmer, the Race Relations Secretary of the FOR, began his job as a "youth field worker" on October 1 and moved to Chicago. That autumn he spoke to fifteen colleges and universities, six churches, and six local FOR groups in the midwest and South. In a report he wrote to A. J. Muste on November 26 he declared, "I have consistently sought to introduce the Negro college groups reached to nonviolent direct action, and have suggested their further study of such techniques in relation to their application to racial problems in America." Farmer further suggested, "The first step might be to bring to an end the Negro's submission to, and cooperation with, outright discriminatory agencies wherever possible, with such non-support, financial and otherwise, to continue until the discriminatory policies were changed."

This was certainly advocating the Gandhian way if not using in this report the Gandhian name. These techniques went beyond the more conventional techniques used by the National Association for the Advancement of Colored People (NAACP) and the National Urban League.

One evening Farmer and Robinson left Fellowship House for a cup of coffee at a nearby restaurant named Jack Spratt. They were rudely refused service. They got no satisfaction by using the traditional methods of protest to the management through letters and phone calls. The Fellowship House decided to try direct action. After a careful briefing, a group of all whites entered the cafe and sat down. Then a mixed group entered. They were refused service. Still a third group entered—all blacks. They were also refused service. A witness was a reporter from the black newspaper, the *Chicago Defender*. This first sit-in produced much publicity, but no change in practice by Jack Spratt's management.

In February and March 1942 Farmer showed his memorandum, called "The Brotherhood Mobilization," to Muste in New York. The latter was encouraging and arranged for Farmer to unveil this plan for a national effort before the National Council of the FOR meeting in April in Cincinnati. George Houser, Bernice Fisher, and I drove with Farmer to this meeting.

"Only Cause Conflict"

At the FOR meetings, some members felt Farmer's plan would "only cause conflict." The plan was not endorsed, but Muste managed a compromise whereby Farmer could stay on FOR salary while attempting to build an organization along the lines of his plan. In the meantime, the FOR cell in Chicago was independently planning to broaden its Gandhian effort by launching a city-wide group organizationally independent from the FOR whether or not the FOR Council approved.

As our FOR group continued to figure out the best way to attack racism and to adapt Gandhism to the Chicago scene, we finally came up with three principles: interracialism, nonviolence, and direct action. We wanted whites and blacks—all people—to work together. We wanted our actions to be nonviolent, despite great provocation for violence. We wanted participatory direct action, not primarily legal action. We experimented with these principles as Gandhi himself even then and throughout his life experimented with them. Thus Gandhi's autobiography, *The Story of My Experiments With Truth*, was also our autobiography.

In March, a preliminary organizing committee was formed to discuss the establishment of the independent nonviolent direct action group. Included were Kenneth and Polly Cuthbertson, Henry Dyer, George Houser, and Bernice Fisher. Soon Joseph Guinn, James Robinson, and myself also joined this organizing group. It was probably at this point where the "Houser effort" and the "Farmer effort" coincided.

Reports of discrimination against Negroes at the appropriately-named White City Roller Rink at 63rd Street and South Parkway led to the organization of an action in April involving twenty-four blacks and whites. We discovered that Negroes were excluded on the pretext that they were not members of a fictitious private club. Negotiations were held with the management, but it was finally decided to take the company to court for violating the state civil rights laws. After eight months of litigation, the case was lost.

The White City action further stimulated members of the group to discuss further forming a permanent organization. Still in April 1941, a group of fifty people from all over Chicago met on a Sunday afternoon at Meadville House to form a permanent group committed to the use of nonviolent direct action to oppose discrimination. A subsequent survey showed that the initial members were mostly unmarried university students in their thirties, one-half pacifist, and one-third black. A steering committee was elected, with Bernice Fisher as chair. James Farmer was absent, no doubt on an out-of-Chicago speaking engagement.

We took several months to determine a name. Then in June at a meeting at Men's Fellowship House, some suggested that this evolving Chicago group be called the Committee of Racial Democracy. Bob Chino—a University of Chicago student who had been arrested for refusing induction—shouted: "I've got it. Let's call it CORE, because it will be the center of things, the heart of the action." We constructed a name from an acronym. RE easily stood for Racial Equality. CO, after much discussion, stood for Committee of. CORE became the Committee of Racial Equality. Significantly, the prepositions, for or on, before equality, were turned down, since the members felt racial equality was a fact, not a goal.

Sit-In at Jack Spratt

The negotiations to end discrimination at Jack Spratt were slowly continuing. In May began what Farmer records as "the first organized civil rights sit-in in American history." This time we mobilized twenty-eight persons to enter Jack Spratt in parties of two, three and four, and at least one black man or woman in each. None of us was served, although the woman manager offered to serve the Negroes in the basement. We refused. Finally James Robinson, after earlier notifying the police, telephoned them. They came. When the manager asked the police to throw us out on the grounds that "we reserve the right to seat our patrons," a policeman responded: "No, lady, there's nothing in the law that allows us to do that." Then the waitresses were asked by the manager to serve everyone. We ate, tipped the waitresses well, and left. Money was not thrown out after us as it was when we first tried to deal with Jack Spratt.

During these first experiments, many involved were not pacifists. Yet all remained nonviolent, although the debate on whether nonviolent direct action was a tactic or a principle dominated the discourse in Chicago as in India then—and still today.

Soon word about CORE spread around the country, especially as Farmer and Rustin spoke as FOR field workers. We began receiving mail asking how nonviolent direct action could be started in other cities. Some of the first mimeographing I did in the basement of the Meadville Theological School, but we needed an office. The Rev. Archibald J. Carey, pastor of the Woodlawn African Methodist Episcopal Church, and later a Chicago alderman, gave us space in his church.

By June, the second men's fellowship house opened on South Ellis Avenue and the first women's interracial house opened on nearby Kimbark Avenue. A real estate agency tried to evict the men, but their neighbors refused to testify against them in court. The women's house lasted for two years and the real estate agents also could not evict the occupants. Breaches in the restrictive covenants began to occur.

The next academic year, 1942-43, we continued to experiment with nonviolent direct action, including the elimination of segregation at the beaches of Lake Michigan near the University. We often had interracial picnics on the 55th Street promontory. We marched in front of blood donor centers that at that time were segregated. Then efforts were made to induce Stoner's Restaurant in Chicago's loop to serve blacks and interracial groups. This was difficult and led us to do research and compile a CORE leaflet on "50 Loop Restaurants Which Do Not Discriminate." I well remember the discrimination at Stoner's. I was seated at a table with some black and white friends. We waited a long time and were finally served—garbage—as the black waitresses warned us not to eat it!

Congress of Racial Equality

In June 1943, we convened in Chicago a conference of local groups (from New York City to Colorado Springs) and agreed to form a National Federation of Committees of Racial Equality—later called the Congress of Racial Equality.

The conference centerpiece was an effort to end the continued harassment of interracial groups at Stoner's. Some sixty-five persons participated and, for the first time in many months, full service was given to black diners. When this happened, spontaneous applause occurred. It was an appropriate climax to months of persistent testing. The irony was that Mr. Stoner was an ardent churchgoer, but also, alas, an ardent segregationist. At the convention, James Farmer was elected national chairman and Bernice Fisher national secretary-treasurer of the Congress.

During the war CORE militantly opposed the segregation of blood by the American Red Cross, waging a public campaign and issuing a variety of literature. It also attacked the discrimination by the University of Chicago, under the presidency of Robert M. Hutchins, against Negro patients and physicians in their several hospitals.

At the second national congress, in Detroit in June 1944, the name was changed from the Committee to the Congress of Racial Equality. In the summer of 1945, CORE conducted its first workshop (for two months) on nonviolent direct action in Chicago. In this period a statement of discipline for CORE members was put into final shape. It stated the purpose and method of the organization: "CORE has one purpose—to eliminate all racial discrimination. CORE has one method—interracial, direct nonviolent action." The statement asked its members "to commit themselves to work as an integrated, disciplined group" by doing two things: 1) "abiding by all democratic group decisions and accepting CORE discipline for all projects in which the individual participates" and 2) "renouncing overt violence in opposing racial discrimination and using the method of direct nonviolent action." The latter "refuses to cooperate with racial injustice," "seeks to change existing practices," and "endeavors to develop a spirit of understanding rather than antagonism."

Did Mohandas Gandhi ever learn of the experiments with *satyagraha* against racism in Chicago and elsewhere by CORE? It is not known if word about CORE ever reached Gandhi in the six years between 1942-48 before his death. Howard Thurman and his wife visited Gandhi in 1936 when the latter predicted that "it may be through the Negroes that the unadulterated message of nonviolence will be delivered to the world."

The establishment of CORE was a collective task, resulting from the vision and hard work of many blacks and whites, pacifists and non-pacifists, who chose the nonviolent, interracial, direct action route toward racial justice. This pioneering achievement of using Gandhian means to lessen American racism came a decade and a half before Martin Luther King, Jr. and his associates borrowed Gandhi's and CORE's techniques and further evolved them in Montgomery, Alabama.

The several dozen Chicagoans and several hundred Americans elsewhere, black and white, were innocents then, experimenting with nonviolent resistance while, during those same years, and beyond, the world was practicing violence, with the slaughter of the Second World War, the Holocaust, Hiroshima/Nagasaki, and the enormity of massacre during the partition of Gandhi's beloved India. What an audacious man Gandhi was, trying to stem the tide of centuries of human violence! He did not do so significantly during the partition of the subcontinent, yet he planted the seeds of a new way of resolving conflict which must sprout to fruition if humanity is to survive the twenty-first century. And we of infant CORE may have been Gandhi's first American followers to deal with black/white relations. We may have been in some ways flawed, but we were pioneering in our experiments.

13 MIAMI
(1943)

MY FATHER'S LAST DAYS

After three years' retirement in Florida, Homer's father passed away in the spring of 1943. He was sixty-five and had been ailing from heart disease for several years. These remarks are from a sermon Homer preached in memory of his father at the Unitarian Church in Lawrence, Kansas.

I can see Alex now, as I knew him growing up in Rochester, sitting by the drawing board, by the window facing Bread Street. Coat off, sleeves cut short, elbows smudged with dragon's blood—the photo-engravers' standby—Alex would be working over a candy label or a signature for one of the big department stores. Brushes, pens, blotters, celluloid triangles, labels, patterns, catalogues, copy—what a fascinating mess was on the big oak table that spread to the wall. And then Alex would bounce up from the drawing board, make a proof, and then charge a zinc plate at his roll-top desk. For twenty-five long years, Alex worked at the drawing board, stripped negatives occasionally, ran proofs, and charged up half-tones until his health forced him to quit in the autumn of 1940.

But all this is mere detail. The Alex I knew and loved and the Alex hundreds of others knew and loved had no relation to photo-engraving, except for his four-in-hand tie and smudges of dragon's blood on his shirt. The Alex we knew was the self-educated man who had a wise, civilized opinion about little things—and big things, too. The Alex we knew was the man who had to tend to business to support his family, but whose enthusiasms were his avocations: his new house up on Crosman Terrace, his rock garden,

121

his stamps and coins, his chess and checkers, his eighteenth-century books, his wood carvings, his plants, his photography.

Though my father had to leave school when he was only eight years old, his whole life was more of a formal education than most. He was, as many men deprived of their schooling, an avid reader. He read the classics, the American classics, too: Prescott's *Peru* and Bancroft's *History*. He read Sinclair Lewis in the '20s and Stuart Chase in the '30s. He took the *Nation* for many years—and had that common habit of never throwing away an issue of the *National Geographic*. And as a self-educated man, my father saw through pretense and hypocrisy and soon attained a liberal, but infrequent, nineteenth century philosophy. The Right will prevail. The world is slowly getting better and better. And, of course, Emerson's law of compensation.

My father's reading took him, not so far as I know directly to Karl Marx, but at least to socialist literature. Its justice appealed to him, and he soon joined the Socialist Party local in Rochester in the early nineteen hundreds. He took an active part in local socialist affairs. He helped entertain passing socialists: Debs, Steffens, lesser men now forgotten. He helped establish a series of ill-fated socialist social centers in Rochester. During the last war, the high point of organized socialism in this country, he opposed militarism as did most socialists.

And then after the war, when the Socialist Party split, he, for some reason, withdrew from liberal activity. He retained his socialist analysis, his socialist friends, but he became quite a petty capitalist. He built a house in a nice part of the city. He owned a cottage on the shores of Lake Ontario. And, it being the lush twenties, he—as others—dabbled in the stock market. He made money, too, as much as from his business, which was not unsuccessful. I don't know quite why, as I say, Alex did all this—why he even gave me presents of stock certificates of General Motors and Pennread for Christmas—except a resolve perhaps that *his* child should not go through the economic struggle he went through. The long, cold winters he sold newspapers on the street had left him undernourished. And in this respect, my father's wishes came true, for he always provided for me handsomely, whether it was a trip to Washington, an auto in college, a sojourn in Europe, or three years in graduate school. Yet for all his playing the game, my father never fooled himself. He denounced capitalism and once when some workers picketed his engraving plant which went non-union to survive the Depression, his heart was on the side of the workers. And when Roosevelt came into power, my father succumbed to his magic. He probably voted for a winning candidate for the first time in 1936. And he was a Roosevelt man, if a critical one, all the rest of the days of his life.

If my father was a liberal in politics and economics, he was a radical in religion. He had no truck with the church, including the Unitarian Church. He had, of course, a warm spot in his heart for them because of his days at the Boys' Evening Home, but he saw their hypocrisies in his own city. He was a free thinker, the nearest thing to an atheist—unless it be my mother—that I have ever known. He was not concerned with the thing ordinarily called God, and he knew there was no life hereafter. His simple religion was to live well, be human, act justly—and that is all.

A keen, lifelong interest of my father was nature study. In his youth, he would go to the woods in the spring to paint the red trillium or in the summer to the sand hills along Irondequoit Bay to paint lupins. When he was in his twenties, he took a two-hundred mile hike through the Adirondack Mountains, and climbed to the top of Mt. Marcy—highest in the state. On this trip, too, he visited old John Brown's grave above Kean Valley—and took my mother and myself there to see it twenty years later. Though my father appreciated nature, he never knew the species and sub-species like an expert. He never envied the professional, yet he and my mother did all they could to interest me, when very young, in nature. They joined a nature club which had hikes every weekend and soon my father was elected trustee. I was very proud of him—up in front there with the leading botanist from the University and the entomologist from Ward's. And later, when I studied the natural sciences in college and graduate school, my father vicariously enjoyed the experience. When, after leaving Cornell, I decided to go into the liberal ministry, my father was mildly disappointed; but then, as always, he gave me my complete freedom and his moral and financial support. Several times afterwards, he tried to induce me to weave my nature-study more into my ministry.

Because of heart trouble, he retired to Florida in 1940. Carefully, he began a series of quarto-size watercolors of the Florida flowers. And then one summer he started the flowers of New York State. And the second winter, when he was on his fifty-fifth plate—when he was on the eve of his sixty-fifth birthday—he laid down his brush and was rushed to the Ft. Lauderdale hospital.

It was there, that I saw him for the last time. During that last week together—and it was truly a passion week—I alternated between walking under the Florida pines and palms and visiting his bedside. I would bring him a lily. And he would immediately name it as a turks-cap. And we would be off remembering about the Turks and Hindus I would bring to our house in Rochester from the Cornell Cosmopolitan Club. I would peel an orange—and in good humor to the last—he would say that it was natural to see me eating. I would read him *PM*—of which he was a charter subscriber. And he showed me an article in *PM* which he read and saved for me to read, just before he went to the hospital. The treatment of the Negro in the South distressed him greatly. And we talked about it, even that last week together. He muttered, when all he could do was mutter, if only they would be treated as human beings. As that week wore on, I promised him I would fight against war and racial intolerance and economic injustice, as he would want me to do, as he did, and as he—in business—was unable to do. And then on a bright Sunday noon, with the deep blue sky making a sharp contrast with the red bougainvillea against the white stucco hospital, Alex died. A year ago this moment, almost.

The next day I called at the crematory—for that was his wish and he never ceased to denounce cemeteries—and there in a small pine box was all that was left, in a physically tangible way, of Alex. Could it be? Could it be? But there it was.

And for the last time Alex rode in the front seat beside me. We drove west of Miami out the Tamiami Trail—the trail we had passed over a year before to go across the Florida peninsula to search for shells at Naples Beach. Yes, for the last time we drove deep into the Everglades, past where Homestead Road comes on the trail. And there, beside the canal, trafficked by Seminole canoes and floating hyacinth and egrets, we scattered Alex—fine white dust on the deep blue waters and everglade grass.

But Alex is not only there—he is all over the world in the hearts that have been lighted and lightened by his life and by countless persons that have been inspired by his example. And if, in my six months here in Lawrence, I have been able to inspire anybody by my determination to make this a better world, it has been due to my promise to Alex—and also the example of my dear mother.

14 CHICAGO (1944-48)

RACE RELATIONS SECRETARY

Returning to Chicago from Lawrence, Kansas, Homer became executive secretary of the Chicago Council Against Racial and Religious Discrimination (CCARRD). In 1945, a son, Alex, was born and named after Homer's late father. Two years later, a daughter, Lucy, was born, named after Esther's mother.

My four and one-half years with the Chicago Council was the first important position in my life—really the first of four major positions spanning the forty years 1944 through 1984. This position was largely an uncharted field—no real job description—and thus I had to find my way in what was then the second largest city in the U.S. I began with a three-month trial, for the organization and for myself. In some ways I wanted to return to the ministry in Kansas after that first summer or perhaps to a larger one that could pay me more of a living wage. Yet I also wanted to make a contribution to race relations in wartime.

During my years with the Chicago Council I performed multiple tasks which can be disentangled into five. First, I tried to build a coalition of organizations, some in the field of race and religion, and others in more general fields. Second, I realized that I must deal with the biggest racial or religious problem in Chicago—discrimination against Negroes—but without neglecting other racial and religious minorities and problems, especially Mexican-Americans, Japanese-Americans (coming from the relocation camps), and anti-Semitism. Third, I wanted to discover a way citi-

125

zens' groups could apply effective pressure on the City of Chicago and its official Commission on Human Relations. Fourth, I wanted the coalition to be able to respond quickly to emergencies—yes, race riots. There were several in Chicago and "Chicagoland" in that period. Finally, I wanted to document both the racism and the efforts to counter it. I believed in good communications to "civic leaders" and the media.

I lived almost a lifetime—an exciting and creative one—in the four and one-half years with CCARRD. This autobiography could be filled entirely with what I did—and learned at the Chicago Council. However, I will confine this section to some of the more important events chronologically.

1944-45—War Years!

While minister in Kansas, I received a letter from Frank W. McCulloch on February 2, 1944—my mother's birthday—asking if I would be interested to become Executive Secretary of the Chicago Council Against Racial and Religious Discrimination, an organization that I helped organize while a theological student a year earlier. I had no immediate desire to leave Lawrence and, as a matter of fact, my friend from CORE, Bernice Fisher, was already its secretary. I did not know that she, a radical theological student, was having a feud with its president, Ernest F. Tittle, a Methodist minister in Evanston. By May, the offer from the Chicago Council was renewed. In the end, I decided to take the job at least for the summer of 1944, since I had a three-month vacation from my Lawrence ministry. I was hired for a trial period for $250 a month as Executive Secretary. In the meantime, Dr. Preston Bradley had been elected president, with Earl B. Dickerson, president of the Chicago Urban League "Co-Chairman." Edward J. Sparling, president of the YMCA College in the Loop was its treasurer. Another key leader was Frank W. McCulloch, head of the Union of Democratic Action, forerunner to Americans for Democratic Action.

During the first 18 months as Executive Director of the Chicago Council, I faced the following local headlines: "Cemetery Refuses Tom Chan's Body". . . "Negro Woman's House Burned and Torn Apart" . . . "Gerald L. K. Smith Threatens Chicago Jewry" . . . "Realtor Says People Have Right To Exclude Negroes, Jews, Children, Dogs" . . . "Japanese-American Girl Denied Admittance at Jackson Park Hospital" . . . "Association of Commerce Fights Illinois FEPC"

. . . "Synagogue Attacked Five Times in South Shore" . . . "Negro Youth Killed By White Hoodlums" . . .

Yet there were also some good headlines: "Negroes Integrated in Many War Industries" . . . "Gentile Association Charter Revoked" . . . "Sixty Organizations Testify in Springfield for Illinois FEPC" . . . "Minister and Congregation March to Protect Negro Family" . . .

I came to the Chicago Council with little experience in running an organization, let alone a coalition, and only moderate experience in race relations. I found that the Chicago Council really was in its infancy. To make some order out of its continuing projects, and to give a widening constituency a feeling for our work and priorities, I established a modest, mimeographed newsletter, *Against Discrimination*, and have since found that—if I may say so, like Mohandas Gandhi—some kind of newsletter if not newspaper is essential to organize individuals or groups. This was the precursor of all my subsequent newsletters, *The Evanston Unitarian, Africa Today, SANE World, Beyond Kyoto,* and *Religion for Peace.*

An important task already begun was to give major support to efforts to legislate fair employment practices on local, state, and national levels. One of my first opportunities was to appear before the Platform Committee of the Democratic National Convention, meeting in July, 1944, at Chicago, and make a plea for a FEPC (Fair Employment Practices Commission) plank. Arnold Aronson, of the Bureau of Jewish Employment Problems, helped considerably until he left Chicago for New York to do similar work on a national scale. Anti-Semitism became a headline issue with the formation of the Gentile Cooperative Association and the meetings in Chicago, as elsewhere, of Gerald L. K. Smith.

While we managed to raise the number of organizations affiliated to the Chicago Council to fifty by the end of 1945, our income was minuscule. We ended the calendar year spending only $2,871, with a $492 deficit being "principally the executive director's salary."

I concluded the 1944-45 report of the organization by pointing out that "the continued discriminations outweigh the gains, discrimination in employment, housing, education, health facilities, and recreation." I urged closer cooperation and coordination among our member groups, reminding them that our adversaries, "un-American hate groups in Chicago, whatever their differences, close their ranks for action."

1946 Restrictive Covenants

At the end of 1946, I wrote in my annual report: "Chicago is heading toward a race riot." I continued that this is not idle talk and certainly it is not wishful thinking. It is the conclusion of many of those closely associated with race relations in Chicago. Like a Greek tragedy, many of Chicago's leaders see the violence coming and yet feel they cannot do anything significant to stop the catastrophe. We of the Board of the Chicago Council at least tried. We faced several obstacles: the failure to provide at once some new unsegregated housing units; the active racism of some sixty self-styled neighborhood "improvement" associations; and "the complacence of the civil leadership of Chicago with grass-roots prejudice and a resultant dependence upon the false security of improvisations." Also the federal government withdrew during that year from the wartime FEPC and the War Relocation Authority (WRA).

The most serious setback was the cumulative terroristic attacks on Negroes moving into so-called "white" neighborhoods. We kept a running chart of the attacks against black housing in peripheral areas beginning in 1944. This map of Chicago was widely published in the media, with keen interest shown by TV newscaster Clifton Utley, father of NBC's Garrick Utley. This random violence culminated in the autumn of 1946 at the Airport Homes Veterans Housing Project (*see next chapter*).

Another activity was our fight against racial restrictive covenants or enforceable legal instruments which kept Negroes from buying property. Appeals were on their way to the U.S. Supreme Court and we felt the need to educate Chicagoans on this issue. The Chicago Council sponsored a two-day Conference for the Elimination of Restrictive Covenants on May 19-20, 1946. A total of 300 persons attended, with the banquet speaker being Bishop Bernard J. Sheil, who soon became co-chairman of the Chicago Council. We published a 92-page, illustrated booklet giving the speeches delivered at this event and easily sold 10,000 copies (but not one found its way into our archives!). A young Catholic conscientious objector, John Doebele, aided greatly in this and other fair housing efforts.

Our Conference at least gave cause for the racist Federation of Neighborhood Associations to raise funds. They addressed a "danger—urgent—important" letter to their constituents about our meeting. "Well they have done it. The entire program was directed at the WHITE property owner and Neighborhood Associations." Their letter urged "adequate financial support at once" since "the Negroes and their crackpot White leaders have sold their [souls] to enough nitwits to create the most destructive force this country has ever known."

Working on housing during those post-war years, I belatedly realized that I had my personal housing problems, now that we had one child, Alex. Housing was tight. However, Charles Liebman, a friend who was treasurer of the Illinois ACLU (and a founder of the Free Press), owned an apartment on Juneway Terrace, the last street in Chicago before Evanston. He rented us an apartment at 1820 Juneway Terrace. It was a long drive to Fernwood and other neighborhoods of tension on Chicago's South Side, but we were happy to live in a slightly larger home, especially when our daughter, Lucy, came along in 1947.

The Chicago YMCA had a small college in its building on La-Salle Street. Edward J. Sparling, Treasurer of our Chicago Council, was president of the Chicago YMCA College since 1936. He turned this small school into a thriving college right on LaSalle Street near the financial district. The Board of the College, appointed by the Board of the Central YMCA, was uneasy about the number of blacks attending the school. They wanted some restrictions which Sparling refused to countenance. Indeed, he felt it strange that black college students could not use the swimming pool and other gym facilities in the YMCA building. Sparling was asked to resign; when he refused, he was fired. The faculty, by a vote of 43 to 15, declared that "the real cause of Dr. Sparling's dismissal was a desire to impose racial restrictions upon the student body." Many faculty also resigned. The students supported the faculty statement by a vote of 448 to 2.

Sparling decided to establish a nonracial college. He called it Jefferson College until Franklin Delano Roosevelt died, and then this dream was renamed Roosevelt College. In a small rented office, initially furnished with an orange crate and a chair, Dr. Sparling received help from liberal Chicagoan Marshall Field and from Edwin Embree, head of the Rosenwald Fund. Roosevelt mushroomed in the postwar era and soon had its own building, the site of the old Auditorium, on Michigan Avenue. I was in the midst of the birth of this institution. I documented some of Sparling's problems in a Chicago Council memorandum, and helped him in other ways. Today Roosevelt University remains in the Loop, and has served several generations of minority students—and faculty. Harold J. Laski, the well-known British socialist, taught at Roosevelt shortly before his death in 1950. I ended my memorandum on the establishment of the college by asking: "Does the C in YMCA stand for Christian or Caucasian?"

Many smaller projects were undertaken. We successfully urged the *Chicago Sun* to drop race labelling. If John Jones was arrested, he was not thereafter labelled as a Negro, since James Jones when arrested was routinely not labelled a white! On the eve of Thanksgiving, we induced several prominent Chicagoans to issue a statement on the necessity of liberalizing existing U.S. immigration laws. We worked on many aspects of employment discrimination. We both criticized and supported the Mayor's Commission on Human Relations, by the end of the year urging that its budget be increased. We protested the injection of racism in national discussions of the statehood of Hawaii. We urged legislation repaying relocated Japanese-Americans for loss of property during their evacuation. We issued documented memorandum on "Gerald L.K. Smith Comes to Chicago," based on my observations attending his rallies.

Our public relations activities increased. I spoke widely and wrote many reviews on race relations books in Chicago and national media. Yet our finances lagged. Our total budget for the year was $13,363, and this included four months' back salary for 1945!

The Fernwood Riots

In the summer of 1947, riots occurred at the Fernwood Emergency Veterans Housing Project. I was at the Project almost continuously for five days and many times thereafter in the southern part of Chicago. Our role was primarily to present timely facts about this major crisis in Chicago human relations and to coordinate citizen action to quell the violence. Daily meetings of concerned local and city representatives were convened by Tom Wright of the Mayor's Commission and myself. We also conferred with the new Mayor, Martin H. Kennelly, the State's Attorney, the superintendents of public and parochial schools, and local clergy. "Fernwood" consumed our entire attention for six weeks.

Isolated attacks continued against Negro families and we monitored carefully the sixty-three reported attacks during the year. We tried unsuccessfully to induce the Police Department to start an in-service training program on intergroup relations. I went to Gary, Indiana, to observe the strike of white high school students there and also tried to help quell the strike of 500 white students at Wells

High School in Chicago in September 1947.

The Mayor's Commission on Human Relations continued under attack and we compiled a memorandum defending this agency. Also the Chicago Housing Authority, and Elizabeth Wood its director, came under severe criticism, especially from white neighborhood groups. Again, we came to its defense. The nicest Christmas card I received in 1947 was from Elizabeth Wood who wrote, "with the deepest affection and respect for a most helpful and valiant warrior in all good fights."

We also tried to induce the Illinois legislature to adopt a law outlawing the enforcement of racial restrictive covenants. We worked for an Illinois fair employment practice law, and I made many trips to downstate Illinois to engender support for this unattained goal. I went to Washington twice to support different aspects of our program: a national FEPC, admitting displaced persons from Europe, and safeguarding the property and naturalization rights of Japanese-Americans and others of Oriental ancestry.

At the invitation of CORE, we joined in the formation of a Council on Equal Job Opportunity on State Street—meaning more jobs for black salesclerks in the principal department stores (many of which at the time refused to hire any blacks). We helped student groups at the University of Chicago oppose discrimination at Chicago Lying-In Hospital (where my son, Alex, was born) and thus admit black mothers. Earlier we sponsored a Conference on the Unsegregated Church which resulted in an interracial, interdenominational Protestant group being formed. For some time the office of the Chicago Fellowship of All Christians was in our offices. We also gave space to the Chicago Committee on Displaced Persons.

I undertook a number of church-related projects, working half-time from July through September as the research secretary of the Commission on Planning and Review of the American Unitarian Association. Also I became National President of the Unitarian Fellowship for Social Justice. In the secular field, I was named Vice-Chairman of the new National Association of Intergroup Relations Officials.

Also I had to juggle constantly the Council's finances—and my own. I was the chief source for the Council to borrow short-term loans—through not writing regularly my own salary checks. I always received my salary, but often months late. This was an experience which continued in many other organizations of which I was an employee, including the American Committee on Africa, SANE, and the World Conference on Religion and Peace. Only when I worked with local churches and the Unitarian Universalist Association did I have financial security. Yet in all of these jobs, I felt honored to work and really wondered whether I should not pay for the opportunity I was given.

Interracial Balance Sheet

In 1948, the Chicago Council issued a national honor roll. The first was the President's Commission on Civil Rights for its uncompromising, specific report on the state of minority relations in the U.S. The second was to Branch Rickey and Jackie Robinson of the Brooklyn Dodgers for pioneering in the removal of the color line in professional baseball. Among the national defeats was the acquittal by an all-white jury of twenty-eight white defendants accused on ninety-six counts of participating in a lynching near Greenville, South Carolina. Another defeat was the refusal of the U.S. Congress to pass legislation creating a FEPC, outlawing lynching and poll taxes, and indemnifying Japanese-Americans for losses incurred during the evacuation from the Pacific Coast. Among the ten best books of 1947 were the *Report of the President's Commission on Civil Rights* and the novel, *Gentleman's Agreement*, by Laura Hobson.

In those days in Chicago, houses were not only burned out, but also race relations executives. After a few years I realized that I had to take another kind of job. All during my work with the Chicago Council, I had a desire to return to the parish ministry. I was offered the ministry of the Unitarian Church of nearby Evanston and I eagerly accepted. In a farewell address given to the Chicago Council in November 1948, I recalled that its founders had a "dream that intergroup relations is more than the sum of all its parts and that the effectiveness of the various organizations could be significantly increased by studied coordination." Some constituent groups were understandably suspicious about cooperation while others were skeptical. While no organizational sovereignty was perhaps abrogated, I felt more selfless cooperation did result. The campaign for an Illinois FEPC was lost, but organizational unity won. Because of the veterans homes riots, organizations forgot their rivalries, politics, and approaches, and worked very closely together to save the city from falling apart.

I was given a farewell reception by the Chicago Council two months after I left—on January 18, 1949, in Altgeld Hall of Roosevelt College. Several hundred Chicagoans were present to hear speeches by Dr. Sparling, Dr. Bradley, and the Rev. Archibald Carey (by then also alderman of the Third Ward). The Chicago Council board gave me a TV set—a rarity in those days. Our family kept the small RCA black and white set in daily use for over thirty years.

I treasured most several letters. Lucy P. Carner, a senior staff member of the Council of Social Agencies of Chicago, wrote that it was "a sad piece of news" that I was leaving, since "we have appreciated more than we have ever expressed your unfailing cooperation and help." Russell Ballard, head of Hull House, wrote: "I just want to say how much I regret your leaving the Council, but I won't have to worry any more about your getting your monthly salary on time." Most of all, I heard from Elizabeth Wood, Executive Secretary of the Chicago Housing Authority. (This was the era when Robert R. Taylor was still its Chairman and only a few months later Elizabeth herself left, being forced out for her tenacity in insisting on non-racial housing.) She wrote: "I think very few public officials could have had the rich and sustaining experience that I have had in working with you and your organization." She added: "I don't think that the line that has been held in the City of Chicago could have been held if it had not been for your tireless energy, your unmatchable zeal, and very remarkable skill in letting people know what is going on." She remembered "too vividly the sleepless nights and the terrible strain you went through in some of our recent struggles."

15 CHICAGO (1946)

THE AIRPORT HOMES INCIDENT

In the post-war years, Chicago was the site of several race riots. In the face of rising expectations on the part of black G.I.'s who had fought for their country and new government ordinances and laws on discrimination, white neighborhood associations often took the law into their own hands. Here is Homer's report on one such incident written while he was director of the Chicago Council Against Racial and Religious Discrimination.

Airport Homes, a project encompassing two square blocks on the far southwestern part of Chicago, was planned some time after V-J (Victory over Japan) Day. Owned by the Board of Education, the property was reportedly reserved for a community park, and a previous effort to build a stadium on the site was successfully opposed by community residents. Thus when the establishment of the temporary veterans' housing project was announced shortly after the end of the war, there were again objections from the community, both on the grounds that the plot was reserved for a community park and that even temporary veterans' units would seriously depreciate the surrounding property. Also objections were raised that some of the veterans moving into the project might be Negroes who, it was alleged, would also depreciate property values and make the community unsafe and unfit to live in. Petitions were signed and sent to appropriate city and federal authorities on several of these objections.

Despite these hindrances, work began on building the Airport

134

Homes by the Federal Public Housing Authority. This agency then turned the units over to the Chicago Housing Authority (CHA), which would then have full charge of them, including the selection of tenants. To prepare for this, the CHA had conversations with various interested parties in the neighborhood on tenancy. Among other items, the possibility of Negro occupancy was raised again, and the CHA reiterated that it was a public agency without discriminatory policies.

When some of the units were finished in September 1946, the first group of veterans were moved in and some 125 were in the project by November 1. The project was planned for 186 apartments and about fifty-nine of these were delayed in being finished and thus in being turned over formally to the CHA for rental. While these were being completed (and seemed habitable except for minor repairs), a number of veterans, largely from the immediate neighborhood, decided to take over the vacant apartments. It is clear that they were not discouraged by local politicians and other community leaders, who hoped to forestall a possibility that some of the units would be rented to Negroes. In fact, most of the veterans who planned to take over the apartments were badly in need of housing—as were those who had been selected, Negro or white—and only secondarily, it is believed, was their motivation anti-Negro. The *Chicago Sun* first raised the racial implications of this situation in an editorial.

Whatever the reasons, the veterans forcibly obtained keys to eighty apartments from the project caretaker and moved in on November 4. Their efforts immediately made nation-wide headlines. Community leaders and neighborhood and city officials, including police, made no attempt to dislodge the squatters. After trying by persuasion to eject the squatters, the CHA finally had warrants served on six squatters and they appeared in court. The trial was adjourned, as the squatters garnered local community support.

The CHA has maintained a splendid record of integrating all kinds of people into its temporary and permanent projects. No Negroes were moved into the Airport Homes initially. Then on November 9, four Negroes on the master CHA list of veterans were advised that apartments for them would be available. For varying reasons, all refused to accept the apartments except Theodore Turner and his family. Mr. Turner is a veteran of the European theater and was the last man to be discharged from Camp Grant in 1945. He has a wife and two children, one only three weeks old, and is employed at the U.S. Cold Storage Company.

Mr. Turner signed his lease and said he would move in as soon as he could buy some furniture. In the meantime, police had been alerted and a 24-hour detail stood guard in front of the apartment he was going to occupy. A petition was hurriedly drawn up by residents of the community and delivered to the CHA. It read in part: "We, the undersigned, vigorously protest the renting of flats in the Veterans Housing Project at 60th and Keeler to Negro families. We believe that the indiscriminate mixing of white and colored families will not encourage racial tolerance, but on the other hand will create ill-feeling." On November 15, the tenants' council held a meeting in a local church and agreed to take into the Council all residents of the project, squatters and nonsquatters, and resident veterans of all backgrounds. Mr. and Mrs. Turner were present at the meeting and it was clear that most of those assembled welcomed their presence, though ten veterans and their wives left the auditorium on their arrival.

However, after subsequent threats of violence, the Turners decided that it would not be safe for them to live in the Airport Homes and they turned in their keys and were given a refund on their deposit. "Watchers" from the community continued to stand vigil all weekend in front of the apartment to be occupied by a Negro. Bonfires were lit to warm the hands of the watchers, who seemed able to mobilize a crowd on short notice. On November 17, a former marine illegally moved into the apartment reserved for Mr. Turner.

On advice of counsel, the squatters began to move out of the Airport Homes soon after November 20. By December 1, all but five families of squatters had vacated the property. Meanwhile, at least 700 West Lawn residents met at Marzano's Palace of Pleasure, a bowling hall, and demanded that the squatters be kept in the housing project or that only veterans from the local ward be admitted to the project. During the meeting it was evident that the real purpose was to keep Negro tenants out of the project, and at the conclusion of the meeting a delegation was appointed to visit Mayor Kelly and the City Council to demand a public hearing. The City Council agreed to a hearing and, in a raucous atmosphere dominated by local residents, heard testimony, pro and con. I spoke in favor of the CHA on behalf of the Chicago Council. At the conclusion of the hearing, the chairman announced that matters would be taken under advisement and considered at further hearings.

On December 4, some thirty veteran tenants were authorized by CHA to move into apartments formerly occupied by the squatters. Among these were six Negro families. In anticipation of possible violence, CHA, the Mayor's Commission, the Chicago Council, and possibly other groups, alerted the police. Families began moving into the project at 9 a.m. A force of thirty-two policemen and a variety of city officials, representatives of citizens' organizations, and local clergy were present.

The Riot Begins

The situation during the first part of the morning was orderly, except for a growing crowd of persons, mostly women, who gathered on the south side of the project opposite the project office. They booed and hissed recognized civil leaders, talked with newspaper photographers, and made numerous threats. At about 11:30 a.m., a truck containing a portion of the furnishings of John R. Fort and Letholian Waddles—two accredited Negro tenants—entered the housing project. The truck had some difficulty turning from the street into the project road and police rushed up to protect it and prevent the mob from following the truck. After receiving a broken windshield, the furniture truck stopped about 300 feet inside the project, and the two tenants left it to go to the project office to secure their keys. The father of one of the tenants and three movers—all Negroes—stayed by the truck until it became clear they were in danger, and I asked them to go to the project office for greater protection. In the meantime, police were desperately trying to prevent a breakthrough of the crowd from rushing the truck. Women were in the front of the mob fighting and kicking police and men were in the back throwing stones and clumps of dirt at police, photographers, and civic leaders. Acting Commissioner Crane was in the thick of the melee and Lt. Anthony De Grazio was struck in the temple while preventing a woman from taking away his police club. Three other policemen were hit by missiles. As the disorder continued, Thomas Wright, of the Mayor's Commission on Human Relations, and myself demanded immediate police reinforcements.

Stones continued to be hurled at the furniture truck and it was decided to move the truck farther into the project and nearer the apartments to be occupied. To avoid danger to the Negro movers, Rev. Erwin Gaede agreed to drive the truck several hundred feet north; however, the truck became mired in mud. The mob ran around the project, followed the truck faster than the police did, pelting it with stones and trying to slash the tires. The crowd was forced back only when additional police arrived. To protect the fur-

137

niture, a group of ministers volunteered to carry the furniture into the apartment. Stones occasionally flew around us, and there was much booing, as we did so, while the crowd desperately tried to break through the lines. Despite the violence, no arrests were made.

More police protection was demanded by CHA, the Mayor's Commission, and the Chicago Council Against Discrimination. The Mayor's Commission and CHA arranged a conference with Mayor Kelly later in the afternoon. During the middle of the afternoon, Kenneth C. Kennedy—a Negro—of UNAVA drove to the project, was intercepted on the street, and his automobile was overturned although he was not injured. He was immediately rescued by police and taken to the project office.

The six Negroes vainly waited for a tow wagon to pull their truck out of the mud so they could return for a final load of furniture. No private tower would come into the project, and the driver of a grader-tractor on the project (under contract with CHA) refused to push the truck out of the mud. Since some of the Negroes wanted to leave, it was decided that five of them would be escorted out of the project in a paddy wagon by police. I accompanied them to make sure the police wouldn't leave them too near the project, and they were finally taken to a point where they could safely continue.

Crowds continued to gather on various sides of the project in late afternoon, and the crowd swelled to about five thousand persons at its peak: perhaps at 9:30 p.m. Additional details of police were demanded and assigned (several Negro police appeared but were sent away immediately) until about 10 p.m. when nearly 500 were on duty. Several attempts were made during the evening to break through the police lines, and twice the mob surrounded the water-pumping fire truck which was on hand in case of arson (which was freely threatened). CHA and Chicago Council had to insist that the mob be pushed back off the project and across the street bordering the project. The Chicago Council also continued to demand of Capt. Crane that those inciting to violence or committing violence be arrested, but no arrests were made. During the evening, my automobile, parked at 61st and Tripp, was overturned and looted by the mob. Late in the evening, a paddy wagon carried CHA officials, the representative of the National Public Housing Agency, and myself out of the project.

Friday morning, at 1 a.m. the Chicago Council sent the following telegrams to President Harry S. Truman and Mr. Charles Wilson, head of the General Electric Company and chairman of the newly-appointed President's Civil Rights Committee: WE INVITE THE

NEWLY-FORMED PRESIDENT'S CIVIL RIGHTS COMMITTEE TO BEGIN ITS AC-
TIVITIES BY INVESTIGATING IMMEDIATELY MOB VIOLENCE AGAINST NE-
GROES AT AIRPORT HOMES PROJECT IN CHICAGO ON DECEMBER FIFTH,
THE DAY THE FORMATION OF YOUR COMMITTEE WAS ANNOUNCED. SERI-
OUS HATRED FOMENTED BY ORGANIZED GROUPS IN CHICAGO CAN PRO-
VIDE SIGNIFICANT BACKGROUND FOR RECOMMENDATIONS YOUR COM-
MITTEE WILL MAKE TO PROTECT CIVIL RIGHTS MORE EFFECTIVELY
THROUGHOUT THE NATION.

The Chicago chapter of the American Civil Liberties Union announced a $250 reward for information leading to the arrest and
conviction of anyone who conspired or acted to deprive any other
person by reason of race or color of the civil right to rent and occupy any dwelling place and in a telegram to the Justice Department
demanded an FBI investigation of efforts to keep Negroes from the
project.

On Friday, the following morning, violence continued as two
Negroes returned to complete their moving. Observers reported
that some women were pushing baby-carriages in the area carrying
sticks and bricks. The police were uncomfortable, inexperienced,
and reluctant to investigate such reports or make any arrests in the
face of overt violent. Police discipline was especially poor whenever
a senior officer was absent. The police attitude appeared to be that
they were personally opposed to the city policy of nondiscrimina-
tion in the project and didn't understand why the Mayor was doing
what he did. They talked to the crowd in an apologetic manner.

On Friday noon, the Church Federation of Greater Chicago
held an enlarged meeting of its Commission on Interracial Relations
and issued a statement signed by eighteen leading clergymen. The
statement read in part: "We give full moral support to the position
that Mayor Kelly has taken when he said, 'These homes are and will
continue to be available to veterans and their families without regard to race, creed, or color.' We feel that all citizens, and particularly religiously-minded citizens, ought to support the Mayor in this
stand." Later that afternoon, a delegation representing organizations affiliated with the Chicago Council spent 45 minutes discussing the situation with Mayor Kelly and Congressman Dawson. We
asked for more police to be assigned to the Airport Homes and that
more adequate handling of the situation be made by the police
there. We specifically asked that arrests be made of those inciting to
violence and actually committing violence, that the crowd he kept
moving and kept in better control although in a nonviolent manner,
that the police keep all people two blocks away from the project,

and that the police not fraternize with the crowds. Mayor Kelly replied that he would put 500 more police there if necessary and would protect the Negro families in any way possible. He indicated that he didn't know we had people in Chicago who would create such a disturbance. He admitted that it was pretty hard to do anything with a frenzied mob, but he had given orders for the police to go the limit on the whole thing. He felt the excitement was bound to drop off and hoped to deal with the situation as temperately as possible and minimize the thing in the eyes of the public. He expressed fear lest the Negro community be aroused and the violence would spread. He indicated that with 500 policemen, some are bound to be bigoted—as would be some individuals among any 500 churchgoers.

On Friday evening, about 500 policemen were on hand and the crowd was estimated at three thousand. At 8 p.m., a four-foot wooden cross, drenched with gasoline, was burned at 61st St. and Kedvale. Reporters' and photographers' cars were molested. The police, in an attempt to force the crowd back on the sidewalk, used a squad car in cavalry tactics. The crowd retaliated by throwing bricks and attempted to overturn the squad car. To control the situation, the police used clubs for the first time. Six persons were injured and taken to nearby hospitals, and six patrolmen were also said to be hit by blows or bricks. One patrolman was subsequently reported to have lost an eye in the melee.

On Saturday morning, December 7, the Mayor's Commission on Human Relations in cooperation with the Chicago Council called an emergency meeting of representatives from about 120 citizens groups to discuss the situation and come up with a plan of action. After much discussion, it was decided that while commending the Mayor's position, organizations should put pressure on him to have the police make arrests and not to hesitate to call upon other officials or agencies to maintain law and order. Newspapers that helped ease the situation were to be supported, and in lieu of police support, the possibility of arranging private security was to be investigated.

The situation was relatively quiet all Saturday, although a cross was burned for the second time, several bonfires were set, and one man was arrested for disorderly conduct while drunk. Sunday was also relatively quiet. Thurgood Marshall, legal counsel of the NAACP, flew into Chicago to be near the situation and conferred with city and civic leaders. On Sunday evening, after hearing recurring rumors of planned arson at Airport Homes, we sent the follow-

ing telegram to the Fire Commissioner: REPORTS OF REPEATED
THREATS OF ARSON AT AIRPORT HOMES. DEMAND MORE ADEQUATE FIRE
PRECAUTIONS IN FACE OF MOB SPIRIT, CONGESTED STREETS AND FRAME
DWELLINGS. THIS REQUEST NOT RELEASED TO PRESS.

Tension and violence continued at Airport Homes during early 1947. We were unable to help form a "goodwill council" in the
area. Those whites arrested in December 1946 for "creating distur-
bances" were discharged in February 1947. Two shots at night just
missed the two Negro families still living in the project. The police
could not find the perpetrators. The Negro families understandably
decided to move. Airport Homes became a "white" housing project.

16 NASHVILLE • KNOXVILLE • LOUISVILLE
(1947)

JOURNEY OF RECONCILIATION

*In the spring of 1947, Homer participated in the first Freedom Ride to inte-
grate interstate buses and trains in the Border States and South. According to a Gallop Poll of the period, the nation as a whole was about evenly
divided over whether public transportation should be integrated or segregated. In the South, those who favored segregated transportation numbered
84 percent. Freedom rides were later employed during the civil rights
movement in the 1960s. Homer's account originally appeared in* Common
Ground, *published by the Fellowship of Reconciliation, in autumn 1947.*

Several years back, Mrs. Irene Morgan boarded an interstate
bus in Gloucester County, Virginia, for Maryland. She was asked to
sit in the "colored" section of the bus. Instead of acquiescing to this
segregation or even reluctantly accepting it, Mrs. Morgan refused to
move from a seat in the "white" section and was arrested for breaking the Virginia Jim Crow laws. Her objection became the substance
of a long legal battle (Irene Morgan vs. Commonwealth of Virginia),
which eventually reached the United States Supreme Court. On
June 3, 1946, that court announced an historic decision penetrating
the iron curtain of Jim Crow in the South: it decreed that state laws
demanding racial segregation of interstate passengers on motor carriers were unconstitutional since segregation on buses was "an un-
due burden on interstate commerce." In a later decision, the Court
of Appeals of the District of Columbia interpreted the Morgan decision to apply also to interstate train travel.

This was one of the few successful legal attacks on Jim Crow in the South. Several bus companies immediately announced that they reserved the right to seat passengers and would continue to segregate Negroes to ensure the public safety. A Southern governor threatened to stop every interstate bus coming into his territory and make the passengers walk across the state line, then buy intrastate tickets.

Customs precede legal decisions or customs follow them—and some customs follow some legal decisions more slowly than others. It was on the hunch that Southern customs were not following the Morgan decision very quickly that the Fellowship of Reconciliation (FOR) with the aid of the Congress of Racial Equality (CORE) decided to sponsor a "Journey of Reconciliation" through the upper South.

The Journey was not meant to be just another testing of existing laws. It was primarily to ascertain whether an unpopular court decision could be enforced by using the spirit of aggressive goodwill or, more accurately, nonviolent direct action. Both sponsoring organizations were pledged to this method. Thus the participants in the Journey took with them a technique as old as Jesus and as contemporary as Gandhi, one which is much more concerned with transforming the wrongdoer than with inflicting retribution. The participants were concerned more with justice than with pride or even personal safety, and they tried to avoid bitterness and to maintain a spirit of self-giving love. In short, they were not passive nonresisters of the evil of segregation, but were active resisters of segregation in a nonviolent manner. They used laws whenever possible, yet did not depend upon them. Thus the designation of the trip, Journey of Reconciliation.

The leaders of the Journey were George Houser, white, a Methodist minister and full-time secretary of the Racial-Industrial Committee of the Fellowship of Reconciliation, and Bayard Rustin, Negro, staff member of the Fellowship of Reconciliation and part-time lecturer for the American Friends Service Committee. The two leaders went, Jim Crow, over almost the entire itinerary several months beforehand to make the necessary preparations. Lawyers were retained in fourteen communities, thousands of dollars of bail money were secured, and more than thirty speaking engagements were scheduled. Besides Houser and Rustin, fourteen carefully selected men also participated in the Journey. They included an attorney, a musician, a scientist, four ministers (three Methodists, one Unitarian), and several editors, students, and executive secretaries. Almost a third of the participants were Southerners, and about half were Negroes. At least four members of the group had had their courage pre-tested as federal prisoners for being conscientious objectors during World War II.

First Arrests

I joined the Journey at Knoxville, Tennessee, on April 17. The group had been traveling since April 9, when they left Washington. Their itinerary had taken them to Richmond and Petersburg, Virginia; and Raleigh, Durham, Chapel Hill, Greensboro, Winston-Salem, and Asheville, North Carolina. On each lap, members of the Journey traveled interracially, often dividing into two groups to take different bus lines (Greyhound or National Trailways). Between Washington and Petersburg, they encountered no trouble; indeed, there was evidence that the Morgan decision had begun to take effect. At Petersburg, however, one of the Negro members of the Journey was arrested for sitting in the second seat from the front of a bus. The charge was "disorderly conduct for not obeying a reasonable request of the bus driver." The trial has been indefinitely postponed pending a state supreme court decision on a similar case.

Two Negro members of the Journey were arrested at Durham. One white member was arrested at the same time, also for breaking the Jim Crow laws. All were later released and the charges dismissed. In Chapel Hill, where the only incident of violence occurred, two Negro and two white members of the Journey were arrested, the Negroes for "disorderly conduct for refusing to obey the bus driver," and the whites for "interfering with arrest."

At the trial several weeks later, the two white men received sentences—to be appealed—of "thirty days on the road" while one of the Negroes arrested was fined court costs only—about eight dollars—and the other was fined $25 and costs. At first, the judge sentenced one of the whites to six months, but when the prosecutor pointed out that the maximum sentence was thirty days, the judge reduced the sentence with the remark, "I can't keep all these things in my little head."

After the arrest in Chapel Hill, members of the Journey were chased by a group of taxi drivers to the house of a friendly white Presbyterian minister, Charles Jones. The taxi men threatened the minister and his family, and the men on the Journey decided to leave immediately for Greensboro. Later, in Asheville, a Negro and a white member of the group were arrested, this time frankly for vi-

144

olating the state Jim Crow laws. Subsequently, the two men were convicted and sentenced to thirty days under the supervision of the highway commissioner. The sentence will naturally be appealed.

It was a group of men exhibiting the somewhat taut morale of ten arrests that I encountered in Knoxville. The whites were beginning to know the terror that many Negroes have to live with all the days of their lives. All members of the party were dead-tired, not only from the constant tenseness, but also from participating in many meetings and conferences at every stop. There were press conferences, public rallies to secure expenses for the Journey, and conferences with liberal white and Negro leaders for follow-up work by local residents. After a typical day of these activities in Knoxville, Nathan Wright, a young Negro church social worker from Cincinnati, and I were selected to make a bus test from Knoxville to Nashville. George Houser went along as an unidentified observer.

Wright and I bought separate interstate bus tickets reading Knoxville to Louisville, Kentucky, via Nashville. I was one of the first to board the bus shortly before midnight. I took the fourth seat from the front. Wright entered the bus five minutes later and sat down next to me. Slowly heads began to turn around and within five minutes the driver asked Wright to go to the back of the bus. Wright answered, "I prefer to sit here." I said Wright and I were friends, that we were riding together, that we could legally do so because of the Morgan decision. The bus driver then pleaded, "Wouldn't you like to move?" We said we would like to stay where we were. The driver left the bus, apparently to talk to bus officials and police. After much ogling by passengers and bus employees (although it was then midnight and the departure had been delayed almost half an hour), the driver finally reappeared and started the bus, without any more words to us.

We had overcome the first obstacle—arrest by Knoxville police—but as we were riding through the outskirts of Knoxville, we realized that the hard part of the Journey was still ahead. Ours was the first night test of the entire Journey. The Southern night, to Northerners at least, is full of vigilant justice and the lynch rope from pine trees if not palms. We wondered whether, despite the current long-distance telephone strike, the bus company—or one of its more militant employees—would telephone ahead for a road block and vigilantes to greet us in one of the Tennessee mountain towns. Neither of us slept a moment that night. We just watched the road.

At the two rest stops, we kept our seats. Police squad cars were on hand at both places, but nobody questioned us. Early in the morning, a half hour before we arrived in Nashville, the bus filled with city commuters. White women, and a few white men, stood in the aisle while Wright and I sat in our fourth seat from the front. The flower of Southern womanhood, if she rode the bus at all, stood in the aisle that morning while a young Negro sat up front! Yet the reaction of the passengers on the trip was not one of evident anger and certainly not of violence. It was first surprise, then astonishment, and even tittering. On that bus, anyway, there was only apathy, certainly no eager leadership in preserving the ways of the Old South.

Midnight Rail Journey

We arrived in Nashville early in the morning, exhausted, relieved, and with a bit of the exhilaration of the adventurer. Ours was probably the first interracial bus trip made between Knoxville and Nashville. Once in Nashville, Wright and I spoke before classes at three colleges and planned the second stage of our particular part of the Journey: the first train test from Nashville to Louisville. I secured two coach reservations on the Louisville and Nashville's *Hummingbird*, an all-reserved coach. We left just before midnight. We entered the coach separately, and Wright had no difficulty. Few passengers noted his presence. The conductor took our tickets without incident. Soon thereafter he tapped me on the shoulder, pointed to Wright, and whispered, "He's your prisoner, isn't he?" I said he was not. Then the conductor asked, "Why, then, is he sitting here?" I replied that we had reservations together. The conductor said that was impossible and asked Wright to go back to the Jim Crow coach. Wright said he preferred to sit where he was, and the recent interpretation of the Morgan case made it legal for him to do so. The conductor muttered that he never had had to face this situation before and that if we were riding back in Alabama he wouldn't have to face it: the passengers would throw us both out of the window. In the end, he conductor merely took our names and did not put us off the train at Bowling Green—the only stop. A white passenger passed me a note indicating that we could get in touch with her as a witness if we encountered any legal trouble.

I had to leave the Journey at Louisville, but most of the men went on: Roanoke, Lynchburg, Charlottesville, and back to Washington. Several other train tests were made, again without trouble. Two more arrests occurred, however, on bus tests in Amherst and Culpepper, Virginia. Both trials were postponed pending the outcome of the Virginia Supreme Court decision on a similar case.

Before enumerating the significant conclusions of the Journey, I would like to give my personal reaction toward trying to challenge Jim Crow in the South, a challenge which had the sanction of the supreme court of the land notwithstanding. This was not my first trip to the South, but it was my first sustained flouting of Jim Crow in the South. In the North—in Chicago—a white person can easily enough become embroiled in racial violence perpetrated against him by his fellow whites: stonings, assaults on property, anonymous threats. Yet in the North a white person challenging discrimination always feels the law is on his side, if not always the police. And a white person can easily seek refuge after his forays for justice in the relative safety of his own house, certainly in the houses of his white or Negro friends—or, in an extremity, the protective custody of a jail.

Yet when a white traveler reaches the South—and is prepared to do no more than question the need for a colored waiting room—he feels completely on his own, isolated. In these situations, the traveler can feel only the strength of his convictions plus the support of preciously few Negro and white citizens. There is no refuge for the stranger in the South—not even deep in the Negro community and not in the white one. It is probably like a visitor living in a totalitarian state—without an American passport! So, in the South, a white person on a project such as the Journey gets that cold sweat within him which makes him both constantly fearful and everlastingly fearless, an emotion a white feels only fleetingly in the North, an emotion perhaps not unlike that experienced by those on the Underground Railroad. But why look for comparisons? It is an emotion most of the 14 million Negro Americans experience every waking hour of their day, and doubtless in their dreams, too.

Perhaps the most important factual conclusion of the Journey is simply that the Morgan decision in terms of unsegregated interstate bus travel has not penetrated the South much beyond Richmond, Virginia. Where the decision is elsewhere understood, various attempts are made, principally by bus companies, to circumvent it. At least the experience of the Journey shows that Southern practices vary widely both with law-enforcement officers and with bus companies: there were no arrests in Tennessee and Kentucky and no arrests from incidents on Greyhound buses.

147

Sociological Lessons

The sociological conclusions of the Journey are tentative. With the barrier between the races down, if only for one bus trip, confusion reigns in the attitudes and habit-patterns of both whites and Negroes. This often leads, on the part of the dominant group, to frustration and frequently to aggression. During the entire Journey, however, there was no overt violence initiated by any of the bus passengers. The chief source of danger is apparently from onlookers who generally get their information secondhand, from rumors, and are incited by them.

It is difficult to assess the Southern reaction to the Journey. Many Southern white students and most Southern NAACP branches welcomed it. Some Southerners, including some self-styled liberal Southerners, felt that the Journey "stirred up trouble"—which it did! Any significant attempt to lessen segregation in the South will stir up trouble—a trouble which has been created by segregation and which will probably not be eliminated without a great deal of stirring.

What, finally, did the Journey of Reconciliation accomplish? It showed progressive Americans that the Morgan decision must be implemented by constant "testing"—in the spirit of goodwill—and by subsequent law enforcement. The Journey helped implement the decision at least by spreading knowledge of it to bus drivers and some law-enforcement officers (both policemen and judges) in the upper South. The Journey also showed whites and Negroes living in that area that the Morgan decision could be enforced, without disastrous results, if the proper psychological and legal techniques—and accompanying inspiration—to thousands of whites and Negroes in the South; and a simple manual for Southerners who want to make their own journeys of reconciliation is in the process of preparation. Already, spontaneous, often one-man, testing expeditions have been undertaken. Already, and much more important, local committees are being formed. In one Southern city, as a direct result of the Journey, a committee of lawyers has been established to offer free legal aid to any person who observes the law according to the Morgan decision and thereby breaks the customs. And there is talk of an interracial team of young women, recruited from North and South, invading the South even further sometime soon to extend the Morgan decision into the land of Talmadge, Rankin, and Bilbo.

But that surely will be material for another story!

PART **THREE** 1948-1954

PARISH MINISTER

THE EVANSTON YEARS

"The world's great age begins anew.
The golden years return,
The earth doth like a snake renew
Her winter weeds outworn;
Heaven smiles, and faiths and empires gleam,
Like wrecks of a dissolving dream . . .
A new Ulysses leaves once more
. . . for his native shore."

— Shelley

As minister of the All Souls Unitarian Church of Evanston, Homer lived in that beautiful tree-lined city north of Chicago through the end of the 1940s and during the 1950s. Staunchly conservative, Evanston was home to the national Women's Christian Temperance Union (WCTU), Northwestern University, and, in 1954, the international assembly of the World Council of Churches (which Homer attended as a correspondent since Unitarians were barred from membership). In the 1952 and 1956 presidential elections, Evanston voted overwhelmingly for Dwight D. Eisenhower against Adlai Stevenson, the Democratic candidate and Illinois' own governor. During this period, Homer and his family lived in the parsonage at 2026 Orrington Avenue, several blocks from Northwestern's Deering Library (where he researched his sermons) and Lake Michigan (where the children swam). In this setting, during the height of the McCarthy, Norman Vincent Peale, and Ozzie and Harriet years, the Unitarian Church, under Homer's auspices, served as a cauldron of innovative ideas and social change. From his pulpit, Chicago area committees, and the local ministers' association, Homer waged a steady campaign to desegregate Evanston and the North Shore and introduce revolutionary ideas of freedom and independence for Africans and Asians.

Photograph: Homer at the Unitarian Church of Evanston

17 EVANSTON
(1948-59)

THE GOLDEN YEARS

Perspective: In 1948, violence and the threat of war intensified with the as-sassination of Mohandas Gandhi in India, the Soviet blockade of Berlin and the American Airlift, the first peacetime draft in U.S. history, and a hard-ening of racial attitudes. The State of Israel was founded, and the year marked the first commercial transatlantic flight and the popular introduc-tion of television. Entertainers who made their debut on the new medium included Arthur Godfrey, Ed Sullivan, Milton Berle, Perry Como, and Kukla, Fran, and Ollie. The year's new books include Camus' The Plague *and Alan Paton's* Cry the Beloved Country. *And, as a portent of things to come, in California, two brothers, Maurice and Richard McDonald, opened a new hamburger stand, and in Japan, Soichiro Honda started a small motor company with $7000.*

I became minister of the Unitarian Church of Evanston, then at 1405 Chicago Avenue, in the autumn of 1948. The world was only three years removed from the end of World War II, only three years into the atomic era. In 1948, the church was fifty-seven years old. I, myself, was only thirty-two years old. I left the ministry of the church, by then at 1330 Ridge Avenue, in 1959, on my own volition. Much happened during those eleven years—to the world, to the church, and to myself as its minister.

In the world, these years witnessed the beginning of the Cold War, the hot war in Korea, the invasion of Suez, and colonial wars in Indo-China, Kenya, and Algeria. In this period the U.S. devel-oped a large atomic arsenal and the Soviet Union became a nuclear

151

superpower. The H-bomb was manufactured by three nations. Mt. Everest was conquered and the Soviet Union sent Sputnik I, the first satellite, into space.

In our own nation, this period fell within the full presidential term of Harry Truman and the two full terms of Dwight Eisenhower. Joseph McCarthy came and went. Television came and stayed. The U.S. Supreme Court outlawed separate but equal schools. In Evanston, alternate street parking was introduced and disappeared, but along the North Shore such newcomers as Edens Highway and Old Orchard came and remained.

At the Unitarian Church of Evanston, membership rose from 175 to almost 600. About 700 persons joined the church in this period. Average Sunday morning attendance climbed from 100 in 1948 to 355 in 1959. We outgrew our building on Chicago Avenue and built on Ridge Avenue. During this period we also helped develop a new Unitarian Universalist congregation in Deerfield.

334 Sermons!

Church Covenant

Minister: Love is the spirit of this church
and service is its law.

Congregation: This is our great covenant:
to dwell together in peace,
to seek the truth in love
and to help on another.

During my ministry in Evanston, I performed 124 marriages, dedicated 88 children, and conducted 60 funerals. In this period my family went through ten pets (including Siamese cats, a Dachshund, and a St. Bernard) and five automobiles. I took my first airplane ride (not until 1955), swallowed my first tranquilizer, reached forty, and wore my first bifocals—all duly recorded in my sermons. Indeed, by actual count I preached 334 sermons, on everything from flying saucers to white whales, from trinity to eternity. I especially liked controversial themes and provocative titles. Typical sermons included: "Does Protestantism Need a Reformation?" "Is Science a Sacred Cow?," "Is It Socialism That's Creeping?," "How Original Is Sin?," "Who Ought to Investigate Whom?," "What Is Hell and Where Is

It?," "How Red Are the Clergy?" My sermons were mimeographed and often reprinted in magazines and newspapers. In 1951 a sermon on hospital segregation appeared in *Modern Hospital* which went out to 11,000 hospital executives. The *Christian Register* reprinted my "Sunday at 11: The Segregation Hour." My 1954 sermon "Is McCarthy a Concealed Communist?" went through several printings and sold thousands of copies.

Many distinguished visitors spoke from our pulpit, including South African leader Z. K. Matthews; Albert Schweitzer's associate, Mme Emma Haussknecht; Gandhi's friend, Muriel Lester; British laborite, Fenner Brockway; and American socialist, Norman Thomas.

Somehow, in this period, I had time to edit three books (two on Gandhi), wrote some 200 articles for periodicals, and visited Africa three times and Asia twice. I brought interviews into the pulpit that I made with Albert Einstein in Princeton, Bertrand Russell in Wales, Jawaharlal Nehru in Bandung and Delhi, Albert Schweitzer at Lambaréné and Günsbach, and Coretta and Martin Luther King, Jr., in Montgomery.

Organized religion cannot be remembered, or measured, by old statistics or new buildings. How to transmit over more than three decades a flavor of the dynamics of our tiny, then burgeoning, congregation, especially during those ten years on Chicago Avenue? Perhaps these vignettes will help:

Vignettes

• The congregation had originally been founded in 1891 by a mother in South Evanston who was not satisfied with the Sunday School training offered by traditional Protestant churches. She gathered a few mothers in her living room, and out of their efforts, the church was born. From the start of my ministry, I emphasized the role of women in social change. "Dr. Jack made the statement at the close of his report . . . that only the women could bring about the abolishment of wars," one member wrote me in 1950. "There are several of us who want to know to what lengths we can go and what the contact is that Dr. Jack would suggest for our maximum effectiveness."

• Rev. James Vila Blake (1842-1920), longtime minister and guiding spirit of the church, composed the Church Covenant (quoted above) that was later widely adopted throughout the denomination. He also composed a Covenant of Belief noting that "Religion is

Natural, Helpful, Needful, witness within us of the Infinite and Eternal . . . That the Universe is beautiful and beneficent Order. That we ought to give reverence to all Prophets of Religion who have wrought Righteousness whose teachings are holy and inspiring Scriptures. . . . " Along with other early members of the church, he was inspired by the World's Parliament of Religions held in Chicago in 1893.

• The small stone church on Chicago Avenue, constructed in 1904, bore the accents of Frank Lloyd Wright. Indeed, its designer, Walter Burley Griffin, was an associate of Wright and later gained fame as the designer of the Australian capital city of Canberra. Hayford Hall was added in 1924-25. After we moved in 1958, the gem of a building was demolished and is today a Presbyterian Church parking lot!

• On the first Sunday of my ministry, after preaching my first sermon, a member came up to me and declared that I was much too radical for him. He said that he would quietly leave and transfer his membership down the block to the First Presbyterian Church. He is still there—billionaire insurance executive W. Clement Stone!

• All during our Chicago Avenue years, a library of Sacred Books was placed on the altar, a symbol of inclusiveness. Our religion was an open book, with insights from all the scriptures of the world. However, from time to time some unholy books found their way into this Library.

• Evanston, in 1948, was a stronghold of conservatism. Yet something happened in the 1950s. Political and intellectual liberalism moved from Hyde Park in Chicago to the North Shore, greatly benefiting our church.

• The Fireside Forum in Hayford Hall on Sunday evenings provided stimulating analyses of national and world problems, decades before the MacNeil-Lehrer Hour. Among the speakers were Professor James Luther Adams, community organizer Saul Alinsky, and Albert Bigelow, captain of the *Golden Rule*, the ketch which sailed into the Pacific nuclear testing zone. Muriel Lester and William Worthy spoke on their respective visits to Communist China— in a decade when any contact with the People's Republic was considered subversive. Once we had a special three-week forum on "How Can We Attain World Government?" with special speakers, an international dinner, and talk-backs. We also participated in a Model United Nations in Evanston, with delegations from different churches and civic institutions representing different countries. Our church represented Tunisia, and at another time the Soviet Union!

• In the autumn of 1950, after President Truman indicated that he was considering using the atomic bomb in Korea, we organized a Prayer Vigil for Peace in Chicago attended by a thousand persons of all faiths. From this a new, broad regional organization, Peace, Inc., was formed. I was named chairman, and we issued a 10-point statement on "American Foreign Policy Toward Asia," calling for an immediate cease-fire in Korea and the admission of Communist China to the United Nations.

• My condemnation of the Korean War from the pulpit incurred the displeasure of a church member who was Vice-President of Northwestern University. I submitted an undated resignation, but the church overwhelmingly supported my right to speak out on the great issues of the day. Northwestern—the largest and most influential institution in Evanston—had then only recently desegregated its women's dormitories. At Northwestern, a colleague on the Board of Chaplains was Alan Watts, erstwhile writer on Eastern religions. A graduate student occasionally attended our Unitarian service—George McGovern.

• African freedom fighters Tom Mboya of Kenya and Eduardo Mondlane of Mozambique spoke in our church. Alas, both were later killed by terrorists, although today in Nairobi Mboya Street intersects with Mondlane Street!

• The World Council of Churches held its Second Assembly (and first in the United States) in Evanston in 1954. We Unitarians were theologically excluded, but we did play host to Czech Protestant leader, Joseph Hromadka. When none of the 1,300 Protestant churches in Chicago invited him to speak on "World Council Sunday," we did, despite—later we learned—the FBI eavesdropping from every house and tree on Chicago Avenue. It was the McCarthy Era.

• Evanston experienced a bitter battle over the construction of a million-dollar Community Hospital, just as the two existing hospitals were on the verge of desegregating staff and patients. I found myself pitted against all of the white clergy of Evanston, and half of the black ones.

• Our church budget in 1949-50 was $12,555, of which $4,300 was for the minister's salary and parsonage! Later our church held several capital fund campaigns, stimulated by some of the pioneer hucksters in church fund-raising. These brought mixed financial results and often psychological trauma. I learned, as a poor minister, how to to make "a pace-setting, sacrificial gift," and was carefully taught that "money, like water, always runs down hill!"

• I received, in my little study on Chicago Avenue, strange visitors, occasionally FBI agents. I was vice-president of the Illinois branch of the American Civil Liberties Union during my whole ministry in Evanston. Also I was a member of the boards of Evanston, North Shore, and Chicago race relations organizations. I tried to project the need for civil liberties and racial equality into our growing congregation.

• I also spoke widely to what I called our "larger parish." For example, during a typical early spring, in 1956, I spoke at Antioch College in Yellow Springs, Ohio, the International Forum of Cincinnati, the Institute of International Relations at Syracuse, the League of Woman Voters of Lincoln, American Association of University Women of Springfield, United World Federalists of Oak Park, Channing Club of the University of Chicago, Kappa Alpha Theta and Alpha Epsilon Phi sororities at Northwestern, Beth Emet Synagogue of Evanston, the Hillel Foundation at Northwestern, Central Methodist Church in Detroit, and the Indian Club of Notre Dame University. An active Unitarian minister does not preach to just the converted!

• While I had the reputation for being "a social activist," I spent long hours on two projects as we became a larger institution: first-class music and professional religious education. We succeeded in both.

• I was very much a pastor, making many parish calls. I remember having a monthly "toddy" with H. Rea Hixson who told me how he rented a private railroad car for his annual vacation to go to the Rockies! Also I was among the chaplains of Mather Home when it was planned and opened. However, I recognized early my professional limitations as a guidance counselor. In 1951, a psychiatrist was added to the church staff and his services were freely available to any congregational member.

• A number of church families, including ours, were members of the North Shore Co-operative. In addition to lower costs, the co-op provided "foods of integrity," including church member Earle Bronson's locally famous whole wheat bread.

• As I often stated, "Ours was a laymen's (and laywomen's) church." Over the years, I was blessed with the leadership of many capable men and women, who helped make the church a beehive of activity. Board chairs over the years included Pauline Galvarro, John Weston, Ken Fullerton, Ken Russ, and John Grenzebach. Malcolm Knowles, Wilbert Seidel, Fred Urban, Stewart Cremer, and Charles Worthington distinguished themselves presiding over the

Fireside Forum. Mrs. Charles Martin, Mrs. John Weston, Mrs. Wendel Hance, and Mrs. Eric Fantl tended the Women's Alliance and an endless smorgasbord of picnics, dances, sales, and dinners. Charles Martin and Richard Lassar, among many tasks, oversaw finances. Eric Leander and Ernest Knuti took charge of maintenance, and Mr. Knuti, a lawyer and Chicago Counsel for Finland, handled the sale of our old church building. Richard Saunders chaired the new building committee, and Dale O'Brien organized the dedication. Mrs. Weaver, Mrs. Violet Knuti, and Mrs. Karjola saw that beautiful flowers were in the sanctuary every Sunday, and Earle and Mrs. Bronson served as head ushers and church historians. The annual Church Picnic in June at the large dairy farm of Nate and Betty Ladenson near Kenosha, Wisconsin, was looked forward to eagerly by the whole congregation. My old classmate, Paul Henniges, minister of the Universalist Church of Racine, often joined me in a dialogue sermon in the cow pasture before bringing out the soft drinks and barbecue grills and choosing up sides for a spirited softball game. Many others—too numerous to mention or too modest for me to remember—devoted themselves wholeheartedly to the church, and made my job so much easier.

• Church committees and clubs proliferated during my tenure. In addition to various youth, young adult, and choral clubs, the Sateve club held regular square dances with some of the best country and western callers in the Midwest. The drama club sponsored a reading of Alan Paton's *Cry the Beloved Country*, and Mrs. Helen O'Brien organized many wonderful arts and drama events.

• Following World War II and communist uprisings in Eastern Europe, the plight of DPs—displaced persons, or stateless refugees—was critical. Our church was a pioneer in helping to place individuals and families from Czechoslovakia, Hungary, and other parts of Europe through the 1950s. Thanks to the capable leadership of Paul Aicher, scores of individuals and families were settled on the North Shore, many sponsored by members of our church.

• The Unitarian and Universalist ministers of Greater Chicago met regularly, with merger of the two denominations always high on our agenda. We did joint newspaper advertising and occasionally preached on identical sermon topics (once against McCarthyism). We held annual banquets, one featuring Vice-President Radhakrishnan of India.

• Within several years, it became apparent that our little church on Chicago Avenue was too small for our growing congregation. Intermittently for several years, I delivered two identical sermons on Sunday mornings, and a new PA system provided sound to the overflow in Hayford Hall. The building of our new church on Ridge Avenue began when Nate Ladenson found our corner lot. The rejection by our church board of Frank Lloyd Wright to be our architect broke my heart. We finally hired a prominent architect from Yale, and a construction company which was also building the huge Pan American hanger at Idlewild Airport in New York. Our new church—which bore more than a slight resemblance to an airline hanger—had five pairs of concrete bents that weighed 75 tons each and jutted out on each side. Due to bad weather and a steel shortage, there were construction delays, and the building committee spent many hours hoping the concrete beams would not collapse. On one windy Sunday morning, amid deepening doubts, I delivered a sermon "Tilting Up One's Own Faith." Meanwhile, a church treasurer was caught putting building fund money into his new business. Yet somehow we survived, with Dana Greeley, president of the American Unitarian Association, sociologist Pitirim A. Sorokin, and Gov. Adlai Stevenson dedicating our new building on Ridge Avenue in 1958. Not only did the new structure "fly," but based on the historic Golden Section, it also won several top architecture awards!

• Our parsonage at 2026 Orrington Avenue was as nice as any minister could desire, close to Garrett Seminary Library and with ample space for Alex, Lucy, and our various pets. A noisy fraternity house opposite reminded us constantly that we were part of the Northwestern University community.

Golden Years for those of us privileged to be part of the Unitarian Church of Evanston in that period, those were truly golden years. Most of us were the same age. Our hopes for the post-war years were similar. We felt our country and the world would get better—fast. The U.N. was only three years old when I arrived in Evanston. We church members, as other Americans, were only beginning to come out of our personal provincialism. We were expanding intellectually and geographically, if not financially.

These were among the best years of our lives. We were temperamentally on the verge of what became the 1960s. The closeness of the members of the congregation, still in the early 1950s, was precious. Small was beautiful and we feared our relationships might be fractured as our congregation grew bigger and we moved to the new building. In some ways, things were never the same.

Yet if liberal religion is good for the few, it must be good and made available to the many. That is the story of those eleven years as our institution moved from Chicago Avenue to Ridge Avenue—and into the world.

My One Sermon

Joseph Fort Newton, a preacher of another era, once declared: "Every preacher has but one sermon to preach, no matter how many subjects he may select or how many titles he may use. It is the story of his own heart, the truth made real in his own experience and vivid in his vision, and he can tell no other story triumphantly. Whatever text he may take, whatever art of exposition he may employ, he is ever telling the one truth he has learned by living."

Only four years after coming to Evanston, I preached on the inevitable title, "If I Had Only One Sermon to Preach." Let me quote from that sermon: "If I have one sermon to preach, it is simply this: We must outlaw war or else all other problems fall into insignificance. In the past four years I have tried—and largely, I suspect, in vain—to convince each of you that war is the big problem, the number one problem on humanity's agenda. Yes, there are problems of civic corruption, ill-housing, and bigotry. There are tragic problems facing individuals in an era of cancer, of sudden death on the highways, of mental disease. There are domestic problems, vocational problems, and theological problems. Some of these may not be neglected, but none of these problems affects the future of so great numbers of our people as does World War III."

Then in 1952 I continued: "In the past four years I have tried to get you excited to do something about war. But our generation has lived with war: World War I, World War II, World War 2 1/2—Korea—and hot wars, cold wars, civil wars. Our generation has taken in its blasé stride blockbusters and saturation bombing, rocket weapons and jelly bombs. Our generation has yawned at the atomic bombs and 'perfected' atomic bombs, and thermonuclear explosions and hydrogen bombs. But I have failed to shake you out of your comfortable, suburban lethargy. And I have failed more than you have failed, because I have failed to communicate. . . This is my one truth—the prevention of war—which I have tried to utter in many different ways, under many different circumstances, but this is it."

This is my one truth—uttered before the Cuban Missile Crisis, before the Vietnam War, before the Gulf War.

18 PRINCETON
(1952)

AN HOUR WITH ALBERT EINSTEIN

For many years Homer admired Albert Einstein, especially for his pacifism and outspoken opposition to the nuclear arms race. In spring 1952, he was getting ready to make the long trip to meet the "other Albert"—Albert Schweitzer. One of his Evanston friends, Paul Schilpp, suggested that he visit Einstein in Princeton before taking the boat to Europe and Africa. Schilpp, a professor of philosophy at Northwestern University, had recently published Albert Einstein: Philosopher-Scientist, *and allowed Homer to use his name in a letter asking for an appointment.*

Perspective 1952: A year of nuclear firsts: The U.S. detonated the world's first hydrogen bomb, Great Britain detonated its first atomic bomb, the world's first nuclear accident, at the Chalk River in Canada, released 1 million gallons of radioactive water, and the U.S. Air Force authorized combat aircraft to be equipped to carry atomic weapons for the first time. Adlai Stevenson—running for President on a platform of "Let's talk sense to the American people. Let's tell them the truth, that there are no gains without pains,"—lost to Dwight D. Eisenhower, who promised to end the war in Korea. The polio epidemic reached a height, and in Kenya, British troops put down a rebellion by Mau Mau Kikuyu tribesmen, fanning flames of a race war in Africa. On a positive note, the Security Council formed the U.N. Disarmament Commission. In the world of art, new books include Ralph Ellison's The Invisible Man, *Norman Vincent Peale's* The Power of Positive Thinking, *and E. B. White's* Charlotte's Web. *On*

TV, the Today Show, Dragnet, *and* Our Miss Brooks *debuted, and one of the most popular songs was "I Saw Mommy Kissing Santa Claus."*

I arrived at Princeton on April 21, 1952, and asked several people as I walked from the train station where I could find Mercer Street. I passed Trinity Church, Post 76 of the American Legion, the Princeton Theological Seminary, and then came to number 112. This was a nice house, fairly close to the street, painted cream with green shutters.

It was not quite time for the appointment, so I went to the baseball diamond diagonal from the house. There I talked with two small boys. I raised the subject of Dr. Einstein and one boy said that his cousin lived next to Dr. Einstein. And then the boy volunteered, "Einstein can't even add up his laundry bill!" When I pressed the boy for evidence, he admitted that was just a little joke. They see Einstein walking at 11:00 a.m. every morning and he says "hello" to them. The girls ask him for his autograph and he gives it to them. Everybody greets him with "Hi, Einstein." He owns an old dog. He doesn't work in the garden, but has a gardener. He's too busy to watch baseball games, at their diamond or anywhere else, for his mind is on atom bombs and the like—not simple things. Einstein is just another citizen of town, said Chris and Sandy, both aged eleven, both wearing Confederate caps and owning two-wheeled bicycles.

At 4:30 p.m., I knocked on the door of 112 Mercer Street. A woman opened it and asked, "Dr. Jack?" She said that it was such a nice day that the doctor would see me outside. She took me through the long hall to the back porch, overlooking a well-kept garden. I looked at it for several minutes—Japanese quinces in blossom, a dogwood just flowering, a large elm tree, many narcissuses. And suddenly the door handle turned. Albert Einstein entered and shook my hand. He sat down in a porch chair. I sat on the porch bench.

He began the conversation by asking, "So you're going to Africa to see Schweitzer?" I asked him if he had ever known Schweitzer. Einstein said that they had seen each other briefly on several occasions. I said that I had just learned that Schweitzer might visit the United States again. Einstein replied that he knew and Schweitzer could do more good in America than in Africa. He was respected by American church people who, except for the Catholics, are divided.

I suggested that if indeed Schweitzer does come to America again (his only visit was in 1949), the two might meet again and issue some kind of statement on the world situation. Einstein replied that he doesn't issue many statements any more, except on occasion, on an appropriate occasion, since statements are not valued if made too often.

I then somehow turned the conversation to Mohandas Gandhi. Einstein volunteered that he read Gandhi's *Autobiography* in English. He first heard of Gandhi at the time when Gandhi was early involved in India. They never met, although Einstein stopped briefly in Ceylon on a trip by boat to the Far East. Gandhi and he never corresponded, although he wrote several letters for inclusion in volumes honoring Gandhi. The most well-known was written for the Indian's seventy-fifth birthday: "Generations to come will scarce believe that such a one as this ever in flesh and blood walked upon the earth."

Einstein praised Gandhi's *Autobiography, The Story of My Experiments with Truth*, for being so simple. Einstein felt, however, that there were two difficulties about Gandhi. First, Einstein didn't understand the meaning and purpose of Gandhi's fasts. Were they to prepare Gandhi or his people, or were they merely magic—mystical? Also Einstein admitted that he didn't understand completely Gandhi's attitude toward science and machinery. He understood the problem Gandhi faced in India, with millions of people. But science cannot be disregarded.

I suggested that Gandhi had written much about his regard for science. He was against the exploitation of human beings by machines and in the name of science. He was not opposed either to machines or to science in themselves.

I then asked Einstein if and when he personally departed from the Gandhian way of passive resistance, of nonviolent direct action. He said he had to, briefly, because of Hitler. Einstein said that Gandhi never contemplated Hitler. He admitted that he had not read Gandhi's writings on this point, on how he—Gandhi—would have opposed the Nazis with nonviolent action.

Einstein said that Hitler was a beast who had to be checked, but there were few beasts like him in history. Einstein admitted that, in most cases, passive resistance can be used. Einstein said that Gandhi in dealing with the British was dealing with a people who had . . . At this point, I broke in and added, "had a conscience?" Einstein answered, not as much as that, but the British would go just so far and did not mean to exterminate the Indians.

Einstein said that he now feels that he is a pacifist again and that passive resistance or nonviolent direct action is an important tool with which to oppose evil. Then I asked Einstein if passive resistance could be used against the evils of communism. He said that Stalin (who was then still alive) is different from Hitler. Stalin has no aggressive designs. True, the Russians are in Czechoslovakia, Rumania, and Hungary, but this is a reaction to the maneuvering of the West.

Einstein said that he considered the Russians to be "barbarians" in the sense that they never knew the democratic way of life. He admitted that Soviet science is in a bad way. Some of the confusion is due to some Russian scientists who are afraid of their own colleagues. However, Einstein insisted that some Soviet science is good—in his own field, mathematics.

I then asked Mr. Einstein if his religious ideas have changed recently. He knew that I was a Unitarian clergyman and replied: "I am an agnostic, close to you Unitarians." He said that he felt the concept of a personal God has done damage to many people and to society. He said the Quakers are doing a very fine job. They are the real Christians.

At this point, Einstein's secretary appeared with a tray with tea. As we had tea, I noted Einstein's white full mustache and his long gray hair and his almost pink nose and pink under his sad eyes. He wore a cream shirt, with fountain pen attached on one pocket. Over this was his well-known gray sweatshirt. He wore sandals—with no socks. Einstein spoke in quiet, good English, with but a trace of an accent and without any loss for words.

I pointed to the lovely surroundings—overlooking the campus of Princeton University's graduate school. I then asked him if he ever came to Chicago. He replied that there is so much commotion every time he travels that he stays here and will do so for the rest of his days. I recalled that he had then been in Princeton for almost twenty years. He replied that America had deteriorated since that time. I asked, how? He replied, in civil liberties.

I then asked Einstein what a citizen can do about the restrictions on civil liberties. (Those were the times when Senator McCarthy and McCarthyism were at their height!) Einstein replied: "Speak out against this trend whenever you can." He speaks whenever he feels he must. He doesn't try to calculate the effect. He speaks out whenever he has to.

I asked Einstein about the decision he made, in 1919, to speak out on world issues and not confine himself to science and mathematics. Einstein minimized this decision. He had to speak and because he was well-known, people had to listen. He added that what any one person can do is but little. The military has too much power today in America. He likes the United World Federalists, but feels that even they have degenerated to where they are supporting the United Nations uncritically—they are supporting the power struggle within the world organization.

Once more I changed the subject, this time to India. Einstein said that Jawaharlal Nehru is a fit successor to Gandhi, although not the man that Gandhi was. He added that he felt that Nehru is holding high the Gandhian standards with India's role in the U.N. and in the world. He observed that Nehru has a difficult job to do internally, for he has not too many to work with, except those who are naturally his enemies. (Einstein did not mention that Nehru once came to Princeton to visit him, in 1949).

In our closing minutes of conversation, Einstein said that American scientists are too mechanistically-minded. They don't show social concerns. He likes the Society for the Social Responsibility of Science.

Finally, I asked Einstein to try to compare Schweitzer with Gandhi. He said that Schweitzer is more contemplative. Gandhi knew hundreds of people and thus could develop a movement. He was a politician. If civilization survives, Gandhi will go down as the greatest man of our time.

I suggested to Einstein that, although I am a Unitarian, I do have a trinity. This consists of Gandhi, Schweitzer, and himself. Einstein shrugged his shoulders and said, "Not me, but the other two."

With that, our conversation, on the porch, overlooking the garden at 112 Mercer Street, soon came to a close.

Postscript

There is a postscript to this visit. After returning from my visit to Albert Schweitzer in Africa, I edited a volume observing the eightieth birthday of Schweitzer. I invited a number of world citizens to write tributes, including Albert Einstein. He kindly wrote an engaging essay. This book—a Festschrift—was published in 1955, on the eve of Schweitzer's eightieth birthday. Only years later did I realize that, upon receipt of this volume, Schweitzer wrote a letter of thanks to several contributors, including Albert Einstein. Einstein replied—just before his death in April 1955. Einstein's essay, Schweitzer's letter to Einstein, and Schweitzer's letter to me thanking me for compiling the volume follow:

His Simple Greatness by Albert Einstein

I have hardly ever met a person in whom kindliness and a yearning for beauty are so ideally fused as in Albert Schweitzer. This is particularly impressive in someone who is blessed with robust health. He enjoys using his arms and hands in order to bring into existence what his nature urges him to achieve. This robust health which demands immediate action has kept him from succumbing, through his moral sensibility, to a pessimistic resignation. In this way he has been able to preserve his joyfully affirmative nature, in spite of all the disappointments which our time inflicts upon every sensitive person.

He loves beauty, not only in the arts proper but also in the sphere of the intellect, without being impressed by sophistry. An unerring instinct helps him to preserve his closeness to life and his spontaneity in everything. Everywhere he shuns hardened and rigid traditions. He fights against it whenever an individual by himself has any chance of succeeding. It can be clearly felt in his classical work on Bach where he exposes the dross and the mannerisms through which the guild has obscured the creations of the beloved master and impaired their direct and elementary impression.

It seems to me that the work in Lambaréné has been to a considerable extent an escape from the morally petrified and soulless tradition of our culture—an evil against which the individual is virtually powerless.

He has not preached and he has not warned and he did not dream of it that his example would become an ideal and a solace to innumerable others. He simply acts out of inner necessity.

There must be, after all, an indestructible good core in many people. Or else they would never have recognized his simple greatness.

Dr. Schweitzer's Letter to Einstein

Dear Albert Einstein,

Thank you from the bottom of my heart for your dear letter of 6 December 1954, which took a long time to travel from America to Africa. I was deeply moved by the donation of medicines in memory of a deceased woman who is fondly remembered in Princeton and whom I knew when she was a student in Switzerland. I have written a letter of thanks to the responsible parties. Please tell those of them whom you know that this donation means something very special to me. I am also sending a letter of thanks to the Squibb Company, which contributed to the donation.

Here is a line of thanks from Dr. Cenateen, who took the lovely picture of you and the two boys with the packages of medicines in the background. I'm very fond of it.

During the past few years I have sometimes written to you mentally, but I have never managed to do so physically. I have much business correspondence for the hospital, I've been weary for long months, and I suffer from such a serious writer's cramp (inherited from my mother) that many personal letters that I would like to write never get on paper unless something special happens.

We are mentally in touch even without corresponding, for we both feel the horror of our dreadful time and are mutually afraid for the future of mankind. When we met in Berlin, we could never have dreamed that such a bond would ever exist between us. . . . It is strange how often our two names are mentioned together publicly. I find it lovely that we have the identical first name.

In regard to new experiments with the modern atomic bombs, I am at a loss to understand why the U.N. cannot make up its mind to discuss the matter. I receive letters asking you and me and others to speak up and demand that the U.N. do so, but we have spoken up often enough. We cannot tell the U.N. what to do. It is an autonomous body and must find within itself the incentive and the sense of responsibility to try to stave off an imminent disaster. From a distance I cannot judge what prevents it from pulling itself together and doing so. Even if its efforts were futile, the attempt would have been made, and it would expose the points of resistance.

During the second half of 1954 I spent some time in Europe. My main task was to write my speech for Oslo on the problem of peace. By thus studying the history of the idea of peace, I was amazed to discover that Kant's essay on everlasting peace deals purely with the legal and not the ethical aspect of the problem. However, for Erasmus of Rotterdam, the ethical aspect is at the center of discussion. The more one studies Erasmus, the more one appreciates him despite his failings. After all, he is one of the most important pioneers of a civilization based on humanitarianism.

Now I am back in my many-faceted African work. For many weeks I will have to spend most of my time completing the village for the 250 leprosy patients being treated in my hospital. I have to do a lot of excavating to level out the construction site of the village, which is to be built on a hill near the hospital. It has to be on a hill because mosquitoes spread malaria in the valley. The terracing work is taking almost more time and money than building the residential barracks with corrugated iron roofs and hardwood rafters (because of termites). I have to supervise the work myself because the sixty still able-bodied lepers who have to build the village obey only me as the supreme chieftain of the hospital. There is no way of coping with this attitude. I have two capable doctors with me. I have nine white nurses (Alsatian, Swiss, Dutch). If the construction work advances nicely, then a few weeks from now, alongside the hospital work, I hope I can find time to complete writings that have been waiting for a long while. Like you in Princeton, I try to live as quietly as possible in the jungle, but I cannot manage to do so because Lambaréné has now become a landing point for airplanes. My sole relaxation is practicing the organ on my pedal piano. At the moment I am working on César Franck's last organ works. I assume that you relax with your violin. Well, this has turned into a long letter. My hand with writing cramp has held out decently.

In conclusion let me thank you warmly for your lines about me in the book for my eightieth birthday. They were the first thing I read when I got hold of the book and opened it up. I was deeply moved by your text. I could see that you appreciate my work on Bach. I cannot grasp or understand the possibility that I have exerted an influence in our time It haunts me like a secret on the final stretch of my life . . .

With fond thoughts,

Albert Schweitzer
Lambaréné
February 20, 1955

Letter from Schweitzer to Homer A. Jack

Dear Friend,

The fine volume which you had written by friends and acquaintances has been in my hands some weeks. Do not be astonished that I write you only now to tell you how much I am touched at your enterprise. I arrived in Africa in a state of extreme fatigue after a sojourn very crowded and very difficult in Europe. The second day after my arrival in Africa I had an unfortunate fall that put my right knee out of joint. It hurt very much and I was obliged to rest, reclining in bed for a series of days rather tediously. It was impossible to be at my table to write. And then when it was possible for me to write, I was not able to do so, for I had to supervise the construction of the village for lepers. Thus all my correspondence has become chaotic. And it has been only a few days since I made the effort to commence again the most pressing of my correspondence. The knee is healing slowly. Just now I walked around the courtyard of the leper village to see how the work is coming. We are finishing the construction of the last part of the village. We can soon see the finish of this very great enterprise. It is because of this that I can set about to write you this evening. Be indulgent for my tardiness. You know how difficult and complicated it is here.

I do not know how to tell you my gratitude at the initiative that you have taken in publishing this volume. How many hours you must have devoted to the correspondence which was necessary! I know something about that. The correspondence is always more than one at first imagines. Whole days you must have given up for me. But the result is remarkable. I wonder how you succeeded in reaching this great number of personalities and in having them write that which is of great interest. They explain my ideas and define their attitude toward them and all the articles show the sympathy which they feel for them. I find among the collaborators friends who are familiar and others of whom I was ignorant of their sympathy for me. I will thank each one for the words which they have written. But first I must tell you my gratitude for the instigation of this enterprise. I am profoundly touched that you would do this for me. Then there is the fine bibliography which ends the volume. It is very complete and instructive. I have learned of writings which I have been ignorant of their existence. The volume was for me a great surprise and a beautiful surprise.

Mlle Emma has told me about her stay with you. She was happy to be in Evanston, to become acquainted with your wife, and to learn about your activities. And I am grateful for how much you have done for my hospital. Thank you for all that you have done for me.

With my best wishes to you and your wife, your devoted,

Albert Schweitzer
Lambaréné
March 9, 1955

19 JOHANNESBURG (1952)

THE DEFIANCE CAMPAIGN

From Dr. Schweitzer's hospital, Homer proceeded to South Africa to observe and support the fledgling African freedom movement. In this article, part of a series published in the Christian Century, he describes the Defiance Campaign—the first mass campaign against apartheid—and the early leadership role of the African National Congress. Homer's prophetic conclusion that "the Africans hear the drums of freedom beating through the whole continent of Africa," and "out of this leadership will rise a man who, with imagination and dedication, will tap the deep frustration and rich energies of the Africans, the Colored, and the Indians"—was later fulfilled by Nelson Mandela. As a result of his articles and involvement in the freedom movement, Homer was barred over the next four decades by the South African government from again entering the country.

South Africa has been described as a colonial nation maintaining its colony within its borders—a nation of two and a half million whites encompassing a colony of ten million nonwhites. Subject peoples, the nonwhites have no real citizenship and less grounds for hope than the peoples in many of the colonies in Africa. Even the few rights they have had are diminishing. From the Cape of Good Hope to the Limpopo river, there are multiple signs of deterioration.

A symbol of the oppression dealt out to these subject peoples was furnished by a Johannesburg newspaper when—probably by inadvertence—it carried the two following stories in adjacent columns:

169

Ill-Treated Animals: Fined £25. A colored man, William Mulder, was fined £25 with the alternative of six weeks' imprisonment with hard labor when he pleaded guilty in the Roodepoort magistrate's court of ill-treating a horse and a mule.

The other story:

Guilty of Assault on Native: Fined £20. A constable stated in Roodepoort magistrate's court that a miner, William P. O. Prinsloo, brought a native to him with his hands bound with wire, which was also tied to his neck. The native was bleeding from the mouth, nose, and ears. It was alleged that Prinsloo had hit a native, Danuel Mothaung, who was in his employ, with his open hand and fist, and with an iron pipe on the head. Prinsloo was fined £20 with the alternative of a month's imprisonment.

The history of South Africa is chiefly three centuries of "keeping the kaffir in his place." That place was for many years in the rural areas and native reserves; but as gold mines needed labor and as urban life developed, Africans increasingly came to the cities. The mines developed the compound system, where men live for months without their families. The Africans who came to the cities for domestic work and unskilled jobs were soon herded into segregated "locations." A few locations have been built by municipalities and may be tolerable—within the intolerable context of apartheid—but many are shanty towns, as bad as the worst human housing anywhere in the world.

The most heartening sign on the South African veld today is the joint action of Africans and Indians in defiance of certain unjust racist laws. Begun only June 26 this year, the campaign has spread to most of the major cities and is beginning to involve some of the rural areas as well. By mid-August, 2,500 Africans and Indians had been arrested (400 in a 24-hour period). White South Africa is suddenly realizing that it has a new weapon with which to deal—curiously enough, a weapon first perfected by Mahatma Gandhi in South Africa in the decade before 1914 and later used by him with spectacular results in India. This resistance campaign, the most important current political movement in Africa south of the equator, deserves careful examination, if only for the almost religious fervor and sacrifice it is engendering.

170

The present defiance campaign has a long history, going back to the organization of the African National Congress in 1912 and of the South African Indian Congress in 1920—the latter as an outgrowth of the Natal Indian Congress founded by Gandhi in 1894. These congresses (unofficial bodies not unlike the American National Association for the Advancement of Colored People) never had the leadership or support they deserved; it was not until after World War II that they began to gain in effectiveness. The Indian Congress, spurred by Gandhi's success in 1913-14 and by his later victory in India, has shown more initiative than the African Congress. In 1946-48 it launched a passive resistance campaign against the Asiatic Land Tenure act which took away certain elemental land ownership rights from the Indians in South Africa. After the anti-India riots by some Africans in Durban in 1949, special efforts were made to forge new cooperation between the Indian and the African Congresses. They culminated on June 26, 1950, in a nationwide demonstration against discrimination.

At the invitation of the African National Congress, a joint conference of the national executives of the Indian and African Congresses, together with representatives of the Coloreds (the half castes or mulattoes), was held in Johannesburg in July 1951. It was decided to form a joint planning council of the two congresses, with sixty-year-old James S. Moroka, a physician in the Free State, as chairman. At the annual conference of the African Congress in Bloemfontein in December 1951, a detailed plan of defiance was acted upon. The next month the plan was enthusiastically endorsed by the twentieth session of the South African Indian Congress in Johannesburg.

The plan was coolly and brilliantly conceived. So far it has been remarkably carried out. It was not a secret plan; in the tradition of Gandhi, it is available for inspection by anybody. Its preliminary step was a communication addressed to Prime Minister D. F. Malan by Dr. Moroka, as president of the African National Congress, calling upon the government to repeal certain racist acts not later than February 20, 1952, or face a united resistance movement. The prime minister took no heed of this request. On April 6, 1952, as a prelude to resistance, non-Europeans all over the union held impressive, if restrained, demonstrations, boycotting the Jan van Riebeek celebration commemorating the day in 1652 when the Dutch first landed in South Africa. The beginning of the defiance campaign itself was not scheduled until June 26, the second anniversary of the National Day of Protest.

171

In Port Elizabeth, where the campaign has been especially successful in its first two months, a public worship service was held the
Sunday before resistance was to begin. Two thousand natives stood
in the cold rain to pray for those who had volunteered to defy the
laws. An African clergyman told them: "You have undertaken a sacred and touching task. You have started to write a new page of history."

The night before the campaign actually started, a thousand
women held an all-night prayer service in the African location
(ghetto) of Port Elizabeth. The next morning thirty African volunteers, including three women, defied the apartheid regulations by
entering a suburban railroad station through the door marked "Europeans." On their sleeves they wore the African National Congress
colors—black, green, and gold ("black people on the green land under which is gold"). They occasionally chanted the African national
anthem, "N'kosi Sikelele Africa," and gave the clenched hand and
thumbs up salute (the hand a symbol of determination and the
thumb a symbol of freedom), yelling as they did so, "Afrika, Afrika."
They were arrested by police as they cried "Mayibuyee Afrika"
(Come Back, Africa). The volunteers offered no resistance whatsoever, and cooperatively entered the police van. They did not accept
the services of an attorney, refused to be released on the small bail
set, and for several weeks remained in the crowded, segregated jail
awaiting trial.

The Jails Are Filled

These scenes were repeated in selected centers in the Cape and the
Transvaal. During the first week 150 volunteers were arrested. Almost every day the English-language newspapers carried accounts
of the arrest of a new batch of volunteers or the trial of an old
group. Some Africans were tried for breaking the pass laws (regulations requiring certain papers to be carried by all African males),
and some Indians were tried for entering an African location without permits. Others were charged with flouting apartheid in railroad stations and post offices. Initially, the plan was for the principal campaign leaders not to be arrested, but within the month those
arrested included Nana Sita, president of the Transvaal branch of
the South African Indian Congress, and Mrs. J. L. Z. Njongwe, wife
of the president of the Cape Province branch of the African National
Congress.

Most resisters pleaded not guilty, one seventeen-year-old girl telling the court, "Even if I'm released I am going to use the same European entrance again, for I did so because these laws break friendships between us and the Europeans." Magistrates usually found those arrested guilty. The leaders of each group of volunteers received heavier sentences, those in Port Elizabeth being sentenced to two months of hard labor or a fine of 10 pounds (about $28 or the equivalent of six weeks' salary), with half the sentence suspended for six months for good behavior. The rank and file were sentenced to shorter terms, but uniformly they refused to pay the fines. Early in August, as the jails in several cities became full, the government resurrected an old law which permitted the authorities to use any money found on prisoners to help pay their fines. In a few cases, the volunteers were not convicted. In Johannesburg, fifty-two resisters who were arrested for breaking the 11:00 p.m. curfew laws for Africans were released because the police neglected to ask each volunteer separately for his pass. In Port Elizabeth, seventy-three volunteers were freed when it was belatedly discovered that there are no laws compelling segregation in post offices. After eight weeks, more than 2,500 volunteers had defied the laws, and in at least two cities—Port Elizabeth and East London—the jails were filled.

No Support from the White Clergy

One might expect that the Christian church in South Africa would support or at least show interest in this campaign. So far, not one white clergyman in South Africa is known to have endorsed the campaign. A Methodist minister was reported in the newspaper as saying: "A campaign of this sort is negative. We seek something positive. The church cannot condone anything that seeks to break the law." One Anglican bishop said privately, "I'm watching it closely to see if it grows, but of course I can't endorse it because later I might have to repudiate it." Anglican Michael Scott did, of course, send the campaign his support from his exile in London, and a few white churchmen are privately wishing for its success.

The African clergy, however, are much more friendly to the campaign. Several have volunteered, and one—Johnson Sambu—actually was arrested in Port Elizabeth for breaking the post office regulations. Upon arrest he stated: "As a Christian and a minister of the Church of England I have for many years preached and prayed that 'Thy will be done in earth as it is in heaven.' But on the con-

173

trary, government after government has passed unjust laws that make it impossible for such a state of affairs to come about. I therefore have no other alternative than to defy the unjust laws."

General reactions to the campaign have been varied. Prime Minister Malan early warned the African Congress against action. In doing so shortly after the abolition of the Native Representative Council, he unintentionally gave recognition to the congress as the prime spokesman of the African people. Another evidence of misunderstanding of the campaign came from the liberal Johannesburg English-language newspaper, the *Star*. In an editorial written less than two weeks after the campaign opened, it said: "From the outset the whole defiance movement was ill devised in conception and could do nothing but harm to South Africa and the non-Europeans themselves, [alienating] those who are well disposed towards the non-Europeans and hardening the hearts of the reactionaries and their sympathizers."

The campaign has not lacked more legitimate criticism. That the whole movement is the result of white domination and therefore of a black and brown nationalism cannot seriously be denied. Yet the leadership of the National Action Committee constantly emphasizes its nonracial nature. Before the campaign began, the leaders declared, "The struggle is not directed against any race or national group, but against the unjust laws." Dr. J. L. Z. Njongwe, an African physician who is president of the Cape Province branch of the African National Congress, stated: "What is the use of substituting one form of racial arrogance for another? Our people understand the evil results of hatred. The problems of peace are always greater than the problems of war. I am quite certain that we will succeed in our struggle against white domination; but to win what comes after our struggle, we must begin now to be free from hate."

Probable Future Course

The significance of this campaign is initially that South African's Indians and Africans, and increasingly other dark-skinned people, are belatedly uniting to fight their common foe, white supremacy and domination. This alone is a powerful enough factor, but it is made doubly so by the fact that the resisters are experimenting with the religious weapon of nonviolent direct action (the telegraphic address of the National Action Committee is "Satyagraha, Johannesburg!") and because for the first time hundreds of Africans are being initiated into a method much newer to them than to the Indians. In the process, much is being learned. As an English-language newspaper shrewdly admitted: "The present seemingly ineffectual phase is being used by the leaders for several calculated purposes— to test their organizational machinery, to gain experience in direction and liaison, to assess European reaction and, above all, to 'politicise' the non-European peoples, to educate them in the use of that immensely political weapon—passive resistance."

It is impossible to predict the future of this movement. The immediate plans are for the action to spread to most of the urban centers and then to the rural areas, including the native reserves. Future plans call for industrial demonstrations (Africans are legally forbidden to strike). The final step is for the campaign to spread to great masses of people, perhaps when the new Population Registration Act goes into effect.

The reaction of the government once it realizes the serious nature of the campaign is difficult to predict. One wise leader of the African Congress has said: "The way the Europeans react to this campaign will determine the future of race relations in South Africa. If they react with violence [some of the extreme Nationalists have already suggested flogging, and youths already arrested have been given the usual punishment of caning], they will sow seeds of hatred which will take centuries to heal."

This is not the talk of an African too primitive to have a major share in the political control of South Africa. It represents the intelligence and hope of the new leadership in Africa. Out of this leadership will rise a man who, with imagination and dedication, will tap the deep frustration and rich energies of the Africans, the Coloreds, and the Indians. Then apartheid will go—unbelievably fast.

20 JOHANNESBURG • DURBAN • CAPETOWN
(1952)

IN THE FOOTSTEPS OF
MAHATMA GANDHI

On his visit to South Africa, which lasted six weeks, Homer retraced the legacy of Mohandas Gandhi who lived in the country for over twenty years. After completing his studies in London and a brief trip home, Gandhi settled in South Africa in 1893 and practiced law until he was invited to return to India and lead the independence movement in 1914. During this period in South Africa, he developed satyagraha—*truth power—the nonviolent direct action technique that he would later use to win India's Independence. Homer's visit to Tolstoy Farm and the Phoenix Community, as well as friendship with Manilal Gandhi, Gandhi's son who was still living in South Africa, made a lasting impression on Homer and influenced his future development. Homer's account appeared in* Friends Intelligencer.

In April 1893, Mohandas Gandhi arrived in Durban, South Africa, after the long sea trip from India. He stepped off the boat as an obscure attorney who could not make a living in his chosen profession in India. He stepped off the boat as a twenty-four-year-old, inexperienced man without confidence, completely unknown.

In July 1914, Mohandas Gandhi left Cape Town for London. He boarded the boat as a well known person not only throughout South Africa but in his native India. He had led his fellow Indians in an historic struggle for justice and had even bested General Jan

Smuts, the white governor of South Africa. He was already a brilliant lawyer, an editor, a civic worker, and something of a religious leader.

Gandhi returned to India, by way of London, to become the Mahatma and the leader of his nation. For thirty-four years he worked for the freedom of his country and lived to see the day—and to see himself revered by his countrymen and by peoples the world over as one of the saints of all times.

I went to South Africa this past summer to follow the thread of Gandhi's life in this formative period covering the two decades from 1893 to 1914. I went to uncover the trail of this remarkable man, to talk to those still alive who could recall events of four and five decades past. I went to trace, if not to walk in, the footsteps of the Mahatma. In a sense I felt as if I were in early Christian times, in the first century, going over the ground Jesus covered: Bethlehem, Galilee, Jerusalem. But there was this difference: Gandhi's trail was more recent than Jesus' trail could ever have been even for most of the writers of the New Testament.

I mean to make this analogy, not for my part but in respect to Gandhi, for Gandhi will be remembered universally as Jesus is remembered. If a special religion does not grow around Gandhi, he will be the increasing concern and inspiration of a number of world religions. So I felt privileged that I could take this journey before all traces of his life in South Africa were eradicated by apartheid, death, and time. My first full day in Johannesburg was on a Sunday.

Everything is closed in South Africa on Sundays. I knew, however, that there was a Gandhi Hall somewhere in the city. I found the address in the telephone book and without too much guidance reached the hall on the edge of the financial district bordering the Indian quarter. Luckily a man inside the hall heard pounding at the door. He let me in and told me that the building is now a Hindu school, with the auditorium—containing large pictures of Gandhi and Nehru—used for all kinds of civic events. It is one of the few auditoriums in downtown Johannesburg which is open to unsegregated audiences. I told this man, one of the Hindu teachers, of my quest, and he told me to see Mr. P. S. Joshi, a leading Indian author and teacher. He gave me his address, and I walked almost two miles, passing the Indian shops down Bree Street, with its wholesale markets deserted on a Sunday afternoon.

Soon I arrived at Joshi's little house and was greeted warmly by him. He didn't know me, but any disciple of Gandhi's was a friend of his. He had actually come to South Africa after Gandhi had gone back to India, but he was one of the leaders of the Indian community in South Africa and a confirmed Gandhian, still wearing a homespun Gandhi cap. He took me around the corner to visit the secretary of the High Commissioner for India (British Commonwealth countries exchange commissioners and not ministers or ambassadors). The secretary told me that because of the great segregation and discrimination against nonwhites in South Africa, the government of India withdrew her High Commissioner, and he is the only man in attendance at their office. Then Mr. Joshi made arrangements for my visit to the sites of Gandhi's activity in and around Johannesburg.

Tolstoy Farm

My most unforgettable trip with Mr. Joshi was out to Tolstoy Farm. This was a community 21 miles south of Johannesburg which Gandhi established in the spring of 1910. It was, with his smaller community of Phoenix outside Durban, the center of Gandhi's political activity and of his many experiments in health, education, and community living. Gandhi named this farm after Count Leo Tolstoy, the Russian novelist and religious leader, whom Gandhi so admired and with whom he was corresponding. We went out to visit Tolstoy Farm in an old auto with six or seven Indians who went along for the pilgrimage. These included Mr. Ratanjee, who hadn't been at Tolstoy Farm since he was a small boy of thirteen, a pupil in Gandhi's school before 1914. Mr. Joshi had not visited the farm site for many years, but he remembered that it was near the rail junction of Lawley. We reached Lawley, and I knocked at the door of several farmhouses. The Indians were not inclined to ask directions of whites. Finally an ancient lady pointed to some trees past a hill and said, "Over that way Gandhi once had a place."

We went past the hill and, sure enough, on grounds now belonging to a brick and tile factory was the plot with pine and eucalyptus trees which housed the tiny community that played such an important part in South African history. Mr. Ratanjee assured us that this was the spot (cows browsing and all), pointing out how some of the boys would go over the highest hill to the store of an Indian trader to buy sweets—when Gandhi was away! He also told us that Gandhi on occasion would arise at 2 a.m. in order to walk the 21 miles to Johannesburg and, after a day at his law office, he would on occasion return by foot. The residents could only take the train into Johannesburg if their trip was for business.

I told my Indian friends that it was a pity that this site of Tolstoy Farm could not be set aside as an historical monument, and they looked at me queerly. Didn't I know that nothing about Gandhi was preserved by the South African government, any South African government? As we drove back to Johannesburg past gold mine dumps in the twilight on the veld, I told them that someday soon there would indeed be monuments and statues to Gandhi in South Africa.

The Johannesburg Home

I had a pleasant surprise my first week in Johannesburg when Manilal Gandhi came from Durban. I spent a day with Manilal, one of the Mahatma's four sons, visiting some of the places associated with his father. Again with some difficulty, we found the double-story house at 112 Albemarle Street in Johannesburg, where the Gandhi family lived at the turn of the century, before the establishment of Phoenix and Tolstoy Farms. With some hesitation, Manilal went to the door of his old home. It turned out to be the parsonage of a Methodist missionary, and so we were well received. We went through the house, room by room, as Manilal pointed out the places "where father and mother slept" and how the house had not really changed much. This was the house in which Gandhi first put into practice some of the ideas on simplicity which he received from reading John Ruskin. He wrote about this house in his autobiography as follows: "I introduced as much simplicity as was possible in a barrister's house. It was impossible to do without a certain amount of furniture. The change was more internal than external. The liking for doing personally all the physical labor increased. . . . Instead of buying baker's bread, we began to prepare unleavened wholemeal bread at home." And so Manilal pointed to the alcove off the kitchen where the handmill stood and where "Mr. Polak, father, and I would grind our own flour." He told how the living room was used for a reception after Mr. Polak's marriage and how, when a painter dirtied all the walls while painting the ceiling, his father testily ordered the walls done within 24 hours.

Valliamma Munusamy

Soon we left this house, which served to gather together the joint family under Gandhi's paternal care, and by auto we went to downtown Johannesburg. We passed the place where Gandhi was beaten up by one of his own fellow Indians and then we stopped at the corner of Anderson and Rissik Streets, where for so many years he had his law office. Then I told Manilal that I wanted to visit the grave of Valliamma Munusamy, a girl written up in one of Gandhi's autobiographical volumes. He wrote of her as follows: "Another (woman) returned from jail with a fatal fever to which she succumbed within a few days of her release. How can I forget her? Valliamma was a young girl of Johannesburg only seventeen years of age. She was confined to bed when I saw her. As she was a tall girl, her emaciated body was a terrible thing to behold. 'Valliamma, you do not repent of your having gone to jail?' I asked. 'Repent? I am even now ready to go to jail again if I am arrested,' said Valliamma. 'But what if it results in your death ?' I pursued. 'I do not mind it. Who would not love to die for one's motherland?' was the reply. Within a few days after this conversation Valliamma was no more with us in the flesh, but she left us the heritage of an immortal name. Condolence meetings were held at various places . . . to commemorate the supreme sacrifice of this daughter of India."

Most Indians in South Africa today have forgotten all about Valliamma, but we headed for the cemetery, picking up an old associate of the Mahatma, Mr. Medhon, en route. Before reaching the cemetery Mr. Medhon showed us the Hamidia mosque, on August 16, 1908, where Gandhi supervised the burning of two thousand identification cards which the Indians refused to carry. At the cemetery, we found a pervasive, lingering sense of segregation; we walked through the Christian section, the Jewish section, the Moslem section, the Parsi section, and finally found the Hindu section.

Still we did not see Valliamma's grave, although old Mr. Medhon remembered visiting it years ago. In the deepening evening shadows of tall eucalyptus trees, we searched every weathered gravestone. After I was prepared to give up, Mr. Medhon came across it with his cane. We paused for a moment in memory of this young girl and of all people everywhere who gave their lives nonviolently for freedom. The crumbling gravestone read: "In loving memory of our sister who died 22nd February, 1914, aged 17 years, of illness contracted in the Maritzburg gaol, to which she went as a passive resister."

Herdsman Kallenbach

While in Johannesburg, Manilal put me in touch with Hanna, whose uncle was Herman Kallenbach, one of the closest friends and co-workers of Gandhi in the first decade of our century. Kallenbach was born in East Prussia and came to South Africa at the age of twenty-five to become an architect. He met Gandhi in 1903, became a vegetarian, and soon became his lieutenant in the passive-resistance campaign. Being a German citizen, Kallenbach wasn't allowed to go with Gandhi to India at the start of World War I. After being interned in the British Isles, he returned to South Africa, where he became one of the leading architects and builders. The Mahatma and Kallenbach didn't see each other again for almost twenty-five years, when Kallenbach finally paid a short visit to India in 1937. I asked Hanna, his niece and longtime companion, why Uncle Herman waited so long. She said that he was ashamed to confront Gandhi since he had gone down in his own estimation by continuing his profession and thus becoming again a man of the world with money and possessions. Their first reunion in Gandhi's ashram in 1937 is movingly described by Gandhi, who "thought friend Kallenbach too fat and immediately I put him on a strict mango diet, on which he lost 26 pounds." In 1939, Kallenbach paid a second visit to Gandhi, again to renew their friendship and also to solicit Gandhi's help to establish Palestine as a homeland for his people. Kallenbach preceded Gandhi to the grave by three years, dying in South Africa in 1945.

Kallenbach is largely an unknown man—he never did any writing—and so I enjoyed the evening with Hanna and Manilal in Kallenbach's house atop a high hill in the Johannesburg suburb of Linksfield, which Kallenbach developed completely and to which such guests as C. F. Andrews and Muriel Lester frequently came. Kallenbach tried to name a street in this development after Gandhi, but the authorities wouldn't consider it. So he named a street Hannaben, the affectionate term Gandhi used for his niece when she visited Gandhi in India in the '30s. Hanna recalled incidents in her uncle's life and showed me an amazing collection of letters from Gandhi to Kallenbach, not only during their period of closest association, but down through the years. Especially of interest was a letter from Gandhi to Kallenbach on the occasion of the death of the latter's mother. This was written from jail by Gandhi—prisoner No. 777—on April 5, 1909. He ended the letter by these words: "I have read *David Copperfield*. I finished it yesterday. I am quite happy.

Yours sincerely, Your Upper House." It seems as if Kallenbach called Gandhi "Upper House," and' Gandhi called Kallenbach "Lower House" all through their lives.

I saw a good deal of Hanna while I was in Johannesburg; she had access to one of the richest untapped lodes of Gandhiana in South Africa. I encouraged her to continue to edit the letters of Gandhi for publication and arranged with the executors of the Kallenbach estate for a collection of Gandhi's books and eventually of his letters to be deposited in the Hebrew University in Israel, which was so close to Kallenbach's heart. He originally made Gandhi his principal heir and executor, but after Hitler, Gandhi told him to give his possessions to those in whose faith he was born, to his own people.

Pretoria Prison

I had many other experiences in the Johannesburg area relating to Gandhi. In nearby Pretoria Mr. Joshi introduced me to a few of the men who still remembered Gandhi. We visited some of the places in that capital city of South Africa where Gandhi stayed and spoke. With Mr. Joshi I went to the Pretoria prison, hoping to see the cell where Gandhi stayed while serving his third prison sentence in 1909. We found two entrances to the prison, one labelled "European" and the other labelled "Non-European." We knocked at the European entrance, but only I would be allowed to enter, so I retreated and told the guard that I would see him at the non-European entrance. Then Mr. Joshi and I entered the prison this way. This introduction hardly recommended us, and the prison warden hurriedly claimed that he did not know that Gandhi was ever a prisoner there, and in any event we would have to get permission to visit the cell blocks from the general superintendent of all South African prisons. I had a more successful experience at Diepkloof which is now a boys' reformatory but decades ago was a prison. I went with a Johannesburg judge to visit this reformatory, which for many years was headed by Alan Paton, author of Cry, The Beloved Country. The authorities here not only knew the exact cell where Gandhi stayed, but proudly showed it to us, a cell where six juvenile offenders, all Africans, now sleep.

I missed seeing Olive and C. M. Doke, the two children of the Rev. Joseph Doke, Baptist clergyman and first biographer of Gandhi. Olive is a missionary somewhere in Northern Rhodesia, and I especially wanted to meet her and ask her how her life was affected by the close contact with Gandhi she had as a girl, when she sang "Lead, Kindly Light" outside his door in her father's house as Gandhi was recovering from an attack on his life. The last night in Cape Town, however, after a speech in the Unitarian Church, a stranger came up to me and stuck a book under my arm and said, "Keep this." It was an autographed copy of the first edition of Doke's biography of Gandhi, a rare book, with probably only a handful of copies existing here in America.

One of my most unusual experiences was the day I spent in the tiny town of Volksrust, on the border of Natal and the Transvaal. This was the site of the famous march led by Gandhi which was climaxed by his settlement with General Smuts after Gandhi was arrested three times in four days. Manilal Gandhi told me to see Essop Suleman in Volksrust and he would show me around. I sought out Suleman early one morning, and he turned out to be a Moslem fruit merchant, white-bearded, with a red fez and a limp. Apparently nobody in recent years had asked to see the route of the Gandhi march, but Suleman remembered it. He saw his duty and commandeered a car, which one of his nephews drove.

We went from Volksrust across the border to Charleston. The border did not look historic, but it was here, in the autumn of 1913, that Gandhi led his marchers—some 2,000 Indian women, men, and children—across the border in violation of the law. After inspecting this ground and the spot where the nonviolent army encamped at Charleston, it was time for the noonday service of the Moslems. Suleman invited me to the mosque with him, and so I went, first depositing my shoes at the door. It was a moving service. Afterwards we went on another drive on the other side of Volksrust, first passing two different courthouses where Gandhi was tried and sentenced.

After leaving my Moslem friends, I went to the Volksrust library and asked the librarians if they had any historical material on Gandhi. They had none. Then I asked them if Indians could borrow books and use the reading room. "Don't you know," the women in charge explained, "that this library is for Europeans, whites only?" That evening at the hotel around the fire—it can be cold in the Transvaal in late July—I asked the hotel keeper what he would do if Gandhi walked in the door. He told me that as a South African he would have to exclude Gandhi, but that as a liberal he would admit him. The fact is that the hotels of South Africa are for whites only.

Sitting around the fire, I asked if anybody remembered Gan-

183

dhi. Soon two men came up and said they did remember him. One was the town clerk. He said that he was a small boy when the Indians led by Gandhi tried to cross the border, and he remembered his father riding on a horse in an effort of the villagers to keep the Indians out of the Transvaal. He said that a history of Volksrust mentioned this incident, and he went to his office across the street to fetch the volume.

The other man, a Scotsman who was on the eve of returning to his birthplace after long years on the veld, said that he also remembered seeing Gandhi. He told me that he had followed Gandhi on the pages of the newspapers ever since, and by his way of reckoning, Gandhi was a great man, as great as Smuts. This is high praise indeed from any white South African. But a woman who was listening replied, "But how can Gandhi be as great? He has a brown skin." Luckily, it was time for me to take the night train to Durban. I left with the feeling that this tiny town had not completely forgotten the only man, a brown-skinned one, who had however briefly turned on Volksrust the spotlight of world attention and thus made history.

Manilal Gandhi

The next morning I arrived in busy Durban. Manilal Gandhi and his son were at the station with their Dodge sedan to meet me. They whisked me through this seaport town, along the Indian Ocean for awhile, past tall, ocean-front apartments. About fifteen miles north of the city, after passing through sugar-cane fields, we came to the village of Phoenix and to Phoenix Farm. This the Mahatma founded in 1904 after reading John Ruskin's *Unto This Last*. Gandhi wanted a place in which to indulge some of his experiments. For ten years he edited and printed here his weekly newspaper, *Indian Opinion*, and ever since Manilal Gandhi has continued this tiny community and has continued to edit and publish this newspaper.

It was a pleasant week with Manilal, his son, and his two daughters, aged twelve and twenty-three. Mrs. Gandhi was away in India, but we had large, long, and spicy Indian meals, all vegetarian. Outside the one-story house were mango groves and papaya trees; donkeys were running in the fields. I spent one day going through the old file of *Indian Opinion* and reading the original accounts of that march through Volksrust. Another day we spent in Durban itself, passing the home, still standing, where the Gandhi family lived in 1896. We also passed the dock area where the Mahatma was chased by an ugly crowd when he came off a ship from India in 1896.

Most of the time at Phoenix I spent talking to Manilal. He is the son of a great father—and undeniably feels the inability to walk in his father's shoes. Yet Manilal has done so, more than any other of the Mahatma's four children. Mohandas Gandhi, for all his saintliness, was not an especially good parent. He had the tendency to treat all children as his children and his children in no special way. The result was that the Gandhi children had not a very secure upbringing. Indeed, Manilal told me that the most he ever saw of his father was in 1945-46 when he returned to India to accompany him on trips through Madras and Eastern Bengal. Manilal himself went to India in 1914 when his father left South Africa, but returned to Africa in 1916 and has been at Phoenix and attached to *Indian Opinion* ever since, except for short visits to India and, in 1949, to America.

I asked Manilal how many times he was in jail. Rather proudly he made the enumeration for me. The first time was in 1910, when he was eighteen, in Johannesburg as part of his father's civil disobedience campaign. He was given ten days, broke the law again, was rearrested, and spent another ten days in prison. In 1913 he crossed the border at Volksrust and was imprisoned for three months. Again in Durban in 1919, after returning to South Africa, he was arrested. In 1930, while on a visit to India, he participated in the famous Salt March with his father and was sentenced to a year in jail by the British authorities. In 1946 he spent one month in jail as part of an Indian passive resistance campaign in Durban, the same one in which the Rev. Michael Scott was arrested. Also he has, like his father, engaged in hunger strikes, one for two weeks in April 1951, and one for three weeks this past March. The latter, well publicized in America, was to gain spiritual strength to play his part in the nation-wide passive resistance struggle and also to try to bring about a change in the heart of the South African government.

As I talked at length with Manilal, I saw how great the burden is on the nonwhite in South Africa, including the Indians who, in a sense, are more despised than the Africans. The third of a million Indians living in South Africa have few rights, and the official policy of the government is to repatriate them to India as fast as they can be made to go. They are even given money by the South African government to pay for most of their passage. The Indians are also segregated almost as much as the darker-skinned Africans. Manilal has tried to resist this apartheid by going into the white sections of Durban buses, libraries, and railroad stations. A few years ago he took his daughter on the prohibited—to Indians—lower level of a doubledecker bus. The conductor urged them to go upstairs, but they refused. Finally the bus was stopped, and a telephone call made to headquarters. Instructions were received not to arrest Manilal and his daughter. The city of Durban did not want another Gandhi on its hands!

Manilal told me that he last saw his mother, Kasturba, in India in 1939, five years before she died in prison in February 1944. Manilal last saw his father in the summer of 1946. Manilal was in the Indian bazaar section of Durban on that fateful day of January 30, 1948, when he heard rumors that Mahatma Gandhi had been shot. Hurrying back to Phoenix by auto, Manilal was met by Indians near the farm coming up the hill to bring him the news: his father had been shot dead—in far-away Delhi across the broad Indian Ocean.

The World Will Continue to Remember

On October 2, the world celebrated the eighty-third anniversary of the birth of Mohandas Gandhi. Little groups of unforgetting persons around the world remembered this half-naked, brown-skinned man, with loincloth, infectious smile, big ears. They remembered him and will continue to remember him as the father of his country, of a free India. The world will continue to remember him as the creator of the tool of nonviolent resistance, a religious tool in a militaristic, anything-but-religious world. The world will continue to remember him as a man who insisted that ends can never justify means, that freedom can never justify war, that independence can never justify violence. Christians will continue to remember him as one of the most Christlike men who ever lived. Non-Christians will remember him as the man who wedded creed and deed. As Louis Fischer, his biographer, so well said, "Gandhi took words and ideas seriously, and when he accepted an idea in principle he felt that not to practice it was dishonest."

It was during the two decades in South Africa that Gandhi conceived and first tested his ideas, that he first began to bridge the gulf between idea and action. It was the Mahatma's two decades in South Africa that prepared him for his work in India. His South African interlude made a difference to India today, and will make, we pray, a difference to the whole world tomorrow.

NEW YORK
(1953)

IS McCARTHY A CONCEALED COMMUNIST?

In the early years of the Cold War, Senator Joseph McCarthy of Wisconsin launched an anti-communist witchhunt that effectively silenced the White House, the State Department, and the Congress and mobilized the American people to look for suspected communists in their schools, workplace, and churches. As Vice Chairman of the Illinois Civil Liberties Union, Homer vigorously opposed McCarthy and his smear campaign. In 1953, Homer served as summer minister of the Community Church of New York and, at the height of the hysteria, delivered this powerful sermon speculating whether McCarthy, the chairman of the Permanent Subcommittee on Investigations, was a concealed communist. Supporters of the Senator threatened to sue him for libel, but the following year Congressional hearings began and McCarthy was finally toppled from his throne.

Is Senator Joseph R. McCarthy a concealed communist?

This seems . . . I know . . . a preposterous question, preposterous because the American who is today making a one-man crusade against communism is the junior senator from Wisconsin, Joseph R. McCarthy.

Yet in a world of spy and counterspy, of cynical methods for cynical ends, could it be that McCarthy, the anti-communist, is really a concealed communist?

Senator McCarthy himself, in the case of James A. Wechsler, editor of the *New York Post*, warned us not to depend upon what a man says or does. He warned us to look beneath his actions to what he really is. During McCarthy's questioning of Wechsler, the Senator said, "If you or I were a member of the Communist Party, and we wanted to advance the Communist list, perhaps the most effective way of doing that would be to claim we deserted the party." Although an admitted ex-communist, Wechsler for the past decade has had an enviable record of being an anti-communist. Yet McCarthy feels that Wechsler is really a concealed communist! And if he feels the anti-communist Wechsler is a concealed communist, might not there be other concealed communists, including Senator Joseph R. McCarthy himself?

I was toying with this possibility for many months when, a few weeks ago, through a strange set of circumstances which cannot be fully divulged here, I was given a document which—and, I know, this sounds implausible—was found in a secret cavity in a huge wheel of Wisconsin cheddar cheese which was being exported from Milwaukee to Liverpool. This document was apparently addressed to Premier Malenkov, by a top-level recruiting agent of Soviet Russia who was still in America. This document is apparently a plea to spare the life of Beria who headed this espionage apparatus in Moscow. Anyway, here is the deciphered fragment just as I received it:

> On direct orders from comrades Stalin and Beria, at the end of the Second World War, I was sent over to America—under the cover of a Scandinavian businessman—to recruit someone to the concealed apparatus of the Party. None of our American comrades knew of my mission and none knows of it even to this day. Our beloved leader, J. Stalin, conceived this strategy of using anti-communism to promote the party of the proletariat.
>
> The politician worked out beyond our greatest expectations. When I found him, he had just returned from the Pacific war front. I spent some months studying his habits of behavior and his mode of thought and I finally reached him through a friend. Through a combination of circumstances he agreed to join the apparatus. He took money, of course, and he still costs the Peoples' Democracy a great sum yearly. He didn't join us primarily for money, but he is something of a gambler and he became convinced that our side would ultimately win and he wanted to be on the winning side—and on the top. He felt that he really had nothing to lose, since he could always deny that

he belonged to us and it was the kind of gamble in which he could only win. We, too, had little to lose, for we knew he would never tell and we had undeniably selected a man with energy and a reckless spirit, just reckless enough to be lucky—and win.

It was the plan that he would get elected to the American Parliament, probably the lower house first and, in a decade, to the upper house. The Soviet would help finance his considerable political and other expenses. Other than this, there would be no contact whatsoever—not even with the other members of the apparatus. Once he would establish himself in Washington, he would begin to weaken capitalism from the inside. We were initially surprised when he won a primary election for the Senate and didn't even have to do a term in the lower parliament.

For several years he established himself carefully and only after four years did he begin his work. For this purpose, he called together some of his friends in 1950 and told them that he was in need of an issue in order to seek reelection two years hence in 1952. His friends suggested all kinds of issues. He rejected them one by one. Then a crusade against communism in government was suggested and somewhat reluctantly he agreed. He began some researches and within a month launched his campaign—which has only grown in dimensions. Overnight he made and kept the headlines. He has made America hysterical with fear of communists. He has even aided the party directly in attaining sympathy toward our people in some ruling circles because of his reckless charges. And he has not exposed one of our agents on the espionage level, although of course he is not in a position to know who they are.

This technique has been proven a success in America and we must recommend that similar agents in the concealed apparatus be immediately sent to England, France, Africa, and India. But Comrade Malenkov, this technique is a joint result of the brilliant work of our late leader, J. Stalin, together with comrade Beria, and I suggest you spare his life, for this project alone has made Comrade Beria valuable to the heritage of Lenin.

I cannot, of course, vouch for the authenticity of these Wisconsin cheese papers. They might be a fantasy. Indeed, I believe they are a forgery, created out of thin air by this clergyman. They need not be, however, the fiction they are, for, the point is, they could be true. These Wisconsin cheese papers are fiction but could be true because there is so much in the present demeanor of the junior senator from Wisconsin which would lead well-informed persons to conclude that he is indeed a concealed communist.

Therefore I would like to put Senator McCarthy on the stand this morning . . . before his own committee, using the hit-and-smear tactics of his own committee. So step down from the podium, Senator, give the gavel to your distinguished colleague from Illinois, and sit in the witness chair after, of course, swearing to tell the truth and nothing but the truth.

Chairman: Senator, isn't it true that your opponent, Senator Robert LaFollette, in the Wisconsin primaries in 1946 was so uncompromisingly anti-communist that the communists in Wisconsin felt that you would be less dangerous than LaFollette?

Witness: Yes, on the other hand . . .

Chairman: On the other hand, isn't it true that there were many thousands of communists among the 75,000 members of the Wisconsin CIO (Confederation of Industrial Organizations, a major labor union) in 1946 and that you beat LaFollette only by 5,400 votes and these came from the CIO districts in Milwaukee? Isn't it true, therefore, that you won the primary with communist votes?

Witness: No, I deny . . .

Chairman: Wait a minute, isn't it true, Senator, that when you were asked by reporters about this support by the communists you replied, "Communists have the same right to vote as anyone else, don't they?"

Witness: Well, I meant . . .

Chairman: What did you mean? Isn't it true, Senator, that you once said that "Stalin's proposal for world disarmament is a great thing and he must be given credit for being sincere about it?" Did you call Stalin "sincere"?

Witness: I feel you are making a studied effort to twist . . .

Chairman: Which reminds me, talk about studying, isn't it also true, Senator, that soon after moving to Washington as a freshman senator you actually began the study of Russian?

Witness: I can explain that.

Chairman: I'm not interested in your explanation. You admit you did study Russian. What for? Our committee has evidence that you had ideas about making peace with the enemy, with Joe Stalin. Your campaign manager has said that, if you were president, you would end the Cold War by flying to make a deal with Stalin. Right or wrong?

Witness: Wrong.

Chairman: But, Senator, your manager has quoted you as saying, "The first thing I would do if president is to pick up the phone and call Joe Stalin and say, 'This is Joe McCarthy. I'm coming over tomorrow to talk about things. Meet me at the Moscow airport at one o'clock.' And then when you arrived in Moscow, you said you would sit down with Stalin in a closed room. And, then, with your knowledge of Russian, couldn't you pull another Yalta? Do you deny this attempt at appeasement?

Witness: I deny every . . .

Chairman: We won't accept your denial. And, for another thing, to show how much of a communist you have been, is it not true, Senator, that you voted the straight communist line on every major issue of foreign policy, as laid down by the communist *Daily Worker*, since the outbreak of the Korean War?

Witness: I don't read the *Daily* . . .

Chairman: Senate voting records show that you tried to sabotage in Congress measures to oppose the spread of Russian communism such as the Marshall Plan. And is it not also true that in 1950, you voted along with the pro-communist congressman, Vito Marcantonio, against Point IV, again sabotaging plans for the free world to oppose communism?

Witness: Yes, but . . .

Chairman: Well, you do admit it. Genet in the *New Yorker* magazine for May 30, 1953 in her "Letter from Paris" writes that "of all the Paris press this last fortnight, the communist *Humanité* alone has not lifted one stick of type against you." Do you deny that the communist press is on your side?

Witness: But the *Daily Worker* . . .

Chairman: I will not allow the *Daily Worker* to be quoted at this hearing. The hearing will now be adjourned to another day since the television networks have other programs. Thank you, Senator. We are only doing this because of the necessity of exposing communism in the highest places. We are hurting nobody's reputation. You will be given a further chance to reply.

Having displayed a sample of the McCarthyization of McCarthy, I must again return to the question of the morning: Is McCarthy a concealed communist?

By his own standards, by the rules of the game, he and his reputation could be seriously and rather easily shattered.

We must not, however, do unto McCarthy what he would do

unto others. We must not stoop to his methods to answer his kind of question.

There are, however, more objective criteria, which can be used in answering the question of the morning. Whatever his associations, whatever his voting record, whatever his speeches, what have been the results of his actions over the past three years? Could we find light to our question from this more objective source?

I would reply that McCarthy's actions have lead to three things: first, a serious curtailment of civil liberties in America; second, a serious damaging of America's reputation abroad; and third, a strengthening of the communist party here at home.

I am not one who minimizes the danger of communism to our institutions, to our nation, to our whole free world, to all mankind. Communism is an evil, a double one, since it masquerades as a good. Make no mistake, there are communists in our country. Indeed, a few communists—but by no means 7,000—have wormed their way into the clergy, into the churches, into our liberal churches, but we in the church can take care of them, and the McCarthys only make it harder for us to do so.

Just what is McCarthyism? It is nothing especially new. It is an American adaptation of the big lie of Nazism and the smear of communism. To smear, McCarthy uses the big lie with a new twist. He buttresses one lie with another and outruns the public, if not the reporters. He uses what Richard Rovere has called "the multiple untruth." He inserts a misstatement in a side remark, a subordinate clause, or even in an adjective. Truth can never catch up with McCarthy to correct the distortion, for when it does, McCarthy is hot on another investigation and completely disinterested in the old one.

McCarthyism damages reputations and McCarthy, himself, is absolved either through congressional immunity or verbal gymnastics. The *St. Louis Post-Dispatch* once pointed out that McCarthy has frequently had to hedge by admitting: "It appears that (so-and-so) never actually signed up as a member of the Communist Party, and never paid dues . . . " That is, concludes the *Post-Dispatch*, "the same as saying McCarthy does not eat human flesh . . . " That is—McCarthyism!

McCarthy and McCarthyism have lead, first of all, to a fear in America which is similar in kind, if not yet in degree, to the fear we are opposing in communism. Fifteen years ago I visited Soviet Russia. (I am almost afraid to admit it today.) I visited Russia and found a miasma of fear everywhere. People were afraid to talk to me—a foreigner. The Russian people were afraid to talk to each other. Fear stalked the land. When I returned from my month in Russia, I vowed I would help prevent this silent, cruel, totalitarianism from every coming to my land. Alas, it is coming.

The fear is in our public schools. Teachers are afraid to teach controversial subjects.

The fear is in our colleges and universities. Students are afraid to express opinions or to join organizations, lest something go into their records.

The fear is in our government, with civil servants immobilized, refusing to make decisions, refusing to subscribe to certain magazines.

The fear is in our churches, with even courageous clergymen afraid to discuss controversial issues for fear a public discussion will reflect on the jobs of some of their parishioners.

The fear is in our United States Senate, with, until recently, only two gallant warriors daring to speak out: Senator Herbert Lehman and Senator Mike Monroney.

The fear is even in our United Nations, with the former director-general dancing to the tune of our Congress in matters of security and passports.

This fear did not begin with McCarthy and it is wrong to pin the blame exclusively on him, when it has had a long—if dishonorable—history in America, going back in our generation to Martin Dies and the Hearst Papers. It is also wrong to pin the blame exclusively on McCarthy, the Republican, when this fear is of bipartisan origin, with Pat McCarran, the Democrat, also being an accomplice. Yet somehow McCarthy symbolizes these reckless, self-seeking charges, and his name will now and forever nestle ingloriously in our dictionaries, along with that of Quisling.

But McCarthy and McCarthyism have not only weakened American internally. His antics have seriously damaged our American reputation abroad for freedom, fairness, and democracy. You have read what American world travelers, such as Mrs. Roosevelt and Adlai Stevenson, have said about the effort of McCarthyism on our friends abroad. The free world fears this evil mushrooming in our midst and the free world, from London to New Delhi, may see America today in truer perspective than we ourselves can.

McCarthy's investigations of authors of books in our American Information Service Libraries, his investigations aided and abetted by Secretary of State John Foster Dulles on a political trapeze, made us look silly as book-burning directives were followed by take-'em-off-the-shelves directives.

Yes, Molotov or Vishinsky—the old red hands—could not have done a better job in wrecking our reputation abroad than McCarthy has done . . . and all in the last nine months.

McCarthy and McCarthyism have also had the effect, ironically, of strengthening the American Communist Party and actually making it more difficult for communists to leave the party. How could this be?

Morris Ernst and David Loth recently made a study of 300 ex-communists in the volume entitled *Report on the American Communist*. The authors found that, not only party blackmail, but the fear of McCarthyism keeps communists today in the party. Listen: "Smears of non-communists . . . adds to the strength of the party. It seems to identify communism with worthy measures and good men. It tends to keep people in the party through fear of being smeared if they leave."

And so I ask again: Is McCarthy a concealed communist?

Some Americans who oppose McCarthy believe that we must not play up McCarthy, since—they say—he is only a creature of the liberals who built him up. I believe this is a complete misreading of current history. No matter, today McCarthy is so much in the headlines that he can't be ignored. He must be opposed, and opposed with all the urgency, all the wisdom, all the effectiveness that the American people possess and without—I insist—descending to his level.

What can you and I do to oppose McCarthy and McCarthyism? First, we must oppose McCarthy, the man not vindictively, but squarely for the danger his is. We must do what Arthur Eisenhower, the President's brother, did when we called McCarthy what he is: "The most dangerous menace to America."

I have lectured extensively in the Midwest and in the East and in the past six months and everywhere I go I hear many people say, "Where there's smoke, there's fire; McCarthy has performed a useful service." I say to you, don't let anybody get away with saying these things. There is fire, all right—our Bill of Rights is being burned!

Ask the defenders of McCarthy just what service he has performed. Remind them that the labor movement and many liberal organizations got rid of the communists in their midst long before McCarthy's sudden interest in communism bloomed. As a matter of fact, with all his ballyhoo, his game of 205, 81, 57—the various numbers of communists he swore were in the State Department—his game has hardly uncovered a communist who was not known long beforehand by the FBI. Call the lie to those who say, "We don't like McCarthy's methods, but he is getting the commies." He is not.

Second, we must squarely oppose McCarthyism, the method, in all its manifestations wherever we are. Wherever there is fear or suppression, censorship or silence, we must speak out and act to regain our precious liberties, our freedoms and not only for liberals, but even for communists. We must protect freedom not only for ourselves, but even for those we despise. An individuals, we may find this difficult to do, but we must. As groups of individuals, we may find this easier to do and so we may want to join chapters of the responsible, non-communist American Civil Liberties Union. Through group action we can oppose those who would curtail liberty . . . in the name of liberty.

Third, we must be sympathetic with those who, by a kind of civil disobedience, are testing the right of irresponsible Congressional committees to go on political and headline expeditions. I hope we would all agree that Congressional committees do have wide powers of investigation . . . and should have these powers. When they abuse this power, however, is there no way for the concerned or injured citizen to help call a halt? I like the advice Dr. Albert Einstein has recently given. After asking the question, "What ought the minority of intellectuals to do against this evil?" Einstein answered, "Frankly I can see only the revolutionary way of non-cooperation in the sense of Gandhi's. Every intellectual who is called before one of the committees ought to refuse to testify, i.e., he must be prepared for jail and economic ruin, in short, for the sacrifice of his personal welfare in the interests of the cultural welfare of his country."

I think Einstein is correct, only I wish that these persons who do refuse to testify would stand on the first amendment to our Constitution instead of the fifth, would refuse to testify because they feel Congress has no right to abridge freedom of speech and thus delve into their personal convictions instead of not wanting to incriminate themselves.

Is McCarthy a concealed communist?

My considered answer is: I do not think that McCarthy is or has been a member of the Communist Party. However . . . his activities could well be compared to the undercover communist, for no communist in America has done as much damage as McCarthy has done to our American civil liberties and to our whole American democracy.

22 EVANSTON
(1955)

FESTIVAL OF LIGHT

At the Unitarian Church of Evanston, Homer delivered an annual Christmas Eve service for the children of the congregation emphasizing world religions. During the service, the children would leave their shoes in front of the huge fireplace in Hayford Hall with an offering. The money collected went to a worthy cause, such as Dr. Schweitzer's hospital in Africa or to subsidize an Asian or African delegate to a liberal religious congress. After the service, the children would race out to retrieve their shoes and find a shiny penny in each one. After refreshments, they would bundle up and head off with their parents—often in a snowstorm—to dream of reindeer and rooftops, presents and Christmas cheer, and joy and peace for all.

Candlelight Service

All lights in the church auditorium are extinguished, except for seven candles on the podium. A phonograph starts to play a prelude from a Schweitzer recording of Bach. Dr. Jack speaks:

In the Book of Genesis, in the Bible, it is written:

"When God began to create the heavens and the earth,
the earth was a desolate waste,
with darkness covering the abyss."

There is the darkness of the forest.

196

There is the darkness of the eclipse.
There is the darkness of the tornado.
There is the darkness of ignorance.
There is the darkness of the prison cell.
There is the darkness of death.
But darkness need not be desolate.
There is also the darkness of the crisp winter night, the solstice.
There is the darkness to give growing things a rest.
There is the darkness welcomed by lovers.
There is the darkness needed to cool off the earth.
There is the darkness so necessary to those who must sleep.
There is the darkness just before the light.

And light is good, too.
Also in Genesis we read that:

"Then God said, 'Let there be light,' and there was light,
And God saw that the light was good.
God then separated the light from the darkness."

Now seven candles of the candelabra are lighted, one by one, as the following sentences are read:

There is the welcome light—and warmth—of the sun.
There is the light of the stars, of lightning, and of the northern
    lights.
There is the light of the fire, the candle, the lamp, the bulb.
There is the light of lighthouses and of traffic lights.
There is the light of the welder's arc and of the miner's torch.
There is the light, the imperishable flame, of the human spirit.
There is the light of festivals—symbolic thankfulness of the gift
    of light.

Tonight, this Christmas Eve, we would remember three festivals of light: the Divali festival from far-away India, the Hanukkah festival of the Jews, the Christmas festival of Christendom—one Hindu, one Jewish, one Christian, all festivals using light.

Divali

The festival of Divali had its beginnings probably four thousand years ago. It occupies the last three days of the Indian year—and the year ends, not in December, but usually around the first of November. Divali is a festival commemorating the time the gods supposedly destroyed the demons inhabiting the earth. In honor of the gods descending to earth and destroying these demons, this feast of lamps is held.

The first of the three days of the festival is the luckiest. No astrologer need be consulted about a child beginning school that day, or a bride being sent to her husband's home, or gold being given to a goldsmith to become fashioned into jewelry. This first day the houses are whitewashed, the metal vessels are polished until they shine like gold, the bills are called in and paid, the children set off firecrackers, the boys tie white strings and clips to the end of sticks to make buzzers. And on this first day the people illumine their homes by putting lights on the gates and every high place.

Small Divali lamps are lighted at this point.

And there is universal rejoicing this first day of Divali that the debts are all paid, that the harvest is all in, that the rains are all over, that everybody seems all happy.

In some Indian communities, each girl makes a special lamp of her own, decorated with special markings. She will set this lamp on a tiny raft in the river to float in the current. If the lamp burns until it reaches the farther shore, this is a sign of good luck until the next Divali festival.

The second of these three days of Divali is a day for dressing up, a day for calling on relatives and friends. On this day the brother goes to the home of his sister for a Divali visit. On this day the sister takes a lamp and moves it in front of her brother. And then the brother gives his sister a Divali gift.

A boy and a girl stand up. The girl lights a lamp and moves it in a clockwise motion twice and then both sit down. A few bars of Indian music are again played.

The third of these Divali days is the greatest. The whole family arises at five in the morning. Everyone bathes. The children set off firecrackers to their heart's content. They make Divali lamps and go around from house to house begging oil for their lamps that their dead ancestors may get light.

And, on the third day, there is a private worship service—

arati—often in front of a little child. *Child comes in front.*

First some Indian scripture is given, such as this modern scripture from the greatest of all modern Hindus, Mahatma Gandhi: "There is something radically wrong in the system of education that fails to arm girls and boys to fight against social evil. That education alone is of value which draws out the faculties of a student, so as to enable him or her to solve correctly the problems of life in every department."

More Indian music is played, and then the lamp is moved clockwise in front of the child as Indian prayer music is sounded. The narrator moves the lamp clockwise twice in front of the child.

After listening to this Indian music, the Hindus say one to another, "May you be happy all the year." And everyone gathers round to eat grains and sweets and to send trays of it to friends as—outside—the children continue to set off firecrackers. Meanwhile, everyone in the house has kept awake during the long evening and with the beginning of the New Year, each goes forth to wish his friends all happiness.

Hanukkah

The festival of Hanukkah had its beginning more than two thousand years ago, more than a century and one half before the birth of Jesus, when a Syrian emperor captured the Temple of Jerusalem and forbade the Jewish people to worship their God. The Jews treasured their religious freedom, and so they battled the Syrians. Three long years they fought, led by Judah of Maccabee. At last, the Maccabees won, and they cleansed the Temple and made it once again a place for the worship of their God.

The rededication of the Temple was celebrated for eight days by prayer and song. And Hanukkah—meaning *dedication*—is this festival. And it is celebrated in December today for it was at that time of year that the victory and thus the first Hanukkah took place. This festival was celebrated in the time of Jesus. Indeed, in the Book of John in the New Testament it is written, "And it was the feast of the dedication at Jerusalem; it was winter; and Jesus was walking in the temple in Solomon's porch."

This feast of dedication—Hanukkah—is also called the "Feast of Lights," because of the custom of lighting candles on each of the eight nights. These are lit because of a miracle which is said to have happened when the Temple was taken back from the Syrians. Only a small jar of holy oil—just enough for one day—was left, but this tiny jar of holy oil burned for eight days and eight nights until new oil could be made with which to fill the sacred lamp, the Menorah. And thus, today, candles are lit for eight days to remind generation after generation of Jews that the candles stand for the light of freedom and liberty won by Judah of Maccabee.

The important event of this holiday is the candle-lighting ceremony, using the special Hanukkah Menorah, with places for eight candles and for the *Shammash* by which the others are kindled. The father usually lights the Menorah each evening, just after nightfall, in the presence of the entire family. And each successive evening another candle is lit, until the last night when the full eight are kindled. A prayer of thanks to God is recited as the candles are lit and then the Hanukkah story is retold to the children:

Candles, O candles of dedication, now shall you be relit.
Again to dedicate your nation, your shining row is set.

The Temple lies in desolation, but we are living yet,
And this is our reconsecration, a people that cannot forget.

Dr. Jack lights the Shammash, or center candle. He returns to pulpit. A boy takes the center candle out of holder and uses it to light the candle farthest to the left, first saying:

I am the oldest of candles, of our people in our land,
When Abraham came from Aram, I burned at his right hand.

He lights the first candle, returns the center candle to holder, and then sits down. A girl takes center candle out of holder and uses it to light the candle, second from left, and so on, alternating boys and girls for the third, fourth, fifth, six, and seventh candles:

I am the second candle, of a people on its soil,
For I have burned to light the way, of the farmer at his toil.

I am the candle of making things, of stone and clay and wood;
For God, when first He made the world, and saw that it was good.

200

I am the candle of learning things, of light that fills the mind,
Of passing on from man to child, all tasks of every kind.
I am the candle of purity; I made the Temple clean,
Before again its lamp could shine, or sacrifice be seen.

I am the candle of service; our new born nationhood
Again needs many hands to toil, for our ancient people's good.

I am the candle of brotherhood, whose brightness shines afar,
Whose light gives strangers welcome, wherever my people are.

I am the candle of that faith, that kept our people whole,
The light of worship and of trust, whose flame is Israel's soul.

And, after the candles are lit, the Jewish hymn, translated as "Rock of Ages," is sung, both in home and synagogue. A recording of this hymn is played. After two minutes, it plays softer as Dr. Jack reads one stanza of the song. After the singing of "Rock of Ages," one of several psalms from the Hebrew Bible is recited. Then members of the family may exchange gifts. There may be special foods as Hanukkah comes to a close.

Christmas

Young people now pass out lighted candles to persons on aisle seats in the congregation.

The festival of Christmas had its beginning with the First Christmas as given in the Gospel According to Luke in the New Testament. After the birth of the baby Jesus, the shepherds went back, glorifying God and praising him for all that they had heard. And Christians in Palestine then, and the world over today, pause to glorify God and praise him for all that they and we heard.

People—the ignorant and educated alike—have striven for centuries to comprehend the life and the message of Jesus. They have tried—but they have never quite succeeded. They have tried through biographies and novels. They have tried through dogmas and creeds. They have tried through hymns and carols. They have tried through pictures and sculptures. They have tried through poetry and plays. And yet, the whole Jesus eludes them all.

Among the ways we try to learn Who He is is through candle-light services on Christmas Eve. And all over the world tonight the

201

memory of Jesus—indeed, the presence—of Christ is celebrated by candles. And when we think of Jesus, we think of the light of lights, a light greater than our darkness, a light which continues despite efforts to extinguish it. And in connection with these candlelight services everywhere, there are Christmas carols. And so, let us listen to the carollers this Christmas Eve.

In lower Austria, early on Christmas Eve, when Santa Claus appears, each child kisses his ring. Then Santa bids each child to put his shoes outdoors and not look in them until the clock strikes ten. After this, Santa Claus lays on the table a rod dipped in lime, solemnly blesses the children, sprinkling them with holy water, and noiselessly departs. The children then steal out into the garden, clear a space in the snow, and set out their shoes. When the last stroke of ten has sounded, they find their shoes filled with nuts and apples and all kinds of sweet things. And in Germany the gift is a shiny apple with a coin in it.

Before we hear the stroke of the Evanston clock, let us blow out the candles, in the pews, symbolizing as we do so, the passing of the light into our hearts this evening.

Light of light, we humbly pray,
Shine upon thy world today.
Break the gloom of our dark night,
Fill our souls with love and light.
Send thy blessed word again,
Peace on earth, good will to men.

Now let us join hands:
Ah friends, dear friends, touch hands, touch hands,
Strong hand to weak, old hands to young.
The false forget, the foes forgive,
For every guest will go and every fire burn low,
Forgive, forget, for Christmas Sunday may never come to host
   or guest again.
Touch hands . . .

If you listen, you will almost hear the last stroke of the Evanston clock. Now it is time for the North Shore children noiselessly—noiselessly—to steal out into Hayford Hall and find their shoes.

Good night . . .

Schweitzer's music plays until the sanctuary is empty.

PART **FOUR** 1955-1959

WORLD TRAVELER

THE EVANSTON YEARS II

*"Not fondness for my son, nor reverence for my aged
father, nor Penelope's love could drive out of my
mind the desire to experience the far-flung world
and the failings and felicities of mankind."*
 –Divine Comedy

The second half of Homer's years in Evanston
was characterized by increased travel and ministering to a
wider congregation. In 1955 he took his first round-the-
world trip. In 1956, the Montgomery Bus Boycott erupted,
and Homer journeyed to Alabama to support its young
leader, Rev. Martin Luther King. In 1957, Homer journeyed to Ghana, French Equatorial Africa (where he saw
Albert Schweitzer for the second time), England, and Japan. In addition to supporting Asian and African independence, he became a leader of the emerging worldwide
movement against nuclear testing. Because of overflow
crowds at his Sunday sermons, the Unitarian Church in
Evanston embarked in 1954 on a new building campaign.
Four years later, the congregation moved into its striking
new building. Over 1200 people participated in dedication day ceremonies, the highlight of which was a speech
by Adlai E. Stevenson, Illinois Governor and twice Democratic presidential candidate. Six months later, at the pinnacle of his career as a parish minister, Homer resigned to
devote himself to social action and world affairs in New
York.

Photograph: Homer with Prime Minister Nehru of India

23 BANDUNG (1955)

WHAT ASIA WANTS

On his first round-the-world trip, Homer journeyed from Chicago to Indonesia in April 1955 to observe the Asian-African Conference. Held in the beautiful mountain city of Bandung, the Conference not only galvanized the freedom movements and foreshadowed the imminent end of four centuries of European colonialism, but it also marked the beginning of the nonaligned movement and an important stepping stone in slowing the nuclear arms race. Homer's account is drawn from a sermon he delivered to his congregation in Evanston and articles he wrote for the Bulletin of the Atomic Scientists *and* Toward Freedom.

Perspective 1955: In January, Congress gave President Eisenhower discretionary power to use force—i.e., atomic weapons—to settle Taiwan's claims to two small islands off the coast of China. Premier Zhou Enlai's flexibility and willingness to negotiate prevented a probable U.S. preemptive nuclear strike on coastal cities that Pentagon experts predicted would have killed millions of civilians. Following up its historic Brown vs. Board of Education decision the previous year, the Supreme Court ruled that segregation in public schools was unconstitutional. Race relations in the South continued to worsen, however, with the murder of young Emmett Till in Mississippi and the arrest of Rosa Parks for refusing to give up her seat for a white man on a bus in Montgomery, Alabama. Disneyland opened in California, Davy Crockett mania swept the country, and Gunsmoke, *the* Lawrence Welk Show, *the* $64,000 Question, *and the* Honeymooners *debuted on TV.* James Baldwin *wrote* Notes of a Native Son. *Top movies included* On the Waterfront, Marty, *and* East of Eden.

America was conceived, as a nation, by revolution, but today the word—revolution—is kind of subversive, and you can go to jail for daring to think or talk revolution, quite apart from promoting one.

But revolutions—against colonialism, against tyranny, against poverty—are continuing in South America, in Europe, in Africa, in Asia—all around the world. One of the biggest revolutions of our time has occurred in Asia. Asia was a colonial continent with huge English, Dutch, and French colonies. Today, most of Asia is free. Only tiny pockets of colonialism remain: West Irian, Malaya, Singapore, Goa. And the young countries which are independent want to continue to finish this revolution—and to spread it to Africa.

And so the leaders of five of these children of revolution—Burma, Ceylon, Indonesia, India, Pakistan—met last year in Colombo, Ceylon, to explore the possibility of an Asian-African Conference. The five so-called Columbo powers finally agreed to call a conference in April, in the mountain city of Bandung, Indonesia. Its purpose was to explore and advance the mutual interests of the invited countries. These five nations agreed to invite twenty-five other nations. Most of the independent countries of Asia and Africa were invited. There were some notable exceptions: both Koreas, Nationalist China on Formosa, Australia and New Zealand, Israel, Union of South Africa.

The unspoken hope of the conference was to drive a wedge of sanity and restraint between the two atomic giants—the United States and the Soviet Union, although the Columbo powers asserted that it was not their desire to "build themselves into a regional bloc."

Two thousand delegates, journalists, and observers descended on this mountain city only a few degrees below the equator. The city was built as a vacation place for the families of Dutch colonials, but colonialism has never in this century been more unanimously denounced than in the made-over Dutch club where the plenary sessions were held. The Conference was opened with an address by President Sukarno of Indonesia. He demanded that "a new Asia and a new Africa be born," asserting that "the unconventional has become the conventional, and who knows what other examples of misguided and diabolical scientific skill have been discovered as a plague on humanity."

While colonialism and world peace were the recurring themes in almost every opening speech by delegation heads, perhaps the clearest call for world peace came from Sir John Kotelawala of Ceylon. He charged that the great powers are "hag-ridden by the demon of progress, the monsters their scientists have created, (but) neither their science nor their statesmanship can afford them any protection." By contrast, Sir John continued, the Asian-African nations came to the conference table weak and relatively unarmed with "no thermonuclear bombs in our pockets, no weapons of chemical or bacteriological warfare up our sleeves, no plans for armament factories or blueprints for ever more deadly methods of genocide in our brief cases." Sir John insisted that the Asian-African nations possess something which the mighty lack, and that is the strength of their weakness: "The ability which our very defenselessness confers to offer ourselves as mediators in the dispute between the giants of communism and anti-communism which, if fought out to an end, will deluge the world in blood and leave the earth infected with atomic radiation for generations yet unborn or never to be born."

Chinese Prime Minister Zhou Enlai was the most sought-after figure at Bandung—perhaps because he so infrequently comes from behind the Bamboo Curtain—yet in no way was he able to dominate the delegates. In his opening remarks, Zhou reminded the delegates that "the peoples of Asia shall never forget that the first atomic bomb exploded on Asian soil and that the first man to die from experimental explosion of a hydrogen bomb was an Asian." He insisted that the overwhelming majority of the people throughout the world demand the "prohibition of atomic weapons and all other weapons of mass destruction" and "that atomic energy be used for peaceful purposes in order to bring welfare to mankind."

As the Conference broke up into closed committee sessions, there were dinner parties and receptions almost every night, for participants and visitors. At the reception given by President and Mrs. Sukarno in the Governor's residence, Javanese and Balinese dances were given under the Banyan trees in the garden as *gamelan* and *angklung* orchestras played. The Chinese delegation gave a cocktail party to the press as Chinese wine, champagne, and communist postcards and books flowed freely. The Saudi Arabia delegation put on a sumptuous buffet in the Savoy-Homan Hotel, and the table groaned with baked swan and other Eastern delicacies. The five Colombo prime ministers gave a farewell reception on the last evening, with Prime Minister Nehru of India and Ali Sastroamidjojo of Indonesia hand-in-hand walking down the wet street toward the hotel to the cheers of the crowds.

At one reception I saw a diplomat who looked familiar, and he

207

turned out to be my old friend, El Amroussi, third secretary of the Egyptian legation in Athens, eighteen years ago, but today Egypt's ambassador to Indonesia. I later saw much of him in Djarkarta, the capital of Indonesia, the following week. I had breakfast one day with James Michener of *South Pacific* fame, and I saw much of Richard Wright, the author, who was writing about the Conference for a German magazine.

Einstein's Death

The Conference was saddened when, on the second morning, news filtered into the flag-bedecked conference hall that Albert Einstein had died. When a journalist whispered the news to Nehru, he immediately scribbled this tribute:

"It is with profound grief that I learn of the death of Prof. Albert Einstein. The greatest scientist of the age, he was truly a seeker of truth who would not compromise with evil or untruths. He was a beacon of light in a world of the shadows of darkness and a strength to those who grow weak in the strain and stress of circumstances. I offer my homage to his memory, and my deepest sympathy goes to his family who shared his joys and sorrows with him in a life that knew both."

Before Einstein's death, I communicated with him once more by letter indicating that I was about to attend the Asian-African Conference at Bandung, Indonesia, in mid-April. He replied that he felt this was to be an important event and he would like to receive my observations. Two weeks after the Bandung Conference, in Djakarta, the capital of Indonesia, a university held a memorial service for Albert Einstein, and I was invited to be one of the speakers.

Results of Bandung

What were the results of Bandung? The communiqué is an interesting, important document: a summary of what Asians and some Africans want. By prior agreement, it had to be a unanimous document. There are long paragraphs on economic and cultural cooperation among the various countries—to build up their economies and also to build up their cultures, so long fragmented by colonial occupation. There are also long paragraphs on human rights and self-determination. These new countries are not content to bask in their new-won freedom; they have not forgotten those peoples in the world still under tyranny. Finally, there are long paragraphs on world peace. These new countries realize that all their hopes will disappear in an atomic flash if there cannot be world peace, and to get enduring peace they suggest a strengthened United Nations, disarmament, the prohibition on the use of atomic weapons, and a ten-point program for the conduct of one nation toward another.

In addition to this communiqué, there were certain important byproducts of the Conference. First, the offer of China to negotiate with the U.S., which has since resulted in the current talks in Geneva and the current release of prisoners from the Korean War. Second, the partial solution of the problems of dual nationality—of the allegiance of millions of Chinese living in Asia outside China or Formosa. Third, the friendships developed which have already culminated in a number of state visits since Bandung.

But what was the real meaning of Bandung? Pundits from all over the world, at Bandung and at home in their studies, read all kinds of meanings into Bandung before, during, and especially after the Conference. Most agreed that it was historic and unique. All differed on almost everything else. Was Bandung, as *Time Magazine* predicted, "a communist road show" or just "a vague but portentous political communion"? In terms of what Asians want, let me say right here that I found *Time Magazine* the most hated American magazine in Asia. Was Bandung, as *Newsweek Magazine* said during the Conference, just "a vast, illumined soapbox where the malcontent of the world could have their say"?

Initially, there were some disappointments at Bandung. For one thing, there was no continuing or implementing organization set up. This was perhaps in response to a fear that Bandung would supplement, for the East, the United Nations. On the other hand, there was agreement that a second Conference would be called. A second disappointment was to find that the presumed unities, among the Middle Eastern nations or even among the five Colombo powers themselves, were premature. A third disappointment was that the African delegates were strictly junior partners. Fourth, the new state of Israel was given shabby treatment, a country which should have been invited to attend, except for the deep hatred of her by the Arab nations. Fifth, no new directions of peace-making emerged at the Conference; there were the same old formulas, if important ones, of negotiation and disarmament.

But if there were disappointments, there were real gains, too. First, a new bloc, a third camp, was created at Bandung which encompasses two continents and almost two-thirds of humanity. Second, this new unity produced the equivalent of a non-aggression pact at Bandung between China and her neighbors. Third, stronger economic and cultural ties were begun at Bandung which are sure to grow. Fourth, Bandung sounded the death toll to colonialism—in bits of Asia and in most of Africa. The nationalists today in French North Africa know that they have the solid support of Asia, if not the United States. Fifth, Bandung showed that the colored peoples of the world need not be as racist as their fellow whites. The fears of any colored war completely fizzled. Sixth, Bandung showed that communism in Asia and Africa is by no means inevitable. I made a special study of communism in Asia and talked to the top communist leaders of Indonesia, Burma, and India. If some of the Asian leaders feel that they must live with and work with communist China as an important neighbor, many of the Conference leaders, including some of the Colombo prime ministers themselves, gave real evidence that they have no illusions about communism, be it Chinese or Russian or "indigenous."

Finally, Bandung has already forced the U.S. to reexamine her whole attitude and policies toward Asia and Africa. The fears that Bandung would be an anti-American demonstration happily were unfounded. Secretary Dulles was forced repeatedly to revise his own attitude toward Bandung and the last report I heard he praised the Conference, which was not exactly his initial attitude which was one of great hostility. President Eisenhower felt called upon to unveil his Asian aid program during the very week the Conference was in session. A completely new American policy toward Asia may well develop. In any case, the Asia of American support can no longer be the Asia of Chiang Kai-Shek or Syngman Rhee.

From my own travels in eight countries in Southeast Asia and from talks with hundreds of its people, I can attest that the plea of the Bandung communiqué was an accurate if sophisticated reflection of the deep desires of the common people of Asia.

Asians want the end of racism. Positively put, they want a new dignity, a new equality.

Asians want the end of colonialism. Positively put, they want freedom everywhere.

Asians want the end of poverty and disease. Positively put, they want prosperity and all that accompanies it.

Asians want the end of war. Positively put, they want enduring and just peace.

Come to think of it, what Asians want is no different from

what Americans want. The only difference is that we Americans for the most part already have freedom and prosperity, if we do not yet all have dignity and permanent peace.

But the sooner we know that Asians only want what Americans have already had or what we are also aspiring toward, the sooner we can understand Asia and cooperate with her one billion people.

Bandung made world peace more possible. It gained time. It formed a moral if not a military wedge between the two great giants—the U.S. and U.S.S.R. It cleared the air for the Summit Conference in Geneva on European issues and was a prelude to an inevitable Summit Conference on outstanding Asian issues.

Bandung was at least five hundred years in the making. Not by arms, but by moral persuasion—nourished by the world's great religions—will this third force help keep the peace the world so desperately desires?

Bandung somehow caught the world's imagination. Conscious of history, the delegates adjourned hopeful that history will, in the end, become conscious of Bandung. As Sir John Kotelawala of Ceylon hoped, "Bandung will be a name to reverberate in history and earn the gratitude and blessings of ages to come."

24 NEW DELHI
(1955-1992)

MY PASSAGE TO INDIA

Homer visited India at least fifteen—and possibly twenty times—during his life. His longest visit was the first, almost three months in 1955. In this memoir he wrote towards the end of his life, Homer describes his early fascination with India and his later visits over the decades.

As an American, attending high school in the early 1930s, during the great world economic depression, I had only a vague concept of India. It was a large British colony in Asia. I did possess some Indian postage stamps, since my father and I were stamp collectors. The Indian stamps at the time were adorned with pictures of the kings of England or an occasional camel or tonga.

In high school in the 1930s we learned nothing about the Indian freedom struggle. Our debating club discussed the desirability of the recognition of the Soviet Union by the U.S.A., but not Asian or African freedom from colonialism. I do not remember, in that period, hearing anything about Mohandas Gandhi or Jawaharlal Nehru.

If most Americans knew little about India and Indians between the two world wars, they often knew much about the American Indians, the "red" Indians, the native peoples whom Christopher Columbus mistook for East Indians. Growing up in Rochester, New York, I learned about the habits of the Indians who lived in the Genesee Valley south of Lake Ontario, in the eighteenth century before and after the U.S.A. became independent from British rule.

I never met a person from India until I entered Cornell University in 1933. Then my horizon expanded rapidly after I moved into

212

the Cosmopolitan Club—the international house—where I came into contact with several Indians who also lived there—Desai and a Patel and a Singh. H. M. Desai—His Majesty we laughingly called him—was an older graduate student from Gujerat. We had many talks and often wandered into the "collegetown" section of Ithaca for meals. I tried to keep in contact with H. M. later, but failed. Also I never heard from his friend, Patel. Not so with Sardar Singh, who came from the Punjab to study entomology at Cornell. One weekend he came to my home in Rochester. Occasionally Sardar allowed me to wear his white turban—in the confines of the upper floors of the Cosmo Club. I can still recall the rich perfume from his hair. From Sardar I learned much about the people of the subcontinent. We remain in close touch to this day.

At the University of Chicago, I worked with other students to oppose British colonialism in India. Our Free India Committee grew from several influences. One came from reports about the Indian freedom movement from several Indian professors teaching in the Chicago area. One was Tarini P. Sinha who later taught at Roosevelt College. Another influence was a visit to Chicago by Krishnalal J. Shridharani, whose books were popular reading at the time. A third stimulus to our group was an occasional visit by A. J. Muste, U.S. Secretary of the Fellowship of Reconciliation (FOR), a world pacifist organization with close contacts to the independence movement in India. Muste and other F.O.R. speakers came to Chicago with tales of the remarkable spirit, and accomplishments, of Mohandas Gandhi.

Indian Independence

In June 1942 our Free India Committee participated in the worldwide observance of Quit India Day which was decreed by Gandhi. We picketed the British consulate on Michigan Avenue in Chicago. In our opposition to what the British were doing in India, some of us had our photographs printed in the *Chicago Tribune*. President Sidney Snow of my theological school felt that this act of mine was not exactly preparing me for the ministry. Yet it was a harbinger of lifelong protests for racial, religious, and human justice. Out of our early interest in Gandhi and Gandhian techniques was born CORE, the Congress of Racial Equality and through the 1940s we employed *satyagraha*—truth force—to oppose segregation against blacks in the university environment and other parts of America's second largest

213

city, as well as making forays into the South.

During the months of the independence and partition of India and Pakistan in 1947, I must confess that my attention was much more local. The turmoil on the Indian subcontinent seemed to occur on the other side of a large planet. Of course I cheered when I read that the British finally relinquished control of India, but this relief was always conditioned by my opposition to the partition of the subcontinent. Yet I did not follow closely the events as they occurred—and as I did trying to piece together the history many years later.

During the Bengal famine of the early 1950s, many Americans banded together to help send grains to India. Writer Pearl Buck headed the American effort, and I was among her co-workers as pastor of the Unitarian Church of Evanston. While editing my first book on Gandhi, *The Wit and Wisdom of Gandhi*, I began to collect books by and about the Mahatma. This hobby eventually took me to bookstores, not only in the U.S., but to London, Paris, and Asia. I eventually acquired a library of 500 or more volumes.

In the mid-1950s, during the Eisenhower Administration and especially under the foreign policy of Secretary of State John Foster Dulles, India was under constant diplomatic pressure from the U.S. I came to know well Indian Ambassador G. L. Mehta. Several Americans, including Sydney Hertzberg, tried to work for better Indian-U.S. relations. What was needed was an India Society, similar to dozens of American groups relating culturally, economically, and even politically to other countries. As hard as we tried, we could never put together such an organization, although we received obvious encouragement from Ambassador Mehta. Eventually, the Asia Society in New York City helped in some ways to fill the need.

First Visit

In 1955, from the mountain city of Bandung after the completion of the Conference on Asia and Africa, I travelled almost half across Asia for my first visit to India. For me this was a belated visit. I regretted that I never journeyed to India in the 1940s and thus that I never met Gandhi. Yet in 1955 the legacy of Gandhi, and many of his associates, was still fresh. I wanted at least this second-best experience. I visited many of Gandhi's co-workers who were alive seven years after his death. Arriving at Calcutta, I went north to Assam and visited Unitarian Margaret Barr in the Khasi Hills near Shillong.

I then went south to Orissa and walked for a few days with Vinoba Bhave as he walked around India gathering land for the landless in his Bhoodan movement. I visited Gandhi's former ashrams in Sevagram and Ahmedabad. I went to Kashmir to visit Mirabehn. I crossed into Pakistan to talk to Abdul Ghaffar Khan—the Frontier Gandhi—north of Lahore.

On that first visit, I spent some time in Delhi. I paid more than a ceremonial visit to President Rajendra Prasad who was installed in what was the Viceroy's palace. Prasad was an "old Gandhian" who led one of the first *satyagraha* campaigns, in Bihar, in 1917. Also I had talks with Prof. Sarvepalli Radhakrishnan, then Vice-President of India and soon to be elevated to the presidency. (In Chicago in 1958 I headed a committee which sponsored a large event honoring Dr. Radhakrishnan.)

That summer of 1955 I met frequently with Pyarelal, Gandhi's secretary, who was then engaged in writing independently several monumental volumes on the Mahatma. I imbibed India as best I could from my tiny room in the Marina Hotel, just off Connaught Place. I traced the whereabouts of my Cornell friend, Sardar Singh, and went to Ludhiana to visit him and his family. He had a distinguished career as an entomologist with the central government and later with the Food and Agricultural Organization of the United Nations.

Also in Delhi I met Devadas Gandhi, another son of the Mahatma, who was the editor of the *Hindustan Times*. This encounter began my writing for that daily newspaper for a number of years, especially from Africa (during the Ghana independence ceremonies in 1957) but also from the U.S.A. when I covered Nehru's visits.

Later Sojourns

In the 1960s, I belatedly had encounters with C. R.—Chakravarty Rajagopalachari. He was the first Governor-General of India and later an impressive critic. He came to the U.S.A. with R. R. Diwakar to try to stop American nuclear weapons tests. We met in New York City and later in Madras and also in New Delhi, the latter at the apartment of his son-in-law, Devadas Gandhi, on Connaught Place.

Over several years I was able to develop a working relationship with the Gandhi Peace Foundation, an independent group attempting to implement the philosophy of Mahatma Gandhi on both the domestic and the international levels. At the Foundation's headquarters in New Delhi, I came to work with and admire Shri R. R. Diwakar, its dynamic, ageless president, and Shri G. Ramachandran and then Shri Radhakrishna, its secretary. Their broad concerns kept alive many aspects of Gandhi's "constructive program" which the Foundation sponsors from its many branches throughout India. The Foundation also deals with Gandhi's philosophy through its periodical, *Gandhi Marg*, to which I occasionally contributed articles. The Foundation has the merit of interpreting the living legacy of Gandhi. It is not content merely to repeat his aphorisms.

There was a hiatus in the mid-1960s when I did not visit India. I was busy in the U.S.A. helping as I could the civil rights movement headed by Martin Luther King, Jr. I saw King repeatedly and was one of many who encouraged him to take his own trip to India in 1965. In the 1970s and '80s, I visited India on numerous occasions in connection with my work for the World Conference on Religion and Peace. In 1988 my wife and I spent six weeks in India on a speaking tour under the auspices of the University Grants Commission, lecturing at universities in Tamil Nadu, Ahmedabad, Varanasi, Lucknow, and New Delhi. At the end of that journey, we stayed for a week in the extended family of my Cornell classmate, Sardar Singh. It was a rich experience to observe how upper middle class Sikhs live in Lucknow. I loved reading *India Today* in the air-conditioned house while eating mangos taken from the tree on the front lawn. In 1992, I received the Jamnalal Bajaj Award for Gandhian service outside of India and again made a tour of the country, with many speeches, banquets, and meetings.

Why India?

My early relationship with India was not an intentional one. I never planned the way it turned out. If there were any models during my younger years, one was American and two were British. John Haynes Holmes "discovered" Gandhi early—in 1922. In that year, he preached a sermon at Community Church in New York City on the topic: "Who Is the Greatest Man in the World?" Holmes interpreted Gandhi and India to the U.S.A. for several decades. Holmes worked with Norman Thomas and Roger Baldwin to help the India League of America become an effective organization until its director, J. J. Singh, returned to India after independence. I knew Holmes and Singh, and the former influenced me greatly.

A second influence on my life was C. F. Andrews, a British

clergyman who was a longtime friend of Gandhi. I never met Andrews (who died in 1940 and is buried in Calcutta not far from Mother Teresa's headquarters.) Again, Andrews influenced my life. So did Reginald Reynolds, with whom I attended a peace conference in 1957. Reynolds, a British Quaker and writer, had a brief encounter with Gandhi. He served, for me, as a living bridge carrying the mystique of Gandhi.

I know and love India more than any other country in the world, except my own—the U.S.A. I am often asked why this is so—my regard for India. I could conjure up several answers, but the law of parsimony is applicable in answering this question as so many others. The simplest answer may be the best. I happened to be attracted to the Indian freedom struggle and some of its personalities and, above all, Gandhi. I came to know a few of the leaders of that struggle. My vocation coincided with my avocation—India— and so over thirty-four years I visited India more frequently than my birthplace of Rochester, N.Y.

Also the English language retained by so many leaders of India is undoubtedly one factor influencing my continuing interest in India. Except for the British Isles, Nigeria, or other outposts of British colonialism, what large country could I begin to understand without having first to learn another language? Language study was never my forte and so I did not have to learn Russian or Chinese or even Hindi to read contemporary Indian history—or even the fascinating Indian press.

My interest in India is not primarily because it has been the mother of so many world religions. Also I have not cherished India because it is the world's largest democracy. In addition, I have not chosen India to denigrate its two chief rivals, Pakistan on the subcontinent, and China in the world. I do not dislike Pakistan and I do not hope that China rather than India falters. Indeed, the results of the half-century race between the two most populous countries on earth to end poverty and oppression are not yet evident, at least to me.

Another frequent question from my friends, especially in the U.S.A., is this: "But how can you 'take' the poverty of India?" Long ago I simply resolved to accept that poverty as a price for dealing with India. Gandhi "took" the poverty and tried to reduce if not eliminate it. He tried to remind even Indians that India is not the great cities, but the 700,000 villages. It still is. Each visitor, in his or her own way, can attempt to remember the poor of India. I do this by calling attention to the continuing problem of the untouchables—to the consternation, still, of many of my Indian friends.

I must confess that I know little about Indian religions. Over the years, I had a unique opportunity to meet with the many religious groups in India, from the Buddhists (both "old" and "new," the latter being the untouchables) to the Zoroastrians. However, I was so busy following the arcane politics of some religious groups that I had little time to become acquainted with their practices, let alone their theology. I regret this lost opportunity.

I did, however, try to establish contact with those groups in India related to my own Unitarian Universalist denomination. The Brahmo Samaj has long been related to British and American Unitarianism, beginning with Rammohun Roy (1772-1833) and including Rabindranath Tagore. I often visited the Brahmo Samaj meetings in Calcutta or Bombay. I also visited the Unitarian Church in Madras, dating from nineteenth century. In the 1960s I spoke several times to the Unitarian Fellowship then flourishing in New Delhi, its members being mostly expatriates. In 1968 Dr. Dana McLean Greeley, then president of the Unitarian Universalist Association of North America, convened a meeting in Delhi of representatives of these Unitarian-related groups. No such meeting was held earlier; today such groups, and others, convene under the banner of the Indian chapter of the International Association for Religious Freedom (IARF).

Always Right?

In my passage to India, I have often identified with India as if it were "my country, right or wrong." Sometimes India has been wrong and I have been slow to recognize this wrong, or refused to do so altogether. Yet when I come to realize and then admit my rationalization—my defense of the indefensible—I feel very sad.

There came a time when I, like many others, became disillusioned with India. Actually, there were several occasions—and, for me, these were all political.

While one can easily overlook the more pedestrian mistakes of world leaders, I at least expected more from the successors of Gandhi and Nehru. Yet when one suddenly witnesses India act like any other member of the U.N., looking closely at its interest and not beyond, a certain disenchantment for me set in. This happened for me when India, in 1961 and still under Nehru, "took" Goa from Portuguese control. This act was not according to any international norm of law. Likewise, disillusionment set in when the Emergency was declared by Indira Gandhi in 1975. Also I was amazed when India in 1974 detonated its "peaceful" nuclear explosion. Only slowly did I reconcile myself to reality: India was just like any other nation. It was I who had illusions, not the Indian people or their current leaders.

Were my illusions about Indian foreign policy the result of blind infatuation or based on more rational phenomena? My illusions began obviously with Gandhi and easily extended to Nehru. Even some of the early secondary leadership comprised persons who would have been extraordinary in any society, including C. Rajgopalachari and S. Radhakrishnan. With such early leadership, I expected probably more from India than from other nations, including my own.

And so, I have come reluctantly to conclude that India is like any other big nation—"only more so." This, to me, is still a tragic realization, yet of course it is true. My reflections have helped make India and Indians, for me, human—for all of the Indian gods.

25 BOMBAY
(1955)

MASS SATYAGRAHA IN GOA

During Homer's first trip to India open conflict broke out between India and Goa, a tiny Portuguese enclave on the west coast of the subcontinent about 300 miles south of Bombay. A contingent of satyagrahis—*Gandhian peace soldiers—crossed the border in August in a nonviolent attempt to free the last European colony in India. As a journalist, Homer was allowed into Goa to report on the encounter. From Bombay, he filed this account for newspapers in India, Europe, and America.*

I had the tragic experience to cover one of the strangest wars in history, the march of four thousand unarmed *satyagrahis* into Goa on August 15. *Satyagraha*, the marvelous tool used by Mahatma Gandhi first in South Africa and developed here in India against the British, was never before used on an international scale. But on August 15, for the first time in history, *satyagraha* was directed by the nationals of one nation against the governor of another.

Both sides prepared carefully for the battle. For Portugal, the arrangements were traditional: more troops from Portugal and Africa (their huge colonies of Mozambique and Angola), all kinds of war equipment except atomic weapons, and a full-blown propaganda campaign from Lisbon. The Indians' preparations were more novel. Beginning in May they sent small batches of *satyagrahis* to "liberate" Goan villages—symbolically, to be sure, because they could not retain a foothold for many hours. After these initial experiments, the All-Party Goan Liberation Committee recruited almost five thousand nonviolent volunteers for August 15, and they came

220

from all parts of India, from all political parties, and from many vocations. The nonviolent army converged at Belgaum on August 13.
This is a railroad junction a few miles from the Goan border. Each
"soldier" signed a pledge of nonviolence: "I will not under any circumstances adopt violence." Then each man was assigned to a
group, under the direction of a leader, which was given at least one
Indian flag to plant on Portuguese territory. The *satyagrahis* rode by
bus or walked to various places along the 150-mile frontier and secretly entered Goa some time after midnight on August 15 at more
than two dozen places.

Part of Portugal's strategy was to invite foreign correspondents (but not Indians) to see for themselves "the peace, calm, and
indifference of the Goan people." Some accepted the government's
invitation to travel gratis from Karachi. Others of us preferred to
pay our own way, to witness at least the battle preparations from
India, and to reach Goa the long way around—48 hours by train,
bus, boat, bicycle, bullock-cart, and foot via the Karwar border. The
press was given the freedom of Goa, but this didn't mean very
much because time and nature (deep jungles) prevented our reaching many areas of the frontier. Also, because Goa is obviously a police state, we didn't want to jeopardize Goanese we knew were opposed to Portugal by visiting them. By 3:00 a.m. of the 15th we were
riding toward the northwestern border of Goa and by 6:00 a.m. I
was in the back seat of a jeep driven by two Portuguese soldiers
hunting for *satyagrahis*.

It was a grim business, although I at least never felt the dangers of snipers as one feels it on patrols in violent warfare. Half an
hour of searching brought us to a road where the fences contained a
dozen red-and-white posters with an outline map of the Indian subcontinent and the legend "Quit Goa." This was the work of a band
of *satyagrahis*. The soldiers immediately pulled the posters down,
only to find that the invaders had put up an Indian flag high above
one of the houses. This they also confiscated, but with more difficulty. Soon we encountered our first batch of forty-six *satyagrahis*,
marching with a large Indian tricolor. The soldiers immediately re-
trieved the flag but—no doubt partly because of our presence—they
used no violence. The *satyagrahis* continued to shout slogans: "India
and Goa are One," "Freedom for Goa," "Victory for Goa," and the
like. This batch of *satyagrahis* was completely unarmed and did not
resist the soldiers but squatted silently on the ground when ordered
to do so. After spending most of the day, unfed, under the shade of
cashew trees, they were taken to the border in the evening and

221

freed.

In another hour we passed an ancient, moss-covered Hindu temple, guarded by three soldiers. Inside we belatedly found fifty silent, grim Indians squatting on the stone floor around the dead body of one of their comrades, shot an hour before by a Portuguese solider after the group had put an Indian flag on top of the temple. A swami, the leader of the group who himself was shot in the hand, insisted that the group was peaceful and that his comrade was shot in cold blood in the back. The Portuguese insist that the *satyagrahis* advanced menacingly toward a soldier who "nervously" shot at the agitator's leg but hit his body instead. Never shall I forget the slain *satyagrahi*, Panna Lal Yadav, the thirty-two-year-old *harijan* (untouchable) and socialist, father of four children and trade union official, staring stiffly at the bells on the temple rafters and at a cheap lithographed print of Lord Krishna above.

Slowly, precisely, the spokesman told me the tragic story. They crossed the border early in the morning. Around 5 a.m.—when it was still dark—they entered this village in a formation of three abreast. They put the Indian flag on top of the Hindu temple. Then they began to shout slogans for the villagers to hear. Shortly, four military men appeared. At least one had a sten-gun. They began to fire in the air and asked the *satyagrahis* to stop shouting slogans. They continued to chant in a peaceful manner.

Then one of the soldiers struck one of the *satyagrahis* with the butt of his gun and then moved back and fired, one blank into the ground and then one at Panna Lal Yadav, from the back. When he fell, they asked for medical aid, but none was forthcoming. As we were talking, one *satyagrahi* said, "They fired like a hunter hunts animals." I asked them if they remained nonviolent throughout. One replied: "We believe in nonviolence and that is why we came one thousand miles to participate and that is why we walked twenty miles." Another said: "This method is given in the Bible and in the Buddhist books, but people are losing faith in it, and we want to show the world that there is a force greater than these bullets."

Back in Panjim, the capital of Goa, the Portuguese military commander called a press conference just before midnight. Life-sized oil paintings of ex-Governors looked down on the handful of khaki-clad Portuguese Army officers as they tried to preserve their four-century-old empire from crumbling. Major Hormes Oliveira, Chief of Staff of the Commander-in-Chief, presiding from a high dais, admitted that some 3,600 *satyagrahis* had entered Goa that day, but added that there were no uprisings as anticipated by the Indi-

222

ans. In his long communiqué he made not a single mention of casualties. This stunned the assembled pressmen and one sarcastically asked the major if he hadn't forgotten something. Finally the major said that "on the part of the journalists here there is a certain preoccupation with the number of persons dead." The hitherto slick propaganda machine of the Portuguese broke down completely at this point. The spokesman looked at his papers and said that two Indians were killed during the day and three were injured. This was a preposterously low figure, since the chief of police of Goa had just told some reporters that thirteen had been killed.

As I walked along the river and into the hotel, I wondered what all this talk, this double—and triple—talk meant to Panna Lal Yadav, who, for all I knew, still lay stiffly on the floor of the Hindu temple. He truly sacrificed for loyalty, sincerity, and love for truth, and I knew his life and the life of twelve of his comrades all around the border would not be given in vain.

As for uprisings within Goa, there were several small ones, as the government was belatedly forced to admit. There have constantly been uprisings and the prisons are filled with Goans who, in the last years and months, have opposed by word or deed continued Portuguese rule. The prison doors were briefly opened to the visiting journalists, and I visited several leaders awaiting trial.

After I returned to Indian territory I learned the truth of that horrible Monday. As many as twenty Indians were probably killed and hundreds were injured, mostly at places that were difficult for the foreign correspondents to visit. In a Belgaum hospital I saw sixty injured *satyagrahis*, half with bullet wounds, half suffering from savage beatings. That more did not die is a credit to the corps of physicians and medical students at first aid stations hurriedly set up all along the border.

The next steps for India are hard to foresee. Portugal may be goading India into violence so that she can leave Goa under the pretext of being driven out by an erstwhile peace-loving India. It is doubtful if Portugal can hold on many years longer. Indeed, Portugal won't even negotiate with India toward the freedom of Goa, since that would establish a precedent for the subject peoples in her larger African colonies. Also, since Portugal is a totalitarian state at home, any such negotiations might make the Portuguese people themselves want their freedom.

Whatever the future, August 15 will go down as an important, if tragic, date in the history of human efforts to combat injustice by creative means.

26 EVANSTON
(1956)

THE DEEP SOUTH AND
THE NORTH SHORE

The landmark Supreme Court decision against segregated schools and the bus boycott in Montgomery, Alabama, galvanized the modern civil rights movement. Throwing himself into the struggle, Homer reported on his visit with Martin Luther King, Jr. to theologian Howard Thurman, editor Norman Cousins, and author Lillian Smith. In July, Homer visited Dr. King's father in Atlanta, and in August Dr. King invited him to preach to his congregation in Montgomery. In September, Homer invited Rev. D. J. Simms of the Montgomery Improvement Association to meet with Negro tenants from the Trumbull Park Homes in Chicago, site of one of the most dangerous racial situations in the country. In December, Homer gave a main address to an Institute on Nonviolence and Social Change organized by Dr. King and Ralph Abernathy. Homer delivered the following remarks in Evanston after his first visit to Alabama.

"The Southern revolt" is on everybody's mind just now, and rightly so, for it constitutes the greatest challenge to the democratic process since the McCarthyism of several years ago.

Although the news is bad—the manifesto signed by 100 congressmen, the white citizens councils, the Emmett Till murder, the Lucy affair—it is not all bad. Indeed, the *New York Times* in a remarkable survey showed that five border states and the District of Columbia have made remarkable progress toward desegregation in two short years since the Supreme Court decision of May 1954.

All over the South, there is a new Negro, a courageous, re-strained but fearless Negro emerging in the big cities, but especially in Montgomery. The eyes of the world are on Montgomery, for here is a Gandhi-like campaign against bus segregation which is breath-taking in its discipline and leadership. It has given new hope to the Negroes in the South and new hope, too, to all who believe that seg-regation is a sin against humanity, religion, and democracy.

The Deep South continues to be defensive. There can be no compromise on ends—a completely unsegregated society and in the words of the Supreme Court, with "all deliberate speed." There can be, however, "practical flexibility" as to method. Northerners must be patient, compassionate, reasonable and not vindictive toward the white Southerners. We can, with novelist William Faulkner, "stop now for a moment,"but only a moment, since to acquiesce—as col-umnist Walter Lippman has said—"and not to protest would make the middle position unprincipled and, in the end, untenable."

It ill behooves us Northerners to look down our noses at the South unless we, up North and in our own North Shore communi-ties, work equally to lessen segregation and discrimination in our midst. That the North is also discriminatory does not make segrega-tion in the South or North one bit less immoral or irreligious. But this great debate should give us greater initiative to clean our own backyard. In fact, the *Montgomery Advertiser* is putting stories of bad race relations up North on its front pages in retaliation for Chicago and Detroit papers putting Alabama on its front pages—and rele-gating the Trumbull Park riots in Chicago to their back pages, if at all.

The Southerner insists that he "knows" the Negro and "loves" the Negro—and he is even beginning to learn to say Negro—more than the Northerner. This allegation was once debatable, but no more so. The new Negro wants neither to be "knowed" or "loved" but to be treated like any other human being with free access to the institutions of our society. This is a challenge for us Northerners not to fret at what's going on down South, but to do something more than any of us have been doing here up North. That means, in our neighborhood, welcoming Negroes to live anywhere in our sub-urbs, getting qualified Negroes into the Evanston High School facul-ty, opening the Evanston Y.M.C.A. to Negro members, and urging the Evanston banks to lend mortgage money to financially qualified Negroes to buy outside the Evanston Negro ghetto. As we achieve some of these victories, we can in better conscience encourage Ne-groes and whites to make their own victories in the Deep South.

27 ACCRA
(1957)

FREEDOM RINGS IN GHANA

In April 1957, Homer attended the independence of Ghana, the first of four dozen former African colonies to attain its freedom after the Second World War. In addition to Prime Minister Kwame Nkrumah and other African leaders, Homer met with Dr. Martin Luther King, Jr., who was making his first visit to Africa to attend the ceremonies.

On the very first day of Ghana's independence, there was a state reception and ball at the new State House in Accra, the capital. During the very first dance, Her Royal Highness, the Duchess of Kent and the personal representative of Queen Elizabeth, her diamond tiara glittering, danced with Prime Minister Kwame Nkrumah, dressed in his green and gold *kente* toga. This symbolized more than anything else the birth of a new order in West Africa.

One American Negro whispered that to see the Duchess and the Prime Minister together on the dance floor was worth the 16,000-mile round-trip journey. It was worth, as a symbol, the 113 years to the day of the struggle of the people of the Gold Coast for independence.

There are many signs, both dramatic and colorful, of the birth here of this new nation. The new red, gold, and green flag (with a black African lodestar for hope) flies where the British Union Jack will never fly again. Women in the streets dance the uninhibited "high life" often wearing dresses made from material with huge life-sized portraits of Nkrumah. Crowds shout "free-dom, free-dom" whenever Nkrumah comes into view.

226

The opening of the first national assembly was a solemn affair, with the Duchess of Kent and the new Governor-General participating. The parliamentary system seems firmly established, although the members look like ancient Roman senators in their bare-shouldered togas.

One of the debates of the old Legislative Assembly in recent weeks had to do with the colonial Accra Club, almost opposite Parliament. This has never admitted Africans or Asians as members or as guests. After great pressures, the club reluctantly voted to lift the color bar several weeks ago.

Four hours before independence, some 150 journalists from all over the world, including West Africa, had supper and a briefing in this club; Accra Press representatives privately testified that it was the first time that Africans had even entered the last stronghold of racism, in other than a menial capacity.

Now that Ghana is free, its five million citizens have much work to do and the whole world will be watching. First it must face economic problems. While Ghana does not have the lowest standard of living in Africa, one actually higher than Nigeria or India, it is unbelievably low: fifty pounds per head per year.

Unfortunately, Ghana has a one crop economy—cocoa. The price of cocoa is declining. It is difficult to diversify agriculture quickly and industries are few. Hydro-electric power is plentiful if the Volta River can be dammed.

In an important foreign policy statement, Nkrumah on the eve of independence stated that his country "does not intend to follow a neutralist policy in its foreign relations, but it does intend to preserve its independence to act as it seems best at any particular time." This means that Ghana will probably be more pro-English and pro-American than the Asian members of the Commonwealth, but more non-aligned than the United Kingdom.

Already Russia and the United States are courting Ghana. America won the present round with the presence of Vice-President Nixon in Ghana for five days and the presentation of several gifts including a two thousand volume technical library. The Russians sent to Ghana only an unknown Minister of State Farms, and the rumored Russian airplane and motorcar fleet has not materialized.

The leaders of Ghana want to fulfill their promises of a decade to help the pan-African movement. Yet with power comes responsibility, and Nkrumah indicated that the first step will be a conference of the independent countries of Africa. Surely the birth of Ghana will hurry the gestation period for Nigeria, Uganda, and Algeria.

Conversation with Rev. Scott and Dr. King

Of all the clergymen in Africa, one has symbolized in the past decade the best of the church working for justice and against colonialism: Michael Scott. In the past year the best of the church working for justice and against segregation: Martin Luther King, Jr. Ironically, Scott of Africa is a white man while King of America is a black man. Appropriately, both were personal guests of Prime Minister Nkrumah to witness the independence celebrations of Ghana.

It had been arranged that the two clergymen should meet for the first time the day after the independence celebrations, at the bungalow on the Achimoto College campus where Dr. and Mrs. King were staying. I had the privilege of being present. Father Scott arrived at 7:30 in the morning, a tall figure in flowing white robes. He found Dr. King suffering from a fever. He went into King, knelt at his bedside and prayed for his recovery. First he recited an old prayer of the Herero people of South West Africa, then some prayers of the Church of England, and finally the Lord's Prayer. After that they talked.

This was King's first sojourn on the continent of his fathers. Scott had spent many years in Africa, but had never before visited the Gold Coast. What most impressed the Englishman during the celebrations was the pledge that Ghana would "not become apartheid in reverse. This is not an exhibit of black nationalism, but of democracy and cooperation on a multiracial basis."

King was surprised at the material development of the Gold Coast. Accra was less primitive than he had been led to expect. What most impressed him—fresh from the battle of Montgomery—was that the independence of the Gold Coast was gained largely by nonviolent methods and with a minimum of force. A testimony to this fact, he felt, was "the aftermath of friendliness and community and well-being toward the English and a sense of good will and not bitterness."

I asked King what would be the parallel, in his American South, of the taking down of the colonial flag—which impressed him so much. He thought for some time, then said: "When the hardcore whites come to admit that the way of segregation is not only dead legally but morally wrong, and then work out a formula for adhering to the law of the land." Lying there in a far land, he wondered whether such a day will ever come in the American South, when the segregationists admit what the British have admitted in

Ghana. He quickly added, however, that segregation in the schools will disappear even in the Deep South, whether the Southern whites admit it or not.

The discussion turned to religion and their own vocations as clergymen, as well as the role of the church in meeting the current challenge. As for the future, both men are optimistic. King said the new, and initial, reaction always tends to be bitter; moreover, "privilege won't give up without strong resistance." The Montgomery experience, however, convinced him that "when suppressed people begin to march, there is no stopping point short of full freedom." Scott affirmed that he, too, is ultimately optimistic, that "the future holds enormous possibilities, although we may go through many tribulations before we reach it."

King expressed admiration for the bus boycott outside Johannesburg, with thousands of Africans actually walking ten to fifteen miles a day. King recalled that most of the people in Montgomery did not walk, since they had the services of a car pool. What counts in the end, he said, is not lack of weapons but the presence of faith. Nonviolence in India and in Alabama "did something to the oppressors; so it will even in South Africa." The willingness to suffer "will eventually make the oppressor ashamed of his own method," and "the forces of both history and Providence are on the side of freedom."

The drums of the royal *durbar* sounded down the road. Scott and I took our leave of Dr. King, promising to seek a physician. Scott shook King's hand and touched his forehead. The *durbar* was a colorful affair. Sixty chiefs and their retinues under bright umbrellas waited to be presented to the Duchess of Kent. Prime Minister Nkrumah was seated next to Vice-President and Mrs. Nixon. We ran into Lord Hemingford, formerly a principal in the Gold Coast and chairman of Scott's Africa Bureau in London. Scott told him of King's illness, and Hemingford immediately secured a physician attached to the royal navy. I took the physician to the Kings' bungalow and then returned to the *durbar* with Mrs. King (whom earlier I had danced with at the Inaugural Ball). Fortunately, by Sunday, King was well enough to attend the service in the Anglican Church.

28 LAMBARENE
(1957)

REUNION WITH ALBERT SCHWEITZER

From the Independence Day celebrations in Ghana, Homer traveled to Lambaréné—about a thousand miles south—to visit Dr. Schweitzer. He gave this sermon in Evanston on his return.

This morning I would tell you about my reunion with Albert Schweitzer. This is Palm Sunday, I know. But what more appropriate topic is there than Albert Schweitzer truly amid the palms in Lambaréné!

After leaving the small airplane at the gravel runway near Lambaréné, and going to the river in an Air France truck, four boatmen from Schweitzer's hospital met me for the trip three miles upstream. The sun was beating down, just past midday, and I eagerly opened the blue umbrella provided for my protection.

As our boat approached shore, two women in white could be seen. They were undoubtedly Mlle Matilda and Ali—the chief nurses. I took off my white sun helmet and waved to them and they waved back. Then the head boatman said, *"le grand docteur."* Sure enough, Schweitzer was coming down the hill to greet me!

I waved at him, also, but did not take off my helmet, for I know that he disapproves removing one's helmet in the equatorial sun. (As a matter of fact, I didn't wear the helmet until that very day, although I had been in Africa then almost three weeks. Sun helmets are no longer worn in many parts of Africa. I would have been considered an "old colonial" if I wore one in Ghana, but Schweitzer insists that the visitor wear one, and he even has a supply on hand for unhelmeted visitors. Sentimentally, I brought along mine all the way from Evanston, the one I acquired five years ago in Africa for this purpose.)

Soon we reached shore and I jumped out of the boat. I greeted the two nurses and then Albert Schweitzer. He looked quite the same as when I left him in Frankfurt in August 1955: unruly gray hair from under his white pith helmet, large ears and nose, broad smile. He asked me how my journey was, then something about the festivities in Ghana. He lead me to my room—a tiny cell in a building housing some staff members. Then he accompanied me to the dining room for a late meal. He put his hat on the hook above the old piano and sat down as the meal was served to me: rice, tomatoes, eggs, fresh guavas, and pineapple. We spoke of old friends, including Norman Cousins who had visited there only recently. Before I had finished eating, Schweitzer excused himself and I continued to talk with Mlle Matilda and Ali.

The following day I tried to indicate to Schweitzer and his associates that I would like to be put to work. I hated to stay at the hospital as if it were an equatorial hotel, with my merely coming to meals and not doing any work. Most visitors don't stay even as long as I planned to stay—two weeks—and Schweitzer tends not to want visitors to work. Perhaps he knows from experience that it is more bother, in any case. But I insisted on doing something, so they first put me to work typing. Then there was a need for somebody to meet several visitors at the airport. I did this gladly—although it was a hot journey back and forth on the Ogowe River. The planes were invariably late, and it thus became a five-hour round trip. Jokingly, I told Schweitzer I was his "chief du protocol." When I finally left Lambaréné, he excused himself for not going to the airport with me, saying that I could act as my own chief du protocol!

My duties gave me much time to wonder—during my trips up and downstream—why the world, including myself, beat a path to Schweitzer's door. What is Schweitzer's magic—his universal appeal, to Protestants, Catholics, Jews, Hindus, to Americans and Europeans? Why does the world pay homage to Schweitzer at Lambaréné. I decided that it is not primarily because Schweitzer is a multiple genius. It is not primarily because he lived an intentional life. It is not primarily because he has worked in fabulous Africa.

The world pays homage partly because Schweitzer went, early, to atone for what white men did to colored men, and thus he is repaying a collective racial debt of guilt for all of us white Westerners. It may be partly because Schweitzer appears to have made an act of renunciation, when so many of the alleged instances of renunciation since Buddha and Jesus have been contrived and self-seeking. It may be partly because in Schweitzer twentieth-century man sees what twentieth-century man may become. We are only partial men; he is universal, an integral whole.

In any case, I had plenty of time to ponder why so many Westerners are so completely moved about Schweitzer, as I met a steady stream of Westerners who dropped by to see him, if only in between planes. In one case I had to be an interpreter for an American talking to Schweitzer, as this visitor was giving Schweitzer a check at the end of a noon visit. Schweitzer very graciously thanked the donor and took out a little white cheesecloth bag in which he put the check. The American kept talking and switched to very bad French—worse than mine. Schweitzer in desperation finally said, "please speak English" which was one of the very few times I ever heard Schweitzer talk English!

In addition to typing and being chief du protocol, on several occasions I helped out with the children in the leper village. Since 1948 there has been a leper village at the edge of the hospital. After Schweitzer received the Nobel Peace Prize, he took the $31,000 in prize money and bought corrugated iron and concrete and built a new village and clinic for the lepers. Some 150 lepers live in the village today, some with their families. These include some fifteen children, about half with leprosy, the others children of lepers. The one European nurse assigned to the clinic—Trudi Bochsler—tries to keep an eye on these children, although the older and brighter ones go a mile downstream to the mission school.

For several afternoons I tried to teach the children something—and in my bad French. I told them about my own children here in Evanston and their pets. We sang songs—I remember "Frère Jacques." I introduced them to Wrigley's chewing gum—half a stick each. I was going to buy them some candy in the village, but Trudi told me that they would like bread better. So one day en route to the airport I bought fifteen small loaves of French bread, and later that afternoon the children ate the bread while I tried to teach them.

I hope our church school again prepares packages for these children and sends them cards. There is one leper boy there—Albert—whom I remember when I was there in 1952. His was a pathetic case—one leg completely without feeling. In the meantime,

Albert had to have this leg amputated. Now he hops around the village on one foot, a bright twelve-year-old virtually orphaned by his family. I left Albert that last afternoon vowing to raise the necessary funds so that Albert could have a wooden leg.

Mrs. Schweitzer is now at Lambaréné. I first met her in 1952 in Günsbach. She is almost as old as her husband. Dr. Schweitzer appears today in fine health. He eats well, talks vigorously, and walks about the hospital from early morning to sunset and often works in his study-bedroom past midnight. But Mrs. Schweitzer is ailing and only comes to the table now for noon dinner, and then with greatest difficulty. Perhaps the most poignant sight today at the hospital is to see this little lady, dressed all in white and with a white helmet, wait on the porch in front of her husband's door at 12:30. He appears, helps her down the concrete steps, and slowly they walk together across the courtyard between the big palms. She is so breathless that she sits on the bench in the staff dining room and does not take her seat to her husband's right until the meal has started. Then she eats lightly, but as I sat opposite her, she would talk to me in English—which helped a lot. Afterwards, she would have coffee in her chair by the screens in the corner—the coolest place in the dining room. I had several fine talks with her. She told me that she knew Schweitzer fifty-four years; they have been married for forty-four years.

At table Schweitzer himself seemed more silent than in 1952, but frequently he would tell a story. Table talk at Lambaréné or Günsbach is of high interest. Schweitzer told the story, which I had heard before, of how when he visited America in 1949, two youngsters asked him for an autograph, saying, "Albert Einstein, can we have your autograph?" He said he was taken aback, but suddenly realized that his hair and Einstein's hair had certain similarities, and so without batting an eyelash Schweitzer took the autograph book of these two children and wrote: "Albert Einstein, by his friend, Albert Schweitzer." This is typical humor of Albert Schweitzer, often shaking his head knowingly and winking his right eye.

Reverence for Life in Action

At table, also, I saw an instance of reverence for life in action. Schweitzer spotted a moth at midday. He motioned to one of the nurses who quietly arose and took a tumbler and a piece of cardboard from a special place on a shelf. With some persistence she caught the moth alive and then took it outside in the tumbler and released it. One tends not to crush ants at Lambaréné and one never picks flowers for the table. The last night there, when one of the hospital physicians was in my room to bid me farewell, I spotted what looked like a human hand crawling along the wall. It was a huge spider. The physician advised me to kill it. But I couldn't kill a spider on my last night at Lambaréné, and so bravely I told him—and myself—that I would merely pull the bed a little from the wall. Somehow I survived the night—which is reverence for life at Lambaréné!

At table, Schweitzer eats from small dishes of especially prepared food—cooked without salt, He eats almost twice as much as most people, but occasionally he would pass tidbits to others. On several occasions he passed me the whites of hardboiled eggs. He would eat the yellow yokes, but pass the whites to me in a little dish, saying, "This is for you because you went to the airport for me today." I appreciated it more when he gave me, as he did on two occasions, little dishes of unsweetened fresh guava.

One morning at table Schweitzer sat down without nodding to me, although I continued to sit across the table from him. And he never nodded to me at the table again. Later I wrote in my daily diary: "I have arrived. Schweitzer no longer nods at me. He is treating me now just like any other member of the hospital family."

During one of our conversations at table, Schweitzer and I talked about building a new church. He told me that I will age ten years in three in the process. I couldn't agree more. He warned, "Don't build your new church too big; it is better to have a small church full than a large church half-empty." He winked to me knowingly as he said this. I said that I was making plans for a new organ. He said to bring in an organ consultant early, for the architect will put the organ in the basement if he can get away with it. He said that the art of organ-building everywhere is at a low ebb.

I did not go to Lambaréné, as so many tend to go, to sell Schweitzer some pet idea. Every panaceaist hopes for Schweitzer's endorsement. I am not without pet projects, but I know enough now not to bother Schweitzer about them. I also did not go to Lambaréné, as I myself went in 1952, to ask him questions. It would be presumptuous on my part to assert that I know Schweitzer's mind. I do not. But I have a sufficient idea of his attitudes on enough subjects so that I did not arrive with a list of questions.

Once, during my two-week stay, he asked me to visit him for a talk. We must have had at least an hour's conversation, with Mlle

Ali as interpreter. I asked him about his unfinished volumes—the three or four books he has promised in past years to publish. He responded that a chicken only makes a noise after it has laid an egg. When he finishes another book, then it will be time enough to talk about it. He has learned not to predict any more publications.

Then he told me that I could stay at Lambaréné as long as I liked, but I told him I would have to be in my pulpit the following Sunday unless he would like to use my ticket and preach for me. He didn't accept the offer, but he did ask me what text I would use for my first sermon. I told him that Unitarian ministers usually no longer have preaching texts. Then Schweitzer gave this theological student a lesson. He insisted that it is good for every sermon to have a text, for then the layman can return home from church with some words in his heart, even if he returns home from church with nothing else! Schweitzer said that the best texts are biblical—from Jesus or Paul. I told him that I appreciated this lesson in practical theology, and he said that he was never too good in practical theology himself, and now is glad that he no longer has to sit for examinations. Once he said he taught practical theology—homiletics. He told his students to preach from their heart and from life experience. All else is mere technique.

He asked me in detail what the American people are thinking about atomic warfare. We discussed atomic disarmament, and I understand that Schweitzer might soon release a statement on nuclear tests and the effects of radiation.

The name of Soviet Premier Khrushchev came up in our conversations, and it reminded me that some years ago Schweitzer told me how he was frequently mistaken for Stalin. When the Council of Europe met in a hotel in Strasburg, one delegate raised a point of order. He pointed to a statue in the main hotel room and said that his delegation would withdraw if they had to meet in front of a bust of Stalin. Of course, it was a statue of Schweitzer, not Stalin, in this Alsatian hotel!

There are bits of quaintness at the hospital which characterize it as Schweitzer's own establishment. For one thing, he has his own time, about half an hour slower than the time at the town of Lambaréné. For another, he does not allow an outdoor thermometer in the establishment, so none of us can know just how hot it really is. He is also against mechanical contrivances: they always break down in the tropics. He has no motorboat at the hospital. If he had one, he told somebody, he would always have to use it to take friends and visitors about. He prefers to use canoes for this purpose. When, rarely, he needs a motorboat, he has neighbors at Lambaréné who will gladly lend him one.

Schweitzer is characteristically as frugal as an Alsatian peasant. He saves every nail, every old envelope. He has animals everywhere. The hospital looks more like an alpine courtyard than a jungle hospital, with sheep, goats, chickens, roosters, ducks, geese, cats, dogs, parrots, chimps, and young gorillas everywhere.

Schweitzer carries a little cheesecloth bag filled with corn and he feeds the chickens wherever he goes. One new physician told me that he never knew he could attract chickens before, until he realized that he was being mistaken by the chickens for Schweitzer. So now this new physician also carries a cheesecloth bag of corn!

Have there been any important changes in five years at Lambaréné? None too significant. There are more visitors. He seems to play the piano less, although when I was there five years ago, he was getting ready to cut records. He still keeps his hands on the administration of the hospital, but at the moment of my visit he was not constructing any new buildings. He has ceased the active practice of medicine since the age of seventy-five, and now has four physicians helping him.

His is not a traditional mission station. He operates this clinic and village in a nonsectarian manner. There is a voluntary Protestant worship service. Being nonsectarian, no one mission finances the hospital. It is supported by individuals and local churches from many denominations and faiths. It is expensive to feed one thousand persons resident in the hospital community. While the clinic is nonsectarian and, in a sense, Schweitzer is nonsectarian also, he is still a member of the church of his father: the Augsburg Confession Church of Alsace—a Lutheran body. His father was minister in this denomination and he was ordained by them. He is considered theologically left and unreliable by many Lutherans, as he is considered theologically safe and reliable by many Unitarians, but technically he has never left the Lutheran church of his fathers.

A certain number of persons die at the hospital as they do at hospitals around the world. Several died while I was there. I attended one burial—of a girl who was long ill with mental illness. Although I think it is fair to say that Africans tend to be better adjusted than people in our own civilization, this woman died—without friends. One of the European nurses said a few words over her grave in the deep recesses of the jungle, just above the Moslem cemetery. The only mourners were the three grave diggers—and myself.

What does the visitor do at Lambaréné in his spare time? I tried to get impressions of Schweitzer from those who know him best: members of his hospital staff. I had long sessions with each physician. The question all at Lambaréné, and in the world outside, ask is what will happen to the hospital when Schweitzer goes? There are evidences that he wants the hospital to continue. On the other hand, there is some logic, if little sentiment, to discontinuing the hospital when he dies. Its future depends upon Schweitzer's wishes. Those closest to him insist that they do not know what his plans are in this regard. Fortunately, he is still young at heart, humorous and vigorous, though well past his eighty-second birthday.

There are innumerable pictures in my memory of Schweitzer at Lambaréné. Early during my stay—I believe the first afternoon at sunset—I asked Schweitzer to show me the grave of Emma Haussknecht. She was his longtime co-worker and preached in this church in January 1954. He touched my hand as if to say, "follow me." We passed the cage of jungle antelopes and went down a short incline below his study-bedroom window. There it was: a white cross with handlettering: "Here are the ashes of Mlle Emma Haussknect, associated with the hospital from October 1925 to March 1956."

Schweitzer's pet bird, a large parrot-like creature, alighted on my shoulder at this very moment. Schweitzer pointed to a small date palm planted beside the grave. If I understood his French he said that though the palm was not native to Africa, it thrives here, like Mlle Emma, who although also not native to Africa, also thrived at Lambaréné.

Once a visitor asked Schweitzer what message he would have, if any, to young people going into the world today. He said that he was too tired to formulate any message, rubbing his eyes as he talked. He thought a moment, however, and added, "There is only one message: always follow your heart. That is the great message: always listen to your heart. All flows from this."

That is Albert Schweitzer at Lambaréné in his eighty-second year.

29

LONDON • PENRHYNDEUDRAETH

VISIT WITH BERTRAND RUSSELL

In the summer of 1957, Homer went to New York to gather materials on peace and lobby for a nuclear test-ban treaty on behalf of a group of American peace activists which would soon found the National Committee for a Sane Nuclear Policy. In London, Homer spent a week observing the U.N. Disarmament Subcommittee negotiations, met members of Parliament, and traveled to Wales to interview Bertrand Russell, the grand old man of British science and letters, who at age eighty-five was leading the campaign against nuclear testing in Britain.

The telephone operator in my London hotel got me the telephone number—in Wales—and within ten minutes I was speaking to the secretary to Bertrand Russell. I asked if I might come to Wales for a half-hour talk with Mr. Russell about his views on the cessation of nuclear bomb tests. She interrupted me, "Lord Russell," and then said that she would find out. Soon he was on the telephone and said that he would be glad to see me if I wanted to make the long journey. He would arrange for a motorcar to meet my 11:11 train.

I left Paddington Station in London at five past midnight. I managed at the last moment to get a sleeping berth for the first six hours of my journey. There were no sheets, but two pillows and a welcome blanket. One of my compartment companions, a Welshman, told this American the etiquette of addressing an earl: "How do you do, my Lord." After that, he is addressed as "sir." At the end, it is "Good day, my Lord." This Welshman said that Lord Russell does not stand on ceremony, but it was good to be correct if I wanted a favor.

Soon I was asleep, fitfully, with the great blanket wrapped around me in the wind. There was welcome tea at 6:00 a.m. and by 6:15, I was on the station platform at Ruabon, waiting for a smaller train to take me to the Welsh seacoast. The trip was long and tedious, the train stopping for every town en route and, it seemed, often for no towns. The scenery was what I had imaged Wales to be—it was my first visit—but I confess I stretched out in the second-class compartment and slept until we reached Barrouth—the sea. Then I began to notice the late morning scenery—clouds hovering over ragged hills, various shades of green, sheep everywhere, rock outcroppings, and stone fences. The little seaside towns, with ancient stone houses, made me resolve to come again when I had more time—and a better mode of conveyance than the slow train. Soon we were arriving at my destination, as the names of towns became more unpronounceable: Harlach, Tygwyn Halt, Talssrnau, Llandecwyn, and then Penrhyndeudraeth. A girl who came into my compartment gave me the correct pronunciation: pen-rin-dyed-rats. She admitted that they usually leave the dyed-rats off and the town becomes pen-rin.

A taxi driver met me at the station and drove me the two miles to the home of Lord and Lady Russell. They had been living there for about a year. They often have visitors from London, even from abroad. He said the name of the town means "a point where two estuaries meet."

In five minutes' time, we had arrived at the house, after driving up a long shale-cropping lane. In no time I was ushered into the living room of Lord Russell. He looked much as recent photographs—a triangular face with white hair. He seemed young for eighty-five. He sat in a high-backed upholstered chair and smoked. He wore a greenish tweed jacket, blue shirt, and red slippers. I gave him the greetings of Prof. Paul Schilpp, a colleague, who edited the volume on Russell in the Library of Living Philosophy. I then told him of our American efforts to form a group to ban the nuclear bomb tests.

Lord Russell said that he was most keen on banning the tests now because a ban could be largely self-enforcing. There need be no fear of surreptitious bad faith. The banning of the bomb itself or the banning of further nuclear bomb production were too complicated to control. Indeed, this might increase rather than lessen tension. He talked of three stages of arms control: 1) banning the tests, 2) taking political settlements, and 3) banning the production of bombs.

He showed me an article he recently wrote for the *New Scientist* in which he listed three reasons for banning tests. The abandonment of the tests would also allay the resentment of neutral countries. Also such action would be an important step toward the peaceful co-existence of East and West—a necessity with the existence of nuclear weapons. Lord Russell took the pipe from his mouth and emphasized that the most urgent problem is not the prevention of tests, but the prevention of war. Everything else is insignificant beside this problem.

Would he be in favor of the unilateral cessation of tests by his own country? Emphatically! He felt that if the United Kingdom did so it would put Russia so much in the wrong—propagandistically— that it would acquiesce to an international agreement. Beyond this, Russell would be in favor of the unilateral cessation of H-bomb production by Britain. There may be a risk in this, of course, but he prefers a risk in the pursuit of something ennobling to the risk of something leading to the destruction of humanity.

I asked Lord Russell what Albert Einstein would be dong about the testing issue if he were alive today. He felt that Einstein would, of course, be talking against further tests. He recalled how, when he was en route by plane from Rome to Paris in April 1955 the chief pilot told him that Einstein had just died. When he arrived later that day in Paris, there was a letter from Einstein saying that he would sign a joint appeal against nuclear war—an appeal which Russell late released to the press.

Talking about scientists, Russell felt that scientists made the bomb and scientists must now stop war—and nothing less. He dismissed all talk of so-called "clean" bombs, saying that any such talk was a pack of lies. However, he did not dwell on the biological dangers of fallout and implied that the political dangers of the tests were the greater evil. He did say that it would be prudent to assess the hazards at the worst possible level—which some governments might not be doing.

Russell said that he had met Albert Schweitzer and admired his statement on the tests. He felt that nothing would be accomplished by Schweitzer and himself joining in an effort or even a statement, since they probably would issue stronger statements separately. But Russell vowed to "stir things up" until the tests ceased.

We talked of the plan of Harold Steele to go to Christmas Island to try to stop the British H-bomb tests. He wondered what prevented Steele from going through with his plan. He admired the courage of Gandhians in risking their lives with radiation in an effort to stop the tests. He himself had never met Gandhi and acknowledged that this method helped free India from British rule.

How will the tests be stopped? Russell says they will cease when enough facts and knowledge are presented to the people, when enough people know what nuclear war will do to them and to their families. He felt that the National Council to Abolish Nuclear Weapon Tests in Britain was doing a good job. I then asked him about his signature to a statement by the communist-dominated British Peace Committee. He said that he has a rule of not working with communist organizations—although of course one has to work with Russia on an official scale to prevent war—but he will sign an occasional specific statement even if some communists sign it. He admitted that communists are very devious and he has had problems working even with communist scientists.

Would the "clean" bomb alter the deterrent value of nuclear stockpiles? He did not put much stock in the deterrent theory, since wars are often started by the hearts of people—and nations—and not by their heads. He was scornful of present British policy regarding the H-bomb. He said that British policy is motivated by national prestige and a desire not to play second fiddle to America. Laughingly, he said that Prime Minister Macmillan wanted the Christmas Island tests to be completed so he could face President Eisenhower, one criminal to another!

Soon I took my leave of Earl Russell. He showed me the garden with red sweet william and faded rhododendron. It overlooked a large estuary—the Glaslyn. Port Madoc was in the background. He pointed to a little white house on the opposite side of the estuary and said that that was where Shelley, the poet, once lived. We talked about the current Commonwealth Prime Ministers Conference, and he said that while United Nations membership should be compulsory, Commonwealth membership is, of course, voluntary. He questioned whether South Africa should be kept in the Commonwealth with her racial policies.

The taxi soon came and I shook hands with Bertrand Russell and went back to the train station. Within two hours after arriving, I was on the slow train heading for London. I arrived at Paddington Station at 10:15 p.m. It was a twenty-two-and-a-half hour journey into Wales for a forty-five minute conversation, but with one of the encyclopedic men of our times. It was well worth the effort, especially to hear Lord Russell speak with conviction and urgency about this "vast atrocity" which threatens humanity with disaster.

30
TOKYO • HIROSHIMA
(1957)

NO MORE ATOMIC WAR

On returning from Britain, Homer settled down with his family for the month of July in Long Island, exchanging homes for the summer with Joe Delibert, his old friend from Cornell. He commuted to his office in Community Church—in the shadow of the Empire State Building—to edit a weekly newsletter on disarmament. In meetings with Norman Cousins, Clarence Pickett, and Norman Thomas in New York, it was decided that Homer would attend the Third World Conference Against Atomic and Hydrogen Bombs and For Disarmament in Tokyo. "This meant hurried reservations, a few more inoculations, and the important decision of taking along my almost-twelve-year-old son, Alex," Homer recalled. "My family only vicariously shares my trips. This was an opportunity for at least my son to share some of my adventures, and at a moment just before he would have to pay full fare." After giving some speeches in San Francisco and Los Angeles, Homer and Alex took a long flight across the Pacific, with brief stopovers in Hawaii and Wake Island. Upon returning home, Homer reported on his first visit to Japan to his fellow Evanstonians and discussed the morality of using the atomic bomb—a controversial subject even within his own liberal church.

We arrived at the World Conference as delegates came from twenty-five countries, from all continents. I did not quite anticipate what I found. The conference was even more anti-American and more pro-communist than I feared, partly because most noncommunists from America and the West refused to attend. Only two others came from America and only three from England. On the other hand, there were large and well-disciplined delegations from Russia and China and communists from many other countries.

During the opening days of the Conference, I almost gave up. I asked myself, "What am I doing here?" I could have taken a walk, but I decided to put first things first—to help stop nuclear tests and nuclear war, and not to pursue my personal battle against communism and communist intrigue in liberal organizations and conferences.

The Tokyo Conference was a furious round of speeches, committees, receptions, and taxi rides. In addition I had to play mother and father to my boy, who was taken every day to the suburbs to play with Japanese boys. We capitalist Americans stayed in the inexpensive Tokyo YMCA near the Conference headquarters, while the proletarian Russians and Chinese stayed in the expensive Grand Hotel. I made the most of opportunities, and this meant delivering many speeches, and this, in turn, meant rising at 5 a.m., to turn out yet another speech which had to be ready for translation into Japanese hours before it was scheduled to be delivered. I averaged almost a speech a day.

While I was dropped from the Conference Steering Committee, no doubt for my ideological independence, for some reason on the penultimate day of the Conference I was put on the important drafting committee for the so-called Tokyo Declaration. This was my most difficult task in Japan. We began our meeting at 8:20 p.m. one evening and never broke up until 7:20 the next morning. There were about twenty members of this drafting committee, eight Japanese and the rest from other countries, including Australia, China, Russia, West Germany, Japan, and America. We were given a preliminary draft of the Tokyo Declaration, and I found myself objecting to almost every sentence. Early in the negotiations the Chinese delegate, speaking in Chinese, which had to be translated into Japanese and then into English, called me "a Dulles" for trying to prolong the negotiations. But I insisted on making the statement a responsible one even if we had to stay up all night—which we did.

About midnight, we had to move to another hotel. I rode in a taxi through the streets of brightly-lighted Tokyo with the head of the Russian delegation and his interpreter. This was an interesting half-hour conversation, but our sharp debating resumed as soon as the committee reconvened. Indeed, toward morning, one of the Russian delegates shook a finger at me, saying, "Jack, you talk more like a diplomat than a peace-lover." No doubt he thought I was an agent of our State Department, little knowing how critical I am of American foreign policy, but I am also critical of Soviet foreign policy, and so I resisted for almost 12 hours making the Tokyo Declaration a carbon copy of Kremlin policy.

I argued, bargained, pleaded, often over single words, and in the end we got a more responsible document. I don't mean to take credit, but the tragedy is that I had almost no help from anybody in the committee. I was all alone, and political isolation can be tough, even though I tried to retain some humor and passed out American chewing gum at 4 a.m. The Russian never tasted gum before, but the Chinese delegate knew Mr. Wrigley's product when a student at Columbia University. It was after 7:00 a.m. when we finished our work. The statement was not as I would have worded it. As a matter of fact, it is not a very inspiring or a very sophisticated document—but it has the virtue of being made in Tokyo, not Moscow.

Later that same day—the last one of the Conference—the huge plenary session, attended by some four thousand Japanese delegates as well as the one hundred foreign delegates, unanimously passed the Tokyo Declaration. In the evening we had a farewell garden party, and the head of the Russian delegation decorated my son with some kind of peace medal, but I doubt if he wanted to decorate my son's father! He did give me a billfold—but without containing a single ruble.

As a matter of fact, we Americans must have more experience working with Russians and Chinese, on an unofficial level, and my tentative conclusion is that they are easier to deal with than the communists in other countries, who tend to be more royal than the king, more communist than the Russians.

My Son on the Go

During the first few days of the Conference, Alex accompanied me to the plenary sessions and soon became known to newspaper readers. When he learned the Japanese game of "go"—something like checkers—he became well-photographed. He also learned quickly how to use the abacus, the ancient hand adding machine of Asia, and this intrigued his Asian friends. Delegates from India and Australia, as well as a former Evanston house guest from England, writer Reginald Reynolds, made much of Alex, and it seemed for awhile that he preferred the conference to playing with Japanese boys or staying at the Tokyo "Y."

A member of the Japanese Upper House, the Diet, came to our rescue, and for a number of days her auto called for Alex each morning and took him to a far suburb, where he played with children of his age—her relatives. There Alex learned something of the politeness of Japanese family life and of the custom of taking one's shoes off before entering the house.

Later in the week, Alex visited the grandchildren of the Unitarian minister in Tokyo, Rev. Imouka. He stayed overnight and had his first opportunity of sleeping on the floor, Japanese style. He survived this experience—and a Japanese bath. On a Saturday evening in Tokyo, we went to a twilight doubleheader. Alex brought his baseball mitt to Japan, but neither of us was prepared for the popularity of this American sport there. At the game we found all 44,000 seats occupied and were lucky to be able to sit on the steps of one aisle.

During our stay in Tokyo, Alex and I were invited to appear on a TV program. Alex was asked how Japanese baseball compared with American baseball. Patriotic to the core, Alex replied that American baseball was better! This bit of candor probably did not permanently imperil Japanese-American relations, but Alex's father was not at all happy at his reply.

In discussing the Tokyo Conference, there is much I have necessarily omitted. There were many fascinating sessions with the Buddhists. Indeed, I was invited to participate in a Buddhist ceremony on the exact moment of the twelfth anniversary of the bombing of Nagasaki. A Hindu and myself were the only non-Buddhists invited to talk in this impressive Buddhist temple in the center of Tokyo. It was a high religious moment.

In Tokyo, I also made contact with the religious liberals. We found several Unitarian and Universalist churches. The ministers gave a pleasant dinner in my honor, in a restaurant off Ginza Street, the Broadway of Tokyo. One Sunday I was invited to preach at Unity Church which meets in a pleasant chapel attached to a private school. I can't report that the congregation was huge—it was held in humid August—but hand fans seemed to flutter constantly, as I talked in English which was then translated sentence by sentence into Japanese. Several American Unitarian visitors were there—Army personnel. The after church coffee hour, so popular in our liberal churches in America, has invaded Japan, although if I remember correctly it was tea and not coffee. And just as I was about to leave at 12:30 on came the rice and chopsticks. I think this is a custom which ought to invade America, and I commend it to you!

245

Also in Tokyo I had a long visit with the famed Dr. Kagawa at his home in the suburbs. He, too, feels the urgency of preventing World War III and is personally working through world federalism.

Pilgrimage to Hiroshima

After two weeks in Tokyo, my son and I took to the excellent trains for a quick tour of southern Japan. We stopped at Osaka where I gave a speech at a large anti-bomb rally. Then we spent three days in Hiroshima. I knew that I had to made a pilgrimage to Hiroshima and Nagasaki. It was not hard to fathom my emotions as we approach the city early in the morning. To me I was approaching the saddest city in the world, And yet as we approached by train, I saw no signs of devastation. Hiroshima looked like any other city in Japan or in the world: freight yards, warehouses, slums. Yet I realized that it is not like any other city in the world, except Nagasaki.

Soon we got on the station platform and were taken in a 70-yen taxi toward the New Hiroshima Hotel. We passed the built-up business district, with several six-story department stores. I kept looking for signs of devastation—even twelve years after—but saw none. We were taken over the graceful new Peace Bridge, with striking concrete railings, designed by the Japanese-American sculptor Isamu Noguchi. Across the bridge we found a spacious Peace Park with but three buildings, breathtaking in their imaginative modernity. One was the new city auditorium. Another was the Peace Museum—a huge building on concrete stilts that would put even Chicago architect Mies van der Roh to shame. The third was the elegant Hiroshima Hotel.

One of my reasons for going to Japan was to express my regrets, as one American, to the Japanese people for the bombing of Hiroshima and Nagasaki. I have for twelve years considered this use of the bomb by my country as one of the enormities of the war. As most of you know, I am a conscientious objector to war—and so am against all wars. I am against the use of all instruments of war. I was, however, especially concerned during the last war about the obliteration or saturation bombing of German and Japanese cities by so-called conventional bombs. And above all, I was concerned about our atomic bombing of Hiroshima and Nagasaki.

Trying to analyze my reactions, I felt and now still feel that the use of the atomic bomb lessened any morality we had on our side. The end—victory—justified any means. I suppose that is true with

246

any war. I suppose that is war. My concern twelve years ago was basically a moral revulsion against the annihilation of a whole city. But there were also political concerns. I felt, at the time, and this has been confirmed by my experience in Asia since, that our use of the bomb would be construed a discriminatory act on our part. We would be accused of having less qualms about dropping the bomb on colored peoples—Japanese—than on our fellow whites—Germans. Many Japanese and many other Asians and Africans feel this way, rightly or wrongly. The events in Arkansas and Tennessee this past week—resistance to desegregation—make it harder for them to believe that this is not so. I also felt twelve years ago that once we used the atomic bomb, it became a legitimate weapon for any nation to use in any future war. There were, of course, some who didn't want to use the bomb, but wanted to keep its existence secret, for its eventual use against Russia.

But I wanted the bomb not to be used for different reasons. I felt that, if it were once used, it could be more easily used again. Later Dr. J. Robert Oppenheimer confirmed this point, although in 1945 he was apparently in favor of its use. Oppenheimer later wrote, "Every American knows that if there is another major war, atomic weapons will be used. We know this because in the last war, the two nations we like to think are the most enlightened and humane in the world—Great Britain and the United States—used atomic weapons against our enemy which was essentially defeated."

But what about the assertion that we used the bomb to shorten the war and to save American and even Japanese lives? And, in any case, why should this clergyman, himself safe in America in 1945 because of ministerial exemption from war duty, suggest that the atomic bomb should not have been used, and thus condemn husbands, some here in this auditorium, to more war service and perhaps death itself on the beachheads of Japan? How have I a right to question this policy, especially since President Truman who made the ultimate decision no doubt had more facts at his disposal than I have now or then?

Since returning from Hiroshima I have continued my research on why the bomb was dropped. President Truman in his memoirs is, understandably, very defensive. He had the almost unanimous recommendation of the so-called Interim Committee which urged that the bomb be used against Japan as soon as possible and without prior warnings of the nature of the weapon. And so Harry Truman wrote, "The final decision of where and when to use the atomic bomb was up to me. I regarded the bomb as a military weapon and never had any doubts that it should be used." Secretary of War Henry L. Stimson is, if anything, even more convinced that it was right to have used the bomb. The thinking of Stimson is reported in his memoirs as follows: "If victory could be speeded by using the bomb, it should be used; if victory must be delayed in order to use the bomb, it should not be used . . . Once that decision had been made, the timing and method of the use of the bomb were wholly subordinated to the objective of victory." In another place, Stimson wrote, "No man . . . could have failed to use it and afterwards looked his countrymen in the face. To end the war in the shortest possible time and to avoid the enormous losses of human life which otherwise confronted us . . . the bomb seemed to me to furnish a unique instrument for that purpose." Even Winston Churchill, according to Harry Truman, "unhesitatingly told me that he favored the use of the atomic bomb if it might aid to end the war."

How, then, can I dare voice regrets in Japan or America in the face of this historic evidence? There is always another side. A group of atomic scientists, headed by Dr. Jerome Franck of the University of Chicago, made a report to the Secretary of War on July 11, 1945. They warned against the use of the bomb against Japan. The Franck Committee argued that the use of the bomb would make postwar international control of atomic weapons much more difficult. They urged a demonstration of the bomb before the eyes of the world, on a barren island, with America telling Japan and the world, "You see what sort of a weapon we had but did not use. We are ready to renounce its use in the future if other nations . . . agree . . . to international control."

Indeed, it is reported by Alexander Sachs that President Roosevelt himself favored some such preliminary demonstration of the bomb's power rather than its unannounced military use. But he died before he faced this decision. Hanson Baldwin, military editor of the *New York Times*, and a man with whom I usually do not agree, called the dropping of the atomic bomb one of America's "worst blunders in the war." Baldwin wrote in 1950: "The military defeat of Japan was certain. The atomic bomb was not needed." Baldwin says the bomb "may have shortened the war by a day, a week, a month—but not more." Thus the price we paid for using the bomb was too great.

Even our own Armed Forces may have had second thoughts about using the bomb. The U.S. Strategic Bombing Survey—after the war—concluded: "Certainly prior to December 31, 1945, Japan would have surrendered even if the atomic bombs had not been dropped, even if Russia had not entered the war, and even if no invasion had been planned and contemplated." Baldwin calls this report "a reasonable judgment."

But why, then, was the atomic bomb dropped—and not once, but twice? There are several theories. Most important is that we wanted to occupy Japan before Russia, which promised to enter the war against Japan, and before she could get her troops into Japan proper. In the summer of 1945 American leaders sensed that if Russian armies entered Japan, it would be difficult to get them out, as it has been difficult to get them out of Germany still today. And so it is thought that we dropped the first bomb just two days before Stalin promised to enter the war, and Stalin lived up at least to this promise—and did enter the war—but our troops had occupied Japan by the time Russia overran Manchuria.

There are other surmises about why we dropped the bombs. Each bomb cost more than one billion dollars. Those responsible for the project had to show some tangible result for the great expenditure of time and money. They had to justify this great expense. In some eyes, they did. For these and other reasons—and certainly some thought that American lives would be saved—the two bombs were dropped.

But I regret more strongly today than even in 1945 my country's using these bombs. I can't speak for the rest of my fellow Americans, but I hope gradually they will have deep regrets, too. I reflected these ideas on several occasions in Japan and I must confess one point: Only on two occasions—one was with Mr. Fuji in Hiroshima—did any Japanese ever return my atonement—so to speak—and express to me their sorrow at the attack on Pearl Harbor. Indeed, as more than one Japanese has confessed, they would have used the bomb on America had they discovered the secret, but surely that is no reason why we should have used the bomb on them!

Meeting with Survivors

Toward the end of my stay in Hiroshima, Mayor Tadao Watanabe had a small dinner in my honor. He had convened the Atomic Patients Treatment Council so I could have their thinking on future projects which private American groups might support for the Hiroshima survivors. Most of all they would welcome financial help, some 5,000 yen or $15 a month per person so that the very poor survivors could go to the Atom Bomb Hospital for treatment who otherwise could not go because of financial responsibilities as housewives or breadwinners. Perhaps one third of the six to eight thousand survivors needing medical treatment are in this category.

We had an interesting dinner party together, and I made a speech once again expressing regrets at the death of more than 100,000 citizens of the Mayor's city. Mayor Watanabe had a ready answer, no doubt because he met an occasional American like myself. He arose and, in the course of his remarks in Japanese, said: "An atomic bomb is a bad thing, but war preceded this particular bombing. It is war that has to be blamed. We do not think that the American people have to be blamed, but all human beings who cause conflicts between nations. War is the root of this evil and modern wars make the use of uncivilized weapons common."

Alex's twelfth birthday fell during our stay in Hiroshima. In lieu of a party with his Orrington School friends, Alex had a birthday supper at the New Hiroshima hotel, where we were staying. We had sirloin steak and apple pie a la mode. Then one of the Japanese physicians connected with the Hiroshima Maiden's project took us to a professional baseball game, in a new stadium, just a few hundred yards from the center of the atomic bombing. Hiroshima lost to Tokyo that night, 3 to 1, but the residents of that city were still happy that the day before their high school baseball team for the first time in seventy-two years won the all-Japan championship.

My purpose in visiting Hiroshima was to seek out additional projects whereby individual Americans could be of help to the more than 97,000 survivors of the bombing. The Council of Atomic Bomb Survivors asked Alex to visit a victim of his approximate age in the new Atomic Bomb hospital. We visited a thirteen-year-old boy who was badly hurt by the bomb when an infant of one year. He is now hospitalized for plastic surgery so he can have better use of one arm. Alex and this boy played Go for almost an hour, much to the delight of the other patients, including some girls from the second Hiroshima Maiden's project. In gratitude for our visit, the mother of the boy, a farmer's wife, gave Alex a present of five hard-boiled eggs.

We also visited with several other patients. The first was a girl aged sixteen. She was a student from a poor family. She was 1,800 meters from the hypocenter. (This statistic—distance from the atomic explosion—is more important among all the survivors, in a hospital or outside, than age or sex or occupation. It is the universal statistic of all survivors.) She had three skin grafts since May, but now she can stretch her arm. She cried as Dr. Harada pulled out the sutures, but he whispered to me in English, "I think the result is not bad."

The second patient was Toyoto Fusako. She finished junior high school and wanted to enter high school. Her family is poor. She had one operation and needs two others. The third patient, Misuhatta, was an older girl. She was 1,300 meters from the center. She has a disfigured ear and big scars on her arms. She needs another transverse skin graft. Koramoto Sacheko was an unmarried dressmaker, twenty-four years old. She was twelve at the time of the bombing. She had a goldfish bowl at her bedside. One hand looked horrible, but Dr. Harada said, "Not bad, she can now move her fingers, but another operation is needed." The fifth patient was twenty-three, unmarried, and worked as a clerk. She was 1,700 meters from the center. She had four large skin-grant operations and now feels better, but needs two more. She had an electric toaster near her bedstead. As I looked at her, I asked what the hundreds of colored paper cuttings were on strings above the three beds in the room. I was told that they are paper cranes, made by the patients themselves. If there are one thousand, it brings good luck.

From Hiroshima, we went to Nagasaki and Kyoto and then back to Tokyo. I hope every American boy can have someday, when still young, the month's experience Alex has had. Some memories will leave him fast and other experiences will probably leave no imprint whatever. Yet, I predict these twenty-eight days in Japan will make an enduring impression on his whole life.

31

EVANSTON

(1959)

HAIL AND FAREWELL

On Sunday, June 7, 1959, Homer delivered his last sermon as minister of the Unitarian Church of Evanston. In resigning to take up social action fulltime in New York, he confessed, "I am no longer a doctrinaire human-ist. Indeed, I now believe that I would have little difficulty becoming a practicing Quaker or Congregationalist or Zen Buddhist." Warning the church not to hanker after respectability, he noted, "The Unitarian Church should never be the fashionable church in town, yet it can easily enough be-come a kind of non-golfing country club for intellectuals with the minister a kind of an educated pro." The most important thing he concluded, was inclusivity: "Ours should try to be a church of the people, not a church of the best people." On June 16, at a farewell party for Homer and Esther, Homer made the following remarks after an evening of tributes by church members, civic officials, and special guests including Dana Greeley, presi-dent of the American Unitarian Association, Dr. Harold Fey, editor of the Christian Century, Dr. Charles Lyttle of Meadville Theological School, and Shigeo Wakamatsu of the Japanese-American Citizens' League.

Before this memorial service closes, the deceased would like to say a few words. Dear Friends, I am moved that so many of you in this church, but especially so many of you outside this church, would come for such long distances, for such a long program, on such a summer night, and contribute so generously to this so-called purse!

Your magnificent tributes could make me feel vain. I know

that they are really not directed toward myself, but to the system of voluntary organization which has become so important as a medium for the growth of our democracy. We are here this evening to recognize the potential of individuals working in our society to improve our society. Thus you are largely honoring, through me, these organizations and institutions and the individuals who work through them. This Evanston church deserves honor for demanding that its minister give much of his time to work in society. But our whole society deserves honor, too, for allowing the full scope of individuals who want to change social practices through community organizations. Our American society, for all its faults—and they are many—has fluidity and thus is changing and can continue to change.

Since it is these organizations and our society we are honoring, I will personally discount your tributes, although I must confess that I am glad that both my congregation and my family can hear them. Now my church knows, however belatedly, exactly what I have been doing from Monday through Saturday! Now my family knows what I have been doing at those interminable meetings at the Central YMCA cafeteria—and elsewhere! My eleven-year-old daughter Lucy made a New Year's resolution: "I promise, daddy, to love Gandhi and Schweitzer." This is a poignant reflection of the price we so-called reformers pay. We try to reform the world, but do not remember to change ourselves, and we almost completely ignore our families.

I leave the North Shore and Chicago area optimistic about the progress in race relations. When I first came to the Chicago area in 1941, Negroes had difficulty—for example—eating in many restaurants, and the Northwestern University dormitories were closed to them. We have come a distance in race relations in these eighteen years. There is much farther to go, especially in integrated housing, and we no longer, if ever, have the luxury of time. There are still unbelievable areas of prejudice and discrimination, even among liberals, but I perceive a great fluidity in our racial patterns. The direction in American race relations can only be up, although the pace might be fast. I am equally optimistic, but more impatient, about the American South. I have high hopes, however, for the so-called New Negro in the South, and even for the too-slowly-awakening Southern white liberal.

I am not optimistic about the prospects of world peace, and the avoidance of World War III. War is the prime problem mankind must solve, and I feel that all other social problems, including race relations, including civil liberties, including African colonialism, are quite secondary, however contributory. I wish I could somehow mobilize each person here tonight to work actively and continuously for world peace. If there is not more peace activity in Chicago and in America than there is, we might as well have a farewell banquet for us all.

I want, in conclusion, to show my gratitude this evening by giving thanks. I want to thank this church for its continued generosity in urging me to work in the community and in the world, and for not once restricting my freedom in pulpit or marketplace.

I am grateful for the leisure this church has given me to study and to write and for the generous leaves of absence for extended visits to Asia and Africa. I know of no other Unitarian church which has been so generous and understanding of the needs of its minister.

I want to thank my mother, who is present, for the heredity and environment which made me what I am. This may surprise some, but I am really an old conservative. I have merely been conserving the radicalism of my parents who were socialists in the pre-World War I era. I have not progressed in my thinking much beyond my boyhood environment where Eugene V. Debs was worshipped more than Wilson, Harding, and Coolidge.

I want this evening especially to thank my wife, for her gentle criticism and loving support these many years. She is the one who has used the blue pencil late Saturday nights. She is the one who has given me ideas. She is the one who has encouraged my action in community, often at no little danger and tension to herself. She has had to combine the burden of being a minister's wife with that of being the wife of an actionist and a traveler, and I know that it has been lonely for her. I propose to use the generous purse given this evening for only one purpose: to take Esther to Europe where she again wants to go—on our way to Africa and Asia where I want to go!

And so one chapter of my life comes to an end, after eighteen years in greater Chicago and eleven years here in Evanston. I don't know how long I will last in the jungles of Manhattan or Africa, and India is still the principal land of my dreams. Whatever my fate will be, a large part of my heart will remain with you in Chicago and Evanston. It is in your midst that I found myself, and now, it is from your midst that I steal away. Hail and farewell!

PART FIVE 1960-1964

PEACE LEADER

THE NEW YORK YEARS

" . . . Force will fail . . .
The missiles none may avoid, that carry death."
— Sophocles, Philoctetes

In the summer of 1959, Homer began working for the American Committee on Africa, a New York-based organization devoted to supporting independence for the continent's many European colonies. The Jack family—including Homer, Esther, Alex, Lucy, a St. Bernard and a Siamese cat—moved to Scarsdale, a spacious suburb about 20 miles from Manhattan, and Homer commuted to work every day. With the election of John F. Kennedy as president in 1960, the geopolitical landscape suddenly altered, and prospects for reversing the arms race, especially halting the testing of atomic and hydrogen bombs, improved. Homer's colleagues at SANE—the National Committee for a Sane Nuclear Policy—asked him to take the helm of the nation's most innovative and influential peace organization and find a way to turn the tide against atomic testing. Over the next five years, Homer threw himself into the campaign to achieve a test-ban treaty and promote initiatives toward disarmament. His work frequently took him to London, Geneva, Belgrade, Moscow, and other world capitals. During this period, he also paid his fourth—and final—visit to Dr. Albert Schweitzer in Africa and, continuing his race relations work, served as chairman of the Association of Fair Housing Committees in metropolitan New York.

Photograph: Homer at the White House to observe President Lyndon Johnson sign an arms-control bill, 1965

32 NAIROBI (1959-1960)

THE AFRICAN FREEDOM STRUGGLE

Between 1957 and 1979, forty-eight countries in Africa became independent. In this article, adapted from a keynote address given a generation later to an assembly of African religious leaders in Kenya, Homer reviews his own involvement in the African freedom struggle.

Perspective 1959: The Cuban Revolution triumphed on January 1, catapulting Castro into power, the Dalai Lama fled Tibet following the Chinese occupation, and new Prime Minister Verwoerd intensified apartheid in South Africa. The U.S. set up the Ballistic Missile Early Warning System with giant radar screens in Thule, concern for Strontium-90 led to the creation of the Federal Radiation Council to set safety standards for fallout, and following the death of Secretary of State John Foster Dulles, Premier Khrushchev visited the U.S.A. The first xerox copy machine was introduced, Alaska and Hawaii became the 49th and 50th states, and the St. Lawrence Seaway opened. The first U.S. soldiers died in Vietnam, and a tainted cranberry scare—one of the nation's first environmental crises—spread at Thanksgiving. In arts and entertainment, the quiz show scandal broke, Lady Chatterly's Lover was banned from the mails and then permitted, and top movies included Hiroshima Mon Amour, The Mouse That Roared, *and* North By Northwest. *On American television, twenty-seven Western shoot-'em-ups dominated prime time.*

I did not live in the eighteenth century to observe the American revolution. Born in the second decade of the twentieth century,

I missed by a decade being old enough to witness the revolutions for freedom in much of Asia, especially on the Indian subcontinent. However, I was old enough—in my thirties and forties—to witness, if once removed, the African freedom decade and share in some of the spirit, the joy, and the exuberance of some of the African leaders in these heady years of the 1950s and early 1960s.

I first came to Africa in 1952. I went from Chicago to Cape Town and returned without flying—by train, ship, truck. En route I spent a week in London. In many ways the British capital was the seedbed of the African freedom revolution, at least for the British colonies and South Africa. How many years did Jomo Kenyatta—or Kwame Nkrumah—spend in England?

There was, even in 1952, a rich array of organizations and personalities in London devoted to Africa. There I first met Michael Scott, a white Anglican priest who had been exiled from South Africa for strong opposition to the separation of the races. Scott was to represent at the U.N. some of the people of Southwest Africa (Namibia) until some of its leaders fled that huge colony of South Africa, once German, to represent themselves.

Still en route to Africa, one April evening I left Bordeaux, France, by a French ship, third-class as befitted a young pastor's pocketbook. The French soon felt sorry for me, and suggested that I spend each day in the second-class sitting rooms (when not on deck looking without success for whales). Toward the middle of the two-week voyage, off the west coast of Africa, I invited two of my fellow passengers—who were African—to accompany me to the second-class quarters. I was sternly reprimanded—in French! What kind of trouble-maker was I? Was I trying to upset the colonial pattern? I recall this incident because then the French in Africa had a reputation—false—of not drawing the color line.

We stopped at the French ports en route—Dakar, Conakry, Abidjan, Douala—but significantly not British ports. Colonial Africa was like that. French ships touched only French colonies. Then I disembarked at Port Gentil, French Equatorial Africa. I went up the Ogowe River overnight in virtually a dugout canoe to visit Dr. Albert Schweitzer.

I could write a book on Schweitzer and have; but in this address I will only discuss this universal man briefly. It is, I know, the fashion in Africa and elsewhere to demythologize this musician/philosopher-cum-physician. He was a nineteenth century colonialist who lived in Africa from 1913 to 1965. He never subscribed to the freedom decade and I had many private discussions on colonialism, even arguments, with him. Yet he established and maintained a village hospital (in what is now the Gabon) which was decades ahead of modern hospital practices. It was a facility that worked, that was used, long after more modern hospitals fell into disrepair and disuse. Don't believe all the attacks you read about Albert Schweitzer; don't believe all the adulation either. Yet he was a rare soul, a universal man, and the nineteenth and twentieth centuries have produced too few such giants.

From Lambaréné I went by truck overland, and then by railroad, to Brazzaville (and then Leopoldville from Kinshasa). There I lived in the Union Mission House of the Belgian Congo. One evening, while having dinner with missionaries and ex-missionaries (old colonialists all), some small stones were thrown at the screen in front of where I was eating. I thought nothing about this incident, but after dinner the superintendent told me that some "natives" were outside who knew my name and wanted to speak to me. What Africans knew my name? I went outside, tentatively, and several Africans told me that Roger Baldwin and the International League for the Rights of Man at U.N. Headquarters had indicated that I was travelling through Africa.

In this manner I met with some African freedom fighters who were to lead the struggle against Portuguese domination in neighboring Angola. Here, in Leopoldville, I first met Holden Roberto of the Union of Populations of Northern Angola (UPNA) which later became the National Front for the Liberation of Angola (FNLA). Roberto gave me a picture of some of this initial political activity. Two days later I was en route by train and coastal steamer to Lobito. Later I took a wood-burning locomotive across Angola, the Benguela railroad, to what was Northern Rhodesia, now Zambia, and eventually a train to Johannesburg.

Returning to the United States from South Africa, I realized that even the most enlightened of my countrymen were ignorant about the colonialism that shackled Africa and the emerging efforts of some Africans themselves to break the European chains. The United States, founded by revolution, had become a counterrevolutionary society and a provincial one. (I am afraid it still is!) Then, with some friends, Americans for South African Resistance was established in 1952 and—including George Houser and Donald Harrington—we established an American Committee to help the Defiance Campaign in South Africa, and also educate the American people generally about Africa—not so much about its culture as its politics.

In the meantime, I resumed my church duties outside Chicago, but took every occasion to invite itinerant African leaders to speak from my pulpit. One was Z. K. Mathews, a leader of the South African National Congress and inspired adviser of a generation of freedom fighters as principal of University College of Fort Hare, the only institution of higher education which, at the time, Africans could attend in South Africa.

Also a young Kenyan labor leader, Tom Mboya, came to our parsonage for a week. I was to see much of this vibrant leader until he was killed in 1969. I knew both of these assassinated heroes. Eduardo Mondlane was seeking his doctorate at Northwestern University outside Chicago in this period, and he spoke at our church often. Eduardo finished Northwestern, taught at Syracuse University, and also worked in the Trusteeship Division of the United Nations. But always his heart, and mind, were in southern Africa, in Mozambique. He was leader of the Front for the Liberation of Mozambique (FRELIMO) until he died when a parcel exploded in his face in Tanzania in 1969.

Mboya was always bright, always young, always in a hurry. Also he always had excellent connections with the International Confederation of Free Trade Unions in Brussels. He was always political, in the best sense. One of his notable projects was Airlift Africa, an effort to bring hundreds of young Kenyans to U.S. colleges and universities. With the British limiting higher education, Mboya conceived of an airlift, chartered planes in the late 1950s, and his American friends somehow found scholarships for hundreds, if not in the best universities, in some. I remember meeting the first planeload at the airport in New York and transporting them by bus to a hotel in New York City. Then the future leaders of Kenya scattered to many of the forty-eight American States (and to Canada). This was one of Tom Mboya's finest hours.

In the meantime the American Committee on Africa was established in New York, with George Houser as its director. It served a succession of African petitioners who came to U.N. Headquarters to seek their country's freedom. One such person was Julius Nyerere of Tanganyika.

In 1957 the Gold Coast became the first colony in sub-Saharan Africa to attain independence. I was invited to witness the change over on March 6, and from Accra, I took the plane to Leopoldville with Julius Nyerere. We were to meet with some of the African leaders of Angola. However, the Belgian police traced our movements. It was a cops-and-robbers chase through the outskirts of Leopoldville before we outdistanced our colonial supervisors. Only then, outside Leopoldville, deep in the bush, did we talk with the Angolans, including Holden Roberto. Nyerere was giving them wise advice on achieving a viable freedom movement.

I was present at the Accra Conference along with three other officers of the American Committee on Africa. One afternoon, in our room in the Ambassador Hotel, as we were trying to take a siesta, there was knock on the door. In came Patrice Lumumba. He asked if we could contribute funds to purchase a Jeep for his emerging movement for the freedom of the Belgian Congo. In another eighteen months, he was head of the independent Congo. We saw him once at U.N. Headquarters, but soon he was murdered.

On another occasion, during the All-African Conference—the first big pan-African assembly in Ghana in 1958—I went to visit nearby French Togoland instead of attending the Ghana-Guinea football match in the afternoon. My three companions from the American Committee on Africa and I decided to visit the prime minister of Togoland, Sylvanus Olympio, for he came to New York yearly to present the pleas of his country, formerly a German colony and now a U.N. Trust Territory. We had known him in the halls of the U.N. and I had also seen him at the Ghana independence celebrations in 1957. His country had elections the previous April and his party won the election. The French authorities bowed to the inevitable and made Sylvanus Olympio prime minister.

We started out merrily at ten on Sunday morning. Our Ghana government auto, we belatedly learned, could not go beyond the Ghana border. We went to the Accra airport to hire a plane, but the only one for charter was a four-motor affair which would have cost us a fortune. We found a taxi that regularly took passengers the almost 200 miles to Lomé, the capital of Togoland. It was a hot, but interesting ride, near the coast and as we drove we were somewhat concerned about our being able to cross the borders, since we had no visa. We had wired Olympio that we were coming, but we had no great confidence in cables being prompt in Africa.

After crossing the great Volta River on a small auto ferry, we arrived at the Ghana border and flashed the pin of the All-African Conference. That worked magic, as we had hoped, and our Ghana visa clearly marked "good for one visit only" was not invalidated, so we could return. But that was only half of our problem; we still had to get into Togoland. At that border, we pulled rank and said, in bad French, that the prime minister was our friend and, moreover, he was expecting us. That again worked—although it turned out that he never did get our cable!

By three in the afternoon we were in Lomé and soon inside the Prime Minister's drawing room, recalling old days. I asked Olympio how he got started. He told the fascinating story of how he was a businessman, managing the powerful Lever Brothers agency in Lomé. They didn't like his political activity and transferred him to their Paris office. This was the very year the U.N. General Assembly met in Paris, and Olympio arrived in time to testify against the French authorities.

Olympio was scheduled to speak at a political rally that Sunday afternoon, and he invited us to attend. We sat for three hours in the waning sun, as there were long speeches in the Ewe dialect, and shouts of *"Abloude"*—freedom—and responses of *"Mequay"*—We've got it! Ten thousand Togolese were present, the women segregated in front, the men along the edges. There were even singing commercials, from a loud speaker, plugging Olympio and his party, techniques he no doubt learned from his long years in America and France. After the rally we returned to Olympio's house and talked politics with him some more. He told us of a recent visit with President Charles de Gaulle in Paris when the petulant general tried to wipe his hands of Togoland since by U.N. decree it was to be a free country and no longer under the French mandate in April, 1960.

We left Olympio after eight in the evening, had supper in a French hotel near the waterfront, then started the long drive back to Accra. The ferry over the Volta River closed down after dark, so we had to make a hundred mile detour, and we didn't arrive back in Accra until three in the morning.

The following morning the All-African People's Conference officially opened, and it was an emotional event. The Conference headquarters was in the Accra Community Centre, given to the people of Accra in 1951, ironically by the United Africa Company, a colonial exploiting company if ever there was one. For weeks the decorations committee made the most of the relatively tiny auditorium. The Centre is located almost opposite the Parliament House, with the statue of Kwame Nkrumah gracing its outside. On either side of the private roadway leading the Centre were flags of the nine independent Africa states: Liberia, Tunisia, Sudan, Ethiopia, Morocco, Libya, United Arab Republic, Ghana, and Guinea. The Guinea flag—red, yellow, and green—is the same as that of Ghana, except that it is without a black lodestar in the middle. The roadway that first morning was lined on each side with a huge crowd of Ghanaians.

262

Boys carried painted placards reading: "Down with Tribalism." "Hands Off Africa." "Free Kenyatta Now." "Keep Religion Out of Politics." "*Abloude.*" On the outside of the Community Centre was a huge sign reading, "Ghana Welcomes Africa's Freedom Fighters. Long Live the Union of African Republics."

I tarried outside, to take some pictures and to watch some delegates arrive, but I wanted to be sure of a seat inside. I passed through the porticoed courtyard where delegates were conversing. Inside the hall, also on the walls, were these slogans: "Hands Off Africa," "Africa Must Be Free," "Down with Racialism and Tribalism."

Behind the podium were seats for about fifty persons, for the secretariat and the heads of various delegations. It was an interesting sight as they gathered: some dressed in fashionable Western clothes, others in so-called national dress, meaning Nigerians in grey robes, Ghanaians in multi-colored *kente*-cloth togas with one shoulder bare, Tunisians in white *djellabas,* and many kinds of headdress.

Tom Mboya, member of the legislative council in Kenya, was earlier elected Conference chairman by the steering committee. Although he came to the podium briefly, he soon disappeared. Members of the diplomatic corps stationed in Ghana began taking their seats, as did Lord Listowel, the Governor-General of Ghana. Then at ten o'clock Prime Minister Nkrumah, host of the Conference, walked down the center aisle with Tom Mboya, followed by George Padmore, Ghana adviser on African Affairs, and Kojo Botsio, foreign minister of Ghana. They took their seats near the podium as the first All-Africa Peoples Conference began.

On the day before the Conference ended, our American Committee representatives had a special interview with Dr. Nkrumah. We met him in his rooms in Parliament House at noon, shortly after he led a debate on the union of Ghana with Guinea. We found him affable and friendly, especially so since our Committee organized the huge banquet for him the previous July at the Waldorf-Astoria Hotel.

One of the most interesting delegates to the Conference was Rui Ventura. I had first met him in Leopoldville in 1952. Ever since he and his colleagues had been in contact with our committee. They were expatriates from neighboring Angola, a Portuguese colony of almost fuedal conditions. Ventura was sent by his colleagues to Accra. He could not get a passport and so he left Leopoldville without identification papers. By boat, bus, train, and through one border forty miles on foot he made his way to Ghana, starting three months early so he would be sure to arrive, the first representative of the people of Angola actually to attend any inter-African or international conference. The Portuguese police sent a man, disguised as a journalist, to trail him, but this man was discovered and ousted from Ghana. Ventura—that was an assumed name, he was really Holden Roberto—was afraid of reprisals and his speech to the Conference was read by another so he would not be photographed. One of the last things I did in Accra was to help arrange for Ventura to visit America and plead his case at the United Nations.

One afternoon we arranged for the chief Russian observer to come to our rooms for a talk. Professor Ivan Potekhin has been an African scholar for thirty years, although this was only his second visit south of the Sahara. He complained of the difficulties Russians have to visit Africa, even for scholarly studies. He said that when he visited Ghana for three months recently, there were rumors of Russian penetration of the continent, when we Americans have, by comparison, hundreds of diplomats, scientists, and travelers all over Africa. He told us frankly that there is not as much interest in Africa on the part of both the Russian people and the government as he would like.

One of my tasks at Accra was to send daily cables of from 500 to 1000 words to the *Hindustan Times* of New Delhi. Because of the time difference, I had to file the story by 1:30 p.m. for the next morning's newspaper. This was an exacting responsibility, especially to find news pertinent to India so early in the day, every day. Usually at noon or 12:30, I would leave the plenary session, go to nearby Legion Hall which was converted into a press room with typewriters, somehow develop my story, and then walk the three blocks in the hot sun to the cable office. Thence I would take a taxi back to the Ambassador Hotel for lunch, usually with the delegates at long tables. During one cab ride, I found myself with several other delegates or observers. One lady turned out to be Mrs. Paul Robeson. She said that she had often read my writings but, until the Conference, she did not know that I was not a Negro! I considered this a compliment!

At the American Committee on Africa, where I began working fulltime in 1959, I edited its monthly *Africa Today*. I worked on the independence of Algeria, going to Washington to try to convince a skeptical Congress, although John Kennedy—then on the threshold of his presidency—was friendly to the cause. I wrote a pamphlet on a free Angola. We took both Banda and Kaunda on speaking tours. I showed Kaunda for the first time the Lincoln Memorial in Washington. I took Banda to visit his former landlady of a rooming-house when he was a medical student in Chicago. Joshua Nkomo of Southern Rhodesia, now Zimbabwe, was an occasional visitor to New York. I went to Brussels to meet Tom Mboya. Throughout we worked against apartheid and helped launch the worldwide memorials after the massacre at Sharpeville in March 1960. We arranged a dinner in New York City honoring Sekou Touré of Guinea. And we continued to help both petitioners from Africa at the U.N. and African heads of state making their first visit to the U.N. in their official capacities.

I was employed with the American Committee on Africa less than two years, although I continued to be related to the U.N. system in the field of disarmament. Indeed, I returned to West Africa in 1962 to attend Nkrumah's Ban the Bomb Conference and renewed contacts with many African friends. In that period I tried to visit East Africa, but the British refused to give me a visa, apparently because I knew Tom Mboya.

During this whole period I shared, eagerly, the heady excitement of peoples and their leaders on the verge of freedom. Nothing could hold the forces of history back. "The winds of change"—the words were of Harold Macmillan in Cape Town in 1960—were blowing strong. All Africa would be free, united, prosperous after the degradation and poverty of various brands of European colonialism. One could compare the varieties, perhaps, but no form of colonialism was benign. All were evil—and collapsing from their own evil. Exploitation would give way to cooperation, poverty to prosperity, isolation to one continental family. Education would displace ignorance, literacy years of privation. Come back Africa—to its new-found old civilizations.

In my lectures during the 1950s and early 1960s, I spoke to many American audiences about the coming changes in Africa. My thesis was not original, but it remains important: "A people, a continent, is ready for its freedom when it takes its freedom."

33 NEW YORK
(1960-1964)

SANE—THE VOICE OF SANITY

Perspective 1961: Outgoing President Eisenhower warned of the "military-industrial complex," while incoming President Kennedy vowed to "pay any price, bear any burden" to defend the West. JFK established the Peace Corps in March, but the year as a whole was marked by tension and big power competition: the failure of the Bay of Pigs invasion of Cuba, the resumption of nuclear testing by both Russia and America, the first direct U.S. military support in Vietnam, the first cosmonauts Yuri Gagarin and Alan Shepard, and the launch of the first nuclear-powered device in space. A B-52 crash in North Carolina resulted in near explosion of a nuclear bomb, when five of six fail-safe mechanisms triggered on impact. Following the summer's Berlin Crisis, the Administration distributed 31 million copies of a civil defense brochure "Fallout Protection: What to Know and Do about Nuclear Attack." CORE organized a series of twelve Freedom Rides in the South—the first since 1946—and Attorney General Robert Kennedy sent 400 federal marshalls to Montgomery to protect blacks led by Martin Luther King. The Non-Aligned Conference convened in Belgrade. Top movies included West Side Story, Judgment at Nuremberg, *and* Breakfast at Tiffany's. *Roger Maris hit 61 home runs, eclipsing Babe Ruth's record, and ballet dancer Rudolf Nureyev defected to the West.*

For nearly twelve years after the atomic blasts of 1945 that ended World War II, U.S. and Soviet nuclear testing proceeded virtually unopposed. It wasn't until 1957 that public opposition to the deadly practice was organized.

The first protest of note occurred following the ill-fated U.S.

hydrogen bomb test at Bikini on March 1, 1954, when the "ashes of death" fell on the Japanese fishermen of the *Lucky Dragon*. Indian Prime Minister Nehru called for an immediate moratorium on atomic explosions. The following year, the Asian-African Conference at Bandung demanded that the nuclear powers suspend testing. A United Nations subcommittee tried unsuccessfully to negotiate the discontinuance of nuclear testing. Pope Pius XII called for an end to nuclear explosions. Adlai Stevenson raised the issue in the 1956 presidential campaign. Nevertheless, by the end of that year, the U.S. had conducted eighty-six nuclear explosions and the Soviet Union twenty-eight.

The slow growth of world concern was accelerated in April 1957 by Albert Schweitzer's "Declaration of Conscience" against nuclear testing. In May, the Joint Congressional Subcommittee on Radiation began holding hearings on fallout. In June, 2,000 scientists led by Linus Pauling asked for an international agreement to end tests. In July, the first Pugwash Conference of Scientists was held. Increasingly, groups of people in Japan, Western Europe, and North America gathered to discuss the crisis created by increasing global levels of radiation.

Identifying the Problem

In this political climate a new American organization—SANE—was born. On June 21, 1957, a cross-section of American leaders met at the Overseas Press Club in New York City to discuss nuclear politics. The meeting grew out of many people's efforts, but one who stands out was Quaker peace activist Lawrence Scott of Chicago. In April he had convened a meeting of pacifists in Philadelphia to discuss the testing and proposed creating a Committee to Stop H-Bomb Tests. In the meantime they contacted Norman Cousins, editor of the *Saturday Review*, and Clarence Pickett of the American Friends Service Committee to give leadership. On May 29, Scott, Pickett, and myself met with Cousins in his office and decided to convene a meeting of individuals of national stature concerned with the end to nuclear testing. Pickett, who presided over the meeting of the Provisional Committee to Stop Nuclear Tests—later to be named SANE—suggested that "something should be done to bring out the latent sensitivity of the American people to the poisoning effect of nuclear bombs on international relations and humanity."

Lawrence Scott reported that non-pacifist groups all over the country were looking for national leadership to end testing. Poet Lenore G. Marshall (who met independently with Cousins and Pickett and later came to be viewed as a co-founder of the new organization) suggested arranging a meeting with President Eisenhower. Socialist leader Norman Thomas felt any ban on tests should be "but a first step to universal disarmament." Other participants included Earl Edwards of the American Friends Service Committee, Lawrence Mayers and John Swomley of the Fellowship of Reconciliation, Henry Hitt Crane, Rabbi Edward S. Klein, Harold Oram, Earl Osborn, Ralph Sockman, James Warburg, and Catholic Bishop (later Cardinal) John J. Wright. After five hours of discussion that first day of summer, the twenty-seven persons present appointed a smaller steering committee to take the next steps. In July the group established a clearinghouse for information on the cessation of nuclear tests. In the meantime, the group sent me to London to observe the negotiations of the U.N. Disarmament Subcommittee and then to Japan to evaluate the growing world movement to end nuclear testing.

A Committee Is Formed

On September 24, the full committee met again, also in New York. Cousins volunteered that he had recently visited Albert Schweitzer in Europe and found him "with low spirits—heartsick at what is happening in the world." Lenore Marshall urged the group to "think of projects on a much larger scale," such as gaining a court injunction against further American tests. Psychoanalyst Erich Fromm observed that the "normal drive for survival has been put out of action" by Cold War propaganda, and that the group must "try to bring the voice of sanity to the people." It was Fromm who proposed the group's name: the National Committee for a Sane Nuclear Policy—afterwards usually abbreviated to SANE.

Co-chairman Clarence Pickett reminded the group that it was not yet officially organized. He asked whether existing organizations could effectively stop nuclear tests, and the group responded that a new national organization was genuinely needed. These pioneers decided to hire an executive secretary and select a board of directors that could represent many interests and organizations.

By October the new organization had defined its broad purposes as preventing nuclear war and creating a global order of peace with justice. Its first task was "the immediate cessation of nuclear weapons tests by all countries, including our own, through a U.N.-monitored program."

At a committee meeting on October 1, Cousins suggested placing a prominent advertisement to "define the issue in its purest form and provide the people with an action program." On November 15, 1957, the *New York Times* carried a full-page advertisement with the headline: "We Are Facing a Danger Unlike Any Danger That Has Ever Existed." The text called upon all nations to suspend nuclear weapons tests. Published shortly after the launching of Sputnik, the advertisement declared that "the test of a nation's right to survive today is measured not by the size of its bombs or the range of its missiles, but by the size and range of its concern for the human community as a whole."

The copy was largely Norman Cousins' work, and the ad was endorsed by a diverse group of American intellectuals, including Cleveland Amory, John C. Bennett, Harrison Brown, Harry Emerson Fosdick, Oscar Hammerstein II, John Hersey, Stanley Livingston, Lewis Mumford, Eleanor Roosevelt, Howard Thurman, and Paul Tillich. The advertisement soon appeared in twenty-three U.S. newspapers, reaching a total circulation of more than 3 million, including the *Washington Post*, the *Chicago Sun-Times*, and the *Los Angeles Times*. National SANE received 2,300 responses from thirty-six states and more than $12,000 in contributions. (The original advertisement cost $4,700.) Almost overnight the ads created SANE groups in fifteen major cities and informal ones in forty-one others.

Joining SANE

I served as Executive Director of SANE from October 15, 1960, through September 15, 1964. My "tour of duty" encompassed the entire 1,037 days of the presidency of John F. Kennedy (January 20, 1961 through November 22, 1963). When people ask me why I went to work for SANE, I would say glibly that "Norman Cousins wanted me to get SANE from out of the shadow of dealing with Senator Dodd." (Dodd was accusing SANE of being communist-influenced.) Yet in reviewing the archives of SANE today, I realize that was indeed an idealized answer. SANE was in deep trouble that summer of 1960, facing a crisis of confidence and finances. Records also show that both Cousins and Pickett wanted to be relieved of their chairmanship. That summer the debt was $9,000, with a balance in the bank of $174.71. Also I was just beginning my work with the

American Committee on Africa and enjoyed my tasks. Yet Cousins and others on the SANE Board convinced me that I must come to "save SANE."

Once, several years earlier at an African freedom conference in Africa, Michael Scott, the Anglican priest who represented the Herero people of South West Africa and was the conscience of white South Africans, brought me some clippings of English pacifists who had been beaten up by the police a few days before for picketing an atomic missile base in England. Scott was a sponsor of the committee and had received a cable urging him to return to give personal leadership for a second protest at the base. He asked me what I thought of this activity in relation to his work in Africa, and I told him that opposition to atomic war is more important—if one must choose—than opposition to African colonialism. Whether my words had effect or not, Scott cut short his tour of Africa and returned to England. I later learned that he and forty-five others had been arrested at a missile base in Norfolk and had elected to spend Christmas week in prison. In leaving the American Committee on Africa to work for SANE, the same kind of priority weighed on my mind.

SANE was only three years old when I became director. It had two previous directors for brief periods: Trevor Thomas and Donald Keys. I felt my first task was administrative. In place was an excellent staff: Sanford Gottlieb, a former newspaperman and labor official, living in Washington; Donald Keys, one of SANE's founders and a world federalist; and Edward Meyerding. I knew Ed from Chicago, where he was director of the Illinois Chapter of the American Civil Liberties Union, of which I was vice-chairman. (Ed later died from a fatal fall while cleaning the roof of his home in Westchester County.)

We assigned staff responsibilities in our little office at 17 East 45th Street, only one block from Cousins' office at the *Saturday Review*. Gottlieb handled dealing with the Administration and Congress as political director. Keys dealt with program. Meyerding dealt with finances and fund-raising. I assumed other responsibilities, including dealing with both the Board and the chapters, working at the U.N., and relating to overseas test-ban and disarmament organizations. We held frequent staff meetings and made written reports to the board, often every two months. I emphasized communications and in 1961 we changed over our periodical, *SANE U.S.A.*, to *SANE World*—which lasted into the 1980s. We also were able to hire two or three able secretaries. We became a good team, despite a low budget. We began to evolve an enlightened employee policy and, in time, welcomed unionization.

One of my most pleasant tasks was to help relate SANE to the U.N. system. Our office was only 15 minutes' walk to U.N. Headquarters. We soon obtained U.N. credentials, despite their preferring to deal with international non-governmental organizations. Thus we became a NGO and, since the term can be used interchangeably, I also became a NGO. My year's experience at the U.N. with the American Committee on Africa helped me considerably.

I soon found that the First or Disarmament Committee of the General Assembly, meeting every October and November, was a splendid place to meet the disarmament ambassadors of the principal countries testing nuclear weapons: U.S.S.R., U.K., and U.S.A.— and later France and China. While the disarmament secretariat of the U.N. was located in New York, it also became apparent that any significant test-ban negotiations—bilateral or multilateral—would take place at Geneva.

Despite the costs, we occasionally flew to Geneva to obtain political information on the course of the negotiations, news we could not obtain in New York or Washington. In 1961 the McCloy-Zorin negotiations took place in New York, but I must honestly admit that I knew nothing about these historic talks until they were announced. We were elated with what we heard, for the next step appeared to involve new negotiations for a test-ban.

In March 1962, the Eighteen-Nation Disarmament Conference (ENDC) started to meet. SANE collected a useful array of disarmament books and gave this library to each of the eighteen diplomatic missions. Each contained a SANE bookmark. They were appreciated and some of the volumes were in use, or at least available, in some diplomatic missions in Geneva more than two decades afterwards!

I had known some of the U.S. delegates in Washington and New York, and I talked with them more leisurely at their offices in the U.S. Disarmament Mission at Geneva. I also met the principals of other key delegations, especially the Soviet Union, Sweden, France, the U.K., India, and Japan.

Public Education Campaign

In the campaign against nuclear testing and on behalf of peace initiatives, SANE made increasing use of the mass media—especially full page advertisements—to educate the public on the issues and pressure national and world leaders. Doyle, Dane and Bernbach, our advertising agency, was one of the most creative at the time. (They masterminded the Avis car rental campaign—"We're #2, So We Try Harder" by appealing to the public's desire to side with the underdog.) They contributed their services in our continuing series of full-page advertisements. (We still had to pay the newspapers for space!) Between 1957 and 1964, we ran over thirty ads focusing attention on the issues. Banner headlines proclaimed:

"No Contamination Without Representation"
"Nuclear Bombs Can Destroy All Life"
"Of Candidates and Cranberries"
"An Open Letter to President Kennedy"
"Berlin: There Is an Alternative"
"Soviet Nuclear Tests, a Crime"
"Is This What It's Coming To?" (with the picture of a contaminated milk bottle)
"Mr. President, Help Us to Get Behind You"
"The Next Time Madness Strikes"
"Nuclear Tests Must End"

As world public opinion turned against testing, the U.S. and U.S.S.R. observed an unofficial moratorium for about 18 months. Following the Berlin Crisis and resumption of nuclear tests in 1961, however, SANE went back on the offensive. "It is never too late," we declared, "nor too unpatriotic to tell the President that he should postpone atmospheric tests until a test-ban treaty can be negotiated in Geneva." We organized student conferences and convened panels of scientists and other experts to voice their opposition. We called on the American people to bombard the President with letters, telegrams, and calls for an end to atomic and hydrogen weapons testing. In early February 1962, the heaviest mail on any single issue during the whole Kennedy Administration was received at the White House. Western Union called it "a flood," and the tide of telegrams against testing remained at the top of the list of citizens' concerns for sixteen weeks.

Dr. Spock Is Worried

SANE was always looking for new, visible personalities to add to our National Board or our National or International Advisory Committees. We did well and our National Board included such members of the cultural elite—a term not yet coined—as writer and psychoanalyst Erich Fromm, actor Robert Ryan, and TV personality Steve Allen. Our National and International Advisory Boards contained Bertrand Russell, Albert Schweitzer, Pablo Casals, Martin Luther King, Jr., and Harry Belafonte. We could always add new names and several persons suggested that we invite the Cleveland pediatrician, Benjamin Spock, author of the best-selling *Baby and Child Care*.

In 1960 someone at SANE approached Dr. Spock. His biographer, Lynn Z. Bloom, reproduced his original letter of refusal: "I am in agreement with (your) policy . . . I have no expert knowledge at all about the relationship between radiation and health. If I were to take any official part in the work of the Committee I think that many parents would assume 1) that I was, to some degree, an expert and 2) that as an expert I was alarmed by the present dangers of radiation. To put it another way: I have tried as parent educator to be non-alarmist, and I want to save my influence to use in areas in which I feel I have competence. To put it a third way: I'm always under pressure to participate actively or nominally in many children's causes. I have to limit myself strictly. I join the cause only if it is clear to me that it is one that will make appreciable use of my knowledge and experience. So you can see from my protesting I feel ashamed to turn you down, but I have to. I hope you . . . will forgive me."

We did forgive him and did not pursue him at that time. However, on January 15, 1962, I wrote Spock, still teaching at Western Reserve University in Cleveland, inquiring again whether he might become a national sponsor of SANE. I explained our mission in one sentence: "We were established in 1957 and have tried ever since to lead American public opinion in favor of an inspected ban on nuclear weapons tests and substantial steps toward disarmament." I enclosed some materials. I suggested that the "duties of a national sponsor are minimal, but you would be kept informed of the policies and program of the National Committee and will be consulted occasionally on special problems." I ended by indicating that "we would cherish your cooperation by becoming a national sponsor," pointing out the long column on the letterhead of "the company you would be keeping."

Two days later Spock responded to my letter: "I appreciate being invited to be a sponsor of SANE. I believe I was asked before. I am much in favor of what SANE is doing. But I do not wish to be listed because I think that some anxious parents will assume that as a physician I have expert knowledge on radiation and that I am alarmed about present levels from fallout."

This time I did not forgive Spock, and I did not file away his refusal, but kept it in my very active file—my head. How could I change his mind? Suddenly I realized that Albert Einstein faced the same dilemma that Spock faced. After Einstein received the Nobel Prize in physics in 1921, he asked himself: should I use my new fame only in my field of physics or should I transfer it to my deep concern for human affairs? I remember preaching about Einstein's dilemma in a sermon I delivered when I was minister of the Unitarian Church in Evanston in the 1950s.

I looked up that old sermon and found I had quoted Philipp Frank in his biography of Einstein:

> Einstein realized that the great fame that he had acquired placed a great responsibility upon him. He considered that it would be egotistic and conceited if he simply accepted the fact of his recognition and continued to work on his researches.
>
> He saw that the world was full of suffering and he thought he knew some causes. He also saw that there were many people who pointed out these causes, but were not heeded because they were not prominent figures. Einstein realized that he himself was now a person to whom the world listened, and consequently he felt it his duty to call attention to those sore spots and so help eradicate them.
>
> He did not think of working out a definite program; however, he did not feel within himself the calling to become a political, social, or religious reformer. He knew no more about such things than any other educated person. The advantage he possessed was that he could command public attention and he was a man who was not afraid, if necessary, to stake his reputation . . . It was always clear to him that anyone venturing to express his opinion about political or social questions must emerge from the cloistered halls of science into the turmoil of the market place, and he must expect to be opposed with all the weapons common to the market place. Einstein accepted this situation as self-evident and included in the bargain. He also realized that many of his political opponents would also become his scientific opponents . . .

In a week, actually on January 29, I replied to Spock's refusal. I began: "I must accept your opinion not to become a sponsor of SANE, but your reasons sent me to my books on Albert Einstein. I have not been able to find the passage in his own words, but his biographer, Philipp Frank, paraphrases what I remember Einstein somewhere put in his own words." Then I gave that long quotation in my letter.

I ended my letter to Spock this way: "If I may say so, I think there are some parallels here in your case. SANE is not primarily an anti-fallout organization. Our central theme is controlled and comprehensive disarmament, although we are concerned about fallout if atmospheric tests continue. But we desperately want and need leaders such as yourself 'to whom the world listens.'"

I sent this letter to Spock. Within a month, and I am sure due to influences beyond my letter (including a speech by President Kennedy trying to defend his resumption of tests), Spock wrote me on February 28: "As a result of a number of factors including your letter and the drift of events I have changed my mind and am ready to be listed as a sponsor of SANE."

I immediately responded, expressing delight that he had become a sponsor. I enclosed a form for sponsors to sign, "because we do business in New York State." And we did business quickly with Spock. On April 16—barely six weeks after Spock came aboard—the full-page advertisement appeared in the *New York Times*. Most of the page was devoted to a picture of Dr. Spock—dressed in a business suit—with a child. The heading of the page read: "Dr. Spock Is Worried." Then followed seven short paragraphs, boiled down from 4,000 words which Spock carefully wrote for the public service message.

This was the most successful public education ad SANE ever inserted. It cost $5,000 and soon reappeared in eighty papers and magazines around the world, all paid for by local SANE and other peace groups. Thousands of copies of the advertisement were reproduced and circulated.

By June, the public was so wrought up over nuclear testing and its potential harm on individual and family health, especially that of children, that columnist Drew Pearson wrote that President Kennedy's resumption of testing was the most unpopular thing he had ever done, "The nuclear letters are running about four to one against the President." In the autumn, we ran posters following up the Spock appeal in New York subways with a picture of a pregnant woman and the stark message: "1.25 million unborn children will be born dead or have some gross defect because of nuclear bomb-testing." It took another year for the test-ban treaty to be concluded. But Dr. Spock's public appeal, like that of Albert Einstein, Bertrand Russell, and Albert Schweitzer, must be regarded as a turning point in awakening the conscience of the world to the effects of nuclear testing and the imperative of ending the arms race.

Other Aftereffects

After the April ad appeared, SANE was identified with Spock and Spock with SANE. He increasingly became a part of our whole organization, speaking and also devoting himself to policy. Within a year after Spock identified with SANE he became co-chair of the organization with H. Stuart Hughes, a professor of history at Harvard University.

Norman Cousins by then was increasingly working with the Kennedy Administration on the test-ban treaty and he wanted to separate himself at least temporarily from the leadership of SANE. I watched with fascination as he acted as courier among President John F. Kennedy, Secretary Khrushchev, and Pope John XXIII. While relaying messages between Washington and Moscow, Cousins told the President that strontium-90 had been found in milk all over the world after the last round of Soviet and American tests and that the people wanted an end to nuclear testing. In the Soviet Union, he showed Khrushchev a copy of SANE's advertisement proclaiming "We Can Kill the Russians 360 Times Over . . . The Russians Can Kill Us only 160 Times Over . . . We're Ahead, Aren't We?" Clarence Pickett, the co-chair of SANE with Cousins, as the retired head of the American Friends Service Committee, felt it was time for him also to be supplanted.

Spock did his homework—on radioactive fallout, nuclear testing, and nuclear disarmament—and increasingly became a spokesperson for SANE. He traveled widely, delivering speeches—and raising funds for the organization. During the two years I remained as Executive Director of SANE, we worked closely and were involved in the some of the earliest protests against American military involvement in Vietnam. We were together in Rochester, N.Y., on the Saturday morning after President Kennedy was assassinated. By the time I left the staff of SANE in September 1964, the test-ban treaty was signed, ratified, and entered into force—and President Kennedy had died and been replaced by President Johnson.

34 BELGRADE (1961)

THE AMERICAN PEACE MOVEMENT

Homer delivered the following speech at a disarmament conference in Yugoslavia attended by representatives of non-aligned countries. It gives a panoramic overview of the American peace movement in the early 1960s, relations with the Kennedy Administration, and the forces arrayed against arms control and disarmament.

Is there indeed a peace movement in America? It is true that the signs of such a movement may not appear overwhelming to an outsider. The talk for several years by John Foster Dulles of massive retaliation and the immorality of neutrality, the U-2 incident, and the U.S.-aided invasion of Cuba all have tended to blur any image of a peace movement in America, for if there were a strong movement, these things could not have easily occurred.

There are other elements missing as one surveys—from a distance—peace efforts within the U.S. The two American citizens to be awarded the Nobel Peace Prize in the past decade have acted in an official capacity: Ralph Bunche (1950) with the U.N. and Gen. George C. Marshall (1953) with several departments of the U.S. Government. Also, no Americans have been prominent in large, international, nongovernmental peace conferences. Probably no single American individual or organization comes to mind when American work for peace is mentioned. There is nothing in the U.S. of the magnitude of the British Campaign for Nuclear Disarmament and, since the death of Albert Einstein in 1955, there is no prophetic American citizen capturing the attention of Bertrand Russell.

Is there, then, no peace movement in America? There is and, in addition, America's image in the world in the past decade in many ways has been distinctly positive. Some American missionaries have been engaged in nonsectarian service for decades and now there is the official U.S. Peace Corps. The U.S. has played host to the U.N. and has, by and large, supported it more consistently than any other major power. Further, after World War II, when it possessed a nuclear monopoly, the U.S. did not use it. Also nine out of every ten books published anywhere in the world today on disarmament are written by Americans. Finally, America has given huge amounts of economic and technical assistance to almost 100 nations, including nonaligned nations and without strings.

There are also some signs that the American peace movement itself is becoming visible outside the U.S. Americans have played a prominent part in the international congresses of the World Association for the U.N., the World Movement for World Government, and the Women's International League for Peace and Freedom, not to mention the series of Pugwash Conferences on Science and World Responsibility and the series of bilateral intellectual conferences between the U.S. and the U.S.S.R. The reputation of a few American peace leaders is beginning to circle the globe, such as editor Norman Cousins and scientist Linus Pauling. Other individual Americans, by their creativity and courage, have come into the world headlines, such as Albert Bigelow and his voyage of the *Golden Rule* and Earle Reynolds and his voyage of the *Phoenix*, both into the nuclear testing areas of the Pacific. Finally, several American peace organizations are known increasingly in many parts of the world, such as the Committee on Non-Violent Action which sponsored the San Francisco to Moscow Peace March and the National Committee for a Sane Nuclear Policy which has sponsored similar walks inside the U.S. and also inserted large advertisements into the American and European press against nuclear tests and related subjects.

The actual peace movement in the U.S. can first be discussed in terms of government, then in terms of private organizations, and next in terms of program. Finally I will mention several key problems facing the American peace movement in these crucial months ahead.

Before listing the more important private American peace organizations, let me record that, since September 1961, there is an official U.S. Arms Control and Disarmament Agency. The whole American government and especially the whole State Department is actively working to promote a peaceful foreign policy, but something more has been needed and when President Kennedy was running for office he said there was something wrong with a U.S. Defense Department spending at the rate of almost $50 billion a year and not even a half dozen specialists working in the whole field of disarmament. Last autumn such an official, partly separate governmental agency was created. Next year it will have a budget of $6 million; this is small enough, but already some able diplomats and scientists have been assigned to this department. It will itself undertake research on various aspects of disarmament and it will also ask qualified individuals or institutions to undertake certain research studies. In addition, the Department will have charge of the negotiations for the U.S. at the Geneva Disarmament Conference as it had charge of the negotiations since September on reaching a test-ban agreement.

Among the many nongovernmental peace organizations, one could first list the world affairs or foreign relations councils in many American cities. These are primarily educational in nature and are aided by the Foreign Policy Association located in New York. They focus community concern on a host of international issues, help the Institute for International Education in welcoming foreign students and visiting dignitaries, and in general relate Americans to a shrinking world, although these foreign relations councils seldom take positions on controversial issues.

The second category includes the general action organizations. There are three principal ones in America: AAUN, UWF, and SANE. Founded in 1945 as an outgrowth of the League of Nations Association, the American Association for the United Nations (AAUN) does an important educational task on the U.N. within the U.S. and acts in crisis situations, such as currently urging the passage of the $100 million U.N. bond issue now before the U.S. Congress. Mrs. Eleanor Roosevelt is one leader of the AAUN which has offices in principal American cities and has a wide individual membership.

The United World Federalists (UWF) is a more specialized group, being concerned with world government. Fifteen years old, it has about 100 chapters and is part of the World Movement for World Government.

The National Committee for a Sane Nuclear Policy (SANE) is much younger, being founded in 1957. Today it has 125 local chapters from Massachusetts to California. The purpose of SANE is to stop all nuclear weapons tests and to obtain general and complete disarmament, at the same time strengthening the U.N. in order to keep the peace in a disarmed world. Norman Cousins, editor of the *Saturday Review*, is co-chairman of SANE, with Clarence Pickett, who received the Nobel Peace Prize on behalf of the American Friends Service Committee, also as co-chairman.

A third category is specialized nongovernmental organizations. The Committee on Non-Violent Action (CNVA) uses Gandhian techniques to oppose nuclear tests and war. The War Resisters League (WRL) consists of those Americans who refuse to participate in war and enter conscientious objectors' camps or prison rather than join the U.S. Army. The Federation of American Scientists (FAS) influences American policy in Washington and Albert Einstein was one of its early sponsors. The Society for the Social Responsibility of Science (SSRS) is composed of scientists who refuse to work in laboratories doing research directly connected with war. The Women's International League for Peace and Freedom (WILPF) consists of women who have worked for peace for decades and two of its leaders have received the Nobel Peace Prize in another decade for their activity.

A fourth category includes religious-related organizations. The Quakers are most active through the American Friends Service Committee. They have a world-wide program, but also a strong peace education program in thirteen centers in the U.S. Other Protestant groups, especially the Methodists, have strong peace action, and the Catholics and Jews have smaller peace societies. Religious pacifists are banded together as the Fellowship of Reconciliation (FOR) which has had an important program since the First World War.

A final category of nongovernmental organizations for peace is a new grouping called Turn Toward Peace. This consists of some twenty-five cooperating and communicating organizations which have united on specific peace action. Its most successful activity was a youth mobilization for two days in mid-February in front of the White House in Washington with about 5,000 students.

Quite apart from organizations for peace, there is research for disarmament and peace in America. For years such research was confined to a small group of pacifist professors. Then the RAND Corporation, a research agency financed by the U.S. Air Force, launched major studies on arms control. Suddenly several dozen universities held seminars on disarmament and research in this field became very popular. In 1960 the Peace Research Institute was started in Washington as an outgrowth of a study of the needs for peace research made by the International Institute for World Order. For years, the AAUN sponsored the Commission for the Study of Peace and the Carnegie Endowment has financed research on international issues. Also, the U.S. Arms Control and Disarmament Agency is increasing the speed and area of disarmament research. All this research is available through an increasing number of pamphlets, periodicals, and books. Among the periodicals are the *Bulletin of the Atomic Scientists* and the *Journal of Conflict Resolution.*

Let me now turn to the program for peace pursued by a number of these organizations. I will confine my remarks to SANE, which I know best, but in any case maintains a wide program.

First is education. There is a wide educational program through the sponsorship of public lectures in many cities, radio and TV programs on disarmament and related subjects, and publications. We publish a newsletter, *SANE World,* twice a month, and probably a pamphlet once every two months. Also we insert often full-page advertisements into prominent American newspapers on urgent topics. Our last was in mid-January urging President Kennedy not to resume nuclear tests in the atmosphere.

A second aspect of program is political action. Our committee has an office and a political action director in Washington. He frequently confers with members of the Kennedy Administration and with members of both houses of the Congress. He relates this information to our 125 local committees. Recently we launched an effort to send telegrams to the White House against atmospheric tests. More than 10,000 telegrams on this issue reached President Kennedy on a single weekend, and the proportion was 50-1 against resumption of tests.

A third kind of program is contained in the word "demonstrations." While best known are the Aldermaston marches of the Campaign for Nuclear Disarmament in England, we in America on the Saturday before Easter for several years have sponsored large peace parades in major cities.

Fourth is observing the proceedings of the U.N. in New York, especially on disarmament. Almost daily my colleagues and I visit the U.N. headquarters to listen to disarmament debates and talk to delegates or members of the secretariat. Occasionally we have visited Geneva to observe the test-ban negotiations and no doubt will observe the general disarmament talks in Geneva. Fifth is international liaison. We have close relations with groups throughout Europe, Russia, and the West.

Finally, let me discuss some problems facing the American

peace movement which may be of interest to you.

First, we constantly discuss whether the peace organizations should cater to the mass of the American people or the American elite. Should these organizations have a program for thousands of members or should they be directed primarily for a small group of intellectuals who can significantly influence official policy in Washington? Most of the American peace organizations have decided to try to do both, but no organization has done either very well. For example, no single American peace organization consists of hundreds of thousands of persons, although together all of American peace organizations may enroll a million participants.

Secondly, we constantly discuss whether the peace organizations should be crisis-oriented or confine their study and action to longer-term international issues. Should they deal with a Berlin crisis or a Geneva test-ban crisis or should they deal with the ebb and flow, for example, of U.S.-U.S.S.R. relations? Again, many of the organizations have tried to do both: to set a course of longtime education on longtime problems, but not ignore a current flashpoint, be it a Suez or a Congo.

Thirdly, we constantly discuss how the peace organizations should both cooperate with the U.S. Government and oppose it. For example, should we endorse the U.S. resumption of underground tests or should we oppose these tests—and how? In general, ours turn out to be non-aligned peace organizations within a very much aligned nation. There are many actions in the field of international relations of our U.S. Government which we can and have enthusiastically endorsed. Let me name just a few in the past year: the creation of the new U.S. Arms Control and Disarmament Agency, President Kennedy's policy of putting the U.S. on record for complete and general disarmament, and the vigorous pursuit by the Kennedy Administration of a test-ban agreement in Geneva.

On the other hand, many of our groups do not hesitate to make informed criticisms of our U.S. Government policy when we feel it to be wrong. Let me also name a few such policies which we have opposed during the past year: We strongly protested the resumption of American nuclear tests, even underground, even after the Russians first broke the three-year moratorium. We strongly protested the emphasis of the Kennedy Administration on civil defense and fallout shelters. We protested certain votes of the Kennedy Administration on disarmament issues during the last session of the U.N. General Assembly.

Before concluding, I must say a word about those forces within the U.S. opposing the American peace movement. They are better known and need no extensive description. First, the "military-industrial complex," a phrase not from Karl Marx, but Dwight Eisenhower, used in his Farewell Address to the American people on leaving office. President Kennedy has reaffirmed the existence of this combination of the military, industry, and science which depends upon a huge military budget and cannot contemplate substantial reductions. This is not saying, as one could say in the 1920s and 1930s, that a small group of capitalists wanted profits and thus manipulated the world toward war. Rather the whole fabric of U.S. society is tied to a huge military budget and there is a big economic problem to convert the economy to peace without affecting the military, some industry, and much science.

Second, the radical right also opposes the American peace movement. There are the extreme reactionaries. They are not quite fascists, but the next thing. They constitute the John Birch Society and other groups. They call Dwight Eisenhower a communist. Their slogan is "Better Dead Than Red."

Third, a group of intellectuals, some of whom were formerly American communists, but who are now bitterly anti-communist. They feel there cannot be an American détente with Russia because of Russia's determination to make the whole world communist, by force if necessary.

Fourth, a group of members of the U.S. Congress who are provincial and cannot comprehend a world under disarmament and law. Most of the U.S. Congress is more conservative than either Presidents Eisenhower or Kennedy in wanting peace.

How to assess the strength of these groups vis-a-vis the American peace forces? They are much stronger, yet the peace forces have achieved some recent victories: 1) U.S. policy toward colonialism is changing, such as the U.N. vote against Portugal on Angola; 2) establishment of the U.S. Arms Control and Disarmament Agency in the midst of the Berlin crisis; and 3) restraint of the Kennedy Administration not to test atomic weapons in the atmosphere.

I suppose our greatest weapon against the anti-peace forces in the U.S., as elsewhere, is the truth about modern war. Wars may have solved some problems in the past, but not today. The truth, acknowledged universally today except perhaps by the Chinese, is that nobody can win an atomic war.

35 LAMBARENE
(1962)

FINAL VISIT WITH ALBERT SCHWEITZER

In the course of a visit to Africa to attend a disarmament assembly in Ghana, in July 1962, Homer traveled to Lambaréné for his fourth and final visit to Dr. Schweitzer. In the five years since their last meeting, Schweitzer had spoken out publicly against nuclear testing and—in between supervising new construction at his hospital—had become an expert on thorny arms control and disarmament issues. Homer's account of the journey originally appeared in the Christian Century. *(Chapter 38 details Schweitzer's evolution into a peace activist, his famous Declaration of Conscience, and his efforts to influence President Kennedy and his administration.)*

Now into the second half of his eighty-seventh year, Albert Schweitzer is on the eve of the fiftieth anniversary of the establishment of his hospital at Lambaréné, in Gabon. He has seen many changes through his half-century in the African continent, never more so than in recent years. The fears of the French settlers for the future of Gabon proved groundless when independence came peacefully to the nation in August 1960. So fully has Lambaréné taken to life in the new republic that one of its African residents is now a Gabonese representative at the United Nations.

To Dr. Schweitzer's hospital independence has meant that mail arrives less frequently and that red tape is more extensive. Otherwise life goes on much as heretofore. Leon Mba, president of the republic, has paid two visits to the hospital and bestowed a high decoration on the jungle doctor, who has since seen a new postage stamp issued in his honor. Though Dr. Schweitzer accepts the quick turn African events are taking, he laments the woeful extent to which most of the newly independent nations are still financially dependent on the former colonial powers.

Modern Techniques Arrive

Even before independence, the modern world had begun to impinge on Albert Schweitzer and his hospital. Though he has never been slow to make use of new drugs and other healing techniques, modern innovations have come more rapidly in recent years: portable X-ray equipment, a new electric blood-count machine, a completely equipped dental clinic. New techniques are being adopted, too, as medical specialists from around the world visit the hospital, talk with the staff, and continue to send advice by mail after they have returned home. The winds of change have also affected the lives of the patients. Today accidents are likely to be caused by auto traffic rather than by charging elephants. Though most of the patients still arrive at the hospital after several days' journey by river canoe, many now come by truck, some from as far away as Libreville, the capital, and one recently arrived by plane. And there have been personal changes for the doctor; from the desk in his study-bedroom he can look out at the new grave of his wife, Helene, who died in June 1957. It is marked by a crude concrete cross with a black hand-lettered inscription and is next to that of Emma Haussknecht, Schweitzer's longtime helper, who died a year earlier.

Though he still does not have an outboard motor—unlike many Africans who have attached them to their dugout canoes—Dr. Schweitzer recently acquired a large truck and a jeep. Use of such new means of transport has become possible with the building of a road from the hospital to the Libreville-Brazzaville highway. The need for a road arose when France's withdrawal from Asia made it impossible for her colonies to obtain rice cheaply. Since the plantain and manioc chosen to supplant rice in the patients' diets were unobtainable in sufficient quantity along the Ogowe river, the hospital staff could find them only through foraging by truck. Hence the road.

All last summer Schweitzer was at work personally supervising construction of a concrete bridge on the road leading to the highway. It was only five meters high and eight meters from end to end, but months of devoted labor went into its creation. The doctor had hoped to get away last August for a visit to Europe, where he has not been since December 1959, but he stayed on to see the bridge completed. A visit this summer is evidently out, too; again construction has intervened: a new operating theater, for which the concrete foundation has already been poured, and a guest house.

On the Monday morning of my visit, Dr. Schweitzer arose at his usual early hour and worked for some time on his voluminous correspondence; one particular task that morning was to compose a letter of thanks to be sent to a dancing school which had given a recital and sent the proceeds to the hospital. When the breakfast gong sounded at 7:30, he and his present helper, Mlle Matilda, went to the dining room. There he sat down at a table opposite Rhena, his only child. Wife of an organ builder in France and mother of four children, Rhena is spending the summer at the hospital as a laboratory technician.

A Foreman's Morning Work

At 8 o'clock the African workers gathered in the courtyard outside Schweitzer's room to be assigned their tasks for the day. Then the doctor put on his cheesecloth-covered helmet and walked with fifteen of the men to several piles of rock ready to be cleaned of dirt, chipped into shape, and sorted for use as a foundation of the planned guest house. Though two foremen were on hand—one a veteran French pastor who had been at the hospital for years, the other a University of Arkansas student working at Lambaréné for the summer—Schweitzer did not hesitate to supervise the work unceasingly. From time to time he reached into his pocket to hand out bits of food: grains of rice from a small white bag for a chicken, bread crusts for a pet monkey, a pregnant goat, and a tiny African boy watching the proceedings with wide and wondering eyes. He kept steadily at this foreman's work until noon—except for a ten-minute break at midpoint and a brief detour in his study to show me copies of two manuscripts (in German) on disarmament problems which he had just sent off to publications in Russia and Japan.

Though he no longer practices medicine or performs operations, Dr. Schweitzer keeps a close watch on the administration of the hospital. In the afternoons he is usually to be found at his little desk in the corner of the pharmacy near the long queues of African patients waiting to receive their medicines. In an average week, the hospital serves about 400 patients, the out-patient clinic about 300. The adjacent leper colony has some 160 permanent residents.

Dr. Schweitzer spends so much time supervising construction work about the grounds or observing hospital proceedings from his desk at the pharmacy that he apparently has little time left for progress on the several manuscripts he has promised to prepare. Nor does he devote time to the music which formerly occupied his spare moments. When his son-in-law visited Lambaréné recently the doctor asked him to crate and ship to his home in Günsbach, France, the piano, equipped with pedal attachments and a zinc lining to protect it from white ants, which the Paris Bach Society presented to him many years ago. He does, however, take his place at the battered piano in the dining room each evening to play the accompaniment for the hymns which form part of the brief after-supper worship service. Each Saturday evening there is a concert provided by a battery-run record player.

Lest Atomic War Come

With an Austrian nurse as interpreter, Dr. Schweitzer spent two hours one afternoon talking with me about disarmament and international affairs. It was obvious at once that he follows international events closely. He promulgated what he called political heresies, pointing out with a laugh that they can match only his theological heresies. But he is loath to voice his heresies in public—at least in large quantity. Occasionally, on request, he writes articles dealing with issues of peace and war. When I asked if several of the manuscripts he has prepared recently might be published as a collection in the United States, he replied indignantly that as a physician he "mixes his own poison" and knows just what dose should be given each nation separately!

Schweitzer is deeply concerned because members of parliaments throughout the world seem reluctant to debate significant international issues, and he has a similar indictment for the world's press. He is pessimistic about the possibility that the churches might help prevent future war, believing mainly in the working of the spirit of Jesus through individual men. Some months ago, he consented to become an honorary member of the Unitarian Church of the Larger Fellowship. That action brought down on his head attacks by Continental churchmen, but he remains firm in the faith of his Alsatian fathers.

Writing on the failure of recent disarmament negotiations for *Yomiuri*, a Tokyo publication, Dr. Schweitzer saw hardly any hope that negotiations will ever bring about renunciation of atomic weapons. "The question of confidence among the negotiators and rulers has not been solved," he wrote. "All important political agreements presuppose the existence of mutual confidence guaranteed by something moral among those who conclude agreements and those who govern their countries. Only if we give ourselves up to the spirit of humanity, what used to be impossible will become possible."

On a visit several years ago, I had asked Dr. Schweitzer what the average person can do to prevent war. He replied that "one can bark out against atomic tests and atomic war like a dog in the African night." This time, when I asked the same question, he declared that barking out is not enough. "It is not enough to talk," he said. "One must bite like a dog in the African night. And two-legged dogs—men—*can* bite. Men must act, not merely talk. These remain dangerous times. The possibility that atomic war may break out is not as small as people are inclined to think. The possibility is great. By some carelessness, by some error, by some misunderstanding, by some accident, some contingency, the world may stumble into atomic war."

36 MOSCOW (1962)

A HERETIC IN THE KREMLIN

In 1962, Homer traveled to Moscow to present a major statement to the world capital of communism on behalf of a cross-section of American peace activists. "[T]o most of those in his audience," noted New York Post *columnist James A. Wechsler, "he was reciting an almost unbearable anti-Communist heresy." Accompanying Homer was Erich Fromm, the psychoanalyst and writer. In addition to describing this controversial speech in the Kremlin, Homer gives a profile of Fromm and a brief account of a visit to the grave of the censored Russian poet Boris Pasternak, author of* Dr. Zhivago.

In many ways, Erich Fromm was a universal man. He contributed genius to the wide range of activities he touched. Fromm, who maintained an apartment in New York, was among the intellectuals who founded SANE. In fact, Fromm made an essential contribution to the new group by suggesting the name, SANE. This was not an acronym—a word formed by initial letters. SANE was simply the adjective Fromm felt best described rational opposition to the atomic arms race.

Fromm's contribution came two years after he published his book, *The Sane Society.* Although Fromm in that volume expressed what he felt about the atomic arms race, it was not primarily about nuclear disarmament. In it he did declare that "our dangers are war and robotism" and "the first condition is the abolishment of the war threat hanging over all of us."

Fromm was a member of the inner circle of strategists in

SANE from early 1957 until at least the Partial Test-Ban Treaty was completed in 1963. He was listed as a sponsor, but his role was greater. He contributed many shrewd insights, especially at policy meetings in the apartment of Lenore Marshall in the Dorset Hotel in mid-Manhattan. He also lent his increasingly prestigious name to the national SANE advertisements.

Of the many contributions Fromm made to disarmament in this period, one was the essay he wrote in 1960-61 on unilateral disarmament. This was published in an issue of *Daedelus* devoted to arms control and then included in the well-known volume, *Arms Control Disarmament, and National Security* edited by Donald G. Brennan. This 11-page chapter went beyond some of the seminal writings in the field. Fromm discussed both graduated and complete unilateral disarmament. He asserted that "taking seriously the reasoning which supports the unpopular position of complete unilateral disarmament can open up new approaches and viewpoints which are important even if our practical aim is that of graduated unilateral action or even only that of negotiated bilateral disarmament." Fromm concluded that "it is imperative to shake off the inertia of our accustomed thinking, to seek for new approaches to the problem, and above all to see new alternatives to the present choices that confront us."

Mission to Moscow

The major contribution of Fromm to disarmament in this period was a Mission to Moscow in order to present a statement to the World Peace Council (WPC) on behalf of a group of American peace activists. The latter believed strongly in disarmament, but held the U.S.S.R. and the U.S.A. both culpable for the rising potential of nuclear holocaust. The energetic action of Erich Fromm on this trip demonstrates, even today, many of his qualities.

The WPC was founded in 1949. By 1961-62 few sophisticated world citizens had doubts about its ideological bias. WPC was an uncritical, well-financed creation of Moscow foreign policy. Yet there were always non-communist individuals who gravitated to its world congresses and other events. When the WPC announced that a World Congress on Peace and Disarmament would be held in Moscow in July 1962, the divided receptivity within the non-communist peace movement around the world was predictable. The WPC early found well-known sponsors for its Congresses: Martin

Niemöller, Bertrand Russell, and Albert Schweitzer. On the other hand, such American organizations as SANE and the American Friends Service Committee refused to endorse the Congress or send official delegates.

Professor J. D. Bernal, a distinguished British scientist and communist, was President of the WPC. He visited the United States in the spring of 1962, partly to deliver some lectures at Yale University. During that trip he came to my home in Scarsdale to meet with a group of U.S. peace leaders, including Norman Thomas and A. J. Muste. Prof. Bernal pled with us to send representatives to the Moscow Congress. He said that he wanted participants who were known independents, including social democrats. He pledged that several representatives from an independent group of Americans could attend as his personal guests and they would be invited to make a joint statement to the Congress from the podium.

Several weeks later it was decided that Erich Fromm and I would attend the Congress, on the basis indicated by Prof. Bernal. We would pay our own travel expenses and go as individuals, but represent a larger group of America peace leaders. In the meantime, the controversy continued about the advisability of Western peace leaders to attend. Prof. Linus Pauling, also a sponsor of SANE, publicly criticized the organization for not sending an official delegation to Moscow. The WPC inserted its own advertisement in the *New York Times*, urging "all American friends of peace" to come to Moscow. During this period the sponsors of the Mission met in New York to plan strategy and the outline of the joint statement.

Early in July, I met with Fromm, who was living at the time in Paris. Over several days we polished the statement. Fearing a breakdown in Prof. Bernal's commitment that we would be able to deliver the statement, and that it would be translated like others into several languages, we hurriedly had ours translated into at least Russian and the other languages. During this period, Fromm proved to be a hard worker and tried to anticipate all contingencies. I took the multiple copies to Moscow by airplane, while Fromm, normally not travelling by air, took a train to Moscow, via Berlin, accompanied by his wife.

In Moscow, we found ourselves two among almost 2,500 Congress participants, including 110 Americans who were "more concerned about peace than ideology." In this environment, Fromm worked incessantly in many informal meetings, in the hotel and elsewhere, and around the formal meetings held in the Palace of Congresses in the Kremlin.

When it came our turn to deliver a message, Fromm asked me to take the podium and speak for both of us. Prof. Bernal was as good as his word. We were given "prime time" at a plenary meeting, if not at the same one as Nikita Khrushchev. Copies of our address were circulated in the several conference languages.

The Statement

The nine-page, 54-paragraph declaration to the World Congress was a joint composition. Many of the fourteen signers contributed insights to it, and these especially included those of Fromm.

The preamble began by indicating why Fromm and I attended as individuals and not as representatives of any American peace organization. We admitted that we shared with the WPC the conviction that nuclear war would be an "unprecedented disaster." We asserted that "every sane person knows the utter folly of war." We pointed out that "here in the Soviet Union, we sense the strong desire for peace." We demonstrated that all relationships between the U.S.S.R. and the U.S.A. were not negative. Yet there existed "a threatening side," the resumption of nuclear testing, the stalemate in the disarmament negotiations, and the sharpening crises at political trouble spots on four continents.

Then we turned to a controversial section on communications among the peace movements in different countries. We suggested that we would "speak with compete frankness," and "without any feeling of antagonism or hostility toward anyone." We then expressed happiness in there being a "strong peace movement in the Soviet bloc countries." But we noted a "basic difference" between the peace movements in the U.S.A. and the WPC. We stated that U.S. peace organizations "openly criticize and oppose policies of our own government with which we do not agree." Moreover, "we try to use the same criteria and principles in judging all governments." We tried to maintain a single standard of judgment.

Our statement continued by condemning both American and Soviet nuclear weapon tests. We did "not look for the approval of our government first and only then come out for peace." We felt that the basic difference between communist peace movements and American peace movements was that one speaks *to* its government while the other speaks *for* government. We concluded this section pointing out a decisive difference: "The peace organizations of the Soviet bloc espouse the policies of their governments, whether these

292

policies happen to be developing greater bombs or calling for disarmament." We said that peace organizations of the WPC and those in non-communist countries "must not use the peace issue as a propaganda slogan and thus make it suspect and frustrate the longing for peace which is shared by all peoples of the earth."

This was strong fare for delegates to hear—in several languages simultaneously. The leaders of the WPC had heard it many times previously, but to many present, the questioning of the independence of the WPC must have been novel, coming as it did from the podium within the Kremlin.

We turned then to the second preliminary section and discussed the main factors preventing disarmament. We criticized both superpowers, for using disarmament negotiations for propaganda, for putting their "own ideology first and disarmament second." We then examined the slow progress in reaching general and complete disarmament and the differences in the current Soviet and American blueprints. We discussed the slow progress toward a test-ban treaty. When I declared that the WPC "has raised its voice, as we have done, against the [current] American nuclear weapons tests," there was much applause. When this subsided, I then asked, "Will the WCP also join us in speaking out unequivocally against the forthcoming Soviet tests?" Now there was stony silence, almost hissing.

Then came a section on "initiatives toward disarmament," largely written by Fromm. The statement indicated that "even if there is no immediate reciprocation, the steps should nevertheless continue." At least initiatives could reduce suspicion of a nation's motives and—as Fromm often insisted—"strengthen the internal power position of the 'moderates' in each bloc." We also suggested that the "way in which the Non-Aligned countries conduct themselves is crucial." This was less than a year after the non-aligned movement itself began with its first Summit in Belgrade in September 1961.

In the final section we discussed the interdependence of disarmament and political settlements. We expressed "misgivings" about post-war developments in Eastern Europe. We again took a leaf from Fromm's thinking and writing in asserting that "the arms race cannot be ended unless both sides are willing to accept the frontiers that have arisen as a result of World War II." We urged that the Oder-Neisse line be recognized as "definite." We also called for the seating of Beijing in the U.N. and that China be brought into "active disarmament negotiations." (The Chinese were still participating at the time in the WPC, but later withdrew.) Finally, we again expressed our "sense of appreciation" for the opportunity to present these views at length to the Congress."

The twelve other signers were William C. Davidon, Robert Gilmore, Alfred Hassler, Sidney Lens, Stewart Meacham, Seymour Melman, A. J. Muste, David Riesman, J. David Singer, Emily Parker Simon, Harold Taylor, and Norman Thomas. Norman Cousins, usually associated with this group of peace leaders at the time, was conspicuously absent, since he was already involved with Nikita Khrushchev, President Kennedy, and Pope John XXIII in efforts which culminated in the Partial Test-Ban Treaty signed and ratified the following year.

A Visit to Pasternak's Grave

During my sojourn in Moscow, I undertook several non-Congress activities. One was to participate in a brief demonstration against all new nuclear weapons tests, both Soviet and American. (It lasted less than 60 seconds before broken up by the authorities!) Also I decided to visit the grave of Boris Pasternak. He had been dead only a couple of years and it seemed that this was another period of relative relaxation in the Soviet Union. Thus, during some of the social affairs connected with the conference, I tentatively and discreetly asked several of my interpreters if perhaps I could visit Pasternak's grave. Each to whom I individually put the question answered, "And why not?" I was told that Pasternak had lived just outside Moscow, in the writers' colony of Peredelkino, and that he is buried there. One of my interpreters told me that if I went to the Kievski railroad station, I could reach Peredelkino by suburban train in half an hour. He even wrote out the word, *Peredelkino*, for me on a slip of paper in Cyrillic script, for I hardly knew two words of Russian.

One morning, after the conference had adjourned, I began my journey to Peredelkino. Grasping the slip of paper in my hand, I found a bus to the Kievski station. I was helped to buy a round-trip ticket and was taken to the correct train platform. I even had time to buy a Soviet ice cream pie! Soon the train started. We left the railroad yards, passed the skyscraper University of Moscow, and soon reached open fields and pine woods. In less than thirty minutes my solicitous fellow travelers told me that we had reached Peredelkino.

Here, I realized that, after Pasternak had been announced as the Nobel Prize winner for literature, his fellow writers in this town obediently wrote Mr. Khrushchev: "We cannot continue to breathe the same air as Pasternak." On the station platform, I suddenly realized that I still had the task of locating Pasternak's grave. Then I noticed two young men in their early twenties who had also alighted from the Moscow train. I asked if they spoke English, and they replied in unison: "Can we help you?" I told them my mission, and they said that they would be glad to take me to the town cemetery and find the grave, which they themselves had never visited.

The three of us walked down the dirt road, just below the station, toward the cemetery. Suddenly one of the men turned to me, stopped and asked, "Do you dig Ginsberg?" I had to shift my thoughts quickly, and realized that I was being asked about the American beat poet, Allen Ginsberg. As a matter of fact, I didn't "dig" Pasternak very well, let alone Ginsberg, and I had difficulty parrying their question. Somehow I managed to bring the conversation at least back to Pasternak.

My Soviet friends told me that they read Pasternak's poetry and translations, freely available in the bookstores and libraries. One of the men told me that he had read *Dr. Zhivago* in English.

By this time we had reached the cemetery. With the help of two old grave diggers, and after several false turns, we reached three tall pine trees at one edge of the graveyard. There was the grave, with a plain black marble marker: "Boris Pasternak, 1890-1960."

I thanked my guides and erstwhile beatnik poets, and they disappeared. I then realized that I had forgotten to buy flowers at the railroad station to decorate the grave. Instead, I went to a nearby open field and gathered an international bouquet of bluebells and Queen Anne's lace. I put them in a small vase at one side of the marker. As I did so, a visitor—a woman—arrived. She bent low over the grave, crossed herself, and then departed as quietly as she arrived.

Soon I left the plot and made my way back to Moscow. On the train back, I suddenly no longer felt sad about Pasternak. He was, it is true, not allowed by Mr. Khrushchev to accept the Nobel Prize in literature. He died almost as he once predicted to a reporter: "I am an old man; the worst that can happen to me would be death." In an important sense, however, Pasternak has triumphed—the Communists call it being rehabilitated. His poetry and translations of the classics are increasingly being read by the Soviet people. Pasternak's hope—for a general relaxation, and for an end to terror—was ' lowly being realized only shortly after his death.

In the novel *Dr. Zhivago*, Pasternak wrote that after Dr. Zhivago died, his friends still had hope. Pasternak further wrote: "Although the enlightenment and liberalization which had been expected to come after the war had not come with victory, a presage of freedom was in the air throughout these post-war years, and it was their only historical meaning."

In this visit to the Soviet Union I found the presage of freedom in the Soviet air, although two decades after Boris Pasternak had hoped. But it was and is in the Soviet Union and with it a growing appreciation, not only of Pasternak's prophetic writings, but a likelihood of a firmer détente between the Soviet Union and the West.

37 GENEVA (1963)

THE TEST BAN:
JFK'S GREATEST LEGACY

In the aftermath of the Cuban Missile Crisis and the deepening Sino-Soviet split, the 100 days from June 11 to September 21, 1963, saw the climatic breakthrough between America and Russia on a treaty to ban nuclear testing in the atmosphere. From his pulpit and through SANE and other organizations, Homer had been mobilizing public support against atomic and hydrogen testing for nearly a decade, and he flew to Moscow for the signing of the treaty on August 5. The euphoria of the agreement was marred shortly thereafter by the tragic death of President Kennedy in November. Here is Homer's account of these historic events drawn from articles and speeches of the time.

In late May and early June, it appeared to be just another summer. The Cold War continued, the promise of progress in lessening world tensions after the Cuban Missile Crisis had not materialized, and about the only achievement was the Hot Line between Moscow and Washington. Diplomats, journalists, and concerned citizens anticipated a quiet summer and planned accordingly.

A further disarray in both Cold War blocs was about the only anticipation for the summer. The communists were at each other's throats, and the disarray in the West was growing also. No longer were the Chinese denouncing the Yugoslavs when they really meant the Russians; they forgot the amenities in the communist family. No longer were the Russians denouncing the Albanians

297

when they meant the Chinese; they, too, ignored this fiction. In the West, President Charles de Gaulle of France was strictly alone and Chancellor Konrad Adenaueur of Germany in his last months of power wavered between de Gaulle and President John Kennedy. Italy was politically unstable and the Profumo scandal in Britain made the coming to power of Labor closer. A pro-American was elected prime minister of Canada, but American-Canadian tensions had not completely healed. In Latin America, the front against Castro was hard for the U.S. to hold.

Then on June 10, President Kennedy gave a commencement address at American University in Washington, D.C. Only on the eve of the talk did news leak out that this might be "something special." Indeed, the address turned out to be a clarion call for a new beginning in U.S.-U.S.S.R. relations. The speech may be remembered by history as heralding the end of the Cold War just as Winston Churchill's speech at another American institution of higher education, Westminster College, in Fulton, Missouri, signaled its beginning.

I have chosen this time and this place to discuss a topic on which too often ignorance abounds and the truth is too rarely perceived—yet it is the most important topic on earth: world peace . . . . I speak of peace because of the new face of war . . . in an age when a single nuclear weapon contains almost ten times the explosive force delivered by all of the allied air forces in the Second World War . . . an age when the deadly poisons produced by a nuclear exchange would be carried by wind and water and soil and seed to the far corners of the globe and to generations yet unborn. . . . I speak of peace, therefore, as the necessary rational end of rational men.

Some say that it is useless to speak of world peace or world law or world disarmament—and that it will be useless until the leaders of the Soviet Union adopt a more enlightened attitude. I hope they do. But I also believe that we must reexamine our own attitude—as individuals and as a Nation—for our attitude is as essential as theirs. . . . In the final analysis, our most basic common link is that we all inhabit this small planet. We all breathe the same air. We all cherish our children's future. And we are all mortal.

President Kennedy's address was some months in the making. He, as some other Western leaders, was frustrated because no progress was forthcoming from the Soviets in the one area of longest negotiations: the test-ban talks in Geneva. Despite the genuine misunderstanding over the number of on-site inspections, Premier Khrushchev would not move and a test-ban treaty appeared less likely in April than in January. Norman Cousins, at this time, was serving as an unofficial intermediary between the superpowers, shuttling between the White House and the Soviet Premier's dacha on the Black Sea. There appeared signs on the horizon that the deepening split between the communist giants would be healed. In a meeting with the President at the end of April, Cousins urged JFK to speak out before the Central Committee of the Soviet Communist Party held its annual meeting in mid-June. "The moment is now at hand for the most important speech of your Presidency . . . in its breathtaking proposals for genuine peace, in its tone of friendliness for the Soviet people, and its understanding of their ordeal during the last war," Cousins advised. President Kennedy was determined to offer Mr. Khrushchev a new deal, and Prime Minister Macmillan, for more domestic political reasons, also wanted to offer Mr. Khrushchev a new venue for test-ban negotiations. Following his speech, the President announced that Premier Khrushchev had invited the U.S. and U.K. to discuss a comprehensive test ban in Moscow and that the U.S. would not begin a new round of atmospheric tests. "We will not be the first to resume," Kennedy declared. This voluntary moratorium was especially surprising as the U.S.S.R. had conducted two recent series of atmospheric tests and the U.S. had matched the Russian explosions with only one series of its own.

Four days after President Kennedy's speech, the Chinese released their now famous letter to the Russians. They even distributed it widely, if surreptitiously, inside the Soviet Union, much to the embarrassment of the Soviet leadership. Here was a documented, lengthy challenge to "certain persons"—meaning Khrushchev—who were no longer walking the orthodox Marxist-Leninist pathway to world revolution.

In late June, President Kennedy went to Europe and, in West Germany and Berlin, almost undid everything he started at American University. Almost, but not quite, for also in Europe he realized that the MLF—multilateral force—was at least temporarily unacceptable to the British and Italians. He shelved, if not buried, the MLF. This, too, helped the U.S.-U.S.S.R. climate.

Also in June, Harold Wilson, new head of the British Labor Party, visited Moscow and talked to Mr. Khrushchev, as earlier he had visited Washington to talk to Mr. Kennedy. What Mr. Wilson said on leaving Moscow was hard for many observers to believe: Mr. K. was withdrawing his "two or three on-site inspections," but would settle for a more limited test-ban treaty. (For years, the Soviet Union had refused to consider any treaty which allowed underground tests to continue.) Wilson's words were discounted as being the imprecise reporting of an aspiring prime minister. Yet on July 2 in East Berlin, Mr. Khrushchev asserted that he was indeed interested in a limited test-ban treaty, although he suggested that he would like to see a non-aggression pact signed simultaneously.

Hopes for success of the mid-July talks in Moscow rose, doubly so with the release of the Soviet Communist Party's answer to the Chinese letter. The Sino-Soviet split, replete with broken windows at the Chinese Embassy in Moscow, was real and perhaps Khrushchev would hesitate no longer in making a beginning of a détente with the West.

On July 5 the long-awaited Sino-Soviet negotiations opened in the Lenin Hills just outside Moscow. Nobody predicted success, and some predicted that the talks would never be held. They did open, but in gloom and with much bickering in both the Moscow and Beijing Press. Mr. Khrushchev paid the talks scant attention. On the final day—July 20—he ate curry with China's enemy, India, at an Indian trade fair in Moscow, but he also held a feast for the departing Chinese before they sped to Beijing where they were warmly received by Mao Zedong at the airport.

In the meantime, Secretary W. Averell Harriman and Lord Hailsham arrived for the July 15 opening of the test-ban talks. Harriman said later that he knew he had a treaty as soon as he again met Mr. Khrushchev; indeed, Mr. Khrushchev in the opening session playfully offered to sign a treaty before the talks began. A limited test-ban treaty, excluding underground tests, was concluded in ten swift negotiating sessions, much to the amazement and relief of the waiting world. Ten days after the initialing of the new treaty on July 25, foreign ministers Dean Rusk and Home arrived in Moscow, accompanied by U.S. Secretary-General U Thant for the impressive signing ceremonies in the Kremlin. Afterwards there were brief Big Three Foreign Ministers' talks, and Secretary Rusk also conferred—and played badminton—with Mr. Khrushchev in his glass-enclosed dacha along the Black Sea.

Non-nuclear powers were elbowing each other for the opportunity to sign the treaty in London, Moscow, and Washington. India was rightly the first nation to do so in Moscow, since Prime Minister Nehru was the first world statesman, back in 1954, to call for an end to tests. Only France and China announced nonparticipation in the test-ban treaty. Both felt, however, that it was necessary for them to offer alternatives. President de Gaulle announced that he would invite the nuclear powers before the year's end to a conference to discuss the scrapping of the carriers of nuclear weapons. China sent notes to all heads of state urging the calling of a world disarmament conference, since a partial test-ban treaty was too small a step to be of significance.

In the U.S., a week after Secretary Rusk signed the treaty in Moscow, he was the first witness in Senate hearings in Washington for its ratification. In the first five days of testimony, little opposition was expressed. It appeared that the ratification vote would be at least twenty above the necessary sixty-seven. Indeed, on the one hand the Kennedy Administration went to strange lengths to insure passage, even punctuating the hearings with occasional underground tests, no doubt to show sceptical senators that the Administration would continue testing. On the other hand, Administration witnesses warned repeatedly of euphoria—a feeling by the American people that the Cold War was ending and that the national defense could languish. Even normally tongue-tied generals from the Pentagon were using this word, common to Harvard graduates.

The Geneva Disarmament Conference quietly resumed on July 30. The foreign ministers in Moscow gave Geneva no clear agenda. Indeed, Secretary Rusk returned home asserting that the Russians did not seem to him to be eager to explore second steps except a non-aggression pact, and even Mr. Khrushchev did not seem in a hurry about that. However, there were several items on the agenda of Geneva, and delegates from seventeen nations (France has still not taken her seat) will be exploring control posts to prevent surprise attack and other collateral measures. However, it is not expected that talks will resume on a comprehensive test-ban treaty for some months, since the Soviet Union has apparently withdrawn her offer of on-site inspections and the U.S. apparently wants time to see how the limited treaty will operate.

The hundred days between President Kennedy's American University speech and the opening of the 18th General Assembly—by which time 100 nations will have signed or are expected to announced their willingness to sign the Partial Test-Ban Treaty—have found international relations more fluid than at any time in recent years. Those inside governments, and outside, who want the Cold War to end are trying to sustain the fluidity of events to prevent the rigidity of the Cold War from recurring.

The Assassination of John Kennedy

In the 100 days from June through September, a détente between the U.S. and the U.S.S.R. had definitely been established. But during the final 100 days of 1963, the biggest event, even for the Soviet Union, was the senseless assassination of John F. Kennedy. The unfolding, if fragile, détente rested on the hard-won mutual confidence of two men, Nikita Khrushchev and John F. Kennedy, as much as the need for a world to turn toward peace. With the sudden death of President Kennedy, the team is split, and détente is imperiled.

As a matter of fact, even before the death of the President, it appeared that the momentum of the hundred days from June could not continue. In the glow of the "spirit of Moscow," both Moscow and Washington suddenly discovered that they had other problems beside the problem of war and peace. President Kennedy had internal and alliance preoccupations. His attention necessarily was riveted to the civil rights revolution and to the efforts to shore up the American economy. He was preoccupied with a Western alliance in almost complete disarray. Besides, there was the 1964 presidential election.

But if President Kennedy was preoccupied in the early autumn of 1963, so was Premier Khrushchev. His attention was rivitted to the continuing shortage of consumer goods and the extraordinary shortage of agricultural products. His western alliance, the Warsaw Pact, was also in disarray. He had no election coming up, but he was running hard with Mao Zedong for the loyalty of the communist world in between Moscow and Beijing. This open Sino-Soviet split took his time.

As summer turned to fall, there were predictions of a slowdown in the momentum, not a stoppage, but at least a slowdown of the momentum toward détente. At least, it was felt, it would take the shape of ad hoc arrangements, certainly not additional partial disarmament steps.

In the early weeks of the 18th General Assembly, a new partial disarmament measure was arranged. First Soviet Foreign Minister Andrei Gromyko and then the next day President Kennedy spoke to the opening debate indicating that neither country would send nuclear bombs into orbit. This parallel declaration of intent resulted in a U.N. resolution, passed by acclamation, urging all states to refrain from sending nuclear weapons or others of mass destruction into orbit. This was not an iron-clad treaty, but it was a powerful U.N.

resolution and should be listed alongside the Hot Line and the Test-Ban in the succession of steps down the long road to détente through disarmament.

But the road to détente is paved by many steps. One was the wheat deal. President Kennedy struck a hard bargain—that the wheat would be shipped, if possible, in the more expensive American freighters—but this was another sign of relaxation. And the U.S. and U.S.S.R. in this period were negotiating the exchange of consulates in Chicago and Leningrad and the opening of a direct airline between New York and Moscow.

Other problems continued if not proliferated. Southeast Asia was still an enigma, despite the ouster of the Diem regime in Saigon and the immobilization of Madame Nhu. Malaysia and Indonesia were still shouting at each other. In Africa, the area of colonialism and apartheid had narrowed, but no clearcut end of the latter was in sight, despite increasing U.N. pressures and boycott. In Latin America, Castro was less strident, but the virus of Castroism had taken hold on the South American continent and the Alliance of Progress was not exactly progressing. In Europe, the Common Market was still in trouble. In Cyprus, Greeks and Turks reestablished bad relations.

This was a period of transition. New men appeared. Alex Home for Macmillan, ousted by sickness scandal-cum-sickness. Erhardt for Adenhauer, ousted by age-cum-conservatism. And then Johnson, for Kennedy, replaced by the assassin's bullet.

In the U.S. itself there was a great show of continuity. Not only did President Lyndon Johnson see more world leaders, speak to them, phone them, or cable them, than any president in any space in history, but also he went before the U.N. to give personal evidence of continuity—the same U.N. at which his predecessor spoke only a few months earlier. However, in politics as in love, continuity is not convincing. It appears that, in the New Year, despite all logic against it, the U.S. will make new probes for further East-West relations.

38 OSLO • LAMBARENE
(1957-1965)

SCHWEITZER'S PEACE JOURNEY

Unlike other great tragedies of the twentieth century—including the Holocaust in Europe, the purges and totalitarian rule in the Soviet Union, and the Great Leap Forward in China—world public opinion was mobilized effectively to demand an end to atmospheric nuclear testing and thus safeguard the lives of millions of people. President Kennedy and Premier Khrushchev deserve credit for concluding the Partial Test-Ban Treaty, but without the groundswell of public opposition over the previous decade, the accord might never have been achieved. Countless individuals and organizations—influential and little known—contributed to this historic turning point—the first arms control agreement in the nuclear age. But among all the voices raised, Albert Schweitzer's was one of the most electrifying. The story of Schweitzer's conversion from a reticent, mid-European professor into an outspoken critic of governments and a well-informed peace and disarmament activist is adapted from Homer's book Albert Schweitzer on Nuclear War and Peace *(Brethren Press, 1988).*

In the first decade after World War II, Schweitzer became a world-acclaimed figure, yet he refused repeatedly to use his accelerating fame for "political" ends. As more honors were given to Schweitzer and he was stimulated by the international press to respond publicly to them, he still hesitated to go beyond delivering his philosophical, non-activist views.

In October 1953, the Nobel Committee in Oslo, Norway, announced that Schweitzer would become the Nobel Peace Prize laureate for 1952. Schweitzer received news of the award in Africa. He could not leave his work at his hospital to journey to Europe to receive the prize in 1953. At the award ceremony on October 30, Gunnar Jahn, head of the Nobel Committee in Oslo, delivered an address about Schweitzer. The French Ambassador, M. de Monicault, was authorized by Schweitzer to accept the medal and citation. It was understood that Schweitzer would deliver his acceptance address on another occasion. The funds received for the prize ($31,000) Schweitzer used immediately to begin construction of a leper village adjoining the hospital.

Going to Europe in May 1954, Schweitzer worked on his acceptance speech to be given in Oslo on November 4. En route by train from his European home in Günsbach, he was treated by the public as if he were a movie star. He travelled first class, at the insistence of the Nobel Committee, and he commented about his Oslo hotel: "What do I need running water for? Am I a trout?" So many people desired to greet Schweitzer that a Norwegian newspaper suggested that everyone who wanted to shake hands with him should instead give a *krone* to his hospital. As a result, the amount given to him by the Nobel Committee was doubled.

Friends urged Schweitzer to take the rare opportunity of his Nobel address to shock the world out of a lethargy which accepted atomic tests and even the prospect of atomic war. Yet Schweitzer was not ready to break with his European academic tradition and his own inclinations.

Schweitzer delivered his acceptance address on November 4. The distinguished audience included King Gustav Adolf, Schweitzer's wife and daughter, and many friends and co-workers. He spoke in French. What Schweitzer wrote was, at the time, vintage Schweitzer, interwoven with history, philosophy, ethics, and religion. He did mention nuclear politics, but not extensively. He did assert that large-scale atomic "experiments might provoke a catastrophe that would endanger the very existence of humanity." He added that "we can no longer evade the problem of the future of the human race."

Resisting Pressures

Schweitzer took very seriously the meaning of his being awarded the Nobel Peace Prize. He resolved to fit into the shoes of the handful of peace laureates then alive—such as Ralph Bunche, Lord Boyd-Orr, Viscount Cecil, and John R. Mott—and such deceased ones as

305

Jane Addams, Fridtjof Nansen, and Woodrow Wilson. Schweitzer was quoted as saying: "They gave me the Peace Prize—I don't know why. Now I feel I should do something to earn it." But he carefully considered the several options available to him.

The indirect influences on Schweitzer to speak out on atomic issues were accumulating, including encouragement by U.N. Secretary-General Dag Hammerskjold and Bertrand Russell. Peer pressure mounted. Before Einstein died, Schweitzer in 1954 wrote: "Just look at the influence Einstein has because of the anguish he shows in the face of the atomic bomb." Also the activity of Bertrand Russell on nuclear politics affected Schweitzer deeply, although they did not correspond between late 1955 and Schweitzer's letter to him on the last day of 1957.

Still a third instance of peer pressure was from Pablo Casals, the musician. Schweitzer once chided his friend, Casals, for the latter's controversial public utterances. Schweitzer at the time insisted that it was better to create than to protest. "No," Casals replied, "there are times when the only creative thing we can do is to protest; we must refuse to accept or acknowledge what is evil or wicked." Later, when Schweitzer did protest nuclear tests, Casals commented: "I am glad my old friend is protesting too against nuclear weapons tests."

Then the American editor and critic, Norman Cousins, entered the scene. He arrived at Lambaréné early in January 1957 accompanied by Mrs. Clara Urquhart, an Englishwoman who was much more than an interpreter. A friend of both Schweitzer and Cousins, she played a useful role as an aide to the former on several occasions, including the trip to Oslo. One of the purposes of Cousins' trip was to urge Schweitzer to make some statement on world peace and atomic tests. In their initial conversation at Lambaréné on this topic, Schweitzer indicated that his concern about atomic matters had increased when he met with some of the Nobel laureates at Landau in 1955. Many spoke with urgency and gravity about the growing atomic problem. Alongside the problem of peace, everything seemed small. Schweitzer felt that a very high order of public understanding was necessary to deal with peace. "It is a serious thing that the governments have supplied so little information to their people on this subject." Cousins responded that it was precisely Schweitzer who could educate the world public. He was among the very few individuals in the world who would have an audience for anything he might say. Yet Schweitzer, several years even after delivering his Nobel address, responded: "All my life I have carefully stayed away from making pronouncements on public matters. Groups would come to me for my views on certain political questions. And always I would feel forced to say no." Schweitzer added: "It was not because I had no interest in world affairs or politics . . . It was just that I felt that my connection with the outside world should grow out of my work or thought in the field of theology or philosophy or music. I have tried to relate myself to the problems of all humankind rather than to become involved in disputes between this or that group. I wanted to be one man speaking to another man."

Thus Schweitzer insisted to Cousins that he was not the person to educate the world on atomic issues, even though the world admittedly had to be educated in lieu of the governments doing the task. He said that it was really a problem for scientists. It would be too easy to discredit any nonscientist, including himself, who spoke out on this topic. He doubted the propriety of his making any statement.

Cousins persisted and the next day Schweitzer seemed more agreeable to working on some "declaration or statement or whatever it is you want to call it." Schweitzer had no reason to believe that anything he might do or say "would or should have any substantial effect." But if there were "even the smallest usefulness that I or anyone else might have on the question, it would seem almost mandatory that the effort be made." Then Schweitzer discussed the parameters of any statement. One addressing itself to the dangers and consequences of war would be too broad. Perhaps "the place to take hold is with the matter of nuclear testing." He felt that "the scientific aspects of testing may be complicated, but the issues involved in testing are not." He was inclined to settle for "a fairly limited objective." Then they reviewed how the statement might best be issued. Cousins felt a statement could be released to the news agencies. Schweitzer had little faith in the press, but concluded that "our first job is to bring the baby into the world."

Almost overnight Schweitzer became the recipient, even in Lambaréné, of a stimulating dialogue on atomic matters. Prominent intellectual leaders were corresponding with Schweitzer, some old friends, others new: Martin Buber, J. Robert Oppenheimer, Pere Dominique Pire, Aneurin Bevin, and many others. Some made the long journey to Lambaréné. Marshall and Poling describe the situation aptly: "The visitors came to see Schweitzer as students to learn; as promoters to enlist; as politicians to exploit; as journalists to profit; as thinkers to probe; and as sceptics to be convinced."

The Declaration of Conscience

Between the time that Norman Cousins left Lambaréné on January 12, 1957, and when Schweitzer released a major statement in Oslo on April 23, there was much activity. Cousins returned to the United States via the Middle East and in Israel he talked to Martin Buber about his visit to Schweitzer. On February 13, Cousins wrote to his friend, Indian Prime Minister Jawaharlal Nehru, discussing his visit to Lambaréné. He asked Nehru if a meeting of world leaders in Vienna, presided over by Schweitzer, might be useful to stop nuclear weapons tests. Nehru quickly replied that he doubted "if there is anyone in the world today whose opinion can carry more weight in these matters than Dr. Schweitzer." Nehru added: "No one can accuse him of partiality, and whatever he says will at least command world attention. I welcome, therefore, his intention to try his utmost to deal with the present crisis." Elsewhere in the long letter Nehru wrote: "Anyhow, Dr. Schweitzer is the one man who can take the lead." As for strategy and tactics, Nehru said: "I would like Dr. Schweitzer to trust his own judgment or, if I may use Gandhiji's phrase, his 'inner voice,' since that will be a better guide than anything that I can say."

Schweitzer in a letter to Cousins, dated February 23, vetoed any meeting of the world leaders, since it was "much too complicated." So he "returned" to the idea of writing a message to be broadcast by radio. He asked the rhetorical question in this letter: "But to which radio can the mission of the publication be charged, without others feeling indisposed?" Then he responded to his own question: "Answer: Radio Oslo, of the city of the Nobel Peace Prize!" Leaning heavily on Cousins, Schweitzer ended his letter thus: "If you approve of it [the Oslo broadcast], please cable me 'Hospital Schweitzer Lambaréné. Agree with you.' You can cable in English. . . . But all this remains between you and me." Cousins immediately responded affirmatively, sending a copy of Nehru's letter to Lambaréné.

Nehru, although governing a subcontinent, was not too busy to continue writing long, discursive letters to Cousins. On March 16, Nehru wrote: "I entirely agree that Oslo will be the right and appropriate place for an appeal by Dr. Schweitzer and it would certainly add to the value of the appeal for peace if it was made under the auspices of the Nobel Committee."

The Nobel Committee, through its president, Gunnar Jahn,

and the director of Radio Oslo cooperated completely and arrangements were quickly made. Schweitzer wanted ample air time "to develop the facts very carefully. I don't want to be criticized for leaving large gaps in the argument." On the other hand, he wrote, "Don't ask me to come to the microphone myself." In the end, it was agreed that Mr. Jahn would read the text in Norwegian, with the Declaration in other European languages—English, French, German, and Russian—being broadcast from Oslo later the same evening. Radio Oslo hoped for a date in May to broadcast the statement, but Schweitzer cabled that it would be "too late." He wanted the broadcast to coincide with a major campaign against nuclear tests which he knew would take place in the Federal Republic of Germany around April 20.

In this manner, what became known as the Declaration of Conscience was broadcast on April 23, 1957, and released to the world press the next day. It was widely reprinted. In a letter to Cousins, written actually a day before the broadcast, Schweitzer wrote that "what's essential is that what was due to your initiative has succeeded and that the attempt to awaken the attention of humanity . . . is being undertaken under the best of conditions." In another letter written to Cousins early in May, Schweitzer reported that the statement was aired from 150 transmitters throughout the world.

The response to the broadcast was widespread, if often intangible. Dr. Willard Libby, an American scientist who was a member of the Atomic Energy Commission, wrote Schweitzer an open letter, claiming the radiation involved in nuclear weapons tests was insignificant compared to normal quantities from other sources. But a more positive result of the broadcast was that individuals on both sides of the Atlantic were becoming much more concerned and militant, making their first tentative plans to establish citizens' movements against nuclear tests. These beginnings led later in the year to the formation of the National Committee for a Sane Nuclear Policy in the United States—with Norman Cousins as one co-chairman—and of the Campaign for Nuclear Disarmament (CND) in England. Prime Minister Nehru in a letter to Cousins on June 6 wrote: "I agree with you that there is now a far greater realization all over the world of the effect of these test explosions than there was previously. I am sure that Schweitzer's statement has helped in this process."

One person reached by the Declaration was Adlai E. Stevenson. In 1956, Schweitzer wrote Stevenson, when the American was running for the second time for president, that "I read with great interest everything that concerns you, and I admire your courage in throwing yourself into the electoral struggle." In June 1957, Stevenson visited Lambaréné. During their conversation, Stevenson filled twelve half-sheets of paper with notes on everything from philosophy to hydrogen bombs.

In June 1957, Schweitzer went to Europe and stayed there until December. Writing a short letter to Cousins from Günsbach on October 14, Schweitzer complained about the speech United States Ambassador Henry Cabot Lodge made at the United Nations minimizing the dangers of nuclear tests. In another letter to Cousins, presumably written while still in Europe, Schweitzer discussed creating a worldwide movement against nuclear tests. He wrote: "The fire must be lighted in the U.S.A., and I will then be able to help other men of other lands to bring the wood to throw onto the fire and give it the importance it should have to enable it to create a different atmosphere."

Final Days

From 1957 until the end of his life, Schweitzer took an active role in opposing nuclear testing and the nuclear arms race. He engaged in an extensive correspondence with President Eisenhower, President John Kennedy, and other leaders, as well as Cousins and Russell. He was extremely concerned during the Cuban Missile Crisis in 1962 and the Berlin Crisis in 1963.

Schweitzer celebrated his ninetieth birthday on January 14, 1965. Russell and many others sent congratulatory cables. Schweitzer replied to Russell that he spent much time supervising building new additions to his hospital, but he also occupied himself "with the great problems of peace and atomic weapons." He wrote that it is "very fortunate" that the United States and the Soviet Union "walk together." He concluded "unfortunately, it does not look that I will come once more to Europe and we will see each other again."

In the summer of 1965, Schweitzer felt a new deterioration in the world situation, with Vietnam only one of the pressing issues. He commented to his confidants at Lambaréné : "Perhaps I should make another worldwide radio appeal, as I did in Oslo." He began talking to his daughter, Rhena, about preparing another appeal: "I should make one more effort, if only I can have the time and am not too tired." This was not to be, for on September 4, 1965, Schweitzer died at Lambaréné and was buried along the banks of the Ogowe River.

PART SIX 1965-1969

DENOMINATIONAL OFFICIAL

THE BOSTON YEARS

"Also there was a herald . . . who went with him . . .
He was round in the shoulders, black-complexioned,
wooly-haired, and had the name Eurybates.
Odysseus prized him above his other companions,
for their thoughts were in harmony."
                              —The Odyssey, Book XIX

As the Cold War thawed, Homer left SANE to become Director of the new Department of Social Responsibility for the Unitarian Universalist Association in Boston—the parent organization for nearly a thousand churches and several hundred thousand members in the United States and Canada. Once again, the family moved—to an apartment on Beacon Hill convenient to UUA headquarters at 25 Beacon St., next to the State House and Boston Commons. As the civil rights revolution and soon the Vietnam War reached a crescendo, Homer was constantly on the move, and Alex and Lucy were now away at college. During these turbulent years, Homer coordinated the denomination's support for an end to segregation in the South, including the March on Selma during which a fellow Unitarian minister was slain. But the racial caldron—especially after the assassinations of Martin Luther King and Malcolm X—bubbled over, and soon liberal bulwarks of integration, including the Unitarian church, were under siege by proponents of Black Power. Amid this turmoil—which took a heavy personal and professional toll in his life—Homer exerted leadership in mobilizing the religious community against the war in Vietnam, in support of draft resistance, and in support of human rights in Eastern Europe.

Photograph: Homer in front of Brown Chapel in Selma, 1965

39 SELMA
(1965)

MARCHING TO THE PROMISED LAND

Taking up his new position with the Unitarian Universalist Association, Homer soon found himself in the thick of the civil rights revolution in the Deep South. This account of the historic March on Selma—the Gettysburg in the new American civil war—is drawn from his sermons and articles of the time, as well as a biographical essay, "Martin Luther King Jr.—We Shall Overcome," published in German in 1992.

Perspective 1965: In March, the first American combat troops landed in Danang, and by the end of the year, 180,000 G.I.'s were in South Vietnam. The air war on North Vietnam also began, and by the end of the year the Air Force was conducting 1500 bombing sorties a week. President Johnson launched his Great Society program, and Congress passed Head Start and Medicare. Despite the Civil Rights Act of 1964 and the Voting Rights Act of 1965, rising expectations and declining will to address the needs of the inner city led to riots in Watts, the predominantly black ghetto in Los Angeles, and other urban centers. The Beatles were at the height of their fame, My Fair Lady *won Best Picture Award, and Sandy Koufax pitched his fourth no-hitter.*

Selma, 1965, was an authentic American epic, a folk play with religious dimensions. All the elements of high drama were present. The hero was Dr. Martin Luther King, Jr., fresh from receiving the world's highest honor—the Nobel Peace Prize of 1964. He was also the symbol of all the disenfranchised, brutalized Negroes in the American South. He led, Moses-like, his children out of Egypt—

Selma—to the Promised Land of equality and with the right to vote. The sources of evil in this epic were several: Governor George Wallace of Alabama, Sheriff Jim Clark of Dallas County—with a "Never" button on his lapel—and the numerous Alabama rednecks to whom Wallace and Clark gave license to murder. There was also the Ku Klux Klan.

The martyrs were at least three: Jimmie Lee Jackson, a young black from Marion, Alabama; the Rev. James J. Reeb of Boston; and Mrs. Viola Luizzo of Detroit.

Violence was a part of this epic; so was law. Violence included beating, whipping, clubbing, tear-gas, murder. Law emerged finally by putting U.S. troops once again on Southern soil.

Big government was involved, including a message by the President of the U.S., Lyndon B. Johnson, to a joint session of Congress and to the American people. This was in response to the outraged conscience of a nation, a response that took the form of demonstrations in almost every Northern and Western city in our land. Religion was an ingredient, in the nightly prayer meetings at Brown Chapel A.M.E. Church, and the hundreds of ministers, priests, rabbis, bishops, and nuns who became completely involved both in Selma and back home in their own neighborhoods.

The chorus to this epic included at first only Dallas County Negroes. They were joined suddenly by a swelling interracial band of persons from all walks of life.

Finally, chants and songs gave folk humor to the scene. These included not only the recurring theme of "We Shall Overcome . . . Some Day," but "Ain't Gonna Let Nobody Turn Me 'Round," with improvised stanzas on how "Reverend Reeb gave his life."

Thus Selma, 1965—Martin Luther King's civil rights march of 55 miles—will indelibly be written into the fabric of American history, as Dandi, 1930—Mohandas Gandhi's march of 200 miles to the sea to obtain salt—is forever written into Indian history.

This Alabama drama which began more than a century ago exploded into our present to become one of those rare hinges of history and was visible almost as it occurred. Indeed, President Johnson explicitly told the nation: "At times history and fate meet at a single time in a single place to shape a turning point in man's unending search for freedom. So it was at Lexington and Concord . . . So it was in Selma, Alabama."

Background to the March

Fifty miles west of Montgomery, Selma was a city of almost 30,000 persons, more than one-half black. There was rigid segregation. Only one per cent of blacks were on the voting list. However, there was a new Mayor, Joseph I. Smitherman, and a new Public Safety Director, Wilson Baker, a professional police officer. Soon Baker worked out an uneasy agreement whereby he would be in charge of law enforcement in the city, except around the Dallas County courthouse where the more volatile Sheriff Jim Clark would have control.

On January 2, 1965, King addressed a rally of 700 people in Brown Chapel. He reported that SCLC chose Selma because it "has become a symbol of bitter-end resistance to the civil rights movement in the Deep South." King then gave what turned out to be a correct scenario for the campaign: "Today marks the beginning of a determined, organized, mobilized campaign to get the right to vote everywhere in Alabama. If we are refused, we will appeal to Governor George Wallace. If he refuses to listen, we will appeal to the legislature. If they don't listen, we will appeal to the conscience of the Congress." Andrew Young suggested that the campaign would benefit by sending potential voters to the downtown courthouse since "we want to establish in the mind of the nation that a lot of people who want to register are prevented from doing so." SCLC and SNCC (Student Nonviolent Coordinating Committee) staff then met with the Committee of Fifteen, composed of local black leaders, which earlier had invited SCLC to lead the movement in Selma.

On January 18, King and John Lewis of SNCC led 400 blacks from Brown Chapel to the Dallas County courthouse. Sheriff Clark refused them entry, and had them wait in an alley until the county registrars would call them one at a time in order for each to take the difficult voter registration literacy test. During the two-hour wait, not one black applicant was registered. The leader of the American Nazi Party, George Lincoln Rockwell, was present and tried to converse with King. That same day King and ten aides went to the segregated Albert Hotel, were given rooms, and became the first blacks to spend a night in that hotel. While King was registering, a member of the Nazi Party punched King, but he was pulled away by John Lewis and not hurt.

On January 19, King and the marchers refused the Sheriff's demand that they go into the alley as before. Clark then ordered them off the courthouse sidewalk. When they refused, sixty were arrested, with Mrs. Boynton roughed up personally by the Sheriff. Later King said that it was "one of the most brutal and unlawful acts I have seen an officer commit." Sheriff Clark yelled at the marchers: "You are here to cause trouble . . . You are an agitator and that the lowest form of humanity." (One clergyman defended the agitator label: "An agitator is a part of a washing machine that gets the dirt out!")

On January 22, 100 black teachers, led by the Rev. Frederick D. Reese, President of the Dallas County Voters League, marched to the courthouse to oppose the sluggish voter registration system. On January 30, there were three successive marches to the courthouse, and a total of 226 demonstrators were in jail.

On February 1, King with Ralph Abernathy submitted to intentional arrest. They set out from Brown Chapel with 250 blacks and fifteen whites. All were arrested. That same day another 700 persons were arrested by Sheriff Clark near the courthouse. Some sang, "I love Jim Clark in my heart." Also 20 miles away in Marion, the seat of Perry County, there was a large protest demonstration.

King Imprisoned

While in prison, King heard that 300 were arrested in Selma and 700 in Marion. King asked Andrew Young, not in jail, to telephone singer Sammy Davis, Jr., and ask him to appear later at a benefit concert in Atlanta. King confessed: "These fellows respond better when I am in jail." Outside, Malcolm X, the black nationalist Muslim, arrived in Selma and talked to Coretta King. He told her that he wanted her husband to know that he "didn't come to Selma to make his job any more difficult . . . If the white people realize what the alternative is, perhaps they will be more willing to hear Dr. King." (Eighteen days later, Malcolm X was fatally shot in Harlem, New York City.)

At this time President Lyndon B. Johnson released a statement saying that "the problem in Selma is the slow pace of voting registration for Negroes who are qualified to vote." On February 5, 500 marchers were arrested at the Dallas County courthouse. Also that day a full-page advertisement from SCLC appeared in the *New York Times*, with the headline: "A Letter from Martin Luther King, Jr., from a Selma, Alabama Jail." The letter began: "When the King of Norway participated in awarding the Nobel Peace Prize to me he surely did not think that in less than 60 days I would be in jail. He,

316

and almost all world opinion, will be shocked because they are little aware of the unfinished business in the South . . . This is Selma, Alabama. There are more Negroes in jail with me than there are on the voting rolls . . . "

Also on February 5, King gave bond and left jail in order to confer with advisers in New York City and arrange for pending legislation in Washington. In the process he secured an appointment with Vice-President Hubert Humphrey and Attorney-General Designate Nicholas B. Katzenbach. On February 9, Humphrey took King to the White House for a brief talk with the President. The latter promised that a voting rights bill would be sent to Congress soon. The President had a "deep commitment to obtaining the right to vote for all Americans."

Back in Alabama, Sheriff Clark (wearing a large lapel button, "Never") and his aides used cattle-prods to make 165 marchers run three miles into the countryside. King addressed two mass meetings. In a strategy session later, explorations were made to arrange demonstrations for voting rights in several rural black-belt counties, such as Lowndes. Sensing that the people of Selma might be growing tired of constant marches and arrests, King declared that one "should not only know how to start a good movement," but one should "also know when to stop." King also had to give time to lessening rising conflicts between SCLC and the more youthful and militant SNCC. C. T. Vivian led a demonstration in Marion and the state troopers hit the 400 marchers after lights went out. Some marchers and journalists were injured, and young Jimmie Lee Jackson was fatally hurt when shot in the stomach by police.

The next two weeks were both typical and atypical of the schedule King was juggling. On February 22 King led a march in Selma and visited Jimmie Lee Jackson in the hospital. February 23 saw him still in Selma, where he spoke at an evening rally and then left for Atlanta. On February 24 he flew to California for some speeches and other SCLC fund-raising activities, finishing at Victory Baptist Church on Sunday. On Monday, March 1, King was back in Selma where he led a registration caravan by auto through several rural counties. On March 2, he flew to Washington to speak at Howard University. On March 3, he was back in Selma and spoke at Jimmie Lee Jackson's funeral. He flew to New York City still that day and spent March 4 there consulting with advisers about his meeting the next day with President Johnson. At the 75-minute meeting Johnson felt that the prospects for the civil rights bill looked good. King returned to Atlanta on March 5 and preached at

Ebenezer Church on Sunday morning. In the afternoon, he heard by phone and then saw by television the battle of Edmund Pettus Bridge. Those were but two weeks in the life of King.

Earlier, back in Selma, seventy-two whites from various cities in Alabama, led by the Rev. Joseph Ellwanger of Birmingham, paraded to the courthouse protesting white violence. Vague plans were in the air for a march from Selma to the Alabama capital in Montgomery, but these plans became specific after the funeral of Jimmie Lee Jackson. King returned to Selma and SCLC officials discussed how to escalate their campaign. Then James Bevel on March 3 announced that King would lead a mass march to Montgomery on March 7—less than four days thereafter.

As SCLC staff prepared the march to Montgomery, Governor Wallace announced that he would use "whatever measures are necessary to prevent a march." King by phone wondered if it should be delayed, or postponed a day so he could be present. (He felt he had to preach in his Atlanta church that Sunday.) James Bevel and Hosea Williams felt that postponement would only dampen enthusiasm. Thus on Sunday, March 7, 600 blacks gathered at Brown Chapel, including some activists from Perry County. They walked in the afternoon through Selma and up the ramp on the west side of Edmund Pettus Bridge.

When the demonstrators reached the crest, they could look down the four-lane Highway 80 and see blue-uniformed state troopers standing about 300 yards ahead to block the road. Some police were mounted on horses. The commanding officer, Major John Cloud, declared: "Your march is not conducive to the public safety. You are ordered to disperse and go back to your church or to your homes." When Hosea Williams asked to speak to the Major, the latter replied: "You have two minutes to turn around." After a minute or more, Cloud gave the orders: "Troopers advance." Then followed "the bloody battle of Pettus bridge." A flying wedge of troopers went through the marchers. They used nightsticks, as white spectators on the sidelines cheered. The mounted policemen rode into the retreating blacks. Then tear gas was used. John Lewis was felled with a blow on his head. Mrs. Boynton became unconscious. Black marchers fled back into Selma and sought protection in black homes, pursued by state police. Seventy-five people were treated at Good Samaritan Hospital and seventeen had to remain there. Before entering the hospital, John Lewis declared: "I don't see how President Johnson can send troops to Vietnam. . . and can't send troops to Selma, Alabama."

News of the attack spread fast that Sunday afternoon in early March. The ABC television network interrupted its showing of *Judgment At Nuremberg* to give actual scenes of the violence at Pettus Bridge. The role of the storm troopers in both societies was not lost on most viewers. King and other leaders made a conference telephone call and decided to urge civil rights supporters from throughout the country to converge on Selma for a second March to Montgomery beginning on Tuesday, March 9. In a telegram to religious leaders King stated: "In the vicious maltreatment of defenseless citizens of Selma, where old women and young children were gassed and clubbed at random, we have witnessed an eruption of the disease of racism which seeks to destroy all America." He continued: "It is fitting that all Americans help to bear the burden." Clergy "of all faiths" were urged to come to Selma.

Unitarian Involvement

At the Unitarian Universalist Association—as at other denominational offices across America—we received a telegram from Martin Luther King, Jr. inviting us to send clergy in numbers to Selma on Tuesday March 9. As newly appointed Director of the Department of Social Responsibility of the Association, I immediately notified our regional network and urged numbers of our ministers to go to Selma. I arrived in Alabama later that Monday. I also attended the final rally in front of the State Capitol in Montgomery almost three weeks later, on March 25. Viral pneumonia prevented my walking on the march itself. Let me recall some of my most vivid, poignant memories of Selma, 1965:

• The Monday evening when we arrived in Selma's Brown Chapel, among the first whites to do so, we were greeted eagerly, warmly, by the overflowing church full of Negroes, some of whom were brutalized by state police only the day before. They welcomed the presence and concern of some white clergy.

• The Negro community of Selma absorbed, without visible effort, up to several thousand white civil rights workers for sleeping, eating, just telephoning.

• At a kneel-in outside Selma's First Baptist Church, the white deacons proudly pointed to their new brick edifice: "We built it. It is ours. We can exclude whomever we choose."

• President Johnson spoke to Congress, as we crowded around a TV set in the home of a Negro family in the public housing project near Brown Chapel. When the President said that "their cause must be our cause, too . . . And we shall overcome," we suddenly realized with tearful eyes that Monday evening—the evening of Jim Reeb's funeral—that indeed we had overcome, that this particular battle for voting rights was won, if not completely over, in nine days.

• Members of the large interracial demonstration saluted the American flag at the start of the final rally in front of the State Capitol in Montgomery, with hundreds of American flags unfurled by the marchers to offset the Confederate flag atop the State House.

Selma, 1965, the American epic, was an amalgam of heroism, evil, martyrdom, and much more. It was also a combination of chant and hymn and song. Many sang all night at the so-called "Selma Wall"—plaintive, improvised songs. The grim, helmeted state troopers kept time to the music with one foot. One of the favorites of Martin Luther King, Jr. and his lieutenants was the antiphonal chant:

"What do you want?" "FREEDOM! "
"When do you want it?" "NOW!"
" How much do you want?" "ALL OF IT!"

Then there was the popular folk song, "Oh Freedom":

Oh Freedom, Oh Freedom, Oh freedom over me
And before I'd be a slave
I'll be buried in my grave
And go home to my Lord and be free.

There was the parody on the "Battle of Jericho":

We've got a line that's a Berlin Wall, Berlin Wall, Berlin Wall
We've got a line that's a Berlin Wall in Selma, Alabama.
Hate is the thing that built that wall, built that wall, built that wall
Hate is the thing that built that wall in Selma, Alabama.
Love is the thing that'll make it fall, make it fall, make it fall
Love is the thing that'll make it fall in Selma, Alabama.

En route to Montgomery from Selma, the marchers sang loudly:

Ain't gonna let nobody turn me 'round, not Jim Clark, not Al
Lingo, not George Wallace
Ain't gonna let nobody turn me 'round
I'm gonna keep on walkin,' keep on talkin,'
Marching up to freedom land.

Although ours was only part of a much greater interreligious
witness, Unitarian Universalist involvement in Dr. King's campaign
began several months earlier, in January, when our denominational
team went to Mississippi to explore new opportunities for volunteer
service in the civil rights struggle for ministers and laypersons. After travelling 1,000 miles inside Mississippi, Orloff Miller, Clifton
Hoffman, and myself returned by way of Atlanta and there made
contact with the SCLC. We arranged at that time for denominational participation in the so-called Black Belt Project, extending to those
counties with more Negro than white population, from Arkansas
through Louisiana, Mississippi, Alabama, Georgia, and South Carolina.

In mid-February, two of our Boston ministers, Ira Blalock and
Gordon Gibson, went to Selma to represent the denomination. They
were arrested, and their subsequent description of the treatment of
black prisoners in Southern jails made nation-wide headlines.

On Saturday, March 6, Seventy Concerned White Citizens of
Alabama marched for the first time in Selma. Approximately one-
half of these whites were members of our Unitarian Universalist
churches in Birmingham and Huntsville, Alabama.

On Tuesday, March 9, forty-five of our ministers and at least
fifteen of our laymen responded to Martin Luther King, Jr.'s call to
come to Selma. We attended the morning meetings in Brown Chapel and held several Unitarian Universalist caucuses. By mid-
afternoon we marched, led by Dr. King, to the center of Edmund
Pettus Bridge.

Tangled Legal Situation

King returned to Selma on Monday, March 8, to face a tangled legal
situation. Federal Judge Frank M. Johnson, Jr., was hearing a plea to
ban a state injunction against marches and to allow the March to
Montgomery. He had not yet made a ruling. Washington officials
wanted a waiting period, if only a day or two. Attorney-General
Katzenbach phoned King from Washington and urged him not to

march.

King responded: "Mr. Attorney-General, you have not been a black man in America for 300 years." On the other hand, SCLC and SNCC staff wanted the march to go ahead on Tuesday. King was occupied much of Monday night and all of Tuesday morning trying to reconcile these tactics. Hundreds of marchers in the meantime from all over the U.S. were converging on Selma and waiting in Brown Chapel to march. Finally, King appeared early on Tuesday afternoon and told them to "put on your walking shoes."

At 2:30 p.m. King led an interracial march of 3,000 persons to Pettus Bridge. In the front line with him were Ralph Abernathy, Ralph Bunche (another Nobel Peace Laureate on the staff of the United Nations), and Rabbi Abraham Heschel of the Jewish Theological Seminary. Of the marchers, half were white and an estimated 15 percent were clergy. Col. Al Lingo, Commander of the State Police, was describing the march in an open telephone line to Governor Wallace in Montgomery while a Justice Department official, John Doar, did so to Attorney-General Katzenbach in Washington. King stopped some 50 yards from the state troopers on the bridge and prayed. Then representatives of several faiths made brief speeches. Together they sang, "We Shall Overcome." Then King turned around and led the demonstrators back to Selma. Most marchers did not know, or understand, the compromises which led to this "Tuesday turnaround."

Back in Washington and elsewhere, focus was still on "Bloody Sunday." President Johnson said that "Americans everywhere join me in deploring the brutality with which a number of Negro citizens of Alabama were treated when they sought to dramatize their deep and sincere interest in attaining the precious right to vote." Six hundred persons picketed the White House, asking for federal intervention in Alabama. Sympathy marches took place in Boston, Chicago, Detroit, New York City, Toronto, and elsewhere.

In Selma, shortly after the march concluded, and before the evening rally, three white Unitarian Universalist ministers were assaulted when leaving a black cafe. One, James J. Reeb—employed to develop interracial housing in Boston by the Quakers—was mortally wounded by some whites and had to be taken by ambulance to Birmingham (*see next chapter "James Reeb's Ordeal"*).

On Thursday, March 11, Judge Johnson held a hearing on SCLC's demand that the March to Montgomery be sanctioned. On news of Reeb's death late Thursday evening, President Johnson telephoned Reeb's widow. Two groups of religious leaders met with the President, on Friday, demanding stronger federal action in Alabama and legislation in Washington. Three thousand persons rallied at the Lutheran Church of the Reformation on Capitol Hill in Washington.

On Saturday, March 13, Governor Wallace flew to Washington to confer with President Johnson, with 1,000 demonstrators outside. On Sunday, Johnson phoned King and invited him to hear him speak to both houses of Congress on Monday evening. King declined, because on Monday he had to speak at Reeb's funeral in Selma. On Monday, two thousand religious, labor, and other civil leaders from all parts of the U.S. and Canada participated in an interreligious service and then followed King as he marched to the courthouse for another brief service. King asked, "Why must good men die for being good?" He hoped that Reeb's death "may cause the white South to come to terms with its conscience." Then King laid a wreath on the Dallas County courthouse door.

Monday evening President Johnson spoke to Congress, with perhaps 70 million Americans listening on television. He described Selma as a milestone in the nation's development, like Lexington, Concord, or Appomattox, where "history and fate meet at a single time in a single place to shape a turning point in man's unending search for freedom."

Johnson was given two standing ovations and applauded on thirty-six occasions. Then the President mouthed a civil rights slogan never uttered before publicly at the time from the White House: "We shall overcome . . . the crippling legacy of bigotry and injustice." With these words, King and millions of others realized that they had won. King later wrote in the *Saturday Review* that Johnson "made one of the most eloquent, unequivocal, and passionate pleas for human rights ever made by a President of the U.S." But the struggle in Alabama was by no means completed.

On Tuesday, March 16, a group of demonstrators, led by SNCC, near the capitol building in Montgomery, was attacked by police who were on horses and used nightsticks and whips. Again the civil rights movement was in an uproar. King spoke that night at Beulah Baptist Church in Montgomery and led a march to the state capitol the next day. Montgomery County Sheriff Mac Sire Butler publicly apologized for the violence. On Wednesday, Judge Johnson granted SCLC the right to march from Selma to Montgomery: "It seems basic to our constitutional principles that the extent of the right to assemble, demonstrate, and march peaceably along the highways and streets in an orderly manner should be commensurate with the enormity of the wrongs that are being protested and petitioned against." It would be a five-day, four-evening event, with the state of Alabama prohibited from hampering the march and with the federal government providing whatever Governor Wallace would request to protect the marchers. Governor Wallace supplied "insufficient personnel" and President Johnson then federalized 1,800 members of the Alabama National Guard.

On Sunday afternoon, March 21, King led three thousand demonstrators across Pettus Bridge and into rural Alabama. Walking with Martin and Coretta King were the leaders of the U.S. civil rights movement: A. Philip Randolph, Roy Wilkins, Whitney Young, Bayard Rustin, Ralph Bunche, and John Lewis. It was rightly called a "miniature March on Washington."

Just before the march began, King told the demonstrators: "Walk together, children, don't get weary, and it will lead us to the Promised Land. And Alabama will be a new Alabama, and America will be a new America." The marchers sang freedom songs as they passed the spot where there was bloodshed two weeks before and where the Tuesday turnaround occurred. They marched 7 miles the first day, with 300 staying in camp and the others riding back to Selma. There was no violence, protected by nationalized guardsmen, even by helicopters overhead.

On Thursday, March 25, King led 25,000 marchers into Montgomery, passing near his former parsonage and next to his former church, Dexter Avenue Baptist, before arriving at the state capitol which was flying a Confederate flag. Governor Wallace would not receive a petition from the marchers and the gates and doors of the state house were closed, but reportedly he peered at the demonstration from behind a curtain. King delivered one of his historic speeches.

Coretta flew back with Martin that evening to Atlanta, only to learn that, after the rally, Viola Liuzzo of Detroit, a white housewife and Unitarian, who was driving demonstrators from Selma to Montgomery, was shot and killed while driving through Lowndes County.

This was the climax, and anti-climax, of King's and SCLC's foray into Selma in 1965. Although SCLC's work in Selma and the rural countries continued, attention was soon focused elsewhere—to the North. King told a Cleveland audience that the Selma March "may turn out to be as important an event in American history as Gandhi's march to the sea was in Indian history."

40 SELMA (1965)

THE ORDEAL OF JAMES REEB

Among the many martyrs of the civil rights movement in the 1960s was James Reeb, a young Unitarian Universalist minister based in Boston. Homer was with Reeb the evening he was fatally attacked in Selma. (On hearing news of the attack on a group of Unitarian ministers, Alex, Homer's son, a student at Oberlin College, drove to Alabama and joined Homer in the vigil at Brown's Chapel.) Homer wrote this account based on his own field notes at the time and contemporaneous accounts by other Unitarian Universalist participants in the march.

In the autumn of 1964, the Rev. James J. Reeb concluded his work as Associate Minister of All Souls Unitarian Church in Washington, D.C. and began a new job as Community Relations Director of the Boston Metropolitan Housing Program. This was sponsored by the American Friends Service Committee.

Reeb was working at his office on Monday, March 8, when he received a telephone call from the the Rev. Theodore Webb, director of the Massachusetts Bay District of the Unitarian Universalist Association. Webb as other regional Unitarian Universalist directors throughout North America had quickly been told that morning of the request of the Southern Christian Leadership Council and of Dr. Martin Luther King, Jr., to urge clergy to come to Selma on Tuesday and finish the march that was so brutally stopped on Sunday afternoon. Reeb was asked if he wanted to drop everything and go to Selma. He and his wife, Marie, had heard the eleven o'clock news on Sunday evening of the "bloody battle of Pettus Bridge" in Selma.

Reeb rapidly explored the possibility of going to Alabama, first with John Sullivan, his immediate superior in the Quaker agency, and the Rev. Virgil Wood, the black head of the Blue Hill Protestant Center. He also called Unitarian Universalist headquarters, and as director of the new Department of Social Responsibility (and the one who made the original call to the regional directors), I talked to him briefly, urging him to go. Later, Reeb consulted his wife, who reluctantly agreed to his quick trip to Alabama. Reeb left his wife and four children and appeared at the Logan Airport that Monday night. As he waited for the charter flight to Atlanta, he met many Unitarian Universalist colleagues, including three who were working at denominational headquarters: Orloff Miller, Robert Hohler, and Henry Hampton (who later produced *Eyes on the Prize*, the award-winning documentary of the civil rights movement).

They left Boston at 11:00 p.m. and arrived at Atlanta early in the morning. They slept for a few hours in an office at the airport and then took an early one-hour flight to Montgomery and found transportation with SCLC the 50 miles to Selma. Reeb and his associates left their small suitcases at Brown Chapel A.M.E. Church and soon talked with old and new friends from all over the nation. As they milled around Brown Chapel, without bothering for much breakfast, word came that Dr. King and his associates were negotiating with state and federal authorities about the intended march from Selma to Montgomery. They faced a legal and moral dilemma. There was an injunction prohibiting them from marching. Should they break this injunction or should they defy it. Strong pressures came from Washington to obey the injunction and postpone the march by several days, but strong pressures came from Brown Chapel that the thousand or more clergy from all over America begin to march! Finally a deal was struck whereby King would take the marchers to the middle of Edmund Pettus Bridge, hold prayer meeting, and then turn the group around to march back to Selma.

During the long wait, Reeb as others discussed the dilemma of breaking a court injunction: when was civil disobedience applicable and when not? Finally, at 3:00 p.m. Dr. King gave the order that they would march. Reeb joined the others to the crest of the bridge where King and other leaders held a brief interreligious service. Then Reeb went with the marchers back to Selma and Brown Chapel. Rev. Clifton Hoffman, district director of the Mid-South Unitarian Universalist District, encountered Reeb and asked him if he wanted an auto ride back to Atlanta that evening. Reeb put his suitcase in Hoffman's auto, but later told him, "I think I'll stay," and re-trieved his suitcase.

In the meantime, Reeb realized that he had not had a full meal since the previous evening. He walked with the Rev. John Wells, a Washington colleague, to the headquarters of SCLC which was in the office of the Boynton Insurance Agency. There they asked for a good place to eat. Mrs. Diana Bevel asked if they wanted a Negro restaurant or an integrated one. She directed them to Walker's Cafe. There Reeb found many other Unitarian Universalist ministers.

I myself was at that restaurant. After finishing, I had to make a telephone call to President Dana McLean Greeley of the Unitarian Universalist Association—to tell him that the march was a success!—but the line of clergy waiting to use the one telephone was very long. The Rev. David Johnson, eating at my table, said he had a rented auto and would be glad to take me back to Brown Chapel where it might be easier to phone. We bid good-bye to our colleagues, including Reeb, and said we would see them at Brown Chapel where King was scheduled to speak later that evening. After leaving the cafe, we were immediately chased by some white youths. We ran quickly to David's car and somehow managed to lock the doors and speed away.

Reeb made a call to his wife in Boston, and then left the cafe soon after we did with Orloff Miller and Clark Olson, minister of the Unitarian church in Berkeley, California. They had no auto and were not as lucky as we were. They saw several whites cross the street who followed them. Reeb, Miller, and Olsen quickened their steps, and did not run. One of the whites called out, "Hey, niggers." One white took a heavy stick and hit Jim's head. Orloff immediately dropped to the sidewalk to protect himself, especially from the kicks of another of the whites. Clark, in front, was attacked by another white, who broke his glasses. Soon the white ruffians disappeared. Jim was lying on his back, dazed if conscious. Clark and Orloff pulled up Jim and they walked with him to the SCLC office. An ambulance-cum-hearse from a Negro funeral home next door took Reeb to the Burwell Infirmary, a small Negro hospital.

In the meantime, I was at Brown Chapel when a state trooper came to me, asked my name, and said he would quickly take me to Burwell Infirmary. Reaching there, I found Olson and Miller standing at the back of an open ambulance, with Reeb on a stretcher inside. They told me what happened and said that the Dr. W. B. Dinkens, head of the Infirmary, realized that a major brain operation was necessary and had made arrangements. Soon the ambulance started for Birmingham, as I was asked to go with the state policeman to their headquarters to oversee efforts for police protection en route so the ambulance would not be stopped and could reach Birmingham—90 miles away—as fast as possible. However, the ambulance had a puncture just outside Selma, and had to return before Reeb was transferred to a second vehicle. There was no interference en route, but they did not reach University Hospital until 11:00. The operation began at 11:30—more than four hours after they left Walker's Cafe.

The specialists found Jim's skull had been crushed on the left side, resulting in a large blood clot. The physicians early on could predict no recovery.

Forty-Eight Hours

In the meantime Marie Reeb had to be notified, if possible before the late night news. From Selma I telephoned the Rev. Jack Mendelsohn, minister of Arlington Street Church in Boston, which the Reebs attended since moving from Washington. Mendelsohn immediately talked with Marie. Close friends came to the Reeb home. Marie phoned Jim's parents and her parents, as the four children slept.

On Wednesday Marie flew to Montgomery, accompanied by John Sullivan of the American Friends Service Committee. They met the Rev. Duncan Howlett at the Atlanta airport. Arriving in Birmingham, they immediately went to University Hospital where Marie visited her husband—still unconscious. The authorities told her: "in critical condition—prognosis poor." Soon Marie saw some friends, including Olson and Miller, and also Rev. Gerald Krick, Rev. Lawrence McGinty (minister of the Unitarian Church of Birmingham), two Unitarian physicians on the hospital staff, and myself.

At 7:00 p.m., Marie had the strength to face the press. Questions were asked about the children. She replied: "I told the children this morning as soon as they woke up that their father had been hurt. The younger ones did not fully understand, but the 13-year-old was quite upset." She was asked if the cause was worth the risk of death. She paused and asserted, "I don't believe I could answer for myself, only for Jim. For him, any consequence that might occur would merit his coming." When she returned to her suite in the hospital, a bouquet of yellow roses stood on the table, from President and Mrs. Lyndon Johnson.

Marie Reeb then asked that Clark Olsen and Orloff Miller give her a detailed description of the previous evening in Selma. Jim's father arrived, and they went upstairs to visit Jim. He realized the end was near.

Back in Selma, civil rights workers heard of the attack on Reeb, but none knew its seriousness. The nightly rally was held in Brown Chapel. Martin Luther King, Jr., spoke about the attack on the three ministers. He said that the day had gone too well. "The beast had to strike back. Now our [white] brethren know something of what it's like to be a Negro in Alabama." He led a silent prayer for all three ministers.

On Wednesday morning the civil rights workers decided to march to the Court House, but Sheriff Clark and Public Safety Commissioner Baker said there would be no march that day. The police set up a kind of barricade (the marchers called it "the Selma Wall" or "the Berlin Wall") to prevent the march, using parked cars as a second line of defense. There were no attempts to breach the line, and the demonstrators returned to Brown Chapel for another rally.

On Thursday, March 11, in Birmingham there were further consultations with the physicians and further visits of Marie and Jim's father to Jim's room. At 7:00 p.m. Jim's heart stopped, as it did earlier, but this time it was agreed by Marie that no attempts would be made to restart it. He was declared dead, and soon a telephone call came to Marie from President Johnson. He talked to both Marie and Mr. Reeb, expressing his own deep personal feelings about Jim's death. He said a White House plane would take Mrs. Reeb on Friday morning back to Boston and another would take her and the children to Wyoming whenever they wished.

In Selma, it was just 48 hours since Jim was fatally injured. News of Jim's death reached the line of march at 9:00 p.m. All singing stopped, and the Rev. Richard Leonard of the Community Church of New York gave a short eulogy.

I myself went to Birmingham and then Montgomery and stayed in a motel with Dr. King and his senior staff and conferred with him often on Wednesday and Thursday, making contingency plans for a nationally televised, interreligious memorial service from Brown Chapel for Monday, March 16—just a week after the fatal attack.

Mourning

In many places, especially Washington, mourning about Jim Reeb's death took the form of protest. Picketing, which began with the attack on Jim Reeb, continued at the White House after he died. Indeed, on Friday, March 12, several thousand clergy gathered in Washington to protest. They sent a delegation to confer with President Johnson and he spent two hours talking with them. The protests outside and inside the White House stimulated the President to make final the draft of a voting rights bill and also schedule a speech to the nation at a special session of Congress the following Monday evening.

Also on Friday an Air Force Jet Star took Marie Reeb and John Sullivan back to Boston. The Boston Symphony Orchestra that afternoon, in memory of James Reeb, played "Dance of the Blessed Spirits," which they selected 18 months earlier on the death of President Kennedy. Also a series of ecumenical and interreligious services were held honoring Jim, not only in the cities he served, but throughout the nation, even overseas. The Catholic diocese newspaper in Worcester, Massachusetts, proposed James Reeb for sainthood! Actors and entertainers in New York City put on a special show, *Broadway Answers Selma*, and raised $100,000 for civil rights activity. More money was raised for Marie and the four children than they felt could be used!

On Sunday, March 14, the National Board of Trustees of the Unitarian Universalist Association, which the previous Friday and Saturday was holding its regular meetings in Boston, recessed out of respect for James Reeb. It agreed to reconvene in Selma that Sunday afternoon. It was an unforgettable sight, the Board and senior national staff members of the Association arriving in the compound of St. Elizabeth's Catholic Church in Selma. Later that Sunday evening, various board and staff members stayed with Negro families and took their turn on the all-night demonstration line at the Selma Wall. UUA President Dana McLean Greeley indulged in a shouting match with the heads of the racist state troopers.

Many of the Northern civil rights workers stayed in Selma after Jim's death in order to attend the service on Monday. They were determined to march to the Courthouse honoring Jim. Dr. Greeley and C. T. Vivian of SCLC led a group down Sylvan Avenue to the "Selma Wall"—a solid wall of policemen. The Police Commissioner asked the demonstrators to disperse since there was a ban on marches in the city. Dana made an eloquent speech asking that the march be allowed to continue to honor Reeb. Commissioner Baker said he had to uphold the constitution of Alabama, to which Greeley replied, "But what about the Constitution of the United States of

America, Mr. Baker?" A negotiating committee was formed to deal with the authorities, including Dana, Rev. Vivian, Hosea Williams, Elder William Greer, and myself. We made little headway that morning, but hoped there might be a breakthrough, perhaps after the afternoon memorial meeting.

On Monday, March 15, more than 100 Unitarian Universalist ministers, and perhaps an equal number of laypersons, attended the memorial service for James Reeb in Brown Chapel, telecast nationwide. Martin Luther King gave the principal eulogy, with Dana giving one of the prayers. When the service was finished, King led three or more thousand worshipers to the Dallas County Court House. The "Selma Wall" of state troopers at last dissolved. King laid a wreath in memory of James Reeb. Dana and Walter Reuther, head of the United Automobile Workers, walked just behind King, as did a cross-section of the heads of American Protestant, Catholic, and Jewish denominations.

At 9:00 p.m. that Monday evening, the President of the U.S. spoke to a special session of Congress. Millions of Americans listened and twice President Johnson was given a standing ovation. When he uttered the phrase, "We Shall Overcome," tears came to the eyes of many, especially those several thousand who answered King's call to come to Selma.

On March 16, there was a memorial service in Reeb's All Souls Unitarian Church in Washington, led by Duncan Howlett, conducted by Dr. William Stuart Nelson of Howard University. Dana participated and Hubert Humphrey, Senator Edward Kennedy, and others attended. Marie was present as were her parents and Jim's.

On March 18, a memorial service was held at Arlington Street Church in Boston, conducted by the Rev. Jack Mendelsohn, with words from John Sullivan, Rabbi Roland B. Gittleson, and a representative of Cardinal Cushing. Marie Reeb and her family were also in the audience.

The next day, a plane provided by the President flew Marie and her four children to Casper, Wyoming. Two days later, on March 21, the Selma-to-Montgomery March began once more. When it concluded on March 25, thousands of marchers rallied in front of the Alabama State House on March 25.

Soon James Reeb's ashes were scattered, as he wished, on the prairie in Shirley Basin at the petrified forest of Wyoming, a world away from Selma, Alabama.

41 ATLANTA
(1955-1968)

THE SOURCES OF GANDHISM
IN MARTIN LUTHER KING, JR.

Homer began his association with Martin Luther King, Jr. during the Montgomery bus boycott in March 1956 and preached at his church in Alabama later that summer. He visited King in Harlem Hospital after he was stabbed and joined King in civil rights marches in Washington in 1957 and 1963, at the independence celebrations in Ghana, in appeals against nuclear testing for SANE, and on the Selma March. As the author of two books on Gandhi's life and thought and as a founder of CORE, Homer helped influence the development of King's nonviolent philosophy. He encouraged him to go to India and to speak out against the war in Vietnam—which King did in 1965 and was bitterly criticized by other civil rights leaders. In June 1966, Homer joined King on his second visit to Philadelphia, Mississippi, during the Meredith March and delivered a prayer at the courthouse as hundreds of state troopers looked on. "This was a dangerous mission," Homer recounted. "Ralph Abernathy recalled that it was one of the few times that he prayed with his eyes open! Somehow we survived the white hatred." Following King's assassination in April 1968, Homer flew to Memphis and accompanied the slain civil rights leader's body back to Atlanta with Coretta Scott King in a chartered airplane and served as a guard at his bier in the chapel of Spelman College. In this lecture—first given in longer form in India and published by the Gandhi Peace Center in Madras—Homer traces the sources of Gandhism in King's life and thought.

Dr. and Mrs. Howard Thurman of Howard University in Washington, D.C., had an interview with Mohandas Gandhi on February 21, 1936. According to Gandhi's secretary, Mahadev Desai, the meeting was the "first engagement of an important nature undertaken by the Indian leader after the breakdown in his health." Nevertheless, he wanted to meet this "American Negro delegation." Gandhi began by asking Dr. Thurman—a professor of comparative religion and philosophy—if "the prejudice against color" was growing or dying out. Dr. Thurman replied that it was "difficult to say because in one place things look much improved, while in another the outlook is still dark." Then the Thurmans asked Gandhi if the South African Negroes took any part in his earlier movement. Gandhi replied, "No, I purposely did not invite them. It would have endangered their cause. . . . " When Dr. Thurman asked Gandhi if nonviolence was a form of direct action, Gandhi replied that "without a direct active expression of it, nonviolence to my mind is meaningless." He added that "one cannot be passively nonviolent."

The interview went along in this manner until both the Thurmans declared, "We want you to come to America." Mrs. Thurman added, "We want you not for white America, but for the Negroes; we have many a problem that cries for solution, and we need you badly."

Gandhi answered, "How I wish I could, but I would have nothing to give you unless I had given an ocular demonstration here of all that I have been saying. I must make good the message here before I bring it to you. I do not say that I am defeated, but I have still to perfect myself. You may be sure that the moment I feel the call within me I shall not hesitate." Dr. Thurman changed the subject and declared that "when one goes through the pages of the hundreds of Negro spirituals, striking things are brought to my mind which remind me of all that you have told us today." Gandhi concluded the interview: "Well, if it comes true it may be through the Negroes that the unadulterated message of nonviolence will be delivered to the world."

At the time that Gandhi made this prophetic statement, Martin Luther King, Jr., was only seven years old. Yet King grew up to be called "the American Gandhi" during his lifetime and especially after his death. King was born on January 15, 1929. He received the Nobel Peace Prize on December 10, 1964, when he was thirty-five years old. He was assassinated on April 4, 1968, when he was but thirty-nine years old. Indeed, his whole ministry was short, less than fourteen years from the time that he became pastor of his first church in Montgomery, Alabama, on September 1, 1954, until he died in Memphis, Tennessee.

Gandhi and King Compared

There are obvious parallels in the lives of Mohandas Karamchand Gandhi and Martin Luther King, Jr. Both were colored men. Both came out of the middle class of their people. Both were well educated. Both married and had four children (all sons for Gandhi, two sons and two daughters for King). Both led large political movement, using the method of nonviolent action (*satyagraha*). Both held no public office, yet both exerted more power and gained more adulation than most elected statesmen of their time. Both were charismatic. Both ironically died by the bullet, although they were votaries of nonviolence. Both were acknowledged in death, and even in life, as the greatest humanitarians of their time. The world truly grieved at the passing of both. Both died in the very midst of battle. Both had premonitions of death, and both died feeling a sense of disappointment, of a lack of fulfillment, not of victory.

Yet the parallels in the lives of Gandhi and King are not complete. Gandhi was an Asian, although he spent several decades in Africa and studied in England. He never visited America. King was an American, of African ancestry. He visited both Africa and Asia (India), but never lived outside the United States. Gandhi was forward-looking, but distinctly a nineteenth century man. King was twentieth century. Their lives overlapped twenty years: 1929— when King was born—to 1948 when Gandhi was assassinated.

Gandhi and King never corresponded. They had several mutual friends (Stuart Nelson and Amiya Chakravarty), although Gandhi could not have known even at his death, that the twenty-year-old King existed.

Gandhi was a Hindu and King was a Christian. Gandhi was a lawyer by training and King studied to be a clergyman. Gandhi lived to seventy-eight years; King was cut down at thirty-nine. Gandhi was the leader of the majority in his nation; King was the leader of a minority. Gandhi was revered the world over, yet only King received the Nobel Peace Prize.

The Intellectual Framework

King was a formal student from the time he entered Morehouse College in 1944 through his years at Crozer Theological Seminar and until he left the Boston University School of Theology in 1954 to assume his first pastorate in Montgomery. King has become such an important personality in history that even the course work in these institutions of higher learning has been carefully studied, far beyond what he himself has written about them.

Many intellectual influences have been found in King's student years which later contributed to his more mature thought and action. Gandhi was only one influence. Also important were George W. Davis, a Crozer professor, and the latter's evangelical liberalism; Walter Rauschenbusch and the Social Gospel Movement; Reinhold Niebuhr and Prof. L. Harold de Wolf of Boston University and his personalism. Thus Systematic Christian thinking, quite apart from the Black Church of his father and his fathers had a major influence on King's life, thought, and actions. Yet among the intellectual influence there was indeed Gandhism.

During the three years—beginning in 1948—King spent at Crozer Theological Seminary outside Philadelphia, he became acquainted with Gandhism on several levels. He took a course with Prof. George W. Davis on the psychology of religion. This apparently included a discussion of Gandhi. Also A. J. Muste, the Secretary of the American section of the Fellowship of Reconciliation, visited and talked to the students of Crozer as he did to those at other theological schools. In addition, King went to nearby Philadelphia and heard Howard University president, Mordecai W. Johnson, talk about his recent visit to India and about Gandhi.

While at Crozer, King was impressed with a description of Gandhi given by President Mordecai Johnson in the spring of 1950. King wrote: "Then one Sunday afternoon I travelled to Philadelphia to hear a sermon by Dr. Moredecai Johnson, president of Howard University. He was there to preach for the Fellowship House of Philadelphia. Dr. Johnson had just returned from a trip to India, and, to my great interest, he spoke of the life and teachings of Mahatma Gandhi. His message was so profound and electrifying that I left the meeting and bought a half-dozen books on Gandhi's life and works."

Montgomery and Gandhism

During the 382 days of the Montgomery Bus Boycott, King and his associates stumbled into using Gandhian techniques. Their tactics began to be called Gandhian and they had no reason to contradict the label; indeed, they were helped by fellow Americans outside the South, both blacks and whites who had independently if earlier experimented with the use of Gandhian techniques in American race relations.

As much as fourteen years earlier—in 1942—some Americans had intentionally used Gandhian techniques to lessen segregation in Chicago and later, in 1947, in a Journey of Reconciliation to end segregation of interstate buses in the middle South and elsewhere. If King did not have direct contact up to that period with CORE, he did have an adviser who was involved in CORE: Bayard Rustin. The latter by then was on the staff of the War Resisters League. A second adviser was a white member of the FOR staff, Glenn Smiley, who was quietly sent to Montgomery. Both Rustin and Smiley in different ways helped King and the Montgomery Improvement Association to become Gandhian in more than name.

Initially, the movement was not called Gandhian except by Juliette Morgan in her letter to the Montgomery newspaper (*see Chapter 71*). When King's house was bombed on January 30, 1956, the Police Commissioner asked King to reassure an assembling group of Negroes at nighttime. King addressed the crowd, urging them not to retaliate against the white community. He said: "We are not advocating violence. We want to love our enemies. I want you to love your enemies. Be good to them. Love them and let them know you love them."

The next day, however, King applied to the county sheriff for a pistol permit so that the watchmen at his home could be armed. At a speech in Chicago, King emphasized that the protest "is a movement of passive resistance." Because of the bombing, King's father put strong pressure on him to leave Montgomery because of further threats, but King in the end replied, " I would rather go back and spend ten years in jail than not go back."

Late in February when a number of Negroes were arrested for breaking the state anti-boycott law, King at a mass rally said: "If we are arrested every day, if we are exploited every day, if we are trampled over every day, don't ever let anyone pull you so far as to hate them. We must use the weapon of love. We must have compassion and understanding for those who hate us."

The mass indictments brought national attention to the Montgomery protest. One national TV commentator compared the protesters to Gandhi and the position of the white leadership of Montgomery to that of the British in India.

Bayard Rustin visited Montgomery on February 21. Rustin did not stay long in Montgomery, but kept in close touch with King. He wrote friends in New York that "King is developing a decidedly Gandhi-like view" and was "eagerly learning all that he can about nonviolence." Yet on a visit to the King parsonage Rustin and Negro journalist William Worthy were startled to find a pistol on the armchair. King said the gun was intended to harm no one unless they were violently attacked. Rustin, according to King biographer David Garrow, "attempted to persuade King that even the presence of guns was contrary to the philosophy that he was increasingly articulating."

King was tried for breaking the state's anti-boycott law—and convicted. He was fined $500 and court costs. When he left the courthouse, King told 300 cheering people: "We will continue to protest in the same spirit of nonviolence and passive resistance, using the weapon of love."

Some days later King spoke to 2,500 Negroes at the Concord Baptist Church in Brooklyn, telling them how Gandhi used "passive resistance" to break loose from "the political and economic domination by the British and brought the British Empire to its knees." He added: "Let's now use this method in the U.S." In an interview King stated, "I have been a keen student of Gandhi for many years. However, this business of passive resistance and nonviolence is the gospel of Jesus. I went to Gandhi through Jesus."

Early in December 1956, the Montgomery Improvement Association sponsored a week-long Institute on Nonviolence and Social Change. King delivered the opening address, almost a year after he addressed the first rally of the bus boycott. He said that the real goal of the campaign was not to defeat the white man, but "to awaken a sense of shame within the oppressor and challenge his false sense of superiority." He said that "the end is reconciliation; the end is redemption; the end is the creation of the beloved community."

Before Christmas the U.S. Supreme Court decision affirming a lower court ruling ending bus segregation in Montgomery was implemented. The bus company welcomed King as the first passenger in an early morning bus, with the white minister, Glenn Smiley, seated next to him.

Visiting Gandhi's India

Some of King's friends—especially Bayard Rustin and Harris Wof-
ford—suggested that he visit India. They and others asked, "Why
don't you go to India and see for yourself what the Mahatma,
whom you so admire, has wrought?" Indeed, both Prime Minister
Nehru and former U.S. Ambassador to India, Chester Bowles, urged
King to go. One planned trip was postponed, but after King was
stabbed in Harlem and recovered, it appeared possible for the Kings
to leave for India in January 1959. This was several years after the
Montgomery campaign was successfully concluded and several
years before the March on Washington and the Nobel Peace Prize.

The Indian connection was forged early when Shri R. R. Diwakar visited for three days Montgomery in mid-August 1956. A longtime Gandhian, Diwakar was president of the Gandhi Peace Foundation. As a result of Diwakar's visit, several Gandhian institutions
in India kept in touch with King.

Lawrence D. Reddick of Alabama State College in Montgomery
accompanied the Kings on the trip. They left New York City on February 3 via Paris and Geneva. In Paris, Reddick introduced the
Kings to American black novelist Richard Wright. Because of
weather problems, they landed in India two days late. King spoke
at a crowded press conference, asserting that "to other countries I
may go as a tourist, but to India I come as a pilgrim."

The one-month visit took the King party to many parts of India.
They made the clockwise visit, beginning in New Delhi and ending
there. In the capital, they dined with Nehru, had tea with Vice-
President Radhakrishnan, and called on President Rajendra Prasad.
Coretta King recalled that her husband remarked that it had been
"like meeting George Washington, Thomas Jefferson, and James
Madison in a single day." They laid a wreath at the Rajghat (where
Gandhi's ashes lay at rest), and King spoke to the Delhi University
Student Union. Then they flew to Bihar to visit Jayaprakash Narayan at his ashram. From there they rode to Shantiniketan, Tagore's
ashram and school. Then they moved on to Calcutta, Madras where
they met C. Rajagopalachari, and Madurai. There they visited several Gramdan villages—on land given during Vinoba Bhave's movement—and also went to Gandhigram where they saw students in
the Shanti Sena, the "peace army." The King party visited Trivan-
drum, Bangalore, Bombay, Ahmedabad, and then walked with Vinoba Bhave who was attending an All-India Shanti Sena Confer-

ence. Jayaprakash Narayan was also in attendance. Back in Delhi, King gave a farewell press conference and advocated unilateral disarmament (after his talks with Vinoba). He regretted that the U.S. and the U.S.S.R. had not disarmed themselves. He asked India to do so, since it had demonstrated that a nation can win independence nonviolently.

King summarized his impressions of his visit to India in an article in *Ebony* magazine, a large picture periodical especially for black readers. He wrote that it was "wonderful to be in Gandhi's land, to talk to his sons, grandsons, to share the reminiscences of his close comrades, to visit his ashram." King felt that they were "looked upon as brothers with the color of our skins as something of an asset." But he quickly added that "the strongest bond was the common cause of minority and colonial peoples."

King admitted that the visit was "one of the most concentrated and eye-opening experiences" of their lives. He met some untouchables and later wrote, "There is, even here, the problem of segregation. We call it race in America. They call it caste in India." King concluded that "in both places it means that some are considered inferior, treated as though they deserve less." He probably had a higher opinion of the results of the official efforts to outlaw untouchability than was warranted, even though he was tutored in this matter by Nehru.

King left India "more convinced than ever before that nonviolent resistance is the most potent weapon available to oppressed people in their struggle for freedom." King came back to America convinced that India needed help. Again he wrote in *Ebony*, "Today India is a tremendous force for peace and nonviolence at home and abroad." He called it "a land where the idealist and the intellectual are yet respected." He asked his fellow Americans "to want to help India preserve her soul and thus help to save our own."

Coretta King later wrote that King, as a result of his Indian visit, "constantly pondered" how to apply simplicity of living to America. She reported that her husband "even considered the idea of changing his style of dress to a simpler one, but he decided that since his main purpose was to attract people to the cause, unusual dress might even tend to alienate followers." She concluded that "dress was really a superficial form rather than the spiritual quality he was aiming for."

339

Six Basic Aspects

Gandhi is mentioned in several places in King's autobiography, *Stride Toward Freedom*. After discussing the evolution of his own thought, King in the chapter on "Pilgrimage to Nonviolence" lists six "basic aspects of this philosophy." It may be productive to examine these six "aspects" and compare them with some of Gandhi's writing to ascertain what King and his collaborators included in this early stage of King's public career.

First, nonviolent resistance is "not a method for cowards." He called the method "passive physically, but strongly active, spiritually." It is "not passive resistance to evil; it is active nonviolent resistance to evil."

Gandhi made similar comments. Indeed, King declared that "Gandhi often said that if cowardice is the only alternative to violence, it is better to fight." Elsewhere Gandhi said,"We shall have to give up even verbal violence and learn dignified ways of dealing with our opponents."

Second, nonviolent resistance "does not seek to defeat or humiliate the opponent, but to win his friendship and understanding." The end is not boycott or noncooperation, but redemption and reconciliation. King felt the aftermath is the "creation of the beloved community," not "tragic bitterness."

Gandhi also had similar themes: "Whilst we may attain measures and systems, we may not, must not, attack men. Imperfect ourselves we must be tender toward others and be slow to impute motives." Coretta King in the introduction of *The Trumpet of Conscience* asked that her husband be remembered "as a man who refused to lose faith in the ultimate redemption of mankind."

Third, nonviolent resistance is directed against forces of evil rather than against persons who happen to be doing the evil. As King told the people of Montgomery, "We are out to defeat injustice and not white persons who may be unjust." Gandhi asserted: "A *satyagrahi* is always prepared for but does not anticipate repression. He imputes no evil in his opponent."

Fourth, nonviolent resistance includes the willingness to accept suffering without retaliation. The votary of nonviolence is willing to accept violence if necessary, "but never to inflict it." He does not seek to avoid jail, but enters it "as a bridegroom enters the bride's chambers."

King quoted Gandhi as declaring: "Rivers of blood may have to flow before we gain our freedom but it must be our blood." Gandhi wrote in *Young India* that "the secret of nonviolence . . . lies in our realizing that it is through suffering that we are to attain our goal." In 1927 Gandhi remarked that "'Hate the sin and not the sinner' is a precept which, though easy enough to understand, is rarely practiced, and that is why the poison of hatred spreads in the world."

Fifth, nonviolent resistance not only avoids external physical violence, but also "internal violence of spirit." The votive refuses to shoot his opponent and he refuses to hate. One must not succumb to the temptation of "becoming bitter or indulging in hate campaigns." Here King discusses at some length the ethics of love, using the concept of love called *agape* or "love in action."

Gandhi likewise declared that "nonviolence begins and ends by turning the searchlight inward." Elsewhere Gandhi said that "nonviolent action cannot be sustained unless it goes hand in hand with nonviolence in thought."

The sixth and last point King discussed was nonviolent resistance that is based on the conviction that "the universe is on the side of justice." The resister "knows that in his struggle for justice he has cosmic companionship." King wrote: "Whether we call it an unconscious process, an impersonal Brahman, or a personal being of matchless power and infinite love, there is a creative force in this universe that works to bring the disconnected aspects of reality into a harmonious whole."

Gandhi declared in *Young India* that "my noncooperation has its roots not in hatred but in love."

The six principles hardly constitute a definitive delineation of nonviolent resistance. Yet it is the way by 1958 that King and his close associates viewed some of the elements of this complex, evolving strategy.

Between 1958, when King wrote *Stride Toward Freedom*, and 1968, when he was assassinated, he acquired many additional insights about nonviolent resistance. For example, King went out of his way to insist that his goal was freedom for all human beings, not only for Negroes. Nonviolence was universal, nonracial, even in the days of Black Power. In May 1956 King wrote, "When we speak of love we speak of understanding, goodwill toward *all* men." He added that "we see that the real tension is not between the Negro citizens and the white citizens of Montgomery, but it is a conflict between justice and injustice." Thus the "victory will not be merely for the Negro citizens and a defeat for the white citizens." In 1958 King wrote that a successful nonviolent movement would demonstrate "to the white community that if such a movement attained a degree of strength, it would use its power creatively and not vengefully." In his 1964 Nobel address, King emphasized that his American movement did "not seek to liberate Negroes at the expense of the humiliation and enslavement of whites." It sought "no victory over anyone." In an article published after King's death, and another context, King declared that "we have not given up on integration. We still believe in black and white together."

Gandhi also did not eliminate the English people from his universe. In 1909 in South Africa, Gandhi declared that "I bear no enmity towards the English but I do towards their civilization." Also in 1921 Gandhi said that "I did not consider Englishmen nor do I now consider them to be as capable of high motives and actions as any other body of men and equally capable of making mistakes."

King also believed in the utility of nonviolent resistance to achieve democracy in the U.S. He also believed that this method could be used worldwide to solve problems in other nations and among nations. King, in his book, *The Trumpet of Conscience*, asked: "Can a nonviolent direct-action movement find application on the international level, to confront economic and political problems?" His answer was positive: "I believe it can." He revealed that "it is clear to me that the next stage of the movement is to become international." Referring to Latin America, he predicted that "one of the most powerful expressions of nonviolence may come out of that international coalition of socially aware forces operating outside governmental framework." After apartheid, he felt that "it is obvious that nonviolent movements for social change must internationalize, because of the interlocking nature of the problems they all face, and because otherwise those problems will breed war." He added that "we have hardly begun to build the skills and the strategy, or even the commitment, to planetize our movements for social justice." Facing the number one problem in the world then, King commented: "We live each day on the verge of nuclear co-annihilation; in this world, nonviolence is no longer an option for intellectual analysis; it is an imperative for action."

Gandhi always considered nonviolent resistance to be universal. He used it both in South Africa and India. He suggested, "Its universal applicability is a demonstration of its permanence and invincibility." Elsewhere Gandhi declared that "a soldier of peace unlike the one of the sword has to give all his spare time to the promotion of peace alike in war time as in peace time." Gandhi was suggesting that nonviolent resistance goes beyond national borders.

Conclusion

After visiting India, King called Gandhi "one of the half-dozen greatest men in world history." He did not elucidate further on his criteria for this judgment. Indeed, while King mentioned the Indian people and nonviolence in his Nobel acceptance address, he did not specifically mention Gandhi. King's admiration of Gandhi was not limited to Gandhi's "discovery" of nonviolent resistance. In a sermon delivered to his Montgomery congregation immediately after visiting India, King enumerated three "commendable" characteristics of Gandhi. He had a great capacity for self-criticism; his avoidance of material possessions was almost total; and he had "absolute self-discipline" and thus there was "no gulf between the private and the public." By implication, King admitted that Gandhi bettered him on all three counts.

Though Gandhi influenced King mightily and rightly, King was very much his own man and many other individuals and movements understandably entered King's thoughts and actions. We are all a product of our intellectual environment, whether we admit it or not—and, to his credit, King freely admitted his dependence upon Gandhi.

Let Martin Luther King have the final words, taken from the last paragraph of *Stride Toward Freedom:* "It may even be possible for the Negro, through adherence to nonviolence, so to challenge the nations of the world that they will seriously seek an alternative to war and destruction . . . Today the choice is no longer between violence and nonviolence. It is either nonviolence or nonexistence. The Negro may be God's appeal to this age—an age drifting rapidly to its doom. The eternal appeal takes the form of a warning: 'All who take the sword will perish by the sword.'"

42 STOCKHOLM • SAIGON
(1967)

WHAT VIETNAM WANTS

Since his days with SANE (on whose Board he remained from 1964-1984), Homer had actively opposed America's military intervention in Vietnam and through the UUA helped organize the religious community to speak out against the war. In 1967 he visited South Vietnam and met with Thich Tri Quang, the charismatic leader of the Buddhist movement and a student of Gandhi, Ambassador Henry Cabot Lodge, and his son, Alex, who was reporting the war in South Vietnam and Cambodia. At a conference in Stockholm in July, American peace leaders met as a group with representatives of the National Liberation Front (the Vietcong) and North Vietnam for the first time. Although he found their rhetoric and platform extreme, Homer recognized—years before negotiations began and the war finally concluded—the inevitability of their victory. Homer filed an account of the conference and his changed perspective for War/Peace Report. *The following year, in January 1968, Homer returned to Vietnam with an interfaith delegation and met with General William C. Westmoreland, commander of U.S. forces, and Vietnamese leaders. In May 1971, Homer made his third and final visit to Saigon. In September of that year, he planned to return for an interreligious consultation but was denied a visa by the South Vietnamese government. Following the Christmas bombing of Hanoi in 1972 by President Nixon and Secretary Kissinger, Homer called upon the U.N. Secretary-General to convene the Security Council and condemn the attacks, but the U.N.—as throughout the conflict—took no action.*

The Stockholm Conference

It was a Sunday noon in Stockholm. In the Folkets Hus, Swedish peace leader and journalist Bertil Svahnstrom asked the three representatives from the National Liberation Front of South Vietnam and the two delegates from Hanoi to come to the platform of the closing plenary session of the World Conference on Vietnam. Then he asked the American delegates—some forty persons—also to take the platform. What followed—a public exchange of greetings by persons who had worked together for four days while their governments were still battling—was undoubtedly the emotional high point of the Stockholm Conference, as Vietnamese and Americans hugged each other unrestrainedly. This was a genuine display, in a highly charged political atmosphere, of humanity overarching nationalism.

Convened by the Swedish Peace and Arbitration Society and sponsored principally by the communist-aligned World Council of Peace (WCP) and the nonaligned International Confederation for Disarmament and Peace (ICDP), this July 10-12 conference brought together more than 400 delegates and observers from twenty-two international organizations and countless national organizations in sixty-two countries.

The biggest political headache was the representation of the Vietnamese. The organizing committee initially voted to invite representatives from the Democratic Republic of Vietnam (DRV) and the National Liberation Front (NLF) since such representation would insure Soviet participation, make criticism of the conference from China less credible, and give a rare opportunity for an expected large U.S. delegation to fraternize with non-Saigon Vietnamese.

With acceptances received from the DRV and the NLF, ICDP members then attempted to urge Buddhist representation. This produced the threat of an NLF pull-out, which would have triggered a withdrawal by the DRV and no doubt by the Russians as well. Hard-pressed ICDP representatives made a compromise: The Buddhists would be asked to submit a working paper instead of appearing in person, but it was considered too anti-communist and neutralist by the WCP and the ICDP retreated again, so there was no Buddhist representation. Swedish economist Gunnar Myrdal did not open the session as planned partly because of the absence of Buddhists. When he did speak at the close of the conference, he expressed regrets that the Buddhists were not invited and commended them for their continued opposition to the Ky regime in Saigon.

If the Buddhists were absent, the other Vietnamese were very much present. The leaders of both the NLF and DRV delegations made long speeches at the opening plenary. They took an active part in commission deliberations and many private meetings. The American participants, a contingent more than a unified delegation, included Dr. Benjamin Spock, Rev. James Bevel of SCLC, Dorothy Hutchinson, David McReynolds of the War Resisters League, Prof. D. F. Fleming, and Sidney Lens. There was little moderate or even pacifist representation. The American continent held daily caucuses and its members were active in many commissions and work groups. They met separately with the NLF and the DRV delegations in friendly but political hour-long meetings.

Much of the work of the conference was carried out in eight commissions and several vocational work groups. Commission 1 on International Law, headed by Krishna Menon of India, reflected the general assertion of the conference that U.S. action in Vietnam was leading to genocide. It condemned the U.S. for transgressing "the generally recognized principles of international law." Commission 2 on the Face of the War declared that "the erosion of the long-standing conventions against the use of weapons of mass destruction and ill-treatment of prisoners have paved the way to the violation of these standards elsewhere, notably in the Middle East."

Commission 3 on the Struggle for Independence and Development sought to define the precise role of the NLF in Vietnam. Dinh Ba Thi of the NLF called the Front "the only genuine representative of the South Vietnamese people." A few delegates, notably David McReynolds of WRL and Amy Swerdlow of Women's Strike for Peace, felt that it was not the business of the conference to decide who represents the Vietnamese people. However, there were strong pressures for designating the NLF. A new formulation was worked out: "The Front, alone, authentically represents the fundamental aspirations of the people of South Vietnam."

This group also devised a three-point basis for settlement, which did not replace the previous formulas of the NLF and DRV: "1) There must be a definitive and unconditional cessation of bombing and all other acts of war against the DRV; 2) A genuine, durable solution can be obtained in the South only by the cessation of the U.S. aggression, the unconditional, total and permanent withdrawal of American and allied forces and their equipment, and the dismantling of their military bases, and 3) It is up to the Vietnamese people to settle their own affairs, on the basis of independence, democracy, peace and neutrality, that is to say, according to the principles of the

Geneva Agreements and the program of the NLF."

Calling U.S. initiatives since 1965 "in effect . . . demands for surrender," Commission 4 on Peace Initiatives asserted that the U.S. has shown "no real desire" for a just and honorable solution of the conflict. Commission 5 dealt with the Growing Isolation of the U.S., and Commission 6 was concerned with Material Aid for North Vietnam. Commission 7 on Coordination of Activities suggested future actions including a boycott of U.S. goods and leafleting of U.S. tourists. Commission 8 on War and World Peace declared that the U.S. intervention in Vietnam was part of a "vast plan to create a strategic U.S. zone of influence in Asia."

Work groups were held for parliamentarians, housewives, students, teachers, and religionists. The latter included Martin Niemöeller of Germany, Abbé Pierre of France, Bishop Juvenalius of the Soviet Union, and James Bevel of the U.S. No rabbi attended the conference and the one Buddhist monk present (from Ceylon) did not attend this work group. The religionists declared that Christians "cannot remain silent or inactive in the face of the immense suffering being inflicted on the people of Vietnam."

The major accomplishment of the conference was to provide an opportunity for forty U.S. citizens working against the war in Vietnam to talk to representatives of the NLF and the DRV for four days. They got a sustained, noncombatant measure of each other.

The greatest limitation of the conference was the exclusion of the militant Buddhists, which left bitterness in the hearts of a minority of Stockholm delegates. Perhaps a different solution should have been found, with at least one Buddhist monk attending as a delegate from an international organization.

A second limitation was the absence of moderation in representation and language. This turned out to be a revolutionary conference. Most moderate individuals who oppose the Vietnamese war did not attend, and probably they would have felt out of place amid the constant references to "American imperialism," "American aggression," and "nothing less than genocide." It was too bad the conference could not have included a greater spectrum of anti-war positions.

Illusions Dispelled

Most persons attend conferences from habit or duty. They have a harried, usually interesting, experience, and return to write a report.

They generally also go home without having immediately changed their minds. This conference was different for at least this reporter. Here are four illusions I carried to Stockholm—all of which were dispelled, some quickly, others slowly, all painfully:

1. *Nothing is more important to the people of Vietnam than peace.* While it was amply established that Washington and Saigon do not want peace in Vietnam at any price, I learned that the Front and Hanoi have also put one priority above peace: independence, the right to choose their own government without American or other interference.

2. *An armistice, negotiations, and a permanent settlement have been held up primarily because of the U.S. and Saigon governments.* At Stockholm it became obvious that not only the U.S. and Saigon fear negotiations; so do the NLF and DRV. They feel that negotiation spells compromise, and that military victory will come to them even if they must fight for another decade. So why negotiate? They believe the Geneva Agreements need to be enforced, not "negotiated down," because there is nothing to negotiate about.

3. *The militant Buddhists in Saigon and Hue can play an important role in the future of South Vietnam.* The truth is that the militant Buddhists could at most be members of a transitional, caretaker regime. The NLF constitutes the prime political entity in South Vietnam today, whether or not it "authentically represents the fundamental aspirations of the people." The NLF has fought, bled, and died for too many years to be shunted aside by the Buddhists, however much the latter are viewed by liberals in the West as humane, reasonable, democratic, and socialist. The Buddhists are too much a "third force" in a long civil war; in such a political atmosphere—as in Algeria before independence—neutralism is expendable.

4. *The NLF and the DRV should be willing by now to compromise because of the military punishment they have received.* Actually, the morale of the NLF and the DRV is surprisingly high, despite the military punishment they have received. They are keeping the huge American, Saigon, and allied military machines at least at a stalemate. From this position of relative psychological and even military strength, they are not about to give away positions at a negotiating table.

This is the painful reality I perceived during the Stockholm Conference. Many perhaps have gained such insights without leaving home through careful reading. I myself did not acquire such understanding even on a short visit to Saigon. Yet at this conference, with only five Vietnamese present, it suddenly became clear to me why President Johnson seems so trapped. He has a more formidable opponent than at least I ever dreamed—the militant, confident nationalism, for good or ill, of the Vietnamese people.

Return to Vietnam

In January 1968, the American delegation to a WCRP symposium in New Delhi flew to Saigon. In four days we held extensive talks and were welcomed especially by the An Quang Pagoda. Thich Tri Quang was in the hospital when we arrived, but saw Dana McLean Greeley and me when he returned to the pagoda. The American group also conferred with U.S. General William C. Westmoreland. The latter asserted, "We want an honorable peace, but we can't be trapped into a position here where we will be the losers." After the one-hour interview, General Westmoreland volunteered that he was listening to a perspective—with sharp questions from Dr. Greeley, Bishop James K. Matthews, and Rabbi Eisendrath—that was new to him; at least never before had he heard it through face-to-face contact.

The American delegation also talked to U.S. Ambassador Ellsworth Bunker who admitted that "military victory is not possible without . . . rural reconstruction." He said that "the U.S. is waging a limited war for limited objectives and therefore [is] using limited resources." Before leaving, the American group gave a press conference and stated that we had "stopped in Saigon because the war in Vietnam represents probably the greatest current threat to the peace of the world." We asked President Johnson to reevaluate U.S. policy and "give serious consideration to an immediate halt, on moral and political if not military grounds, of the bombing of North Vietnam." We further asked the President to be "continually open to negotiations, including the use of the services of the Secretary-General of the U.N." Less than one month after our visit, the National Liberation Front's Tet offensive occurred, with attacks on more than 100 cities and bases. In May of that year, the Nixon regime in Washington started negotiations with Hanoi in Paris.

43 BOSTON (1969)

SANCTUARY AT MARSH CHAPEL

During the Vietnam War, Boston served as the nation's crucible for dissent and protest, following a tradition going back to the Boston Tea Party and the Abolitionist movement against slavery. Homer's son, Alex, a Unitarian seminarian at Boston University School of Theology, was a founder of the New England Resistance, a radical anti-war, anti-draft group that organized a large rally on Boston Common and mass draft-card burning ceremony at Arlington Street Church on Oct. 16, 1967 (for which Rev. William Sloane Coffin, chaplain at Yale, and Dr. Spock were indicted for conspiracy in a major protest trial during the war). Alex and his friends also organized the first sanctuary in support of G.I.'s who refused to go to Vietnam, also at Arlington Street Church, in May 1968. Here is Homer's report of a subsequent sanctuary that his son, Alex, helped initiate at Boston University's historic chapel the following spring.

Perspective 1969: Newly elected President Richard Nixon pledged to end the war in Vietnam, but by autumn over a million Americans mobilized in Washington against the war, and the Trial of the Chicago Eight opened. America sent a man to the moon, Golda Meir became prime minister in Israel, and Yassir Arafat was elected chairman of the PLO. The nuclear Non-Proliferation Treaty was signed, SALT talks opened in Helsinki, and Soviet and Chinese forces clashed on the Manchurian border. The first SIPRI yearbook came out and described the arms race as "runaway," doubling every fifteen years. Nineteen sixty-nine was the year of Woodstock, My Lai, the Weathermen, Chappaquidick, and the films Easy Rider *and* Butch Cassidy and the Sundance Kid.

For six days and nights recently, Boston University's Marsh Chapel (where Howard Thurman was chaplain for more than a decade and where Martin Luther King. Jr., worshiped as a graduate student) became the site of a vigil against the war in Vietnam.

It all began when five B.U. School of Theology students turned a regular nine o'clock chapel service into a symbolic sanctuary for eighteen-year-old Raymond Kroll, AWOL since July from Fort Benning, Georgia. Speaking from the pulpit, Kroll said, "Only after I came to the decision that I could not take part in the armed forces without going against my moral conviction did I turn to the New England Resistance."

School of Theology and university officials were told of the project, not asked; they were hesitant, then overwhelmed. Though they did not sanction this declaration of war resistance, they did not appear as petulant and frightened as did the Harvard authorities across the Charles River during a similar but much shorter attempt at sanctuary a few weeks earlier at that university's divinity school.

In its long history, Marsh Chapel had probably never been so completely occupied (the committee declared it "liberated"). At times lines of students waited outside for an opportunity to enter. They packed the pews, and filled the aisles in the hope of preventing federal marshals from getting to Kroll. Students slept all night in the pews, attempted to do some homework, and ate three meals a day (at one point a nearby restaurant donated 500 hamburgers).

Outside the chapel, student "security" patrols operated; inside, marshals roamed the aisles, some wearing "theo" badges or medical or legal observer armbands. Many wore the "Omega" symbol of the growing Resistance movement. Underground newspapers were sold and read. Slowly the "Marsh Chapel Community" evolved, as more than 5,000 students and dozens of faculty members participated in one way or another.

At the pulpit was an open, well used microphone, with a theolog in charge. Students were given a phone number to call if they should be imprisoned and in need of bail money or legal aid, were told how to fend off police blows, how to deal with MACE and other chemicals. Leaders repeatedly underlined the primacy of nonviolent resistance in case of a "bust" involving campus, city, and/or federal authorities. Many worship services were held—Protestant, ecumenical, Jewish. A peace symbol appeared on the altar. Untraditional communion services were held. The kiss of peace was exchanged. Chants were recited: "Hell, No. We Won't Go," "End the War," "Peace Now." Occasionally, Ray Kroll talked from the pulpit while a rock band gave several concerts. A guerrilla theater performed. One professor took his government class to the chapel and taught it there. Movies of the sanctuary last May in Boston's Arlington Street Church were shown.

Suddenly, at 5:30 Sunday morning—before the chapel pastor was scheduled to give the weekly service—church bells chimed, signifying that the "bust" had begun. A hundred or more federal agents and Boston police swept down on the chapel, so quickly that the 400 sleeping students scarcely had time to begin singing "We Shall Overcome" and attempt to form a human cordon to protect Kroll. Agents moved reclining students from the aisles to the pews; none offered resistance. They found Kroll in a room off the sanctuary and dragged him outside. Many students followed, standing on the curb with their hands raised high and two fingers held up in the peace sign. Leaders lowered the American flag outside the chapel to half mast. Then the students, only a few left, returned to the chapel for a special service. Many remained for the regular Sunday worship service.

Declared the students: "Our thoughts and our love go to Ray as he must pay the penalty for showing a mirror to our society." They pledged to stay together as a community and to work toward the ending of ROTC on the campus and the cancellation of government-supported research.

During the episode, Arland Christ-Jenner, B.U.'s new president, sent the students no message. Later, in an address to students assembled in the chapel, he said:

"In the past ten days a number of the members of the Boston University community expressed as a matter of conscience their protest of a war which sheds a dreadful shadow upon the world. . . . Throughout the event the university acknowledged its obligation and its responsibility to observe the laws of the land. At the same time, without itself engaging in civil disobedience, Boston University maintained the principle of freedom of assembly and freedom of speech. The university respected the right of peaceful protest."

Today Boston University is decidedly on the left bank of the Charles—to the left of both Harvard and MIT, which have yet to be "liberated" by students pledging themselves not to participate in this "military nightmare." At long last, for 116 hours the chapel of this Methodist-established institution was indisputably "where the action was."

44
BOSTON
(1967-1969)

BLACK POWER AND WHITE
LIBERALS

*The legacy of racism in America—especially after the deaths of Martin Lu-
ther King, Jr. and Malcolm X and the interminably slow progress toward
racial equality—gave rise to Black Power. The new militancy rocked the
nation and its institutions, including the churches—even the liberal
churches such as the Unitarian Universalists. As social action director of
the UUA, Homer found himself in the middle of a firestorm that threatened
to engulf the denomination and those, like himself, who had led the struggle for racial justice for many years. Under attack by both militants and
moderates, Homer tried to be sympathetic to the overall goals of the Black
Power movement and put the confrontation into wider social and historical
perspective. He delivered this speech to a Unitarian fellowship in New Delhi in early 1968.*

Last summer civil rights leader Bayard Rustin wrote that the
United States is in the throes of a historic national crisis: "Its ramifi-
cations are so vast and frightening that even now, shocked in numb-
ness and disbelief, the American people have not yet fully grasped
what is happening to them." I must confess that I am among those
Americans who still feel shocked at the intensity of the hate and violence of the U.S. during the summer of 1967, and I like to believe
that I do not shock easily. For more than twenty five years, I have
worked professionally, if impatiently, in what used to be called
"race relations" and more recently has been termed "civil rights."

Our Unitarian Universalist denomination in the U.S. and Canada has long had a concern in this field of black/white relations. Theodore Parker and other Unitarian Universalist clergymen more than a century ago helped lead the movement for the abolition of slavery. One of our laywomen early in this century was a founder of the NAACP. Another layman, Whitney Young, Jr., is today executive director of the National Urban League. One percent of our denomination's membership—more than 1,500 persons—participated in the March on Washington for civil rights in August 1963. Several hundred of our ministers marched at Selma, Alabama, in March 1965. One of them, James J. Reeb, was martyred there. For almost two years our Association employed an itinerant James Reeb Civil Rights Worker to relate our largely white and suburban churches to the inner city ghetto. Many of our local churches and fellowships have pioneered in their communities, even in the South, for equality of opportunity and for desegregation.

Yet I think it fair to confess that our denomination felt powerless to be relevant or even helpful during the rebellions in Newark, Detroit, and elsewhere last summer. We sent a few small checks to these smoking cities from our Unitarian Universalist Freedom Fund for relief. We have no Unitarian Universalist Church in Newark itself and most of our churches in Greater Detroit were apparently closed for the summer! I myself felt it futile to fly to these two cities during the rebellion; such a presence, helpful perhaps in earlier situations, seemed useless last summer.

While the smoke was still arising from Detroit, our Unitarian Universalist Commission on Religion and Race decided to hold an Emergency Conference on the Unitarian Universalist Response to the Black Rebellion. (We called it a rebellion, because the situation was somewhere between a race riot and a full-scale revolution.) We decided to bring together about 150 Unitarian Universalists, laymen and ministers, Negro and white, from all parts of the United States and Canada, to assess our denominational role in the changing situation of black/white relations.

Simultaneous with our Association efforts to convene this Conference, a small group of Unitarian Universalists gathered in Los Angeles last summer to form BURR: Black Unitarians for Radical Reform. They informed the Association that they would create a Black Caucus at our Emergency Conference. On the very first evening that the 150 registrants gathered in New York City early in October, many of the blacks did go off into a separate hotel room to form a Black Caucus. By the end of the three-day conference, thirty-one of the thirty-seven Unitarian Universalists registered identified themselves as members of this Black Caucus.

Some of us white Unitarian Universalists were taken aback by this development of a Black Caucus. Certainly as director of the conference, I was surprised. Yet in retrospect we should have anticipated this development. If, as some of us hope, our denomination is still vital, still a microcosm of the dynamics and tensions within American society, these cannot but be reflected in our own religious society. Many other institutions in American life, including some religious groups, were experiencing Black Power. Why should we religious liberals be exempt? We were not. The experience hurt many—indeed, it still hurts.

Let me describe something of what happened during those three days of the Emergency Conference. Most of the blacks present held their own meetings—the Black Caucus. Most of the scheduled meetings and panels of the Conference, as a consequence, were mainly attended by whites. White liberals had come to New York City, some from as far away as California, just to have a continental dialogue with their black co-religionists to create a hard-hitting program as a total denominational response to the Black Rebellion. Instead, there was little or no dialogue, but our whole denomination felt one unmistakable response to the Black Rebellion: our brother black Unitarian Universalists rebelled and separated themselves into a Black Caucus!

In the process of separation, some blacks no longer talked to their friends at the Conference, even those from their same church District or even their same church. Some blacks no longer smiled; some were serious, often grim, even secretive. One or two white delegates, half seriously, perhaps half in fun, tried to enter the Black Caucus. They were firmly shown the door. Yet inside that door, by the final hours, the Caucus included most blacks present at the conference.

Some reports are now available on what happened inside the Caucus. It was apparently a historic, exciting experience for many of the blacks participating. One man present described it as the first effort of black Unitarian Universalists to find themselves, to explore collectively why they joined a basically white denomination. One middle class Unitarian Universalist admitted that he was sceptical about the whole Emergency Conference and questioned whether he should attend. But then, he observed, he walked into the Caucus a Negro and came out a black man! Indeed, one of the signs of the Black Caucus and of Black Power is semantic. The word, *Negro*, is out; *black* is in. The term, *integration*, is also out.

The tactics of the Black Caucus came to a climax at this Emergency Conference during the final plenary session. The three commissions made their reports without benefit of much dialogue with the blacks. Still, these were rather good reports, outlining new suggestions for future work by the denomination on the problem of the cities. During this plenary, a Youth Caucus and the Black Caucus were also asked to present their reports. That of the Black Caucus was also good, indeed fairly restrained. It catalogues some of the racial sins of omission and commission of our denomination, the chief of which has been the failure to settle qualified black ministers in so-called white churches. The main proposal of the Black Caucus was the creation of a Black Affairs Council as an affiliated agency of the denomination, something like the Laymen's League or the Women's Federation, with a majority of blacks on the Board, but presumably with a few whites. The Caucus also asked for $250,000 a year for each of four years from denominational funds, capital funds if necessary, for Unitarian Universalist work in the black ghetto.

More controversial than the contents of the report of the Black Caucus was its demand that "these proposals be given unqualified and total endorsement by this Conference to be transmitted directly to the Board of Directors of the Unitarian Universalist Association . . . any discussion of changes or revisions (taking place) only between the Unitarian Universalist Association and the Steering Committee of the Black Caucus." This tactic was immediately puzzling to many of the whites present—and still is. Religious liberals don't give "unqualified and total endorsement" to anything—not to the Bible, not to Sophia Fahs, not Paul Blanshard, and not to a Black Caucus. There was an immediate parliamentary skirmish to tone down and plead for total endorsement. In the end, the blacks had the vote, since about one-half of the whites present went along, for a variety of reasons, with the Black Caucus formula. The resolution for total endorsement was carried by the necessary two-thirds vote of those participants present.

The Emergency Conference with its Black Caucus was a traumatic experience for most whites who participated; for the blacks, who have traumatic experiences daily for just being black, the conference was an additional evidence of the distance continuing between themselves and even white liberals.

This issue has simmered in this fashion much of the past autumn and into the winter. In the midst of the trauma and name-calling, three honest questions have recurred about the Black Caucus. First, are the members of the Caucus really Unitarian Universalists? The answer is unqualifiedly yes. Indeed, some of these blacks have been or are chairmen of the boards of their churches.

A second frequent question is the representativeness of the thirty-one members of the Black Caucus at the Conference. Are they typical of the black members of our denomination, estimated to number no more than one percent of our total adult membership, or some 1,750 persons? The answer is that nobody knows. However, Black Power is taking hold in many sections of the black community in the U.S. today, and the Black Caucus is the nearest thing in the denomination to Black Power (although some members of the Caucus deny any close relationship to Black Power). I would estimate that at least a large minority of the black members of our denomination would endorse the Caucus and its demands—not a majority perhaps, but a sizable, certainly articulate minority.

The most frequent question asked is this: aren't the tactics of the Black Caucus undemocratic? Much controversy has revolved around these tactics. "Abrasive" is one critical term often used. The Caucus has also been called "un-Unitarian" which some feel is far worse than even being un-American! These tactics of the Caucus break down into two categories: Are the tactics totalitarian? And are they separatist?

Some have alleged that the secrecy of the Caucus has given it a totalitarian flavor which is foreign to democracy and certainly to the Unitarian Universalist denomination. Knowing something of church politics for three decades, I can attest that some of these tactics are strangely familiar. Perhaps they have not been as concentrated into as small a group of people over such a short period of time, but most of the elements are not new in a denomination which has seen all kinds of machinations by political and theological extremists, as theoretically undesirable as such tactics may be whether practiced by whites or blacks, humanists or theists.

It is also alleged that the tactics of the Caucus are separatist. They may well be separatist, but they are not segregationist. The one is voluntary; the other is imposed. Black Power has used separatism both as a tactic and as a goal. So far the Black Caucus in our denomination has used separatism as a tactic, chiefly to enhance group solidarity, for the blacks to "find themselves." If the Black Caucus uses separatism as only a tactic, I doubt if it is profitable to call a Black Caucus "racism in reverse."

Lessons for the Denomination

What lessons can we, as a denomination, already learn from the experience of a Black Caucus in our midst? First, we have learned the depth of the problem, the intensity by which it is felt by nearly all blacks. The social distance between black and white religious liberals and the inner hate—these are all greater than even the most sensitive whites may have heretofore guessed. It should not have taken a Black Caucus to make us white Unitarian Universalists realize the enormity of the problem, but it should not have taken the Black Rebellion in the cities to make white Americans realize the problem either.

A second lesson from the Black Caucus is that our American society continues to be racist and our Unitarian Universalist denomination, for all its liberalism, also encompasses great areas of racism. This is again hard to believe and it may not be universally true, but we white liberals are more racist than we like to think.

A third lesson derived from the Black Caucus is that the elimination of racism in the U.S. is still basically a white problem. We whites have to change our ideas and our actions, lessen our prejudices, and eliminate our discriminations. There are things, many things, which blacks can do to cooperate, but we whites must do more.

A fourth and final lesson brought to us vividly by the Black Caucus is that efforts to change American racial patterns have, in our time, been basically unsuccessful. They have been too little, too late. There have, of course, been qualitative, often spectacular, gains for a few blacks, such as membership on the U.S. Supreme Court and in the presidential cabinet. And there may be many more white Americans, despite talk of white backlash, who at least intellectually know that equality must cost. Blacks are more quantitatively segregated today than a decade ago—in schools, housing, etc. We whites who have given leadership to the race relations and civil rights movements in the past must admit our overall failures, despite the occasional victories. Black leadership may turn out to be no more successful, but we whites have had to change and, by and large, we have failed.

If we have learned some of these lessons, what does this mean for the outcome of this Black Caucus controversy developing in the midst of our denomination? Certainly the controversy has been good for us. It has educated some blacks among us as it has certainly educated more whites. We Unitarian Universalists will not come out of this controversy with one mind, but then we never do. Indeed, this may not be like past controversies among us. There may be no neat resolution; the problem will and probably should plague us for years and decades.

As we continue this debate, let us white and blacks try to do several things. Let us chiefly listen, with compassion and with sensitivity. If chiefly whites must listen to the innermost feelings of blacks, also blacks should know that whites hold deep feelings which they must find ways to work through.

Let us also value pluralism. There is no one path to racial justice any more than there is only one path to God. We must respect individual differences, varying temperaments, past experiences, present circumstances. In the end, there may be tempers lost, withdrawals of funds, even walkouts. Yet in a denomination which is observing the four hundredth anniversary of the edict of toleration, I would hope that both the black and white succesors to Francis David would maintain something of this spirit of liberal toleration. Yet perhaps this is too much to expect when radical changes in church and society are overdue.

Whatever the negative price this denomination must in the end pay for the rise of the Black Caucus movement, I think the positive results will be greater. The tactics of the Black Caucuses have shaken us as a denomination in a way that rational, reasonable pleas have not done in a decade and perhaps in a century. The program of the Black Caucus movement so far does not appear excessive; certainly no other program for our denomination appears better.

I would personally hope that the Board of Trustees of the Association would soon concur in the establishment of an independent Black Affairs Council as an affiliated or associated agency of the Association, in a manner similar to that of the Unitarian Universalist Service Committee. I think we whites should eagerly and enthusiastically help blacks at this moment in history obtain a power base within our denomination as they should also do within our society. And this base within our denomination, by their own suggestion, will not be entirely black, but will contain certainly a majority of Blacks.

Can we religious liberals afford an adequate budget for a Black Affairs Council, let alone a reorganized Commission on Religion and Race? We can afford that to which we give highest priorities. Although we are a tiny denomination, I am convinced that we can as a denomination find hundreds of thousands of dollars a year for such activities. A dynamic program in black/white relations and urban affairs would contribute to a total denominational dynamics which would increase fundraising even for the more mundane, bread-and-butter aspects of our denominational life. In fact, we might even then have adequate funds to welcome the formation of still another group; a Peace Caucus. Surely there is little point to reordering our attitudes and our cities if we will all be burned some day soon by the atomic bomb!

Religious liberals need not choose between these two methods of consensus and confrontation. On some issues we can continue to work for consensus. But we American Unitarian Universalists may not have this present luxury of choice forever. The polarization in society and in denomination is growing. We in the liberal "middle" may find our areas of experimentation lessening; we may soon be forced to make choices. Just because our denomination is a microcosm of basically a counterrevolutionary country in a revolutionary world, we cannot expect business as usual or institutionalism as usual. If war and peace, if black and white, tear apart our country and our world, can we expect our institutions to continue their relatively Brahman tranquility and not be torn apart? In the meantime, let us use this moment of experimentation wisely, let us not be too quick to make more than provisional judgments, whether about Black Caucuses or draft card burners. Let us listen, contemplate, observe, ponder. Let us remember what that great Unitarian of more than a century ago, William Ellery Channing, observed, roughly in a similar period in American if not world history: "The great interests of humanity do not lose their claims on us because sometimes injudiciously maintained."

At the UUA General Assembly in Cleveland in May 1968—"the year of ministerial turtle-neck shirts and of buttons"—the delegates recognized the Black Affairs Council and authorized $250,000 in funds. The following year, the General Assembly in Boston, despite a walkout by sixty blacks and 250 white supporters, rejected the BAC's demands for $6.5 million in reparations investments and endorsed the UUA's own social investment policy calling for a commitment to invest substantial funds in enterprises with high social value."The Unitarian Universalist world has not ended," Homer observed, "though many conservatives feel alienated, many liberals are confused and confounded, most black and white radicals are dispirited and restless." Years later, a leader of the Black Caucus and one of his staunchest critics at the time told Homer that he was essentially right in trying to steer a middle way during the crisis.

45

BOSTON

(1970)

REFLECTIONS OF AN EX-DENOMINATIONAL BUREAUCRAT

In 1969, Robert West was elected president of the Unitarian Universalist Association, succeeding Dana Greeley. West—a fiscal conservative— abolished the Division of Social Responsibility of the UUA and fired Homer. This action followed closely the Black Power struggle in the denomination and coincided with personal crises in Homer's life. At home family strains multiplied as Homer's mother, Cecelia—probably suffering from Alzheimer's disease, which was not a recognized disorder at the time—moved to Boston from Miami and had to be institutionalized; Homer's mother-in-law, Lucy Adams Williams, and father-in-law and mentor, David Rhys Williams, passed away within a year of each other; Homer's son, Alex, was dismissed from theological school following the sanctuary at Boston University, moved into a commune, and became involved with the counterculture; and his daughter, Lucy, went through a personal crisis. Amid these pressures, unemployment, and loss of income, Homer and Esther's marriage started to collapse. Homer delivered this sermon at Arlington Street Church (where he was a member) on January 4, 1970, "before I felt the separation from the UUA."

In the third chapter of Ecclesiastes it is written: "To everything there is a season and a time to every purpose under the heavens . . . A time to keep silence and a time to speak . . ." And the time has now come for me to speak, as an ex-denominational bureaucrat. I have had several careers in my life: student, teacher, parish minister, secular social action executive, and—for almost the past six years—a denominational bureaucrat. Now that this last phase of my life is coming to an end, let me discuss briefly the life of a bureaucrat in our Unitarian Universalist denomination and then make some reflections for the future of our churches and denomination.

I use the word reflections advisedly. I have no confessions, no memoirs—nothing that spicy, that salacious, that sensational. If there are skeletons in the old closets at 25 Beacon Street, denominational headquarters, I have not yet found them, no more skeletons—that is—than in any closet on Beacon Hill! I also use the word, *bureaucrat*, advisedly. I was an executive, director of the late Division of Social Responsibility of our Unitarian Universalist Association. Really I was a denominational bureaucrat, but I do not mean that to be a pejorative term either.

I had the privilege of working for our denomination during what history will record as its golden era, the last term of the Greeley Administration. I also use this term—the golden era—advisedly. I am confident that it will be so regarded, not only because of the style and prophecy of President Dana McLean Greeley, but because of the recent obvious decline of denominationalism, beginning to be apparent at the end of the Greeley regime but even more evident during the five months since that time.

How did it feel to work at Unitarian mecca? in the Universalist Vatican? Denominational bureaucracy was not that bad—from the inside. Even radicals can become seduced into accepting certain administrative chores if there are curtains on their office windows if not rugs on the floors! The fact is that I came to enjoy working for the Greeley Administration. I was a member of his small cabinet—eight persons—carrying out the policies of a small denomination during a dynamic moment in its history and that of the nation and world. I came to cherish working as a member of a denominational team, each with special tasks, but also all together dealing with whatever problem at the time seemed overriding—and there were always problems, even crises.

Dana McLean Greeley, former minister of this church, was an ideal denominational president. He delegated authority, demanded innovation, and always backed up his staff. He was always busy, but also always accessible. He was a compulsive worker and expected equal hard work from his staff. He worked almost 24 hours a day, seven days a week, even when away from Boston, and he expected his senior staff to do likewise—and we did! Dana Greeley always wanted to hear the truth from his staff; he wanted no yes-men, even if—in the end—his mind was not changed. He never asked his staff to lie to protect the Administration; he gave us freedom to differ publicly with him, and even with Board policy. He was humane, even religious. One felt that one was working for a church, not a business. There was little, certainly a minimum, of office politics associated these days with all denominations.

There was style at 25 Beacon Street, such as leisurely teas for important visitors. I would put on my jacket as I walked down one flight to tea in the President's Office. The Association was not just another Boston business, but we did return long-distance calls with dispatch, and we did answer our voluminous mail promptly.

That genial Greeley era is gone, probably forever, and there is no point in mourning the past. Also my role in the denomination has evaporated. The UUA Board, at the recommendation of President Robert West, has liquidated the almost six-year-old Division of Social Responsibility and my position as its director. I can take care of myself vocationally, but I grieve for the cavalier annihilation of the Division, one which was carefully created through a decade of planning. I understandably mourn the passing of this arm of our denomination which must surely be reestablished unless we make a mockery of our prophetic history. But liquidation is one of the perils of agreeing to serve. I now have a full-time position in fascinating Japan for the next ten months while I look for another venue for my training and experience, perhaps in a local parish again, perhaps on the international scene. Horrors—an international bureaucrat!

Turning Agonies into Ecstasies

Out of these and other denominational experiences, I want to draw some conclusions. Recently I was in Japan, and there I discussed our denominational dilemmas, first with the largely-American fellowship in Tokyo and then the largely Japanese church there. Later this month I will speak to our fellowship in New Delhi. Not only religious liberals overseas, but those here at home, are all fascinated, often intrigued, occasionally affronted, by the turmoil occurring within our denomination. Let me try to sort out a few of the problems, make some order, then some meaning, and all from my vantage point—now—of an ex-denominational bureaucrat.

The first agony of Unitarian Universalism has been over black/white relations. A few years ago it all seemed so simple: "We Shall Overcome" through "Black and White Together"; James Reeb; integration; Martin Luther King. Then along came the Black Unitarian Universalist Caucus (BUUC). We white Unitarian Universalists were challenged as never before. We have been torn asunder, not only white from black, but white from white and black from Negro. The uneasy tranquility of our liberal denomination was broken by caucuses, name-calling, walkouts, microphone occupation. BUUC and FULLBAC won overwhelmingly at our Cleveland Assembly. The Black Affairs Council (BAC) got its funding and began its program. Black empowerment was reaffirmed at the Boston Assembly, but by a smaller margin, and in the process Black and White Action—BAWA—became empowered. The controversy has percolated into local churches, even into church families. Our candor, I think our learning, about race relations has never been greater. Our wounds have never been deeper. Our denomination will never be the same again because of this racial agony.

The second agony of Unitarian Universalism has been over denominational relations. A few years ago, just a few months ago, it seemed so simple: 1,000 churches and fellowships in the U.S. and Canada working as a team for Unitarian Universalist Advance, for our Annual Fund, for denominationalism. There were jokes, to be sure, about Boston—we didn't believe them, but perhaps we should have—and there was some coolness in strange quarters, but denominational morale seemed remarkably high. Then came deficits with the phasing out of our development funds. Then came a new administration. And now the budget has been drastically cut. Confidence has been reduced. Program and personnel have been liquidated. The very purposes of our denomination have been called into question. Scepticism toward 25 Beacon Street has never been greater; wounds in districts and departments never deeper. Our denomination may never be the same again because of this internal agony.

There are other current agonies in our denomination: the continuing controversy over the Saigon project of our Unitarian Universalist Service Committee by ministers and laymen who rebel at any kind of denominational social action; and the continuing revolt of youth, women, and Canadians who all want a bigger share of denominational power.

What are the basic causes of these agonies? Some have recently said that all our troubles were caused by the wild spending of the Greeley Administration. From the accusations of BAWA, one could conclude that I personally and single-handedly brought the virus of Black Power to our denomination. But what are the real, underlying

364

causes?

For some years I have held a sociological theory about our denomination. We Unitarian Universalists, for all our history, for all our smug liberalism, are only a microcosm of American society, a little more liberal perhaps, but only because we are a little more affluent, a little more educated, a little more suburban, a little more white. In making this evaluation, I did not mean to be negative, but a distinguished Canadian Unitarian minister, reading this assessment of mine in a recent issue of the *Christian Century* magazine, replied: "I find that all the more rather than less disturbing. I don't expect to find Unitarians being a microcosm of society as a whole, I expect to find them distinctively different. Our entire history has been one of nonconformity . . ." Well, ask our Black Caucus how different we are today, or ask our Unitarian theological students, or ask our folk who deal closely with the ecumenical movement. It may be more disturbing, but we are not that different.

If we are to look at the basic causes of our agonies, I think they lie in the dynamics of contemporary American life, of which—thank God—we are so much a part. The cause of our agony over black/white relations is because what is vital in American society is caught up in this controversy. It is not endemic to liberal religion. We are not alone; indeed, now almost every denomination has its own Black Caucus. The cause of our agony over denominational affairs is a loss in other denominations. Again, we are not alone in an era of declining attendance and declining budgets in much of organized religion in the United States.

Given the current agonies in our household of faith, and some reasons for their development, is there a way out? Can we turn our agonies into ecstasies, our traumas into triumphs? We as a denomination, and probably much of American religion, are at a crossroads. Will the American denominations, including our own, hold together; or will they begin even further to fly apart, and ultimately form new combinations?

The handful of blacks in our denomination might one day walk out and either form a black liberal denomination or become part of a much larger black ecumenical church. I doubt if we whites or we as a whole denomination can do very much to influence this trend either way. The outcome will depend upon forces greater than our own, especially if the walkout goes in an ecumenical direction.

More likely several handfuls of blacks and whites in our denomination might one day soon walk out—whether to join a nonracial ecumenical radical church or to form small cells which will be loosely connected into an underground church movement. Again, I doubt if we as a denomination can do much to influence this trend.

This trickle of blacks, or of whites and blacks, can quickly become an avalanche unless we do some clear thinking about the purposes of church and denomination resulting, I would insist, in the adoption of new philosophies and new social strategies. We must, I feel, soon bury the Old Liberalism of the nineteenth century and of the twentieth century in much of New England Unitarianism and in some of our churches in the rest of the continent. We must also, I feel, turn our backs on the New Left of the last half-decade in a few of our churches, especially in California and Canada, but also right here in New England. I do not, unfortunately, have time to give here a critique of the Old Liberalism or the New Left as it appears in our denomination, but I would plead for the adoption of what I would call a New Radicalism.

What will this New Radicalism encompass? Let me quickly enumerate the demands of the New Radicals for rapid social change, for new goals, for new methods, for new levels of participation, and for new styles. If we can painfully work through to this New Radicalism, I do believe our agonies can turn into ecstasies, but the very process I acknowledge will be agonizing and some of our people will be permanently offended. But let me enumerate the demands of this New Radicalism.

The New Radicalism

The New Radicalism demands rapid social change. In our kind of world, talk is not enough, action is not enough, indeed individual change is not enough. The pragmatic test is the creation of institutional social change. The arteries of our institutions, from church to state, are hopelessly clogged. All kinds of institutional changes must be made: the structure of the United Nations, the relations between nations, the role of the Pentagon, municipal/county relations, teaching in the universities, the role of the local church, the function of the religious denomination. Norman Cousins recently wrote that "the biggest problem lies not in change itself but in the absence of enough awareness that change is necessary."

The New Radicals demand new goals also. These are not rigid goals. The New Radicals yearn for no easy utopias of the past, no packaged ideologies. Their goals are highly eclectic. But they transcend both tinkering with the present system in the manner of the

Old or New Left. If man, with priority, can walk on the moon in a decade, he can with more justifiable priority, learn to walk in brotherhood on earth, without war, even granting that the social sciences are more difficult to harness than the physical ones.

The most important goal of the New Radical is a warless world, yet a changing one. Change would not be suppressed to suppress violence. The goal is the most far-reaching transformation of our institutions, beginning with the Pentagon, perhaps, and then the United Nations. The goal is also domestic: to reorder race relations and the cities. The goal is also economic, but neither simplistic capitalism nor doctrinaire communism. Neither works very well in human terms, although capitalism has apparently produced more economic goods than communism in the past two decades.

The New Radicals also demand new methods. The old no longer function, whether electoral politics in the nation or the present General Assembly in the denomination. (If you think we have troubles with our General Assembly, read about the chaos at the recent meetings of the National Council of Churches in Detroit!) The New Radicals will continue to experiment with confrontation, profiting more perhaps from its immediate benefits than fearing its lingering perils. The New Radicals will continue to debate what in ecumenical circles is called the "theology of violence." The concealed violence bolstering the status quo in society has been, and continues to be, massive. However, the New Radical will also take a new look at neo-Gandhism in this centenary of the Mahatma's birth.

The New Radicals also demand the acceptance of more participation by blacks, by women, and by youth. This is a revolution against oppression, for enfranchisement. The New Radicals, may I add, appear to have little time for some of us white, middle-aged males!

The New Radicals, finally, demand acceptance of a broad spectrum of styles. They are beginning to welcome what somebody has called "ecstatic transgressions of the older norms" or, in more common parlance, "doing one's thing." They obviously value people more than institutions. They abhor the hypocrisy, the cant, of the present older generation. Indeed, much of the New Radicalism is generational, of persons around thirty years of age, if not always under it. The New Radicals have a broad tolerance for people, for all lifestyles. They do not wince at the straight life of some of us over fifty. However, they will not be censorious, and neither should we, of the relatively new drug-rock-sex syndrome existing in world society.

These, then, are some of the values, methods, and goals which must emerge in our local church and our total denomination if we are to survive, or at least continue to be relevant, and not become ecclesiastical dinosaurs. These values cannot be arrived at easily, again in local church or denomination, not by fiat or decree, but by group processes. They certainly cannot be accepted merely by the urging of a leader, however charismatic. The local church and denomination must remain pluralistic. Ours cannot become only a hippy church or only an under-thirty denomination. Ours cannot become only a black church or only a T-group denomination. We need the pluralism of age, of interest, of temperament, of styles, even of Gods: Goodman, Ginsburg, Marcuse, yes; but also Channing, Parker, and Albert Schweitzer. This diversity makes the church the church and not a school or forum. Yet in social action our local churches and denomination cannot afford the wide accordion spread of extreme pluralism mirrored in American society. I submit we must come down toward the radical side. However, we must never excommunicate, for social or theological stances. On the other hand, we can understand if not welcome self-pruning: certain members will suddenly realize that their church is not theirs and quietly or unquietly move out.

If we Unitarian Universalists do some fundamental thinking, and out of this thinking adopt some new social philosophies and new social strategies, I think we can indeed change our temporary traumas into tenacious triumphs. But the process will be painful. The pain felt in many Unitarian Universalist hearts during the past two years, indeed in this very church, will only be a prelude to the pain which may have to be endured for a whole generation. But free religion has never been easy: in early New England, in contemporary Czechoslovakia, or anywhere on earth today. The New Radicalism may just preserve, through change, that Old Liberal church and denomination of ours. At least it should be worth trying.

PART SEVEN 1970-1983

DISARMAMENT & HUMAN RIGHTS ACTIVIST

THE UNITED NATIONS YEARS

"But when the planets,
In evil mixture, to disorder tend,
What plagues and what portents! What mutiny!
What raging of the sea! Shaking of earth!
Commotion in the wind frights, charges horrors,
Direct and crack, rend and deracinate
The unity and married calm of states . . ."
—Shakespeare, Troilus and Cressida

As the new decade began, Homer assumed the post of Secretary-General of the the World Conference on Religion and Peace, a new interfaith organization that he helped found in the 1960s with Rev. Dana Greeley, Rabbi Maurice N. Eisendrath, and religious leaders from Japan, India, and Germany. After the success of its first assembly in Kyoto, Japan, in 1970, WCRP set up permanent offices, and Homer piloted the organization through the seventies and early eighties. From Boston, he moved to New York to set up headquarters at the Church Center across from the United Nations. After their divorce, Esther remained in Boston with Alex and Lucy, continuing as a librarian at Brookline High School. In 1972, Homer married Ingeborg Kind, a German-born Quaker who worked for Amnesty International in Geneva and who had three daughters from a previous marriage. At the United Nations, Homer also founded the NGO Committee on Disarmament and undertook human rights initiatives around the world. During this period, Homer and Ingeborg lived in a small apartment on East 43rd St., 5 minutes' walk from the U.N. and his office.

Photograph: Homer speaking at the United Nations, 1980s

46 DACCA (1971)

DEATH IN GOLDEN BANGLADESH

On behalf of WCRP, Homer went to the Indian subcontinent twice to observe the civil war in East Pakistan—site of one of the worst human massacres since World War II. In May 1971 he went to refugee areas and to Calcutta, where he met with the Gandhians, led by his old friend Jayaprakash ("J. P.") Narayan who organized a peace march to the Indo-Pakistani border. In September, Homer returned to Dacca, capital of East Pakistan, in the midst of the siege and massacre and to Karachi, the capital of West Pakistan. In Washington, he testified before a hearing of the U.S. Senate Judiciary Subcommittee in support of independence. In New York, WCRP lent their offices to a delegation of Bangladeshis who came to the United Nations to lobby for independence and gave NGO credentials to Justice Abu Sayyed Choudhury. In an article for the New York Times *Op-Ed page in November, Homer lamented the indifference of the world community to events in this distant, poverty-stricken region.*

Perspective 1971: Opposition to the war in Vietnam escalated with the publishing of the Pentagon Papers, the conviction of Lt. Calley for the My Lai Massacre, and Muhammad Ali's appearance in court for refusing to serve in the army. The Seabed Treaty was signed banning nuclear weapons in the oceans, a nuclear alert was accidentally triggered in Colorado, and Canada pledged to dismantle all nuclear weapons. President Nixon announced plans to visit China, the trade embargo was lifted, and the world's most populous nation joined the U.N. 1971 was the year of hot pants, waterbeds, EST, Jesus Christ Superstar, Columbo, *and* All in the Family.

Poet Rabindranath Tagore wrote many years ago: "I love you my golden Bangla Desh . . . O Mother, during spring the fragrance of your mango groves maddens my heart with delight . . . " This spring there is only the stench of death in the mango groves of East Pakistan/Bangladesh as many hearts are maddened by massacre.

Firm figures of massacre in East Pakistan, as anywhere, are hard to verify. Some say thousands, others insist on two hundred thousand. Probably 50,000 is a conservative estimate. Numbers of refugees are more obtainable: 650,000 in four Indian states on May 1.

The refugees from East Pakistan insist that those massacred were Bengalis—Moslems, Hindus, Buddhists, Christians living in East Pakistan who were systematically eliminated by the Pakistan Army immediately after March 25 when negotiations for the autonomy of East Pakistan broke down. The West Pakistanis insist those massacred in the "east wing" were Biharis—Moslems originally from Bihar and other Indian states who migrated to East Pakistan after partition but had not yet been absorbed into the Bengali culture.

A visitor to Karachi finds the Pakistan economy going downhill, martial law declared in the West and East, and a Government desperately trying to show a return to normalcy among the 75 million people in East Pakistan. All in Karachi are deeply upset about the massacre of the Biharis, not by the army, but by some members of the autonomy-cum-successionist Awami League; however, almost all deny any massacre of the Bengalis by the army.

West Pakistanis feel the whole situation is an Indian plot— Indian "infiltrators" (soldiers without uniform), Indian ammunition, even Indian (not Pakistan) refugees—aided by a few "antistate elements."

A visitor to Delhi finds an India united as seldom before in recent history with the people pressing Prime Minister Indira Gandhi to recognize Bangladesh (the independent state of East Bengal) and to give the "freedom fighters" arms. The India press emphasizes the massacre of Bengalis. India is obviously taking every political and psychological advantage of the situation, yet so far is acting with great restraint.

In Calcutta and especially at the border, one sees thousands of recent refugees—only one-quarter in camps. Optimistic cabinet ministers of the Bangladesh Government plead for recognition and arms. Refugees show how West Pakistan has treated East Pakistan as an internal colony for twenty-five years. They feel their country can no longer remain as part of an integrated, two-wing Pakistan.

Sheik Mujibur Rahman's Awami League won 98 percent of the seats for the National Assembly in East Pakistan during the first national election since independence in 1947. Sheik Mujib campaigned on a six-point platform calling for autonomy, not secession. Apparently the military rulers of Pakistan, aided by the powerful bureaucracy and some industrialists, refused to submit to this major transfer of power. On March 25 they declared martial law, banned the Awami League, arrested Sheik Mujib, and their army began the massacre. Before and after this army action, some elements in East Pakistan apparently indulged in their own massacre in this seldom nonviolent subcontinent.

Why the unconcern about East Pakistan in the U.S., the U.N., and the world? Are Americans unconcerned merely because Moslems are again killing Moslems and, in any case, no white Americans are involved? Or because, for once, no ideology appears involved, at least not communism? Or are Americans unconcerned because East Pakistan could easily become a second Vietnam?

Why the unconcern at the U.N.? In an era of norms against genocide, are events in East Pakistan merely an "internal" matter and not a clear violation of the rights of man? Is this situation still "domestic" if it endangers the peace of the world, with Indian and Pakistani armed incursions into each other's territory, not to mention possible intervention by the big powers?

Why the unconcern from the non-aligned nations? Does each nation have its own Bangladesh in its belly? Can no process be devised by the international community to face squarely the "autonomy plus" of peoples in the 1970s, so a people, such as the East Bengalis—separated by language, culture, and one thousand miles—can opt for freedom if it is truly a free choice?

Bangladesh struggles to be born. The green and red flag, with an outline of the country's borders in gold, flies over the headquarters of Pakistan's former deputy high commissioner in Calcutta. And the "freedom fighters" have adopted Tagore's song for their national anthem: "I love you my golden Bangladesh . . . "

Will the U.S., the U.N., and the world do nothing?

In the face of continued repression in East Pakistan and the reluctance of the global community to become involved, India intervened militarily, and after a short conflict East Pakistan was freed on December 16, 1971. Justice Choudhury, who was working out of Homer's office, was named first president of Bangladesh.

47 ROME
(1974)

DISARMAMENT AND HUNGER

In the face of adverse weather conditions and sharply rising grain prices, the World Food Conference convened in Rome in November 1974 to develop a global strategy to solve the world food crisis. Homer attended the two-week assembly on behalf of WCRP to put forward the view that in an increasingly complex and interdependent world, the production and distribution of food could not be separated from other economic, social, and political problems, especially disarmament. Homer wrote several long reports on the conference for WCRP and this brief analysis for the bimonthly journal, Church and Society.

Perspective 1974: Richard Nixon resigned, Gerald Ford succeeded him as president, and the Watergate Coverup Trial opened before Judge Sirica. India developed a nuclear bomb, Karen Silkwood died investigating abuse in the nuclear industry, and the superpowers signed a ten-year agreement limiting strategic and offensive nuclear weapon and delivery systems. Turkey invaded Cyprus, OPEC lifted the oil embargo, Britain outlawed the IRA, and the authority of the South Vietnamese government collapsed. 1974 was the year of the first test tube birth, the exile of Solzhenitsyn from the U.S.S.R, the discovery of "Lucy" in Africa, the Patty Hearst kidnapping, streaking, and Hank Aaron's all-time home run record.

Two stark sets of facts confront the world community and the religious conscience: the arms races are escalating at a time when hunger and malnutrition are also increasing. Hundreds of millions of children, young people, women, and men are painfully hungry because many of the world's governments are more prepared to destroy human life than to develop and sustain it. While the minds of citizens, like the policies of governments, tend to relegate disarmament and hunger to separate fields of action, the relationships between them are extensive, critical, and complex. Our awareness of these relationships and our attitudes toward them are of incomparable urgency in our common responsibility for the security and welfare of the world's peoples.

A recent United Nations report stated: "The developed countries' appropriations for military purposes are some twenty times their appropriations for developmental aid. There are many reasons why the level of resources devoted to development assistance is so low; the high level of resources devoted to military expenditure may be one explanation."

Linkages between disarmament and hunger include the following:

1. *Costs.* The most massive and direct relationship is suggested by the savings that could result from curtailing military expenditures and reallocating them to a world food effort. If only 10 percent of present world military expenditures were redirected to development, including food aid to the Third World, the sum of $25 billion would be made available.

2. *Nuclear Proliferation.* The larger countries in the Third World have a special stake in avoiding nuclear weapons systems of their own. Then scarce resources for their own economic development could be allocated to develop a capacity for self-sufficiency in basic foods.

3. *Energy.* The power required for irrigation and other aspects of agricultural development, including the production of fertilizers, may also raise the spectre of nuclear weapons spread. India justified its nuclear explosion of May 1974 in terms of the need for new sources of energy. In doing so, India may have weakened the inhibitions of other states about "joining the nuclear club."

4. *Raw Materials.* Military forces consume large proportions of scarce resources which are important to economic development. The military account for about 14 percent of the world's consumption of both bauxite and copper. The military consume about 5 percent of the world's petroleum and this contributes to both inflation and fertilizer shortage.

5. *Defoliation.* The deliberate resort to environmental warfare for purposes of denying cover and crops to an adversary may seriously impair the capacity of a country to feed itself when hostilities

have ended. Even if the war in Vietnam were to cease altogether tomorrow, the environmental damage would last a century.

6. *Fallout.* The contamination of food (especially milk) from past and continuing nuclear testing will poison the nutrition of untold millions in unborn generations. It is *"le crime dans l'avenir"*—the crime projected into the future.

7. *Shelter Stocks.* The fallout shelters reflecting the nuclear hysteria of the early 1960s were stocked with vast food supplies now threatened with spoilage. About 150,000 tons of food remain in these stockpiles after the 1973 distribution of whole wheat crackers to Bangladesh and countries in Africa and Latin America. What food remains in U.S. shelters could feed 10 million people for 60 days.

8. *Economics of Conversion.* The daily bread of millions of American workers and their families is dependent upon defense contracts and military installations. An adequate disarmament strategy must plan for alternative patterns of production, employment, and income.

9. *The Arms Trade.* Industrial nations confronted with inflation and balance of payment problems are especially tempted to relieve these problems, at least temporarily, by aggressive arms sales abroad. The U.S. and France have responded to the inflation of oil prices by selling vast quantities of military hardware to Middle East oil-producing states whose treasuries suddenly permit such purchases. This may seem to help with bread and butter at home, but it is accelerating the regional arms race in the most dangerous part of the world today.

Implicit in our approaches to both disarmament and hunger is the conviction that security—a most distorted and misunderstood concept—is ultimately the result of humane and constructive policies and not of military technology or mutual terror. Disarmament may contribute more to meaningful security among the nations than so-called "defense." A global victory over hunger—assuring the survival of half a billion people who would otherwise face starvation—may do much more for authentic international security than any combination of offensive and defensive nuclear weapons systems.

48 MANILA (1975)

HUMAN RIGHTS OF THE MUSLIMS

On a trip to Southeast Asia, Homer went to the Philippines to observe the human rights of the Muslims, who constituted about 5 percent of the population and were being oppressed by the government of President Ferdinand Marcos and the nation's predominantly Christian population. Homer and Ingeborg, who accompanied him, spent nine days in Mindanao, the principal site of the conflict, other Moslem areas, and Manila, the capital. Homer's full report for WCRP was promptly translated into an indigenous language and circulated in Mindanao. This is the first of a short two-part article that appeared in Impact International, *an Islamic periodical in Britain.*

Islam was founded in A.D. 622. With the help of Arab traders it spread to the Philippine archipelago. By 732 Muslim forces conquered the Spanish peninsula in Europe. It took the Spanish seven hundred years to drive the Muslims, Moors, or Moros out of the peninsula with the battle of Granada in 1492. When the Spanish took control of the Philippines in 1564, much to their surprise they found the Muslims already present. They declared a holy war against the Moros—the Moro Wars. Moro influence was gradually eliminated from the central and northern Philippines, but not from Mindanao and Sulu. It was more than three hundred years before the Muslim sultanates there acknowledged Spanish sovereignty. When the U.S. took over from Spain at the turn of the century, warfare continued to "pacify the Muslims."

Today there may be as many as 3 million Muslims in the Philippines, and they come from various cultural backgrounds. The word *Moro* is a legacy from the Spanish conquerors. This name was used first for the Islamized North African Mauritanians (Moors) and then for all Muslims from Africa and Asia who came to Spain and conquered them for almost eight centuries. When the Spaniards came to the Philippines they found that the people of Mindanao and Sulu organized against them were also Muslims; so they called them Moros and Moriscos—words which were intended to be derogatory. At first they resented being called Moros. They later preferred being called Filipino Muslims. When violence escalated in the 1970s, the appellation of Moro suddenly did not become pejorative and is increasingly used by the Muslims themselves as indicating unvanquished peoples who resisted conquest and conversion.

There are four main groups of Moros: 1) the Maguindanaos or "peoples of the flooded plain." They number about 500,000 and live in the three Costabato provinces. 2) The Maranaos or "people of the lake." They number from 450,000 to 500,000 and live around the shores of Lake Lanao. 3) The Tausugs or "people of the current." They number about 180,000 and are found in the Sulu province. 4) The Samals comprise up to 180,000 people in Siasi, Jolo coasts. In addition there are smaller groups of Muslims and two non-Muslim groups. The Badjaos or sea gypsies are originally Borneans who came to Sulu in search of fishing grounds. They are 30,000 people. They have never become Muslims. The Yakans live in Basilan Island and amount to 110,000 persons. They are of Polynesian stock and Arab blood, but again are not Muslims.

Discrimination

There is a catalogue of grievances and discriminations about which the Muslims today complain. The more important are:

A. *Land.* One aspect of colonization has always been settling people on the land. The Spanish and later the American colonialists of the Philippines always tried to "develop" agricultural areas and, incidentally, "civilize" the "natives." This occurred especially in Mindanao which was called "the land of promise." While such colonization began before World War II, it continued markedly after the war, partly to relieve land and population pressure in central and northern Philippines. In 1965 there was a massive influx from Luzon, diluting the Muslim majorities. The way the Christians have acquired land has been under severe Muslim attack. Moro bin Quadarat writes that "these settlers get homestead grants from the government on lands being occupied by Muslims for generations and easily obtained titles to lands while the majority of Muslims, whose ancestors have worked in the land, remain without titles." The Muslims did not wait long to resist this process. In many cases Christian owners were forced off land they purchased by violence or threat of violence.

B. *Employment.* As part of the colonization process, now called the developmental process, large agricultural and industrial enterprises have been encouraged by the government to come to Mindanao. These extract economic and human wealth, but seldom employ many Muslim workers, certainly not to their percentage in the population.

C. *Religion.* The Muslims feel that they lack complete religious freedom. In recent years they have been able to observe their religious holidays, but only a few years ago they had to request the authorities each year to proclaim them even in preponderantly Muslim areas.

D. *Overt Prejudice.* The whole Filipino nation looks down on the Moro people. Evidence of this prejudice is abundant. Senator Domocao Alonto has written: "Our history books, for instance, tell only of the heroism and patriotism of northern Filipinos. No mention is made whatsoever of the patriotic exploits and heroic deeds of the Filipinos of the south. Why is patriotism a monopoly of the Christian Filipinos? Have not the Moros fought—and successfully, the Spaniards . . . the Americans and the Japanese? Why are the Muslim Filipinos' blood spilt for nothing, and their lives meaningless? Why are the Muslim Filipinos known only in history books as bandits, pirates, and cut-throats, and these books are silent on everything good and creditable to the Muslims?"

Governmental Action

During Spanish and American colonialism, the approach to the Muslims was one to "civilize" or "Christianize" them. U.S. President William McKinley declared that the U.S. had assumed sovereignty of the Philippines in order to "develop, to civilize, to educate, to train in the science of self-government." The policy of the Republic of the Philippines for many years was that of "integration." In recent months the government has accepted, if with reluctance, the concept of autonomy. But so far this concept, embedded in the new Constitution, has hardly been implemented.

In the late 1960s, violence broke out in Mindano-Sulu. The government appeared unable to stop it. When in September 1972 President Marcos announced martial law, one reason was the widespread disorder resulting "in the killing of over 1000 civilians and about 2000 armed Muslims and Christians, not to mention more than 500,000 of injured, displaced, and homeless persons, as well as the great number of casualties among our government troops, and the paralysis of the economy of Mindanao and Sulu."

President Marcos embarked on an ambitious reconstruction and development program. Grandiose plans were made—on paper. Large sums were allocated to projects. Some programs were undertaken and some people—Muslims—were helped. By and large these programs so far have been failures, because they were rhetorical gestures more than completed projects, partly because the violence has continued. Also the Muslims have never accepted this planning in Manila for their development.

The pattern of government-induced violence is multiple. One beginning was when the government attempted to call in all firearms. It is said that Christians in the northern and central Philippines complied, and perhaps also in the south, but not the Muslims who felt that firearms were a way of life and, in any case, that they constituted their own protection. Also as members of the Philippines Constabulary and other armed groups were sent to Mindano-Sulu, they were often ill-trained and badly disciplined and, as predominantly Christians, they tended to cooperate with the Christians. In some cases, the Philippine armed forces, with aeroplanes, were put into battle against the Muslim rebels. There were strong allegations that napalm was used in 1974—and from American planes. The U.S. State Department declared that while it had not supplied napalm to the country, Philippine military forces "could have procured from other sources or manufactured napalm." It also said the use of American planes for bombing was "entirely contrary to the understanding under which the planes had been made available, and was stopped in response to our representations." Thus it is clear that napalm has been dropped from planes of the Philippine military forces.

The Muslims of the Philippines must remain on any worldwide enumeration of acts of religious discrimination.

49 SEOUL
(1975)

SOUTH KOREA: ANOTHER VIETNAM?

Homer and Ingeborg visited South Korea in August 1975 to meet with religious leaders and report on the long, harsh repression in that country. Coming on the heels of the fall of Saigon and the end of American military involvement in Vietnam earlier in the year, Homer's article appeared in an autumn issue of America, *the Catholic magazine.*

In April, eight "members" of the so-called People's Revolutionary Party were found guilty of subversion—despite the absence of real evidence—and sentenced to death by the repressive regime of President Park Chung Hee. They were executed the next morning. Protesting against the silence of Washington in the face of this tragedy, seven missionaries wore black hoods and demonstrated in front of the U.S. Embassy and were detained by Korean immigration authorities.

Thursday morning ecumenical prayer meetings continued in the Christian Building, headquarters of many Protestant groups, despite increasing government surveillance. Saturday prayer meetings were held by the National Association of Catholic Priests for the Realization of Justice. Students in many Seoul universities were restive if not actually demonstrating. At least one newspaper, *Dong-A-Ilbo*, continued to print news of repression, despite government pressures on advertisers.

Then the Park regime cracked down, especially on students and Christians—the two least controllable groups in modern Korean history. Many universities were closed, with students impris-

381

oned, under house arrest, or expelled; the latter were not even able to study in college libraries. The government forbade the holding of further Thursday prayer meetings in the Christian Building, driving them underground (and to several countries overseas, including the Interchurch Center in New York). The Catholic bishops were persuaded to ask the Catholic prayer meetings to terminate. By the end of April, the Maryknoll missionary Fr. James Sinnott was in effect expelled since his expiring visa was not renewed.

Why this increasing repression? The fall of Saigon in May sent a political shiver through several East Asian states, and through South Korea in particular. President Park skillfully used certain events in South Vietnam (and Cambodia) to draw particular parallels with South Korea. He selected the lack of unity and the widespread criticism as causing the fall of "democracy" in South Vietnam. To legislation, in March, against persons at home or abroad who "slander" the government, President Park in May added a new emergency decree—the ninth—providing imprisonment up to fifteen years for dissemination of "falsehoods."

The stepped-up government propaganda worked, at least for a while, especially on the masses of the people who still hated communism and remembered well the Korean War and their experience with Communist aggression and invasion. Park's agencies mercilessly rooted out demonstrations in the universities. One Korean priest who allegedly helped the students was given the choice of prison or study in Rome! Hankuk Theological Seminary could not resist government pressure to fire two outstanding professors and expel twelve students. Murder, execution, torture (authenticated by two reports of missions to Korea by Amnesty International), imprisonment, and house arrest were used in the name of anti-communism. Press, academic, and religious freedom were increasingly denied.

While ninety-three Protestant leaders met in early May to reaffirm their commitment to the militant National Council of Churches in Korea and to the World Council of Churches (the Vatican has so far been silent), other church people were pressured into a show of national unity. In June, a huge prayer rally was held with a half-million persons to demonstrate the religious backing of the government. This effort culminated in "the Korean churches" making a declaration on August 15 for the thirtieth anniversary of Korea's liberation. Signed by eighteen members of the Korean Christian Leaders' Association, but by no Roman Catholic, this statement could have been written in President Park's "Blue House."

Despite the current erosion of human rights in South Korea, it would be a mistake for Premier Kim Il Sung of North Korea, or the world at large, to conclude that South Korea today is, like South Vietnam yesterday, ready if not eager for a communist takeover. There are several important differences. There is no fighting war between the two Korean states, although severe tension does persist. Also, the separate geopolitical interests of China and the Soviet Union today actively discourage North Korean aggression. Yet if economic injustice (which goes on despite South Korea's "economic miracle" of development), corruption, and repression continue, the existing line of difference between Park Chung Hee's totalitarianism and Kim Il Sung's communism will blur in the hearts and minds of the literate, politically sophisticated South Korean people.

To this totalitarianism, the U.S. is once again heavily committed, presumably in the name of anti-communism. Such commitment is huge. Since World War II, America has spent $36 billion on Korea—more than the Marshall Plan and the Apollo space programs together! In addition, it has put one million Americans in uniform on the Korean peninsula. As recently as 1970 America pledged $1.5 billion in military aid over five years. Today the U.S. still has 42,000 servicemen in South Korea and only weeks ago Defense Secretary James Schlesinger refused to say this country will not use its nuclear weapons to defend South Korea from aggression from the North.

This autumn there is little active resistance to President Park. The dissidents—students, Christians, intellectuals—appear dispirited, weary, almost resigned. Four Protestants were sentenced in September to prison terms for misappropriating humanitarian relief funds to help the families of prisoners, although the German funding agency had approved the allocation. This sentencing was the occasion for the presence of 300 dissidents inside the courtroom and a demonstration of fifty outside who sang, "We Shall Overcome."

The Catholic poet Kim Chi Ha languishes in solitary confinement. His poignant "Declaration of Conscience" has been smuggled to the world, with the help of the Japanese Commission for Justice and Peace. In a recent letter to the Catholic clergy he wrote, "My hopes for revolution are *not* because I am a communist . . . I am a radical believer and want to be totally loyal to Catholicism."

As for pressure from outside the country, the Fraser Subcommittee in the U.S. Congress is waiting to lead the effort to prune military appropriations as it did in the past, partially because of Park's repression. The "Korean item" is again before the U.N. General Assembly. The people of South Korea need all the help they can get.

50 GENEVA (1975)

BEFORE THE U.N. HUMAN RIGHTS COMMISSION

Human rights is not a new concept. One can find human rights issues in the scriptures of many world religions. The U.N. Charter lists "respect for human rights and fundamental freedoms" as one of its objectives. Eleanor Roosevelt almost single-handedly induced the world organization to draft and vote approval of the Universal Declaration of Human Rights on December 10, 1948, and that date is still observed worldwide as Human Rights Day. Over the years, the U.N. slowly developed more detailed standards for human rights and tried to devise machinery to search for violations and to induce its sovereign states to stop them. Human rights, after disarmament, became the second major issue in which the young WCRP engaged, especially in the U.N. context. Over the years, Homer was active on such issues as racial and religious discrimination; terrorism, highjacking, and hostages; human massacre and genocide; untouchability in India and Japan; and the rights of indigenous peoples. At a meeting of the Commission on Human Rights in Geneva in 1975, Homer's testimony made waves—and almost got him barred from future proceedings.

The U.N. Charter declares that the Economic and Social Council (ECOSOC) shall set up commissions in economic and social fields and for the protection of human rights. The Charter gives ECOSOC authority "to make suitable arrangements for consultation with nongovernmental organizations." Thus the U.N. early on established a Commission on Human Rights, and NGOs observed its workings carefully. However, the Charter declared that "nothing contained in the present Charter shall authorize the U.N. to intervene in matters which are essentially within the domestic jurisdiction of any state."

Thus member states, and especially those appointed to the rotating membership of the Commission on Human Rights, always had difficulty reconciling the authority to promote and protect human rights with the hesitation to intervene in the domestic affairs of member states. Guidelines also limited the authority of NGOs.

In 1967, ECOSOC adopted a resolution that authorized its organs to deal with situations that revealed a pattern of gross violations of human rights. In the end this encouraged public discussion at the U.N. of a wide spectrum of states violating human rights, not only South Africa or Chile. Later ECOSOC adopted Resolution 1503 which allowed its suborgans to consider private communications alleging violations of human rights. This encouraged hundreds of NGOs and thousands of individuals to communicate to the U.N. Secretariat. However, the "1503 process" sealed off violations from public scrutiny, and seemed to hamper NGOs in their oral interventions to both the commission and the sub-commission on violations by member states.

During the thirty-fifth session of the commission at Geneva, on behalf of WCRP I deliberately decided to "name names" of states. On February 11, 1975, I delivered an address on religious intolerance, indicating that NGOs "are disappointed to the point of disillusionment at the lack of progress in elaborating instruments against religious intolerance," since parallel U.N. efforts against racial intolerance had culminated in a historic and useful declaration. I proposed to give an "inventory" of the denials of religious freedom since they were "not confined to any one country or any one continent." My list mentioned:

• The Muslims in the Southern Philippines who had accused the government of genocide
• The Ahmadiyas in Pakistan, an unorthodox sect, which was not recognized by the theocratic Islamic state
• The Jews in Syria who are forbidden to travel more than 2.5 miles from their homes, obtain a driver's license, and observe certain religious rites without police permission
• Christians in Cyprus, the Copts in Egypt, Christian leaders in several African countries, and Christians in Czechoslovakia who suffer various forms of prejudice and discrimination
• Pentacostalists and Jews in the Soviet Union who are not al-

lowed to assemble peacefully, who have been denied religious and cultural rights, and discriminated against in education and employment

• Catholics in Zaire who have spoken out against the political repression of President Mobutu Sese Seko and face having their churches closed and being imprisoned

I also mentioned cases in the Republic of Korea and Vietnam, concluding that "prophetic religion—Buddhism, Christianity, Hinduism, Islam, Judaism, and their many branches—has always been independent of the state, and some of its leaders have been willing if seldom eager to pay the price that independent criticism entails."

Immediately after the delivery of this speech, five members of the commission exerted their right of reply: Egypt, Pakistan, the Soviet Union, Turkey, and Zaire. Two observer states—the Philippines and Syria—also responded. Soviet Ambassador Valerian Zorin, for example, replied, "I regret that I am required to waste the time of this distinguished Commission to refute the words of a representative of a nongovernmental organization who is so bold as to use the meeting of the Commission to make slanderous, deceitful attacks on a number of countries, including my own." Some ambassadors asked that WCRP's credentials be withdrawn.

Before the commission adjourned its five-week session, it adopted a draft resolution on written and oral statements of NGOs. In a preliminary paragraph the commission observed that "some NGOs have occasionally failed to observe the requirements of confidentiality" and that "the oral interventions of some NGOs on matters affecting member states have often shown disregard for proper discretion." The operative clauses asked NGOs in the future to "comply without exception" with the rules and warned that any NGO that failed "to show proper discretion in oral or written statement may render itself subject to suspension of its consultative status."

In April 1975 twenty-two NGOs issued a statement to the commission defending their right to be heard. Several ECOSOC bodies, including the Committee on Non-Governmental Organizations, discussed the matter. In 1978, Argentina urged that the U.N.'s Joint Inspection unit investigate five NGOs—WCRP, the International University Exchange Fund, Pax Romana, the International Federation for the Rights of Man, and the International Commission of Jurists. In the end ECOSOC sustained the consultative status of all five NGOs. Today in these U.N. organs, NGOs have a much freer ability to "name names."

51 JERUSALEM (1975)

IS ZIONISM RACISM?

On November 10, 1975, the U.N. General Assembly adopted a resolution that labeled Zionism "a form of racism and racial discrimination." A coalition of Arab countries, the Soviet Bloc, China, and OPEC members garnered seventy-two votes in favor; the U.S., members of the European Economic Community, and Israel obtained thirty-five votes against; and there were thirty-two abstentions and three absent. Homer—who visited Jerusalem in 1975 and met with Martin Buber and other religious leaders—had been a longtime supporter of Israel, while at the same time supporting the right of the Palestinians to self-determination and an independent state. In this article, published in Gandhi Marg *and reprinted widely in other publications, he explained why the U.N. resolution should be resolutely rejected.*

A. *How did the equating of Zionism with racism arise in the U.N. system?* For several years Arab and later some non-aligned states used the terms "racism, apartheid, and Zionism" in succession in speeches and non-U.N. documents. In 1973, the U.N. General Assembly adopted a resolution condemning the "unholy alliance between South African racism and Zionism." In 1975 the twinning of racism and Zionism was approved in one resolution of the International Conference of International Women's Year.

B. *Why was this definition injected into the thirtieth session of the U.N. General Assembly?* Some radical Arab states were undoubtedly frustrated by the refusal of the Organization of African Unity in July, 1975, and the Foreign Ministers of Non-Aligned States in August to recommend the suspension of Israel from the U.N. in September. Also some Arab states may have used this device to undermine the interim Sinai agreement on the Middle East.

C. *What is the definition of "racial discrimination" in the U.N. system?* The International Convention on the Elimination of All Forms of Racial Discrimination, signed in 1965, contains a very broad definition of racial discrimination: "Any distinction, exclusion, restriction, or preference based on race, color, descent, or national or ethnic origin which has the purpose or effect of nullifying or impairing the recognition, employment, or exercise, on an equal footing, of human rights and fundamental freedoms in the political, economic, social, cultural, or any other field of public life." This definition goes far beyond anthropological definitions of "race."

D. *What is the definition of "racism" in the U.N. system?* This is apparently of more recent origin, with racism used perhaps for the first time in the U.N. system in the title of the International Year for Action to Combat Racism and Racial Discrimination (1971). No legal or other definition, as far as is known, has been given to racism within the U.N. Racism may, however be considered the doctrine or ideology behind the practice of racial discrimination. Thus, within the U.N. racism goes beyond race or color to include descent, and national or ethnic origin. *Webster's Third New International Dictionary* defines racism as "a belief in the inherent superiority of a particular race and its right to domination over others." Within the U.N. usage, racism would extend beyond a "particular race" to descent, and national or ethnic origin. Thus discrimination against a group based on ethnic origin would be racism as well as that based upon color or "race."

E. *What is Zionism?* While the concept is not precise, Zionism is the historic longing of the Jewish people to create a homeland. Late in the nineteenth century Zionism became a specific nationalist movement, a kind of ideology, which led to the creation of the state of Israel as that homeland.

F. *Is Zionism Judaism?* While some, and perhaps many, Jews today believe in Zionism, all Jews do not believe in Zionism. Some who do not may still support Israel. Indeed, not all who support Zionism are Jews.

G. *Does Israel practice racial discrimination—in terms of the International Convention?* Terence Smith writing in the *New York Times* (November 16, 1975) reported: "The Arabs are full-fledged Israeli citizens with the same rights and duties as the 2.6 million Jewish residents of the state. They vote, sit in Parliament, pay taxes, own land, run business, go to their own public schools, hold union cards, participate in the national health scheme, carry Israeli passports and, occasionally, even die in the same indiscriminate terrorist attacks in the streets of Jerusalem. There are two exceptions to this legal equality: Israeli Arabs are not called to serve in the armed forces . . . and their kin are not entitled to automatic Israeli citizenship, as Jews are, under the Law of Return . . . But the legal status of the Israeli Arabs is only part of the story. In practical economic, human, and social terms, they are demonstrably second-class citizens." Thus within the terms of the International Convention (which Israel, as the U.S.A., has not ratified) Israel does discriminate against Palestinian Arabs.

H. *Why, then, was the U.N. resolution wrong and did it constitute a political attack on the state of Israel?* Given this definition of racial discrimination and the practices of other nation-states, all ideologies would find a place in any catalogue of those practicing discrimination—Nazism, apartheid, but also communism, capitalism, democracy, and Zionism. Also all nation-states would be in any catalogue of those practicing racial discrimination, beginning with Afghanistan and running through each of the 143 member states of the U.N., ending with Zambia. The U.N. resolution was wrong because the extent of racial discrimination which can be attributed to Israel—while in itself to be deplored and condemned—is relatively small compared to that of many states, including some of the co-sponsors of the U.N. resolution. Because Zionism was singled out, this was a political attack and an unjust one.

I. *Is the allegation that Zionism is a form of racial discrimination an "obscene" concept and an "outrageous lie"?* It is in the sense that the Jewish people, who have been discriminated against and decimated in history through the racism of anti-Semitism, are themselves in this resolution also called racists. It is this irony that many people rightly resist.

J. *Is there, however, an ethical ambiguity within Zionism?* Zionism is a form of nationalism which many Palestinian Arabs feel is occurring at their expense. In this sense Zionism can be considered a kind of colonialist intrusion if not a classical example of colonialism. The ethical dilemma is that the need for a homeland for the persecuted Jewish people conflicts with the rights of some of the Arab people who also claim the same territory as their homeland (and thus have never accepted the U.N. division of Palestine). The world community responds to this dilemma in varying ways. This is why some Jews and some other persons oppose Zionism.

389

K. *Is opposition to Zionism anti-Semitism?* To label ethical opposition to Zionism, or Israel, as anti-Semitism is really no more helpful than to label Zionism as racism. On the other hand, some anti-Zionism is anti-Semitic.

L. *Will the resolution hurt the whole U.N. system?* Immediately, the U.N. has come under attack, especially in some of the states which voted against the resolution. Yet further consideration should direct blame towards those member states which voted for the resolution, or abstained, and not to the U.N. itself.

M. *Will the resolution cause anti-Semitism in various parts of the world?* Already some anti-Semitism has occurred as a result of the discussion of this resolution, in the U.N. and in some member states, such as Brazil. Yet the by-products of this resolution and the U.N. and public debates are not wholly negative. The discussion of this cluster of issues in the U.N. and the world community will in some ways be useful.

N. *Has the state of Israel been hurt by this debate and the final vote?* In many ways Israel has been strengthened and many of its wavering friends—states and individuals—have come to its aid. The previous trend of the increasing isolation of Israel in the world community has certainly been sharply reversed—at least for a period.

O. *What results will passage of the resolution have on peace in the Middle East?* This may not have a major effect on the unstable peace. If anything, the controversy should put additional pressure on the several parties, and the negotiators, to continue and indeed hasten their efforts to find a permanent solution to the chronic tensions there.

52 WASHINGTON (1976)

THE EMERGENCY IN INDIA

Following the crackdown on political opposition and the suspension of civil liberties in India, Homer worked with Jayaprakash Narayan and other Gandhian leaders to help restore democracy. As Prime Minister Indira Gandhi's rule in India became more dictatorial, Homer felt compelled to testify publicly. He presented the following statement to the U.S. House of Representatives, Committee on International Relations, Subcommittee on International Organizations, on June 23, 1976, in Washington.

I have been involved with India and Indian-American relations for almost thirty-five years. I was born here in the United States, but I have come to know India better than any country other than my own. Despite this long, admittedly subjective, tie with India, I am today prepared to criticize the violations of human rights in India today. I last visited India for a short period in December 1975 and January of this year, after the emergency was declared. Finally, I am acting chairman of the Ad Hoc Committee for Human Rights in India, with headquarters in New York City.

During this brief oral testimony on human rights in India, I would like to attempt to answer five questions. And the first question is to what degree have human rights in India—called fundamental rights in the Indian Constitution—eroded since the emergency was declared on June 26—one year ago Saturday?

Mr. Chairman, when I returned from India in January, I wrote an extensive memorandum on this topic which, somewhat updated, I would like to place in the record of these hearings as Exhibit 1. Let

391

me outline this material very briefly. I believe, Mr. Chairman, you have a copy of this Exhibit 1.

The declaration of the emergency by the President of India on June 26, 1975, was preceded by events of several years, and I present a chronology in Section 1 of the exhibit. The most recent date is June 16—when the Government of India extended for one year its right to hold political prisoners without trial or formal charges. The emergency decree itself was all very legal, and I discuss that at some length in Section 2. However, the emergency cannot be separated from Mrs. Indira Gandhi's own emergency, her conviction on June 12, 1975, of two charges under the India election laws, and I discuss this situation in Section 3. There are some parallels between the predicament of Richard Nixon and Indira Gandhi. Both were involved with minor infringements of the law which symbolized their far greater misunderstanding of the essence of their respective political traditions. Both Nixon and Gandhi sadly identified—almost using the same accents—their personal future with that of their nation. However, Mrs. Gandhi was a far better politician in her ability to survive; or, perceived in another manner, the American people were far more jealous of their prerogatives and far less able to be manipulated than the Indian people.

A week after the emergency was declared, on July 1, 1975, Mrs. Gandhi promulgated her 20-point economic program, and I give the outline of that in Section 4. The emergency, and its aftermath, is a complex political phenomena for India and it cannot be regarded in simplistic terms. Some of its effects, including that of the 20-point program, were positive. I can only list some of the positive aspects: more discipline, less corruption including fewer economic offenses, less inflation, and lower prices. I discuss these at some length in Section 5 of appendix 1. I would warn, however, that the discipline is external, based on fear, not internal, that corruption continues but may be more expensive, and that what economic indices are rising are the result of many factors, including good weather, and thus it is difficult to determine how much is due to the emergency.

I turn now to the legal erosion of fundamental rights. In Section 6 I provide a list of some of the legal measures taken to whittle away human rights. In Section 7, I discuss the problem of political prisoners and make a conservative estimate of at least 50,000. One should not be conservative, however, in reflecting evidences of torture, and later I will put into the record of this hearing several documents in this regard. In Section 8, I discuss press censorship. In Section 9 I discuss postponement of national elections earlier this year and other problems facing the Indian Parliament. In Section 10, I discuss surveillance and fear which is pervasive in India today. In Section 11, I discuss the lessening of the rights of workers. The rest of the paper deals principally with the opposition and other efforts to oppose the growing totalitarianism. Appendix A contains a discussion on "Fundamental Rights in the Indian Constitution." Efforts are continuing to amend the Constitution, but perhaps not as drastically in its human rights provisions as originally feared.

I believe that the United States should, initially, at least speak out in world forums against the loss of civil liberties in India. I am glad that the United States has begun to find its voice, and conscience, beginning once again to condemn its friends, its allies, its adversaries, any nation in the world community which is flaunting the standards enshrined in the Universal Declaration of Human Rights. We must speak out—the President, the Secretary of State, the Congress—and there is no more appropriate time to do so than in our own Bicentennial Year. Speaking out constitutes pressure of world public opinion and the effect of this even on the most tyrannical of regimes should not be discounted. And Mrs. Gandhi's is by no means the most tyrannical today.

One type of quasi-military aid being given or sold by the United States to India is nuclear expertise, machinery, and fuels, including uranium and heavy water. Given India's decision in 1973 to go nuclear—whatever India's own description of her nuclear pregnancy—I think all U.S. nuclear aid of whatever sort to India should cease, as Canada rightly, if belatedly, ceased her nuclear aid to India some weeks ago. The U.S. Nuclear Regulatory Commission is currently deciding whether to permit export of 40,000 pounds of uranium to India. This should be denied, for reasons of arresting nuclear proliferation, which is as crucial to human survival as arresting totalitarian proliferation.

What other concrete levels are available to U.S. policymakers? The most obvious is food aid. We Americans are now shipping many millions of dollars and tons of food grains to India, even though at the moment the grain harvest in India is abundant. There will undoubtedly be periods in the near future when we must again ship even much larger amounts of food to India. We should do so—willingly, eagerly—whatever the state of human rights in India. Food should never be used as a political weapon—against any regime, against any people, including our own American poor. The prompt adoption by Congress of the pending concurrent resolutions declaring as national policy the right to food could help insure policy for a continuing flow of food to India and other needy countries.

What about economic aid to India? In March, it was announced here in Washington that the Ford administration was breaking off the embryonic negotiations with India for bilateral economic aid because Mrs. Gandhi sharply criticized some things American. At the time I sent a letter of protest to Secretary Henry Kissinger and received a reply from Adolph Dubs of the Bureau of Near Eastern and South Asian Affairs. He denied that talks were "broken off," but said that they were merely postponed; he also denied that "to defer talks on economic aid" is a "policy of 'economic reprisal.'" He did write, however, that "recent unfounded remarks by high Indian Government leaders which were critical of the United States, have perplexed us and let us to conclude that caution is necessary regarding the pursuit of some programs which require that mutual trust and confidence exist between us before they can be carried out successfully." This finely-wrought sentence confirmed widespread fears that the United States apparently operates on pique—hurt pride—but I would hope that pique would not be decisive in American policy formulation, either in the administration or here in Congress. I would hope that this administration would, in earnest, begin again to negotiate broad economic and social aid to the Indian people, as much through multilateral agencies as possible, but also some bilateral aid in the near future. India is one of the most severely affected nations, especially because of the fuel and monetary crises of the 1970s. India needs and deserves all the economic aid she can find anywhere in the First and Second Worlds.

Finally, there are general positive levers the United States can pull which might impinge on the internal direction India may take. These involve other aspects of American foreign policy. To the degree that we can loosen our alliance with Pakistan, to the degree that we can abandon our effort to build a military base on Diego Garcia, to the degree that we can include Delhi as one of the six or seven world capitals with which we must always confer, to that degree we can exert positive influence which can make democracy more possible in India.

The American experience was one of the ideological bases for the independence of India. While higher education in England was a decisive personal experience for both Gandhi and Nehru, such American examples as Henry Thoreau, Abraham Lincoln, Woodrow Wilson, and Franklin Roosevelt greatly inspired the fathers of India—Gandhi and Nehru—and the literate India people generally.

394

This legacy of America will also not be forgotten over the long run, if sometimes it is not instantly remembered.

Whatever America can do about the violation of human rights in India—will it make a difference? And I can only conclude that whatever America and other nations can do will at least not be counter-productive. And it just might lead to a lessening of the violations of human rights in India today.

A final reason why Americans should be concerned about human rights in India today is the effect this overt concern may have on members of the opposition who are trying to relight the flame of freedom. It is important that their morale be considered and enhanced. If it is right to sustain the spirit of freedom fighters in the remaining colonial lands—and much of the U.N. system is committed to do this—it is also right to sustain the spirit of those fighting for freedom in independent nations which are totalitarian. If the United Nations is buoying the spirit of those fighting for the freedom of Zimbabwe and Namibia, the United States and some day the United Nations should hold high the spirit of a Sakharov in the Soviet Union, a Kim Chi Ha in East Asia, or a J. P. Narayan in South Asia. Perhaps morale-building is a proper function of nongovernmental organizations more than governments. But we know that editorials critical of the Indian Government, news stories of demonstrations in front of Indian consulates, and other evidences of overseas criticism of the erosion of human rights in India are eagerly awaited by members of the opposition who pass such evidences from person to person, hand to hand. I can attest to this practice among the opposition in India.

Since the Vietnam war concluded, many Americans have slipped into the pattern of not feeling deeply about issues. True believers are a vanishing species. This is good in that it eliminates sloganeering, irrationality, and stubbornness. It also encourages pragmatism, accomplishment, and realism. Yet something is missing if advocacy and conviction disappear. I feel deeply about the loss of liberty in India today. I wish more Americans felt similarly. When they do, I hope this concern will increasingly be reflected in American policy. Thank you.

53 NEW YORK
(1976)

AS THEY SAW HIM:
FROM MY CIA AND FBI FILES

Enacted in the wake of the Watergate Scandal, the Freedom of Information Act began to reveal some of the long-buried domestic and foreign secrets of the Cold War, including the fact that the American government was spying on its own citizens. In a sermon delivered at the Brooklyn Society for Ethical Culture on Oct. 31, 1976, Homer described—with a combination of righteous indignation and humor—the reaction to reading his own government files.

I have lived a life on the outer margins of power and policy formulation. I have seldom felt that I was the object of national or international surveillance, although I have been barred from entering South Africa (after 1952) and South Vietnam (after 1971). I have never had trouble obtaining a passport from the U.S. government. I have never felt myself a particular target of the KGB or the CIA, although for twenty-five years I have roamed the world widely and have been involved in international relations for nongovernmental—mainly religious organizations.

When the Freedom of Information Act entered into force, I routinely wrote to both the CIA and the FBI demanding the right as a citizen to see my file. That was in August 1975. Since then I have received an occasional communication from both agencies, suggesting patience. Then on May 17, I received an eight-page letter from the Information and Privacy Coordinator of the CIA. They listed ninety-eight items! In addition, they indicated that "a number of FBI documents" pertaining to me were in their files. Also they indicated that documents also about me were in their files originating from the Department of State, United States Information Agency (USIA), the U.S. Army, and the U.S. Air Force. They assured me that these agencies would contact me "directly concerning the disposition of their documents."

With this letter, the CIA sent me eighteen items in their entirety. Another thirty-seven items were sent along, but with "certain portions" deleted. Alongside the index of these items in the covering letter were symbols indicating the cause of the deletions. They listed six exemptions from the Freedom of Information Act: 1) classified material; 2) information pertaining solely to the rules and practices of the CIA; 3) material which would disclose intelligence sources and methods as well as names and functions of CIA personnel; 4) inter- and intra-agency memoranda only advisory in nature; 5) material that would constitute an unwarranted invasion of the personal privacy of other individuals; and 6) material that would disclose the identity of a confidential source or investigative procedures. Finally, there was an index of forty-three additional items which could not be released, even in part, but with the reason for exemption listed. However, the CIA told me in the letter that I have the right to appeal their actions.

Then on May 19—my sixtieth birthday—came a letter from Clarence M. Kelley, director of the Federal Bureau of Investigation. He said that they processed and had available for release seventy-four pages of documents about me. However, pursuant to Title 28, Code of Federal Regulations, Sections 16.9 and 16.46, there would be a fee of ten cents per page for duplication. The CIA had charged me nothing. I petitioned a waiver of the fee. I resented paying even $7.40 beyond my federal taxes for this information, writing Mr. Kelley that "I ask for this waiver because it is in the public interest since I have reason to believe many of these files refer to my activities as an officer of American organizations which have and do work in the public interest under our form of democracy." I received no waiver, so reluctantly I sent the $7.40. A few days thereafter, I received the seventy-four pages of FBI documents. However, the FBI did not reveal to me the documents they retained, but some they gave me were also heavily censored. I also appealed to them for additional material and have not received a reply.

This Is Your Life

Reviewing the material received is reliving one's life. Some goes back thirty-four years. The FBI reported that in the early 1940s I was known "at Chicago as a liberalist, pacifist, and an advocate of racial equality." In 1942 I visited New York City to attend a national rally to free Earl Browder, then the jailed secretary of the American Communist Party. Returning to the University campus, I spoke at a Free Earl Browder meeting at the First Unitarian Church of Chicago on May 8, 1942, with approximately 140 persons attending, including a representative of the FBI or another informant. The latter secured the full text of my speech which said that Browder was "punished because he was the secretary of an unpopular party." And with Browder's sentence on the books, "now any unconforming citizen runs the risk of receiving a major sentence for committing a minor crime." Yesterday communism was an unpopular cause, "and as the result, Mr. Browder is still in prison on a minor passport violation." Today, anyone who doesn't agree with the Administration "generally runs the risk, in any violation of the law, of getting the limit and the consecutive limit at that."

The FBI further quoted from my speech: "I am a pacifist, yes, a pacifist even in time of world-wide war. . . . It has been said that there are more pacifists in jail today than communists. But perhaps that is as it should be, for pacifism to some of us is a positive philosophy and a practical method much more revolutionary and dangerous to our present-day capitalistic society than even communism, than even Earl Browder. I hope to see the friends of Freedom for Browder also fight by our side in preventing the indiscriminate evacuation of Japanese-American citizens and aliens on our West Coast. These poor souls this very minute are being herded by the thousands into reception centers, just a nice American word for concentration camps. America, as well as Germany, is dumping members of one race together, calling them undesirable, and dumping them into the wilderness of barbed wire, and not one case of Japanese sabotage has been verified even at Pearl Harbor. Lastly, I hope to see the friends of Freedom for Browder fight by our side in behalf of the Negroes. It's glamorous, I suppose, to fight for democracy around the world, but how many are fighting for the rights of Negroes . . . to move into property with a restricted covenant clause?" The FBI memo commented that H.A.J.'s speech was "'out of line' with traditional (Communist) Party policy."

In 1952 when I was minister of the Unitarian Church in Evanston, I took my first trip to Africa, spending three months there. Hardly had I returned when the CIA was in my study, asking me about the leaders of the freedom movements I had visited. I curtly showed the CIA agent the door, telling him that he could read my published writings, but I would not brief the CIA privately. The next year, while preaching at Community Church that summer, I delivered a sermon entitled, "Is McCarthy a Concealed Communist?" This severely offended the friends of Senator Joseph McCarthy and no doubt set off a new series of investigations. Indeed, a patron of McCarthy threatened to sue me for slander. That sermon was not sent by the FBI, but the agency mentioned in a letter that this sermon, and another preached earlier in Chicago on violations of civil liberties, were in their files and would be "furnished upon request."

Given this combination of work for African freedom and against Senator McCarthy, the chief of some section of the CIA on November 13, 1953, requested an investigation be conducted on "Dr. or Rev. Homer A. Jack." He wanted to know 1) the organizations he has been associated with in the past, 2) the extent of his active participation in communist-dominated organizations, 3) the real sources of his income, and 4) whether he is or ever has been a communist or communist sympathizer. There was no immediate answer to this inquiry, at least none put in his revealed files. Also in November, 1953, the files received the name of H.A.J. as among the sponsors of Americans for South African Resistance.

In 1953 I reportedly "wrote to President Eisenhower requesting clemency for Julius and Ethel Rosenberg who were under sentence of death for espionage." I was described as a person of "excellent moral character who enjoyed an excellent reputation in the community." Another person, name also deleted, "never heard anything of an unfavorable nature with regard to Homer Jack." Still another informant said that he "has never known Jack to be a member of the CP [Communist Party] but felt that Jack had the reputation of being a 'liberal.'"

The Office of Naval Intelligence in January, 1957, published a long report on the role of H.A.J. as a part-time correspondent for The *Hindustan Times* of New Delhi. The memo stated that those who "have knowledge of Mr. Jack . . . do not think he is a communist or of a communist leaning but state that his writings may be expected to be in admiration of 'any and everything Indian.'" The memo further states that "the editor of that newspaper, Devadas Gandhi, likes the articles or likes Mr. Jack—as Mr. Jack is a great admirer of the editor's late father." While the preparing officer "firmly believes in every American having right to his own opinion on questions of America's policies, it still seems unfitting for an American citizen to air such disagreements with those policies to foreigners in a foreign press . . . Such Americans are often unwittingly used as tools of un-American organizations to further their aims to harm the U.S."

In 1959 I moved to New York City to become Associate Director of the American Committee on Africa and editor of *Africa Today*. In the latter capacity, I wrote to the well known Soviet Africanist, Professor I. Potekhin, whom I had met in Africa. Potekhin replied on July 21, 1960 that he would be unable to write an article in the future, but reserved the opportunity to submit one later. This letter was intercepted, being returned to me also with a photocopy of the envelope, in 1976—sixteen years later. In November 1960, Professor Potekhin did send an article, and the letter—but not the article—was also intercepted.

The FBI clipped a long biographical interview of me appearing in the *New York Post* in May 1961. The U.S. Information Agency from Geneva on June 15, 1962, indicated that I was en route to Moscow (with Erich Fromm) to speak to the Moscow Peace Conference on behalf of a number of prominent Americans. Also the CIA clipped the article from the August 7, 1962, issue of the *New York Times* when I was profiled as "Man in the News."

I left SANE in 1964 to become Director of the Division of Social Responsibility of the Unitarian-Universalist Association in Boston and dropped out of FBI and CIA concern apparently for several years. In April 1967, however, a CIA memorandum discussed "conversations between American clergymen and militant Buddhist leaders in Saigon on plans for 1968 world peace congress." In April 1967 the CIA produced another short political sketch, indicating that H.A.J. was an "ardent supporter of pacifist organizations and civil rights with reputation of lending his name to liberal organizations he approves of but not known to support extremist groups of either wing." It added: "Knowledgeable source has stated that Jack's views are sometimes divergent American policy but his presentation of views have on the whole been intelligent and fair."

The CIA on July 11, 1968, published an internal list of U.S. nationals who went to North Vietnam with valid U.S. travel documentation. My name was on the list, dated March 28, 1967. This was one of the few misstatements of fact in these government files.

By 1968, the World Conference on Religion and Peace was in

preparation, and I attended the Upsalla Assembly of the World Council of Churches and discussed the World Conference with Metropolitan Nicodim of the Russian Orthodox Church. On July 24, 1968, I wrote on the stationery of the Unitarian Universalist Association a letter to Metropolitan Nicodim in Moscow. This letter was intercepted by U.S. postal authorities in Boston and, with its envelope, a photocopy was returned to me in 1976.

In November, 1969, the code Chaos appeared on CIA memos. This was a CIA project whereby its agents infiltrated domestic organizations and spied and reported on more than 300,000 individuals in order to determine "the foreign contacts of American dissidents." In a page mostly masked, one sentence about H.A.J. stood out: "Chaos implications not involved." Another Chaos memorandum dated November 1969, asked for "any information Jack may volunteer on Americans involved in arranging for the World Conference [on Religion and Peace]." A CIA memo dated December 1969 reported that "Jack places a high priority on the attendance and participation of religious leaders from Communist countries and had refrained from soliciting participation of strongly anti-Communist countries, such as Taiwan, or individuals such as the Dalai Lama in order to avoid discouraging Communist participation." A letter on the stationary of the World Conference on Religion and Peace sent from Boston to the Soviet Peace Committee was intercepted by the U.S. Post Office. So was a letter to General Boris Teplinsky of Moscow, with whom I had several discussions on disarmament affairs.

The opening of the decade found me often in Japan, preparing for the first World Conference on Religion and Peace (WCRP I). While there I was contacted by Japanese peace leaders to help an American soldier absent without leave (AWOL) to surrender. I took this sailor to a naval base outside Tokyo. The Naval Intelligence Service in June 1970 reported that I accompanied him "at the time of his surrender." The memo asked "check files of FBI Boston regarding Dr. Homer Jack and the Unitarian Universalist Society of Boston." An FBI memo dated June 24 indicated that H.A.J. supported "pacifists and civil liberties-type actions subsequent to his arrival in this [Boston] area, such activity was not of a nature to warrant reopening his case. Further, there has been no indication of his acting in behalf of a subversive cause."

In October 1970 a CIA memo indicated "impression is that Jack is very idealistic and likes to maintain [a] position of 'theological independence.' He is ambitious and seeks [the] limelight. He is not pro-U.S. spokesman; not communist either but willing to deal with them. He has attended numerous front meetings and allowed his name to be linked with gatherings hostile to U.S., but in [the] past on substantive issues in meetings has tried to be fair and impartial, to castigate both sides. Recently he appears somewhat less impartial. He is apparently so eager to project himself that he is willing to compromise on allowing Communists to be involved in all planning of meetings which he heads."

A CIA memo dated October 1973 indicated that the World Peace Council—the communist-affiliated group—"will open an office in Geneva in spring of 1974 . . . this probably a move to try to off-set Homer Jack's activities and enable World Peace Council to monitor U.N. activities in Geneva more closely."

Commentary

This was the last memorandum sent to me during 1976 by the federal agencies. Of course there were those two sermons which the FBI promised to send along if I wanted them. It is not every preacher who gets two whole sermons into the FBI archives! Since I know well both sermons, and already have them in my personal archives, I refused to give Mr. Kelley ten cents per page.

While the documentation turned over to me was overwhelming, the deletions and maskings were enticing. What was sent me was the tip, and probably not the most interesting tip, of the political iceberg. I shall probably never know the words, the paragraphs, and the assessments which were deleted. I do know that some of my most political activities did not show up in the files as all, including the founding of CORE, my association with Martin Luther King, Jr., 1968 visits to Moscow and Prague to discuss the Russian occupation of Czechoslovakia, and a 1970 trip—via the Trans-Siberian Railway in the U.S.S.R.—to meet with dissidents in Moscow.

In these CIA/FBI papers, one operative concluded that he could "count on Jack for relatively fair and impartial approach." In concluding this address, I want to be neither fair nor impartial in my assessment of my government for this surveillance. Let me quickly finish with four conclusions.

First, I am chagrined and outraged that my government has violated its law and my civil rights by spying on my activities in the U.S. and abroad, going back at least retroactively to 1937 when, at the age of twenty-one, I first obtained a passport. I am doubly chagrined that the federal taxes I have paid all these years went for such evil and plainly wasteful purposes.

Second, that the CIA evaluated my politics fairly—at least in the memoranda shown me—does not detract from the illegal and immoral action of the CIA and other federal investigative agencies. It is my firm conviction that the CIA should be eliminated as should at least the Internal Security Division of the FBI.

Third, this spying on American citizens by the CIA, the FBI, and other federal agencies must stop. Mail must not be opened, incoming or outgoing. Files should not be kept on citizens doing their work as citizens, attending meetings and otherwise peaceably exercising their right to free speech and free assembly. There must be the most comprehensive oversight by the U.S. Congress. It may be too early to evaluate the new efforts of the Congress to do so. However, I have little confidence that the CIA and other such U.S. agencies have ceased their spying.

Fourth and finally, I am sure that the KGB is also deeply involved in the surveillance of its own citizens and those of other countries in many parts of the world. But their nefarious activities do not make any more ethical the mischief and immorality of the CIA and other such investigative agencies of the U.S. Government.

And with these conclusions, I take leave of the FBI and the CIA and try to resume my small efforts to make democracy work in our country and world and to stave off nuclear war. I know that this sermon is bound to find its place, not only in my archives at Swarthmore College, but in the files of the FBI and CIA in Washington. Will this spying on private citizens never stop?

54 SINGAPORE
(1977)

THE BOAT PEOPLE PROJECT

When the Vietnam war ended in 1975, a large exodus began, including many Vietnamese of Chinese ancestry. Thousands of refugees left in small boats for Hong Kong, Thailand, Malaysia, Singapore, and Indonesia. For humanitarian and religious reasons—some of the people feared religious or racial persecution—WCRP initiated a Boat People Project to rescue refugees from the high seas. Thich Nhat Hanh, a Vietnamese Zen monk living in exile in Paris, was appointed director of the project. The effort quickly turned into a disaster, and the Boards of WCRP and ACRP—the regional Asian Conference on Religion and Peace—asked Homer to take personal charge. Confronted with hundreds of stranded refugees, a mutinous crew, and indifferent government officials, Homer—accompanied by Ingeborg—found himself embroiled in one of the most difficult episodes of personal diplomacy and peacemaking of his career.

Thich Nhat Hanh initially chartered a 65-foot ship, *Saigon 200*, at $450 a day, beginning on December 4. The crew was asked to search for Boat People in the waters of Indonesia and Malaysia. Local fisherman had reported seeing small boats with refugees, but all *Saigon 200* encountered was very rough waters. On December 12, *Saigon 200* returned to Singapore. The Project also chartered a small Piper airplane to survey the coastline and islands off the eastern coast of Malaysia. It was unable to identify any boats coming from Vietnam.

A controversy arose about taking Boat People to Australia and Guam. Thich Nhat Hanh early on had a vision of large ships filled with Boat People going to Guam (U.S. territory) and to Darwin in Australia. He felt that this would be a poignant, nonviolent demonstration of the world's responsibility to accept these refugees more promptly. Although this was an early option, both ACRP and WCRP in their several resolutions confined the Project to rescuing individuals from the deep sea, isolated islands, and shorelines. One resolution declared that the U.N. High Commissioner for Refugees (UNHCR) would be "consulted at every step." Soon it became abundantly clear that the UNHCR as well as Australia and the U.S.A. would not countenance what was in effect illegal entry.

Early in January 1977 Thich Nhat Hanh chartered the 130-foot *Roland*, a former U.S. Navy minesweeper. It weighed 120 tons and cost $15,000 a month plus fuel and other expenses. Soon, at additional expense, *Roland* acquired a barge to carry fuel and other supplies. Beginning January 7, *Roland* went up the east coast of Malaysia. As the ship moved north at sea, a team from the Project moved parallel to it on land. The team distributed leaflets, drafted in Vietnamese by Thich Nhat Hanh, as they moved along the coast, stating that "Refugees will be provided with food, medicines, and transported to various countries such as U.S.A., Australia, Japan, etc., and the budget will be provided by various religious organizations throughout the world. All of you, refugees, don't worry. Please keep patient. This program is under the auspices of the Asian Conference on Religion and Peace. Keep calm and we will look after everybody." The BBC and possibly other radio stations soon were making broadcasts to Vietnam, in the Vietnamese language, about the Project, perhaps based on this leaflet. This effort to gather refugees from the shore was undertaken without consulting WCRP or ACRP officers.

In one month, *Roland* picked up 300 passengers. Among the first to come aboard toward the end of January were fifty-three persons at Tumpat, almost on the Thai border, and Kota Bharu. These were part of a group of sixty-six individuals in five Vietnamese families who had landed in five small boats on the Malaysian shore near Kota Bharu in the late autumn of 1976. First living inside their boats in monsoon weather, the refugees were transferred to land and into a makeshift camp. Father W., a French missionary, wrote to the UNHCR in Kuala Lumpur to inform the agency about the refugees and to ask for help, but no reply had been received. In December, two workers from the WCRP/ACRP project, bringing the leaflets in Vietnamese, contacted the refugees, and also the Buddhist and Catholic representatives in town. In January, Father W. was contacted by the WCRP/ACRP Project office in Singapore and told that a chartered boat would soon come to "take" these people, but he was asked not to say "anything to the U.N. or the government." He agreed to cooperate, but said that he would have to inform the local police.

The *Roland* appeared off the shore of Kota Bharu on January 29. However, a representative from UNHCR now appeared for the first time. He warned the refugees not to board the ship, since it was "a mad idea." On the other hand, the owner of the ship, Mr. Y. (an American businessman domiciled in Singapore and a Vietnam War veteran) urged the people to board the ship. Most of the refugees left the camp, except thirteen who had greater possibility of permanent asylum somewhere else. Local authorities transported the fifty-three persons the 12 miles to Tunpat where hired fishing boats took them to the *Roland*, which was three miles off shore. Some weeks later Father W. managed to sell two of the original boats of the refugees and forwarded the funds to them. They were still passengers on the *Roland*.

In this way the *Roland* picked up still other passengers. At Kuala Trengganu, 145 persons boarded the ship directly from a refugee camp. Here also, some chose to stay in the camp, and did not yield to the temptation to leave. From Kuala Dungun came fifty-seven persons. Their small boat had just sunk on shore. At Pulau Pemanggil, twenty-six persons came aboard after living there for some months. As the *Roland* headed for Singaporean waters, of the 300 aboard, 198 persons had been in touch with the UNHCR, and their papers for permanent settlement were being processed.

The *Roland* stopped in Malaysian waters just east of Singapore. Fuel and other provisions were brought to it by the staff of the WCRP/ACRP Project, which was headquartered in Singapore. Then the *Roland* was ordered by the authorities of Singapore to leave these waters and it anchored in nearby international waters. It lost its anchor and went into nearby Indonesian waters until it was told by Indonesian authorities also to leave. The *Roland* could not land even temporarily in Singapore without posting a huge bond. The ship had nowhere to go but to drift in international waters off Singapore, Malaysia, or Indonesia. All these Project activities were undertaken without consultation with WCRP/ACRP representatives in Singapore.

Leap Dal

Early in January 1977 Thich Nhat Hanh chartered a second ship. This was the *Leap Dal*, meaning "good luck" in Khmer. It was a 30-year-old, 1,500-ton oil tanker, owned by a Hong Kong businessman. This ship cost $22,000 a month plus fuel and other expenses, and was in bad shape. An Indonesian was hired as captain, but most of the other thirteen crew members were stateless Cambodians. The ship left Singapore on January 10, making no stops until it reached Bangkok on January 17. The plan was to take on supplies quickly and then pick up stranded Boat People from some Thai camps which Dr. Cao Phung, Thich Nhat Hanh's associate, had visited earlier. Instead, the *Leap Dal* stayed near Bangkok for one month.

Mr. X., a Bangkok businessman, took charge of the ship on orders from Dr. Cao. He loaded the ship with supplies—but also with Laotians. Of the 254 persons on ship, when it finally left Bangkok on February 16, 208 were Laotians, some of whom had been living in and around Bangkok for some time. Also aboard were seventy-three Cambodians and thirteen Vietnamese. After the ship left Bangkok, some of the passengers admitted to the crew that each had to pay Mr. X. the equivalent of $800 to $1,000 "for the trip to Australia." Had they known, WCRP and ACRP officers would have cancelled such actions.

Controlling the Project

The activities of the *Roland* in January and the status of passengers of the *Leap Dal* in February completely changed the character of the Project. What went wrong?

A principal error was that Thich Nhat Hanh did not consult with WCRP and ACRP officers in Singapore or New York. Perhaps he did not do so because he realized that some of his initial actions would not be approved.

Thich Nhat Hanh was also disturbed because no refugee boats could be located by his staff and himself in the South China Sea, despite the hundreds of Boat People known to be leaving Vietnam at that time. The Boat People they approached were on islands or along the shore of Malaysia and were already in the first stages of rescue and resettlement. The refugees admittedly had to await their turn, because the UNHCR had a large backlog.

The two chartered ships ended up with passengers who were not technically Boat People, most of whom had already been given temporary asylum. Moreover, neither chartered ship was in good enough condition to travel the long distances to Guam or Darwin. Thus for several reasons, any notion of travel to these southern ports was unrealistic and not acceptable, even though passengers had been promised by Thich Nhat Hanh and his assistants that they would be brought to Australia.

Thich Nhat Hanh apparently was too emotionally involved with the Boat People. He was too anti-government in general to administer successfully such a Project. He viewed governments and the U.N. as antagonists when both had to be part of any formula to deal with refugees.

In the meantime, both ships were in international waters off Singapore, having to be supplied several times weekly by the small, harassed WCRP/ACRP staff of Thich Nhat Hanh in Singapore. The 300 Boat People on the *Roland* had many problems obtaining visas for permanent asylum. The 254 passengers on the *Leap Dal* were in deeper trouble, being mostly Laotians and having even less prospect of finding visas for permanent placement.

Back in New York, as Secretary-General of WCRP, I was summoned to U.N. headquarters by the representative of UNHCR, Mr. Virendra Dayal. He read a long UNHCR telex critical of the whole Project. He urged me to fly at once to Singapore. I arrived late in January and found Willie Tay and Mehervan Singh—WCRP/ACRP board members—had been kept by Thich Nhat Hanh out of the decision-making. Soon some other WCRP/ACRP board members arrived and together we quickly started to evaluate the status and modalities of the Project.

We found the Project under siege. The UNHCR was deeply concerned and several consulates in Singapore and Kuala Lumpur irate. Thich Nhat Hanh and Dr. Cao were very secretive. They were also spending funds from a separate account in the Netherlands under their control, for expenses they believed the WCRP/ACRP Board would not authorize. They did not immediately reveal the location of either of the chartered ships.

On January 31, Yasuo Katsuyama of ACRP and I flew to Kuala Lumpur to confer with R. Sampat Kumar and other UNHCR officials. When I returned to Singapore and could not make contact with my longtime friend, Thich Nhat Hanh, I wrote him a note on February 5: "You have been secretive with representatives of the Inter-Religious Organization of Singapore and deeply suspicious of the UNHCR. But why are you seemingly avoiding me, too? We need complete cooperation, and no secrecy or procrastination, from you and Dr. Cao. Truth and openness, I had thought, are part of nonviolence."

Later, on February 7, Mehervan Singh and I were back in Kuala Lumpur, trying to find a way for passengers of the *Roland* to receive permission for transit through Malaysia before leaving for countries of permanent asylum. (Transit through Singapore was prohibitively expensive.) Fortunately, we were able to deal with a friend of ACRP, Datuk Taib, then Minister of Information in Malaysia. A formula was worked out: "For every four persons leaving Malaysian camps for permanent settlement, three persons may leave the *Roland* and be allowed to land at a Malaysian port." Under this agreement the *Roland* could sail to the port of Kuantan, along the east coast of Malaysia, to begin to unload refugees who had permanent visas. The boat with the other refugees seeking visas would remain at sea.

A statement of agreement for the Project was also drafted to provide better guidelines to the Project staff. It called for the two chartered ships to "proceed as soon as possible to a designated port," with the UNHCR attempting to provide some information on the status and future of the refugees at the port of debarkation. Only with great reluctance did Thich Nhat Hanh initial this statement.

On February 17, the eve of the Tet celebrations—Chinese New Year, widely observed in Singapore—Mr. Katsuyama and I were able to board the *Roland*. It was off the Malaysian town of Kukup. We had to break the news to the passengers: the boat was not going to Australia. When we left the ship, we were accompanied by the first fifteen passengers who had just received visas for permanent asylum in Austria.

Back in Singapore, members of the Board of the Project came together and decided that Thich Nhat Hanh and Dr. Cao had to resign. They were asked to do so immediately. The direction of the Project was temporarily put in my hands.

However, the *Roland*—even after Thich Nhat Hanh's dismissal—was a rebellious ship, both passengers and crew. The former director, Thich Nhat Hanh, tried to maintain control of both ships. He stayed in Singapore, attempting to give orders to the captains and even sending announcements in the mail that the project was being continued under different, independent auspices. When his visa in Singapore expired, he was variously reported in Bangkok, Bali, and Melbourne. From a great distance he continued to try to control both ships by radio, and caused serious problems between myself and the captain of the *Roland*.

In the meantime, both ships, filled with passengers, had nowhere to go. They had to be constantly supplied with food and water. The passengers had to be made aware of their realistic future and fate. Many were outraged that Thich Nhat Hanh had made promises to them that he and others could not keep.

Ingeborg Jack, in the meantime, had been willingly granted leave from her post at UNICEF in New York to help with this Project. She met the *Roland* in Malacca and immediately took responsibility for the ship. She purchased daily large amounts of vegetables. She also bought dried coconut shells for cooking, fuel, medicine, and some material to help keep the children occupied. Also she maintained daily telephone contact with Mr. Sampat Kumar of the UNHCR in Kuala Lumpur. She received good advice and assistance from the friendly local Red Crescent Society and by the Marine Police. (She even bought fishing rods for the men on board as well as a much-needed new water pump for the ship.) The *Roland* continued to travel international waters off Malaysia, ending up in Kuala Trengganu. Ingeborg, following the advice of the refugees, traveled always on land, although she would have preferred to travel with them on the *Roland*. She also had to keep in contact with the harbor police and obtain permission for the ship to stay outside various harbors. The captain feared a mutiny by the passengers if he steered the ship toward Kuantan—near where they had originally boarded. The refugees had many justifiable complaints against the captain, who was increasingly violent. Ingeborg often had to act as conciliator between the captain and his crew versus the refugees. The latter recommended that she not spend nights aboard ship. They feared the captain might throw her overboard and then blame the refugees for doing so. Thich Nhat Hanh was intermittently in contact by radio with the captain. Finally the captain became convinced that he no longer could listen to orders from Thich Nhat Hanh coming by radio from Australia where the latter was now located. The *Roland* finally went into waters east of Malaysia.

There actually was a mutiny, on March 19, when the captain of the *Roland* and his crew used iron poles to prevent several Vietnamese boys from climbing back on ship after they swam to an island very close by to pick coconuts. The captain and the crew used the moment when Ingeborg boarded the ship, shortly afterwards, to jump ship. Earlier, the captain had turned off all electricity on the ship and locked all doors. The refugees were very frightened when they realized, as night approached, that they had no lights on their ship. Their concern was that another ship might not see them at night and possibly run into them.

When Ingeborg returned to land, she found the captain and spoke to him. He gave her a flimsy excuse for having left the *Roland*. The following day, the captain and the crew were glad to return to the ship "under Inge's protection," and it seemed to her that the refugees were actually glad to have the captain back. However, there was continuous anger toward the captain by the refugees, and they reported all kinds of harassment by the captain.

Ong Tong Hai of the Inter-Religious Organization of Singapore took charge of supplying the *Leap Dal*, whose captain and owner were both more obedient than those of the *Roland*. Soon there was no danger that the *Leap Dal* would attempt to sail without permission. The captain was aware of the bad condition of the boat. The morale of the passengers continued to be low.

WCRP was trying to make a bad situation better. The UNHCR was assuaged, as were many consulates and some Southeast Asian governments. But the press had a story.

Bruce Grant, in his volume *Boat People*, quoted the UNHCR as characterizing the WCRP/ACRP Project as "misguided philanthropy." Michael Richardson in the *Melbourne Age*, asserted that the mission of the *Leap Dal* "has degenerated into an attempt to smuggle people claiming to be refugees into Australia." Jon Swain in the London *Sunday Times* and *Washington Post* called the Project a "scandal of the refugees on a voyage to nowhere." The *Christian Century* headed a story by Michael Lee, a pseudonym, "Bungled Benevolence in the Far East" and concluded that "subtle political implications follow every benevolent action by religious people." Henry Kamm's article in the *New York Times* was headed "Refugees from Indochina Find Only Further Despair." He called the *Leap Dal* "their floating prison."

554 Visas

Quite apart from "controlling" the two chartered boats, the Project also had to find visas for the 554 passengers. In March and early April, I sought visas in Bonn and the Hague, aided by religious leaders in both the Federal Republic of Germany and the Netherlands. I then visited Ottawa in May and Washington in May, June, and July. WCRP/ACRP retained an attorney, Charles Morgan, to

411

open doors in the Carter administration on this issue.

Slowly these interventions paid off. The resettlement of the *Roland* was as follows: fifteen persons to Austria on February 17; three to France on February 26; seventy-four to Australia on March 16; thirteen to Switzerland on March 16; and one to Hong Kong on March 16. (Australia took many who were refused by other countries.) A group of 196 persons remained on the Roland until April 30, when they disembarked to go to Palau Besar Camp near Kuala Trengganu in Malaysia. Most stayed there until September, when thirty-one persons went to New Zealand and twenty-three to the U.S.A. As of October 1, 1977, forty-six former passengers of the *Roland* remained in the Malaysian camps until they were given permanent asylum.

To find visas for the *Leap Dal* passengers, the vast majority of whom were not Boat People, became an even more difficult task. It took until May 31 for Singapore to allow any of the passengers to transit its territory even if they held valid papers for permanent asylum. On June 16, nine passengers disembarked and went to the Federal Republic of Germany. Australia took fifty-two persons on June 19. Nineteen went to Austria and sixty-five to France. By August 29 arrangements were made for the remaining ninety passengers, mostly Laotian, to go to the Singapore airport and fly to Bangkok—from where they had started on February 16. These passengers refused to leave the *Leap Dal*. It was not until September 22 that they were persuaded to disembark. They spent one night in Singapore, then flew to Bangkok. From there seventy-three Laotians were taken to the Lao Center at Nong Khai, twelve went to a Cambodian center, and five escaped. With the *Leap Dal* emptied of its passengers, its nine-month charter to WCRP/ACRP expired.

Evaluation

The Boat People Project was well-conceived, but initially badly administered. So many administrative mistakes were made during the first three months that it took the next eight months to correct them. The venture was rightly called a flawed project.

The Project did, at the onset, publicize the plight of the Boat People, especially to the multireligious community within WCRP circles and beyond. The Project created additional pressures—in countries such as Australia, Canada, the Federal Republic of Germany, and the U.S.A.—to accept larger quotas of Boat People and to process their settlement faster. It gave new appreciation to many religious leaders and others of the important work that the UNHCR had been doing with refugees for decades. The Project may also have given more focus to the UNHCR in dealing with the Boat People. The UNHCR, like other U.N. agencies, is not without bureaucratic lethargy.

The Project did not rescue any Boat People from the deep sea—its primary purpose. The experience demonstrated that no private organization could successfully undertake such activity, however necessary. Such rescues need the diplomatic and financial resources plus a large navy or merchant marine, which only a large state or an intergovernmental or quasi-governmental organization can command.

Thich Nhat Hanh, the initial director of the Project, was—and is—a well-known Buddhist cleric and a popular author and speaker. His planned action of transporting Boat People to Australia was conceived in a Gandhian context. He felt that the sudden presence of a shipload of Boat People would melt the hearts of the Australian people and government. Gandhi had always emphasized truth and openness, not stealth. However, Thich Nhat Hanh was secretive and not candid with the Australian government, with the UNHCR, or with his WCRP-ACRP colleagues. He soon became detached from the real world of visas and intergovernmental organizations. He was a prophet, but he could not lead his fellow Vietnamese or his brother and sister Laotians to the promised land. More than 500 Southeast Asians were forced to remain Boat People for months because of Thich Nhat Hanh's miscalculations in what was a problematic project at best. In the end, he took no funds, but some of the "helpers" with whom he dealt enriched themselves.

The Project demonstrated that leaders from several world religions can work together effectively on a specific task despite differences in culture and country. They can also raise a modest budget for a necessary task; money was not a major problem, at least for this Project. Above all, these religious leaders were not afraid to reveal the shortcomings of their handiwork.

55 PRINCETON (1979)

THE NEW ABOLITIONISM

At WCRP III, the third world assembly of religious leaders held in Princeton, New Jersey, Homer called for a new moral crusade against nuclear weapons and nuclear power based on the absolutism and moral urgency of the nineteenth century anti-slavery campaign.

In October, I will observe the tenth anniversary of being your Secretary-General. This is a pretentious title; in reality, I am General Secretary. I have actually performed, and have been paid to perform, at least the following tasks in the past ten years—and in strict alphabetical order: academic, accountant, detective, diplomat, editor, expert, fund-raiser, ghost writer, intellectual, journalist, mediator, money lender, publisher, recruiter, speaker, taxi driver, tour guide, travel agent, and typist. All this, and more, for a salary exceeding that of a cabinet minister in India, but less than that of many truck drivers here in the U.S.

In my decade as your Secretary-General, I have been privileged to observe closely the U.N. scene and the continuing, global U.N. agenda. This contains many serious, chronic problems, few capable of easy solution. Yet I am generally an optimist and feel that even the most difficult, intractable problems can be solved by humanity: energy, poverty, racism and apartheid, torture, population. I am not, however, optimistic about stopping the arms race, about preventing major war.

We human beings have been extremely lucky that a nuclear device has not been detonated since Nagasaki by accident or terror-

414

ism, by calculation or miscalculation. Many observers insist that we cannot be lucky much longer. Many predict that there will be a nuclear detonation long before the end of this century. It might be confined, and kill tens—or perhaps hundreds—of thousands of people. On the other hand, a nuclear weapons detonation could spark a nuclear war which could kill tens of millions, hundreds of millions of people. It would be nuclear holocaust.

To prevent nuclear explosions and nuclear war, we must put an end to the arms race—and to many of us this can only spell disarmament, in the first instance nuclear disarmament. Yet the traditional approaches to putting "the atomic genie back into the bottle" all seem to be failing. Disarmament negotiations since 1946, from the presentation of the Baruch proposals to the U.N. Special Session on Disarmament, have yielded almost no tangible results. Indeed, nuclear weapons have proliferated to five and perhaps seven nations, with the stockpiles of the superpowers alone measured in tens of thousands of strategic and tactical weapons. Certainly SALT II, whatever its merits as an exercise in military détente, is not disarmament. Indeed, under SALT II, the U.S. can increase its present strategic nuclear stockpile of 9,994 warheads to 13,054 by 1985.

New approaches are needed if we are to prevent nuclear explosions and nuclear war and begin and complete nuclear disarmament. Above all, organized religion must massively and unequivocally oppose the obscenity which is called the nuclear arms race.

The churches must say "no" to U.S. Poseidon submarines, any one of which carries sufficient nuclear warheads to obliterate every Soviet city with a population of 150,000 or more—a third of the Soviet Union.

The mosques must say "no" to nuclear war which would demolish every city in the Northern Hemisphere with the equivalent of 1,000 Hiroshima bombs and the bulk of the inhabitants would be killed instantly, with millions in the Southern Hemisphere also dying from radioactive fallout.

The synagogues and temples must say "no" to Henry Kissinger who recently observed that "nothing in the [SALT II] treaty diminishes the need for a substantial build-up by the U.S. In fact, the situation which SALT reflects makes such a build-up imperative." This is the kind of logic which made one of Kissinger's contemporaries in the Vietnam War suggest that a village had to be destroyed to be saved!

The pagodas must say "no" to counter city strategy, as when the U.S. Secretary of Defense admitted that "cities cannot be excluded from such a list [or targets] not only because cities, population, and industry are closely linked, but also because it is essential at all times to retain the option to attack urban industrial targets."

The New Abolitionism

I ask WCRP today, here at Princeton and beyond, to launch a great new movement: to begin to build a worldwide moral and religious crusade which will say "no" to nuclear war and "no" to the nuclear arms race as the Old Abolitionism launched a crusade to say "no" to slavery. This New Abolitionism against this new form of slavery can be a religious crusade; it can be a winning crusade. In any case, it is a necessary crusade.

The New Abolitionism is based on this single proposition: the development, production, stockpiling, threat to use, and use of nuclear weapons by any nation or any group of individuals or nations is a crime against humanity.

This is not a fuzzy moralism meaning all things to all people—and nations. This proposition means that all nuclear weapons are immoral. This means that for any nation to continue or to begin to stock strategic and tactical nuclear weapons is criminal. This means that nuclear deterrence—Mutual Assured Destruction or MAD—must be completely abandoned. This means that the U.S. bombing of Hiroshima and Nagasaki was wrong.

The New Abolitionism rests on this corollary: the development, production, stockpiling, threat to use, and use of nuclear weapons must be abolished.

This is also not a fuzzy moralism meaning different things to different people—and nations. This corollary means that all nuclear weapons laboratories must be abandoned. This means that all nuclear weapons assembly plants must be closed. This means that all nuclear weapons—the stockpile of 50,000 or more in five nations—must be dismantled. This means that the use of nuclear weapons must never be threatened again.

A Seven-Point Program

The New Abolitionism must proceed along two tracks. One is moral, absolutist. Its advocates must oppose every aspect of the nuclear regime, from research to threat of use, from stockpiling to dependence upon nuclear deterrence. This is the religious dimension to the crusade which has many implications, including direct action.

The second track is diplomatic, pragmatic. Its advocates must suggest what the world community, the disarmament community, might do in the next few years to bring the world from here to there—from massive nuclear stockpiles to zero nuclear weapons.

Let me discuss this second track briefly, or else the statesmen might dismiss us as ignorant religionists, once again talking about which we know little or nothing. Let me discuss the next steps of the New Abolitionism. I will suggest very succinctly seven actions for the world community.

First, the U.S. could supervise the drafting and signing of a U.N. convention against the use of nuclear weapons, declaring that such use is a crime against humanity.

Second, many nations and people have been waiting since 1963 for the completion of a comprehensive test-ban agreement, preventing further nuclear weapons tests in all environments and supplementing the existing partial test-ban agreement now ratified by more than 100 countries (but not by China or France). Until this new treaty is finished, signed, ratified, and enters into force—which unfortunately may be another year at least—individual nuclear weapon States could unilaterally cease all tests in all environments.

Third, States members of the Nuclear-Free Zone in Latin America (the Treaty of Tlatelolco) under Additional Protocol II of this Treaty have been promised by all five nuclear-weapons States that the latter will not use or threaten to use nuclear weapons against them. Since it appears unlikely that additional nuclear-free zones will be established in other parts of the world in the near future, other means must be found to commit the nuclear-weapon States to pursue efforts—in the words of the U.N. Special Session—"to conclude as appropriate effective arrangements to assure non-nuclear weapon States against the use or threat of use of nuclear weapons."

Fourth, States members of the NATO or Warsaw Pacts could decide at what point membership in the military alliance is no longer worth the price of being targeted by nuclear weapons. They could abrogate their membership in the pact and sign bilateral non-use agreements with the nuclear weapons States.

Fifth, the nuclear weapon States, together or individually, could participate in what former Canadian Prime Minister Pierre Trudeau at the U.S. Special Session called a "strategy of suffocation." The two aspects especially pertinent here for joint or unilateral action are an agreement to stop the flight testing of all new strate-

417

gic delivery vehicles—which could use nuclear weapons—and to prohibit all production of fissionable materials for weapons purposes.

Sixth, the U.S. and the U.S.S.R. could sign a bilateral agreement, or could each make parallel undertakings, as follows: 1) To reduce its total nuclear megatonnage 10 percent each year, scrapping whatever mix of strategic and tactical weapons it chose, and inviting the International Atomic Energy Agency to authenticate the destruction of its weapons; and 2) To reduce its testing, production, and deployment of nuclear weapons by 20 percent each year, again inviting the International Agency to inspect this commitment.

Seventh and last, in this itemization of practical steps toward the New Abolitionism, each State, nuclear and non-nuclear, could make parallel declarations as follows: 1) To cease construction of new nuclear power plants and those less than one-third complete, with the International Agency inspecting these declarations; 2) To pledge that all existing nuclear power plants would be phased out by the year 2000; and 3) To stop the construction of nuclear fuel reprocessing plants by any State, with nuclear fuel to be furnished regularly to existing power plants by the nuclear weapon States until each nuclear power plant is phased out after being in operation for twenty years. This would mean that the nuclear power industry, world-wide, would be phased out before the year 2000.

Three Principles

The New Abolitionism must be worked out carefully, by religious and scientific leaders, but let me suggest three initial principles.

A cardinal aspect of abolitionism is absolutism. There is a moral rectitude, a certitude of being on the side of truth, of righteousness, yes, of God. The New Abolitionism, like the old, does not countenance the compromises of liberalism. It is black or white, not in between. Abolitionism is not polite. It is not remedial, not palliative, not partial, not provisional. It is fierce, determined, all the way, in a hurry. Abolitionism is radical—getting at the roots of nuclear war. Leo Tolstoy, the great Russian, described the principle well: "When we utter the truth, we utter it all, without compromise, concession, or modification."

A second principle of abolitionism is that it opposes both the sin and the sinner. It goes beyond the admonition of Mohandas Gandhi to hate the sin but not the sinner. The New Abolitionists mean to convert or, in the end, condemn all who cooperate with the nuclear system, from the pure scientist to the computerized field soldier with tactical nuclear weapons. Abolitionism means to convert the accomplice or, barring that, to harass him or her. As the old Abolitionists hated the slave owner and rescued the slave, today the New Abolitionist hates the Henry Kissingers and the Edward Tellers of all societies and rescues those jailed for civil disobedience against nuclear institutions. Leo Tolstoy called the military profession "as shameful a business as an executioner's and even more so." Are we of the New Abolitionism ready to name names and cease being civil?"

A third and final principle I will discuss here—and many others must be sought—is one which insists that the means pre-exist in the ends: one does not use bad means for good ends. This is a principle enshrined in many world religions. Some of the Old Abolitionists were not above justifying the use of bad means (violence) to attain the good end—the abolition of slavery. However, we who live in the century of Mohandas Gandhi and Martin Luther King must be more sensitive to means. We believe in both the principle and the pragmatism of nonviolence. Nonviolent resistance—*ahimsa* of the Jains—is right, but it also works. Thus we condemn those who would use deterrence to prevent nuclear war, including those who would have our nation make a first strike with nuclear weapons to prevent an adversary from supposedly first using nuclear weapons—first or second or anytime. Is this too self-denying a moral principle for a nation to accept? Nations make all kinds of sacrifice, why not one of principle—of high religious principle? To use right means for an entire nation's military policy may be difficult, but it is not impossible. Nothing is impossible for the New Abolitionism, for human survival.

Genius to Capture this Genie

We religious people in WCRP are seeking a significant project for education and action on a worldwide basis. We of the 1980s need an urgent project with human dimensions, something like our WCRP/ACRP Boat People Project of the 1970s. In a sense the New Abolitionism is a nuclear people project—to rescue humanity from drowning in its own nuclear folly.

The New Abolitionism will require the best brains, the most adroit strategy, the largest fund-raising, the greatest sacrifices, and—above all—the deepest prayers and meditation. We might not succeed, but we must surely try. Nothing is more important for peace and justice today than to put the atomic genie back into the bottle. Perhaps world religionists do have the genius to capture this genie.

Let me close with the words again of Leo Tolstoy. In 1909—70 years ago—he told the Swedish Peace Congress: "We have met here to fight against war . . . Private people gathered from the various ends of the earth, possessed of no special privileges and above all having no power over anyone . . . We have only one thing, but that is the most powerful thing in the world—Truth."

We of the Third Assembly of WCRP have met here to fight against war, gathered from the various ends of the earth, possessed of no special privileges and above all having no power over anyone. We, too, have only one thing, but that is the most powerful thing in the world—truth. And the truth today is that we must abolish nuclear weapons and nuclear war.

56 BEIJING
(1980)

THE REEMERGENCE OF BUDDHISM IN CHINA

While neither Homer's speech at WCRP III in Princeton nor keynoter Rev. Jesse Jackson's speech made worldwide headlines, the arrival of a delegation from China did. For the first time since the founding of the People's Republic, Buddhist and Christian leaders met with their counterparts in the West—a further stage in the resumption of normal relations between China and the U.S. following President Nixon's visit in 1972. Following their successful participation in the conference, the Chinese invited Homer and his family to visit China, especially to observe the revival of religion after the death of Mao and the end of the Cultural Revolution. On a nearly three-week tour of Beijing, Nanjing, Hangzhou, Suzhou, and Shanghai, Homer—accompanied by his wife, Ingeborg, his son, Alex, and stepdaughter, Renate—met with the leaders of Buddhism, Catholicism, Islam, Protestantism, and Taoism. The following article, focusing on the reemergence of Buddhism, appeared in Dharma World, *a Buddhist journal published in Japan.*

Although Buddhism is one of the three religions—together with Islam and Christianity—imported into China, it remains the largest. The indigenous religions of China—ancestor worship, Confucianism, and Taoism—are also still practiced, but Buddhism in many ways overshadows them. Indeed, Confucianism, with its ups and downs in Chinese history, is now in an ascendancy phase, but is considered more of a philosophy than an organized religion.

421

Christianity, also reemerging, is considered in China today as two religions: Protestantism and Catholicism.

Thus of the five recognized religions in China today, Buddhism is the largest. Nobody knows how large, but the figure of a hundred million adherents is still widely used.

There were golden years—centuries—of Chinese Buddhism, but it was in decline long before the advent of Chairman Mao Zedong. In the 1928-33 period, the nationalist government severely limited Buddhism, although there was a revival in the early 1940s.

Buddhism Under the Gang of Four

While the road to religious freedom for Buddhism and other religions was uneven after Liberation, the worst period was between mid-1966 and 1976. The Cultural Revolution and the Gang of Four played havoc with all Chinese religions, led by the students in the Red Guards.

Clergy were dismissed and often persecuted. In the Jade Temple in Shanghai, only one monk was allowed to remain. In some cities, Buddhist monks were forced to parade through the streets wearing the garb of Christian ministers. Monks were secularized. Monks were ordered to "abandon superstition," shred their robes, eat meat, and marry.

The Buddhism Association of China, established at Beijing in 1953, was closed. The periodical, *Modern Buddhism*, was closed even before the Cultural Revolution began. Many temples were closed. The Kuang-shi Ssu in Beijing was closed and occupied by soldiers. The Tien-chu monasteries of Hangzhou were closed and locked in July 1966.

Religious images were removed or defaced. At the Dragon Hill Pagoda in Hangzhou, the rock carvings were defaced. At the Kwag-si in Hunan, the Buddha images were destroyed and replaced by statues of Chairman Mao. At the Ling Yin Temple in Hangzhou, Red Guards pasted revolutionary posters over the Buddha images. Temples were converted to other uses. The Fa-Tsang Ssu in Shanghai was converted into an apartment house. The Temple of the Six Banyans in Beijing became a warehouse and a refuse dump.

It must be recorded, however, that certain religious institutions were protected. The People's Liberation Army expelled the Red Guards from the Ching-an Ssu in Shanghai and locked up the temple for protection. Most Buddhist monks were not publicly molested. No important Buddha image was apparently broken.

The wreckage—physical and psychological—was aptly described in a poem written by Zhao Puchu, chairman of the Buddhist Association of China, in 1977 after travelling to the Trigram Mountains in Shanxi Province and visiting the Xuan-zhong Monastery:

The empty halls and carved images are wonderfully excellent
Yet in recent years they have suffered cruelly at the hands of
    the vicious four
The Party Secretary has been virtuous in the affairs of Jiao-
    cheng
The vicious four have been harmful in more than this. . . .

Emergence

With the arrest of the Gang of Four in 1976, religious leaders spent as much as two years trying to understand the emerging situation. They finally decided that the religious freedom was genuine. Slowly the various leaders decided to bring back their various institutions.

The Buddhist Association of China resumed its operation in its old quarters, the seventh century Fa-yuan Temple, not far from the Forbidden City in Beijing. The temple and the Association offices have been restored. The adjoining Buddhist Study Center and museum are now functioning.

Zhao Puchu continues as chairman of the Buddhist Association of China. He is undoubtedly the most important lay Buddhist in China today as well as a well-known civil leader, poet, and calligrapher. (His poems in an elegant hand are inscribed on small hand fans given to passengers on Chinese airlines).

He feels that he has three tasks for the future: to help in the restoration of destroyed Buddhist temples; to restore and preserve old Buddhist texts and artifacts; and to compile a glossary of Buddhist terms commonly used in China.

Buddhist temples have reopened, or are reopening, in various parts of China. Tai Ching Tae Buddhist Monastery in Shansi Province: Once forty monks and two thousand others were associated with this temple. Now it has reopened after being closed and damaged, with four monks and twenty other persons.

Fa-Jing (Da-Ming) Temple in Yangzhou: In 1980, the Japanese Government approved the temporary loan, to this temple, of a lacquer statue of the Chinese monk, Abbot Jian Zhen, who visited Japan in A.D. 754 and died there in 763. When the statue was exhibited in May 1980, more than two hundred thousand Chinese visited the temple which has become a place of pilgrimage for Japanese visitors.

Cold Mountain Temple in Suzhou: No longer receiving income from land holdings, the temple derives income from contributions of believers and the sale of rubbings. Ten monks reside in the temple, with large numbers of believers coming on special days.

Jade Temple in Shanghai: The temple was fully reopened in 1976 and today there are thirty monks in residence.

Nanputo Temple, Drum Mountain, in Fijian Province: This several thousand year old temple and monastery was reopened in 1979 after being closed and damaged for eight years. It was repaired by the state at great cost and now fifty monks are in residence.

Ling Yin Temple: The history of one temple is illustrative of Buddhism in China today. This is one of the largest and best known Buddhist temples, located in Hangzhou. First built in A.D. 326, it was burned or destroyed, and rebuilt, fourteen times. The rear temple houses a sixty-foot-high carved Buddha. After Liberation, the temple was found to be in need of repair and the government helped in its restoration during 1952-57.

After 1966, the temple was attacked by the Red Guards. Some nearby college students wanted to preserve the temple for historical reasons but middle school students wanted it destroyed because of its religious significance. The impasse was referred to the municipality which took the problem to the State Council. A telephone call from Premier Zhou Enlai to the Religious Affairs Bureau helped preserve the temple. The municipality built a protective wall at its entrance. Still, there was some damage and one of the carvings of the Laughing Buddha was painted black by the Red Guards.

After the downfall of the Gang of Four, Premier Zhou Enlai ordered that repairs to the temple begin. Only the government could contribute the funds necessary to repair such a large temple.

As with other Buddhist temples in China, this does not have a regular "membership," but believers flock to it on auspicious occasions, such as the birthday of the Buddha each spring. In 1980, more than one hundred and twenty thousand persons came on that day.

More than forty monks are now attached to the temple. (There were one hundred and fifty in 1949.) The temple maintains a vegetarian restaurant and may soon build a hotel. The abbot is chairman of the Provincial Association of Buddhists and was a delegate to the Provincial People's Congress. He meets and cooperates with other religious leaders of Hangzhou—Catholic, Protestant, Muslim, Taoist.

The Future

Buddhism is not reemerging in China as rapidly as some other religions, especially Protestantism. It is not believed that the Buddhist Association of China has yet held a national conference (as have the Catholics, Protestants, Muslims, and Taoists).

The problems all Chinese religions face in the future are formidable, despite the current religious freedom. The Chinese Catholics have not yet come to terms with the Vatican. The Chinese Government has not yet come to terms with the Dalai Lama, although relations may be less strained than they were previously.

All Chinese religions do not know how to handle religious education of minors in an avowedly Marxist society.

As for the future of Buddhism in China, Zhao Puchu made this observation: "For Buddhism to survive in any situation, it must continuously change and adapt. This is fine, for change is the essence of what Buddhism is. The future of Buddhism in China lies with the laypeople and with the penetration of Buddhist ideas into society. There are young people today who are practicing Buddhists, even some who are willing to leave home and become monks and nuns. This is a very recent development, and their numbers are not great."

57 NEW YORK
(1981)

THE U.N. DECLARATION ON
RELIGIOUS DISCRIMINATION

During his years with WCRP, the cause of religious freedom remained high on Homer's agenda. At the United Nations, he worked to get the world body to adopt a declaration against religious intolerance. When that was finally achieved, he lobbied to follow that up with an international legal convention guaranteeing religious liberty as a universal human right. Homer delivered this address, reviewing the campaign against religious discrimination, at the Biennial Assembly of the American Ethical Union on June 21, 1991, at the C. W. Post Campus of Long Island University.

There is plenty of evidence that organized religion, through history, but even in the twentieth century, has been the cause of all kinds of tragedy—and death. The history of religion is the history of one religion fighting another religion. In our century we have seen the massacre of the Christian Armenians by the Muslim Turks in 1915-17. The tragedy was not that simple, for culture and nationality were also involved. Then it was the massacre of the Jews, and others, in Europe by the Nazis, the latter being largely Christians. The world gave a special name to this outrage—the holocaust. Then during the independence and partition of the Indian subcontinent, in 1947-48 there were more mass killings: Hindus versus Muslims, and also Sikhs. On every continent we have had religious bigotry and religious discrimination. In 1951 a new treaty entered into force and a new crime in world law and language—genocide. This meant "intent to destroy, in whole or in part, a national, ethnical, racial or religious group."

Religious discrimination continues: Christians versus Muslims in the Southern Philippines; Christians, Jews, and Muslims in the Middle East; Christians and Muslims versus other Christians and Muslims in Lebanon; Christians (Armenians) versus Muslims (Azerbaijanis) in the Soviet Union; and Protestants versus Roman Catholics in Northern Ireland.

The U.N. Charter, when it was adopted in 1945, did not contain a bill of rights—a section on human rights. Mrs. Eleanor Roosevelt induced the U.N. General Assembly in 1948 to adopt the Universal Declaration of Human Rights. This historic document in Article 18 declared: "Everyone has the right to freedom of thought, conscience and religion; this right includes freedom to change his [or her] religion or belief, and freedom, either alone or in community with others and in public or private, to manifest his [or her] religion or belief in teaching, practice, worship and observance."

The world community realized that, as important as that Declaration was, further world law had to be adopted. Thus almost each article of the Universal Declaration was spelled out in a separate U.N. Declaration, followed by a separate U.N. convention (or treaty).

A Declaration Against Religious Intolerance

In the early 1950s, the U.N. Commission on Human Rights—and its Sub-Commission on Prevention of Discrimination and Protection of Minorities—became concerned about religious discrimination and authorized a study of discrimination in religious rights and practices. A historic study was made by Arcot Krishnaswami of India. His report included one sentence of some interest to this Ethical Union: "There is also an increasing recognition of the rights of those who do not hold a theistic belief, like agnostics and atheists, in countries where the majority of the population adhere to one or more religion." His report was published at the time when there were manifestations of anti-Semitism, including swastica-painting, occurring widely in Europe and elsewhere in 1959-60. Krishnaswami's report stated basic rules were necessary to assist governments in eradicating discriminatory measures and the debate to adopt such rules would be useful since those who "practice or condone discrimination will be placed on the defensive."

Because of this public anti-Semitism in Europe, the U.N. Economic and Social Council (ECOSOC) and the 1960 U.N. General Assembly asked the Sub-Commission to deal with this topic. Delegates hoped that perhaps a single legal instrument might deal with the elimination of both racial and religious intolerance. ("Intolerance" is not an ideal word, but it was used early in the debates and, once used, such key words stick and can't easily be dropped for better language.) Soon, however, it became evident that there was much more immediate support in the U.N. system for dealing with racial discrimination than with religious discrimination. A U.N. Declaration on the Elimination of All Forms of Racial Discrimination was completed and adopted in 1963. This was advisory to member states, and so a convention or treaty was immediately drafted. The U.N. International Convention on the Elimination of All Forms of Racial Discrimination was adopted in 1965. It entered into force in 1969 and today the convention against racism has been ratified by 130 countries—but not yet by the U.S.A.

It was not until 1963 that the Commission on Human Rights asked its Sub-Commission to prepare a draft declaration on religious intolerance. Already almost a decade had passed, with the U.N. only intermittently seized with this issue. Then began a series of desultory actions and drafting that showed the U.N. system at its fumbling worst. In the meantime the U.N. completed drafting the International Covenant on Civil and Political Rights. This put in treaty form the material in the Universal Declaration of Human Rights. Thus Article 18 of the International Covenant contained four sections on religious freedom. This Covenant entered into force in 1976. However, once again, the Covenant has still not been ratified by the U.S.A.

But back to the drafting process for the declaration against religious intolerance. The snail-like pace was getting nowhere. Some governments began to ask if the result would be worth the effort. Then in 1972 a group of representatives from nongovernmental organizations (NGOs) met and decided to give some leadership to this lagging effort. Four organizations—out of several hundred NGOs—were involved and they should be remembered: Caritas International (a Catholic group), Agudas Israel World Organization, the International League for the Rights of Man (later renamed the International League for Human Rights), and the World Conference on Religion and Peace.

Four causes for this chronic lack of progress were found. One was the negative stance of the Soviet Union and the various Eastern

European states members, at various times, of the Commission and its Sub-Commission. They took turns sabotaging the effort. A second cause of failure was that most African, Asian, and Latin American states showed no interest in the issue. They had different priorities, especially the elimination of apartheid. Third was the opposition on several substantive issues by some Islamic countries. Fourth was the failure of some Western states to show sustained interest in the issue.

Of the many substantive differences, four can be mentioned. First was the political decision to spell out "religious rights" in detail—what detail? Attempts to go beyond the minimum were tempting, but the list could be pushed too far. Finally, certain rights were included, such as teaching and days of rest, while other rights were omitted—such as holding public office, and marriage and funeral rights.

A second polemic issue was the so-called "domestic jurisdiction clause." Was the effort worthless if an article had to allow limitations due to "the protection of public safety, order, health, or morals"? A third touchy issue was "foreign interference in the internal affairs" of states. Some countries did not know how to handle their ambivalence toward organized religion, denouncing it for supporting colonialism in the past, yet praising it for opposing apartheid in the present. A final polemic point, among many others, was "religion or belief." Eastern European states insisted that, if religion should be protected from discrimination, so should atheism. Other states felt that the traditional field of religion was a large enough domain for one U.N. instrument. A compromise was reached whereby atheism would not be mentioned in the title, only "religion or belief."

Progress remained slow and by 1975 the Commission adopted only a total of 238 words toward a declaration. In 1976 an additional fifty-eight words were added! Soon some Muslim states joined the Working Group. Some had real reservations about any declaration, but one state—Senegal—in 1980 produced a Chairman-Rapporteur, Justice Abdoulaya Dieye. By 1981 the Working Group under Justice Dieye held sixteen meetings and completed its task. He was determined to complete the drafting process and, as a Muslim, he had some leverage with some of the more intransigent members of the Group. The Commission on Human Rights approved the draft, by a vote of 33 to none, with five abstentions—the U.S.S.R, Bulgaria, Byelorussian S.S.R., Mongolia, and Poland. There was much more politicking, but finally the 1981 General Assembly adopted the draft on

November 25 by consensus—unanimously. The full title was *The Declaration on the Elimination of Intolerance and of Discrimination Based on Religion or Belief.*

This Declaration Proclaims

The Declaration contains ten preambular paragraphs and eight articles. Just two small sections are given below:

> In accordance with article 1 of the present Declaration, and subject to the provisions of article 1, paragraph 3, the right to freedom of thought, conscience, religion or belief shall include, *inter alia*, the following freedoms: To worship or assemble in connection with a religion or belief, and to establish and maintain places for these purposes; to establish and maintain appropriate charitable or humanitarian institutions; to make, acquire, or use to an adequate extent the necessary articles and materials related to the rites or customs of a religion or belief; to write, issue, and disseminate relevant publications in these areas; to teach a religion or belief in places suitable for these purposes; to solicit and receive voluntary financial and other contributions from individuals and institutions; to train, appoint, elect, or designate by succession appropriate leaders called for by the requirements and standards of any religion or belief; to observe days of rest and to celebrate holidays and ceremonies in accordance with the precepts of one's religion or belief; to establish and maintain communications with individuals and communities in matters of religion and belief at the national and international levels.
>
> For the purposes of the present Declaration, the expression "intolerance and discrimination based on religion or belief" means any distinction, exclusion, restriction or preference based on religion or belief and having as its purpose or as its effect nullification or impairment of the recognition, enjoyment, or exercise of human rights and fundamental freedoms on an equal basis.

A Convention?

Once the Declaration was adopted, it was translated into many languages. This newest U.N. instrument against religious discrimination was increasingly used by religious and secular bodies in many parts of the world. In 1984 the U.N. Sub-Commission appointed a Special Rapporteur to study "current dimensions" of the problem. In 1986 the Commission appointed a Special Rapporteur to examine "incidents and governmental actions" inconsistent with the Declaration. Also an international secular organization was established further to implement the Declaration. Project Tandem held worldwide conferences in the U.S.A., Poland, and India.

The normal sequence for human rights instruments in the U.N. system has been to follow the adoption of a declaration rapidly with the elaboration of a convention or treaty on the same subject in order to make implementation mandatory and give the subject the force of international law. With an interval of a decade and no attempt to begin to draft a convention, a few NGOs in New York asked, why not? What is holding back this normal practice of a declaration being followed by a convention? Early in 1990 a group of NGOs met, raised $12,000, and hired a staff director to make a study on "The Question of a U.N. Convention on Religious Intolerance." Dr. John P. Salzberg, a human rights expert in the Carter Administration, made the study which was released in November 1990.

The Salzberg report suggests strategy toward a U.N. convention against religious intolerance, for religious freedom. Salzberg concludes that while the drafting and adoption of a convention "remains a long-term objective," it is "not wise to press immediately" to do so. This was disappointing news to me personally, but it is an objective assessment of political reality. But Salzberg makes a second conclusion: interested NGOs can begin to undertake preparations now for the drafting of a convention.

And that is just what has been happening recently at U.N. Headquarters. A small group of us have formed what is tentatively called the Ad Hoc Group Against Religious Intolerance and Discrimination. Our purpose is to help the U.N. draft a U.N. convention against religious intolerance. Our immediate program is to help make that goal more politically possible. We are putting together an executive committee, a two-year budget, and have hired Dr. Salzberg at least on a part-time basis to help us undertake the discussions with religious groups worldwide, with NGOs, and with governments, especially at U.N. Headquarters and in Geneva—where most of the human rights bodies convene.

U.N. conventions do not solve everything. Yet every approach may be useful—international and national, legal and educational.

58 NEW YORK
(1982)

INCHING TOWARD DISARMAMENT

Among many fields and interests, disarmament was closest to Homer's heart. Through the years at SANE, WCRP, and as founder of the NGO Committee on Disarmament at the United Nations, he became a recognized authority on the subject. The following excerpt from his book on the history of WCRP introduces the scope of these prolific activities from the early seventies through the U.N. Second Session on Disarmament in 1982. Behind the scenes, Homer also strategized with U.N. delegations, writing speeches for ambassadors and helping to guide the official pace and content of the decades-long disarmament debate.

Disarmament has always been a major concern of WCRP. When some religious leaders in the U.S.A. first explored the possibility of bringing together a worldwide group, it was the lack of public and religious support for disarmament and peace that helped energize their persistence. The American leaders belatedly realized that, whatever the recklessness of Nikita Khrushchev in transporting atomic missiles to Cuba, church and synagogue in the U.S.A. had not done enough to encourage the Kennedy administration to explore—with equal energy—the alternative to atomic war during the 1962 missile crisis.

WCRP has probably given more emphasis to disarmament than to any other substantive issue and at each of its world conferences, plenary addresses, commissions, and final declarations addressed this overriding global issue. There are three reasons for this emphasis. First, disarmament remains the most important political problem of our time, certainly as long as the nuclear threat to humanity continues. Second, I had earlier acquired expertise in disarmament with other organizations and, as the first WCRP Secretary-General, could easily transfer this ability to WCRP. Third, I made the nuclear issue my personal quest and devoted much of my spare time to writing about this problem. Together these factors produced a high level of concern with disarmament, especially in the U.N. context.

Disarmament Reports

In the 1980s the stockpile of nuclear and conventional weapons appeared to be exceeded only by the pile of reports, memoranda, monographs, and books on all aspects of disarmament, peace, and military affairs. Yet in the early 1970s, there were many fewer publications, especially those issued by religious bodies and those reflecting a non-aligned viewpoint.

To meet this need for more non-aligned disarmament materials produced by and for a primarily religious constituency, Herman Will of the Board of Church and Society of the United Methodist Church in the U.S.A., proposed that his board and WCRP/International together publish a series of memoranda written by me as the new Secretary-General of WCRP. Mr. Will obviously made this proposal not only because WCRP had a mandate to work in the disarmament field, but because I was an expert in the disarmament field, especially in the U.N. context.

The first *Disarmament Report* was issued in August 1971—less than one year after WCRP I was held—and the series was published through May 1974. In 1972, the National Committee for a Sane Nuclear Policy joined in co-sponsoring the publication of this series. Some 300 copies of each report were sent, on request, to religious individuals and organizations in many countries.

The topics were often related to U.N. disarmament issues, but not exclusively so. Some early materials on SALT I, China and disarmament, unilateral disarmament, the relationship between disarmament and development, and a world disarmament conference were discussed in these reports. In total, thirty-one reports were issued, some only nine pages, others more than 30 pages, all in English.

WCRP II

The issue of disarmament loomed large at WCRP II held in Leuven, Belgium, in 1974. Although since 1970 SALT I had been achieved and negotiations were continuing on SALT II, the people of the world realized that the nuclear arms race had not been curbed. (Indeed, India made its "peaceful" nuclear explosion on May 18, 1974, a little more than three months before WCRP II.)

The one redeeming aspect of WCRP II in the field of disarmament was the presence at the entire conference, as a consultant-expert, of the Honorable Philip Noel-Baker, who had received the Nobel Peace Prize in 1959 for his work in disarmament. He used the honor of the award to travel the world to speak and consult on disarmament issues. It was natural for him to come to WCRP II. A longtime U.K. parliamentarian, he was perhaps better known as an athlete and supporter of the Olympic Games than for his religious connections (the Society of Friends). Philip Noel-Baker made an important impact on the Leuven conference, as an active participant in the WCRP disarmament commission. He also made an impression at the conference as a wise British statesman with extraordinary disarmament experience, going back to before the 1931-33 disarmament conference of the League of Nations.

The Leuven Declaration asserted that participants "dedicate ourselves to work together for the total abolition of war." Then it inserted a powerful paragraph on disarmament:

> We plead with all people of faith and good will to recognize that there is no future for humanity if worldwide nuclear war is simply postponed or temporarily avoided. The delicate "balance of terror" has given the superpowers, and all other nations with them, nothing more than a reprieve—a little time to concert action to end the nuclear arms race. We urge that the religions of the world mount every possible pressure on the nuclear weapons governments to halt the proliferation of destructive nuclear armaments and to roll back all existing nuclear weaponry until the stockpiles of nuclear devices have been safely dismantled and destroyed. We also ask all religious bodies to press other governments now capable of initiating nuclear-weapons programs to renounce any such undertaking.

The NGO Committee on Disarmament

The Charter of the U.N. provides for a role for representatives of nongovernmental organizations—NGOs. The role is explicitly confined to the Economic and Social Council (ECOSOC). This council discusses many substantive issues of concern to NGOs, such as human rights and economic issues, but it does not discuss disarmament. Thus NGOs have not had a defined role with most U.N. disarmament organs, as they have had, for example, with the U.N. Commission on Human Rights. NGOs have seldom been aided in their quest for legitimacy by members of the U.N. Secretariat, who tend to be bureaucratically timid and, above all, do not wish to upset any of the major member states. The biggest power in this period was the U.S.A. which did not welcome NGO intervention in the field of disarmament. Consequently, NGOs specializing in disarmament have had a long struggle—which still continues—to go beyond putting a foot in the door both at U.N. headquarters and in Geneva (where disarmament negotiations increasingly gravitated).

To focus and magnify the impact of the small number of international NGOs on disarmament discussions and negotiations in Geneva, the Special NGO Committee on Disarmament was established there in 1969. Duncan Wood, head of the Quaker U.N. Office in Geneva, was one of its longtime leaders; another was Sean MacBride of the International Peace Bureau. As WCRP's Secretary-General, I dealt with this Geneva committee and soon realized the need to bring together a similar group at U.N. headquarters in New York. In June 1973 I convened the first meeting of what became the NGO Committee on Disarmament. This was at a time when the General Assembly and other U.N. organs were still attempting to find an acceptable new disarmament forum so that both France and China might participate. I was chair of the NGO Committee in New York from its inception until I retired and moved away from New York in early 1984.

NGOs often use the words of U.S. President Dwight D. Eisenhower in a BBC interview with British Prime Minister Harold Macmillan on August 31, 1959: "I like to believe that people in the long run are going to do more to promote peace than are governments. Indeed, I think that people want peace so much that one of these days governments had better get out of their way and let them have it."

The First Special Session

In 1957 the U.N. began to explore holding a special session on disarmament or a general disarmament conference. It took until May 1978 to convene the Special U.N. Session on Disarmament (SSOD I hereafter). During these two decades, the purpose of the event changed somewhat, but always it was to involve all member nations, move public opinion (and thus NGOs), and especially those major powers whose absence from the disarmament discussions and negotiations severely limited their universality and relevance.

When WCRP began working in the U.N. community in 1971, there was support for convening a world disarmament conference, and WCRP became active in encouraging this effort. A WCRP Disarmament Report was published in 1972, entitled, *A World Disarmament Conference?* China and the U.S.A. opposed convening such a congress, and over time it became a forlorn effort of the Soviet Union. Another approach seemed necessary; the impetus came from the enlarging Non-aligned Movement at the U.N. At its first summit in 1961, the Non-aligned Movement called for a special session on disarmament or its equivalent. By 1975 the Non-aligned Movement felt that a special session would be the best vehicle to involve a reluctant China and a petulant U.S.A.

Some NGOs, including WCRP, pressed hard for a world disarmament forum, and in December 1976 the U.N. General Assembly adopted a resolution convening a Special Session on Disarmament in 1978.

One of the innovations was to allow selected NGOs an opportunity to address the Special Session, or more precisely, its ad hoc committee. This was to be called "NGO Day." This was held on June 12, 1978, and twenty-five speakers were allowed to address the session. The NGO committees in New York and Geneva and the U.N. Secretariat selected the organizations and research institutions, and WCRP was one. The latter invited the Reverend Nikkyo Niwano, the honorary chairman of WCRP and president of Rissho Kosei-kai, to deliver the address.

President Niwano began by suggesting that "risks must be taken by statesmen for peace as they are obviously taking risks today with arms." He prayed that "some state, out of strength and not weakness, will take a major risk for peace and disarmament." He asked that a "new appraisal be made of national and world security." He underlined the goal of general and complete disarmament.

He also thanked the Special Session "for allowing NGOs to speak and participate so fully," expressing the hope that this relationship of NGOs to U.N. disarmament issues "might be institutionalized."

Some months before the opening of SSOD I, NGOs in New York decided to publish an occasional newspaper to explain disarmament affairs at the U.N. to several publics, including the U.N. community itself. A total of $40,000 was raised for this purpose. Some thirty-one issues of *Disarmament Times* were published before, during, and after SSOD I, with 5,000 copies of each issue printed. WCRP was one of the founders of *Disarmament Times*, and I was a member of its editorial staff and a frequent writer. Today, *Disarmament Times* is still published, and I remain a member of its editorial advisory board and also a frequent contributor.

NGOs, both independently and under the NGO Committee on Disarmament, sponsored many other types of activities during SSOD I. Seminars were held in advance for diplomats and others. A disarmament information bureau was opened, and a coffeehouse was established. Vigils and demonstrations were encouraged. WCRP, with its Secretary-General as chair of the NGO Committee on Disarmament, was heavily involved throughout SSOD I.

Mission to Beijing

When the WCRP governing board met at New Delhi in November 1981 a resolution was adopted to support the Second U.N. Special Session on Disarmament (SSOD II) in 1982. It also resolved to send multireligious missions to world capitals on the nuclear disarmament issue. On December 1, 1981, I issued a "context statement" for these missions. It indicated that "the possibility of nuclear detonation has been felt by humanity in the last few months more than at any time since the late 1950s and early 1960s." The statement asked, "How can one small multireligious organization add its modest influence to the effort to prevent nuclear war?" The purpose of the multireligious missions would be "to show the heads of state or government of the five nuclear weapons states that world religious leaders want a stop to the drift toward nuclear war." A second purpose would be to "demonstrate that religious groups care deeply about the success of SSOD II." On December 15 explorations with all five capitals began, but by the spring of 1982 it became clear that only China was ready to receive such a multireligious mission.

Thus a ten-person mission, including top WCRP officers, visited Beijing on May 7-11, 1982. They came from five world religions and six countries: India, Japan, Pakistan, Singapore, the U.K., and the U.S.A. The Beijing hosts were the five recognized religions of China, headed by Zhao Puchu, leader of the Buddhist Association of China.

The mission was received by Ji Pengfei, member of the State Council, and by Ambassador Kang Mao Zhao, then ambassador to the European Economic Community and the leader of the Chinese delegation to SSOD II. WCRP President Angelo Fernandes and WCRP Vice-president Nikkyo Niwano made four requests of the Chinese leaders in relation to SSOD II: 1) that SSOD II set in motion the drafting of a convention making the use of nuclear weapons a crime against humanity; 2) that SSOD II ask the superpowers to announce an immediate freeze of their current nuclear stockpiles; 3) that SSOD II launch a world disarmament campaign; and 4) that SSOD II ask all states to transfer immediately a portion of their armaments budgets to development projects.

Ambassador Kang's reaction to the WCRP mission was to express excitement in finding "such common language with NGOs and religionists in recognizing the serious nature of nuclear war and the nuclear threat." Also, while in Beijing, members of the mission met many leaders of the religions of China, who meditated for the success of SSOD II and of the mission.

Second Special Session

In New York, the preparatory committee for SSOD II agreed to hear oral statements by NGOs on arrangements for the Second Special Session. Representatives of eight NGOs and three research institutions spoke, including myself for WCRP. I urged that SSOD II "set the date for the elimination of all nuclear weapons by 1990, and general and complete disarmament by 2000," calling this timetable "not visionary; indeed it may be too slow for human survival."

During meetings of the preparatory committee, WCRP also proposed that new groups be invited by the U.N. to participate in SSOD II, "including religious leaders, parliamentarians, and Nobel laureates." An unimaginative U.N. Legal Office reported to the preparatory committee that there was no precedent for such an innovation, and no special action was taken on this proposal, except to include the phrase that the committee expected "a greater spectrum" of NGOs.

At the Second Session itself, a total of seventy-seven NGOs and peace and disarmament research organizations delivered short speeches on "NGO Days," June 24 and 25. I spoke for WCRP, urging the adoption of a "short list" of immediate disarmament measures. These included a comprehensive test-ban treaty, a treaty against any and all use of nuclear weapons, and a verifiable freeze. I called the numerous "marches, demonstrations, and petitions . . . desperate manifestations of deep public concern." More than 10 percent of those who gave oral interventions were part of the WCRP family.

The NGO Committee on Disarmament, through its liaison group, continued to coordinate a wide range of informal NGO activities. More than 3,000 NGOs registered. Some had their visas delayed and eventually denied. As chairman of the New York-based committee, I filed a lawsuit in the U.S. Federal Court against U.S. Secretary of State Alexander Haig. Both the suit and a subsequent appeal eventually lost, but the U.N. community knew that many Americans felt that Washington's denial of visas to NGOs was a violation of the Headquarters agreement between the host government and the U.N.

Disarmament Times continued to be published, with twenty issues coming out during SSOD II. A disarmament information bureau was established at the UNITAR building opposite U.N. headquarters on street level. A "plowshares coffeehouse" operated in the Church Center, and an NGO media center was established.

On June 12 the largest demonstration in North American history (to that time) took place, with three-quarters of a million people gathering at U.N. headquarters and walking to Central Park in support of disarmament and peace. WCRP was a member of the planning committee and participated. Civil disobedience was undertaken in front of the U.N. missions to the five nuclear weapons states. Some 1,600 persons were arrested, including myself.

SSOD II was an occasion for NGOs to broaden and increase their role in disarmament at the U.N. Whatever progress was made was almost wholly due to united, persistent pressures by the NGOs themselves. Despite some retrospective praise given to the actions of NGOs by member states and members of the U.N. Secretariat, one involved NGO concluded that "the fact is that NGOs have made little impact on the disarmament policies of states as reflected in the U.N., either at the two Special Sessions or in other U.N. bodies."

59 NEW YORK (1982)

WHAT I LEARNED IN NEW YORK

*In one of his most autobiographical sermons, delivered to a Chicago subur-
ban audience, Homer described what he had learned living in New York
and the East Coast for more than twenty years.*

Since living in New York, have my Chicago habits changed?
Let me catalogue quickly some of the superficial changes.

In Chicago, I used to listen to Clifton Utley; now I turn on the
MacNeil-Lehrer Report. In Chicago, I used to watch the *Hit Parade*
every Saturday night. Now I turn on Lawrence Welk every Sunday
night. (At least I do not yet read regularly *Readers Digest!*) In Chicago, I used to watch on TV three or four games of the World Series.
In New York, I am lucky to watch one. In Chicago I used to drive an
auto; in New York, I have not owned one for twelve years and only
keep up my license for fear of failing a written test again. In Chicago, we lived in a house and enjoyed preparing the yard in spring. In
New York, we've been apartment dwellers, and I scarcely know
when spring arrives.

In Evanston, football was in the autumn air, and I always managed to see one Northwestern game. In New York, I do not even
know the names of the professional football teams in New York. In
Chicago, my hit list included Billy Graham. In twenty-three years,
he or I changed, and he has been replaced by the Rev. Sun Myung
Moon. I could go on in this way, but you now understand that the
distance from Chicago to New York can be measured in years as
much as in miles.

Facing My Own Mortality

In New York I came face to face with my mortality. I never really felt that I could defy the laws of nature, the inevitable chain of birth, life, and death, but often I acted that way. The recognition of my own mortality crept upon me from a variety of factors. Part of it was simply the calendar. The years pass so quickly, despite the increased average life span.

Part of this recognition comes from seeing one's own friends pass on. It seems that every week I write a letter to a survivor after the death of a friend. In New York, I have had the occasion to say farewell to many friends. Two you may remember are socialist Norman Thomas in the 1960s and civil libertarian Roger Baldwin in the past year (after the filming of *Reds*). I was with both a few weeks before their deaths, both in old age, Baldwin over ninety-five. The experience of the death of one's friends makes one measure one's own future.

Part of facing one's own mortality is also one's own health. I had what in retrospect was termed a mild heart attack in October 1980. It came without much warning; indeed, it occurred just three days after an annual checkup when the physician pronounced me fit! This attack took me to New York's famed Bellevue Hospital, the first time I was a patient in a hospital since I went to Evanston Hospital in 1952 when my son, Alex, and I had scarlet fever and I was able to make a sermon out of that experience in the isolation ward! In Bellevue, I came to terms with the termination of my existence and I was determined to begin to do some things differently, to live differently. For example, I made better arrangements for all my personal papers to go to the Peace Collection of Swarthmore College Library where they have been deposited for twenty years.

Another part of the recognition of my own mortality came with the death, in New York, of my ninety-year-old mother in 1976. The death of a parent is difficult for anybody, probably doubly so for an only child. My father died thirty years before. Without siblings, I found in my mother's passing that I was cut off from most of my roots. She lived alone in Miami (after two subsequent marriages, one ending in divorce and one in the death of her husband), and was fiercely independent as long as she could be—until past eighty. Then I had to put her into a nursing home—first in Boston, and then later in New York. I dutifully visited my mother two or three times a week, taking the subway to 96th Street and back. A nursing home in New York is not where older people should end up, or their children to place them, yet there appear few alternatives in urban America. It is sad, and expensive, even when Medicare steps in.

One must not only face one's mortality; one must come to terms with it. The best way is, of course, to have both children and grandchildren. I have been blessed with two children who are surviving in an increasingly difficult world. My daughter, Lucy, also has two children. Here is, obviously, one kind of immortality. Yet I wonder if even my children will have my normal life span, given this nuclear age.

Facing My Own Limitations

In New York, my ambition leveled off and I came to the belated self-knowledge that I alone would not save the world. It is hard, publicly, to admit that I once had such grandiose thoughts. But many people do, only most come to the recognition of their limitations much earlier than others. Most who are called to work even in New York, from Chicago, feel that it is not the final step upward. Yet somewhere along the way, but not until New York, it dawned upon me that I had reached my zenith.

Success for me was never money—bank accounts, CDs, autos, real estate, assets. I was, fortunately, never poor, but I never wanted to be rich either. And I never have been. But success for me was a determination to help save the world, or serve it. Along the way I realized that there is only so much that one person can do. Each individual—however hard he or she works, however much favored by God or by his or her fellow human beings—is but a drone bee in a global beehive. Belatedly, I realized that I was not the queen bee!

New York somehow taught me that I might as well relax. And also that I should broaden my interests and concerns. I began to read more widely—and on a greater array of subjects than ever before—away from war and peace, away from politics. I read for the first time something of Dostoevski, Thomas Mann, Joseph Conrad, and also some English-language novels from India and Japan.

Facing Ethics

In New York, the very center of the fast buck, I learned that there is no such thing in life as the moral short cut. There is no free ride in life. When I was a student at Meadville Theological School in 1941, I was asked to participate in a Free Earl Browder Campaign. I got a free railroad ticket from Chicago to New York to attend a conference and rally. I believed then, and still, in the freedom of that communist leader. Ever since I have been on the FBI computer, even before computers were invented! Almost thirty years later, in 1971, I went on a free ride to Iran, to celebrate an extravaganza of the Shah—whose rule was maintained by state terror and torture. It was not all free, however, since even then the fundamentalist Muslims did not want the Shah to deal with non-Muslim leaders. Fifteen of us were kept from the ceremonies for a week, watching them only on TV in a plush hotel several hundred miles way in Tehran. Later we did have a relaxed conversation with the Shah—for which my wife bitterly condemns me!

In the past few months, a friend who is a high official in our denomination, took a free ride to Seoul, to attend a global conference sponsored by the Unification Church. When I protested, my friend replied: "I consider it a responsibility of the UUA to understand all other religious groups with which we come in contact." This is not a satisfactory rationalization. In 1962 I was given a free ticket to Moscow to attend a peace conference. At that time, I had the wit not to accept the free ride. However, Erich Fromm and I went and we both paid our own way. By refusing free transportation, we perhaps had more freedom and were able to mount the podium inside the Kremlin and speak with an independent voice.

There is a more general principle here. Life is not a free ride. One doesn't get something for nothing. There appear enough exceptions to this rule that most people, not only the young, often feel that they can indeed beat the game. They have seen others take a free ride, without visible negative results. They have seen others make the quick fix. They have seen a few men and women live under an unbelievably lucky star—or so it seems from the outside. Yet these are usually deceptions. One may beat the game once or twice, as a few do at Monte Carlo or Las Vegas, but we know that the exception is not the rule. That rule was posited in the various scriptures of world religions, but also by Ralph Waldo Emerson in his essay on compensation:

> Every excess causes a defect; every defect an excess . . .
> Every secret is told, every crime is punished, every virtue rewarded, every wrong redressed, in silence and certainty . . .
> Cause and effect, means and ends, seed and fruit, cannot be se-

vered . . . the end preexists in the means . . . You cannot do wrong without suffering wrong . . . It is impossible to get anything without its price . . .

Certainly my own life bears out this principle. Quite apart from the free ride, I have never in the end beaten the game: in love, in marriage, in vocation, or in human relations. I would not have been human if I had not tried; indeed, at times I may have gone to great lengths in the attempt. Believe me, there is no easy out. Yet it is a lesson which, in our secular world, cannot be easily transmitted from person to person, from generation to generation. It is one which has to be learned individually, personally, painfully, the hard way.

Human beings can learn a lot, but some things, especially in the area of ethics, human beings seem never to learn—before it it too late.

At sixty-five, almost sixty-six, I do not know if I have five years more—or fifteen. I do know that I am still learning, in New York and outside. I am still thirsting, at times still fuming. I still have illusions, still at times feel disillusioned. But this ambivalence is the human condition, both along the North Shore and the East River.

PART EIGHT 1984-1993

ELDER STATESMAN

THE WINNETKA AND
SWARTHMORE YEARS

"Old age hath yet his honour and his toil;
Death closes all, but everything ere the end,
Some work of noble note, may yet be done . . .
Come my friends,
'Tis not too late to seek a new world . . . "
— Tennyson, Ulysses

At age sixty-seven, Homer left WCRP and New York, but he never retired in the usual sense. For three years, he served as minister of the North Shore Unitarian Fellowship in Winnetka, Illinois, near his old parish in Evanston, and in 1987 he moved to Swarthmore, Pennsylvania, to be near his archives. During this period, coinciding with momentous changes in the Soviet Union and the end of the Cold War—he remained active on peace and disarmament issues, especially the Nuclear Freeze, the Middle East, and the Gulf War, and launched community initiatives on race relations, nonviolence, and interfaith harmony. As Secretary-General Emeritus of WCRP, he continued to represent that organization at arms control proceedings and served on the boards of the Dana Greeley Foundation, the Albert Schweitzer Fellowship, and others. He often commuted to New York and the U.N. for meetings, was arrested for the second time in his life (opposing apartheid at the South African Embassy in Washington), and traveled around the world to receive many honors and prizes. He also found time to teach a course on Nobel Peace Prize Laureates, write four books, one play, and scores of articles, and—in 1992—take his first trip to Latin America, to attend a WCRP meeting preparatory to the World Environmental Conference in Rio.

Photograph: Homer and Ingeborg in Japan, 1984

60

WINNETKA

(1983)

WHAT THE LIBERAL CHURCH COULD BECOME

Over the years, Homer missed the parish ministry. After leaving Evanston, he briefly served as visiting minister for the Evansville, Indiana Unitarian Fellowship, flying from New York on weekends to preach and give pastoral advice. While working for SANE in New York, in Boston as a denominational official, and at the United Nations for WCRP, Homer frequently preached at churches in the area and around the country. After retiring from WCRP, Homer decided to return to the local church while he was still able. For three years, until age seventy, he served as minister of the North Shore Unitarian Universalist Society in Winnetka, Illinois. This is the candidating sermon he delivered to the congregation.

Running for the ministry is not unlike running for the presidency. The ministry pays less, but the stress is probably less, too. Many presidential candidates over the years have contracted foot-in-mouth disease, the James Watts syndrome, and as a result some have had to withdraw or, in any case, have been defeated. The same can happen to ministers. Presidential candidates in recent years have appeared to be more cautious in their speech-making, more circumspect; even Jesse Jackson appears more temperate than usual. Presidential candidates have to please all audiences, different publics. They have to be for public spending and also for lower budgets, or for Israel and also for Palestinian rights. Likewise, ministerial candidates in sermons have to be sensitive to the several publics even in a small liberal congregation.

Presidential candidates often bring along their wives. So do ministerial candidates. Sometimes the wife can make a big difference; how she dresses or what she says or doesn't say. Presidential candidates tend to bound up to the podium—and so do ministerial candidates. Have you ever noticed that the older a candidate is, the faster he will leap to the stage—if he doesn't trip? One misstep, and his candidacy may diminish. Thus candidating for the ministry of any church, or writing or preaching a candidating sermon—is not easy. From the clergyman's standpoint, there is something to be said for that kind of manipulation, like the Methodists or the Episcopalians, where the district superintendent or bishop appoints a minister and stuffs him, or her, down the throat of a hungry (or angry) congregation.

In writing a candidating sermon, one tends to say everything one knows. The sermon this morning may exhibit this tendency. However, I am hedging my bets by promising an open-ended sermon next Sunday. I have brought from New York only the title of next week's sermon, "What I Have Learned from You," and nothing else. If I learn nothing this coming week, you will hear nothing. I have brought no back-up, substitute sermon. But the chances are that I will hear much, and you might hear a 90-minute sermon, like the standard Unitarian sermons in the middle of the last century.

When I was a student at Meadville Theological School, one of my professors—I think it was James Luther Adams—commented that "God has no special concern with the churches." In other words, the church is a human, not a divine, institution. The church can do good or evil, and probably does both. The church is not inherently good or godly just because it calls itself a church or a religious institution. I think this is a good text for the sermon this morning: "God—(he or she or it)—has no special concern with the churches," including the so-called liberal churches.

I want to accomplish two tasks this morning. First I want to think through with you what the liberal church might become. Then I want to discuss what it takes to accomplish this goal. Both can be important topics for the meetings every evening this coming week!

In discussing what the liberal church could become, I have to begin by describing what the liberal church now is. Yet to describe the diversity of Unitarian Universalism today would require at least one whole sermon. How to describe liberal religion not only in the American suburbs—where it is perhaps flourishing best—but our Unitarian churches in such diverse places as Vancouver, Honolulu,

Auckland, Sidney and Melbourne, Tokyo, Madras and Shillong in India, Cape Town, Cluj in Transylvania, Prague, Frankfurt, Paris, London, Montreal, and small towns in New England?

What have all of these churches in common? Not too many elements, yet to most of their members our churches can be alternatively pioneering or traditional, exciting or boring, far-reaching or self-centered, creative or predictable, challenging or comfortable, comforting or frenetic.

Also, how do our existing liberal churches differ today from those of other so-called liberal Protestant denominations, such as the United Church of Christ or even the Methodists? My opinion is that we Unitarian Universalists differ from them less and less in the present than in the past. Yet we do have our Unitarian Universalist traditions: much coffee, wayside pulpits, Beacon Press, Sofia Fahs, *UU World*, the nineteenth century triumvirate of Channing, Parker, and Emerson, and of course our unofficial creed consisting of "the fatherhood of God, the brotherhood of man, and the neighborhood of Boston." We do have a few modern prophets, but in New York City today the visible doers are not Unitarians, but Presbyterian William Sloan Coffin and Episcopalian Bishop Paul Moore. In Boston and even in Chicago today it may be the same. And yet, in small but crucial ways, we Unitarian Universalists may still be out front, significant, relevant to individuals as well as to society.

But enough description, let me become prescriptive. What could the liberal church become? It must at least have leadership which is both prophetic and priestly, a combination of both Martin Luther King and Mother Teresa of Calcutta. It must afflict the comfortable and comfort the afflicted. Often these values are placed against each other, when the liberal church of the future must embody both, and more. The role of the prophetic and the priestly was strikingly delineated by Dr. Henry W. Bellows, minister of All Souls Unitarian Church in New York City during the mid-nineteenth century. He declared: "Prophets address communities; pastors, flocks. Prophets cry aloud and spare not; pastors give milk to babes, and meat to strong men. Prophets obey a divine madness; pastors follow the rule of common sense and sober discretion." Then Bellows added (I almost said, bellowed): "It is only when the pastor's and prophet's duties run together that I can temporarily occupy the prophet's place . . . " At times Bellows was divinely mad, but at other times, he was soberly discreet.

Given the prophetic and priestly functions in all churches, but especially in the liberal church, these qualities obviously cannot be confined to the minister, but must permeate the whole institution. That is why we must go beyond this easy dichotomy and discuss in greater detail the liberal church of the future.

Perhaps a place to begin is the report just circulated by the Purposes and Principles Committee of our Unitarian Universalist Association. All congregations recently received two versions of an amendment to the by-laws of the Association. Also it is printed in the current *UU World*. Congregations must choose between these two versions and mail their choice by February 1. In the first alternative, four purposes of our Association and individual congregations are simply and uncontroversially stated. Here is the single sentence: "Unitarian Universalist congregations, enriched by a variety of religious perspectives, gather for worship and celebration, study and dialogue, companionship, and service and social action." This is more inclusive than the pat dichotomy of the priestly and the prophetic. Let me discuss each of the four purposes briefly.

First, the liberal church must be one of worship and celebration. The liberal church can help its members and friends find time, and space, to think about the eternal and one's personal relation to it. (If the term, "the eternal," is not appropriate, there are other terms, several in use in our own tradition.) The liberal church cannot limit itself to being rational, educational. It must make opportunities for its people, if they desire, to be—yes, emotional, mystical, religious. We must put behind us our old Unitarian reputation of being cold, bloodless.

Worship begins at 11:00 a.m. on Sunday mornings. But worship does not end Sunday noon. The liberal church can also make possible more private and even experimental opportunities for meditation and celebration. The range of commemoration and celebration can be wide in a liberal church, and goes beyond weddings, namings, funerals, and retreats. Each liberal church ought to make possible diverse and excellent formal and informal opportunities for worship and celebration.

A second purpose of the liberal church must be one of study and dialogue. The church must be concerned with ideas; it is a teaching, a learning institution. Eleven o'clock on Sunday morning might not be the most important hour of the American week, but it should be the single most important time in the Unitarian week. Here is where the professional—the minister—can make a difference. Here is where the people can learn from the wisdom and insight of the resident minister. This does not exclude a two-way process. The minister can also learn from the church members. On

Sunday is also where there should be an excellent church school program—one that will attract children. I am glad your present priority is for building up a church school.

In addition to the learning situation of the Sunday morning service, there are many other educational opportunities. There are church forums, public meetings, lecture series, small group discussions. These are not necessarily superior to excellent opportunities on educational or even commercial television, or school and other community events. There is, however, one significant difference in church and away from the TV screen. People can interact, they can talk back, and they can learn and grow with persons of all ages and conditions in a diverse church family. This opportunity for dialogue, this interpersonal dimension does make a great difference, and that is why the tempting TV menu from 11:30 a.m. to 1:00 p.m. on Sundays (at least in the East) or Phil Donahue weekdays is really inferior to the liberal church. Each liberal church ought to make possible excellent opportunities for study and dialogue.

A third purpose of the liberal church is, in the words of the UUA Committee, simply "companionship." The church must be a caring fellowship. Our society needs institutions which care for people as individuals. Ours is a society with a high instance of mobility, of longevity, of divorce. Most individuals in our society have lost their moorings if not their roots. There is widespread loneliness, isolation, helplessness, a feeling of not being wanted. This happens in the lives of all of us, at some time if not at all times. We have, in the West, seldom known the solidarity of the joint family as it exists in India and elsewhere. Indeed, the shelter even of our Western nuclear family appears today to be vanishing.

The liberal minister and church is not the only institution that can help this alienated condition, but it is one. There is the normal family, there are many and specialized social service agencies, there are even the secular or country clubs. Yet there is also the church family, including the minister. Some church families really care for people, not only for an in-group, but for anybody in need. A few ministers and churches can develop sensitivity and do have a record of personal service.

Sometimes the conservative church, even the fundamentalist one, is more caring than we are. But we liberals must try harder as personal lives fall apart. None of us, during a lifetime, is exempt from catastrophe and we all, at different times, need help—companionship and fellowship. Each of us, perhaps at different times in our lives, needs to be alert to this opportunity to help, and be helped. The church is a unique, inclusive institution in our autonomous society offering companionship.

The fourth and final purpose of the liberal church, according to the UUA Committee, is service and social action. The self-survey you made last January indicates that you give highest rating to "participation/leadership in national/global issues activity." You also rate highly the function of "social witness" for the minister.

The spectrum from service to social action is a broad one, but the definition of service may be changing. Once it was to collect food and clothes; more recently service meant to help a family from Indochina resettle here in the Midwest. Yet we may be going full circle, for once again service may mean collecting surplus food for hungry Americans.

The definition of social action is also wide. In your self-survey of methods in dealing with social issues, you put "public stands by the minister" next to the last on the list. In a way this is good, for too often the minister is a surrogate for members of the congregation; the minister gets paid to stick his neck out, or even to have his body imprisoned, if only for a few hours. But the best social action is that in which everybody in the church participates, up to one's ability or inclination.

At this point of the sermon, I should make this statement. For the past twenty-four years I have specialized and worked professionally in secular and church social action. I realize that, in returning to the local pastorate, I am returning to being a generalist again. Social action is only one of four purposes of the liberal church. I cannot turn my back, however, on my longtime conviction that action to stop nuclear war is the overriding issue of our time. Yet world peace is admittedly only one goal, one value, for myself and for a liberal church. Still, each liberal church ought encourage, among others, service and social action.

Time is fleeting, and I must deal more rapidly with the concluding aspect of this sermon. It is one task to project a goal. It is another to suggest how that goal may become a reality. Can a vibrant, expanding liberal church be made real—here on the Lake Shore? Or, indeed is the goal already an actuality, however imperfect, in this institution?

What conditions are, at a minimum, necessary? I would name only three. First is a determination that the majority of the present members want a vibrant liberal church. Second is the conviction that the potential for growth in the direction of an active liberal church is possible on the Lake Shore. And third is the acquisition of creative ministerial leadership.

The first condition for possible success is agreement, if not complete consensus, that a viable liberal church can only be created if most of its current members yearn for this goal. From studying your self-survey, I assume that most of you have some such vision of the future. You have listed for the most important present needs of this church as four-fold: You want to increase church membership. You want a broader age base. You want intellectual stimulation. And you want a liberal presence in the community.

Some of you admittedly have other desires, other values. How to allow for institutional pluralism so that those of you who have different priorities and thus legitimate doubts are not alienated? That is one reason why a slightly larger church membership can give more people broader opportunities. Pluralism can create diversity without necessarily bigness.

A second condition for success is an existing potential for growth here on the Lake Shore. I do not know for sure and I certainly can make no easy promise. The religious demography appears favorable. There must be many more religious liberals living in Wilmette, Winnetka, and Glencoe, from the lake to twenty or so miles west. I believe that the kind of active liberal church I have described, if appealing to most of you, ought to appeal to many others. At least we can collectively hope and try. Nothing is easy. Nothing can be guaranteed.

In 1977 a study was made of the unchurched in America. Six rough categories were discovered. One category is the "boxed-in," or those who feel that church membership stifles personal growth or makes intolerable moral and doctrinal demands. The boxed-in ought to flock to our doors. Then there are the "burned-out," or those who have been so heavily involved previously in church work that they simply give up. Again, some burned-outs ought to flock to our doors if we can guarantee no repetition. The "locked-out" are those who feel unwanted or embarrassed by the clothes or manners in church. This is a class difference and here suburban UUs may not be attractive. Then there are the "nomads" or those who are highly mobile and can't make any deep church commitments. Some nomads ought not be put off by religious liberalism. The "anti-institutionalists" are those who complain about church bureaucracy or fund-raising. Again, they ought easily enter our doors! Finally, there are the "pilgrims," or those who are constantly looking for spiritual belief. Again, some pilgrims might find us! These categories may not be entirely helpful, but they do point to the vast unchurched in America, perhaps also here on the Lake Shore, some of whom we might and should attract.

A third condition for success is ministerial leadership. I understand that many of you are now convinced that hiring a full-time minister is a desirable, even a necessary, goal. I know that some of you may still have doubts.

Some of you may still wonder: what can a resident minister do that a succession of good speakers each Sunday—some better speakers than a minister—cannot do? How can a minister possibly work full time for such a small congregation? And isn't it rather boring to have the same minister in the pulpit two out of every four Sundays? These are honest questions and let me quickly give you honest—if perhaps self-serving—answers.

A minister is a professional. By training and experience he or she does not do everything, but can help the church leadership themselves try new things. You who demand, and rightly, the best in medicine, in education, in culture, and in life generally—you know that excellence demands professionals, specialization. A minister is a professional, not perhaps in converting souls—not in our denomination, anyway—but with experience in making a complex institution run better and fulfill some of the agreed goals of its members. And a full-time minister has plenty to do, even in a small congregation. The ministry is not make-work. It is hard work, because it is intellectual as well as institutional.

By your own survey, you want a minister who is intelligent, committed, warm, enthusiastic, humorous, with a strong sense of self, inspiring, communicative, broad in interests and theological posture. Jesus Christ himself might not have fulfilled all your specifications, or the Buddha or Muhammed! But why not aim for the highest?

These, then, are some of the considerations for institutional success. You will note that I have not put the ownership of a church building or a comfortable bank surplus on this list of necessary elements which can make, if not guarantee, success. It will take hard work, by minister and congregation together. It will also take the beneficent grace of the gods of history and of Beacon Hill to make it happen. And I must assure you, warn you—if you do not know—that I have no special password, no special pass key, either upstairs or even to Boston.

In conclusion, let me remind you that, while I have sought to emphasize the role of the resident, full-time minister, I do not mean to overemphasize that role. Indeed, I want to close by quoting William Ellery Channing who 150 years ago put the role of minister in a correct perspective:

> The great error in regard to churches is that we imagine that the minister or the worship can do something for us mechanically; that there are certain mysterious influences in what we call a holy place which may act on us without our own agency. It is not so. The church and the minister can do little for us in comparison with what we must do for ourselves and nothing for us without ourselves. They become a blessing through our own activity. Every man must be his own priest. It is his own action, not the minister's; it is the prayer issuing from his own heart, not from another's lips, which aids him in church. The church does him good only as by rites, prayers, hymns, and sermons it wakes up his spirit to think, feel, pray, praise, and resolve. The church is a help, not a force.

So be it. Whatever the liberal church may become, I can do little compared to what each of you can do for yourself.

61 TOKYO (1984)

HUMANITY'S HIGHEST PRIORITY

A year after leaving WCRP, Homer received the Niwano Peace Prize for promoting "world peace through interreligious cooperation." The new award was named in honor of Rev. Nikkyo Niwano, co-founder and spiritual leader of Rissho Kosei-kai in Japan and a colleague of Homer in international peace and interfaith activities. In April, Homer, accompanied by Ingeborg, Alex, and several friends, went to Japan for the ceremonies in Tokyo hosted by the Niwano Peace Foundation and a speaking tour of Hiroshima, Kyoto, and Osaka. Homer's remarks—especially those touching on Hiroshima and Nagasaki and Japanese-American relations—were widely covered by the Japanese media. He delivered his acceptance speech "Nuclear Disarmament: The Priority for Humanity"—distilling many familiar themes in his life—at the National Press Center Hall in Tokyo on April 27, 1984. The World Without War Council subsequently published the full text of his speech and held a reception for Homer in Chicago.

There is only one priority for humanity today. That is the abolition of nuclear weapons through nuclear disarmament. Such universal goals as "freedom" or "justice," or such ideological hopes as "democracy" or "socialism," these are quite secondary. The prime goal must be to stop turning every city everywhere into another 1945 Hiroshima or Nagasaki.

The nuclear age has not produced a nuclear war for almost four decades. Has not nuclear deterrence, despite its critics, prevented nuclear war? Perhaps luck has so far prevented any nuclear detonation since Nagasaki as much as any strategic doctrine. Yet what of the future, with 50,000 strategic and tactical nuclear weapons in the stockpiles of five or perhaps eight States? The chances of a nuclear detonation by calculation or miscalculation, by accident or terrorism, appear high. The possibility escalates when the leaders of one nuclear State intermittently declares that it can fight and win a nuclear war.

Nuclear disarmament is the only method to prevent the real possibility of nuclear holocaust. The Final Document of the First United Nations Special Session on Disarmament, adopted unanimously in 1978, makes this clear. Humanity is confronted with a choice: "We must halt the arms race and proceed to disarmament or face annihilation." Thus disarmament must be the priority, not alone of the United Nations, but of all States, all organizations, all religions, and all peoples.

Yet is not peace indivisible? Development was called another name for peace by a recent pope and others have said that peace is human rights. A holistic approach to world peace is important, and yet there may be no time to take all steps to create a just world. Some steps are more important, more crucial, than others. Thus disarmament is more urgent than development or even human rights. Nuclear disarmament is more urgent than that involving so-called "conventional" weapons.

Some allege that this concern for nuclear disarmament is provincial, an East/West or "Northern" preoccupation, but not a universal one, at least not "Southern." Some suggest that the so-called "Third World" has priorities—such as development—different from those of the "First" or "Second" worlds, both of the latter being more fearful of the consequences of nuclear war. I assert that peace and disarmament are not East/West or Northern luxuries. They are equally a necessity in the "South." (Japan, as you know, is considered by some quirk of political geography to be a "Western" State.)

Four-Point Prescription

Having suggested the priority of nuclear disarmament, let me indicate what this means in the current bleak political atmosphere where everything seems to be going downhill. There has been no good news for many years to reverse the trend of increasing nuclear stockpiles. Here is a four-point prescription of next steps to begin to get out of the nuclear arms spiral.

First, the developing, testing, and deployment of all new nuclear weapons should immediately be frozen by all countries, initially by the U.S.A. and the U.S.S.R. This means that no additional nuclear weapons and their delivery systems should be installed anywhere. This is the popular, world-wide campaign called "the nuclear freeze." A freeze can be verified by so-called "national" means of inspection to prevent cheating. Also any nuclear State might begin this process, hoping that others might reciprocate.

Second, nuclear weapons tests in all environments should be prohibited by treaty. (The Partial Test-Ban Treaty of 1963 does not prohibit underground tests and it has not been universally signed.) Any of the five nuclear weapons States might immediately stop such underground tests until a comprehensive treaty could be signed and ratified.

Third, the use—and not just the first use—of nuclear weapons should be prohibited by treaty, and their use made a crime against humanity. The non-aligned countries at the U.N., led by India, have persisted toward this goal, but some countries resist, including your own.

Fourth and last, nuclear weapons should be phased out of the arsenals of all nuclear weapon States—those acknowledged and those covert—as soon as possible, certainly by the end of this decade. The whole world must become a nuclear free zone. This means the end to nuclear research and development for weapons purposes, the end to production, and the end to deployment. This means the dismantling of every nuclear weapon in existence.

These steps may be the widely-acknowledged goals of many States, but there is no guarantee that they will be implemented. Here is where unilateralism can be useful, whether under the name of "mutual example" (that was Mr. Khrushchev's term) or "national initiatives." The arms race has proliferated by unilateral steps and it might be lessened also by initiatives independent of treaties. A nuclear weapons freeze could be unilaterally begun as a recent U.N. resolution recommends. Which of the five nuclear weapons States will have the courage to start this necessary process?

Five Steps

In discussing this broad canvass of peace issues, listeners might wonder, "Do you have a formula for attaining world peace with justice?" Alas, I have none! There is no magic to prevent war. There is no short-cut to disarmament. There is no quick fix for world peace.

Let me suggest, however, certain methods which I have stumbled upon over several decades of working for world peace. Here are five steps:

First, know the facts. Study international affairs. Do your homework. One must remain curious and informed about world events. The reading and paperwork are enormous and often overwhelming, but this cannot be avoided.

Second, work with others. Join an existing peace or disarmament organization, if its principles and actions more or less coincide with your own. What one person can do can be multiplied greatly by working in groups. If no adequate group exists, help organize one. I have not hesitated to do so on several occasions.

Third, explore frontier issues. Be out front, but never too far out. Both the priestly and the prophetic approaches are needed. One must bind up the wounds, but one must also change society so that there will be fewer wounds.

Fourth, do not be attached to results. Especially in working for peace, the results are incremental. Be prepared for the long race. If miraculously you can make a small difference, that is an exception.

Fifth and last, sometimes work alone. Work with others when you can; work with yourself, alone, if you must. That was the genius of Mohandas Gandhi and of Martin Luther King, Jr. Yet we need not all be Gandhis or Kings to work effectively alone. And we need not be martyrs either!

This is my own working philosophy. It might not work at all for you. But read the lives of your own heroes—national and international, religious and secular—and see what gives them strength. You can save disillusionment and defeat by learning from others, indeed by working with others, especially in this difficult field of world peace.

Some say the knowledge of how to make nuclear weapons can never be forgotten. In this year of George Orwell's dark vision, 1984, let us say forthrightly that nuclear knowledge is nuclear ignorance. As a result of nuclear war, human history can be ended. In the century of Mohandas Gandhi and Martin Luther King, let us say forthrightly that nuclear disarmament and nonviolence are the only hope for the future.

62 TOKYO
(1990)

APPEAL FOR PEACE IN
THE PERSIAN GULF

In August 1990, Iraq invaded Kuwait, and for several months America prepared for war. Homer tried to prevent what many felt would prove to be an unmitigated disaster, through speeches, articles, signing a letter of protest of 530 Unitarian Universalist ministers in the New York Times, *and community action for the Coordinating Committee of the Delaware County Campaign for Peace in the Middle East. Internationally, Homer mobilized the seven recipients of the Niwano Peace Prize to sign an appeal for peace, including Norman Cousins, his longtime collaborator. Cousins helped draft the statement several weeks before he died on November 30. The Appeal entitled "Restraint, Dialogue, Negotiation, Mediation" was released in Tokyo on December 10. In January, President Bush launched war on Iraq. In other news this year, Mikhail Gorbachev won the Nobel Peace Prize, a spacecraft named* Ulysses *was launched to explore the solar system, and* Dancing with Wolves *won best movie award.*

With the sudden end of the Cold War, the peoples of the world had looked forward to funds saved from the huge world military budget to be redirected to long-deferred social purposes. A portion of the large "peace dividend" of one trillion dollars annually was to be used hopefully for national and international development, especially in Africa, Asia, and Latin America. Also humanity began to look toward a period when ideological tensions would no longer stimulate regional conflicts and the U.N. could for the first time in its history operate more in conformity with its Charter as adopted by the Member States.

Alas, the few months of transition from the Cold War were suddenly truncated by Iraq's invasion of Kuwait. The widespread condemnation of Iraq's invasion was reflected by new unanimity in the U.N. Security Council which adopted a series of resolutions establishing economic and political sanctions against Iraq and some restraints on the multilateral force building up in Saudi Arabia. We trust that humanitarian aid to the peoples of Iraq and Kuwait will continue.

We seven recipients of the Niwano Peace Prize—representing longtime peace activists in Latin America, the Caribbean, China, Japan, Pakistan, and the U.S.A.—hope and pray that military action will not be taken in the Middle East. We hope that the expertise of the U.N. Secretary-General for quiet diplomacy and negotiation may be used to its fullest. Restraint and negotiation are far better than war. Violence is never a solution for national or international differences. War makes the resolution of conflict more distant and more difficult. Peace does not, however, automatically stop conflict, but it does give time and space for compromise negotiations for just solutions. A shooting war will solve no outstanding problems. A war could, however, kill untold numbers of human beings. A shooting war could turn into a longstanding North/South war as devastating as the East/West Cold War. A shooting war could be the beginning of the Third World War.

What began as a Gulf Crisis has become a Middle East Crisis, with the problems of Kuwait and Iraq increasingly linked to a host of other political issues in the region. We believe that an All-Arab Conference followed by an International Conference may be one means not only of helping restore the sovereignty of Kuwait, but of focusing the need for mutual recognition between the Arab States and Israel, as well as the need to resolve the problem of a homeland for the Palestinians. The sovereignty of all States in the region, including Israel, must be guaranteed. Also the creation of a chemical weapons-free zone and a nuclear-free zone in the Middle East is necessary.

We longtime supporters of the United Nations are gratified that the world organization is increasingly at the center of political negotiations and actions to resolve the crisis. The need to develop mechanisms of world law through the United Nations remains the greatest challenge of a civilized world society. The multinational force in

Saudi Arabia is not yet a U.N. force and should be placed under U.N. command, perhaps with more Arab and non-aligned countries participating and fewer Western ones. This crisis demonstrates that the Arab world, as the Christian, Jewish, and Muslim communities, is not monolithic and must not be subjected to careless stereotypes.

Late in October, former U.S. President Jimmy Carter and President Nikkyo Niwano of Rissho Kosei-kai made a joint statement in Japan urging "all parties to the (Gulf) conflict to exercise great restraint and to remain open to dialogue directed toward a negotiated resolution to the conflict." At the same time the presidents of the World Conference on Religion and Peace, representing seven world religions, sent a letter to the U.N. Security Council appealing for "continuing prayer, meditation, and commitment around the world for the peaceful settlement of conflict in the Middle East."

As peace activists, we counsel patience and perseverance. The world embargo against South Africa is working to change apartheid. The world embargo against Iraq can also, given time, result in change without war. We commend those non-governmental individuals, often retired statesmen, and representatives of non-governmental organizations, who have journeyed to Iraq and elsewhere in the Middle East to plead for reasoned solutions. We are convinced that solutions can be found.

We ask for restraint, not retaliation. We demand dialogue, not destruction. We urge negotiations, not name-calling. We suggest mediation, not militarism.

Helder Camara
Homer Jack
Zhao Puchu
Philip A. Potter
Inamullah Khan
Etai Yamada
Norman Cousins

Helder Camara is the retired Catholic Archbishop of Recife in Brazil and has been a longtime activist with the poor. Zhao Puchu is president of the Buddhist Association of China and a well known calligrapher. Philip A. Potter is a clergyman from the Caribbean who was General Secretary of the World Council of Churches. Inamullah Khan is Secretary-General of the World Muslim Congress. Etai Yamada is Chief Abbot of the Tendai Sect of Buddhism at Mt. Hiei, Japan.

63 SWARTHMORE
(1992)

A NEW AGENDA FOR AN OLD PEACE MOVEMENT

The collapse of the U.S.S.R. and the end of the Cold War in the early 1990s diminished the threat of global nuclear war. For nearly fifty years, the world lived under the shadow of a thermonuclear exchange between the two superpowers. Homer addressed the future of the peace movement in a radically changed world in a speech at the Unitarian Universalist Peace Fellowship of Delaware Valley on May 19, 1992, his seventy-sixth birthday.

I welcome this opportunity to think through a new agenda for the old peace movement. The agenda, in one sense, is unchanging, eternal—to end war. I am reminded of this because I have recently started to write my autobiography. In my archives at the Swarthmore College Peace Collection I found remarks I gave in high school on December 15, 1939—almost sixty years ago. The title was "A Common Cause: To Abolish War." I suggested we form a high school "peace and disarmament club" to "help the interested student find out more about war and spread the good-word of peace to' friends, parents, teachers." I also warned against "saddling Germany with the sole guilt in causing the (past) world war." That was only a few months before Adolf Hitler became chancellor of Germany and less than a year before Franklin Delano Roosevelt was elected president. This vignette is one proof that there has been, at least in our time, deep yearning for peace as well as that there is nothing

463

new under the sun, except perhaps nuclear weapons.

If the goal remains the abolition of war, strategies and tactics change, even for the peace movement. Indeed, change has happened so rapidly in the past two years that the peace organizations themselves, not to mention governments and peoples, are breathless and perplexed. What should be our next steps, our priorities, our agenda? And if we appear at a loss, so is our opposition. The U.S. military-industrial-education-science complex also is in a daze, also not knowing which way to turn.

Also our government—indeed all governments—are in a quandary. Earlier this year the Bush Administration sent up two outrageous trial balloons. One suggested scenarios for preparing for half a dozen wars just over the horizon. The other trial balloon was even larger: "to maintain the mechanism for deterring potential competitors from even aspiring to a larger regional or global role." The U.S. would remain the one superpower by further rearming ourselves for that role—and ignore the role of regional security organizations or the U.N. itself. A third trial balloon is the incredible request from the Pentagon that it, too, wants a slice of the peace dividend—up to a billion dollars to refurbish and enlarge the Pentagon!

Let me recall, in the briefest way, how the dangerous—but for some, comfortable—world of the late 1980s collapsed for all of us, including the peace movement. The Berlin Wall went down in 1989, signaling that Soviet Premier Gorbachev was willing for Eastern Europe to go free and for satellite regimes in the developing world (from Vietnam to Angola to Cuba) to make other arrangements. In the meantime, the vast changes in the Soviet Union caused a political vacuum in the world, including the U.N. This made possible the control of the U.N. Security Council by President Bush and thus the Gulf War. Then the Soviet Union dissolved before our very eyes. Former Warsaw Pact nations were invited to associate themselves with NATO. President Bush cut the Pentagon budget ever so gently and still hesitates to buy former Soviet military and space expertise. The START Treaty will soon lessen numbers of intercontinental ballistic missiles, tactical weapons are being reduced, disarmament is being done more through unilateralism than long-winded negotiations, and the U.N. is doing brisk business with peacekeeping operations worldwide.

Our Reactions To These Changes

During these vast changes, what has been happening to our peace and justice organizations? Where do we fit in?

First, some peace activists are quickly receiving the message. They get it! The reason that brought them into the peace movement originally—for some, more than thirty-five years ago—was to try to lessen the danger of nuclear war. The nuclear stockpiles still remain, but the danger of intentional nuclear war has appreciably lessened. The nuclear clock on the cover of the *Bulletin of the Atomic Scientists* has been turned back from a few minutes to midnight to 11:43. This symbolizes this lessening of global nuclear catastrophe. Thus many have sensed this reality and have left to tend their own gardens. Can we blame them? Indeed, the whole peace movement, their movement, owes them gratitude for their dogged persistence. This exodus has especially been felt by nuclear disarmament organizations, such as SANE/Freeze. The latter may be holding its own nationally, but often disappearing locally, as here in Delaware County.

A second reaction to these vast changes is that some peace activists are dividing their time and money into different organizations and issues—even more than previously. Peace is, theoretically, a holistic quest. Yet organizationally and philosophically, peace has been divided into many pieces. Some organizations and individuals still focus on weapons. Others focus on regions, even continents, such as the interreligious group on Latin America in this county, called CASA. Also in this county there is a Committee for Peace and Justice in the Middle East. Other peace organizations are vocational: physicians, teachers, social scientists, and yet others working for peace. Still others focus on environment, such as the Sierra Club and many more. Some are religious, such as our own Delaware Valley Fellowship.

Third, a few peace groups focus on machinery, especially the U.N. The U.N. Association sees its mission as enhancing the world organization. The World Federalists focus on restructuring the U.N. in an entirely new way. Other groups prefer the priority of electoral politics, especially in a presidential year.

Fourth and last, some organizations and individuals at least try to keep up with the vast changes. This is increasingly difficult, even in a computer age. I find yearbooks important, and let me name just three in three fields of peace: disarmament, environment, and human rights. I refer to the *SIPRI Yearbook on World Armaments and Disarmament*. This annual volume is indispensable, although the price is too high except for institutions and libraries. More inexpensive is the annual volume of the Worldwatch Institute, *State of the World*. Also relatively cheap is the Annual Report of Amnesty International. To keep even more current, certain periodicals are vital. I read weekly everything from *Newsweek* to the *Christian Century*, and including the *Nation*. In the field of disarmament, for example, the *Bulletin of the Atomic Scientists* is useful as is *Disarmament Times*, for timely news of U.N. negotiations.

The Global Agenda

In the meantime, the global agenda is under strict review. In May 1990, U.N. Secretary-General Javier Perez de Cuellar issued a creative mid-term report shifting priorities for the world organization. This was at the climax of Gorbachev's years. The Secretary-General wrote:

"The lifting of the deadening weight of the Cold War open(s) enormous opportunities to remedy the sins of omission and commission of the past . . . to ensure peace in all its dimensions." Thus the objectives of the U.N. itself "into the new century must be defined with this heartening circumstance in mind." He pointed to the holistic nature of solving outstanding global problems: "Most of the issues of the U.N. agenda are closely interrelated," and "lack of progress in one area can retard developments in the other." The Secretary-General admitted the "overall linkage between political, economic, social, and humanitarian questions."

Another set of priorities is that negotiated in March at U.N. Headquarters for the Earth Summit, the U.N. Conference on Environment and Development, and to be fine-tuned and approved early in June in Brazil. Even though limited to environment and development, the Earth Charter will loom large in the priorities of most of us. While the long laundry list—originally 800 pages—implementing the Earth Charter deals with North/South relations almost as much as with environment, it is not yet final. Yet we know enough to factor its thrust into our peace agenda.

The New Agenda

Given this background, what is the new agenda for the old peace movement? I am no Albert Einstein of the peace movement. I have no theory to unify this broad field. I have no clever formula and thus can only provide another list. Let me try to reduce the agenda into five points, in search of a slogan.

First, we must respond to electoral politics. A president, some members of the Senate, and all members of the House will be elected after a bitter campaign. We must participate, for there is more possibility of non-incumbents winning as many of the incumbents deserve to lose.

The American people are fed up with leadership in Washington. While their dissatisfaction is basically domestic—economic—this same leadership is also often hopeless on international relations issues. Never has it been possible to turn so many people out of office who have been supportive of cold wars and hot ones. However, better replacements will not be automatic.

Second, we must work for more justice in regional issues or areas. Each one of us cannot take on the whole world. Some of us follow the Middle East, or Southeast Asia, or Eastern Europe, or Southern Africa, or Latin America. There have been unbelievable gains recently, such as in South Africa, but also in the creation of U.N. forces in Yugoslavia and Cambodia, and the lessening of violence in Latin America. We must, if necessary, specialize in watching, working, or helping one area if not all. I am working currently on only one regional issue: to establish a viable Palestinian State alongside a secure Israel. I should also be working to strengthen democracy in the former Soviet Union and Eastern Europe in order for the new fragile democracies to survive. Had President Bush fought this battle in 1990-91, instead of the Gulf War, the world would be in a better condition now.

Third is disarmament. This is no longer first on my agenda with the lessening if not the end of the nuclear threat.

Fourth, we must work on both development and environment, and find a sophisticated relationship between the two, not only in the developing world but in our world—which also must develop if our country is to thrive again economically. Some of the insights of the Earth Summit might be useful.

Fifth, we must now give real time to think seriously about major changes for truly a new world order—world government. This still seems unrealistic among many liberals, but it is necessary. Some of us saw the necessity of world—not coalition—governance before, during, and after the Gulf War. Albert Einstein saw it many years ago. He was always declaring that, as important as work for disarmament was during the Cold War, much more important were efforts to abolish the whole institution of war through world government and a vastly changed U.N. We must devote some time to attaining world government which may be some years in the future, but not decades or centuries.

Changing Styles

Let me comment on the style of the peace movement for the remaining years of the 1990s. Today anything goes; it all hangs out. When I was a young theological student, I once visited famed Unitarian preacher, John Haynes Holmes. He declared: "Jack, if you want to be a social radical, dress conservatively." I took Holmes' advice all my life, but now I realize that times have indeed changed even in this regard.

However, there is one bad habit among many peace people, including at times myself. We have faced defeat so often that we cannot absorb—and exude—good news. Let us relax as a result of all the recent good news: the diminishing of the nuclear threat with the end of the Cold War, the result of the recent plebiscite for whites only in South Africa, and the recent U.N. peacekeeping efforts, however slow, in Cambodia and Yugoslavia. As the once-popular song said, let us accentuate the positive!

Also—and here some of you will differ radically with me—we must not live on conspiracies. Much war, murder, and terrorism can occur in the world without the complicity of the CIA or the White House. The death of JFK and similar phenomena of our time give us pause and, to many of us, have not yet been satisfactorily explained. Yet let us not join that cottage industry of almost welcoming the latest conspiracy theory.

A final word on style. Let us not take ourselves seriously—all the time. Let us continue our sense of humor—or develop one. There was a cartoon in a recent issue of the *Bulletin of the Atomic Scientists*. It showed a general trying to read a book at his desk in the Pentagon. The book was titled, *How To Survive Full-Scale Nuclear Disarmament!*

Eight Disarmament Measures

With the end of the Cold War, and the dissolution of the Soviet Union, the disarmament movement appears unnecessary—and dead—

until one reads the ambitious plans of the Pentagon! Still, disarmament measures appear to take place faster than governmental leaders or citizens groups appear to catch up. Unilateralism seems to become more useful than the more lengthy process of negotiating disarmament treaties.

Yet guidelines are needed for governments to take advantage of the new political atmosphere and for citizens groups, and their members, to continue to make policy-makers honest. Before putting the nuclear disarmament symbol on the shelf, citizens must examine the remaining disarmament agenda. It is formidable.

1. The goal must be made explicit: to eliminate all nuclear weapons everywhere by the year 2000. This could take the form of a U.N. General Assembly resolution, then a Security Council resolution—for one unused function of the Council is to submit plans "for the establishment of a system for the regulation of armaments." Member States could make parallel declarations that they would eliminate all nuclear weapons by 2000. Eventually there must be a U.N. treaty with this goal.

2. A comprehensive test-ban treaty must be signed, ratified, and entered into force. This perennial in the disarmament garden for forty-six years must finally come to blossom. There is a parallel testing moratorium in three or four former Soviet states; the U.S.A. and the U.K. must reciprocate, not to mention the U.K. and France. Once again the world community is on the verge of eliminating nuclear tests.

Once again more interest appears in the Congress than in the White House. The pending Nuclear Testing Moratorium Act has 183 sponsors in the Congress—at the end of March—but only 22 co-sponsors in the Senate.

3. New steps must be taken toward non-proliferation of nuclear weapons. Recently China, France, and South Africa have signed the Non-Proliferation Treaty. Yet another half-dozen States continue to be outside this regime: Israel which stockpiles nuclear weapons, and Pakistan and India which could stockpile nuclear weapons, and other States on the verge of becoming nuclear. New efforts must be made by the States Parties to the NPT to stop the spread. The best method is for the nuclear weapons states to take Article IV of the NPT seriously and continue to disarm down to zero nuclear weapons—even by the year 1995 when the NPT must be renewed and some non-nuclear States are raising justifiable questions.

4. The production of nuclear materials for weapons must stop. This could take the form of unilateral declarations to the Security

Council and eventually by treaty. With the scrapping of hundreds of nuclear weapons, no new nuclear fuel should be manufactured. Indeed, the workers making the stuff should now be employed to clean up, if they can, the nuclear wastes.

5. The reduction of nuclear stockpiles should continue. The START treaty lessening intercontinental ballistic missiles is beginning to lessen these weapons and follow up negotiations have been promised. Also the unilateral reduction of tactical nuclear weapons is beginning. While any minimum nuclear deterrent should be considered only as an interim measure. The reduction of strategic weapons to a minimum deterrent—500 by the U.S.A. and 500 by Russia—would be an interim measure, with smaller ceilings for the U.K., France, and China.

6. The above steps would make the creation of additional nuclear-weapon-free zones unnecessary. Yet if some of these steps are not promptly taken, new nuclear-weapons free zones should be legally created, including Africa, the Middle East, South Asia, and perhaps all of Asia.

7. So-called "conventional weapons" must be drastically reduced. They killed the millions who died from war since 1945. The new U.N. Registry of Arms Transfers has just opened. This will now include statistics on production and stockpiles, not only on sales. Yet publicity or transparency does not prevent arms races. One area to start arms reductions is the Middle East. All kinds of high-tech weapons have come to the Middle East even since the end of the Gulf War. (Arms just don't materialize; they are bought or sold or given away.) An international embargo on arms sales to the Middle East is necessary—however difficult to achieve. Also the arms stockpiles of individual nations can be appreciably lessened if a permanent U.N. force can be established. Certainly U.N. peacekeeping can make individual, national armies less attractive. Likewise, the reduction and eventual elimination of navies is another huge area which is not yet even being negotiated.

8. The military budgets of all countries must be greatly reduced. Governments hesitate to do so, given so much unemployment. Responsible yet rapid conversion can make jobs, not eliminate them. The lessening of the Pentagon budget and allocating the peace dividend for a better infrastructure (and not merely service jobs and debt retirement) are a challenge to the peace movement. And the latter is itself feeling the sting of unemployment.

64 BOMBAY
(1992)

THE GANDHI CENTURY

In the twentieth century, Mohandas Gandhi was the foremost person to challenge the age-old cycle of violence and war. From the Indian independence campaign to the anti-apartheid struggle in South Africa, from the American civil rights movement to the Philippine People Power movement, from the Vietnamese Buddhist campaign to the Chinese student movement in Beijing, Gandhian nonviolence has been employed as a philosophy and practical method to challenge authority and, in many cases, successfully achieve social change. In 1992, Homer received the Jamnalal Bajaj International Award for a lifetime of "promoting Gandhian values outside India." On a speaking tour of India and at ceremonies in Bombay on November 5—in which he accepted the award from K. R. Narayanan, Vice-President of India—Homer addressed Gandhi's enduring legacy inside and outside of India.

Lillian Smith, the American author, wrote that the winners name an age to reflect its triumphs, not its failures. Our century will be remembered, not by the Holocaust or Hiroshima/Nagasaki or the tragic partition of this sub-continent, not as the Age of Hitler or Stalin, but perhaps as the Gandhi Century.

Gandhi has emerged—and stayed—above all his peers, those persons born in the nineteenth century who blossomed in the twentieth. British author George Orwell wrote, "Compared with the other leading political figures of our time, how clean a smell he [Gandhi] managed to leave behind." Historian Martin Marty recently described humanitarian Albert Schweitzer as an *exemplum*—a medieval term for "a clearing in the woods." Mohandas Gandhi was also an *exemplum* and his ashram was not only a clearing in Wardha but in all of India and the subcontinent. Gandhi was the supreme exemplar for the whole world for our century, from Tiananman Square to Red Square, from Stockholm to Cape Town.

The preeminence of Gandhi as the leading symbol of peace for the twentieth century is ironic since he never received a Nobel Peace Prize, first awarded in 1901. Some of us are currently urging the Norwegian Nobel Committee posthumously to award the peace prize to Mohandas Gandhi sometime before the end of this century—a Nobel for the entire century.

What are the "Gandhian values" which might be promoted inside India or outside? They are principally nonviolence and truth. *Satyagraha* or "soul force" or nonviolent direct action is easier to recognize or define than to practice. Truth is more elusive, but it may be what today we might call holistic peace. This might include a Gandhian approach to everything, from simpler lifestyles ("small is beautiful") to equitable, sustainable development, from multireligious dialogue and action to unilateral disarmament and civilian defense against aggression.

Albert Einstein in his greetings to Gandhi on the latter's seventy-fifth birthday gave the best evaluation: "Generations to come will scarce believe that such a one as this ever in flesh and blood walked upon this earth." Two or more generations have come since Gandhi, and they must be reminded that Gandhi indeed walked this earth and made it better, and that they also can do so. Gandhi insisted that "any man or woman can achieve what I have, if he or she would make the same effort and cultivate the same hope and faith."

Amid Gandhi's insistence on truth and nonviolence, there was always a twinkle in his eye. He once insisted that "the woes of Mahatmas are known to Mahatmas alone."

Many Strands

Gandhi was a universal human being. He was the Father of India, but perhaps also of the modern world. He was much bigger, if I may say so, than India. Indeed, his influence may be greater outside India today than inside! Four and one half decades after his death in 1948, Gandhi is alive—and well—throughout the world.

To understand Gandhi's continuing influence, we must try to

472

disentangle the many strands of his comprehensive, complex, rich life. There was an integrity, even beauty, in Gandhi's whole life. One appreciates the whole, more than any part, and indeed the whole of Gandhi—as of any human being—is much greater than its parts. Also we remember Gandhi for what he was, and for what he stands for in the minds and hearts of millions of world citizens everywhere. He also accomplished much that was tangible in his long lifetime, even if he attempted even more.

In 1926 Gandhi wrote to a "persistent" correspondent: "I have no desire to found a sect. I am really too ambitious to be satisfied with a sect or a following." He avoided adulation, including titles. In response to the frequent honorific title of Mahatma—Great Soul—Gandhi wrote: "I assure all my admirers and friends that they will please me better if they will forget the Mahatma and remember Gandhiji . . . or think of me simply as Gandhi." He also said that he loves "to hear the words, 'down with Gandhism.' An 'ism' deserves to be destroyed . . . The real thing is nonviolence . . . I am eager to see Gandhism wiped out at an early date." Again he insisted, "There is no room for 'Gandhism.'" What then shall we today call those individuals, organizations, and institutions trying, however imperfectly, to walk and work in the direction that Gandhi took during his lifetime? In deference to Gandhi's stern warning and wishes, I will not use Gandhism, but it is difficult, if not impossible, not to use the adjective, Gandhian—meaning "like Gandhi."

Popularity

Visitors and admirers, if not pilgrims, continue to gather at places here in India associated with Gandhi: Rajghat and Birla House in Delhi, his ashrams at least at Sabarmati and Sevagram, and of course the many Gandhi margs, statues, museums, schools, and bhavans. However, statues of Gandhi are also prominently placed around the world: London, Moscow, Honolulu, New York, and elsewhere.

As with many popular figures, there appeared a decline in world interest, if not a disillusionment, after Gandhi's death. Yet less criticism of Gandhi emerged after his death than during his often controversial life.

Several resurgences of interest in Gandhi manifested themselves. One occurred in my own country, the U.S.A., in the 1960s when Martin Luther King, Jr., strode the American stage and rightly was called "the American Gandhi." Another new world focus on Gandhi came in 1969 when the centenary of his birth was observed. Still a third resurgence occurred when Sir Richard Attenborough's motion picture *Gandhi* appeared in 1983. This Academy Award film in a true sense brought Gandhi back to India and South Africa and sparked interest in Gandhi for an entire new generation.

The renewed popularity also brought renewed criticisms. Several articles in American magazines, in reviewing the film, attacked the man. American critic Hendrick Herzberg called one article an "exercise in Gandhi-bashing. . . a nasty piece of work, so repellent that there is nothing to do with it but pick it up with a pair of tongs and drop it in the trash." He added, "Gandhi a failure? Gandhi a humbug? The world needs more such failures, more such humbugs."

In the West, and really worldwide, Gandhi has become a pop figure. Young people, but some old people also, regarded and still regard Gandhi as a contemporary ideal. There are Gandhi buttons, Gandhi posters, Gandhi calendars, Gandhi slogans. His picture and name appear wherever there are demonstrations for peace and human rights, against war, against repression, and in those long years against apartheid.

Gandhi has become a symbol that transcends nation, religion, race, and culture. Gandhi certainly did not plan it that way and his friends did not manipulate his image. Yet Gandhi is revered by millions in India and also outside India—elsewhere in Asia, Africa, Latin America, North America, and Europe.

Gandhi's Greatest Contribution

Satyagraha or nonviolent direct action or "soul force" was perhaps Gandhi's greatest contribution to the world. While he discussed the applicability of this method to international affairs, he was preoccupied with applying and perfecting the method for use against the British to produce an independent India and, at the moment of independence, a nonviolent India during partition.

Even before Indian independence and Gandhi's death, lively controversy emerged on the applicability of *satyagraha* beyond the British people and empire. Gandhi insisted that the method could be effective even against the Nazis; also he never agreed that British colonialism was any different or any more lenient than other colonialism. Also discussion began in India and now continues around the world whether Gandhi's methodology was a tactic or a principle, mere politics or a nonsectarian religion. This controversy culminated in the long-time dilemma which Gandhi himself faced: was he a saintly politician or a political saint—or both?

In 1922 Gandhi first used the term, *Shanti Sena*—peace army. He considered organizing one in 1947 and he died a few weeks before a conference of his co-workers was planning a Shanti Sena. Vinoba Bhave and Jayaprakash Narayan managed to create a national Shanti Sena. This inspired the creation of a World Peace Brigade in 1962. In various forms such experiments have persisted in Africa, Asia, and Latin America, including a group called Witness for Peace to oppose the contras around Nicaragua.

Another extension of the use of *satyagraha* was in the early 1940s when Gandhi considered how India might defend itself nonviolently against any Japanese invasion. Scholars in Europe, after Gandhi's death, have written much about nonviolent defense using the whole population of a nation, as a practical substitute for military defense. This has been called civilian defense, and is being actively studied in the Baltics—Sweden, Denmark, even Lithuania.

In 1986 when Soviet Premier Mikhail Gorbachev visited Prime Minister Rajiv Gandhi, a joint communique called for a "world without (weapons of mass destruction) and war, a nonviolent world." Also the Soviet leader enunciated a "defensive" military strategy for his country and the Warsaw Pact States, rather similar to some of the urgings of Gandhi a half-century before. Indeed, unilateral disarmament—so hated yesterday and so effective today—is a type of Gandhian diplomacy.

Gandhi's Environmentalism

Gandhi could be considered a premature ecologist. With his mother a Jain, Gandhi wrote as early as 1920: "Complete nonviolence is complete absence of ill-will against all that lives. It therefore embraces even sub-human life, not excluding noxious insects or beasts." Gandhi's concern for environment showed itself in his lifetime at his ashrams with his deep involvement in village life and agriculture. He once wrote that "earth provides enough to satisfy every man's need, but not every man's greed."

After Gandhi's death, E. F. Schumacher followed some of Gandhi's economic ideas and wrote the well-known volume, *Small Is Beautiful*. The Hug the Trees or Chipko movement along the Himalayas retains Gandhian overtones: "We will not allow the felling of a single tree. When their men raise their axes, we will embrace the trees to protect them."

Also the demonstrations against nuclear-produced power, worldwide, is a reflection of Gandhi in a nuclear age which opened only in the last three years of his life.

Unfinished Legacy

There are many other dimensions of continuing Gandhi interests I must pass over, only for reasons of time, such as his concern about untouchability and about racism. I must, however, say a word about Gandhi's insistence on multireligious action. His father was a Hindu and his mother was a Jain. Gandhi died a Hindu, yet became increasingly eclectic religiously, choosing elements from several world religions for his daily prayer meetings. During the Gandhi centennial observances, the Gandhi Peace Foundation sponsored an international interreligious symposium in 1968. Gandhi would have been pleased as representatives from world religions not only meditated, but also planned for organized religions to work together on United Nations issues. This became the still-existing World Conference on Religion and Peace.

New material almost daily appears as part of the Gandhi legacy. Gandhi just cannot be confined to his lifetime—or to India. His work continues, everywhere. Let me conclude in this quite unfinished manner, since the legacy of Gandhi is astoundingly unfinished.

65 SWARTHMORE
(1993)

ACHIEVING LASTING UNITY
IN INDIA

The 1980s and early 1990s saw a wave of religious fundamentalism sweep the Middle East and parts of Asia and Africa. In India, hundreds of people were killed or injured in the worst outbreak of communal violence since Partition in 1948. In December 1992 a Hindu mob burned down an Islamic Mosque in Ayodhya, and violence flared up throughout India. Invited to speak to a small group of nonresident Indians in Media, Pennsylvania, on the anniversary of Gandhi's death on January 30, 1993, Homer read an open letter to Hindus. The appeal to quell passions and restore peace was later submitted and ignored by an Indian-American weekly, but parts appeared in the Statesman *in New Delhi. The avalanche of opposition he received from Indians caused Homer to compose an open letter to Muslims, also appealing for toleration and calm.*

Dear Friends,

The demolition of the Babri Masjid at Ayodhya on December 6 and its continuing aftermath have been called the greatest tragedy for India since the partition of the subcontinent in 1947 and the assassination of Mohandas Gandhi on January 30, 1948.

This letter cannot deal with the facts about Ayodhya on December 6 and its aftermath. It is clear that an orchestrated plan by right-wing Hindu organizations led to the destruction of the Babri Masjid. The immediate reaction was felt in at least 135 cities throughout India, with an estimated 1,200 persons killed, many more injured,

477

with damage amounting to *crores* [hundreds of thousands] of rupees. Indeed, violence resumed in Bombay one month later with at least 600 more persons killed in an "ethnic cleansing" which recalled the Nazis of yesterday and the Christian Bosnians today. Of the almost 2,000 recorded deaths in December and January, most of those killed were Muslims and killed by local Hindu police. (I write this letter without knowing the motive of the bombings in Bombay on March 12.)

Let me now make six suggestions especially to Hindu friends in India (or elsewhere). I am also writing a letter on this subject to Muslim friends.

1. Oppose the pandering to religious organizations and religious "voting banks" by all the political parties of India. Pandit Nehru did not use the religions of India for narrow political purposes, even if his daughter, Indira, and her son, Rajiv, occasionally did so. The programs of the Bharatiya Janata Party (the BJP), the Vishna Hindu Parishad (the VHP), and the Bajrang Dal are reactionary as are the Rashtriya Swayam Sevak Sangh (RSS), the Shiv Sena, and yet others. Each is trying to make India a Hindu state and to abolish India as a secular state. Each is trying to obliterate the painstaking work of both Gandhi and Nehru who through the Indian Constitution created an integrated, secular state.

2. Cease blaming Muslims for the problems of India. The canards—falsehoods—about Muslims are just that. Substitute blacks in America or Palestinians in Israel—some of the same allegations are used against racial, religious, and ethnic minorities the world over, and for centuries. There is always a grain of truth, but usually only a grain! Professor Sarvepalli Gopal, the son of former Indian President Radhakrishnan, said it best in his three-volume biography of Nehru: "In Nehru's view the responsibility for communal peace rested primarily on the Hindus. Like [Jean Paul] Sartre, to whom the Jewish question was a gentile one, to Nehru the Muslim question was a Hindu one."

3. Help your children understand, cherish, and appreciate their Hinduism, but help them also to respect and accept all world religions. This is a task for the family, for religious education for children, and with care for secular public schools also. Multicultural education is popular today in many societies and it also includes multireligious education. We in the West were taught that Hinduism was the most tolerant of all world religions. Now we know that some Hindus can be as exclusive and cruel as adherents of other religions. Thus Hindus of all ages must somehow learn appreciation

478

for other religions, including Islam.

4. Set for yourself some date, before which you will not blame people for whatever their ancestors did to rule, despoil, and colonialize the Indian subcontinent. The Persians, the Muslims, the British, and others cannot be held responsible today for the imperialism and colonialism—religious and secular—of centuries ago. There must be some statue of limitations. The Muslim shopkeeper in Bombay is not responsible for the Mughul demolition of Hindu *mandirs* [temples] in the sixteenth century, but the right-wing Hindu politicians living today throughout India are responsible for the ruin of the Babri Masjid on December 6.

5. Remain aware of the strong economic, class, and caste system which plays an important role in communal riots. The bifurcated status of India today may help the middle class and the rich, but it is hurting the poor. One might marvel at a middle and affluent class of perhaps 100 million or more persons in India today; but they remain in peril as long as 700 to 750 million Indian citizens remain poor.

Also special attention must be given to the Dalits, Harijans, untouchables—whatever the current politically correct term. Hindus cannot evade their responsibility. The fate of Dalits is related to the fate of caste Hindus on the subcontinent; India cannot rise without the Dalits rising also, and intentionally, not as a by-product of making the rich Indians or the middle class richer.

6. Ponder the best way to regulate the religions of India. The Indian secular state is not an end in itself, Just as the "separation of church and state" in the United States is not an end in itself. Both are methods to regulate deeply held convictions and indeed passions which, now we know, will not shrivel away with several decades of education or affluence. Religion is in India, and the world, here to stay. How best can it be regulated? Perhaps there is a better way, but not just because the BJP or the VHP say so. And do not let them convince you that Hinduism is a minority or treated as a minority by the Muslims (who are truly a minority). You can also be sure that one hundred million Muslims cannot take advantage of 700 million Hindus. This is the big lie which again and again must be exposed. No one is taking advantage of Hindus in India today.

One special word to those of you who are now American citizens. U.S. citizen or not, don't be afraid to praise contemporary India when appropriate, and to criticize it when necessary. India is old and durable enough to withstand constructive criticism, and perhaps your very distance can provide needed perspective.

Friends, remember the glorious history of Bharat—India. Remember the persistent struggle for a modern, independent subcontinent during the past two centuries. Rammohun Roy and Rabindranath Tagore, B. G. Tilak and G. K. Gokhale, Gandhi and Nehru—these were giants. Most of these giants did not struggle for a sectarian Hindu state, but—as the 1950 Indian Constitution proclaims—a "sovereign, socialist, secular, democratic republic." The right-wing Hindu groups are eroding this goal. The effort to regain ground towards a secular India, but one not trivializing any religion, rests primarily with Hindus living both in India and around the world.

I end this letter returning to Mohandas Gandhi, the father of your nation, a very violent nation, as most nations in the world remain violent. Gandhi insisted on nonviolent direct action—*satyagraha*—and Gandhi was right. Few leaders in India or the world today choose to walk in Gandhi's footsteps and that is the principal reason for the violent India and violent world in which we live today. Just because of Gandhi, India is judged by higher standards than most other nations. Muslim-killing and Muslim-bashing are unacceptable behavior in today's world.

India and Hinduism have produced the greatest peacemaker so far in the twentieth century. Gandhi is claimed as such all over the world. We can only honor Gandhiji, and indeed mourn his passing if we genuinely try to lessen resort to violence, on the streets of Bombay or Los Angeles, but most of all in our own hearts. It was Bapu who said in 1924:

"I see no way of achieving anything in this afflicted country without a lasting heart unity between Hindus and Mussalmans [Muslims] of India."

66
CHICAGO
(1993)

THE WORLD'S PARLIAMENT
OF RELIGIONS

The World's Parliament of Religions—the great assembly of spiritual lead-
ers that convened in Chicago in 1893—foreshadowed a century of multire-
ligious dialogue and action. Never again would Eastern religions be at a
disadvantage with the West. The Parliament resulted in the development of
the Hindu Vedanta movement, Buddhism, and Japanese Shintoism and
Zen in America. It also helped establish, in 1900, the incipient Internation-
al Association for Religious Freedom and, in 1970, the World Conference
on Religion and Peace. In the years preceding the one hundredth anniver-
sary of the Parliament, Homer frequently invoked its legacy, writing arti-
cles for selected Christian, Buddhist, Hindu, and secular magazines focus-
ing on each tradition's contribution to the historic congress within the
larger whole. Homer planned to attend the ecumenical centenary of the
Parliament in Chicago—the site of his own earliest interfaith activities—in
the autumn of 1993, but he died in midsummer.

In the late 1880s, the U.S. Congress chose Chicago—not New
York or Washington—as the proper venue to celebrate the 400th anniversary of the landing of Christopher Columbus in the Western
Hemisphere. (Although the anniversary fell in October 1892 the international exposition was not held until 1893). The General Committee on Religious Congresses wanted not only to honor material
progress by building a White City—featuring the new technology of
electric lighting—but also to recognize intellectual achievement.

They conceived a series of meetings that would go beyond agricultural and industrial progress to encompass art, philosophy, labor—and religion. The last was the capstone of the many congresses and the highlight of the entire Columbian Exposition.

The organizers sent three thousand copies of a "preliminary address" worldwide to religious leaders: "We affectionately invite the representatives of all faiths to aid us in presenting to the world, at the Exposition of 1893, the religious harmonies and unities of humanity, and also in showing forth the moral and spiritual agencies which are at the root of human progress."

An advisory committee of several thousand people was soon assembled including Buddhist scholar, Edwin Arnold, Salvation Army General William Booth, British poet Alfred Lord Tennyson, Orientalist Max Muller, and Cornell University President Andrew D. White. If many praised the assembly, some criticized it. The Sultan of Turkey disapproved. The Archbishop of Canterbury could not endorse the "equality of the other intended members and the parity of their positions and claims." Yet many individual Anglican and Episcopal bishops endorsed the effort.

The Parliament began on Sunday, September 11, with 4,000 persons crowding into Chicago's newly built Art Institute on Lake Michigan. Arm-in-arm, representatives of world religions marched down the aisle. Flags of many nations were displayed and the audience cheered. On the stage were seated fifty dignitaries, with the foreign delegates wearing ecclesiastical or national dress. In addition to the many Christians and Jews on the platform, there were seven Buddhists, three Hindus, two Muslims, one Confucian, one Jain, one Shintoist, one "pronounced Theosophist," and one "Idealist." The delegates came primarily from the U.S. and Canada and various parts of Europe, but some from Ceylon, China, India, Japan, and Liberia.

As the Parliament opened at the Hall of Columbus, several miles away at the exposition grounds the new Columbian Liberty Bell rang ten times to honor the ten religions represented. The opening service began with the reading of Jewish scripture, followed by a Christian hymn. James Cardinal Gibbons of Baltimore then led the Lord's Prayer. The official language was English—by the end of the nineteenth century, as a byproduct of British colonialism, many Asian and African religious leaders knew English well.

While the Christian setting was unmistakable, Dr. Charles C. Bonney, as president of the many congresses associated with the exposition, struck the appropriate if pioneering note in his welcoming address: "The very basis of our convocation is the idea that the representatives of each religion sincerely believe that it is the truest and the best of all; that they will, therefore, hear with perfect candor and without fear the convictions of other sincere souls on the great question of the immortal life." He predicted—prematurely, as we now know—that "this day the sun of a new era of religious peace and progress rises over the world, dispelling the dark clouds of sectarian strife."

Then the Rev. John Henry Barrows, chairman of the Parliament, welcomed "O wise men of the East and of the West!" He suggested what, at the time, was a progressive principle of multireligious amity: "Whoever would advance the cause of his own faith must first discover and gratefully acknowledge the truths contained in other faiths."

Then followed a succession of short speeches. The Emperor of China sent a diplomat from his Washington embassy. When the latter was presented, a journalist reported, "men and women rose to their feet in the audience, and there was wild waving of hats and handkerchiefs." Christians from Germany and Russia spoke, as did Hindus from India and a Shintoist from Japan. A monk from Ceylon brought greetings from the world's 475 million Buddhists. A Hindu monk from India, Swami Vivekananda, revealed that in Sanskrit, "the word *exclusion* is untranslatable." He hoped that the bell ringing to open the congress would also toll "the death knell of all fanaticism." A bishop of the African Methodist Episcopal Church welcomed the handful of delegates from Africa on behalf of the 740,000 black people on the North American continent. He reminded the Parliament that, a quarter of a century after Lincoln's Proclamation of Emancipation, "there is not a slave among us today."

Each session opened with a silent prayer, followed by the Lord's Prayer. Four or five papers were read each morning and again each afternoon; sometimes evening meetings had to be added for a third reading. Among the papers presented was one by a Quaker, Aaron M. Powell. He discussed "The Grounds of Sympathy and Fraternity Among Religious Men." He recalled that, among the exhibits at the Columbian Exposition, was the great Krupp gun. He described it as "a marvelous piece of inventive ingenuity," but "absolutely appalling in its possibilities for the destruction of humanity." He predicted that, "if the religious people of the world, whatever their name or form, will unite in a general league against war and resolve to arbitrate all difficulties, I believe that great Krupp gun will, if not preserved for some museum, be literally melted and recast into plowshares and pruning hooks."

The world's press gave immense coverage to the Parliament. Attendance was high during the seventeen days of meetings: an estimated 150,000 persons. Speakers gave their addresses in the Hall of Columbus, then often gave them a second time to an overflow audience in the adjoining Hall of Washington.

Ticket speculators were present outside the final meeting of the Parliament on September 27, where more than 7,000 persons sought admission. Among those on the platform were Julia Ward Howe, author of "Battle Hymn of the Republic," and suffragette Susan B. Anthony. After the hymn "Lead Kindly Light," two dozen speakers participated. A Shinto prayed that "the 8 million deities protecting the beautiful cherry-tree country of Japan may protect you and your government forever." Swami Vivekananda believed the Parliament proved that "holiness, purity, and charity are not the exclusive possession of any one church in the world."

In his closing speech, Chairman Barrows reported a moment during the Parliament when the Ceylonese monk Dharmapala, who was at the top of the giant ferris wheel overlooking the exposition, commented: "All the joys of heaven are in Chicago." His companion, Dr. Alfred Momerie, an English Christian, replied: "I wish I were sure that all the joys of Chicago are to be in heaven!"

Barrows expressed his hope that, as a result of the Parliament, "henceforth the religions of the world will make war, not on each other, but on the giant evils that afflict mankind." Barrow's vision was to be cruelly erased in the twentieth century, which has seen two world wars. Yet the World's Parliament of Religions achieved one of its ten stated purposes: to bring "together in conference, for the first time in history, the leading representatives of the great historic religions of the world."

The Parliament was the culmination of the exposition. When the fair closed its doors shortly after the Parliament adjourned, the *Chicago Tribune* editorialized that Christianity had learned that "there are no longer pagans and heathens." The newspaper went on to bid farewell to "a little ideal world, a realization of Utopia, in which every night was beautiful and every day a festival, in which for the time all thoughts of the great world of toil, of injustices, of cruelty, and of oppression outside its gate disappeared, and in which this fantasy of the artist and the architect seemed to foreshadow some faraway time when all the earth would be as pure, as beautiful, as joyous as the White City itself."

PART **NINE**

MY HEROES

HOMER'S PANTHEON

*"You must endure much grief in silence
standing and facing men in their violence."*
—The Odyssey, Book 13

"We all have heroes," Homer wrote. "Mine have lived mostly during my lifetime. I never met Mohandas Gandhi, but he stands above all human beings of our time." The other dwellers in Homer's Seventh Heaven— Albert Schweitzer, Albert Einstein, and Martin Luther King—are described at length elsewhere in this book. Prophetic and sagacious influences included David Rhys Williams, Eleanor Roosevelt, Roger Baldwin, James Luther Adams, Shinichiro Imouka, Lillian Smith, Bertrand Russell, Andrei Sakharov, and Mother Teresa. Rulers of thrones and principalities Homer greatly admired included Jawaharlal Nehru, Adlai Stevenson, John F. Kennedy, Dana Greeley, and Nikkyo Niwano. Ministers and counselors of church and state—the third and fourth orbits in which he himself largely operated—were Norman Cousins, George Houser, Michael Scott, Bayard Rustin, Philip Noel-Baker, R. R. Diwaker, A. J. Muste, Jayaprakash Narayan, Alfonso Garcia Robles, Donald Harrington, Toshio Miyake, and Reginald Reynolds. Younger or junior associates, including some who made the supreme sacrifice, included James Reeb, various *satyagrahis* and *satyagrahinis*, and Juliette Morgan. Parents, family, friends, parishioners, and the general public constituted the first level.

*Photograph: Adlai Stevenson at the Dedication Ceremony of
the Unitarian Church of Evanston's new building, 1959*

67 HEROES AND MENTORS

Norman Thomas

Norman Thomas, perennial Socialist Party candidate for president, had been a hero of Homer's since childhood. Unlike many childhood idols, Homer not only met Thomas but also got to know him well and work with him in later life.

My first encounter with Norman Thomas occurred when he ran for president of the U.S. in 1932. I was in my senior year in high school. Aged sixteen, I felt Thomas should be president, as did my parents. I remember adorning the front of Monroe High School in Rochester one evening with Thomas-for-President signs. The signs did not last very long after the janitors arrived the next morning!

I may well have heard Norman Thomas speak in Rochester before 1932. My father was a member of the Rochester City Club, chiefly a Saturday luncheon group bringing national speakers to the city. When I got to Cornell in 1933, I also heard Thomas on campus. Some years later, in March 1939 I wrote to a friend: "Norman Thomas was quite in top form, at least I thought so. Perhaps I am a bit prejudiced, for we see eye-to-eye on Russia. Thomas was there a year or so before I was, but our conclusions and disillusionment are identical. I know, for I had the good fortune to discuss politics with him all yesterday afternoon, go to dinner with him, and see him off at the train."

In the 1940s, I must have met Thomas, as I voted for him in 1940, 1944, and 1948. I do remember that he stayed in our parsonage in Evanston in 1954. I recall we went down the street from our home for him to speak to the students at Garrett Theological Seminary. When we returned to the parsonage, a group of journalists were outside the house. Joseph Stalin had died and they wanted to obtain some quotations from Norman Thomas! Thomas was never at a loss for words. He flayed the air with his flapping hands, curled his peculiar tongue, and said something both newsworthy and intelligent. Several years later, in 1958, he spoke at my church on "The Double Standard of Morality." Over 600 persons attended, making it one of the largest—if not the largest—Sunday morning service of my ministry.

In the late 1950s and early 1960s, I saw a good deal of Norman Thomas in New York. We attended national board meetings of the ACLU and worked together at SANE, especially on the campaign against nuclear testing. After the signing of the Partial Test-Ban Treaty in Moscow, I returned to the U.S. and wrote an informal memorandum entitled "The Confessions of an Ex-Anti-Communist." I sent copies of the manuscript—"not for publication in any form"—to fourteen colleagues in the peace and religious community. Two days later Norman Thomas responded. In his four paragraphs, he initially wrote: "I will be blunt and say I appreciate what I think you are trying to say but I also think you could say it better. I am glad that you do not expect to publish this particular document."

Then in a second paragraph, Thomas added: "Did you ever oppose communism because it was revolutionary, rather than because it waged its revolution on somewhat wrong lines? Grant that we ought to be critical of [President Warren G.] Harding as well as Stalin, do you do well to link them? Stalin was carrying out communist dogma; Harding was sinning against the accepted democratic ideals. The philosophical difference is of very considerable importance."

Thomas concluded his letter by admitting that my thinking was "consistent with my general agreement with what I think is your position." He felt, however, that "it should be more carefully and perhaps more deeply explored and expressed." He added that my statement lacked "depth" in its "spiritual thinking."

From the long-time leader of the Socialist movement and master dialectition, I was properly chastised. I never published the manuscript. Perhaps the death of President Kennedy and the resultant turmoil a few weeks later diverted my attention to other problems.

Several years later, I spent a weekend with Thomas in Washington. I led him, half-blind, arthritic, more angular than usual, around a State Department reception. Thomas got into a bitter argument about Vietnam with Dean Rusk, and the Secretary of State left in a huff. Norman Cousins later brought them together at the reception again, and Rusk invited Thomas to drop around at his office the next day. Thomas did, but he was not charmed.

The last time I saw Thomas was in Huntington in a nursing home. We spent almost an hour together that Sunday morning. He asked me how to handle the orthodox clergymen who insisted on seeing him and praying with him. I, a Unitarian Universalist, told Thomas, an erstwhile Presbyterian minister, that it was probably easier to pray than to resist! At his death, a few weeks later, even the President showed sadness. Thomas' big eyes observing Lyndon Johnson eulogizing him would have twinkled, then clouded, and words of righteous indignation would have cascaded from his mouth.

Next to Albert Schweitzer, Norman Thomas made the deepest impression on me of the many great men and women with whom I have been privileged to be associated.

David Rhys Williams

David Rhys Williams, minister of the Unitarian Church of Rochester and Homer's father-in-law, had a profound influence on Homer's career and his development.

I did not plan it that way, but as I gradually witnessed the multifaceted ministerial duties of my father-in-law, I realized that I was more interested in a career in helping people, individually and through movements, than pressing rare species of plants or even doing research in the young field of ecology.

The son and grandson of Welsh-born ministers, David Rhys Williams attended Harvard Divinity School, converted to Unitarianism in his thirties, and became one of the leading social activists of his era. As a pacifist, he served as a noncombatant in France driving an ambulance for the Red Cross during World War I. In the twenties, he served as minister of the Congregational Church in Cleveland and at the Third Unitarian Church in Chicago before being called to Rochester in 1928, where he remained for thirty years (and then becoming minister emeritus for another twelve). He was active in international affairs—especially U.S.-Soviet relations—the labor movement, religious freedom and separation of church and state, the crusade against capital punishment, and world religions.

D.R.W. had a deep, booming voice, a gift of oratory worthy of ancestral Welsh bards, and a keen sense of righteousness. He could recite poetry hour after hour. Many who heard him preach compared him to a Biblical prophet. His prayers and meditations, especially his annual Christmas messages (which Alex later compiled into a booklet) became famous throughout the denomination and were used by many ministers, myself included. At my ordination in Evanston in 1948, he gave my prayer of installation:

> O thou who art the redemptive power in the life of man and human society, who raisest up prophets and teachers and liberators of the people in every age and generation, we invoke a double portion of Thy spirit upon him who has offered himself for the adventurous calling of the ministry.
>
> We pray that the memory of his own brave and civic-minded father may continue to guide his footsteps and sustain his courage. Touch thou his lips with the eloquence of sincere speech. Inflame his soul with a burning passion for truth and righteousness. Vouchsafe to him wisdom to interpret correctly the signs of the times, and insight to see into the deep needs of the human spirit.
>
> May he go in and out among us as a friend to the friendless; as a shepherd to those who have lost their way; as a physician to the mentally and emotionally ill; as a welcome guest in the house of festal joy; as an undiscouraged herald of glad tidings to the hopeless and despairing; as a fearless champion of the despised but noble cause.
>
> May the peace that cometh from truth consecration, and the courage that cometh from singleness of purpose, rest and abide with him and with us all, now and forevermore.

David Rhys Williams' three brothers were also ordained ministers. Albert Rhys Williams, the second eldest, a left-wing journalist in New York, went to Russia in 1917, wrote eyewitness accounts of the Russian Revolution, and became a confidant of Lenin. Only slightly less famous than his colleague, John Reed, Williams' championed the cause of Soviet Socialism throughout his long life and wrote many books on his experiences. The movie *Reds* mentions Albert, and his wife Lucita—who followed him to Russia—appeared as one of the witnesses commenting on the fictional portrayal of those epic days. Howard Rhys Williams, the eldest brother in the Williams' clan, left the ministry after several years and became a businessman in the New York area. In the late 1950s, he became a celebrity on a national quiz show, delighting the audience with his ready wit and razor-sharp mind. Rhys, the youngest brother, died in the pneumonia epidemic during World War I.

The Williams family owned a lovely cottage on Lake Erie near Westfield, N.Y. and for nearly thirty years, Esther and I, and later the children, spent part of each summer there. Grandpa David, as the kids called him, would hold court on the porch, playing checkers, chain-smoking, and reminiscing about the era of Debs and Darrow, Franklin D. Roosevelt and Harry Truman. Lucy Adams Williams, my mother-in-law, also came from an accomplished family, tracing her ancestry to the Adams family in New England. Her parents, hearty Ohio farmers, lived into their late nineties. She served as family historian and was a proficient writer in her own right.

Outside of the social arena and parish concerns, one of the Williams' principal interests was parapsychology. My in-laws were involved in some early psychic experiments at Harvard in the '30s and followed Professor J. B. Rhine's experiments at Duke University with great interest. They held séances, visited trumpet mediums in Lilydale, the spiritualist summer camp near Chatauqua, and were fascinated with the unknown. Partly as a result of his own psychic experiences, David Rhys Williams developed a "Faith Beyond Humanism," as he entitled one of his books.

Like his views on Russia, I did not share my father-in-law's optimism on telepathy and life after death. Nor was I willing to suspend belief in the authenticity of the Shakespearean Canon— D.R.W.'s hobbyhorse in his later years. However, he championed the theory that Christopher Marlowe wrote the plays attributed to Shakespeare, not because of some psychic revelation, but on the grounds that Marlowe was a religious heretic and, to escape impending arrest and certain execution at the stake, faked his own death in a barroom brawl. Will Shakespeare, the actor, then served as a foil for Marlowe who wrote the plays from Italy or somewhere beyond the Alps. Like Sherlock Holmes—though he looked more like Dr. Watson—David Rhys Williams in his later years prowled around ancient English tombstones and manuscript archives in quest of evidence for his hypothesis. Eventually he wrote a small book, *Shakespeare, Thy Name Is Marlowe*, which made out the author of *Hamlet*, *King Lear*, and *Macbeth* to be—in essence—a Unitarian!

Despite these quirks, David Rhys Williams remained a mentor through the years. In 1963, in his mid-seventies and suffering the lingering effects from a heart attack, he and his wife participated in the great March on Washington. I was in the U.S.S.R. when he passed away in 1970. He demonstrated that a minister can be both a social prophet and a parish priest, and at the same time develop an active literary and historical imagination. Outspoken, eloquent, inspired, profound—that was David Rhys Williams.

John Haynes Holmes

John Haynes Holmes (1879-1964), minister of the Community Church in New York, was the foremost Unitarian minister and social activist of his generation. Homer established a lasting association and friendship with Holmes and Holmes recognized Homer's prophetic qualities. "You have proved in New York that you are worthy of the utmost confidence of us all, and thus are rightly headed to a leadership in the Unitarian ministry which will be one of the great sources of influence in our time," Holmes predicted in the early 1950s. Later he wrote, "You were the favorite among the ministers of your generation."

I admired John Haynes Holmes, who in 1922 first introduced Gandhi to the American people. Holmes certainly increased my interest in Gandhi. He wrote the cherished introduction to my *Wit and Wisdom of Gandhi*.

Holmes retired from Community Church on his seventieth birthday, in 1949, the first full year of my own ministry in Evanston. He was a towering figure, not only in our denomination, but in society, and I preached a sermon about him in a series on living philosophers including Schweitzer, Einstein, and John Dewey. Holmes' uncompromising spirit of truth shone through all of his activities and writings. Take this Easter prayer for example:

> There are certain things which are immortal in this world. One is the concept of truth, discovered and proclaimed for the liberation of mankind. You may silence this truth, suppress it, deny it, destroy it; but still, in spite of all, it does not perish. Another is the movement of heroic men and women on behalf of justice, righteousness, and peace on this earth. You may resist this movement, scatter it, persecute it, annihilate it; but still it is carried on into generations yet unborn. Another thing is a soul uncompromising in its ideals and steadfast in the service of those ideals. You may imprison this soul, torture it, kill it, bury it; but it survives, to baffle opposition, and win at last the victory. These are some of the things that can't be removed. The power of eternity dwells within them. Silence, they speak;

kill, they live; buried, they rise again.

In 1953, I had the privilege of serving as summer minister at the Community Church in New York and saw Holmes often. Several years later, when I moved to New York to work in the field of African independence and later SANE, I also saw much of this grand old man. Though he was bent by Parkinson's disease in later life, and had to be wheeled into services at Community Church, his mind remained active and his spirit undaunted.

Adlai E. Stevenson

Adlai Stevenson, Governor of Illinois and twice Democratic presidential candidate, was a fellow Unitarian and longtime friend of Homer.

One of my earliest encounters with Stevenson was at a downstate conference of midwestern Unitarian and Universalist ministers. Along with some fifteen ministers, we stopped off at Springfield, the capital, and were soon closeted with the governor in the executive mansion.

We ministers were interested in fair employment practices, increased state aid to education, and defeating "thought control" bills. Fair employment practices legislation had his active support, and we discussed with him the need for a few more senatorial votes. We spent some time on budgetary problems and he revealed to us the new state budget. (He talked in millions of dollars as our church finance committee talked in hundreds!) Gov. Stevenson was forthright on the civil liberties bills and on the investigation of Roosevelt College and the University of Chicago, and the statement he subsequently released to the press on this inquiry paralleled his conversation with us. All in all, we ministers came out of the governor's mansion greatly pleased with the fellow Unitarian running our state.

I actively supported Stevenson during both of his presidential campaigns, especially his call for a moratorium on nuclear testing by all nations, and covered the 1956 Democratic Convention for newspapers in India. In 1958, Stevenson spoke at the dedication of our new church in Evanston. I introduced him as a "political trinitarian" whom I hoped "once again will seek the presidency." Adlai laughed and responded that "the only thing I am not is a political trinitarian!" In the course of his talk, he said:

I am honored and happy to have this opportunity to share in the dedication of this new church in Evanston. I have known Dr. Homer A. Jack for many years, not only as a Unitarian but also as a citizen. I am happy that I could come here to pay my respects to him and to his congregation on this memorable occasion . . .

A church program, like church architecture, must be responsive to the most searching, functional needs of our contemporary society. I hope the ministers of this country will always speak out their undying hostility to ignorance, to war, and to the afflictions of contemporary society . . .

I would like to congratulate this congregation, speaking of travel, on the way you have encouraged your distinguished minister, Dr. Jack, to roam around the world and to reflect here some of the aspirations of the people, especially the newly-emerging people of Asia and Africa. How he has expressed the aspirations of the underdeveloped people to the overdeveloped suburbs of Chicago! I think this is a wholesome thing and I think of it as an important contribution in this world which is shriveling hour by hour.

It was a great pity, of course, that Stevenson never became president. However, he served with distinction as U.S. Ambassador to the United Nations—which he helped found in 1945 as secretary to the American delegation—under John F. Kennedy, and I occasionally saw him in New York while working for SANE until his death in 1965. Stevenson was a compassionate, eloquent, elegant man with a wry sense of humor; a worthy native son of Illinois and heir to Lincoln; and a prophet on issues of nuclear war and peace.

Jawaharlal Nehru

If Gandhi, Schweitzer, and Einstein constituted the three brightest stars in Homer's firmament, Nehru occupied a throne not far removed from this trinity. Homer met Nehru twice, in Bandung in 1955 and in Belgrade in 1956, reported on his visit to America to talk with President Eisenhower at Gettsyburg in 1956, and corresponded with him until his death in 1964. This essay on Nehru and non-alignment is from an anthology Nehru and His Contributions to World Peace, *edited by R. R. Diwakar, and published during the centenary of Nehru's birth in 1989.*

Few countries of the world could produce a Nehru and a Gandhi within one century. The only other country may have been Germany where both Albert Schweitzer and Albert Einstein were born within four years.

Jawaharlal Nehru, a man of many talents and achievements, was successful both an as architect of national independence, a freedom fighter, and a consolidator of that independence, a nation-builder. He could make a revolution and also build a country. Two of Nehru's peers, Sukarno of Indonesia and Kwame Nkrumah of Ghana, succeeded brilliantly as nationalists, but both failed when they became heads of state or government. Nehru was successful before the independence of India and also afterwards.

During the years when Nehru was prime minister of India, he became a world statesman. His achievements in this field were many. He was the father of the nuclear test-ban movement which resulted in the Partial Test-Ban Treaty of 1963. He was one of the founders of the Bandung movement which resulted, if indirectly, in the establishment of a Third World caucus in the United Nations system known as the Group of 77. He was also one of the architects of the non-aligned movement which still remains a formidable force in the world community.

Non-alignment goes back at least to the Greek city-states. In our time, the term "non-alignment" may first have appeared, according to the dictionary, in 1934. However, the 1976 supplement to the *Oxford English Dictionary* indicates that the word appeared in the *Times* of London of May 5, 1955—a few weeks after the Bandung Conference was held. Yet Jawaharlal Nehru used the concept, if not the full term, as early as September 1945. In a broadcast some months before the independence of India, Nehru declared: "We propose, as far as possible, to keep away from the power politics of groups, aligned against one another, which have led in the past to two world wars and which may again lead to disasters on an ever vaster scale." Here was a fully developed concept, gained from Nehru's experience with pre-war colonialism and World War II, and in the political environment emerging after that war. Non-alignment evolved in Nehru's mind as a practical necessity for national survival in a post-colonial world where institutions of imperialism died slowly, not as an intellectual luxury concocted by exiled freedom fighters in Brussels, London, or Paris.

Talking to the Constituent Assembly after Indian freedom in December 1947, Nehru reminded the delegates that "we have proclaimed during the past year that we will not attach ourselves to any particular group." He added that he had "nothing to do with neutrality or passivity or anything else." "We have sought to avoid," Nehru declared, "foreign entanglements by not joining one bloc or the other." He admitted that the result had been that "neither of these big blocs looks on us with favor" and indeed they think of us as "undependable, because we cannot be made to vote this way or that way."

In June 1952, Nehru in a debate in the Indian Parliament used the word "non-align," three years earlier than recorded in the 1976 edition of the *Oxford English Dictionary*: "So far as our policy is concerned . . . we [India] have not swerved at all from our non-alignment with any group."

Another step Nehru took in getting from Brussels to Belgrade was in March/April 1947 when he convened, even before Indian independence, delegates from twenty-eight Asian nations. The Asian Relations Conference attracted representatives of both aligned and non-aligned Asian nations, many from Soviet Asia. Nehru managed to bring Gandhi twice to these meetings. Gandhi urged, on April 1, 1947, that such meetings of Asians be held "regularly" and hoped that the delegates came together not to "wage war against Europe, against America, or against non-Asiatics." The next day Gandhi told these Asian leaders that "the message of Asia . . . is not to be learned through the Western spectacles by imitating the atom bomb." He asked them to go home "with the thought that Asia has to conquer the West through love and truth." With this admonition, the delegates dispersed to their homes all over Asia. Within a year, Gandhi was assassinated.

Jawaharlal Nehru did not easily agree to participate, let alone sponsor, the Asian-African Conference in Bandung, Indonesia, in 1955. He was juggling many international issues, including souring relations with the United States, delicate overtures to China, and always difficult problems with Pakistan. Also the Indo-China crisis remained volatile. Yet Nehru became slowly convinced that an Asian-African meeting, if it would not be confined to U.N. members, and if it would focus on major and not regional issues, might be very useful.

Jawaharlal Nehru was one of the founders of Bandung as well as one of its shining stars. His only rival at the conference was Chinese Prime Minister Zhou Enlai, although Col. Gamal Abdel Nasser of Egypt received much publicity since it was the first international gathering he attended. Nehru made no plenary address but spoke often in the closed committee meetings. He once observed: "I belong to neither [bloc] and I propose to belong to neither whatever happens in the world. If we have to stand alone, we will stand by ourselves, whatever happens . . . and we propose to face all consequences."

In his closing address to the Bandung Conference, Nehru reverted to the non-aligned theme: "If we are camp followers of Russia or America or any other country of Europe, it is, if I may say so, not very credible to our dignity, our new independence, our new freedom, our new spirit, and our new self-reliance."

After the Bandung Conference, President Tito of Yugoslavia invited Nehru and Nasser in July 1954 to his island of Brionai for political discussions. Yugoslavia was not, as a European nation, invited to Bandung, but during this period Tito was developing his own foreign policy and maintaining a dialogue with his peers. In 1960, Tito, Nehru, and Nasser met again at the opening of the fifteenth session of the U.N. General Assembly in New York. Kwame Nkrumah of Ghana and President Sukarno of Indonesia joined them in discussing the mounting Soviet-American tensions. Tito began advocating a meeting of non-aligned states.

The Non-Aligned Summit opened on September 1, 1961, in Belgrade. At Belgrade, the twenty-five nations staked out positions of non-alignment in the post-colonial world where the two superpowers were competing for supremacy. The definition of non-alignment was not perfectly made, nor was it easily accepted by outside sceptics and critics. Nehru succeeded in deflecting attention at the meeting from continuing colonial problems. As Professor Sarvepalli Gopal has written: "Nehru wrested the Conference out of the old ruts of ritual opposition to colonialism, imperialism, and racism and forced it to face the danger of nuclear warfare." Indeed, the Conference composed and issued an Appeal to Peace, with Nehru and Nkrumah immediately afterwards visiting Secretary Khrushchev in Moscow, and Sukarno and President Keita of Mali visiting President Kennedy in Washington. The Conference also discussed a list of substantive world and regional issues and demanded a strengthened United Nations.

Nehru, Tito, Nasser, and the other leaders may or may not have fully realized the magnitude of the movement and indeed the institution they created at Belgrade. Nehru died only three years later, although preparations were already under way to convene the Second Non-Aligned Summit at Cairo in October 1964 and since then eight others have been held through the 1980s.

Despite many disappointments, including the failure to stop its own members from joining the nuclear club, the non-aligned movement for almost three decades prevented the further polarization of a bipolar world into pro-Washington or pro-Moscow allies. It gave legitimacy to the new nations, or old ones, which preferred to be independent and unlabeled politically. The non-aligned movement gave much impetus to the process of decolonization. Credit must be given to the political forces unleashed by the Second World War and the rise of the United Nations, but the non-aligned helped greatly to lessen colonialism in our time. The non-aligned movement insisted that nuclear disarmament remain on the top of the world's agenda.

The non-aligned movement has become the best protector and defender of the United Nations system. The members of the non-aligned—mostly small states, but also some big ones such as India and Nigeria—need the world organization. The non-aligned, as the largest caucus in the United Nations, have come to dominate the U.N. agenda and, in the General Assembly, sometimes its voting patterns. Indeed, the U.N. caucus may be currently the most effective arm of the non-aligned movement.

The polycentrism in the world community emerging during the past decades has cast some doubt on the future of the non-aligned movement. When there were only two superpowers, both searching for clients or allies and when new nations were being born almost every month, the need for a "third force" seemed clear and welcome. Yet now that there are a third and a fourth and a fifth, and more, centers of economic and political power, non-alignment becomes a more politically complex choice. What happens when some of the non-aligned states, such as India, are also these new powers? Also when Beijing split with Moscow, non-alignment for some nations was to refuse to identify, not with Washington or Moscow, but with Beijing or Moscow. Today, with *glasnost* and the approaching end of the Cold War, it is not clear that non-alignment will survive in a less polarized world.

Once Jawaharlal Nehru, while alive, proposed his own epitaph. He diffidently suggested: "If any people choose to think of me, then I should like them to say, 'This was a man who, with all his mind and heart, loved India and the Indian people. And they, in turn, were indulgent to him and gave him of their love most abundantly and extravagantly." On the occasion of Nehru's birth centenary, it seems appropriate to internationalize and universalize this epitaph: "This is a man who loved the Asian and African peoples."

Michael Scott

Michael Scott was an Anglican priest and outspoken opponent of apartheid in South Africa. Homer wrote this tribute following his death in 1983.

Michael Scott was a man of all seasons. He towered as a saint among many more fragile NGOs. I first met Michael in London in April 1952, some years after he was thrown out of South Africa for identifying with the Africans and Indians in their growing opposition to the separation of races there in the late 1940s.

Returning to London, Michael became part of the very center of Africa work in the British capital. He organized the African Bureau. He helped petitioners during the 1950s when the African freedom decade was just unfolding. He associated with Fenner Brockway, Reginald Sorenson, Bertrand Russell, and Colin Legum. He haunted the vestibule of the House of Commons and wrote in the pages of the *London Observer*.

Michael Scott often came to U.N. headquarters in New York, representing the Herero people in Southwest Africa before any of them could escape and represent themselves. They collected shillings on the desert sand and sent Michael to New York to speak in their behalf. He came to headquarters once or twice a year since 1947, for decades. He haunted the Fourth Committee, the Council on Namibia, and the Special Committee Against Apartheid, and became the best-known white foe of colonialism. Scott was the kind of man who was also ousted, once, from India, for siding with the Nagas, the tribal people on India's borders.

I had the privilege of being with Michael, not only here at the U.N. but in various parts of the world. I saw him sit down, with Bertrand Russell, in London's Trafalgar Square against nuclear arms in the early 1960s. I saw him at Kwame Nkrumah's Ban the Bomb Congress at Accra, Ghana, in 1961, after having tried to prevent the French from testing atomic weapons in the Sahara.

I was with him at the First Summit of the Non-Aligned Movement at Belgrade in 1961. One of my favorite memories of Michael was at this conference when both of us had an appointment with Prime Minister Nehru. The Indian leader came from a meeting and sat with us on a bench, talking to Scott about India and to me about nuclear matters. I saw Michael in Louvain, Belgium, in August 1974 as he met with representatives of various world religions to discuss disarmament, development, and the eternal fight against apartheid and for the freedom of the Namibia people.

Michael was a sweet person, always thinking the best of persons and ideas. But he was also determined, persistent, despite indifferent health. He always brought out the best in men—and women. In his thread-bare clothes, his turned-around clerical collar, always askew, Michael brought out the mother instinct in dozens of women. Broken hearts for Michael can be found all along U.N. Plaza. He never married, but he was wed to a church which never fully appreciated his Christ-like courage.

The last time I saw Michael was last spring, coming into the NGO Lounge at the U.N. He went to the old manual typewriter in the corner and worked on his testimony. Now that typewriter is stilled. But generations to come will hear, and admire, the legend of Michael Scott.

Norman Cousins

Norman Cousins' career as a writer and peace activist went through a major transformation in the early 1980s. The Saturday Review *which he had edited for many years came under new ownership and he developed a debilitating disease—which he overcame with unconventional methods and led him to write* The Anatomy of an Illness. *Moving to the West Coast, Cousins became a professor at UCLA Medical School and wrote increasingly on the mind-body connection, as well as social issues. Homer saw little of him in the '70s and '80s, but collaborated with him in trying to end the war in the Persian Gulf. When Cousins died on November 30, 1990, age seventy-five, Homer gave the following tribute at a SANE/Freeze banquet in New York two weeks later.*

In the mid-1950s, the forty-year-old editor of the *Saturday Review*, Norman Cousins, maintained a significant friendship and correspondence with the sixty-six-year-old Prime Minister of India, Jawaharlal Nehru. In 1954, Nehru was the first statesman to demand a moratorium on nuclear weapons tests, just a month after "the ashes of death" from American tests over Bikini fell on Japanese fishermen. Cousins and Nehru reinforced each other's insistent demands for the end of nuclear testing.

In January 1957 Cousins went to Lambaréné, then French Equatorial Africa, to visit Albert Schweitzer. I myself had visited Schweitzer five years earlier and found the latter to be a typical, tongue-tied European professor, living in the jungle, and silent on urgent world issues. Even after he received the Nobel Peace Prize in 1954 for his general humanitarianism, Schweitzer hesitated to speak out.

Yet during Cousins' short visit, the forty-two-year-old editor-critic motivated the eighty-two-year-old physician-musician. Cousins had that persuasive magic. Within three months, Schweitzer gave his Declaration of Conscience against atomic testing over Radio Oslo. This sparked a world-wide campaign against testing. A few months later, Schweitzer generously wrote to Cousins: "You tried to convince me that I should speak in regard to atomic weapons. Before, others had talked to me, asked me to do so, without my being able to make a decision. Then you came and asked me the same and it impressed me. So it was you who made me do it, to take up the word for the cause."

In this same year, 1957, Cousins with Clarence Pickett, head of the American Friends Service Committee, established the National Committee for a Sane Nuclear Policy, aided by Norman Thomas, Erich Fromm, Lenore Marshall, and many others. An advertisement, written wholly by Norman Cousins, inserted in the November 15 issue of the *New York Times*, was boldly entitled, "We are facing a danger unlike any danger that has ever existed." Yet this single ad created a movement, one which remains active today.

Over six years the international and U.S. anti-nuclear movements kept pressure on President John Kennedy and Secretary Nikita Khrushchev to complete a treaty. Cousins became the confidant of President Kennedy on this issue and shuttled among Secretary Khrushchev, Pope John XXIII, and the White House, especially in 1962 and 1963. This brought a temporary end to the Cold War of that period and, only months later, the Partial Test-Ban Treaty was signed and ratified. This collaboration of Cousins with Kennedy was truncated, as so much else, by the assassination of the President only a few weeks after the test-ban treaty entered into force.

Cousins was a person of many talents and sparked many humanitarian projects. During the past month, it was my privilege to collaborate once more with Norman Cousins. We worked on a public statement on the Gulf Crisis. I close by reading a sentence Cousins insisted be included in that statement: "The need to develop mechanisms of world law through the United Nations remains the greatest single challenge of a civilized world society."

Lillian Smith

Lillian Smith's novels and books on race relations in the South—
Forbidden Fruit, Killers of the Dream, *and* Now Is the Time—*sold
millions of copies and were translated all over the world. On a visit to her
home on Screamer Mountain, overlooking Clayton, Georgia, in 1957,
Homer profiled this amazing woman.*

Of the half-dozen symbols of integration in the South during
the decade before the U.S. Supreme Court school decisions in the
mid-1950s, Lillian Smith of Clayton, Georgia, was the most outstanding. For twenty years and more she worked openly against
segregation, while the Faulkners, the McGills, the Cohns, and the
Carters were silent or, at best, "separate-but-equalers."

Miss Smith was, of course, grateful for the initial Supreme
Court decision outlawing segregation in the public schools. She is
doubtful, however, of the wisdom of the court's own implementation of its decision. "I am by no means sure I am right—it is a complex situation—but I feel the psychological moment to have begun
desegregation was immediately after the first decision, since the initial reaction of many Southerners was a good one," she says. "There
was one golden month when Southern people would have yielded
to reason and conscience."

While many liberals, Northern and Southern, are today striking
tragic poses about the South, Miss Smith is unusually hopeful. She
sees the South, since the Supreme Court's last school decision, as
not apathetic but activated—"activated by the germinal idea of human dignity, its meaning to a man's soul and mind as well as to his
body." She hears the South talking, and talk is good for people, she
says; it tends to bring about change, for better or for worse. What
troubles her is that the angry, hating, frightened people are doing
most of the talking. "Negroes working for integration can get a
hearing in the national press and weeklies; but a white Southerner
who works for integration—well, how many of them have you
heard on television networks?" she laughed and added: "You see, a
Negro working against segregation is working for his freedom; a
Southern white working against segregation is working 'against the
white race,' against Southern custom, sometimes against old family
beliefs. People actually look with suspicion on such a person, doubly so on a woman."

Miss Smith affirms that more people today are speaking out for segregation than for integration. Those who basically believe in de-segregation are afraid of breaking the old taboo of silence. She acknowledges that the curtain of silence is stronger than the wall of actual segregation. As she pointed out in her *Killers of the Dream*, it has always been quite acceptable in the South to cross over the segregation line "if you don't leave any footprints." "Break segregation in fantasy and act," she says, "but as long as you deny you do it, you can convince yourself and your region that maybe you have not." She smiled and added: "I love my region and my people, but they are like the Irish: complicated and lovable, exasperating and illogical, yearning to be good and aching to be bad, and overflowing with fantasies. That is why I like to write about them."

Southern churchwomen, she said, have been speaking out for twenty years—at first only against lynching, but then against discrimination in jobs and voting, and now against the whole system of segregation. Miss Smith believes that the white women of the South speak out much more openly than do the men "not because they have less to risk in personal security, but because their dignity as women was more injured by the white supremacy system, by the tradition of concubinage which became quite widespread during slavery days and afterward."

Miss Smith urges Northerners to work out their own problems. She thinks that racism is easier to fight in the North. When Northerners fight discrimination they are at worst opposing their neighbors; when Southerners fight segregation "they are opposing their own mothers and fathers, often, and their own childhood memories."

She considers love and nonviolence especially powerful weapons in the South, where violence is feared by whites as much as by Negroes. "The Montgomery Negroes have succeeded in keeping the protest on a higher level than I had thought possible," she said. This kind of fighting, she feels, is not fighting but growing; and the Negroes in the South are growing—in hope and confidence and in gaining objectivity. Brave they have always been: "They have quietly endured, and the wiser ones have conquered hate."

Lillian Smith is still the best symbol of integration in the entire South, even though her voice at the moment has been muted because of cancer. "Nobody should dare speak 'for the South,'" she concluded. "The wisest of us can only speak about what is on our mind and heart, what we have learned from our own personal experience and from our study. A writer's strength and validity lie in listening to that small, quiet voice within and speaking its words truly. That is the best we can do. And only this way can each of us find a small fragment of the truth."

Alan Paton

Author of Cry, The Beloved Country *and a practicing Anglican, Paton became the symbol of white opposition to apartheid in South Africa. Homer wrote this brief profile in 1986, before significant changes in Pretoria's racial policies.*

Alan Paton was a white social worker in South Africa, born there, who became the director of a boy's reformatory. The tragedies he experienced there he put into memorable cadences and this became *Cry, The Beloved Country,* published in 1948. He became, in our time, the most famous writer in or from South Africa. Paton entered the political arena and became head of the Liberal Party.

I knew Alan in the 1950s and later. My most vivid memory is going out with him to Kennedy Airport in New York in the early 1960s. We were kept for hours by fog and he was a troubled man. He knew that he would face the lifting of his passport the minute he returned to Johannesburg. It was lifted and almost a decade passed before he was able to leave South Africa again.

Today, Paton is in his eighties, and not at all as radical as he was. Indeed, he wrote an op-ed article in the *New York Times* 13 months ago opposing American divestment of stocks in companies doing business with South Africa. Listen to Alan Paton: "I do not think that damaging our economy will help us to do better . . . I, as a Christian, will have nothing to do with disinvestment. To believe that disinvestment will bring our Government 'to its knees' is to believe nonsense." I repeat the words of my friend, Alan Paton, even if I do not agree with him on this issue.

Desmund Tutu

Among black South African leaders, for thirty years Homer knew Oliver Tambo, the longtime president of the outlawed African National Congress. He met Nelson Mandela, the acknowledged leader of the Africans and future president, at a WCRP gathering in Tokyo in the late 1980s. In this vignette, he describes Desmund Tutu, the spiritual leader of the African people.

Desmund Tutu, Anglican bishop of Johannesburg, was just elected Archbishop of the Anglican Church in all South Africa. I first met Tutu in the halls of the U.N. when he and I were both giving testimony before the U.N. Special Committee Against Apartheid. He has become the outstanding spokesman of the church in South Africa against racial separation. In August, 1984, my wife Ingeborg and I were with him at Nairobi when our World Conference on Religion and Peace held its fourth Assembly.

Archbishop Tutu was dynamic, yet mild. A few months later he was given the Nobel Peace Prize. Even then, he privately advocated disinvestment. He did not advocate it publicly at the time because it was against the law for any African resident to do so. However, Tutu shortly went public in his feeling that the world must pull its companies out of South Africa, even if the African people, his people, might initially suffer because of this withdrawal. Is Tutu radical? He must run fast, for events not to pass him by, as racial violence continues to grow in the African townships.

Reginald Reynolds

Reginald Reynolds was a world citizen and peace and human rights activist, who was born in China, grew up in Australia, traveled to India, and lived on and off in Britain. Homer wrote this appreciation of him in December 1958.

I had not known Reginald Reynolds long, but he made me feel that I knew him well. We first met on a train, preposterously in dust-ridden Kansas, in June 1956, en route to an institute of the American Friends Service Committee. We talked about so many mutual friends and so many mutual loves—chiefly India—that we almost rode past our destination, Topeka. Within an hour, Reginald was speaking to a group of hard-headed (and hard-hearted) American businessmen. He mixed enough humor with his revolutionary ideas that these American executives were rolling in the aisles with laughter—and asking for more. We don't have enough humorists in the peace movement to lose Reg so easily!

I met Reg again in London in 1957. We had supper in a little Indian restaurant near his basement flat in Chelsea. Again our conversations were largely about India, and mainly about Gandhi. As he saw me off on the bus, he shouted, "And where shall we see each other again?" Although Reg was especially mobile in an increasingly mobile world, neither of us realized at the time that in less than six weeks we would be together half way around the world—in Tokyo—at the Third World Conference Against A and H Bombs.

Reg was on the preparatory commission and later had charge of publicity. He was intrigued more by the Japanese way of life than by the taut ideological battles. He did mutter how he discovered that he was brought from England by the secretariat so the Japanese government would allow them to bring in a delegate from China! But Reg did his assigned work, tearing his hair at the translations. He was never too busy or too exasperated to be unable to slip away, towel on shoulder, for a bath—somewhere. And he did introduce my twelve-year-old son to the Tokyo YMCA pool.

As Reg prepared to take the slow boat from Tokyo to London—he preferred this to flying—and I to take the plane to America, we asked each other, "And where will we meet each other next?" Alas, we never did, for when I reached London on December 1, Reg was already in Australia. I received a letter from him some months ago agreeing with my general conclusions about the Japan Conference, but he wiped his hands of all international conferences. Reg was not an organizational man.

When Reg was resting in my home in Evanston for a few days in June 1956 we read that the Indians were about to change the names of some of their streets. Professor Amiya Chakravarty also happened to be at the house at the time, and the three of us wrote a letter to several Indian newspapers suggesting that if the English street names go, one English name should be added: C. F. Andrews, one of Gandhi's associates. Our letters, we heard later, were printed, but we never did hear if our suggestions bore fruit. Now that Reg is gone, I think there is another name which should be remembered in India after those of the viceroys are forgotten. A tiny Reynolds Lane in Ahmedabad would be far more fitting than a huge obituary in the *Times*.

Philip Noel-Baker

Philip Noel-Baker, winner of the 1959 Nobel Peace Prize, was a British MP, Olympic athlete, and longtime peace activist. Homer worked with him intermittently from 1957 to 1982—in the halls of Parliament in London, in Belgium, Greece, Ghana, Hiroshima, and at the U.N. These remarks are from a longer tribute Homer delivered at Haverford College in 1989 celebrating the centenary of Noel-Baker's birth.

Philip John Baker was born in London on November 1, 1889, one of seven children of Joseph Allen and Elizabeth Baker. His father came from a Quaker family which settled in Canada from Ireland and his mother was the daughter of a Scotch clergyman. Philip grew up in London. In 1906 his parents sent him, age seventeen, to Haverford College for one year. Then Philip went to Kings College, Cambridge University, from 1908 to 1912. World War I broke out and, age twenty-five, Philip joined the Friends Ambulance Unit to accompany the British Expeditionary Force to France. There he met Irene Noel and they were married in England in June 1915.

Philip Noel-Baker was a life-long athlete. He was also a long-time promoter and defender of athletics. He once wrote that "there is no reason why athletics and intelligence should become divorced in the general mind." Philip was a runner—and an organizer. He won forty-two races for Kings College. He also arranged for Oxford and Cambridge to run against Harvard and Yale. He joined the British team for the Stockholm Olympics in 1912. He ran the 1,500 meter event and, before a tremendous crowd, allowed his Oxford teammate to forge ahead and win. Philip recalled: "I made him run with me and I got him to the right place for the last lap and he won the gold medal. I was sixth and very pleased to be sixth because I beat four Americans." Much later he also wrote: "I left the sunlit Swedish capital with a deep conviction that international sport and the Olympic movement could become a mighty instrument for making all nations understand that they belong to one Society with common interests, common hopes, and common aims."

After World War I, Philip ran again, at the Antwerp Olympics in 1920 and won a silver medal. Philip regarded sport as part of culture, especially after witnessing, with anguish, a whole generation killed in the world war. He wrote: "To lots of people running means more than any game or any sport. It is on a plane with the great forms of art . . . It has dramatic power that nothing else has; it brings in qualities of spirit that are beyond any price. And what makes it most important is that it is so simple that its appeal is universal."

At war's end, Joseph Allen Baker, just before his death, introduced his son to Lord Robert Cecil, who was forming a League of Nations section at the British Foreign Office. Philip was asked to join the section and in 1919—aged thirty—accompanied Lord Cecil to the Paris Peace Conference. He was joint secretary of the Commission, of which U.S. President Woodrow Wilson and Lord Cecil were principal members, to draw up the Covenant of the League of Nations. Philip was also a member of the Preparatory Commission for the United Nations in 1945, and was one who insisted that the new U.N. be linked to the old League. The constant, at times almost uncritical, devotion which Philip gave to both the League and the U.N. forms the matrix for his more focused concern and activity with disarmament in both international, intergovernmental organizations. The League of Nations in 1924 first called for the convening of a Disarmament Conference, but the political atmosphere was problematic, and it was delayed year after year. Noel-Baker managed to become a member of the British team preparing for the Conference. He then became aid to Arthur Henderson who became president of the sixty-four-nation conference which managed to convene first in Paris in 1931. Philip was also active in England, Austria, and elsewhere, seeking popular, public support. The failure of the League's Disarmament Conference in 1934 was crushing to the hopes of Noel-Baker and, as he later wrote, "the turning-point at which Hitler's war begun." Noel-Baker tried to stave off that war, moving easily for years across Europe.

World War II broke out in 1939 and Noel-Baker's Quakerism was under tension. He was an ardent supporter of collective security through the failing League of Nations to the very outbreak of war and then went along with his Labor Party in joining the war. He did not oppose Churchill; indeed, after two years, he became a member of Churchill's wartime, coalition cabinet, as Minister of Transport. Before the war's end, Philip was drafting plans for the new United Nations. In 1958 his great book, *The Arms Race*, was published—dedicated to his late wife—and the next year he received the Nobel Peace Prize, notably for disarmament. He gave much of the considerable stipend to the U.N. Association of the U.K. for a popular disarmament campaign. He circled the earth promoting disarmament.

Not a conscientious objector to World War II, Noel-Baker showed in the 1950s and 1960s, and subsequently, that he was also not a unilateralist. He believed in large steps of multilateral disarmament, entered into by agreement, by many countries. He parted company with some of us on both sides of the Atlantic who were willing to accept, however reluctantly, smaller steps, such as the Partial Nuclear Test-Ban Treaty of 1963. I remember sharp differences with Philip Noel-Baker on this issue, but he always possessed style and good taste; he was never bitter.

In his Nobel lecture, Noel-Baker asked: "In the age when the atom has been split, the moon encircled, diseases conquered, is disarmament so difficult a matter that it must remain a distant dream?" He then added, "To answer 'Yes' is to despair of the future of mankind."

A self-styled "congenital disarmer," Noel-Baker repeated his disarmament themes before the First and Second U.N. Special Sessions on Disarmament at New York. At the second, in 1982, he was at ninety-two years half blind, half deaf, unable to walk. No matter, friends wheeled him everywhere at U.N. Headquarters.

How to sum up the life and legacy of Philip Noel-Baker? For seventy-five years he was the right person at the right place and at the right time, yet he was never the top person. He always ran second. Perhaps he was too self-effacing, too gentlemanly, too intellectual, too optimistic, too restrained, indeed too much of a Quaker.

Philip Noel-Baker was a politician enough to get repeatedly elected to Commons. Yet he was preoccupied with issues, not tactics. He could not resist an intellectual or political challenge, whether at the Olympic track, in Parliament, or in Whitehall. He often failed, but he usually rationalized the failure with an "if only"—if only certain statesmen acted differently, things could have turned out better. If only public opinion had been mobilized, the failing League of Nations might have been saved and World War II averted.

For these, and other, reasons, Philip Noel-Baker never stayed for long in the inner circles of the British Labor Party. He was chairman of the Labor Party, but only briefly. He was a member of Churchill's wartime coalition cabinet, but only briefly. He was in the cabinet of several labor governments, but never as foreign minister—a task he especially hoped for. Always others quickly took his place, often pushed him aside. Noel-Baker was part of the history of much of the twentieth century, but seldom a prime maker of history. In fairness, this historical judgment must be made.

But there is one important exception—and that is his Nobel Peace Prize. None of his contemporaries received the prize, not Churchill, not Attlee, not Nehru. Indeed, Philip was the first Britisher to receive the prize since Lord Cecil and Arthur Henderson, two close colleagues who received the award almost a quarter of a century earlier. Noel-Baker received the prize when he was sixty-nine years, but made the most of that prize, using the prestige of a peace laureate to circle the globe to lobby for disarmament. A noble man without the prize, Noel-Baker, through the award, became truly immortal.

Philip Noel-Baker's legacy is sports-for-peace and comprehensive, total disarmament, the latter within the matrix of collective security and world law. Beyond this legacy, he adhered to one princi-

509

ple. He believed in large, imaginative steps in anything he undertook; perhaps he learned this from his Olympic experience. I can no better illustrate this principle than to conclude with two paragraphs appearing within Noel-Baker's long address given in Oslo when he received the Nobel Prize:

> Some people honestly believe that small steps will be much easier to take than large ones. They quote proverbs to support their point—the crude English: "Don't bite off more than you can chew"; the elegant French: "The better is the enemy of the good"; the Russian: "The slower you ride, the further you go." Well, in Russia I should have thought it would depend on whether you had a pack of wolves howling hungrily at your horses' heels. We have a pack of wolves, the modern weapons, howling at our heels.
>
> I prefer the words of our great economist and political thinker, John Stuart Mill: "Against a great evil, a small remedy does not produce a small result; it produces no result at all." [The saying was on the title page of Noel-Baker's book on the arms race!] I prefer the saying of Lloyd George: "The most dangerous thing in the world is to try to leap a chasm in two jumps." There is a chasm, a great gulf, between the armed world of today and the disarmed world which we must have on some near tomorrow.

Benjamin Spock

In the chapter on SANE, Homer described how in 1962 he influenced Dr. Spock to join the peace movement. In this reminiscence, he describes his later involvement with Spock during the Vietnam War era.

By 1964, SANE began to shift from affirmation of nuclear disarmament to opposition to the Vietnam War. The tactics of the organization in its opposition split the National Committee of SANE. Benjamin Spock was highly involved in this split. Indeed, he was beginning to work with other organizations on several social issues—in addition to disarmament and the Vietnam War—and using less conventional methods of opposition, including civil disobedience. He wrote in his autobiography, "I had no idea, when I joined SANE in 1962 that I would become a full-time opponent of a war." He also revealed that he had no idea that this would lead him

"to becoming a spokesman for an anti-war movement, to civil disobedience, and to indictment for a federal crime."

Spock became increasingly outspoken against the "conservative" stance of SANE and especially its National Committee. The
struggle within SANE—and indeed the whole growing anti-war
movement in America—on tactics against the Johnson Administration and how to win over the majority of the American people became bitter. Early on, SANE was very much in the tactical middle.
In the end, Cousins and Spock resigned from SANE's Board. As a
Board member (now based in Boston, working for the Unitarian
Universalist Association), I stayed. Donald Keys, my successor as
executive director of SANE, opposed what he called Spock's "ecumenical promiscuity." In retrospect Keys recalled that he "feared
Ben's isolating himself, and feared that he would become a messian-
ic leader of a forlorn and radically irrelevant left."

Spock was always a gentleman and reserved for his 1989 autobiography such comments as "the SANE National Committee had a
relatively conservative majority" who "originally selected themselves." He added: "I thought the standoffishness toward other
groups was dead wrong. The peace movement was a popular
movement, not a country club in which you felt entitled to blackball
other people." He wrote that, for a meeting on SANE policy toward
working with other groups, Keys and I "rallied people who hadn't
been to meetings in years" and "there was a motion to remove me
that didn't quite pass." He admitted that "the conservatives certainly felt very hostile toward me." Though we differed at times, when I
left the organization, Ben wrote: "I'll miss you badly when you
leave SANE as all the rest will too. You've done a terrific job—for
the record!"

I witnessed the radicalization of Dr. Spock. He realized his drift
and wrote in 1989, "I'm politically as radical as ever." But not in the
early 1960s! This personal radicalization of a strong-willed, independent personality I recalled having seen within the SANE organization before—in Linus Pauling a few years earlier.

In 1992, in a commentary for public television, I was asked
what I thought about the development of Dr. Spock since my persuasive letter to him in 1962—thirty years earlier. I honestly replied
that I was both pleased and sad. Much of my life was devoted to
making the American peace movement more acceptable to the
American people. I never felt that civil disobedience was unrespect-
able, and I never opposed Spock for getting arrested for any good
cause. (My son was part of the "conspiracy" which led Spock to a

federal indictment!) But I increasingly felt that while Spock knew the development of eight-year-old children, he never appreciated the annual trauma of eight-year-old liberal organizations.

SANE's parents, some active since 1957, admittedly wanted to create a middle class, indeed bourgeois movement. I increasingly felt that Spock in the late 1960s was running with the wrong crowd in opposing the Vietnam War. He preferred the tactics of Sidney Peck of Cleveland to those of Sanford Gottlieb of Washington, and of lawyer Leonard Boudin to lawyer David Riesman. His associates were not, I felt at the time, persons who could change America's mind on the Vietnam War. Today, I am less sure than I was in 1965-75. Perhaps all approaches to opposing the Vietnam War were needed; on the other hand, perhaps I was correct then. At least these were my musings in trying to evaluate Dr. Spock several decades later. In any case, I had but a very minor and modest part in politicizing Spock, none in radicalizing him. I felt vindicated when, at the very end of his autobiography, Spock asserts that "disarmament is part of child care, not only in avoiding annihilation but in freeing up money for facilities for children—and their parents."

Dana McLean Greeley

Dana Greeley, Homer's colleague, associate, and co-worker for peace for nearly thirty years, was scheduled to preach at Homer's installation at the Lake Shore Unitarian Universalist Society in Winnetka. However, owing to treatment for cancer, he was unable to attend. Homer delivered these remarks on Dana at a service on April 1, 1984.

I have known Dana since 1956—for more than a quarter of a century. I was a member of his staff as Director of the Division of Social Responsibility in the last six years of his eleven years as president of our denomination. I cherished those years at 25 Beacon Street. Under Dana's humane and creative leadership, it was the golden age of the modern denomination. Then for an additional thirteen years, I worked with him closely, since he was the chief American officer, and inspiration, of the World Conference on Religion and Peace.

We have marched together in Selma and Washington. We have been together in Beijing and Nairobi. We were in Saigon arguing with Gen. Westmoreland and at the State Department imploring Secretary Dean Rusk. We have been together with Martin Luther

King, Jr., and, at different times, with Albert Schweitzer. We have visited together small Unitarian churches in southern Mississippi and the southern Philippines.

Yet in some ways, I am not the person to make this appreciation. I did not know Dana at all for most of his life, and only casually until the mid-1950s. Also I have been so close to him that I have no distance, little perspective, almost no criticism.

Dana was a fifth generation Unitarian. His grandfather recalled, in his boyhood, how he sat in the pew back of Henry Wadsworth Longfellow in the First Parish Church in Portland, Maine. As a matter of fact, Dana was born at eleven o'clock on a Sunday morning. How could be not be a preacher?

His family lived in Lexington, Mass., and his father was an architect. (His New England accent remains to this day.) Dana graduated from Harvard in 1931 and continued at Harvard Divinity, with a B.D. in 1933. He was married to Deborah Webster and they have four daughters. Dana was parish minister for twenty-six years before he became president of the American Unitarian Association. The first twenty-one were spent in the Lexington church, the home church of Theodore Parker. He was later minister for twenty-three years at Arlington Street Church in Boston at which William Ellery Channing had his entire ministry. Finally, Dana is now serving the church in Concord that was Ralph Waldo Emerson's home parish for nearly half a century. Parker, Channing, Emerson. How is that for being close to Unitarian history?

Dana was long involved in the International Association for Religious Freedom. For a term he was its president and he managed to widen it, bringing into membership the Buddhist group, Rissho Kosei-kai. Also Dana's role in creating WCRP was an exercise in travelling far down the multireligious road, even past the ecumenical station.

As president of the UUA, Dana gave real leadership against the Vietnam War, both in the Unitarian denomination and among other denominations. He visited Saigon twice. Dana was far ahead of both the UUA Board and the membership of the churches in his opposition to the U.S. role in Vietnam. I was often attacked, as Director of the Division of Social Responsibility, for instigating Dana's opposition to the war when, if the truth were known, he was constantly prodding me!

The most commonly acknowledged characteristic of Dana is his optimism. Dana exudes optimism, because he refused to be deterred by adversity. It is akin to his enthusiasm, and both are highly contagious.

Another thing about Dana: he always looked his part, never losing his dignity. Our colleague Rev. Bob Jones describes this well: "Through all the sixties, when ministers were breaking out with beards and turtlenecks, Dana continued to wear his three-piece suits, white shirts, and conservative ties, and kept his hair cut as it had been in earlier decades." Indeed, some of the conservative stripe ties I wear in this pulpit were Christmas gifts—from Dana!

A further aspect of Dana is his leadership. He leads, yet he includes others. Bob Jones again describes the process aptly: "One trait about Dana is his obvious enjoyment of life. . . . One can always tell when Dana is in a gathering by the boom of his laughter. It sort of peals out. He dominates a room full of people. He would have been a marvelous politician, with his ability to command center stage—not for himself alone, but as a magnet, drawing other people in to share the center with him. In fact, with Dana there are no outsiders. He is gracious in including everyone, without regard to their station."

Dana is not only Mr. Unitarian. He is an indestructible man. And he is already also a legend.

Ranganath Ramachandra Diwakar

R. R. Diwakar, a prominent Gandhian, Hindu, and Indian political leader, was one of the seven principal founders of WCRP and worked with Homer closely for over twenty years. Homer wrote this tribute following his death in 1992.

Shri Ranganath Ramachandra Diwakar accomplished many tasks in his long life. He had many interests. One among many was religion. Like Mohandas Gandhi, Diwakar was a Hindu. Like Gandhi, Diwakar appreciated the spectrum of world religions and was not blind to the values of religions beyond Hinduism. Like Gandhi, Diwakar realized that each religion was but one path to God. Both Gandhi and Diwakar also realized that all religions could be means to attain world peace and justice.

As India and the world prepared for the centenary in 1969 of the birth of Mohandas Gandhi, Diwakar saw the potential of world religions working for world peace. In 1967 some U.S. religious leaders approached the Gandhi Peace Foundation, of which Diwakar was chairman, and asked if some Gandhian group might co-sponsor an international symposium on religion and peace. Diwakar, G. Ramachandran, and others were glad to do so in the name of the International Seminars Committee for the Gandhi Centenary. Together these two groups—Indian and American—co-sponsored the International Inter-Religious Symposium on Peace which was held at the Indian International Center in New Delhi on January 10-14, 1968, and was a forerunner to the World Conference on Religion and Peace.

At the Symposium, R. R. Diwakar said he felt that "it is the very breath and inspiration of religion to give us the strength to wean ourselves away from everything that leads to war and to promote everything that makes us live in friendliness, mutual understanding, and cooperation—in a word, in peace." He stated that the "major responsibility of all religions [is] to put forth their best efforts to establish peace at all levels, because no religion—formal, doctrinal, or ritualistic—can be practiced properly without inner as well as outer peace." He called for "a concentrated effort for peace by a kind of united religious organization of the whole world." Diwakar concluded that "only a peaceful world will help realize the dream of *visva-kutumba*: 'the world as one family.'"

In 1971 South Asia was very much seized with violence in East Pakistan. Shri Diwakar and Shri Radhakrishna, the secretary of the Gandhi Peace Foundation, made available ample documentation for WCRP to understand that there was massacre in that part of Bengal. At a meeting in New Delhi, Radhakrishna and I were asked to make a first draft of "An Appeal on East Pakistan." Diwakar and other officers made some changes in the statement and then it was promptly released. The statement asked U.N. Secretary-General U Thant to use his good offices since "the issue is no longer an 'internal' or 'domestic' issue." We asked the Vatican, the World Council of Churches, and other religious groups to give "urgent attention to this issue." Most of all, we called upon the President of Pakistan, Gen. Yahya Khan, and his Government "immediately to stop violence and repression in East Pakistan. . . not only to save the people of East Pakistan, but to preserve the honor of the people of West Pakistan." This meeting helped make young WCRP active on many fronts to lessen the violence in East Pakistan and, eventually, to help the people establish Bangladesh.

At committee meetings, Diwakar was a memorable participant. He was a veteran in debate, but no stickler for procedure. He was most interested in substance. One could predict that Diwakar, during some part of every committee meeting, would be eloquent,

515

sometimes too eloquent for the small group assembled. Yet he insisted on taking his time to develop a point. He often talked as if he were addressing again the Rajya Saba or the state council in Bihar (of which he was governor from 1952 to 1957). Diwakar was an articulate advocate. His precise use of the English language would have embarrassed most American legislators—and indeed, perhaps today, even many English parliamentarians.

En route in early August 1979 to attend WCRP III at Princeton, Diwakar had an engagement at the International Shivananda Yoga's Ashram in Quebec, Canada. He arrived from India at Kennedy Airport in New York. While catching a plane for Canada, he fell in the terminal and broke or fractured a hip. He was taken to the airport clinic and then to the nearby Mary Immaculate Hospital in Jamaica, a section of New York City.

I immediately visited Diwakar in the hospital. He was in good humor especially when on my second visit he told me that his physician reported that he would "not be incapacitated too long." I communicated to the Gandhi Peace Foundation in New Delhi that Diwakar was coming along "fine, talkative, and beginning to walk." We found an Indian family in New Jersey with whom he could stay during a short convalescence. On August 21, I wrote S. Radhakrishnan of the Bharatiya Vidya Bhavan in Bombay that Diwakar was "doing splendidly—and healing like a boy of sixteen years." I added that "your main job now is to persuade him to slow down." Nothing would deter Diwakar at the end of August from attending WCRP III at Princeton, albeit on two canes. He participated in the discussions.

Shri Diwakar, at ninety, managed to attend WCRP IV at Nairobi. He was a vice-president of the Assembly. He was one of three moderators of the Commission on "Human Dignity, Social Justice, and Development of the Whole Person." Indeed, he delivered a short paper on that topic. He went back to an earlier theme that "mere humanism is not enough." Humanity must look to "ecological humanism." The "ecology of the whole of humanity" is necessary.

Later the same year of 1984, Prime Minister Indira Gandhi was assassinated. I immediately sent a letter of condolences to Diwakar. He replied, calling the assassination "the most brutal and heinous crime committed against one of the most extraordinary women of our times." This was a compassionate response for the death of a person who had caused many problems for Diwakar in the 1970s—including the Emergency and its effect on many of Diwakar's co-workers, including Jayaprakash Narayan, and the Gandhi Peace Foundation itself (and of which Diwakar remained head).

In mid-January 1990, I received a cablegram that "Doctor Diwakar passed away Monday night January 15 in Karnataka Health Institute near Belgaum." Shri Diwakar lived to see the world become a much better place as the Cold War disappeared. The eclipse has indeed gone away. Diwakar also lived to see, in this new international atmosphere, his beloved India make a greater détente with both the United States and China. Yet in this same period tensions between India and its neighbors rose, not only with Pakistan again, but also with Nepal and Sri Lanka. Also, inside India, there were those same "fissiparous tendencies" against which Diwakar's comrade, Jawaharlal Nehru, so frequently warned. These tendencies R. R. Diwakar in his lifetime tried for so many decades also to lessen.

Mother Teresa

On a trip to India in 1976, Homer and Ingeborg journeyed to Calcutta to see Mother Teresa (who later participated in WCRP conferences and activities). He wrote a brief profile on this "living saint" for a Buddhist magazine in Japan. Afterward, Homer seemed visibly changed by the visit—perhaps the nearest thing to a mystical experience he ever had.

Most world religions recognize saints—men and women of their tradition who lead exemplary lives and yet are not gods. Most saints are honored decades or even centuries after they have lived. However, a few persons are regarded as saints while still alive. One such living saint in today's world is Mother Teresa of Calcutta.

Some months ago my wife and I went to Calcutta, partly in the hope of meeting Mother Teresa. Archbishop Angelo Fernandes of New Delhi had given me her telephone number. From the Great Eastern Hotel I phoned. Mother Teresa answered. Yes, she would see us early in the evening at her center at 54A Lower Circular Road. Upon arriving, we rang a high bell, on the side in an alley. We were soon ushered into what appeared to be a convent. We were given chairs in a narrow room. Soon a small woman entered—Mother Teresa. She was short, but not thin, and she wore a white sari. She introduced herself in good English and asked us to sit down.

I began by asking Mother Teresa—who was born in Albania, trained in Ireland, and sent to India to teach—when she first decided to work for the poor. At the age of twelve, she felt that she had a vocation to the poor. But why, I asked, did you decide no longer to teach the middle-class Indian girls at that cloistered, comfortable school? She replied that it was on a train to a retreat in Darjeeling in September 1946 when she first heard a call to follow Jesus Christ "into the slums to serve him among the poorest of the poor."

Within six months, Mother Teresa opened a school in the heart of the Calcutta slums. At first five abandoned children came and she had only five rupees. She taught the children the alphabet and practical hygiene. Soon some of the older Indian girls from St. Mary's School helped and wanted to take up a vocation with her. This small beginning increased until today in Calcutta alone, her institutions take care of more than 500 unwanted children.

I asked Mother Teresa how she was financially able to maintain her many institutions in Calcutta and elsewhere. She immediately replied: "He—Christ—always provides." This is a kind of divine providence. She takes nothing from the Indian Government, because she does not want to be burdened by keeping accounts! But the funds and goods in kind just keep on coming. She feeds more than 5,000 people daily in Calcutta alone. The city tries to help her and has arranged to deliver to her left-over bread and rice. Once she ran completely out of food grains. She had nowhere to turn. Then suddenly she received a large shipment of bread and rice, but just in time. She wondered why, investigated, and found that the schools of Calcutta suddenly—without any apparent reason—closed for two days. This, she called, the "delicate thoughtfulness of God."

When Pope Paul VI visited India in 1964, he was moved to give Mother Teresa the white Lincoln limousine that had been given him for ceremonial use. No doubt he surmised that Mother Teresa would make good use of the automobile in Calcutta. She did. She never rode in it once, but promptly raffled the limousine off for 700,000 rupees—with which she promptly built a whole leper colony!

I asked her why she helped the dying? "First of all," she responded, "we want to make them feel that they are wanted, and we want them to know that there are people who really love them, who really want them, at least for the few hours that they have to live, to know human and divine love." Some are brought into the Home just in time. They mutter "thank you," and then die. But nobody dies without a blessing, which is not necessarily Christian. Hindus receive the waters of the Ganges on their lips. Muslims hear readings from the Qur'an. The few Catholics can be given the last rites.

When I compared her work to that of Catholic Worker activist Dorothy Day in New York, she admitted that poverty in the West is most difficult. In India they can give a poor person a plate of rice and he or she is quite satisfied. Not so in the West. She felt that much of the problem of the West is due to murder—abortion. Mother Teresa insisted that "life is life, whether old or young." She and her Sisters rescue tiny lives from the refuse heaps. In her Home for Unwanted Children, the lives of abandoned children are preserved. She is triumphant about every life of every child she can save. Her reverence for life is as strong, if as differently based, as that of Albert Schweitzer. "The life of Christ," she insists, "is the life of the child." God provides "for the flowers and the birds, for everything in the world that he has created. And those little children are his life. There can never be enough children." She added that "the poorest country in the world is not necessarily India, but that with the highest number of abortions."

I asked Mother Teresa whether Mohandas Gandhi was one of her inspirations? I reminded her that Gandhi's longtime, close Christian co-worker, C. F. Andrews, was buried just down the road from her headquarters. I am not sure that the full weight of my comment registered with her, but she firmly said that Gandhi was not the source of her work. I then asked her if she knew of the work of Albert Schweitzer. Her answer was vague. She said that the inspiration of her work came directly from Jesus Christ.

Finally, I asked, why did she make a vocation to work with the poor and not just with all men and women? Mother Teresa responded that she wanted to "give the poor what the rich get with money." I asked her what is that. "Being wanted." She feels that, more than a fatal illness, being unwanted is "the worst disease that any human being can ever experience." She once told Malcolm Muggeridge that "for all kinds of diseases there are medicines and cures. But for being unwanted, except there are willing hands to serve and there's a loving heart to love, I don't think this terrible disease can ever be cured."

Too soon, we took our leave of Mother Teresa. This very modest woman saw us to the alley, and almost immediately we were on lower Circular Road—in the heart of Calcutta, having talked to a real heart in this most tragic city, in a world of tragic cities.

Jayaprakash Narayan

J. P. Narayan, the Indian freedom fighter, Gandhian activist, and states-man intersected with Homer on several occasions.

Gandhi left several heirs, including Jawaharlal Nehru who piloted the Indian ship of state after independence and became the architect of the non-aligned movement; Vinoba Bhave, the Walking Saint, whose marathon pilgrimages on behalf of the dispossessed moved the whole nation; and Jayaprakash Narayan, the master political theorist and strategist.

J.P., as he was universally known, originally became a Marxist while studying in the United States. In India, he helped found the Socialist Party, was imprisoned by the British for political activities, and made a dramatic escape. He organized violent resistance to imperial rule during World War II, was recaptured, and was active in Congress Party politics, ultimately leaving to found the PSP socialist party. In 1954, he renounced politics to work for Vinoba Bhave's Bhoodan Movement, obtaining land for the poor.

In the early 1970s, J. P. was the leading ideological opponent of Mrs. Indira Gandhi during the Emergency when civil rights were curtailed and thousands imprisoned unjustly for demanding that the results of democratic elections be implemented. Although he had forsaken public office, J.P. was always mentioned in the press and political circles as the most capable person to become chief of state. However, he preferred to preside behind the scenes, as he did when the Janata Party under Moraji Desai, another Gandhian, eventually came to power.

During this period, I saw him frequently on trips to India for WCRP and he participated actively in our symposiums and conferences. At one assembly, for example, he reminded the delegates that he was "not a religious man in the traditional sense of the term." He reminded those present, all religionists, that "whereas religion should unite humanity, it is one of the strongest, divisive forces today, and when religion is linked with the nation-state, then the danger of divisiveness is multiplied tenfold."

Unfortunately, J.P.'s prophetic words came true, sooner than anyone dared to think. In 1980, the massacre of East Bengalis spurred him to assume leadership (at least outside of East Pakistan itself) against mounting repression by the Pakistani Army and the specter of outright religious warfare between Hindus and Moslems.

J.P. organized a nonviolent march to the sprawling refugee camps on the Indo-Pakistani border and used all of his political acumen and skill to achieve an independent Bangladesh. He masterminded the international campaign to win support for Dacca at a time when the superpowers, and India itself, were largely indifferent to the fate of this extremely poor and strategically unimportant region of the world. Although he never held the ultimate office, J.P. was a true statesman, and his legacy on the subcontinent will long endure.

Shinochiro Imaoka

Shinochiro Imaoka, Japanese clergyman and peace activist, studied at Harvard in 1915, the year before Homer was born. On his first trip to Japan in 1957, Homer met Dr. Imaoka in Tokyo, and Alex stayed with his grandchildren. Homer continued to see him regularly whenever he visited Japan, and Dr. Imaoka, who remained active well into his second century, served as a mentor and sage. Homer delivered this tribute at a Memorial Service for Rev. Imaoka in Tokyo on May 15, 1988.

Dear Friend: It seemed that you would live forever, but last month you also died. Yet what was remarkable about you was not your longevity, but how you used constructively your 106 years.

We first met in Japan in August 1957 when you invited me, as a Unitarian colleague, to speak to your Tokyo church. Indeed, you invited our twelve-year-old son to live in the home of your son. In 1967 I met you for the fourth time when I came to Japan to explore convening a world assembly of religionists for peace. You gently reminded us that we were considering what was attempted between the two world wars. You were active with the Japanese section which held a religious peace congress here in 1931. In 1967 you recommended that we meet with President Nikkyo Niwano of Rissho Kosei-kai. You accompanied us to the Great Sacred Hall where we conferred with President Niwano who encouraged us in our worldwide project. In October 1970 when you were eighty-eight years young, you were one of the honorary sponsors of WCRP I held in Kyoto.

The last time I saw you was in July 1986. We then grieved about the recent death of Dr. Greeley. You took my wife and myself to International House to dine. You bounded down the steps to the dining room, talked excellent English as always, ate well, and chain-smoked—at age 104!

Eventually, as all human beings, even you died. We will remember you as a catalyst for the creation of WCRP, as a strong supporter of IARF, as a religious liberal, as a patriotic Japanese, and as a world citizen. We no longer grieve at your death, but glory in your long, rich, and productive life.

Nikkyo Niwano

Nikkyo Niwano, founder and leader of Rissho Kosei-kai, a Buddhist society in Japan with 3 million members, worked closely with Homer for a quarter of a century. In this excerpt from a lengthy tribute, Homer relates Rev. Niwano's role in helping to found WCRP and his leadership over the years.

My first encounter with President Nikkyo Niwano of Rissho Kosei-kai was in 1967. For eighteen consecutive years we met—through 1984. We did not see each other in 1985 and again not in 1987. Over this period, we have met not only in Japan or the United States, but in ten other countries on five continents.

As an American clergyman employed professionally in the field of social responsibility, I was sent around the world in the spring of 1967 for six weeks to ascertain the readiness of religious leaders from Egypt to Japan to work together for world peace, especially by convening a world conference on religion and peace. My companion was another American clergyman, Episcopalian Herschel Halbert.

Our last stop was Japan and one of our last interviews of the trip was with President Niwano. I had first visited Japan ten years earlier to attend a meeting on the twelfth anniversary of the bombing of Hiroshima and Nagasaki and to help, in a minor way, with the Hiroshima Maidens Project of Norman Cousins. Through Dr. Shinochiro Imaoka, the head of the Japan Free Religious Association, we met President Niwano and found him to be especially receptive in helping this embryonic effort to bring representatives of all world religions to discuss world peace.

The International Inter-Religious Symposium on Peace was held at New Delhi in January 1968 on the eve of the centenary observances of the birth of Mohandas Gandhi. This was our first international effort to experiment with convening a worldwide interreligious meeting. Ven. Riri Nakayama of Tokyo was among the participants, and he earlier arranged for the U.S. delegation attending the New Delhi Symposium to return to the U.S. via Kyoto for a one-day Japanese-American Inter-Religious Consultation on Peace.

Thus the U.S. delegation returning from New Delhi stopped in the ancient city of Kyoto on January 22, 1968. President Niwano was one of several Japanese religious leaders present. He told the Consultation that, as a result of our shrinking world, "news of the sufferings of the people in distant regions becomes known to us with immediacy, so that their sufferings are directly our sufferings." That single day began a series of meeting which have continued now for more than twenty years. Together we established and maintained a worldwide movement which came to be the World Conference on Religion and Peace.

The year 1969 saw feverish activity to create a worldwide infrastructure, growing out of the determination at the Kyoto Consultation to attempt to convene a world conference. Our first step was to bring together a more representative group than the American and Japanese religious leaders who met at Kyoto. Already at New Delhi an Interim Committee was appointed. In April this religious leadership, primarily from India, Japan, and the U.S., met at Istanbul, Turkey, an historic crossroads between East and West. There, President Niwano and the other Japanese present, including the Rev. Toshio Miyake and the Rev. Nakayama, first proposed that we meet at Kyoto for the initial world assembly. And so, in the shadow of the famed Bosphorus—the waterway between Europe and Asia—the foundation was laid. Archbishop Angelo Fernandes of India was named president, with President Niwano and Dr. Greeley as co-chairmen. They were to work closely together for more than fifteen years.

A second meeting during 1969 was held at Dedham, outside Boston, Massachusetts. The planning for WCRP seemed earthbound compared to what we, and the world, witnessed that very week during July on television—the first steps of human beings on the moon. President Niwano and all of us marvelled at the technology and cooperation in the heavens which we hoped could also be focused toward world peace on earth. At this meeting President Niwano urged that Pope Paul VI be invited to speak at our world conference since the Prime Minister of Japan told him that a papal visit to Japan would be welcomed. It was agreed for this purpose to obtain the assistance of Cardinal John Wright of the Vatican who had been made a member of the Curia since he attended our Istanbul meeting.

Still a third encounter during 1969 was when we returned to Kyoto in December for the session of the International Preparatory

Committee for WCRP I. Meeting in the new International Conference Hall, we discussed plans for our truly historic assembly. No policy problem was overlooked. President Niwano often presided over our bilingual meetings.

I probably saw more of President Niwano during 1970 than during any year before—or since. He helped supervise preparations for WCRP I. As Secretary-General of this Assembly, I moved to Japan in May and had an office in Fumon Hall, just a few minutes' walk from President Niwano's office. We consulted once or twice a week during the four months before we moved the international office to Kyoto. The Japanese Host Committee for WCRP I, and with Shuten Oishi as Joint Secretary and Japanese Secretary, often met at various Tokyo hotels. There, over elaborate luncheons, we discussed every detail of the forthcoming world congress, often with President Niwano presiding.

On Friday, October 16, our dreams came true as WCRP I opened with 210 delegates from thirty-nine countries on five continents and ten world religions represented. President Niwano, as Chairman of the Conference (together with Dr. Greeley), gave an address in behalf of the host organization, the Japan Religions League. He declared that "the time has arrived when religions, instead of antagonizing each other because of what we once thought was a religious conviction, should cooperate with each other in order to contribute to the cause of mankind and world peace because, in the final analysis, all sectors of religion are and can be bound together by the common aspiration for human happiness and salvation." He closed his inaugural address with the "sincere hope that we, children of Buddha or God, will stand hand in hand and lose no time in bringing harmony into the world that is realizing world peace."

The great achievement of WCRP I was simply that it was held. The dream of millions of people over centuries that religions should try to make peace, instead of often being the cause of war, or surely blessing their nation's side in wars, was fulfilled in that old Japanese city which itself was spared bombing in World War II. Also achieved at Kyoto was the effort to induce the religious leaders not to extol their own particular religion, or try to make converts to it, but to work with other religions by leaping over doctrinal problems to suggest solutions to political and secular obstacles to world unity. The Kyoto Declaration and resolutions on disarmament, development, and human rights were sophisticated documents which U.N. diplomats found useful since they were not the usual unreal preach-ings of religionists.

Hawaii was an ideal site for another Japanese-American Inter-Religious Consultation on Peace (after the first at Kyoto in 1968). In June 1972, some forty persons met at a hotel on the Honolulu beach to discuss emerging tensions and Japanese-American relations. In the five years of working together many Japanese and American religionists became friends. We wanted to use that friendship to develop better relations between our two great nations. On the first morning, Dr. Greeley—head of the U.S. delegation—came into the meeting room dressed in a flowing, colorful Hawaiian shirt. President Niwano entered wearing a three-piece business suit with a tie. They looked at each other—and laughed. Then at noon the Consultation adjourned for lunch. When the meeting resumed, Dr. Greeley arrived wearing his three-piece business suit and tie, while President Niwano entered wearing his Hawaiian shirt. They roared with laughter. Such is humor—with religionists.

The First U.N. Special Session on Disarmament was held at U.N. Headquarters in June 1978. WCRP and other groups worked hard to allow representatives from nongovernmental organizations—NGOs—to address this U.N. body on this survival issue. Finally, a group of NGOs was allowed to speak. President Niwano represented WCRP in a rare appearance for a nondiplomat from the podium of the Great Hall of the General Assembly. After working on his speech in our modest WCRP offices overlooking U.N. Headquarters, President Niwano asked the statesmen to take risks for peace as they are obviously taking "risks today with arms." He prayed that "some States out of strength and not weakness, will take major risks for peace and disarmament." He urged that "motivated by our several religions," we make "a new appraisal of national and world security." He hoped that "the new relationship" of NGOs to disarmament issues in the U.N. might be institutionalized.

In June 1986 we gathered in the capital of South Korea, Seoul, for the Third Assembly of ACRP (Asian Conference for Religion and Peace). My wife and I had just flown from Chicago and reached the hotel when news arrived that Dr. Greeley, who had been ill in the U.S.A., had died. We went up to President Niwano's room. He prayed for the soul of his closest American friend. This death cast a shadow for us on the ACRP Assembly, already problematic because of the repressive Korean political regime.

A week later we met in the suburbs of Beijing to attend the international Council of WCRP. President Niwano seemed at home in China, especially with his friend, the calligrapher, Zhao Puchu, a laureate of the Niwano Peace Prize and head of the Buddhist Association of China. With us were two religious leaders from the Soviet Union, perhaps the first time in several decades that religious figures from Russia visited China. We were all guests of Zhao Puchu at a magnificent banquet in the Great Hall of the People, opposite the entrance to the former Forbidden City.

In June 1988, we met at the U.N. where President Niwano for the third time spoke to a special session of the U.N. General Assembly on disarmament. He urged a 50 percent cut in existing intercontinental missile stockpiles and an end to nuclear testing and to Star Wars research. Dr. Niwano also visited Concord, Massachusetts, to pay his respects to Dr. Greeley's widow, visiting the two gravesites of Dana Greeley amidst historic places in Concord and Lexington associated with the eighteenth century American Revolution.

While most of these encounters were person-to-person, we were seldom alone. Since 1972, my wife usually accompanied me. President Niwano rarely brought any of his children and I rarely brought mine. In President Niwano's retinue were always Mr. Masuo Nezu, his translator, and until recently, Mr. Kinzo Takemura. Mr. Motoytuki Naganuma was often in the background until in recent times he became one of the substitutes for President Niwano when the latter could not travel. Also from Rissho Kosei-kai came Mr. Yasuo Katsuyama, Mr. Koichi Kita, and Mr. Hiroyuki Oshima. Other Japanese aides with whom I worked included Mr. Masumi Goto, Mr. Masatoshi Kohno, Mr. Kojiro Miyasaka, Mr. Yoshiro Ohno, and—in New York—Mr. Katsuji Suzuki.

What did all these encounters, these frenetic comings and goings, really accomplish? Did we mistake activity for action? While I cannot speak for President Niwano, these more than two decades of encounters markedly changed my life and thought. These encounters also brought into the world a new institution, the World Conference on Religion and Peace, and its many subsidiary organizations, including national WCRP groups in Africa, Asia, Australia, Europe, and North America. Also these encounters significantly changed the outlook and program of Rissho Kosei-kai and the Unitarian Universalist Association, and no doubt many other religious institutions. Certainly they broadened the scope and constituency of the International Association for Religious Freedom (IARF). A description of the detailed spiritual, cultural, and political growth of these many individuals and institutions may someday be written. Slowly these encounters changed structures, secular and religious, and always in the context of multiple world religions.

Juliette Morgan

Juliette Morgan, a reference librarian in Montgomery, Alabama, had a profound effect on delineating the modern civil rights movement. In his retirement, Homer traced the fascinating—and tragic—story of this unsung modern heroine. Excerpts from his findings follow:

In his first book, *Stride Toward Freedom*, Martin Luther King explained, "About a week after the protest started [the Montgomery Bus Boycott], a white woman who understood and sympathized with the Negroes' efforts wrote a letter to the editor of the *Montgomery Advertiser* comparing the bus protest with the Gandhian movement in India. Miss Juliette Morgan, sensitive and frail, did not long survive the rejection and condemnation of the white community, but long before she died in the summer of 1957 the name of Mahatma Gandhi was well-known in Montgomery." Who was Juliette Morgan? The history books are silent about the first person to connect the Montgomery civil rights campaign with Gandhian nonviolence—before King himself! In the late 1980s, I went to Montgomery in search of this mysterious woman.

Juliette Hampton Morgan was born in Montgomery on February 21, 1914. Her father, Frank Perryman Morgan, was elected for sixteen years to the Alabama Public Service Commission. Her mother, Lila Bess Olin, was the fourth generation in her family who went to college. An only child, Juliette was early described as "a sunny-hearted, sunny-headed little lass." She grew up in Montgomery, attended the University of Alabama, and graduated in 1933 Phi Beta Kappa. While at the university, her mother applied for a scholarship for her daughter from the United Daughters of the Confederacy, recalling that her great grandfather Richard Olin served in Claxton's Battery, Alabama Light Artillery during the Civil War. She went to obtain a M.A. in 1935 with a thesis on "A Study of Carlyle's Style with Particular Reference to 'Sartor Resartus' and 'Heroes and Hero Worship.'"

The archives reflect little of her early vocational life. She returned to Lanier High School in Montgomery and taught English. She edited a country newspaper, *Cleburne News*, in 1949. She served as a reference librarian at the Montgomery Public Library. She worked at a bookstore and returned to the library where she was chief reference librarian until her death.

She was a constant writer of letters to newspapers, usually in

527

her own name, but sometimes using pseudonyms, sometimes writing letters for others. These echoed wide interests and occasionally she wrote on the care of animals. She was not much of a joiner, but was a trustee of the Montgomery Humane Society.

Rosa Parks refused to move to the back of a Montgomery bus on Thursday, December 1, 1955. The boycott began on Monday, December 5. Just a week after the boycott began, on Monday, December 12, a long letter appeared from Juliette Morgan in the *Montgomery Advertiser*. In brief strokes, she reflected the essence of Gandhi's campaign in India:

> Not since the first Battle of the Marne has the taxi been put to as good use as it has this last week in Montgomery. However, the spirit animating our Negro citizens as they ride these taxis or walk from the heart of Cloverdale to Mobile Road has been more like that of Gandhi than that of the 'taxicab army' that saved Paris.
>
> As you remember, Gandhi set out on his "Salt March" from Sabarmati to the sea—about 150 miles—as a boycott against the government's salt monopoly. He took with him only a loin cloth, a bamboo walking stick, and a consuming idea. He vowed that he would not return until India was independent. Depending on their point of view, people laughed, sneered, or shook their heads, but seventeen years later India was free. Passive resistance combined with freedom from hate is a power to be reckoned with. The Negroes of Montgomery seem to have taken a lesson from Gandhi— and from our own Thoreau who influenced Gandhi.
>
> One feels that history is being made in Montgomery these days, the most important of her career. It is hard to imagine a soul so dead, a heart so hard, a vision so blinded and provincial as not to be moved with admiration at the quiet dignity, discipline, and dedication with which the Negroes have conducted their boycott.

She added that the cause and conduct of the blacks of Montgomery filled her with "great sympathy, pride, humility, and envy." Few white women at that time would have made that identification publicly with the black community, especially with the White Citizens Council carefully watching. That single letter set off an avalanche of hate which, in the end, overwhelmed Juliette Morgan. "Instead of acting like sullen adolescents whose attitude is

528

'Make me,'" she concluded, "we ought to be working out plans to span the gap between segregation and integration, to extend public services—schools, libraries, parks, and transportation to Negro citizens. Ralph McGill's is the best advice I've heard: 'Segregation is on its way out, and he who tries to tell the people otherwise does them great disservice. The problem of the future is how to live with the change.' This may be a minority report, but a number of Montgomerians not entirely inconsequential agree with my point of view."

The chain reaction this missive caused is best described by Professor Jo Ann Robinson of the English Department of Alabama State College. She wrote that Miss Morgan "began to get an unending stream of terrible telephone calls, frightening noises at her door and windows, and, where ever she went, hisses, boos, slurs, threats. Angry white people threatened her night and day, promising harmful retaliation. She was threatened with loss of her job, her friends, her few possessions. For awhile she ignored the threats, thinking they would go away. But instead they increased. The telephone rang almost incessantly. Then her doorbell began to ring, more and more frequently as the sun surrendered its light to darkness. Pebbles were hurled against her window panes far into the night, awakening and frightening her, or preventing her from even getting to sleep."

Reflecting on the attacks, Juliette observed: "I know there are many people, many Southerners, who feel as I do. It's just when it comes to signing their name to something that they back down. I can sympathize with them. The cuts from old friends, the ringing telephone with anonymous voices. I know how it feels when the butterflies in your stomach start turning to buzzards."

The Alabama black newspaper, *Alabama Tribune*, referred to her letter in a front-page column, "Strange As It Seems," four days after her missive appeared. E. G. Jackson wrote: "Personally, I have read many articles in different newspapers and I have tried to write some myself, but I have never read one that hit the point like this article did."

Juliette's letter put the Gandhian label on the movement and its president, Martin Luther King. The letter helped turn, in time and in the public mind, the basically Christian movement growing out of the black churches in Montgomery into a Christian-cum-Gandhian movement. Miss Morgan was perceptive during the very first week of the boycott. She realized that it had the potential, and indeed already the intonations, of a different kind of campaign. Where she picked up her knowledge of Gandhi, beyond that of an efficient reference librarian, I have so far been unable to discover. I even thumbed through some of her notebooks from university, but found nothing on Gandhi.

Except for isolated individuals and small groups of liberals, Juliette Morgan had little protection from the social harassment of her time. She had no husband or other partner, at least to my knowledge, on whom she could lean, especially toward the end. And toward that end, she sought professional help, in Birmingham, but it was apparently too late. Juliette Morgan could "not go on," and died, evidently by her own hand, at age forty-three, in July 1957. She remains a member of that small pantheon of women, white and black, in the South who firmly opposed once slavery, and then segregation.

Bill Lloyd

Bill Lloyd, editor of Toward Freedom, *published many articles and pamphlets of Homer's and was a pioneer world government advocate.*

Bill hailed from a prominent family of Chicago peace activists. His mother, Lola Maverick Lloyd, was the granddaughter of Samuel Maverick, a signer of the Declaration of Independence. For several decades she worked with Rosika Schwimmer and Jane Addams in what became the Women's International League for Peace and Freedom. In1915, she went on Henry Ford's Peace Ship along with three of her children, including Bill, who was then seven. The Peace Ship—a valiant effort to end World War I by mediation—visited Stockholm, Copenhagen, and the Hague and held great peace rallies.

Following in the footsteps of his mother, Bill devoted his whole life to peace and freedom. He interviewed Albert Einstein, worked in a public service camp in California during World War II, and worked tirelessly for a world without war. I worked closely with Bill, his wife Mary, and his sister Georgia—a peace champion in her own right—visiting the Lloyds at their home in Winnetka, Ill., and later in Burlington, Vermont. This gentle, Quaker family contributed their time, energy, and money to humanity for most of the 20th century and, if humanity survives into the new millennium, it will be on account of selfless souls like the Lloyds.

68 PROPHETS AND ICONS

In addition to living models, Homer admired several historical figures and invoked their teachings in his speeches and writings.

Jesus of Nazareth

Homer preached about Jesus on many occasions, weaving contemporary insights and discoveries with timeless truths. This excerpt is from a typical sermon, "Was Jesus a Christian?," given in Evanston in 1953.

To many, including many Unitarians, Jesus was the greatest man who ever lived, even if he was not God. To many, including many Unitarians, the teachings of Jesus were and are the greatest teachings known, even if they cannot be very well defined or observed. But are the teachings of Jesus the same as the teachings of Christianity? Put another way: How did the teachings of Judaism become, through Jesus, the teachings of Christianity?

For centuries, for more than a thousand years, it was generally assumed that the teachings of Jesus were original. Jesus was thought of as a Christian, the first Christian, but a Christian nonetheless. Then in 1905, Professor Julius Wellhausen, a distinguished Protestant scholar in Germany, drew the logical conclusions of almost a century of New Testament scholarship. He asserted: "Jesus was not a Christian; he was a Jew."

In the view of modern Jewish theologians, unlike the eighth century prophets, Jesus had little concern for social justice or for national politics. His total concern was for one's individual belief in God and for the practice of what we would call, and they did call, an extreme ethic. This was a negation of the national life and the national state of the Jewish people. Thus the nation could only see the public ideals of Jesus as abnormal, even fanatical. They felt that, as a nation, they could not be swallowed up by the Roman Empire. They rejected ethical teachings separated from their national life. Thus Jesus' kind of Judaism became so extreme as to lead to non-Judaism. This established the base on which Paul, in the name of Jesus, could organize Christianity.

Unwittingly, Jesus laid the foundation for a new religion by his excessive emphasis on certain radical Jewish ideas. Without Jesus, no Paul. But without Paul, no world Christianity. Rabbi Ernest Trettner makes this fruitful comparison: Like the rabbis, Jesus attacked the impurities of the contemporary religion. Unlike Paul or Luther, who broke with the past, Jesus was like Erasmus who criticized severely the beliefs and practices of contemporary religion and yet died a loyal member of his ancestral faith.

There have been efforts to prove that the insights of Jesus were Egyptian, that his teachings had an origin along the Nile. There have been similar suggestions that he visited India before his ministry. It has even been said that Judaism had a Hindu origin, and that the Jewish word, *Amen*, is similar to the sacred Brahman word, *Aum!* There were theories that the Essenes were really Jewish Buddhists. There were allegations that Jesus spoke not the Palestinian vernacular, Aramaic, but Latin, since as one scholar suggested: "The Lord cannot have used any other language than Latin on earth, since this is the language of the saints in heaven."

What do contemporary Protestant thinkers say? Professor Guignebert of the Sorbonne explains the originality of Jesus this way. Jesus wanted neither to destroy nor to reform Judaism. He wanted to introduce an active principle into it. Jesus was not trained in the rabbinical schools. He was much simpler. He was much more accessible to sinners. He emphasized the need for internal reformation of the individual, rather than on a popular appeal to force. He laid much more stress on the invincibility of love. Jesus crystalized the essence of Phariseeism in a single act of faith: repent—for this is the only door to salvation.

The teachings of Jesus show a tension between law and love. In the religion of Israel, merit lay in observing the Law—the Torah. It was not thought that Jesus ever consciously wanted to break the Law. One evidence is the early church in Jerusalem founded by his closest disciples. This church strictly observed the Jewish law, as opposed to the early churches outside Jerusalem which did break the Law. But Jesus came "not to destroy but to fulfill" the Torah.

But there is much evidence that Jesus wanted to go beyond the Law. He believed in the spirit, not the letter. He substituted inner reality for outward form. Jesus had an attitude of heart which went beyond the arid rules of the Book. He rejected an ostentatious and complacent legalism. His law was the will of God—as he saw it—although he did not overthrow the Torah in the process. Thus to him sin was not so much the breaking of the rules of Torah as going against the will of God. If Jesus made some departures from the Law these detours were in the direction of Love. Morality, ethics, all religion—these are based for Jesus on the law of love. Again, Jesus nowhere provides us with a textbook definition of Love. Indeed, Christian love springs more from the writings of Paul than of Jesus. The Gospel writers provide us with several examples to show that Jesus taught that love towards God is inseparable from, indeed, inconceivable without, love towards one's neighbors. Mark recalls that "to love one's neighbor as oneself" is more than all the Temple sacrifices. It is this area of the relationship of law to love that modern Christian scholars see the originality of Jesus.

What do the Dead Sea Scrolls say? It is really too early to make valid conclusions about these scrolls. There is almost an indecent haste to make the scrolls fit one's religious outlook, whether liberal or conservative. It is too early to draw conclusions, but what are some preliminary theories? There are parallels which have already been suggested. One is the parallel between the Teacher of Righteousness in the Scrolls and Jesus of Nazareth in the Gospels. The other is the parallel between the Essene and the early Christian Church. The two groups—Essenes and early Christians—were organized in a similar manner. In each case, when the group met it was called "the many." From "the many" were chosen "the twelve" to represent, no doubt, the twelve tribes of Israel. In the early church, as in the Essene sect, there was an "inspector-superintendent" or overseer. These and many other parallels are possibly significant, unless there are similar parallels between other sects within Judaism and the infant Christian church.

The scrolls also contribute a new dimension to our knowledge of the life of Jesus. The Gospel of John has heretofore been difficult to reconcile with the three synoptic gospels, and has been regarded as being the most recently written of the four. There are, however, enough similarities between John and the Scrolls to induce some to believe that John could have been written much earlier and perhaps by an Essene.

Whatever Jesus' originality, it did not extend toward founding a new religion. In one sense, Jesus was a failure. His dream of the Kingdom did not materialize. On top of that, he was crucified. Yet it was these very failures which brought success. When he was crucified, his disciples dreamed about His coming instead of the coming Kingdom. And Paul took this dream and created a myth on which he founded a church. Thus Professor Guignebert concludes as we must: "Jesus neither foresaw nor desired the new order which replaced the immediate future of the dream of the Kingdom. And although Christianity may be said to have its origin in him, since the new religion grew out of speculations concerning his person and his mission, he was not its founder. It had never even entered into his mind."

Jesus was a prophet of the Kingdom, not the son of God and probably not even the Messiah, although opinions of modern scholars vary widely on this point. The Kingdom to him was the Jewish concept of the Kingdom—an impending future wherein all men would be judged. As for the ethics of Jesus, they issued directly from his concept of God. His ethics were largely individual, seldom social, hardly systematic, yet relevant just because they are interim ethics.

The quest for the teachings of Jesus is long and difficult, often disillusioning, occasionally rewarding. It is the quest of modern religious scholarship. Even for Unitarians there is the Jesus somewhere between history and faith. This Jesus, however elusive, has been described in the familiar quotation of Schweitzer:

> Jesus comes to us as One unknown, with a name, as of old, by the lake side. He came to those men who knew Him not. He speaks to us the same word: Follow thou me. And sets us to the tasks which He has to fulfill for our time. He commands. To those who obey him, whether they be wise or simple, He will reveal Himself in the toils, the conflicts, the sufferings which they shall pass through in His fellowship. And, as an ineffable mystery, they shall learn in their own experience, Who He Is.

Jesus Christ

In 1952, The Evanstonian, the weekly city newspaper, ran a series of articles written by local ministers on the meaning of Christmas. Homer contributed the following reflections.

Again this year our community is making an all-out effort to put Christ back into Christmas. After the cheap commercialization of Christmas, this is a laudable aim. Yet putting Christ into Christmas surely must mean more than reminding the populace of his birth through high-powered advertising gimmicks and even beautiful creches.

Christians and non-Christians alike must be reminded that to remember that Jesus was born is not enough. The miracle of Christ and thus of Christmas is what Christ had done in the hearts of men—at Christmastide and, we hope, through all seasons of the year.

To put Christ into Christmas must mean to put His love into our hearts. Christ demands that we suspend our differences and our fears, our prejudices and our jealousies—and become humans all. Christ demands that, in our lives, in the community, and in the world, we substitute love for hate, good will for envy, understanding for suspicion. This does not come easy; yet high religion cannot be bought across the counter.

To put Christ into Christmas must mean that we attempt here, in Evanston, to honor the Prince of Peace by doing something which otherwise we as a community would not do. If, each year, we as a community could lessen a specific area of bigotry in our midst—in housing, in recreation, in employment, most of all in our churches which bear his name—Christ would indeed be put into Christmas. To put Christ into Christmas must mean to put a Christ-like spirit into our dealings with people who differ from us because of race, religion, or national origin.

Especially in a community of many denominations and faiths such as ours, we must not forget at Christmas time that Jesus was born a Jew and died a Jew. We must try, as best we can, to observe the twin celebrations of Christmas and Hanukkah. In celebrating the birth of Jesus, we must not do violence to those in our midst who are the direct descendents of His people. In celebrating the birth of Jesus, let us also celebrate the courage of the Maccabees and may the flame of zeal kindle within our hearts together the eternal quest for good will and peace.

John Brown

John Brown, the abolitionist leader who ignited the Civil War, was a long-time hero of the Jack family. Interestingly, Lawrence, Kansas, where

535

Homer had his first church, was the site of John Brown's first assault on slavery. This vignette is from a regular column, "On Democracy's Battlefront," that Homer wrote for the Pittsburg Courier, *the nation's largest black newspaper, in the late 1940s.*

Last Thursday, my wife and I checked our two children with my parents and headed from western New York to Montreal and Quebec. It was a second honeymoon—after almost ten years of marriage. With a good deal of faith in our '41 Ford (which turned out to be justified) we drove toward the Adirondack Mountains. In a carefree manner, we tarried to buy plums, later peaches, and then stopped briefly to see a rural minister friend in the foothills of the mountains. His delightful garden of phlox and portulacas and his 125-year-old church building made up for his tiny congregation! By early afternoon, we passed the well-known Adirondack resorts: Old Forge, Tupper Lake, Saranac Lake, and swank Lake Placid.

At twilight, we paid our respects to John Brown. On the hills above Lake Placid toward Mt. Marcy way lie the remains of old John Brown of Harpers Ferry. The Adirondacks was one of his many homes and his grave is marked by a large boulder. Half a century ago, my father in a walking tour of the Adirondacks camped overnight at the side of John Brown's grave and I remember in my childhood his frequent tales about John Brown. Twenty-five years ago—could it possibly be that long?—my parents took me to the mountains and we paused at the grave of John Brown. Last week again I revisited that hallowed ground.

You and I today might not approve of John Brown's method of violence to settle the slavery issue, but we can surely approve of his courage and his sense of urgency. As the lengthening shadows fell on the grave, I thought that one John Brown in the South in our generation would advance race relations fifty years in a single decade. The marker on Brown's grave indicates that he was taken prisoner at Harpers Ferry on October 18, 1859, and executed for armed insurrection on December 2, 1959. Buried with him are twelve of his followers, including two sons and two Negroes (Dangerfield Newby and Lewis S. Leary). Of those that escaped but were later hanged, two were Negroes: Shields Green and John A. Copeland. Those of his tiny band who escaped included one of his sons and two Negroes: Osborne P. Anderson and John Anderson. I wondered as I read these names (and I would be interested to know) if any of the relatives of these courageous fighters for freedom are living in Chicago at the present time.

In 1959, Homer again visited John Brown's grave and wrote this sentence:

Visiting John Brown's grave—a century to the month after his raid on Harpers Ferry—was to me early one October Sunday morning as religious an experience as visiting any cathedral or even Unitarianism's "mother church" in Boston.

Abraham Lincoln

Lincoln had been a hero for several generations of Homer's family. Homer's father operated the Lincoln Photo Engraving Company, and Homer kept a portrait of Lincoln (without a beard) prominently displayed in his house. The following remarks were part of a sermon Homer gave in Evanston in 1956 on "The Religion of Abraham Lincoln."

Of all our American presidents, none has fascinated people more than Abraham Lincoln. I was surprised in India this past summer to find that Pandit Nehru admired Abraham Lincoln—and knew his works and his biography. I was also surprised that Leo Tolstoy once called Lincoln "a Christ in miniature." But Lincoln was a man who was not without honor in the esteem of his own countrymen. This gauky, sad-faced man has become the greatest folk hero our country has so far produced.

Abraham Lincoln grew up on the American frontier, in a revivalist environment. His parents were members of the Separate Baptists in Kentucky. Itinerant preachers no doubt visited the Lincoln cabin and the Bible loomed large in Abe's early education. Later, in Illinois, in his New Salem days, Lincoln became an agnostic—and a talkative one. In the stores and taverns, if not in the churches, Abe would argue religion. He reflected ideas he had read in Thomas Paine's *Age of Reason*. Somewhat later he prepared an essay in which he made an argument against Christianity. He apparently asserted that the Bible was not inspired and therefore was not God's revelation and that Jesus Christ was not the son of God. He showed this manuscript to his friend and employer, Samuel Hill. Hill read the manuscript and then questioned the wisdom of such a promising man as Lincoln publishing such damaging doctrine. Hill snatched the manuscript away from Lincoln and thrust it into a nearby stove. William Herndon, in recounting this incident, writes: "The book went up in flames, and Lincoln's political future was se-

537

cure."

But Abraham Lincoln never retreated from these heretical religious notions. When, in 1846, he ran for Congress in the Seventh Illinois District, he found that his opponent—a Methodist minister—was whispering charges of disbelief against him. Lincoln had printed and distributed a handbill which in part stated: "That I am not a member of any Christian Church is true; but I have never denied the truth of the Scriptures; and I have never spoken with intentional disrespect of religion in general, or of any denomination of Christians in particular."

In Springfield, Mrs. Lincoln was a member of the Episcopal Church, but her husband seldom accompanied her to services. Later she joined the First Presbyterian Church of Springfield on confession of faith. One of their sons, Tad, was baptized in that church. Lincoln, however, would spend his Sunday mornings in Springfield anywhere but in church.

During this Springfield period, efforts were made to get Lincoln to join a church. He was given a new theological volume by his wife's minister, Dr. James Smith—a volume entitled *The Christian Defense* and subtitled "Containing a fair statement of the leading objections urged by infidels against the credibility and inspiration of the Holy Scriptures." William Herndon, his law partner, writes about this book: "Lincoln brought it to the office, laid it down, never took it up again to my knowledge, never condescended to write his name in it."

Lincoln left Springfield for Washington to become president. In his farewell talk to his townspeople, Lincoln struck a rich vein of religion which continued in his state papers after becoming President. During his Farewell Address he said: "No one, not in my situation, can appreciate my feeling of sadness at this parting. To this place, and the kindness of these people, I owe everything. Here I have lived a quarter of a century, and have passed from a young to an old man. Here my children have been born, and one is buried. I now leave, not knowing when or whether I may return, with a task before me greater than that which rested upon Washington. Without the assistance of that Divine Being who ever attended him, I cannot succeed. With that assistance, I cannot fail. To His care I commend you, as I hope in your prayers you will commend me, and I bid you an affectionate farewell."

The people of Springfield heard him, stood bareheaded in the rain, and watched the train recede. They were never to see their fellow townsman alive again.

On their arrival in Washington, Mrs. Lincoln joined the New York Avenue Presbyterian Church. President Lincoln attended different churches. A tragic experience occurred when one of the Lincoln boys, Willie, died in the White House. Someone recalled that Lincoln, just after the boy died, gazed at the body and earnestly remarked, "My poor boy, he was too good for this earth. God has called him home. I knew that he is much better off in heaven, but then we loved him so. It is hard, hard to have him die." The human benediction of a father who was also a president!

It has been observed that, with the experience of Willie's death together with the tremendous responsibilities of the presidency and the tragedy of the war, the religion of Lincoln became less heretical, more God-centered. But he never did join a church.

A delegation came to the White House and asked Lincoln to put more reliance on prayer. He gently replied, "The rebel soldiers are praying with a great deal more earnestness, I fear, than our own troops." At another time, he said on the same subject: "The will of God prevails. In great contests, each party claims to act in accordance with the will of God. Both may be, and one must be, wrong. God cannot be for and against the same thing at the same time. In the present Civil War, it is quite possible that God's purpose is something different from the purpose of either party." Mr. Henry Luce [publisher of *Time* Magazine] and others who feel that God is on our side in the Cold War, please take note.

The accents of religion were most noticeable in Lincoln's three great addresses: the First Inaugural, the Second Inaugural, and the Gettysburg Address—the last Carl Sandburg called "a piece of the American Bible." In both the Emancipation Proclamation and the Gettysburg Address, mention of God was omitted in the first drafts, but inserted before they were given. William Herndon wrote, "Lincoln's conventional use late in life of the word, *God,* must not by any means be interpreted that he believed in a personal God." Elsewhere Herndon wrote, "I know that it is said that Mr. Lincoln changed his views. There is no evidence of this . . . Mr. Lincoln was a thoroughly religious man, not a Christian, a broad, liberal-minded man, a liberal, a free religionist, an infidel, and so died."

Was Abraham Lincoln a Unitarian? His law partner, William Herndon, corresponded frequently with Theodore Parker, the great New England Unitarian preacher. Often Herndon wrote to Parker about his law partner and observed that Lincoln asked to be remembered to him or Lincoln has read his last address and thanked him for it. At times, Herndon apologized to Parker for Lincoln's relative moderation in some of his speeches on the issue of slavery. Once Herndon received from Parker a sermon entitled, "The Effect of Slavery on the American People." Herndon rejoiced in the hard-hitting sermon and passed it across the desk to Lincoln, and he especially liked Parker's definition of democracy which he underlined for Lincoln to ponder. The definition read: "Democracy is direct self-government over all the people, for all the people, by all the people."

Lincoln was also introduced to that other great Unitarian preacher of the nineteenth century, William Ellery Channing. One of Lincoln's close friends in Springfield was Jesse Fell, the great grandfather of Adlai Stevenson and a founder of the Unitarian Church of Bloomington, Illinois. Fell talked with enthusiasm to Lincoln about the sermons of Channing. Lincoln showed so much interest that Fell presented him with Channing's complete works which Lincoln kept next to a book on *Exercises in the Syntax of the Greek Language.*

There was no Unitarian Church in Springfield, but Lincoln occasionally attended All Souls Unitarian Church in Washington. This was organized in 1821 and during the Civil War it met in the Capitol building, since its premises were offered for emergency use as a Civil War hospital.

It could be said that Lincoln was friendly to Unitarianism and his ideas were basically Unitarian—but in all honesty we Unitarians cannot claim him as one of us, and shouldn't.

One cannot help but admire Lincoln's religious independence. He refused to join a church, even when running for office, even when President. He disliked the dogma and duplicity of the church—all churches—and he did not try to cover up his feelings. One cannot help but wonder what would happen to a man of Lincoln's stature today—in politics? What we lack today in all political parties is more men of principle, of religious, humanitarian, and moral principle who will be unyielding to the crowd, to the latest Gallup poll, who will stick by the most unpopular of convictions. Such men will lead our nation to peace, will lead our nation through the waters which are as troubled in the 1950s as they were in the 1860s.

Perhaps the religion of Lincoln is best summarized in his Second Inaugural Address, given just five weeks before his assassination. He concluded his great speech with the familiar lines: "With malice toward none; with charity for all; with firmness in the right, as God gives us to see the right, let us strive on to finish the work we are in, to bind the nation's wounds, to care for him who shall have borne the battle, and for his widow, and his orphan, to do all which may achieve and cherish a just, and lasting peace, among ourselves, and with all nations."

Karl Marx

Marx had been one of Homer's boyhood heroes. While he engaged in many ideological battles with twentieth century Marxists and communists, Homer retained an affection for their prophet. This excerpt is from a sermon "The Gospel According to Marx" he gave in Evanston in 1954 at the height of the McCarthy era.

Upon graduating from the university, young Karl associated with a group of young Hegelians, and, in a sense, cut his revolutionary teeth in the field of religion. The great debate at that time was whether religion had made man or whether man had made religion. At this time, he wrote his now-famous phrase, "the criticism of religion is the foundation of all criticism."

From Paris, where he worked as a journalist, Marx began a series of exiles to Brussels to Cologne to Paris and thence to England. Along the way, he helped organize an international communist association that opposed utopian socialism and, in 1948, he was asked to write a manifesto for this group. This became the famous Communist Manifesto—written when Marx was only twenty-nine years old.

What did Karl Marx teach? What is the Gospel according to Marx? Marxism—the teachings of Marx—is both a way of looking at the world and a method of changing it. Like many another faith, Marxism believes in joining theory with practice. One of its favorite phrases is "unity of thought and action." Marx once wrote, "The philosophers have only interpreted the world differently; our business is to make it different." Marxism is not embodied systematically in any formal treatise. The Marx-Engels Institute in Moscow is publishing a complete edition of their writings in twenty-eight volumes. Marx's greatest work was *Das Kapital* which is, as one author has written, "as widely quoted, reverently regarded, and little read as the Bible."

Seventy years after his death, Karl Marx is held in veneration by millions of Marxist socialists and by hundreds of millions of communists from Paris to Peiping. His is the official philosophy of the governments controlling today almost a third of the area of the world. It is popular, these days, not to say a good word for Karl Marx. It is subversive, these days, to know who Karl Marx was. Marx and Marxism cannot automatically or easily be dismissed. However much Marxism has become aborted, there is much in Marx and Marxism that one must admire.

Marx foresaw the consequences of technological development and warned of the machine-mindedness of the workers, long before Gandhi or Schweitzer. Marx's emphasis on the economic or material basis of history is to me a correct interpretation of what is, however much we may wish history would have other motivations. The enduring significance of Marx is as a revolutionary prophet. His predictions as an economist and as a sociologist were wrong. But he was a prophet because he gave a vision and a promise to the despised workers in all countries. He showed, he documented from tomes in the British Museum, the evils, the injustices, and inequalities, of nineteenth century capitalism, evils present in twentieth century colonialism and some twentieth century capitalism.

If Marx could not see the future completely, he saw—more than most of his contemporaries—the feudalism transplanted in the new industrialism. Norman Thomas writes that Marx "gave the working class of the world [a] deep sense of its own revolutionary destiny . . . He made socialism appear no longer as merely a beautiful social and ethical hope but a predestined goal in the development of human society." Marx gave workingmen a faith—a faith to replace their diminishing faith in the church.

In *Religion and the Rise of Capitalism*, Professor R. H. Tawney makes this point: "On a narrower stage but with not less formidable weapons, Calvin did for the bourgeoisie of the sixteenth century what Marx did for the proletariat of the nineteenth . . . the doctrine of Predestination satisfied the same hunger for an assurance that the forces of the Universe are on the side of the Elect as was to be assuaged in a different age by the theory of Historical Materialism. He . . . taught them to feel that they were a Chosen People, made them conscious of their great destiny in the Providential plan, and resolute to realize it."

Marx, the revolutionary prophet, was the patriarch, if not the technical founder, of both democratic socialism and communism. It was Charles Kingsley, an Anglican clergyman, and not Marx, who first used the phrase: "Religion is the opium of the people." One does not have to be a Marxist to realize the basic truth of this phrase, not only for the time of Marx, not only in the early twentieth century in Russia, but today here in the suburbs in America. Much of religion is indeed the opium of the people.

Reinhold Niebuhr, one of the top Christian theologians of our time, wrote that "there are concepts of Marxism indispensable for the solution of the problem of social injustice." He listed three concepts:

First, it is impossible to secure justice, as the churches have tried to do, simply by appeals to the conscience. Marx was right in implying that a sufficient number of persuasive sermons on love will not charm laymen in the pews who act through self-interest.

Second, it is impossible to secure justice, as the churches have tried to do, simply by putting social action in the hands of the intelligent. Marx was right in implying, as were the Hebrew prophets before him, that it is often the poor who are the champions of change, of justice.

Third, it is impossible to secure justice, as the churches have tried to do, without power and thus property being more redistributed. Marx was right in implying, as Neibuhr says, that "the present system of property automatically makes for injustice . . . which undermines the very foundation of society."

A heresy arises when a religion, a faith, has omitted or minimized some essential truth. Communism has been called the latest of the Christian heresies, in that it emphasizes, if in a one-sided way, the social criticism and utopianism of the Old Testament. Edward Rogers rightly says that "there would have been no communist heresy if the church had preached and lived the full gospel." The great Lambeth Conference of religionists in England in 1948 made this same point: "Marxism, by an ironic paradox, is at some points nearer to the Christian doctrine than any other philosophy, and this makes its rivalry all the more formidable."

69 FALSE MESSIAHS AND ANTI-HEROES

"Hate the sin, not the sinner," Gandhi admonished. While Homer engaged in many ideological battles over the years, he rarely attacked an individual's character or motives. He tended to see evil as social and impersonal, rather than as individual and personal. Nuclear war and the threat of nuclear war, in his view, constituted the ultimate sin. At the nadir of his cosmos were nuclear warriors such as John Foster Dulles, President Eisenhower's Secretary of State and exponent of nuclear brinksmanship; Edward Teller, father of the H-Bomb; and Senator Thomas Dodd, advocate of a national home fallout shelter network. Homer also vigorously opposed Hitler, Stalin, Mao, and other great dictators of the century; Senator Joseph McCarthy and other enemies of civil liberties; Bull Conner, George Wallace, and other segregationists; and President Johnson, General Westmoreland, Dean Rusk, and other military and civilian warmakers. But perhaps Homer's greatest spleen was reserved for religionists and social activists who preached one set of values and practiced another. Here are verdicts on several perceived fallen angels.

Stephen H. Fritchman

Rev. Stephen H. Fritchman, Homer's slightly older contemporary and longtime ideological opponent, was active in Unitarian denominational affairs in the 1940s and later served for many years as the minister of the Unitarian Church of Los Angeles. This excerpt is from Homer's review of Fritchman's 1978 memoir, Heretic: A Partisan Autobiography.

Before reading Fritchman, I paused and wondered whether

Fritchman was right about the Soviet Union all these years—and I wrong? Was Fritchman truly a prophet—and I but a timid, anticommunist liberal? Is a society that persecutes a Sakharov, a Solzhenitsyn, a Grigorenko, or a Shcharansky really the wave of the future and its sponsor our denomination's prophetic voice?

Fritchman has been an able Unitarian Universalist leader, both as pastor and as denominational official. Since Unitarian Universalism is a denomination, and not a sect, it has been broad enough to include chaplains to the capitalist status quo and other chaplains to liberal and radical ideologies. However, Fritchman's denominational career has been flawed by at least three activities, all of which understandably have not been described with objectivity in this book.

Fritchman politicized the Unitarian youth movement. Fritchman left his Maine pastorate in 1938 to become youth adviser at Unitarian headquarters. He writes that he "tried and succeeded in coming down on the side of the young." But he also came down on the side of involving his young colleagues in almost every "socialist" front and cause in this pre-war and World War II period.

As a theological student at Meadville, I attended some of these denominational youth meetings more than thirty-five years ago. At the time, Fritchman used the tar brush of liberalism and/or pacifism on persons such as myself as he introduced the officers of American Unitarian Youth (AUY) to new vistas in the World Youth Conference and the World Federation of Democratic Youth (WFDY). In 1946 AUY unanimously voted to affiliate with WFDY. The next year Fritchman resigned as youth adviser, but by then the youth themselves were taking another look at WFDY. A young Canadian, Charles W. Eddis—now the U.U. minister in Montreal—in a report warned that AUY would soon be "the only non-communist youth organization in the sea of communists and communist supporters." By 1948 AUY voted to sever all connections with WFDY, charging that it was an "instrument of communist policies." Fritchman's politics had been repudiated, but echoes of the political polarization he produced in these young people continues thirty years later.

If Fritchman spent nine controversial years as youth adviser, during part of this time he slipped into deeper controversy as editor of the denominational *Christian Register* beginning in late 1942. The "Fritchman Crisis" is too long to describe here. He finally was forced to resign his editorship in May 1947. Fritchman took his case to the annual meeting of the Association. His friends asked for his reinstatement, but they lost in the final vote. Why did Fritchman lose in a denomination which prized freedom? Was it merely that "some powerful and politically ambitious ministers" were working to fire Fritchman? Or were readers of the *Register* finally realizing that they had a totalitarian editor who, in the name of freedom, was not practicing freedom? ACLU President John Haynes Holmes criticized Fritchman as did an increasing number of ministers and lay-persons.

The role of Fritchman in the politics of the Unitarian Service Committee (USC) is still murky. His role was surely more than to make "war-time train journeys and flights to several States to raise funds for the project in Europe of our Unitarian Service Committee." I believe that he does not mention Noel Field, but they surely knew each other. This apparent double agent (see *The Man Who Disappeared: The Strange Case of Noel Field* by Flora Lewis, now the *New York Times* columnist) was ousted from the USC in September 1947 after Rev. Jack Mendelsohn went to Europe and confirmed that there was serious communist influence in the European program of the USC.

As Fritchman went international, it was almost inevitable that he would gravitate to the extravaganzas of the World Peace Council (WPC). Based in Vienna—until it was ousted—and now in Helsinki, the WPC was made in Moscow, and is still highly subsidized by the Soviet State. For more than three decades it has promoted Soviet foreign policy without deviation, not hesitating at times to allege that Soviet nuclear bombs bring peace. If Fritchman at the WPC congresses met "some of the finest intellects and most generous spirits of the world," his was a unique experience. The WPC meetings are notorious for being a blend of party hacks and fellow-traveling innocents—generous perhaps, but hardly intellectual. I am sure that there were more fine intellects in Fritchman's Sunday morning congregations that at the greatest of the WPC congresses.

There are many things that liberals can learn vicariously, but not apparently the ruin or rule methods of communists in international and domestic social movements. Every generation of liberals must personally be burned, bitten, hurt, lied to, and maligned before it believes that there is such a thing as ideological deviousness. Most liberals have never had such experiences, and thus dismiss such warnings against communism as red-baiting, McCarthyism, or witch-hunting. However, there are communists as there are capitalists in our society and in our organizations. Both can do good and both can do evil. We must put the Cold War behind us, and Fritchman over the years has performed a useful service in reminding us that the Russians are *not* coming. But in the world of the future, any triumph of the totalitarian communism which Fritchman calls "socialism" would be as exploitive as any final triumph of unfettered capitalism. We need something better than either of them.

Sekou Touré

Some rulers of newly independent states in Africa and Asia proved as repressive as the colonial rulers they replaced. Homer reflected on one such dictator—a former colleague from the African freedom movement—who died in 1984 after a quarter century of human rights abuses.

Last week, at a clinic in Cleveland, President Ahmed Sekou Touré of the West African country of Guinea died of heart trouble. In the 1950s, Sekou Touré was one of the leading freedom fighters of Africa. Guinea was the first country to reject membership in the French community of Charles de Gaulle. French-speaking Sekou Touré of Guinea, as English-speaking Kwame Nkrumah of Ghana, were heroes to some of us Americans and certainly to many Africans. Indeed, one of my first tasks after leaving Evanston in 1959 and going to New York with the American Committee on Africa was to arrange a large banquet honoring Sekou Touré.

Over twenty-six years as president of Guinea, Sekou Touré became a tyrant with his one-party government. Many dozens, then hundreds, then thousands of persons were imprisoned, tortured, killed. Amnesty International condemned his tyranny and his only reply was—"rubbish."

Sekou Touré, dying at the age of sixty-two, was a survivor, with most of his contemporaries in Africa having been deposed or died. Thousands of mourners reportedly came to the Conakry airport and to his funeral, but more thousands are dead because of the oppression and poverty, and one million or more persons felt that they had to leave that well-endowed country.

Did we put too much faith in Sekou Touré? At least I did. Did we put too much faith in the movement for colonial freedom? I still do not think so. The end of African colonialism was inevitable. I still subscribe to the aphorism that a people are ready for independence when they take it. I still believe that Africa had no choice in the late 1950s and early 1960s but become free.

547

Sun Myung Moon

For more than a decade, Homer criticized Rev. Sun Myung Moon, the Korean founder of the Unification Church, for organizing lavish anticommunist conferences to which he would invite and pay the expenses of clergy, professors, and other molders of public opinion. In 1985, Homer decided to succumb to the blandishments of CAUSA, one of Moon's front groups—"free trip and all"—held in Houston. Homer assessed the three-day conference "Communism: A Theistic Critique and Counter-Proposal" in a sermon to his congregation in Winnetka.

My assessment of the CAUSA (Confederation of Associations for the Unity of the Societies of the Americas) conference contains two favorable elements. First, I am impressed by the number of blacks CAUSA has obtained. Black preachers have been largely forgotten by our American society, except in the era of Martin Luther King. The National Council of Churches and often local church and ecumenical councils tend to ignore black churches and their leaders. They remain outside most networks. Not with CAUSA. I commend CAUSA for including so many blacks, and some in leadership positions, even if the conference staff is almost wholly white or Oriental.

My only other high mark for the conference has to do with its seriousness. I brought my bathing suit, thinking that I could spend some—perhaps much—time in and around the swimming pool: Southern Texas in late April! With envious eyes, I looked at the pool daily, but I did not even take out my bathing trunks during the full three days there. We were much too busy. There was, it appeared, full attendance at all sessions, even at 8:20 a.m.

Otherwise, my assessment of the CAUSA conference is all negative. The discussion of communism—its history, philosophy, economics, and politics—was thorough. Yet the emphasis was one of glassy-eyed hate. Not completely, of course, for there had to be some acknowledgment, however grudgingly, that some of Marx's insights were correct. My basic quarrel with the conference curriculum was that it was purposely truncated. The lecturers documented, ad nauseam, the evils of communism. The textbook explicitly states that "Godism [Moon's philosophy] does not advocate maintaining the status quo. It calls for change in the West as well as the communist world." Yet the text and the lecturers never made an inventory, let alone discuss, other evils existing in our world today: the evils of capitalism and other contemporary ideologies. Thus nuclear war, conventional war, world poverty, environmental problems, human rights violations (outside the communist world), even apartheid—these are hardly mentioned. Thus the many needed solutions to the human predicament—except the campaign against communism—were not even suggested, such as work through the U.N., disarmament, and world economic development. They were completely ignored.

I found this huge omission unpardonable. I especially found it bizarre that 300 ministers, 80 percent black and thus numbering more than 200, could spend three full days hardly mentioning racism in America or apartheid in South Africa. Yet it was that kind of conference.

I do not find it profitable to pluck out one ism and mount a crusade. And Mr. Moon's crusade, for all its intellectual pretensions, is not finely-tuned ideologically. He does not even recognize the spectrum of the many varieties of communism today. The Soviet Union is lumped together with China, although the latter was seldom mentioned.

Mr. Moon's crusade would make the Cold War with the Soviet Union hot, right in the ballroom of the Marriott Hotel in Texas, had the opportunity arisen. That was probably what Mr. Moon vowed when he was taken prisoner decades ago in North Korea. Yet we need not help him make his vow come true. We do not want to be taken prisoner by nuclear holocaust or nuclear winter.

CAUSA is determined to introduce 7,000 American clergymen to this experience. I estimate that the conference I attended cost Mr. Moon—who is presently in Danbury Penitentiary for tax evasion—about $150,000 for the 300 persons involved, or approximately $500 for each person. Thus for $3.5 million, CAUSA can accomplish its goal. Where does CAUSA get that kind of money? The sponsors admitted that CAUSA is fully funded, "so far," by the Unification Church. The finances of the latter are unclear, although a church brochure says that "the time-honored practice of tithing is encouraged for all members." Some of the money may still come from street sales of roses and other flowers.

Mr. Moon has also huge commercial holdings, some in South Korea. His Tong II Industries, near Pusan, makes parts for the Vulcan anti-aircraft gun, the M-79 grenade launcher, the M-60 machine gun, and the M-16 rifle. Also Mr. Moon maintains businesses in America, such as fishing fleets in Norfolk, Gloucester, and Kodiak, Alaska. It is said that a large middle-class constituency in Japan contributes much foreign exchange to the movement. Yet the total bal-

549

ance sheet of Mr. Moon and his many fronts remains a mystery. But not apparently to most who attended that CAUSA conference. They rationalized that they earned their keep. They probably did. So did I, especially writing and preaching this sermon, however critical!

In a word, Mr. Moon and CAUSA are eloquent, and often but not always accurate, in cataloguing the evils done in the name of communism and people's democracies. But they are silent in enumerating the evils done in the name of capitalism and the Western democracies. This is a grievous double standard. Thus Mr. Moon becomes a mirror image of what he hates. And he does this in the name of God and Jesus and religion.

The Dalai Lama

The Tibetan freedom movement presented a challenge to WCRP, and through the years the organization supported China's claim to sovereignty over the high Himayalan kingdom. Homer held that this was not just a realpolitik decision—to ensure Chinese religious participation—but a matter of principle. In "A Second Opinion on Tibet: Demythologizing the Dalai Lama," a sermon given to the Unitarian Fellowship in Warrington, Pennsylvania, in 1989, Homer spelled out his objections to recognizing the temporal authority of the Dalai Lama.

The Dalai Lama is, of course, a myth wrapped inside an enigma. Tibet for centuries was isolated, impenetrable. In our time, Tibet was fictionally portrayed by James Hilton's 1933 novel, *Lost Horizon*. Shangri-La was Tibet, where nobody grew old or sick. How to penetrate and understand this alleged Utopia?

What is the legal status of Tibet? Many books have been written on the status of Tibet. A case can be made either way—that Tibet is independent of China or that Tibet is part of China. During the forty years that the People's Republic has been in power, and decades before, no nation in the world has recognized Tibet as an independent state. And no nation has recognized the Dalai Lama as the Government-in-Exile of Tibet—even India. Today, a second opinion about an independent Tibet is that Tibet is part of China. All existing countries in the world, and the U.N., agree on this determination.

The presumptive Dalai Lama came to full power somewhat prematurely in November 1950, the first year after Mao Zedong and the communists consolidated their power. Various myths about the

Dalai Lama have surfaced these forty years and they merit analysis.

The first myth about the Dalai Lama, widely perpetuated, is that he comes from poor peasant stock. Even the Dalai Lama himself had to admit in his autobiography, published in 1962, that "normally, we had five workers on our farm," and during the harvest up to forty men. British officials described them as "a fairly well-to-do family."

The second myth is that the Dalai Lama left Tibet suddenly in 1959 just one step ahead of the People's Liberation Army of China. In his autobiography, he tells the now familiar story about how he made the final trek out of Tibet to the Indian border, "sleeping fully dressed" each night. This is the truth, but hardly the whole truth. The Dalai Lama did not reveal, at least in 1962, that his two brothers dealt over the years in depth with the American CIA. For years, the CIA tried to foment revolution in Tibet after 1949. The CIA trained Tibetans to be able to parachute back into Tibet and this training was done in a camp in Colorado! When the *New York Times* stumbled on the story, Secretary of Defense Robert McNamara successfully persuaded the *Times* to kill it. Yet the involvement of the CIA, and even its initials, appear nowhere in the Dalai Lama's poignant—to some—*Autobiography*.

A third myth about the Dalai Lama is that he is a fair-minded intellectual, a scholar. He and his associates lean heavily on reports of the International Commission of Jurists for their positions on the international status of Tibet and human rights there. How impartial? Minimal research reveals that the ICJ grew out of the Investigating Committee of Free Justice, set up by U.S. intelligence operatives in 1949 to publish anti-communist propaganda for recruiting agents in East Germany to work for the CIA. This committee in 1952 became the ICJ and was supported with grants totaling $650,000 from the CIA in the period 1958-1964.

Still a fourth myth is that the Dalai Lama is somehow a Gandhian. He does write sympathetically about Mohandas Gandhi in his *Autobiography*. Yet it appears that the Dalai Lama is able to work well on two levels. He travels both the high road and the low road. He can appear to be a selfless Buddhist, even a Gandhian, visiting the Vatican or the headquarters of the World Council of Churches. Yet many of the Dalai Lama's followers, in Tibet and outside, use every tool and weapon they can find to oust the Chinese from Tibet. If the Dalai Lama were revered as much as he and some others claim, could he not turn off, shut off, or at least deflect these violent associates?

A fifth and final myth about the Dalai Lama is that he is the head of a neat, New Age religion, Tibetan Buddhism or Lamaism. Perhaps so, but the old religion of Lamaism, practiced by the Dalai Lama's predecessors and by himself until he went into exile, would make an atheist out of most sensitive persons. A Nepalese diplomat stationed in Lhasa in the late 1940s gave this description: "The monastic centers are like college towns with as many as 10,000 monks in one place, whiling away their time, spending the mornings in doing mechanical prayer, supported in parasitic luxury on the meager resources of the country." No wonder it took "hundreds of pack animals loaded with wealth and treasure" for the Dalai Lama to leave Tibet for Sikkim when he went to Southern Tibet almost to exile in 1950! In his *Autobiography*, the Dalai Lama had to admit the excesses of Lamaism and wrote that the "ancient color and splendor" of the ceremonies were "too ornate in the old days, and it may not be a bad thing to observe them more austerely."

As regards human rights in Tibet, this topic needs no second opinion. The first and second and third opinion is that violations of human rights continue in Tibet and must come to a prompt end.

Until the 1950s, Tibet was a feudal society. The people possessed neither civil nor political rights nor economic, social, or cultural rights. The Tibetan people under successive Dalai Lamas had no human rights whatsoever, except freedom to practice primarily Lamaism. When the communists came to power in China in 1949, they treated Tibet with initial circumspection. When the Dalai Lama left Tibet in 1959, China decided that at least serfdom had to be eliminated. The communists at the time complained about the "three lacks" and the "three abundances" in Tibet. It lacked fuel, communication, and people. Tibet was abundant, they insisted, in poverty, oppression, and fear of the supernatural. With the Dalai Lama in exile, Beijing was determined to give the people of Tibet something to make up for these three lacks as well as to eliminate these three abundances. The cost in doing so was much too severe, but perhaps there may be greater economic and social rights in Tibet today than in recent centuries.

Violations of human rights are widespread in Tibet today, but no more so than under a succession of Dalai Lamas—except for religious freedom. But today the measure, the standard, must be the U.N. Declaration of Human Rights, not the feudalism of the "God-King."

By way of a postscript, I believe that Tibet should not become independent in today's world, under the present system of world organization. Yet the present system is not good enough. There ought to be a better system of world organization which would meet the present articulated needs of ethnic, linguistic, and other minorities which feel that they must be free—whether Basques in Spain, Sikhs in the Punjab in India, several groups within the Soviet Union, or Tibetans in China.

One could envision a new process under U.N. supervision. A people could simultaneously petition the "mother country" and the U.N. for special status—U.N. autonomy. A new U.N. organ, perhaps a U.N. Peoples' Council, would then ask the mother country if it is willing to grant the petitioning people U.N. status if the mother country retains overall foreign policy and technical sovereignty. Then a U.N.-sponsored (and monitored) plebiscite would be held to ascertain the real wishes of the people. If two-thirds of those voting agree, then the people could become the Punjab, the Basque, or the Tibetan territory. They would pledge not to raise any armed forces and their police would be under direct U.N. supervision. The could send observers both to the parliament of their mother country and to the U.N. Peoples' Council.

I can see world polity slowly, or even rapidly, moving in this direction. A U.N. solution is of little practical help to those several million Tibetans who want independence from 1.1 billion Chinese. The odds for independence are hopeless, given the demographics. A second opinion I believe is reasonable: not an independent Tibet, but one with the Dalai Lama back without political power. A third possibility, a new world system of national autonomy, is further down the U.N. road an indeterminable distance.

PART TEN

MYSELF

MY PERSONAL LIFE

*"Every life is many days, day after day. We walk
through ourselves, meeting robbers, ghosts, giants,
old men, young men, wives, widows, brothers-in
-law. But always meeting ourselves."*

—James Joyce, Ulysses

Like many public figures, Homer was occupied
with social and community activities for most of his life
and did not devote as much time to his family or his own
self-development as he would have liked. In this section,
Homer reflects on his family relations, his hobbies and
pastimes, and the overall meaning of his life.

Traveling was a lifelong passion, and he usually encountered good fortune. However, on one ill-fated trip to
London, in which he was delayed by an airline strike and
bad weather, he noted in a letter, "I feel like Ahab on his
last voyage." During most of his life, Homer was rarely
alone. However, in Tokyo where he lived for several
months organizing WCRP's first conference in 1970,
Homer turned for companionship to a cicada which he
named *Hawai* (peace). "Hawai-san is still singing—
rounding out his third month, and about his fourth cu-
cumber," he wrote his family back home. "The best investment in my life! But he may go the way of all flesh, insect included, one of these days."

Photograph: Homer in Egypt, 1938

70 SWARTHMORE (1992)

MY FAMILY

My Son, Alex

The week of August 6, 1945, I was in Wisconsin leading a group of Unitarian youth on a week-long retreat at Lake Geneva. We arose on August 7 to read about the atomic bombing of Hiroshima and were stunned. We listened to the radio and could talk of little else that day. By evening we put together a religious service focusing on the bomb. Some of us resolved to do whatever we could to work for the abolition of atomic weapons and for other forms of disarmament. Many of those Unitarian youth, decades later, cannot forget that worshipful occasion.

Two weeks after that tragic event and the bombing of Nagasaki, our son, Alexander, was born on August 21. We informed our friends through an announcement mimeographed on a postcard: "For immediate release. Baby Boy Born to Jacks. Alexander Jack was born in the University of Chicago Lying-In Hospital on Tuesday morning, August twenty-first at eleven twenty-five. Seventy ounce Alexander is doing fine, as are Esther and Homer."

Another family event also happened on that day, of much less importance, but annoying at the time. Our auto, a Ford, parked on the street near our Ellis Avenue apartment, was stolen! The police allowed me to go with them in a squad car for blocks around, hoping to find it. Two weeks later the car turned up, stripped of parts. In those early postwar days, parts were as valuable as cars. Radio, tires, and all moveable parts were stolen. We were insured, but our garage had a hard time locating parts. The cost for all the parts was $128.00! This incident caused me anguish and—hard to believe in retrospect—detracted from the joy at the birth of Alexander.

From the South Side of Chicago, we moved to the apartment on Juneway Terrace. Because of my work in race relations and civil liberties, I was frequently away from home until late at night, but Alex picked up some influence from his father. In a letter to a friend in January 1947 I observed, "Alex, our two-year-old son now says these words . . . daddy, mommie, and commie."

Several years later, in my column for the *Pittsburg Courier*, the black newspaper, I described another experience:

> If there has been any little white boy that his parents have tried to bring up color-blind, it has been our little Alex, aged almost five. We have not told 'race jokes' at table, we have not made slurring remarks in his presence (or out of it, for that matter!), and we have given him at least more opportunity than perhaps the average white boy living in a segregated society to play with Negro children and to see Negro adults. So far, so good. Alex recognizes the fact that some people are white-skinned and some people are dark-skinned, but he has not, like too many people in our racist society, attached any value to the possession of a white or a dark skin. But he is very conscious of race. Last week, on our way to the railroad station to meet a displaced person from Hungary our church is bringing to the Chicago area, little Alex asked whether the man will be white or black. I pressed Alex to tell me why he asked, but all he would say was that he wanted to know. . . . This summer Alex will be living in Jim Crow Florida and next autumn Alex will be going to school in a lily-white environment and it will be interesting, if tragic, to see just how soon he picks up the virus of racism.

Alex spent nine years growing up in our parsonage in Evanston. He did not appear to be too intimidated by being a PK— preacher's kid. He played Cub Scout baseball, with a proud father watching. At age twelve, as I described earlier, Alex went with me for several weeks to Japan where I attended an international conference on atomic issues. His visit to the Atomic Survivors Hospital and poignant talk with young victims his age—injured in the very month and year he was born—made a deep impression. Also, just before we left Evanston for New York, Alex joined me in a peace march in Chicago. He lasted the whole 12 miles, passing out leaflets against nuclear testing and his picture appeared in the *Sun-Times*.

Alex went to Scarsdale High School from 1959 to 1963 and served as editor-in-chief of the *Maroon*, the school newspaper. During a prolonged strike of the *New York Times*, Alex and his staff fanned out through Manhattan and put out several issues of a daily newspaper and distributed it to the commuters on the railroad line to New York City. One issue featured the Kennedy-Macmillan conference in the Bahamas, wire service stories contributed by Tass—they turned to the Soviet News Agency when the American wire services in New York were not forthcoming—and a large advertisement from Bergdorf Goodman's!

One summer Alex went to the Town and Country Camp in Vermont. Alex applied for admission to several colleges and was accepted at Oberlin, his mother's and grandmother's school. In the autumn and winter of 1964, Alex and some other Oberlin students participated in an extension of Mississippi Summer, spending several weeks in Mississippi during the school term organizing voter registration. Over the holiday break, he returned with a campus group called "Carpenters for Christmas" to rebuild a burned-out black church in the northern part of that state. I rented an auto in Memphis and spent a day visiting him.

Alex easily caught my fascination with India and arranged to spend his junior year with the Indian program of the University of Wisconsin. He studied at the well-known Benares Hindu University. He was able to travel extensively around India and visited Jayaprakash Narayan at his ashram in Bihar and Indian President Radhakrishnan in New Delhi.

Alex was managing editor of the *Review*, the Oberlin student paper. The Vietnam War was raging and Alex went to Vietnam in the spring of 1967 to write for the *Review* and other college and university papers. He spent four months there, obtaining journalist credentials and interviewing U.S. pilots on an aircraft carrier off the North Vietnamese coast, and he flew on an aerial combat mission over the South. He had an important visit with Thich Tri Quang, the charismatic Zen priest who took refuge from the authorities in the An Quang Pagoda. I managed to visit Alex in Saigon and we went to a reception at the home of Henry Cabot Lodge. Alex engaged in a spirited argument with the U.S. Ambassador, but didn't change his mind. His anti-war reporting led to a string of "alternative press" journalists going to Saigon.

Returning to Boston, Alex entered the Boston University School of Theology—Martin Luther King's alma mater—as a Unitarian. As opposition to the Vietnam War escalated, Alex became active in the Resistance, which encouraged young men to resist military service. In October, 1967, Alex and his associates organized a peace rally on Boston Common—the largest antiwar demonstration in Boston at the time—and planned the ceremony at Arlington Street Church in Boston. This service—at which several hundred young men turned in draft cards to Catholic, Protestant, and Jewish clergy or burned them at the altar over a candlestick belonging to Rev. William Ellergy Channing, the great nineteenth century Abolitionist—received nationwide publicity and some federal indictments. Somehow, Alex was passed over and he was not a defendant in a federal conspiracy trial with Benjamin Spock, William Sloane Coffin, and others. This non-indictment broke Alex's pro-conspiracy heart.

Later, at Boston University Alex researched and published in the university newspaper a list of professors who had contracts with the Defense Department and organized a sanctuary in the university chapel. This action paralyzed the campus and Alex was dismissed as a student. His not continuing studies for the Unitarian ministry broke my heart. However, he continued to try to reform organized religion—including our own denomination. In the spring of 1969, Alex and his seminarian colleagues "liberated" the headquarters of the Unitarian Universalist Service Committee—several blocks down Beacon Street from my office and the Unitarian Universalist Association. The UUSC (which is independent of the UUA) operated social work projects in South Vietnam that were funded by the U.S. State Department and could be construed as part of the pacification effort. Alex's group occupied the building for about a week and published correspondence documenting this relationship.

As the war dragged on, Alex became increasingly uncomfortable with the violent protests of the peace movement. He eventually quit organizing protests, edited the *Boston Free Press*, an underground newspaper, and moved into a commune in Cambridge. In the early 1970s, he began hitchhiking around the U.S. and went to Europe on a spiritual odyssey. Returning to Boston, he established a small press, Kanthaka (named after the Buddha's horse) and earned a living for awhile as a taxi driver. His first book, *The Adamantine Sherlock Holmes,* recounted the English detective's adventures in Tibet and India and was essentially a literary study of racism and colonialism in the Holmes' canon. In the mid-1970s, Alex married Ann Fawcett, a Unitarian-Universalist seminarian at B.U. and later Harvard, and he and his "spouseperson" lived in Marblehead, Massachusetts, outside Boston.

A vegetarian since his Indian sojourn, Alex eventually gravitated to Michio Kushi and his macrobiotic educational center (originally in the Arlington Street Church). Soon Alex was editor of the *East West Journal*, a vital vegetarian-cum-macrobiotic, New Age monthly. Alex worked at the *Journal* for seven years, eventually leaving to write books full time. With Kushi, he wrote *The Cancer Prevention Diet*, a 460-page work published in 1983 by St. Martin's Press and soon translated and published in a dozen languages. They also collaborated on *Diet for a Strong Heart* (1985), *One Peaceful World* (1987), and *The Gospel of Peace* (1992), a commentary on Jesus' teachings in the long-lost Gospel of Thomas which was found in an Egyptian cliffside in 1945, the year Alex was born. With Aveline Kushi, Alex wrote *Complete Guide to Macrobiotic Cooking* (1985) and several other works. I never expected my son to be an editor of a cookbook! Soon Alex had many more readers than his father ever had!

In 1980, Alex accompanied Ingeborg, Renate (Ingeborg's daughter), and me on a three-week trip in China, guests of the Buddhists and Protestants of that country. Alex tried to convert the billion Chinese to eat brown rice! He did not succeed, but at the end of the trip they produced a package of "home-grown" brown rice for him, demonstrating they could sell it if there were demand. In Beijing, Alex helped organize a macrobiotic banquet for religious leaders at the Fa-Yuan Zen Temple, west of the Forbidden City, dating from the seventh century. The surviving vegetarian restaurant in Beijing catered the affair, with Alex supervising the cooking of the organic brown rice that he brought from America. He also cooked miso soup from bean paste commercially made in the U.S. At the banquet a Roman Catholic recalled that the Lord's Prayer is translated, "Give us this day our daily rice."

In 1982 Alex and Ann separated, and several years later he married Barbara Gale Fields, a macrobiotic cooking teacher from Dallas. She has a son, Jon. For awhile they lived in Texas, working on Gale's autobiography, *Promenade Home*, but soon migrated again North. In 1988, Alex and Gale moved to Becket in western Massachusetts, to manage and teach at the Kushi Institute, which had moved from Boston to a former Franciscan monastery on a beautiful 600-acre site in the Berkshires. In 1990, Alex became director of the One Peaceful World Society, an international holistic information network and friendship society, also based in Becket. OPW has about twenty-five national offices around the world, publishes a quarterly newsletter, and operates OPW Press, publishing books on diet, health, ecology, and spiritual development. Through OPW Press, Alex handled the production and printing of my book *WCRP: A History of the World Conference on Religion and Peace* (1993).

Over the years, Alex has given me the soft sell on diet. For short periods Ingeborg and I have been devotees of whole foods, but not over the long run.

So far Alex has led a variegated life. I am afraid at times I have overshadowed him, but he has in the end carved out a career independent from that of his father. I see him four or five times a year, and talk at rare intervals on the telephone; neither of us is addicted to calling. (He gave me a fax machine for my seventy-fifth birthday, and I don't know what I would do without it!) I do not see enough of Alex and I hardly know him. That is more my fault than his, in this modern society, where there seems time for everything else.

My Daughter, Lucy

Lucy came along on August 26, 1947. We were living on Juneway Terrace, just south of Evanston by then, and thus Lucy was born at Evanston Hospital, with an announcement that did not take the form of a press release. Our auto, parked along Juneway Terrace in Chicago, was not stolen.

Lucy grew up in the Evanston parsonage until she was twelve. This was on Orrington Avenue, one block from the Northwestern University campus, two blocks from Lake Michigan. She went to Orrington School, a mile up Orrington Avenue. She had much support from her two-year-older brother and, in a sense, from a series of pets. We had several Siamese cats—in succession—and a dachshund, and a St. Bernard. We called the latter, Bonzie. (We should have called our dachsy, Umlaut, but we did not.) When we moved from Evanston to Scarsdale in June 1959, Bonzie and two cats were in our automobile.

In the summer of 1954, the whole family went on a month-long trip by auto to Alaska (then still a territory). This was an ambitious journey along the Alcan Highway, 10,000 miles round trip from Chicago to Fairbanks, one-half on unimproved road. Our greatest adventure was when we reached Whitehorse, British Columbia. We were told the highway was closed because of landslides. There was no prediction when the Alcan might be reopened. Tourist traffic was piling up. We were lucky to obtain a motel for the night. We discussed our bad luck with other tourists in our motel. We decided to visit a British Columbian ranger. He told us that there was one detour available to reach Alaska, but it involved several hundred miles of extra driving and the use of several undependable auto ferries. The routing was through the old gold-rush town of Klondike.

When the highway did not reopen early the next morning, ten families formed a caravan and we pledged to stick together for the two-day detour. We did, despite one or two cars being more puncture-prone than most. Lucy and Alex were elated with our adventure and exchanged comic books and often seats with the other children their age in our cars. Driving during the midnight sun was an additional adventure. We survived the ferries and the often-empty gasoline stations. When we returned to the Alcan inside Alaska, we sadly broke up our caravan, only to encounter some of our members days after in other parts of Alaska. Indeed, we wrote Christmas cards to each other for several years afterwards.

Lucy and Alex giggled when we passed the town of Homer. We spent two days in the rustic Camp Denali in a national park. Our Alaskan venture was to be a fond family memory for decades. We followed this adventure several years later with a similar journey to Cuba. We drove down to Key West and put our auto on a ferry to Havana. There we had many adventures, the first as a family in a foreign country. We loved Veradero Beach and Cuban food, especially guava and cream cheese, and occasionally we encountered rebels loyal to Fidel Castro in the provinces.

Since I took Alex to Japan in 1957, I was looking for an opportunity to take Lucy overseas. It came in August 1961—on her fourteenth birthday. We began in Paris, then went to Geneva, and then to Nice. There we visited Ira and Anita Morris in their villa along the Mediterranean. It was a rare moment on the French Riviera, as the Morrises were discussing establishing a home in Hiroshima for the survivors. We then went on to Rome and visited the tourist sights in a Grey Line bus. Lucy had a birthday lunch in Rome and a birthday supper in Athens where I showed her some of the ancient diggings I remembered in my one year in Athens.

We flew to Belgrade where I attended the first Summit of the heads of the Non-Aligned States as an observer. There we saw something of U.S. journalist I. F. Stone and his wife who were also reporting on the conference. In London, Lucy stayed with the family of a British Unitarian minister and his physician wife. We attended the booking, or trial, of Bertrand Russell, charged with civil disobedience in opposing British nuclear policy. Lucy and I had an exciting European trip.

Lucy graduated from Scarsdale High School; I returned from Boston weekends so she could finish high school in Scarsdale. Then she went to Mt. Holyoke College. In the summers, she participated in civil rights activities, painting houses in Roxbury in the summer of 1964 and working on an interracial project in the slums of Newark. After two years at Mt. Holyoke, she transferred to Boston University. After graduating with a major in English literature, she decided to study nursing and commuted to Salem State College.

In 1972 Lucy married a cousin, Jonathan Williams—the son of her mother's brother, George. Lucy and Jonathan took an apartment in Somerville and later in Brookline. Jonathan drove a taxi for several years. On December 10, 1976, their first child, a son, Michael, was born. Molly, their daughter, was born on July 12, 1980.

George and Margery Williams had three children other than Jonathan. Jeremy, the eldest son, left America to live in Australia. I once visited him and his wife, Christine, in Sydney. Portia, Jonathan's sister, married Tom Weiskel, an instructor of English at Yale. They had a lovely daughter named Shelbourne. One wintry day, her husband was skating with the little girl. They went through the ice and both drowned. Portia was pregnant at the time. In addition to this child, a girl, she went on to take in several foster children, become an authority on organic, country-style living, and eventually entered a longtime relationship with a young graduate student who became a professor in the Amherst area. Roger, the youngest Williams' child, became an architect, married, and has several children.

Over the years, Jonathan developed psychological problems and was in and out of several mental hospitals and clinics for severe depression. During his last crisis, he stayed at Gould Farm in western Massachusetts, which had some informal connection with several Unitarian Universalist educators. He was under treatment by the Gould Farm physician who was only later to be found practicing without a license. Jonathan was allowed to go unsupervised to Boston for a weekend. He went to his parents' home in suburban Belmont and committed suicide.

This was a traumatic moment for Lucy, Michael, and Molly. Somehow they survived, if not unscathed. Lucy was working as a nurse in Beth Israel Hospital before Jonathan died. Now she had to be both father and mother to a young family and continue to work. Before Jonathan died, they had bought with Esther a double-family home in Brookline equally distant from a primary school which the children attended and Brookline High, where Esther worked as a librarian. At least Lucy had the help of her mother in this difficult period since Esther lived in the unit downstairs.

I tried to be helpful to Lucy in this period, first from Winnetka, and then when we lived at Swarthmore. Following the establishment of the Dana Greeley Foundation in nearby Concord in 1986, I was able to go to Boston four times a year to attend Board meetings and see them—as well as confer with Esther about their welfare—a few days on each visit, and occasionally at other times.

Michael took up acting in grammar school and beyond, and appears to be a typical American boy, knowing well his Apple computer. Molly is never far behind, playing soccer, the clarinet, and going twice now to a summer camp for girls in Maine. Both children live a busy Brookline life, with many telephone calls, constant TV, and posters. On one visit we took the T to central Boston, thinking I might take the children to tea at the Ritz. The dress code prevented that extravaganza, but that same afternoon we did see presidential candidate Jerry Brown speak on the Boston Common.

Lucy worked for some years for a group of physicians in Chelsea and now for a visiting nurses association. She has had to juggle her job with her two busy children, not to mention the household chores.

Lucy sued Gould Farm for the irresponsible way their physician released Jonathan that unfortunate weekend. It was plucky for Lucy to want to go to court and testify. In the end, they were found partially negligent. After Johnny's death, Lucy met Stanley Rauch, who had lost his wife to cancer. Stan, a financial planner, and Lucy proved to be very congenial and for the last several years have been engaged. Lucy has become increasingly interested in Judaism, especially after she became a nursing coordinator for a Jewish social service agency in Boston.

My Grandmother by Lucy Jack Williams

At the memorial service for Homer's mother, Cecelia, after her death in 1976, Lucy gave an especially appropriate portrait of her grandmother.

When I think of my grandmother, I picture a strong, plucky, vital woman who enjoyed life and believed in the finality of death. She was a believer in life. She loved music, nature, and people. When she came to Evanston and then to Scarsdale when I was a child at the beginning of every summer, it was a supreme event. It meant a permanent, friendly babysitter—my father and mother were often away—a companion, lots of fighting perhaps, but a summer of TV, canasta, dancing, good times. And as summer turned into autumn, she was gone, so quickly it seemed. There we would be, seeing her off, waving and crying at the train station.

One of the best gifts my grandmother had was her uncanny ability to see through things that were false. She hated pretense, conventions, insincerity, dishonesty—and alcohol. Of course, that got her into trouble. She never cared what anyone thought. She never wore makeup or curled her hair. She wore comfortable, competent clothing and brown oxfords.

She also taught us by example to treat people equally, explicitly black people. She was never impressed by status, credentials, position.

She was, however, always impressed by my father. And she was so proud of him! She could never get enough of her son. But she did not hold on to him or any of us. She let people go. She was a courageous lady in many ways. She must have been lonely, living much of her life alone. But she loved herself enough to take care of herself and let it be.

My grandmother, like all of us, was a mystery. She was a feminist, who preferred men to women. She was justice-oriented and often unfair. She was unbelieving, as an atheist, but spiritual in the sense that she was life-giving. She was loving, but did not have a sense of family or permanence, and could cut off family members for years. She was a woman who knew who she was, but never affirmed her heritage.

But I like to remember my grandmother as she was in Florida, controlling her own life, living the only life she believed she could live: tanned, healthy, spontaneous, going to Ethical Culture lectures on Spinoza, visiting her sister daily, writing letters to President Kennedy. When she lived in Florida, she lived simply. She knew the values of a simple life. A flower picture by Grandpa Alex on the wall, a letter from Homer, oatmeal and wheat germ in the icebox, an ocean breeze, writing a letter to her grandchildren sending us her love. She long ago had given her possessions and money away.

My Grandchildren

Michael Williams

On the occasion of the birth of Michael, Lucy and Jonathan's first child, on December 10, 1978, Homer sent a telegram from Australia where he was traveling: "Felicitations to you and your parents generally but also your selection of Human Rights Day to be born and thus the disadvantaged will celebrate the day of your birth. Grandfather Homer." On the occasion of his grandson's sixth birthday, he wrote a letter en route to Scandinavia.

Dear Michael,

Now that you can read, I want to send you this first birthday letter—your sixth birthday, but the first letter from your grosspapa which is written just for you.

You must feel like a big boy now, going to school and learning to read and write. I am sure you will soon do both very well.

I am sure also that you will have a good birthday. I am writing this now because, on the 10th of December, I will be across the ocean in Norway. Look up the capital city, Oslo, on your map. I will be there and in nearby Sweden for ten days, and arrive back in New York just before Christmas.

And so, Michael, I do wish you a very happy birthday. I also enclose a birthday present to you of six dollars. I know how much you like money and take care of your money and so I have no hesitation to give you this present.

Love, Grosspapa

Molly Williams

On July 4, 1981, Homer christened his granddaughter, Molly, who was almost one year old. The ceremony was held at the Old Meadow Farm in Northfield, New Hampshire, recently acquired by Alex. The meadow was wet from intermittent rain and so everyone went inside. "In between the raindrops," Homer recalled, "I picked some black-eyed susans—one of my father's favorite flowers—and three pink clovers. I poured water into a waxed cup from a thermos bottle. I brought from Brookline the tiny, 140-year-old Bible, listing women of three generations of the Pease family on Lucy's mother's side." Following lunch, Homer led the following service:

From time immemorial, young boys and girls have been recognized by society and by religion and welcomed as part of the group. This occurs at different times in different societies and is called by different names. The first kick of the child in the womb, the first cry or scream, the first smile, the first tear, the first bite, the first word—these are all signs by the child affirming individuality. But society, also, gives recognition to the individual in many ways—the birth certificate, the graduation diploma, the voting card, the social security number.

Religion and ethics have played their part, down the ages, by helping to name the child and, in the Judeo-Christian tradition, by baptizing or christening the child. This process not only recognizes the individuality—the uniqueness—of the child, as a son or daughter of the universe and of God, but as part of a tradition. In the ceremony today, we recognize this uniqueness and this tradition. Yet we realize that later, much later, this child, on her own free will, may reaffirm her adherence to this tradition or choose another.

Nevertheless, this is an important infant tradition. We are all honored to participate in this Judeo-Christening of Molly. Just as I annointed Alex and Lucy in the Midwest in the late 1940s, so I am honored to do so to Molly in New England in the early 1980s. This is distinctly another generation.

Now let me read parts of a poem, "A Prayer for My Daughter," by William Butler Yeats, written in 1919:

Once more the storm is howling, and half hid
Under this cradle-hood and coverlid
My child sleeps on . . .

May she be granted beauty and yet not
Beauty to make a stranger's eye distraught,
Or hers before a looking-glass, for such,
Being made beautiful overmuch
Consider beauty a sufficient end,
Lose natural kindness and maybe
The heart-revealing intimacy
That chooses right, and never find a friend . . .

O May she live like some green laurel
Rooted in one dear perpetual place . . .

In the presence of Lucy and Jonathan, of Michael, and of Ann and Alex, I use this water as a symbol of purity, this flower as a symbol of beauty, and this family Bible as a symbol of religious tradition. As an ordained clergyman and as your grandfather, I welcome Molly Miranda Williams to the Judeo-Christian tradition.

Molly, may you continue to be a joy to your parents and grandparents, to Michael and to your friends.

Molly, may your life be one of happiness and yet make a contribution to the slow social evolution of our species.

Molly, may your life live out its term of four score and ten, despite the deep clouds of war and violence on the near horizon.

Molly, may your life benefit from the rich heritage of your parents and grandparents and their parents and grandparents, and may you benefit from the achievements—as well as the mistakes—of others.

Molly, may your robust voice continue to cry out against pain and hunger—everywhere.

Molly, may your vigorous crawl take you to new vistas never dreamt or found by your parents or grandparents.

Molly, may your laughter be infectious and ripple to a whole world in its frequent sorrow.

Before we conclude this service for Molly, I want to say some words to Michael, who was christened by another grandfather.

Michael, we love you.

Michael, we like the way you treat Molly.

Michael, may your life also be rich in experience.

Michael, may you also walk in the firm steps of your ancestors.

Michael, you can relax—we all can relax—for now the ceremony is over.

Jon Beith

On November 1, 1986, when Alex married Barbara Gale Fields Beith, we gained not one, but two additions to our family. Her son, Jon—an avid sports fan, the John Madden of the family—keeps us abreast of the latest dramas of the Dallas Cowboys, the Boston Red Sox, and other teams throughout the nation.

Though he spends most of the year with his father in Irving, Texas, Jon visits Alex and Gale during the summers. In 1992, Jon spent his senior year of school year with Alex and Gale at their home in Hinsdale, and graduated from Wahconah High School. Jon is a very lively, outgoing young man, and everyone enjoys his ready wit and good-natured conversation.

Masha Jack

On February 18, 1992, Gale and Alex adopted a little girl from Russia named Masha (short for Mariya). She was born in Moscow on November 21, 1984. (Earlier Alex had organized an airlift of natural foods to the then Soviet Union, participated in an environmental conference in Moscow, and lectured to medical doctors in Leningrad.) Shortly after her arrival in America, I wrote Masha this letter, though she didn't speak a word of English yet.

Dearest Masha,

You are the second child of Gale and Alex. I welcome my fourth grandchild, to this greater family, to the U.S.A. and to this greater world.

I welcome you for who you are.

I welcome you from the Confederation of Independent States— once the Soviet Union, once the bitter enemy of the U.S.A.

You will not be able to read, immediately, this letter. Someday, you will. And I hope you will sense the great joy I feel, having just learned a few hours ago that you, my new grandchild, are actually with Gale and Alex in their home—your home—at Hinsdale, that you are now part of our family.

I hope to see you very soon—to see your face, and your hair, your nice smile—and to sense the accident of history that you crossed the Atlantic to find yourself in America, in the home of Gale and Alex.

Welcome! Welcome! If only Inge and I knew of your existence when we were in Moscow in June 1987. You would have been only two years old then, but wouldn't it have been nice if we could have known you even then.

The next five years will pass just as quickly. Soon you will be twelve, not seven. I hope both Russia and the U.S.A. grow out of their momentary troubles by then and become, not trouble-free, but hopeful and that this optimism is reflected in the children as well as in your parents and your grandparents. Every good wish from Inge and myself.

Love, Your grandfather

My Wife, Ingeborg and Her Family

My wife, Ingeborg, was born in South West Germany, into a music-loving, nature-loving family. Her parents were Ernst Kind and Franziska Auguste Reichart Kind. Ingeborg had two brothers and two sisters. Her older brother, Ferdinand, died after the war of injuries he had received during the war. Ingeborg's sister, Imelda, is married to Otto Kolb. Her sister, Helma, is married to Manfred Zink. Both families live near their home town, close to their children and grandchildren. Her younger brother, Herbert, lives with his wife, Carmen, and their children in Northern Italy. Ingebord had been married before and has three daughters. Marianne, the oldest, lives with her husband, Christopher Thatcher, and their three children Annemarie, Mark, and Robert, in Vienna, Austria. Renate lives with her husband, Khodr Ahmed Elatab, and their children, Mohammed Sharif and Jasmine, in north New Jersey. Ingeborg's youngest daughter, Sigrid Belck, lives in Geneva, Switzerland.

My Relatives

As a small boy, I was surrounded with family. My maternal grandmother and grandfather were alive as was my paternal grandmother. My father's father died about a decade before my birth. We went to visit my three grandparents often, especially my grandfather and grandmother Davis on Lyndhurst Street. Also I had a number of aunts and uncles—and thus cousins. On my mother's side, three of her siblings lived in Rochester: Jennie, a teacher, married to Al Leve, a chiropractor; Rose, who ultimately ran a small florist shop, married to Eli Berger, who was an antique collector/dealer; and Harry, who helped my grandfather in distributing the cigars which my grandfather made, and then branched out into kindred businesses. They all had children—my cousins. Eunice was Jennie's daughter, a little younger than myself, and Dean—much younger. Of the Berger children, Doris was my age and, looking back, my favorite—almost a sister. Harry had one daughter, Eleanor. In my youth, I saw a lot of my mother's family—especially Doris and Eunice.

My father had eight brothers and sisters. His sister, Elisabeth, or Lizzie, married Maximilian Rappl. I remember we traded postage stamps. Sister Sarah married Henry Higbee who worked in a department store. Sister Emma married Isaac Bloom and they had nine children. Celia married Emil Berman, an accountant, and they promptly went to New York to live. That was an excuse to visit them in Queens or Brooklyn almost once a year. Frances was the youngest sister and she married Herbert LaBarr. Of the boys, Louis became a lawyer with offices in the Powers Building. He married Lena, who worked at Eastman Kodak too much of her life. Emanuel became a rabbi in California, Colorado, and Yonkers. We never went west to visit him and his wife, Sylvia, but we did see him on the outskirts of New York City. Leo never married. He fought in the First World War and became a Rochester policeman. He let me play with his handcuffs.

I had a formidable number of first cousins on my father's side. Somehow, in Rochester, I saw Ellison and Theodore of the Louis Jacks, Lewis and Charles Higbee (although Mildred and Lloyd were also Higbees), Robert and Frances Berman—in New York, but they occasionally came to Rochester—and Douglas LaBarr. Many more cousins were there. We met David and Esther Jack, Emanuel's children, in the Adirondacks one summer in the 1970s and together we climbed Mt. Marcy.

Memories remain of my childhood relatives, including the deaths of my three grandparents. After I left Rochester to attend Cornell in the 1930s, an unfortunate hiatus begins of almost five decades. I kept up with a few cousins, especially the Bermans in New York, and somewhat less Doris and Eunice. My mother had two favorite nieces, Audrey Bloom Kauffman and Mary Higbee, wife of Lewis, and I also touched base with them over the years.

When my kids were growing up, we saw a lot of Esther's brothers and their families. George, my old childhood friend, attended St. Lawrence, became an ordained Unitarian and Congregational minister like his father, and went on to become Hollis Professor of Divinity at Harvard. In that capacity, he became a world renowned scholar, especially of the Radical Reformation and the role of nature—the wilderness—in Biblical thought. In 1967, George participated in the New England Resistance service at Arlington Street Church that Alex organized, accepting at the altar draft cards of young men who refused to fight in Vietnam. Later, George was active in the right-to-life movement, and as a friend of Cardinal Wojtyla in Poland, became an expert—and author of an 800-page volume—on Pope John Paul II after he was elevated to the papacy. George's wife, Margery, was always a gracious hostess, when I came to the annual UUA meetings in Boston and stayed at their home in Arlington. She was also very peace-minded and engaged in many community and global activities.

David, Esther's younger brother, whom we all called Bill, lost his sight in childhood. Despite this disability, he become a successful osteopathic physician, completing medical school with the help of his lovely wife, Polesta, who was also a physician. Bill and Polly's two children, Karen and Gwenyth, were the same age as Alex and Lucy. They lived in Bay Village, a suburb of Cleveland, and our family visited them frequently on automobile trips between Chicago and Rochester or New York. Bill was humorous and inventive, and we all enjoyed our visits immensely. The summer we drove to Alaska, we were shocked to hear on the radio of the Sam Shepherd murder case, involving a colleague of Bill's at the Osteopathic Hospital in Bay Village. Bill adamantly defended Shepherd's innocence, and following one of the most famous murder trials of the century, Shepherd's conviction was overturned and he was released.

On Esther's side of the family, we also saw Rhys Williams from time to time. Rhys, the son of Albert Rhys Williams, followed in the family footsteps and became a Unitarian Universalist minister. I participated in his ordination in Charleston, South Carolina. Later Rhys became minister of the First Church of Boston and, and with his charming wife, Eleanor, at his side, exercised steadfast moral and civic leadership over the last twenty years. Their son, Rhys, Jr., followed in his grandfather's footsteps, traveling to the Soviet Union, learning Russian, and becoming a writer and journalist. The Williams' daughter, Nori, married and settled down in New Hampshire.

Family Reunion

There were long decades when I never set foot in Rochester or maintained contact with my relatives, and I often admitted that, from 1955 to 1990, I visited New Delhi or Tokyo far more often than Rochester. All this changed in 1989 when my cousins Robert Berman and his sister, Frances Ollweiler, and I suddenly decided to try to have a family reunion of the "Jack clan" in Rochester.

This took almost two years of preparation, but we finally set the date for May 23-24, 1992. And we pulled it off. The day before the reunion Robert Berman and I spent hours in the genealogy section of the Rochester Public Library—just across the street from a building—since demolished—where my father had his office for three decades. There we used Rochester Directories and first found the listing of our grandfather for the 1870s. He was listed as a paper-hanger. We went to the U.S. census material and, for 1910, found a fuller description of our family. This gave the place of origin of our grandparents: my grandfather from Austria and my grandmother from Germany.

We later toured that center of Rochester and tried to find two houses where my father's family lived—Eight Wait Street from 1884 to 1906 and then at 156 Delevan Street, from 1907 through 1910. With much difficulty we found both streets. Alas, Eight Wait Street is now a service road to a superhighway and most houses on Delevan Street have been demolished, although number six appears to be a house selling crack! Also we saw our grandparent's graves in Mt. Hope Cemetery.

For our reunion, we had two open houses or receptions where dozens of our relatives—several generations—came. Perhaps a total of fifty persons attended one or both receptions, one at the home of Audrey Kauffman Bernhard in Brighton, a suburb of Rochester, and a second at the home of Mary and Lewis Higbee at Livonia, some 30 miles south of Rochester. It was a poignant gathering, with one eighty-nine-year-old cousin, Sylvia Bloom Kolb, present, and several young children, three or four generations down the family tree.

We found one woman, a second cousin, who was put in a foster home when two years old. In 1992, more than half a century later, we found her name in the Rochester telephone book and phoned her. At first she felt we were not related; suddenly she found that she was and eagerly attended, tearfully, both days of the reunion. Many of us saw each other for the first time in fifty years!

I apologized to my living relatives for not cherishing my relatives and not returning to the family more often to follow their fortunes, their careers, their crises. I pledged to become a better relative and to stay more in touch with each, respecting, of course, their wishes and not clinging. But I do now want to share their moments of disappointment and triumph. After that two-day reunion, I vowed to remember Rochester not as the "four corners" (Main and State Streets), but the Bernhard family in Brighton and the Higbee family at Livonia, among many others. As a result of this reunion, we compiled a genealogy unto the fourth generation, an address list, and vowed to produce a family newsletter.

71 SWARTHMORE
(1992)

MY HOBBIES

Stamp Collecting

I have been a stamp collector—a philatelist—for much of my life on and off, not steadily. My two spurts were when I was young and, since the middle 1970s, when I have been old. Stamp collecting was one of my few hobbies, and it was—and is—a satisfying one. Working all my life in relatively intangible occupations, I found the tangible, concrete nature of the hobby redeeming. I can hold a stamp, find its picture in my album—some stamps almost 100 years old— and hinge it onto its picture. Concrete, tangible, indeed!

If I learned some things in life from my mother's milk, I learned stamp collecting from my father. It must have been in the 1920s, when I was around ten years old. My father was a stamp collector and he encouraged me to become one. He was never obsessed by stamp collecting; indeed, he had many other hobbies. Yet he had many boxes of stamps, often small candy boxes or cigar boxes full. I do not remember that he ever had a stamp album. He kept his stamps, mostly used duplicates, in these boxes. He never said so, but his collecting implied that some day those stamps would go to me, his only child, and some day they might be valuable.

I remember best page after page of duplicates in the 1893 Columbian Exposition Series. They remain in my U.S. album today. (I find that I have earlier stamps than 1893. The earliest I have is 1851-56, although the first U.S. stamp issued was, I believe, in 1847. All told I have twenty-three stamps in my U.S. album before the whole page of pictures of sixteen stamps entitled Columbia Exposition 1893.) These range from one cent to five dollars. The blue one-center features Columbus in sight of land from the deck of the *Santa Maria*. I remember especially the brown, thirty cents design. My father had dozens of these, both mint and canceled.

If I do not remember my father ever having one or two sets of albums, I remember my parents bought one for me—worldwide. My mother made a Cretonne cover and my father pasted old stamps on the cover within a large S. My love for travel in foreign lands may have started as I leafed through the thin album. In time, we bought a set of flags and coat-of-arms for each country and pasted them in their proper place on the front page of the country listed: China, India, Egypt. How strange, how exotic, these places seemed then! Would I ever visit such far-away places? Of course, I did, but such travels were beyond my dreams then.

These are about my only memories of stamp collecting as a child. My father and I never belonged to a local stamp club and we never spent large sums in the hobby. I had two uncles who were stamp collectors, much more professional than we were. We would occasionally visit them and I would admire their collections. As a child, stamps were not my only hobby. I collected rocks and fossils. Over the years I continued to save stamps if not "collect" them— put them into albums. When my son was young, I pointed him toward stamp collecting, but never for long.

In the 1970s, however, my ardor for stamp collecting increased. For one thing, I was working in the U.N. community. Since 1951 it issued stamps and I was an early collector. I have collected U.N. stamps since then. My U.N. collection is undoubtedly my best. For years I had every stamp the U.N. issued, except one. And then I had an opportunity to buy that—at a discount. But it still cost, if I remember, about $250! That is the most I ever paid for any stamp. Today, however, there is another U.N. stamp which has eluded me, and one never catches up—for long.

My new beginning as a collector in the 1970s was occasioned by the frequent overseas travel I did, working with WCRP. Also I had extensive foreign correspondence. Five or more letters from overseas reached me each day and all these stamps found their way into my collection, from all over the world.

For some years in the late 1970s and 1980s a Unitarian Universalist Ministers' Stamp Club existed. We used to exchange booklets of 100 used stamps through the mail. We would keep those we did not have in our collection and replace them with another from our duplicate collection.

The system worked well for almost a decade, but suddenly petered out. When the Stamp Club worked best, I would sometimes receive two booklets each month, often taking as many as thirty stamps from each to add to my collection. In recent years my collection steadily grew. I was, and continue to be, a squirrel. I tend to collect everything and specialize in many countries. Yet I am stingy. I don't like to spend big amounts for anything; rather, I just don't have big amounts of money to spend for this purpose, or any purpose. Yet it all adds up. In the 1970s, I began with a two-volume Minkus Comprehensive Stamp Album.

Minkus issued once each autumn a global supplement. Once it was about 100 pages and sold at a decent price. Recently it contains about 300 loose-leaf pages, with illustrations of stamps on both sides of the page, and now retails at almost $50! Somehow I buy one each late autumn, vowing it will be my last. Today this Minkus collection has spread to twelve bursting red volumes. But I also have almost an equal number of specialized albums: South Asia, especially India; China (People's Republic and Taiwan); Canada; the U.N.

I must have at least 15,000 individual stamps in these twenty volumes. I have few valuable stamps—and no insurance! I really don't know their value and I don't care. I have four thick Scott catalogues (which I bought second-hand) and they list the selling—or buying—price of each stamp, both mint and used. Most used stamps are still worth only a few cents each. Even U.N. stamps are not expensive. I still manage to buy almost every new U.N. stamp and receive their announcements. Also I try to buy every new American stamp, usually at the post office, although I receive monthly the U.S. announcement of new stamps.

When we travel, I keep myself from buying more than a token of mint stamps, except in India. Occasionally I buy from a dealer a whole envelope of used stamps. On my first visit to China I saw boys trading stamps in front of a post office in Beijing. I prepared for my second visit and brought with me little packets of used U.S. stamps which I traded with them for used Chinese stamps. I wrote up this experience, briefly, in a letter published in the Travel Section of the *New York Times*.

Stamps are indeed my hobby, but not my mistress. I am in command—or so I think. At times I would give this hobby, on the average, one-half hour a day. I would sometimes skip days and weeks. Now, as I write this, overseas stamps come in much less frequently, although kind souls on occasion send me an envelope full of used stamps.

I remain very much an amateur collector. I do it for the fun, and not for business, not for profit. It is profit enough for me when, with a stamp in my hand, I can find its picture in my album and hinge it to the picture. Then I press on. Can I find a place for this next stamp? If not, why not? What is the year? My aging eyes often cannot quite read the date, if any, at the bottom. A magnifying glass now adorns my desk, even if I use it with stamps only five or six short times these weeks, months, and years.

Late in my collecting experience, I tried topicals—collecting by subjects rather than by countries. I began with the obvious: birds, butterflies, horses, insects, mammals, shells, trees. Then I chose topics of more personal interest: stamps with pictures of Nobel peace laureates, world religions, blacks, peace, Gandhi, Einstein, Schweitzer. I finally made a category of stamps picturing friends along the way of life: A. Philip Randolph, Adlai Stevenson, Martin Luther King.

Quinces

I begin by admitting that I am an unabashed, unrestrained lover of quinces.

There are, strangely, some persons living today who do not know what a quince is. It is hard for me to believe that there is a human being anywhere in the temperate clime who has not felt one of these yellow, lop-sided, pear-like fruits. It is hard to believe that some persons have never smelled the sweet perfume as a quince is peeled. Or who have never rubbed off the slight fuzz on the golden yellow skin.

I grew up in western New York State and every farmer, it seemed then, had one quince tree. Somehow, quinces have become much less common. One American article has the nerve to say "the least esteemed of all tree fruits for orchards." Not so on the European continent, however, where one still finds a quince tree, really a large shrub, on a farm, or even in a large suburban backyard.

Quinces are found in the temperate zone, worldwide. They may have originated in Asia, possibly Anatolia or Crete, perhaps Iran. (Maybe the Shah in his reconstructed Garden of Eden bit into a quince instead of an apple!) Indeed, despite the books warning that quinces are "almost inedible in the uncooked state," somewhere I got the habit of eating raw quinces, like an apple. The taste is astringent, puckish; the flesh hard and acid. Some call the eating of a raw quince an uncommon, daring adventure. But late October, for me, is not late October, in New York or almost anywhere, without my quota of raw quinces. Indeed, I have purchased quinces on several continents, even in North Africa. And I have tried to learn the several indigenous names; *koinage, coing,* etc.

I read everything I can about quinces. Someday I must write a real essay, if not a book, about these incomparable fruits. I will condemn the fat, flabby, tasteless variety commercially grown in California and shipped East, but I will commend the small, home-grown variety, decreasingly available in many American cities, but still amply available in some places around the Mediterranean.

I have also collected quince jams and quince jelly, with fancy labels and prices, especially in England. I urge my wife, once each autumn, to make quince purée, if I am lucky enough to amass more than three or four quinces beyond my capacity for eating them raw. The flesh when cooked is pinkish, and still, faintly perfumed. And some friends in Baltimore, knowing of my predeliction, almost annually send me a half dozen quinces, carefully wrapped in paper.

On occasion I have put a cut quince in the corner of a closet. Its strong aroma adds fragrance for months to an otherwise stale closet, according to a practice I picked up, I believe, in Czechoslovakia.

My love of quinces extends to the Japanese flowering variety, a hardy Chinese shrub called *maroumerou* in Japanese. Its buds are exquisite. Its fruit is inedible, yet the jam is excellent.

Perhaps my researches so far have been shallow, but I know of no religious connection to the secular quince. But it is truly a fruit fit for the Gods and, for all I know, both favored and flavored by the Gods. So find a quince, search out one, or half a dozen, not the soggy, tasteless kind, oversized, late in September, but the small ones, with often spotted or blighted yellow skins late in October. To me, they are heavenly.

O quince, where is thy pucker? Alas, I must wait for three long months to bite into a raw one again. But in our refrigerator there is an emptying jar of quince jam I purchased a month ago in the open market in Athens.

St. Bernards

On a tour of Europe in the late 1930s, Homer traveled through the Swiss Alps and stopped near St. Bernard Pass, home of the famous St. Bernard rescue dogs. In the late 1950s, his admiration for these oversize animals was realized in a family pet. When he left Evanston, Homer organized a Farewell Pet Show at the Unitarian Church. Along with Alex and Lucy, he inspected the dogs and cats, hampsters and fish, that the church schoolchildren brought to display. "Parents can keep the more energetic pets in their autos in the parking lot and an inspection will be made auto by auto,"the church bulletin announced. "In this manner, Dr. Jack can take his leave of the children in an imaginative way."

Small is beautiful, especially St. Bernard pups. Buy one, a little ball of fur, and it unravels before your eyes, and becomes a huge animal in a very few months. I have had mongrels and thoroughbreds, especially dachshunds, but no dog as nice as Bonzie, our St. Bernard.

Never has any dog been so gentle with children, or so difficult with house-tidy mothers. A long-haired St. Bernard is primarily a hair-producing machine. It manufactures and then sheds seemingly bushels of hair. Also one has to be another St. Bernard to appreciate the smell of its shaggy hair after being in the rain. Yet not even this pungent, yes unpleasant, smell detracts from my memory of Bonzie.

Huge, gentle, cuddly, great slurps of saliva—a St. Bernard is all that a household of children would ever desire. The *Guiness Book of World Records* never listed a single child bitten by a St. Bernard! Dachshunds bite regularly; I remember especially one biting the ankles of the chairman of our Church Board one day when he visited our parsonage!

St. Bernards, despite their size and massive head, do not eat terribly much, only a little more than the much more active, peripatetic dachshunds. With large, adorable drop ears, St. Bernards are lazy, sleep dogs if not exactly lap dogs. When they turn and lie down, floors often tremble. Soon the dog dreams of St. Bernard heaven, snowy climes of Switzerland near an alpine pass. There is, however, no evidence that our St. Bernard especially craved brandy or sought to carry brandy, even in the keg somebody gave us. Only its ample saliva is needed to awake and warm any wayfarer in the snow.

The St. Bernard is a nonpolitical animal—loving, loyal, a conversation piece, but never controversial. He or she will agree on anything, with anybody, lounging in the front room or walking around the block. What delicious joy to encounter one St. Bernard with his owner, on the streets of Tudor City in Manhattan! I look at that dog, invariably with child-like envy. How audacious, to own a St. Bernard in Manhattan! I sometimes wonder how, after twelve years, I can't be that adventurous.

But in 1959 we were adventurous in moving our Bonzie, with two children, a thousand miles from Chicago to Scarsdale in the back seat of a Ford. Somehow our family survived, and Bonzie thrived. What further tribute can one pay to any dog?

I know that if we ever leave Manhattan, we will buy a furry St. Bernard puppy long before acquiring another auto again. How I have missed Bonzie since we parted with him in 1964—almost twenty years without a St. Bernard! Deprivation in the extreme.

Lists

Many people compile lists, especially of daily tasks to start—or finish. In 1969, in Tokyo, I improbably discovered another kind of list, in the thousand-year old *Pillow Book of Sei Shoganon*. I was staying in the International House of Japan with its excellent library and beautiful gardens. On a Friday afternoon, I came across Ivan Morris' translation of this Japanese classic. The title seemed slightly salacious, and I had known Morris' parents in the peace movement, so I checked out the book from the library for the weekend. The volume contained primarily a series of lists which the lady-in-waiting of the Empress composed before retiring at night, She kept her lists in a drawer of her wooden pillow. Let me give just two examples:

Elegant Things:
Duck eggs
Snow on wisteria or plum blossoms
A pretty child eating strawberries

Things That Should Be Large:
Priests
Fruit
Houses
Winter cherries
The petals of yellow roses

Sei Shoganon's lists were so striking that I began to compile my own lists. Alas, mine were more prosaic, less poetic than hers. Yet, since 1969, I have found the habit of compiling such lists useful. Here are some I have put together.

Beyond My Initial Expectations:
Connaught Place, New Delhi
Shinjuku District, Tokyo
Fatherhood
The Great Wall of China
The terra-cotta figures in Xian, China
The Kremlin, especially St. Basil's
The Masai-Mara game preserve in Kenya
Victoria Falls
Igucu Falls, Brazil
Albert Einstein
Sphagnum bogs
The redwoods
The Pillow Book of Sei Shoganon
R. K. Narayan's novels
New Zealand
The Martin Luther King, Jr. national holiday
Both the Parthenon and the Taj Mahal in moonlight

Painful Experiences:
Watching, twice, the defeat of Adlai E. Stevenson
My job abolished by the incoming U.U.A. President, Robert
  West
The suicide of my son-in-law
My divorce
Riding alone in the back seat of a taxi to a New York City
  hospital during a heart attack
My son abandoning theological school
Growing old

Worshipful Situations:
The meditation room at U.N. Headquarters
First Parish, Concord, Massachusetts
Unity Church of Frank Lloyd Wright in Oak Park, Illinois
College Camp at Lake Geneva, Wisconsin, on August 6, 1945

Unforgetable Conferences Attended:
Second World Assembly of the World Council of Churches at
  Evanston in 1954
Church and Society Conference of the World Council of Churches at
  Geneva in 1956
First Assembly of the World Conference on Religion and Peace at

Kyoto in 1970
World Food Conference at Rome in 1974
Second U.N. Special Session on Disarmament at U.N. Headquarters
in 1982

Most Stressful Situations:
Black power confrontation of Unitarian Universalist Association,
Boston, 1968
The WCRP Boat People Project, Singapore, 1977

Regrets:
That, despite my many visits to Asia, I have never been able to fo-
cus on any Eastern religion and learn it in depth.
That I have never lived for at least a year in California

I Have Never Seen Enough Of:
Taj Mahal
Acropolis
London
Tokyo
Great Wall of China
Giraffes in Africa
Peacocks at League of Nations in Geneva
Silberhorn from Wengen, Switzerland

Fragrances:
Lobby of old Grand Hotel in Calcutta
Curry anywhere
Sphagnum bogs
Incense in Greek Orthodox Churches
Alpine meadow
Elementary school classroom on opening day

Longtime Adversaries:
War
Racism
Apartheid
Government of South Korea
The military everywhere
FBI, CIA, KGB
Moscow-brand communism until Gorbachev
American-brand capitalism epitomized by Reagan

Personal Jeopardy.
Sled accident, Rochester, 1922
Airport Homes Race Riot, Chicago, 1946
Visit to Philadelphia, Mississippi, May, 1966
Visit to Saigon, May, 1971
Visit to KPLNF guerrilla camp, Kampuchea, January, 1980
Auto accident, Damascus, Maryland, September, 1989
Street robbery, Sao Paulo, Brazil, April, 1992

Expeditions:
To the Adirondack Mountains to climb Mt. Marcy, 1920s
From Evanston to Cape Town, without flying, 1952
To Alaska along the Alcan Highway with family, 1954
Around the world, 1955
Along the Trans-Siberian Railroad, 1970

Persons I Would Have Liked to Have Known:
Eugene V. Debs
Mohandas K. Gandhi
Abraham Lincoln
Theodore Parker
Alfred Wallace

Magnetic Personalities:
Preston Bradley
Adam Clayton Powell

Geniuses I Have Known:
J. D. Bernal
Kenneth Boulding
Karl Deutsch
Albert Einstein
Linus Pauling

Underrated Women:
Margaret Adams
Cecelia Davis Jack, my mother
Coretta King
Marcia Lyttle
Marie Roberts
Eleanor Roosevelt
Helena Schweitzer

72 SWARTHMORE
(1992)

IF I COULD LIVE MY LIFE AGAIN

To the end, Homer remained an agnostic in his personal faith. He said that he understood "one grand design" to life but could not believe in a personal God. "What I have tried to do—in peace or social justice—has not been to make a correction to fit a plan or purpose," he wrote in concluding notes for this book, "but to help human beings, sometimes individuals, usually groups. But what little I have done is not to fit into some greater scheme. Also what I have done is not because I am an American or a Unitarian Universalist or anything else, but because I am pleased and able to do so." In this essay, composed the year before he died, Homer looks back on his life and what, if anything, he would change.

Toward the end of one's life, but occasionally at times of crisis in between, one often wonders: would I have chosen different paths if I could live my life again? Would I even have chosen different parents? different jobs? different mates?

Thus far in my life, I have no real complaints, but only thankfulness for having been able to live a long life of absorbing and differing interests. I have experienced no deprivation. As I have repeatedly observed, my life—vocational and otherwise—has not consisted of complete or even intermittent drudgery. I have sadly observed that menial, uninteresting tasks are the lot of most men and women on earth.

I was not charmed, but I was perhaps lucky. In some cases I made good choices. In others, the result was pure chance. All told, indeed with every major position I held, I felt grateful for the opportunity. I usually felt I should have paid for the privilege of working, not be paid.

If I could reconstruct my life—and we human beings do not have the privilege, not even of tinkering with the lives of our children—I certainly would have picked the same parents. They gave me much social vision, and a good start educationally. They left me quite free to reach my own vocational and social level. I would not want to have had different parents.

If I could do it again, I doubt if I would have become immersed so soon in geology, biology, and nature study. These gave me a hobby, almost a cause, but it was premature. I did not have to go to Allegany School of Natural History while still in high school or take adult extension courses at the University of Rochester. My parents did not push me; I pushed myself. These courses did give me college credit and saved me a year at university. However, there was no great rush.

I am glad I went to Cornell, not as big as it is today, but even then a large, first-class university. Although I was enrolled in the Ag School, I had access to electives in the liberal arts college and took advantage of this opportunity, especially with Professor Carl Becker, the noted historian.

I was fortunate to find and be able to reside in the Cornell Cosmopolitan Club. This truly opened my eyes to different cultures—to the world. Also the experience made me want to go abroad and, indirectly, to the position at Athens College. Also preparations for my doctoral thesis gave me the opportunity for the five-month swing through Europe on the eve of the Second World War.

My preoccupation with science continued until I received my doctorate. In a way I am sorry that I spent so much time on science education and vertebrate zoology, and on my thesis on biological stations. Yet it was not all a waste. Those were important, life-long learnings—such as an appreciation of the history of science, of a great university library, and of ecology (in its early years).

If I had been able to get a job immediately after receiving my Ph.D., in teaching or at a museum, my life might have been different. But perhaps not completely. Already, on returning from Europe, I was drawn more to sociology and politics, and might have gravitated as an instructor in a college or university to the administrative side. I cannot now imagine myself as a teacher of nature study or mosses or aquatic life, and writing the prerequisite scientific papers, or popular manuals—all my vocational life. Popular manuals, perhaps, for that is journalism as much as science.

In this early period, I married Esther Williams. I would have done so again. As for leaving science and entering the Unitarian ministry, I would also have done so again. The Unitarian ministry is an open door to many paths, within the ministry, several of which I myself have taken. As for having children—of course. Alex and Lucy were just right.

My race relations work in Chicago was fortuitous. I enjoyed every minute of it and I may have helped Chicago not get worse even if I did not make much of a difference. I am glad, after four years, to have left to enter the parish ministry in Evanston. There I could have my cake and eat it, since Evanston was part of Greater Chicago. I continued to be involved in race relations for another decade, if not on a vocational level.

The ministry in Evanston provided me with a launching pad for my several foreign travels—to Africa to visit Albert Schweitzer, to Bandung and later India, to Montgomery to visit Martin Luther King, Jr., and to Japan to visit Hiroshima/Nagasaki.

One of the largest forks in my life's path was whether to continue in the parish ministry at Evanston, or somewhere else, or take an unknown branch of the social ministry. I took that risk in 1959. I still do not know if it was the right judgment. I may not have become divorced had I remained in the parish ministry. Being minister in Evanston turned out to have been the most satisfying job of my life.

My work in New York, briefly with the American Committee on Africa, and four years with SANE, was exciting. So was the work at 25 Beacon Street with Dana Greeley at the Unitarian Universalist Association. The establishment of WCRP and my becoming its Secretary-General was serendipitous. It could not have been planned.

My divorce in 1972 was some years in the making. All I can say is that divorce is always second best. Yet I have been lucky in finding and marrying Ingeborg, despite the vast differences in our culture and resulting tastes. Marriage between two people growing up in two continents—worlds—has both its benefits and its drawbacks. I would marry her again.

If I could do it again, I would have announced my retirement from WCRP after my heart attack in 1980, age sixty-four. I would then have had time to help select and train a successor, with a transition period. I would also perhaps have had more of a choice in selecting a local parish and WCRP would have had more of a choice in selecting my successor.

Also looking backwards, I should have been more concerned

with my personal finances, especially for my retirement years. I should have bought a home in the New York suburbs in the early 1970s, both for better living but also to acquire equity. I did not. Had I not received the stipend from the Niwano Peace Prize, we would be living in retirement even more poorly than we are. Yet poor is a very elastic term, and we really live relatively well.

So far my retirement has been most of what we wanted—a perch from which we could occasionally fly. And also a local environment in which we could pursue our domestic and foreign policy interests.

My regrets about Swarthmore are two. The community is still too segregated. That is a challenge as well as a complaint. Also the weather in Swarthmore, the air quality, is not as nice as are the borough's trees and shrubs. The fumes from industry along the Delaware River Valley seem to gather just above Swarthmore. It is a gem surrounded by foul air.

If I had the privilege of living my life again, I would—without qualifications.

EPILOGUE

TOUCHING HANDS

TIMELESS MOMENTS

"Now the rosy-fingered Dawn would have shone
on their weeping
had not the grey-eyed Goddess Athena held the
the long night back . . ."
— The Odyssey, Book XXIII

In the early spring of 1993, Homer was honored at a community reception at the Swarthmore Friends Meeting-house. The event was sponsored by the Friends and nine other organizations, including the Delaware County Committee for Peace and Justice in the Middle East which he co-chaired, and the ceremonies were presided over by Professor Will Richan. Up until the end of his life, Homer remained active in community affairs. One of his last projects was to organize a memorial for Dr. Martin Luther King at Crozer Seminary, four miles from Swarthmore. While a seminarian at Crozer in 1950, King was refused service at a restaurant in nearby Maple Shade, N.J., and filed charges against the owners. Homer had researched and written up this incident—King's first legal challenge of segregation—in the *Friends Journal*. In May, Homer went to Sweden to attend a WCRP gathering on what proved to be his last international journey.

Photograph: Homer, as leader of SANE, reviewing one of the public service advertisements in the campaign against nuclear testing.

73 SWARTHMORE • BECKET
(1993)

HOMER'S LAST DAYS

Shortly after returning from his trip to Europe, Homer was diagnosed with cancer. In this account, Alex describes his last days and pays tribute to his father.

"Can you cure me?" Homer asked. He had just called with news of his diagnosis. I sensed a mixture of hope and apprehension in his voice.

"Only you can do that, Dad," I replied truthfully, "but I will go over a special diet with you that I think will help."

I drove down to Philadelphia the next day, June 5, and met him in the oncology unit of the Temple University hospital. He had gone to see a world-renowned specialist. Homer looked tired, gaunt, and his color was jaundiced. The doctor confirmed that most pancreatic patients lived only several months to a year. In Homer's case, tests indicated that the tumor had already spread to the lung and the liver. He recommended experimental chemotherapy. Homer was shaken.

Back at his apartment in Swarthmore, I went over the macrobiotic approach to cancer with Homer. Over the years, we have had several impressive recoveries with his primary type of malignancy. Researchers at Tulane University reported that pancreatic cancer patients who ate macrobiotically lived about three times longer than matched controls from a conventional tumor registry. I told Homer about Dr. Hugh Faulkner, a British physician about his same age who had pancreatic cancer. He went to a hospice to die in London and discovered macrobiotics. He was now in his seventh year of remission and had written a book, *Physician Heal Thyself,* which I had edited and published.

Homer and Ingeborg's kitchen had a variety of natural foods—including grains, beans, and sea vegetables—from past forays into more conscious eating. But like most people, my father partook of the modern diet high in fat, low in fiber, and high in refined sugars. In 1980, after a heart attack, I had taken him to see a macrobiotic cardiologist in Hartford, and Homer was impressed by his recommendations to cut back fat and cholesterol intake. However, after he recovered, he gravitated to his former pattern. He was particularly fond of snails and Camambert cheese; fondue; cream cheese, cottage cheese, and buttermilk; Indian food, including curry and other spices; grapefruit, persimmons, and other tropical fruits.

We went to a large whole foods market and stocked up on fresh vegetables, especially carrots, onions, squash, and cabbage to make a sweet vegetable drink that is especially good to relax the pancreas. Generally, pancreatic cancer is caused by longtime excessive consumption of eggs, chicken, cheese, shellfish, and other saturated animal foods, as well as sugar including excessive fruit intake. On his world travels, Homer delighted in mangoes, guava, durian, and other exotic fruits and collected sugar packets the way some travelers collect matchbooks. For several years, he had been borderline diabetic and had restricted his sweet consumption. But because of his lifestyle—traveling and attending many parties, banquets, church dinners, and diplomatic receptions—it was hard for him to follow any dietary recommendations for long.

On a several-mile walk through the beautiful tree-lined streets of Swarthmore, Homer reminisced and said that he had enjoyed "a wonderful life." When we reached the college arboretum, he stopped by a tranquil field of holly bushes—Hollywood as he called it—and said that this is where he would like his ashes to be scattered. I told him not to be so pessimistic, but it was clear that his condition was advanced and his will to live was low.

Over the past year, we had worked together to finish the production on his big book on the history of WCRP. He had been working on it steadily for the last few years. It had gone through several drafts, and Homer was sending me constant revisions by fax and express mail until it went to the printer's in early spring. And then when it came out, there was the matter of distribution—the most difficult part of any publishing venture. Homer arranged to rent storage space in Swarthmore for dozens of boxes of inventory.

592

When the 600-page volume arrived in May, he exclaimed, "I've finally finished my book on WCRP and now I can die in peace."

Of course, his autobiography—the project that originally inspired him to move to Swarthmore to be near his archives—remained unfinished. For the last six years living in the Delaware Valley, Homer had involved himself in a whirlwind of social action projects and scarcely took time to write about his own life.

I returned home in the Berkshires and kept touch with Homer daily by phone, as did my sister Lucy in Boston. He spent his days greeting visitors—friends and relatives who had heard of his terminal prognosis—writing letters, and generally winding up his affairs. In early July, at my suggestion, he and Ingeborg drove to western Massachusetts to attend the Way to Health Seminar at the Kushi Institute where I teach Oriental philosophy and medicine. I was alarmed at how much Homer had declined. He suffered abdominal pain, had little appetite, and was skeptical about going ahead with the program. During the week, he felt too weak to attend classes, but did listen to part of my lecture on healing traditions East and West, including material from the Greek epics. He had no appetite and slept most of the day. Some of the staff administered compresses and prepared special drinks to make him more comfortable. One morning, Paul Aicher, his friend and former parishioner from the Evanston Church who headed a peace foundation in Connecticut, came to visit and they talked animatedly about old times. Aicher's daughter, Sarah, had died in the tragic bombing of Pan American flight 103 over Scotland several years earlier, and Homer had conducted the service, as well as continued his efforts at the United Nations against international terrorism and hijacking.

Michio Kushi, the founder of the Kushi Institute and a longtime supporter of world federal government, was in Becket during the week. They had met several times over the years, but Homer was not impressed. He placed Michio in the same circle with Thich Nhat Hanh, Rev. Moon, the Dalai Lama, and other Eastern teachers whom he felt preached a dubious gospel.

Homer saw Michio for a consultation but rebelled at his recommendations. "I am still enough of a scientist to ask what real evidence is there that macrobiotics works?" Homer declared. Michio gently encouraged him to do the best he could. "This way may help you live another year, another month, another week," Michio replied. "Even one day more will allow you to contribute further to our common dream of world peace." "In the spirit of our mutual friend Norman Cousins," Homer acknowledged, "I will try."

593

One day at lunch, Homer came down from his room and ate for the first time with the other seminar participants, most of whom also had cancer. With some difficulty, he joined in the table talk and delivered a homily on traditional Thanksgiving in New England. For a brief moment, his voice was strong and clear—as I had heard him a thousand times deliver a speech or prayer. It was to be his last sermonnette.

The next day, Homer felt worse and we drove to Berkshire Medical Center, a modern hospital in Pittsfield. An oncologist recommended by his own physician saw him but could find no physical basis for his complaints. During the next week, Homer remained at our house in Hinsdale, while my wife, Gale, and daughter, Masha, helped care for him. Homer called his cousin, Doris, in Rochester, and my sister Lucy and her partner Stanley came out from Boston. Homer found a novel in the house by James Michener—the Pennsylvania Quaker and an old acquaintance from the Bandung Conference—which he read with interest. But he was too weak to listen to the evening news or the *MacNeil-Lehrer Report*—a bad sign since these were as indispensable to him as the air he breathed.

One afternoon, he called me into the room where he was propped up in the bed. "What have you learned from your parents?" he asked me tenderly. "I learned to stand up for what I believe in and to oppose prejudice and discrimination," I answered. "I hope I've been a good father to you and Lucy," he went on softly. "Yes, you have." "I'm proud of you," he continued. "I have not always understood or appreciated what you are doing, but it is really wonderful." I was grateful for his blessing, but sad that I was unable, to help him—to provide, in Milton's words, "that moly that Hermes once to wise Ulysses gave."

That weekend, Homer and Ingeborg returned by auto to Swarthmore. I was in California the following week teaching, but kept in touch daily by phone. Each day Homer's voice grew weaker, but he still hailed me with his customary printer's greeting: "How many fonts do you got?" Lucy and Stanley arrived in Swarthmore the last week in July to be with him until the end. I planned to join them, but Homer told me to wait and come after Masha's Russian reunion. Our eight-year-old daughter was scheduled to attend a get together in Maine of children who had been adopted from Russia. It would have been the first time since she came to America the year before that she could meet some of the boys and girls she grew up with at an orphanage in Moscow. In a barely audible whisper, Homer insisted—in his last gesture of international peace and goodwill—that it was more important for us to go with Masha to the reunion than to be at his side.

After the reunion, I flew to Philadelphia, but by now Homer had slipped into a semi-comatose state. For four days and nights, Ingeborg, Lucy, and myself—with the support of Stanley and Renate, Ingeborg's daughter and Homer's invaluable secretary for several years at WCRP—watched over his bedside. Drugs eased the pain, but he could not speak nor eat, just sip a little water. I promised Homer that I would finish his autobiography, and each expressed farewell in his or her own way. One night, while listening to a tape of an Alpine melody, Homer sat up in bed and mimed an orchestra conductor leading the music. Early Wednesday morning, shortly after midnight, Homer died peacefully as Lucy and I held his hands. We read a few verses from the Bible and prayed for his spirit. It was August 5—but a day later, August 6, in Japan, Hiroshima Day. Homer was always early, so it was fitting that he died on the international day of peace. Hiroshima Day, the day devoted to preventing nuclear war and humanity's hope for the future, symbolized more than anything else his life's work and dream.

A memorial service for Homer was held in mid-September at the Unitarian Church in nearby Media, Pennsylvania. Afterwards we scattered Homer's ashes in the holly grove in Swarthmore. A selection from his book, *The Gandhi Reader*—describing the disposition of Mahatma Gandhi's ashes—was read. There were also memorial services that autumn at the world church center across from the United Nations and at the Unitarian Church of Evanston.

Speaking Truth to Power

Homer lived to see the realization of many of his dreams: the end of the Cold War, the first steps toward nuclear disarmament, an end to segregation and apartheid, the freedom and independence of Asia and Africa, the rise of world religions and multiculturalism, and an active role by the United Nations in international peacekeeping.

It is impossible to assess the contribution of any one person to such sweeping historical changes. However, it is clear that for over a half century Homer devoted himself ceaselessly to the cause of peace and social justice and was one of many—indeed millions of men and women—who helped humanity in the twentieth century turn away from its self-destructive course. The civil rights injunction "speak truth to power" encapsulates his fearless and uncompromising stance. Like his hero, Gandhi, he remained unyielding in the face of superior might and temporal authority.

Homer had a unique ability to make things happen. Not only was he tireless in pursuit of a cause, but he also inspired and motivated others. He was a Ph.D., but he was not an intellectual, content to analyze from the sidelines or merely criticize in print. He threw himself physically into the fray, and more often than not moved others by the strength of his convictions and moral example. He did his homework, thoroughly mastering the intricacy of an issue, and then used his organizing talents to mobilize support. He was not afraid to roll up his sleeves and dig in and do the menial work that had to be done. As minister in Evanston, he often performed the duties of the janitor. As Secretary-General of WCRP, he licked stamps for a mailing and carried out other duties of a general secretary. The *New York Times*, in its profile of him in the 1960s, aptly described him as "a one-man band."

Homer was a good writer—clear, concise, and convincing—but he was a tremendous speaker. He had a magnificent voice—melodious and flowing—that transported his listeners, possibly like the original Homer and ancient Greek bards. More than anything, I miss hearing his voice—and I was overjoyed recently to find lying forgotten in a storage box a cassette that I had taped of him in China. It was a speech that he gave in the Great Hall of the People to an assembly of religious leaders and government officials. The tape is poor quality, and there are interminable sections in which the interpreter translates his remarks into Chinese, but nonetheless Homer's voice comes through shining, clear, and strong. I keep it in my car and play it from time to time—a voice resonant with humanity's endless dream of faith, hope, and peace.

Homer had an unerring pulse—not only for righteousness—but also for seeing through hypocrites and fakes and was seldom taken in by promises that were too good to be true. In the great American tradition, he was at heart a pragmatist. He was a disciple of Gandhi, Schweitzer, and Martin Luther King, but in the end he always went with what worked and could be accomplished at the time. An inveterate list maker, the notes that he left for his autobiography included a list of all the peace activities he had been involved with from 1931, when he proposed a disarmament club at high school, to 1991, when he opposed the Gulf War. The list concluded: "One theme—how to construct a mid-America, midstream, not left, not Gandhian, not passive, but peace [movement]."

Homer also had a great sense of humor. Like his associate Norman Cousins, who healed himself of a serious illness with laughter and reruns of the Marx brothers, Homer found solace in humor and slapstick. When we were living in Evanston, he almost never watched television, except for *Meet the Press.* However, he would come down from his study on occasion to watch Milton Berle, Red Skelton, or an old movie with Charlie Chaplin or Laurel and Hardy. Occasionally, he enjoyed clowning around himself. Once he went to a church party dressed as Gandhi—wearing only a loincloth, a Nehru cap, and carrying a staff—and brought down the house. When he came back from a visit to Africa sporting a bushy mustache like Albert Schweitzer's, everyone—except my mother—was amused.

One of the funniest episodes I remember is at one WCRP assembly when he intervened to mediate between an Indian swami and a Russian orthodox priest whose rooms shared a common bath. It seems the pious Hindu would get up at 3:00 a.m. and proceed to do his ablutions and chanting in the bathtub and drive the long-bearded Russian patriarch to distraction. Homer hastily rearranged the living arrangements and prevented a holy war between two major world faiths. On another occasion, on a visit to Asia, Homer was honored with a long poem extolling his virtues which began: "Homer the Comber of Knotty Tangles . . . " It was hilarious and went on verse after verse, and he treasured it for years. An amateur student of architecture, Homer idolized Frank Lloyd Wright. One of his favorite stories was how Wright was once sworn in by a judge and told the court, "My name is Frank Lloyd Wright and I'm the world's greatest architect." The judge looked up and said, "Mr. Wright, isn't that assertion a little arrogant?" "Not at all," Wright replied, "I'll remind you that I am testifying under oath."

Homer was also unfailingly kind and just. As a child I remember once we were driving to Chicago and a policeman stopped him for making a wrong turn. When he looked at Homer's license and saw that he was a clergyman, he let him go with a deferential warning. Meanwhile, another driver—a black man—had also made a wrong turn, and the cop started to write out a ticket. Homer intervened and said that if he was let off, the black driver should be left off, too—and he was! At home, Homer was always very gentle with us as children. I cannot recall a single instance when he disciplined us physically. Homer was also solicitous of older persons, including his mother, parents-in-law, elder church members, professors, and mentors. He had a strong sense of continuity—"Memories for the Generations" was his family's ancestral motto—and to the end of his days he continued to look after older men and women. Nearly every time he visited Boston, Homer asked me to drive him to Cambridge to see James Luther Adams, his old professor at Meadville who was ailing (and survived him by a year), for a chat about national and international affairs. Homer's kindness also extended to animals. One of my abiding memories is of him in his study typing a sermon or speech with a Siamese cat draped across his desk. He would reach around the cat for paperclips or to answer the phone, but would never disturb its sleeping.

While Homer practiced reverence for life, he was no saint. In the arena of public life, he was abrasive, blunt, impatient, skeptical, proud, and ambitious. He did not suffer fools gladly and made enemies easily. Because of his own strong nature, he repelled others of strong, but opposing principles. In Homer's FBI files, there is the comment that he "likes the limelight"—an assessment Homer conceded was often true. (In addition to enjoying center stage, he was attracted to celebrities. Once, in the airport in Honolulu in the 1950s, he recognized Clark Gable, the actor, and had me get his autograph.) As children, Lucy and I would tease him by answering the phone and telling him it was the White House calling.

Another shortcoming was that Homer did not fully share the Oriental or traditional mind. He was admiring, tolerant, and respectful toward Eastern cultures and their representatives. He worked with Asians and Africans for many years, but his approach was very Western—moralistic, legalistic, constitutional. Over the decades, he came to regard social, cultural, and economic rights as seriously as individual and political rights, but, like most apostles of modern science, he did not appreciate the traditional nexus between a society and its ancestors and the spirit world. One of our biggest disagreements concerned Tibet and the Dalai Lama. Where I saw a traditional society being sacrificed to the *realpolitik* of Chinese expansionism, Homer saw a flawed leader who would lead his people backward to serfdom and superstition.

The roots of this distinction are not cultural or genetic, but biological. Most traditional people have a vegetarian or semi-vegetarian background and orientation so their thinking tends to remain calm, clear, and flexible. They see the unity behind conflicting opposites and do not hold the same rigid, precise, material standards of morality, territoriality, or time as cultures eating the modern diet based on high caloric foods such as meat and sugar. Gandhi, a lifelong vegetarian, understood that violence could never be eradicated solely by legal or political means. It could only be eliminated by reaching people's hearts and elevating their health.

Homer's success—especially his unfailing energy, intuition, and common sense—was in large measure constitutional. His parents were vegetarian when he was born and in the early years growing up, so he had a reservoir of health and vitality which helped to carry him through his entire life. This biological inheritance naturally created a sympathetic attraction to Gandhi, Schweitzer, and Martin Luther King—all of whom ate simply and were vegetarian or semi-macrobiotic. In this sense also, Homer was truly "my father's son" and imbibed social justice with "my mother's milk."

If Homer didn't fully appreciate the East, the East appreciated him. For all his abrasiveness—the proverbial Taurus in a China shop—Asians came to admire his indomitable physical energy, moral strength, and sound judgment. On our trip to China, I remember how Homer was extolling the wonders of the quince, his favorite fruit, at a banquet of religious leaders in Shanghai. The Chinese—Buddhist abbots and monks—could not understand what he was talking about, since the pocket dictionaries they carried did not include the word for this exotic fruit. Finally, further discussion and gestures on Homer's part elicited *satori*: he was talking about the fruit known in China as "Buddha's Hand." The Buddhists seemed awed by this auspicious coincidence and appeared to regard Homer as the reincarnation of a great Buddhist saint who had returned to their land after many lifetimes.

On this or another visit, Homer acquired a large wall hanging of Bodhidharma, the Indian monk who brought Buddhism to China and became the first patriarch of Zen. He kept the black and white rubbing of Bodhidharma in his apartment in Swarthmore and occasionally compared himself to the Indian sage, who was depicted crossing the sea of ignorance on a single reed. According to legend, Bodhidharma became enlightened after living in a cave for nine years and staring at a blank wall. I think Homer's patient attendance at disarmament proceedings in Geneva and New York for upwards of thirty years more than qualifies as the modern equivalent of this feat. After Homer passed away, I consulted the *I Ching*—the Chinese oracle which rested with the Sacred Books of the East by his pulpit in Evanston and which the hard-headed scientist in Homer always dismissed as pseudoscience—and it described his life thusly:

Here life comes to its end. A man's work stands completed. The path rises high toward heaven, like the flight of wild geese when they have left the earth far behind. There they fly, keeping to the order of their flight in strict formation. And if their feathers fall, they can serve as ornaments in the sacred dance pantomimes performed in the temples. Thus the life of a man who has perfected himself is a bright light for the people of the earth, who look up to him as an example.

One of the most auspicious judgments in the *Book of Changes*, I feel it is a truer mirror of his spirit than old sermons and articles, CIA and FBI files, and even the reminiscences of his son.

There have been many changes in the two years since Homer died. Israel and the PLO signed a peace accord, South Africa made a successful transition to full democracy, and Ukraine, Kazakhstan, and Belarus pledged to disarm themselves of nuclear weapons—events that he would surely applaud. However, as a whole, the world has become increasingly violent, with further bloodletting in Bosnia and Kashmir, the massacre in Rwanda, the development of a blackmarket for nuclear expertise, and the assassination of Israeli Prime Minister Rabin. Homer would not want us to recite his laurels, but organize as best we could to solve these problems. On a personal note, his grandson, Michael, enrolled at Swarthmore College, his granddaughter Masha is studying Japanese in elementary school in Becket and learning about the bombing of Hiroshima, and Northwestern University in Evanston became the first college in America to establish a macrobiotic dining hall. Homer was noted briefly in *You Don't Have to Ride Jim Crow*, a documentary about the first Freedom Ride in 1947 by producer and journalist Robin Washington that appeared on public television

One of my abiding memories as a child growing up in Evanston is of our house—the church parsonage at 2026 Orrington Avenue—serving as a constant site of meetings, open houses, church suppers, and visitors from around the world. Our dining room—lined with wooden carvings of elephants, giraffes, hippos, and rhinos Homer brought back with him as souvenirs of his travels—served as a meeting place for nonviolent knights of the round table. My parents played host to a steady stream of pacifists, civil rights activists, civil liberties advocates, vegetarians, emancipated women, and other freethinkers. There were Indians, Africans, black people, yellow people, white people—persons of all nations and creeds. Homer presided over the sparkling conversation, while my mother served exquisite meals and made everyone feel perfectly at home.

Homer's influence was far-reaching. In New York, in high school, I remember taking one call from a man who introduced himself as Robert Maheu, the assistant to Howard Hughes. He said that he was calling from Nevada and that the reclusive billionaire wanted Homer to find a way to stop the government from conducting nuclear tests in the desert. (Apparently, it was bad for business at the casinos.) I don't think anything ever came of it. (Maheu later figured in speculation surrounding the Kennedy assassination.)

Return to Ithaca

Beyond superficial coincidences—such as his name (Homer), his place of birth (Greece, N.Y.), his college town (Ithaca), his interest in biology (the poet Homer was the author of a satire on frogs and mice), and his youthful wanderings (in the Greek isles)—my father's life had epic dimensions. Certainly the campaign to reverse the atomic arms race was the Trojan War of our times—or all time. Never before had the future of humanity itself been at stake. In the 1950s and 1960s, the world came perilously close to self-destruction. The superpowers threatened to use nuclear weapons no less than seven times—in Korea, in China, in French Indochina, in Berlin, in Cuba, along the Sino-Soviet border, and in Vietnam. In the past, humanity had never succeeded in developing a new weapon or delivery system that had not ultimately been used. The prospects for pulling back from the precipice were slim.

In this modern drama, the Trojans—our lower impulses, the U.S. military-industrial complex, the Soviet hardliners—had abducted Helen—the embodiment of peace, beauty, and the earth's safe, clean, natural environment. To get her back, the Achaians—the Greeks, the democratic forces, the ordinary people of the world—set sail, led by Achilles and Odysseus. Norman Cousins played the role of Achilles in this drama. Like his forerunner, he was the most eloquent of mortals and had a special interest in healing. Homer, in turn, performed the part of Odysseus, the most resourceful of men. Cousins' divine pen—like Achilles' shield—delineated the highest literary and cultural values of the era and was readied to slay Hector—the giant, multi-megaton spectre of atomic radiation and the nuclear arms race. However, to gain a foothold on Trojan soil, it was Homer, the master strategist, who came up with the bold plan. The Trojan Horse that finally turned the tide of the arms race was modern advertising, the establishment's own vehicle of propaganda and control. In a brilliant stroke, Homer convinced Benjamin Spock to join the campaign against nuclear testing. In the name of the world's children and generations unborn, Dr. Spock—the high priest of the medical and scientific establishment, the real religion of our time—became the international symbol of an end to atmospheric nuclear testing and humanity's desire for world peace. The leaders of SANE prevailed upon a top Madison Avenue advertising firm to design and execute the media blitz. Practically every family in the modern world was reached. The walls of Troy—the walls of public opinion—were breached. The icons and inventions of modern society were successfully turned against modern society itself.

Following this surprise—mythic—invasion, President John F. Kennedy—playing the role of the enlightened monarch, Agamemnon or, to switch myths in midstream, Arthur—had no choice. The air of Camelot could not remain poisoned. He acceded to the national and global call for peace. Cousins was summoned to conclude the final agreement.

I see the effort to end nuclear testing and reach a partial test-ban treaty—the first arms control agreement in the Cold War and the beginning of détente—as the main drama in my father's life. Interestingly, the campaign—stretching from Nehru's first call for an end to atmospheric tests, to Schweitzer's Declaration of Conscience and Dr. Spock's appeal, with minor forays and skirmishes into occupied territory such as the launching of Albert Bigelow's *Golden Rule* and Earle Reynolds' the *Phoenix* into the testing zone—took just ten years, the same length of time as the Trojan War.

Following the main drama, there was the long journey home. These pages record Homer's encounter with the Cyclops—Senator McCarthy, Governor Wallace, General Westmoreland, and other protagonists whose harmful or hateful policies fed on human flesh; the Sirens of the World Peace Council and Rev. Moon's anticommunist fronts; the Scylla and Chrybadis of black power and white complacency; the Circe of government grants which turned his fellow scientists into swine; and the Antinoos (Greek: anti-mind or insanity) of the military-industrial complex who along with the other suitors was eating up the nation's treasure. Homer's long wanderings came full circle in his later years when he reconciled and resumed his friendship with Esther and with the family reunion in Rochester during which he embraced his ancestral heritage.

Of course, Odysseus represents both everyman and no man. These comparisons should not be taken too seriously, except in so far as all of our lives have archetypal dimensions. Now, Homer's earthly wanderings are over. In the words of the poet, he has joined "the choir invisible, whose music is the gladness of the world."

PICTORAL ODYSSEY
Rochester • Cornell Years

Homer's father, Alexander Jack
1878-1943

Homer's mother, Cecelia Davis
Jack 1886-1976

Homer, age 3

Taking a break from studies
at Cornell University

Homer A. Jack

Esther Rhys Williams

Dr. Schweitzer and boatman on the Ogowe River

The Parsonage in Evanston

A rare evening at home
with the children

Homer and Esther at the ground-
breaking for the new church

Alex in front of the Peace
Memorial in Hiroshima

Left: The old Unitarian Church on Chicago Avenue in Evanston.
Right: The new Church on Ridge Ave.

New York • Boston Years

Homer at the United Nations

Homer and Esther with Tom
Mboya, Kenyan Leader

Presenting Schweitzer medal to
Martin Buber in Israel

Family House in Scarsdale, N.Y.

Editing *Africa Today*

With Norman Thomas (center),
Dean Rusk (second from left), and
unidentified man at White House.

Dr. Martin Luther King speaks at
the March on Washington

Speaking at a SANE rally
in New York

Peace Demonstration in Red
Square, Moscow

Homer doing what he liked
to do best

The First World Conference for Religion and Peace (WCRP I)
Meeting in Kyoto, 1970

Left: Homer on visit to China with Ingeborg, Renate (behind her), and Alex. Zhou Puchu, leader of the Buddhist Association of China, is to Homer's right and high government official to his left

Right: Homer with President Jimmy Carter and Rosalind Carter at White House reception for WCRP III participants

Alex and wife Gale in Dallas

Gale (left) and daughter Lucy
(right) with Masha and Molly

Homer with Rev. Niwano (front
left) and Dana Greeley (right)

Lucy and David Rhys Williams,
Homer's in-laws and mentor

Left: Homer shows his stamp album
to Michael and son-in-law Jonathan

Homer at Gandhi's memorial in
India with WCRP associates

The Gandhi Century

Mohandas Gandhi, whose teachings on love and nonviolence Homer
considered to be the 20th century's greatest achievement

HOMER A. JACK
HONORS, AWARDS, AND ARRESTS

1938—Film confiscated by Soviet authorities in Odessa.

1952—Received the Thomas H. Wright Award for leadership in race relations by the City of Chicago.

1957—Government of South Africa refused to issue a visa at Leopoldville to enter South Africa.

1959—United Kingdom refused to issue a visa to enter Kenya.

1964—Received the Roosevelt Peace Award after resigning from SANE.

1970—Detained by Soviet authorities at the Moscow Airport after visiting the family of dissident General Grigorenko.

1971—Awarded honorary Doctorate of Divinity by the Meadville/Lombard Theological School in Chicago.

1971—Barred from entering South Vietnam.

1975—Testified on human rights violations at the United Nations Human Rights Commission in Geneva, after which several governments demanded that his U.N. credentials be withdrawn.

1976—Detained by Indian police at the Patna Airport in New Delhi after visiting Jayaprakash Narayan.

1977—Received the Albert Schweitzer Award in Ithaca from the North America Committee of the International Association for Religious Freedom.

1981—Delivered the Mahatma Gandhi Lecture in New Delhi at the invitation of the Gandhi Peace Foundation.

1982—Delivered the Essex Hall Lecture in Lampeter, Wales, at the invitation of the General Assembly of Unitarian and Free Christian Churches of the United Kingdom.

1982—Arrested for civil disobedience in front of the Chinese Mission to the United Nations during the Second Special Session on Disarmament.

1983—Received the Josephine Pomerance Award at U.N. Headquarters by the NGO Committee on Disarmament.

1984—Awarded the Niwano Peace Prize in Tokyo by the Niwano Peace Foundation.

1985—Arrested for civil disobedience in front of the South African Embassy in Washington, D.C.

1985—Received the Adlai E. Stevenson Award from the Illinois Division of the United Nations Association of the U.S.A.

1987—Delivered the 1987 Minns Lectures in New York, Rochester, Wilmington, and Washington at the invitation of the Minns Committee of the Unitarian Universalist Association.

1987—Delivered the second Toward Freedom/William B. Lloyd Lecture in Evanston at the invitation of Northwestern University.

1988—Received the Defender of Peace Award in Coimbatore, Tamil Nadu, India, from the Sarvodaya Movement.

1989—Received the Holmes/Weatherly Award in New Haven, Connecticut, from the Unitarian Universalist Association for distinguished service in social action.

1992—Received the Jamnalal Bajaj Award in Bombay for distinguished service of Gandhian values outside of India.

1993—Honored at Swarthmore Friends Meeting by nine Delaware Valley civic organizations.

A NOTE ON SOURCES

Homer wrote original material for the early part of this book, especially Parts I and II, sections of Parts III, IV, V, VIII, and IX and most of Part X. The rest of *Homer's Odyssey* was selected and edited from articles, sermons, speeches, letters, and other published or unpublished material. The sources for these chapters are noted below. Chapters or sections of chapters without citations indicate original manuscript material. The author and editor make grateful acknowledgment for use of copyrighted material.

1. "With Schweitzer in Lambaréné," *Saturday Review*, May 2, 1953. Also in *Saturday Review Reader, No. 3*, New York: Bantam Books, 1954.

2. "Negro Satyagraha in Alabama," *Hindustan Times*, April 8, 1956 and *Indian Opinion*, March 23, 1956, pp. 133-137.

3. "Lessons from the Cuban Crisis," speech, New York, Nov. 1962.

4. "The Kyoto Assembly" and "The Kyoto Declaration (1970)," in *WCRP: A History of the World Conference on Religion and Peace*, New York: WCRP, pp. 53-71, 437-440.

10. "Chicago: Paris of the Prairies," *Indian Messenger*, May 7, 1958.

12. "A Preacher's Prerogative," sermon, Unitarian Church of Lawrence, April, 1944.

15. "Journey of Reconciliation," *Common Ground*, Autumn, 1947, pp. 21-26.

16. "The Racial Factor in the Veterans Airport Housing Project," I and II, Nov. 18, 1946 and Dec. 1946, Chicago Council Against Racial and Religious Discrimination.

17. *The Evanston Unitarian.* Evanston: The Unitarian Church of Evanston. Vol. I (1), Jan. 7, 1949 to Vol. VII (19) to June 3, 1959.

18. Albert Einstein, "Out of Inner Necessity," *To Albert Schweitzer on His 80th Birthday*, Evanston, Ill., 1955. Letter from Schweitzer, March 9, 1955.

19. "South Africa Today," *Christian Century*, Sept. 17, 1952, pp. 1057-1059; "What Is This Apartheid?", *Christian Century*, Sept. 24, 1952, pp. 1092-1094; "Signs of Deterioration in South Africa," *Christian Century*, Oct. 1, 1952, pp. 1122-1125; "Under the Southern Cross," *Christian Century*, Oct. 8, 1952, pp. 1158-1160; "Hope for South Africa," *Christian Century*, Oct. 15, 1952, pp. 1189-1191; "Africans in Gandhian Defiance," *Christian Century*, Oct. 22, 1952, pp. 1220-1222.

20. *Friends Intelligencer*. Eleventh Month 8, pp. 636-38; Eleventh Month 22, pp. 670-671.

21. "Is McCarthy a Concealed Communist?" sermon, Community Church of New York, summer, 1953.

22. "The Asian-African Conference," *Bulletin of the Atomic Scientists,* June, 1955. *Bandung: An On-the-Spot Descripton of the Asian-African Conference,* 37 pp., Toward Freedom, 1955.

24. "American Reporter's Impressions," *Hindustan Times,* Aug. 19, 1955, pp. 1, 12; August 20, 1955, pp. 1, 12.

25. "Stride Toward Freedom," sermon, Unitarian Church of Evanston, 1958. "Newborn Ghana Faces the Future," *Peace News,* March 15, 1957. "Eyewitness in Ghana," *Christian Century,* April 3, 1957, pp. 416-418; "Conversation in Ghana," *Christian Century,* April 10, 1957, pp. 446-448.

26. "The Deep South and the North Shore," speech, Evanston, 1956.

28. "Reunion with Schweitzer," sermon, Unitarian Church of Evanston, 1957.

29. "Visiting Bertrand Russell in Wales," sermon, 1957.

30. *Anti-Atom: The Third World Conference Against A- and H-Bombs and for Disarmament.* Evanston: Unitarian Church of Evanston, 56 pp., 1957. "An American in Hiroshima," sermon, Unitarian Church of Evanston, 1957. "Unitarian Minister Homer Jack Tells of Visit with His Son to Atom Blasted Japanese City," *The Evanstonian,* 1957.

31. "Hail and Farewell!" speech, Unitarian Church of Evanston, June 7, 1959.

32. "Africa in December," sermon, Unitarian Church of Evanston, Dec. 28, 1958. "Inaugural Address by the General Secretary of WCRP/International," speech, WCRP First All African Assembly, Nairobi, Kenya, April 20-30, 1983.

33. *SANE World.* New York: National Committee for a Sane Nuclear Policy. I (1) Feb. 1, 1962 through III (15) Oct. 1, 1964.

34. "The American Peace Movement," *New Politics,* Summer, 1963, p. 127.

35. "Changes at Lambaréné," *Christian Century,* Aug. 22, 1962, pp. 1006-07.

36. "The Moscow Conference for General Disarmament and Peace: A Report to SANE," New York: SANE, 26 pp., July, 1962; "A Visit to Pasternak's Grave," *Penfriend* (New Delhi), August, 1966, pp. 26, 31.

37. "The One Hundred Days from June," *Gandhi Marg,* Oct., 1963, pp. 229-234.

38. "Albert Schweitzer's Activism in Nuclear Politics," in *Albert Schweitzer on Nuclear War and Peace,* Brethren Press, 1988.

39. "Selma: An American Epic," sermon delivered in several churches, spring 1965. "Martin Luther King Jr.—We Shall Overcome," in *Der Friendens-Nobelpreis von 1963 bis 1970,* edited by Michael Neumann, Munich, Germany, 1992.

40. "The Ordeal of James Reeb," *A Sheaf of Papers on Selma and James Reeb,* 48 pp., Swarthmore, 1993.

41. *The Sources of Gandhism in Martin Luther King, Jr.,* Gandhi Peace

Centre, 33 pp., 1988.

42. "Stockholm Conference Reveals Hard Truths," *Christian Century*, Sept. 13, 1967. "The World Conference on Vietnam: An Evaluation from Stockholm," Boston: UUA, Special Report, 14 pp., 1967. "Regional Conflict," in *WCRP: A History of the World Conference on Religion and Peace*, New York: WCRP, pp. 305-312.

43. "Boston University's Marsh Chapel 'Liberated,'" *Christian Century*, Nov. 6, 1968, pp. 1412.

44. "Black Power and White Liberals," speech, Unitarian Universalist Fellowship of New Delhi, Jan. 7, 1968; "The Unitarian Universalist Black Caucus Controversy," Boston: UUA, Special Report, 28 pp., 1968; Black Caucus Controversy II, Special Report, 17 pp., 1968; Black Caucus Controversy III, Special Report, 28 pp., 1968. "Black Power Confronts Unitarian Universalists," *Christian Century*, June 26, 1968. "Confrontations Beset U.U.A. Assembly," *Christian Century*, Sept. 3, 1969.

45. "The Agony and Ecstacy of Unitarian Universalism Today: Reflections of an Ex-Denominational Bureaucrat," sermon, Arlington Street Church, Boston, Jan. 4, 1970.

46. "Death in Golden Bangla Desh," *New York Times*, Op-Ed, p. 41, May 20, 1971.

47. "Disarmament and Hunger: Life and Death for Planet Earth," *Church and Society*, March-April 1975, pp. 45-53.

48. "The Human Rights of the Muslims of the Philippines," *Impact International*, Oct. 24, 1975.

49. "South Korea: Another Vietnam?" *America*, Nov. 8, 1975, pp. 302-303.

50. "Are Human Rights in Jeopardy?" *Liberty*, July-August, 1975, pp. 5-9.

51. "Is Zionism Racism?" *Bulletin of Peace Proposals*, No. 4, 1976, pp. 382-384.

52. Statement to the U.S. House of Representatives, Committee on International Relations, Subcommittee on International Organizations, June 23, 1976, Washington, D.C.

53. "As They Saw Him: From My FBI and CIA Files," sermon, Brooklyn Society for Ethical Culture. Oct. 31, 1976.

54. "Refugees: The Boat People Project," *WCRP: A History of the World Conference on Religion and Peace*, New York: WCRP, pp. 277-292.

55. "The New Abolitionism," in *Religion in the Struggle for World Community*, New York: WCRP, 1980, pp. 57-67.

56. "The Reemergence of Buddhism in China Today," *Dharma World*, Sept. 1981, pp. 42-45.

57. "Drafting a U.N. Convention for Religious Freedom," speech, Biennial Assembly of the American Ethical Union, C. W. Post Campus of Long Island University, June 21, 1991.

58. "Disarmament," in *WCRP: A History of the World Conference on Religion and Peace*, New York: WCRP, pp. 197-219.

59. "From the North Shore to the East River: What I Learned in New York," sermon, Lake Shore Unitarian Society, Winnetka, Ill., April 18, 1982.

60. "What the Liberal Church Could Become," sermon, Lake Shore Unitarian Universalist Society, Winnetka, Ill., 1983.

61. "Nuclear Disarmament: The Priority for Humanity, address, Niwano Peace Prize Ceremony, Tokyo, April 27, 1984.

62. "A Statement on the Middle East Crisis by Seven Niwano Peace Prize Recipients," Tokyo, Dec. 10, 1990.

63. "A New Agenda for an Old Peace Movement," speech, Unitarian Universalist Peace Fellowship, Delaware Valley, May 19, 1992.

64. "The Gandhi Century," speech, Jamnalal Bajaj Award Ceremonies, India, 1992.

65. "A Letter to Hindu Friends," March 15, 1993; "A Letter to Muslim Friends," March 15, 1993.

66. "No Longer Pagans or Heathens," *Friends Journal,* July 1992, pp. 28-29. "Chicago's Parliament of Religions," *Fair,* Oct.-Dec. 1989, pp. 9-10.

67. (Jawaharlal Nehru) "Jawaharlal Nehru and the Rise of Non-Alignment," in *Nehru and His Contributions to World Peace,* edited by R. R. Diwakar, 1989. (Michael Scott) "Michael Scott," tribute, New York, 1983. (Norman Cousins) "Adieu to Norman Cousins: Au Revoir to William Sloane Coffin," speech, Riverside Church, New York, Dec. 11, 1990. (Lillian Smith) "Lillian Smith of Clayton, Georgia," *Christian Century,* Oct. 12, 1957, pp. 1166-68. (Alan Paton, Des-mund Tutu) "The Rise and Fall of Apartheid: Fighting South Africa Since 1952," sermon, Lake Shore Unitarian Society, Winnetka, Ill., May 18, 1986. (Reginald Reynolds) "Reg Was Not an Organizational Man! An Appreciation," tribute, Chicago, Dec. 26, 1958. (Philip Noel-Baker) "Philip Noel-Baker: Olympic Champion, Nobel Laureate, and Haverford Student," address, Haverford College, Haverford, Pennsylvania, Oct. 31, 1989. (Dana Greeley) "Dana McLean Greeley: A Unitarian Legend," sermon, Lake Shore Unitarian Universalist Society, Winnetka, Ill., April 1, 1984. (Mother Teresa) "Mother Teresa of Calcutta, *Dharma World,* Oct. 1976, pp. 10-17. (Shinochiro Imaoka) Tribute, Tokyo, May 15, 1988. (Juliette Morgan) "A Quest for Juliette Morgan of Montgomery, Alabama," sermon, Unitarian-Universalist Fellowship of Montgomery, March 11, 1990.

68. (Jesus of Nazareth) "Was Jesus a Christian? The Originality of Jesus," sermon, Unitarian Church of Evanston, Feb. 24, 1957. (Jesus Christ) "The Meaning of Christmas," *The Evanstonian,* December 1952. (Abraham Lincoln) "The Religion of Abraham Lincoln," sermon, Unitarian Church of Evanston, 1956. (Karl Marx) "The Gospel According to Marx," sermon given to the Unitarian Church of Evanston, 1953-54. (John Brown) "On Democracy's Battlefront," column, *Pittsburg Courier, 1950.*

69. (Stephen Fitchman) Review of *Heretic: A Partisan Autobiography* by Stephen H. Fritchman in *Kairos,* Autumn, 1978. (Rev. Moon) "Moonshine: The Gospel According to the Rev. Sun Myung Moon," sermon, Lake Shore Unitarian Society, Winnetka, Ill., May 5, 1985. Sekou Touré, "Jack Out of the Pulpit," column in the newsletter of the Lake Shore Unitarian Society, April 1, 1984. (Dalai Lama) "A Second Opinion on Tibet: Demythologizing the Dalai Lama," sermon at the Bux-Mont Unitarian Fellowship in Warrington, Pa., May 28, 1989.

BIBLIOGRAPHY

The archives of Homer A. Jack, including manuscripts, articles, correspondence, sermons, prayers, notebooks, and other materials, are located at the Swarthmore College Peace Collection in Swarthmore, Pennsylvania. WCRP and SANE archives are also located here. UUA archives are located at Harvard Divinity School in Cambridge. Bound copies of the *Evanston Unitarian*, the newsletter of the Unitarian Church of Evanston which Homer edited from 1948-1959, are in the personal library of Esther Jack. In September 1991, Homer compiled "A Bibliography of the Writings of Homer A. Jack," listing nearly 1000 of his publications chronologically from 1931 and providing a topical index. He added a supplement in June 1992 and Alex Jack is preparing a final supplement through 1993.

Major Writings of Homer A. Jack

Albert Schweitzer on Nuclear War and Peace. Elgin: Brethren Press, 216 pp., 1988.

Biological Field Stations of the World. Waltham: Chronica Botanica, 73 pp., 1945.

Disarm—Or Die: The Second U.N. Special Session on Disarmament. New York: WCRP, 291 pp., 1980.

Disarmament Workbook: The U.N. Special Session and Beyond. New York: WCRP, 137 pp., 1978.

To Dr. Albert Schweitzer: A Festschrift Commemorating His 80th Birthday. Evanston: Privately printed, 179 pp., 1955.

"Friedens-Nobelpreis 1964: Martin Luther King Jr." in *Die Friedens-Nobelpreis von 1901 bis Heute,* ed. by Michael Neumann. Zug, Switzerland: Edition Pacis. Vol. 1963-1970, 208 pp., pp. 48-151, 1992.

The Gandhi Reader. Bloomington: Indiana University Press, 532 pp., 1956. Reprinted by Grove Press, Vol. 1, New York, 1961 and by Samata Books, Madras, India, 1983.

Nuclear Politics After Hiroshima/Nagasaki: Unitarian Universalist and Other Responses. The 1987 Minns Lectures. Swarthmore: Privately printed, 98 pp., 1987.

Religion and Peace. Indianapolis: Bobbs-Merrill, 137 pp., 1967.

Religion and Peace: Proceedings of the Kyoto Conference on Religion and Peace. New Delhi: Gandhi Peace Foundation. Bombay: Bharatiya Vidya Bhavan, 391 pp., 1973.

Religion in the Struggle for World Community. New York: WCRP, 418 pp., 1980.

WCRP: A History of the World Conference on Religion and Peace. New York: WCRP, 596 pp., 1993.

The Wit and Wisdom of Gandhi. Boston: Beacon Press, 234 pp., 1951.

World Religions and World Peace. Boston: Beacon Press, 208 pp., 1968.

World Religion/World Peace. New York: WCRP, 200 pp., 1979.

Index

in Boston, 370
children of, 442, 564, 567
on Gandhi and Schweitzer, 253
growing up, 158, 256, 312, 562, 580
and Homer's last days, 593-595
Jack, Masha (granddaughter), 570,
594-595
Jack Spratt, 116, 118
Jack-O-Lantern, 85-86
Jackson, Jesse, 421, 447
Jackson, Jimmie Lee, 314, 317, 318
Jacubowitz, Fanny (grandmother), 65
Jackubowitz, Gustave (grandfather), 65,
574
Jahn, Gunnar, 305, 308, 309
Jains and Jainism, 46, 419, 476
Jamnalal Bajaj Award, 216, 471
Japan
religions of, 43, 456, 462, 513, 517,
521, 522, 526
untouchability in, 384
visits to, 42-49, 242-251, 456-459,
504, 521-524, 556
(*See also* Hiroshima, Rev. Nikkyo
Niwano, Risso Kosei-kai)
Japan Free Religious Association, 522
Japan Religions League, 44, 524
Japanese-American Citizens' League,
252
Japanese-American Inter-Religious
Consultation on Peace, 523, 525
Japanese-Americans, 112, 113, 125, 130,
131, 132, 398
Japanese Committee for Justice and
Peace, 383
Jerusalem, 44, 387
Jesus, 199, 201-202, 337, 454, 517, 518,
531-535, 537
Jews and Judaism
and Dr. Jack's ancestry, 68, 72-73
discrimination against, 68, 72-73, 125,
389-390, 427-428
and Gulf War, 462
and Hanukkah, 199-201
and Holocaust, 93, 106, 113, 120, 304,
426, 471
and Jesus, 531-535
and peace, 280
in U.S.S.R., 385
and WCRP, 43, 44, 46, 47
and WW II, 81, 87, 92, 106, 113
and Vietnam, 351
and Zionism, 387-390
Ji Pengfei, 438
Jim Crow, 21, 142-148
Johannesburg, 169-179, 504
John Birch Society, 283
Johnson, David, 327

Johnson, Frank M., Jr., 321, 322, 323-324
Johnson, Lyndon, 276, 303, 314, 316,
317, 319-320, 322, 323, 324, 329, 331,
349, 489, 544
Johnson, Mordecai W., 335
Jones, Bob, 514
Jones, Charles, 144
Jones, Jenkin Lloyd, 104
Joshi, P. S., 177-178, 182
Journal of Conflict Resolution, 281
Journey of Reconciliation, 142-148, 336
Joyce, James, 556

Kagawa, Toyohiko, 246
Kallenbach, Herman, 181-182
Kang Mao Zhao, 438
Kant, Immanuel, 166
Karachi, 372
Karjola, Mrs., 157
Kashmir, 600
Katzenbach, Nicholas B., 317, 321, 322
Kaunda, Kenneth, 265
Keller, Helen, 56
Kelley, Clarence M., 397, 402
Kelly, Mayor, 136, 139
Kelly, Thomas, 77
Kennedy, Edward, 331
Kennedy, John F., 18
and African independence, 264, 497
American University speech, 298
assassination of, 276, 297, 302-303,
330, 468, 486, 488, 501, 601
Berlin visit, 299
and Cousins, 501
and Cuban Crisis, 37, 40, 432
election of, 256, 266, 279
on military complex, 283
and nuclear testing, 272, 275, 281
and test-ban, 10, 276, 294,
297-303, 602
and Schweitzer, 310
Kennedy, Robert, 266
Kennelly, Martin H., 130
Kenya, 155, 160, 257, 260, 263
Kenyatta, Jomo, 258
Keys, Donald, 269, 511
KGB, 403, 583
Khan, Abdul Ghaffar, 215
Khan, Inamulla, 462
Khan, Yahya, 515
Khan, Zafrulla, 43
Khrushchev, Nikita, 18
and Cousins, 501
and Cuban Crisis, 37, 40
and disarmament, 292, 458
and John F. Kennedy, 302
and Pasternak, 295
and test-ban treaty, 10, 276, 294, 299,
300, 301

631

One Peaceful World Society, 561
Oppenheimer, J. Robert, 247, 307
Oram, Harold, 268
Organization of African Unity, 387
Orwell, George, 459, 471
Osaka, 43, 246, 456
Osborn, Earl, 268
Oshima, Hiroyuki, 526
Oslo, 166, 304-305, 306, 308, 501
Oxford English Dictionary, 495, 496

Pacifism, 98, 109, 112, 113, 117, 118,
 120, 162-163, 267, 398
Paine, Thomas, 537
Pakistan, 43, 44, 217, 372-373, 386, 394,
 515, 520
Palestinians, 181, 388-389, 461, 478
Palmer, E. Laurence, 79, 80, 86, 108
Paper cranes, 251
Park Chung Hee, 381-383
Parker, Theodore, 354, 368, 449, 513,
 539-540, 584
Parks, Rosa, 32, 33, 205, 528
Pasternak, Boris, 289, 294-296
Paton, Alan, 151, 182, 504
Paul the Apostle, 532, 533
Pauling, Linus, 267, 278, 291, 511, 584
Peace (*see* Disarmament)
Peace Corps. 278
Peace, Inc., 155
Peace Research Institute, 280-281
Pearl Harbor, 68, 106, 109, 112, 249, 398
Pearson, Drew, 275
Peck, Sidney, 512
Pentagon Papers, 371
Peredelkino, 294-296
Perry, Loren, 77
Philaret, Metropolian, 44
Philippine People Power, 471
Philippines, 114, 377-380, 385, 513
Phoenix, 278, 602
Phoenix Farm, 178, 179, 184-185
Pickett, Clarence, 18, 267, 268, 269, 276,
 280, 501
Pierre, Abbe, 347
Pire, Dominique, 307
Pittsburg Courier, 536, 558
PM, 124
PLO, 350
Poland, 46, 431
Pope John Paul II, 572
Pope John XXIII, 10, 276, 294, 501
Pope Paul VI, 45, 518, 523
Pope Pius XII, 267
Port Elizabeth, 172-173
Portugal, 220-223, 283
Potekhin, Ivan, 264, 400

Potter, Philip, 462
Powell, Aaron M., 483
Powell, Adam Clayton, 584
Prasad, Rajendra, 215, 338
Presbytarians, 108, 114, 144, 154, 449,
 489, 538, 539
President's Commission on Civil Rights,
 132, 138-139
Princeton, 160-164, 414-420
Prohibition, 62
Puerto Rico, 40
Pugwash Conference, 267, 278
Pyarelal, 215

Quakers and Quakerism, 77, 163, 217,
 252, 280, 370, 435, 507, 508, 509, 530
Quinces, 161, 578-579, 599
Quit India, 112, 113, 213
Qur'an, 43, 518

Race relations, 125-141
 North and South, 502-504
Racism
 definition of, 388
 in Montgomery, 31-32, 527-530
 and Zionism, 387-390
Radhakrishna, Shri, 216, 515
Radhakrishnan, Sarvepalli, 157, 215, 219,
 338, 478, 559
Rahman, Mujibur, 373
Rajagopalachari, Chakravarty, 215, 219
Rajayogeendra, J. G., 44
Rajghat, 338, 473
Ramachandran, G., 216, 515
RAND Corporation, 280
Randolph, A. Philip, 324, 578
Rankin, Jeannette, 106
Rappel, Elizabeth (aunt), 65, 571
Rappel, Maximilian (uncle), 571
Rashtriya Swayam Sevak Sangh, 478
Rauch, Stanley, 565, 594, 595
Rauschenbusch, Walter, 60, 335
Reagan, Ronald, 583
Reddick, Lawrence, D., 338
Reeb, James J., 314, 322, 323, 325-331,
 354, 486
Reeb, Marie, 323, 325-331
Reed, John, 490
Reese, Curtis, 110
Reese, Frederick D., 316
Religion
 liberal, 107, 446-455
Religious Discrimination, 426-431
 (*see also* Discrimination, Anti-
 Semitism)
Renckert family, 56, 61
Restrictive covenants, 128
Reuther, Walter, 331

and Schweitzer, 66, 236, 287-288
in Selma, 319-321, 325-331
and Stevenson, 493
Unitarian Universalist Association
(UUA), 22
annual meetings of, 572
and Black Caucus, 356, 359, 360
Department of Social Responsibility,
312-313, 319-321, 326, 353-360,
361-363, 400, 512, 513
and Dana Greeley, 8, 45, 362-363,
512-514, 587
and March on Washington, 354
purposes of, 450-452
and Selma, 319-321, 354
and Vietnam, 344, 513
and Robert West, 361, 582
United Kingdom
nuclear protests in, 241, 281, 499, 506
visits to, 86, 238-241, 499, 505, 563
United Nations
and African freedom struggle, 265
and autonomy for regions, 553
and Bandung Conference, 209
and Bangladesh crisis, 373
Charter, 384-385, 427, 435
and China's admission, 293-294, 371
and end of Cold War, 466, 470
Commission on Human Rights,
384-386, 427, 428, 429
Conference on Environment and
Development, 466
Council on Namibia, 499
Covenant on Civil and Political
Rights, 428
and Cuban Crisis, 38-40
Declaration on the Elimination of All
Forms of Racial Discrimination, 428,
430-431
Declaration of Human Rights, 384,
393, 427, 428, 552
Declaration on Religious Discri-
mination, 426-431
and development, 48, 375
Disarmament Committee of the
General Assembly, 271
Economic and Social Council
(ECOSOC), 384-386, 428, 435
Eighteen Nation Disarmament
Conference (ENDC), 271
founding of, 508
Fourth Committee, 499
General Assembly, 40, 262, 282, 301,
302, 383, 387, 428, 429, 436, 469,
497, 498, 525
and global peace, 465
Group of 77, 495
and Gulf War, 461-462, 501
High Commissioner for Refugees,

406, 408, 409, 410, 413
Human Rights Commission, 384-386
International Convention on the
Elimination of All Forms of Racial
Discrimination, 388
and Kennedy's assassination, 303
and Kyoto Declaration, 49
model, 154
and NGOs, 414
and nonaligned movement, 496-498
Nuclear Regulatory Commission, 393
peacekeeping, 470, 595
and Peoples' Council, 553
Preparatory Commission, 507-508
Registry of Arms Transfers, 470
and SANE, 281
Second Special Session on
Disarmament (SSOD II), 437-439,
509, 526, 583
Secretary General, 40, 43, 193, 300,
304, 344, 349, 461, 466, 515
Security Council, 38, 160, 461, 462,
464, 469, 470
memorial service for Homer, 595
Special Committee Against
Apartheid, 499, 505
Special Session on Disarmament
(SSOD I), 415, 417, 436-437, 457,
509, 525
stamps, 67, 576
structure of, 366, 367
subcommittee to end nuclear testing,
267
and terrorism and hijacking, 593
Trust Territories, 261, 262
and Vietnam War, 344, 349
and weapons in space, 302-303
World Environmental Conference, 446
and Zionist resolution, 387-390
United States
Air Force, 397
and colonialism, 395
Arms Control and Disarmament
Agency, 278, 281, 282
Army, 397
civil liberties in, 187-195
and civil rights, 314, 319, 323
Congress, 281, 383, 391-395, 403,
467, 469, 481, 538
House of Representatives, 391, 467
Information Agency, 397, 400
Senate Judiciary Subcommitte, 371
State Department, 194, 278-279, 380,
394, 397, 488, 512, 560
Strategic Bombing Survey, 248
Supreme Court, 128, 142-148, 152,
205, 224-225, 337, 358, 502
United World Federalists (UWF), 64, 279
Unity Church of Frank Lloyd Wright, 582

RESOURCES

The Homer A. Jack Peace Fund has been established to continue Homer's ideals and support projects devoted to peace and social justice. Contributions are welcome and are tax-deductible. Donations may be made payable to "OPW—HAJ Fund" and be sent to One Peaceful World, P.O. Box 10, Becket, MA 01223.

One Peaceful World is a non-profit educational foundation devoted to creating a world of enduring health and peace. Activities include communications and publishing, seminars and programs on personal and planetary health and world peace. For a free catalogue and membership information, please contact: One Peaceful World, P.O. Box 10, Leland Rd., Becket, MA 01223. Telephone (413) 623-2322, Fax (413) 623-8827.

Mail Order and Bulk Copies of *Homer's Odyssey*: Additional copies of *Homer's Odyssey* are available by mail order from the publisher. Please send a check or money order payable to OPW (in U.S. funds drawn on a U.S. bank) or enclose Visa/MC number and expiration date. Cost: $22.00 for each book plus $3.00 shipping per copy (outside of U.S./Canada, please add $5.00 for surface mail and $18.00 for airmail).

Bulk copies are available at discount to bookstores, peace groups, religious organizations, ministers, teachers, and other institutions and individuals. To order or for further information, please contact: One Peaceful World, P.O. Box 10, Leland Rd., Becket, MA 01223, U.S.A. Telephone (413) 623-2322, Fax (413) 623-8827.